The Earthscan Reader on Adaptation to Climate Change

Edited by

E. Lisa F. Schipper and Ian Burton

publishing for a sustainable future

London • Sterling, VA

First published by Earthscan in the UK and USA in 2009

ISBN: 978-1-84407-530-0   hardback
      978-1-84407-531-7   paperback

Typeset by Domex e-Data, India
Printed and bound in the UK by MPG Books, Bodmin
Cover design by Andrew Corbett

For a full list of publications please contact:

Earthscan
Dunstan House
14a St Cross Street
London, EC1N 8XA, UK
Tel: +44 (0)20 7841 1930
Fax: +44 (0)20 7242 1474
Email: earthinfo@earthscan.co.uk
Web: **www.earthscan.co.uk**

22883 Quicksilver Drive, Sterling, VA 20166-2012, USA

Earthscan publishes in association with the International Institute for Environment and
Development

A catalogue record for this book is available from the British Library

Library of Congress Cataloging-in-Publication Data

The Earthscan reader on adaptation to climate change / edited by E. Lisa F. Schipper and
Ian Burton.
    p. cm.
Includes bibliographical references and index.
ISBN 978-1-84407-530-0 (hardback) -- ISBN 978-1-84407-531-7 (pbk.) 1. Climatic
changes--Environmental aspects. 2. Adaptation (Biology) I. Schipper, E. Lisa F. II.
Burton, Ian.
    QC981.8.C5E186 2008
    304.2'5--dc22

                    2008044577

The paper used for this book is FSC-certified. FSC
(the Forest Stewardship Council) is an international
network to promote responsible management of the
world's forests.

Contents

Part I – Adaptation Theory

Part II – Adaptation, Vulnerability and Resilience

Part III – Adaptation and Disaster Risk

Part IV – Adaptation and Development

Part V – Adaptation and Climate Change Policy

List of Boxes, Figures and Tables

Boxes

Figures

Tables

About the Editors

E. Lisa F. Schipper is an interdisciplinary researcher focused on development and climate change. In particular, her research focuses on social factors causing vulnerability to natural hazards, adaptation policy issues and the linkages between adaptation, development and disaster risk. Lisa is a Research Fellow at Stockholm Environment Institute in Bangkok, Thailand, where she also works on research capacity building in the realm of adaptation and vulnerability reduction. She has worked and consulted for numerous international organizations, including the Southeast Asia START Regional Centre at Chulalongkorn University in Bangkok, UK's Department for International Development, German Technical Cooperation Agency (GTZ), International Institute for Sustainable Development, International Water Management Institute, Oxfam Hong Kong, UN International Strategy for Disaster Reduction, UNFCCC Secretariat, UN Development Programme, UN Environment Programme and the World Bank.
Lisa can be reached at lschipper@climate-adaptation.info

Ian Burton is an independent scholar working on the application of science to policy. His fields of interest include natural hazards and risk assessment, environment and development, and adaptation to climate change. He holds honorary positions as Scientist Emeritus with the Meteorological Service of Canada, and Emeritus Professor at the University of Toronto. Ian is also Advisor to the Red Cross/Red Crescent Climate Centre and Visiting Fellow at the International Institute for Environment and Development in London. He has served as Lead Author in two IPCC Assessments and as a consultant on adaptation to the UNFCCC Secretariat, the World Bank, UN Development Programme, UN Environment Programme, and agencies of the Government of Canada.
Ian can be reached at Ian.Burton@ec.gc.ca

List of Sources

Original publication details, and current copyright holders, are given below for each of the chapters in this book. We are grateful to the copyright holders for permission to reproduce the material.

Chapter 1 Schipper, E. L. F. and Burton, I. (2009) 'Understanding adaptation: Origins, concepts, practice and policy', previously unpublished
Copyright © E. Lisa F. Schipper and Ian Burton, 2009

Chapter 2 Burton, I. (1994) 'Deconstructing adaptation ... and reconstructing', *Delta*, vol 5, no 1, pp14–15
Copyright © Meteorological Service of Canada, 1994

Chapter 3 Smithers, J. and Smit, B. (1997) 'Human adaptation to climatic variability and change', *Global Environmental Change*, vol 7, no 2, pp129–146
Copyright © Elsevier, 1997

Chapter 4 Pittock, A. B. and Jones, R. N. (2000) 'Adaptation to what and why?', *Environmental Monitoring and Assessment*, vol 61, no 1, pp9–35
Copyright © Springer, 2000

Chapter 5 Smit, B., Burton, I., Klein, R. J. T. and Wandel, J. (2000) 'An anatomy of adaptation to climate change and variability', *Climatic Change*, vol 45, no 1, p223–251
Copyright © Springer, 2000

Chapter 6 Burton, I. (2004) 'Climate change and the adaptation deficit', Occasional Paper No 1, Adaptation and Impacts Research Group (AIRG), Meteorological Service of Canada, Environment Canada, Toronto
Copyright © Meteorological Service of Canada, 2004

Chapter 7 Davies, S. (1993) 'Are coping strategies a cop out?', *Institute of Development Studies Bulletin*, vol 24, no 4, pp60–72
Copyright © Institute of Development Studies, University of Sussex, 1993

Chapter 8 Ribot, J. C., Najam, A. and Watson, G. (1996) 'Climate variation, vulnerability and sustainable development in the semi-arid tropics', in J. C. Ribot, A. R. Magalhaes and S. S. Panagides (eds) *Climate Variability, Climate Change and Social Vulnerability in the Semi-Arid Tropics*, Cambridge University Press, Cambridge, pp13–17, 23–48
Copyright © Cambridge University Press, 1996

Chapter 9 Kelly, P. M. and Adger, W. N. (2000) 'Theory and practice in assessing vulnerability to climate change and facilitating adaptation', *Climatic Change*, vol 47, no 4, pp325–352
Copyright © Springer, 2000

Chapter 10 Handmer, J. W. and Dovers, S. R. (1996) 'A typology of resilience: Rethinking institutions for sustainable development', *Organization and Environment*, vol 9, no 4, pp482–511
Copyright © Sage Publications, 1996

Chapter 11 Handmer, J. (2003) 'Adaptive capacity: What does it mean in the context of natural hazards?', in J. B. Smith, R. J. T. Klein and S. Huq (eds) *Climate Change, Adaptive Capacity, and Development*, Imperial College Press, London
Copyright © Imperial College Press, 2003

Chapter 12 UNDP (2002) 'A climate risk management approach to disaster reduction and adaptation to climate change', summary of the UNDP Expert Group Meeting 'Integrating Disaster Reduction and Adaptation to Climate Change', Havana, Cuba, 19–21 June 2002; United Nations Development Programme, New York
Copyright © UNDP Publications, 2002

Chapter 13 Moench, M. (2007) 'Adapting to climate change and the risks associated with other natural hazards: Methods for moving from concepts to action', in M. Moench and A. Dixit (eds) *Working with the Winds of Change*, ProVention Consortium/Institute for Social and Environmental Transition-International/Institute for Social and Environmental Transition-Nepal, Kathmandu, Nepal, pp14–48
Copyright © ISET and ISET-Nepal, 2007

Chapter 14 Kates, R. W. (2000) 'Cautionary tales: Adaptation and the global poor' *Climatic Change*, vol 45, no 1, pp5–17
Copyright © Springer, 2000

Chapter 15 Adger, W. N., Huq, S., Brown, K., Conway, D. and Hulme, M. (2003) 'Adaptation to climate change in the developing world', *Progress in Development Studies*, vol 3, no 3, pp179–195
Copyright © Sage Publications India Pvt. Ltd, 2003

Chapter 16 Huq, S. and Reid, H. (2004) 'Mainstreaming adaptation in development', *IDS Bulletin*, vol 35, no 3, pp15–21
Copyright © Institute of Development Studies, University of Sussex, 2004

Chapter 17 O'Brien, K. L. and Leichenko, R. M. (2000) 'Double exposure: Assessing the impacts of climate change within the context of economic globalization', *Global Environmental Change*, vol 10, pp221–232
Copyright © Elsevier, 2000

Chapter 18 Pielke, Jr., R. A. (1998) 'Rethinking the role of adaptation in climate policy', *Global Environmental Change*, vol 8, no 2, pp159–170
Copyright © Elsevier, 1998

Chapter 19 Schipper, E. L. F. (2006) 'Conceptual history of adaptation to climate change under the UNFCCC', *Review of European Community and International Environmental Law (RECIEL)*, vol 15, no 1, pp82–92
Copyright © Blackwell Publishing, 2006

Chapter 20 Burton, I., Huq, S., Lim, B., Pilifosova, O. and Schipper, E. L. F. (2002) 'From impacts assessment to adaptation priorities: The shaping of adaptation policy', *Climate Policy*, vol 2, nos 2–3, pp145–159
Copyright © Earthscan, 2002

Chapter 21 UNFCCC (2007) 'An overview of investment and financial flows needed for adaptation' in UNFCCC, *Investment and Financial Flows to Address Climate Change*, United Nations Framework Convention on Climate Change, Bonn, pp96–125
Copyright © United Nations Framework Convention on Climate Change, 2007

List of Acronyms and Abbreviations

ABI	Association of British Insurance
AF	Adaptation Fund
AGGG	Advisory Group on Greenhouse Gases
AOSIS	Alliance of Small Island States
AR4	IPCC Fourth Assessment Report
CCA	Common Country Assessment
CDM	Clean Development Mechanism
CFC	chlorofluorocarbon
CO_2	carbon dioxide
COP	Conference of the Parties (to the UNFCCC)
CSIRO	Commonwealth Scientific and Industrial Research Organisation (Australia)
DIVA	dynamic interactive vulnerability analysis tool
DRR	disaster risk reduction
EM-DAT	International Emergency Disasters Database
ENSO	El Niño-Southern Oscillation
EWS	early warning systems
FDI	foreign direct investment
GBD	Global Burden of Disease study
GCM	global climate model
GDP	gross domestic product
GEF	Global Environment Facility
GFCF	gross fixed capital formation
GHG	greenhouse gas
GM	Gent and McWilliams
GNP	gross national product
ha	hectares
ICID	International Conference on the Impacts of Climatic Variations and Sustainable Development in Semi-Arid Regions
ICSU	International Council of Scientific Unions
IDNDR	International Decade for Natural Disaster Reduction (UN)
IEA WEO	International Energy Agency World Energy Outlook
IFRC	International Federation of Red Cross and Red Crescent Societies

INC	Intergovernmental Negotiating Committee
IPCC	Intergovernmental Panel on Climate Change
ITCZ	Intertropical Convergence Zone
LDC	least developed country
LDCF	Least Developed Countries Fund
MDG	Millennium Development Goal
MINK	Missouri, Iowa, Nebraska, and Kansas
MNC	multinational corporation
NAFTA	North American Free Trade Agreement
NAI	non-Annex I
NAPA	National Adaptation Programmes of Action
NGO	non-governmental organization
ODA	official development assistance
OECD	Organisation for Economic Co-operation and Development
PAR	photosynthetically active radiation, *also* pressure and release model
ppmv	parts per million by volume
PRA	participatory rural appraisal
RCM	regional climate model
SCCF	Special Climate Change Fund
SIDS	small island developing state
SPCZ	South Pacific Convergence Zone
SRES	Special Report on Emissions Scenarios
UNCED	United Nations Conference on Environment and Development
UNDAF	United Nations Development Assistance Framework
UNDP	United Nations Development Programme
UNEP	United Nations Environment Programme
UNFCCC	United Nations Framework Convention on Climate Change
UVR	ultraviolet radiation
VCA	vulnerability capacity analysis
WCED	World Commission on Environment and Development (Brundtland Commission)
WHO	World Health Organization

Acknowledgements

The development of this book has been an extended project that has spanned not only time but also continents. The authors are very grateful to Farhana Yamin and Neil Leary who initially provided the encouragement to link us up with Earthscan, after this project had simmered for nearly two years in our heads. A huge thanks also goes to International START Secretariat for providing funding for the production of this book, and especially to Roland Fuchs, Hassan Virji and Neil Leary. We are also indebted to Thea Dickson, who helped provide support in locating electronic versions of papers and keeping us organized.

This book also required input from peers. Neil Adger, Simon Anderson, Richard Klein, Youssef Nassef, Barry Smit, Adam Scott and Katharine Vincent deserve gratitude for taking the time to give us detailed comments to help select the final texts that are included in this book. We would also like to thank the authors of the papers that appear here. Thanks also to Ilan Kelman and Pascha Carruthers who helped us in our struggle to find a cover picture. Thanks to Julia Schipper for proofreading. We also recognize the competent and dedicated team at Earthscan who didn't give up on this project even though it nearly died a few times: Rob West, Hamish Ironside, Jonathan Sinclair Wilson and Alison Kuznets.

Introduction to the Reader

E. Lisa F. Schipper and Ian Burton

After years of benign neglect the idea that humanity must give serious attention to adaptation to climate change has finally come into its own. The cause of adaptation has been kept alive for almost two decades by a relatively small group of scholars, experts and researchers, many of whom are represented in this volume. Now with the wider recognition of the importance of adaptation many more people are being drawn into adaptation science and the adaptation advocacy movement. The purpose of this Reader is to provide this growing number with a careful selection of some of the seminal texts drawn from the literature of the past two decades.

There is currently no other single knowledge source that provides an account of adaptation that adequately reflects the progress and trends in adaptation science, highlights the controversies and policy debates, and, more importantly, outlines the many questions that remain to be answered, while identifying the most influential concepts and thinkers. There is much uncertainty about adaptation to climate change – what the concept means or should mean, how adaptation can be effectively introduced, facilitated and managed, for whom, when and where. These questions apply both within the processes of the United Nations Framework Convention on Climate Change (UNFCCC) and in other domains. While not attempting to offer a completely comprehensive guide, the selection of material in this Reader endeavours to provide an inroad to all those interested in understanding the background to the current state of adaptation science. The selection reflects the great diversity of views about adaptation to climate change, especially in its relationship to disasters and to development.

In presenting these difficulties the Reader sets out to be intentionally provocative and to challenge the expanding adaptation community to contribute to the growing fund of knowledge. This is not an inconsiderable task. Thus, the Reader also adopts a historical perspective and includes material that represents the evolution of thinking and concepts of adaptation.

In this necessarily limited selection from the literature we have tried to provide a representative sample that reflects the range of past and current thinking. The selection process involved an extensive list of potential material that was narrowed down based on personal preferences, with advice and consultation with many Intergovernmental Panel on Climate Change authors and others involved in the UNFCCC adaptation community. The longer list is presented in the bibliography of regrettably excluded texts. The most recent synthesis of the adaptation literature may be found in the Working Group II volume of the IPCC Fourth Assessment Report (IPCC, 2007) especially in Chapters 17–20.

Reference

IPCC (Intergovernmental Panel on Climate Change) (2007) *Fourth Assessment Report*, Cambridge University Press, Cambridge, UK.

1

Understanding Adaptation: Origins, Concepts, Practice and Policy

E. Lisa F. Schipper and Ian Burton

Re-enter Adaptation

Before 1992 the word 'adaptation' was infrequently used in relation to climate change or other environmental risks. As explained by Ian Burton (Chapter 2), 'adaptation' as a scientific concept was largely associated with the Darwinian theory of evolution and the process of natural selection. Adaptation occurred as environmental forces worked on random genetic variations and those individuals in a population with characteristics of greater survival value were 'selected for'. The word 'adaptation' has also been long used in a social context but tended to acquire controversial or negative connotations. For this reason, social scientists have generally preferred to avoid using it. In his well-known pioneering book *Human Adjustment to Floods* (White, 1945), Gilbert White pondered what word to use to accurately capture his message that a better way to cope with floods was not to rely exclusively on flood control engineering, but to consider a broader range of options including land-use regulations, building codes, watershed management, flood forecasting, warnings and evacuation, and relocation. After considering the use of the word 'adaptation' he rejected it in favour of 'human adjustment'. In the years following, the concept of human adjustment was elaborated in various ways and other expressions such as 'coping', 'risk management', 'vulnerability reduction' and 'resilience' came into widespread use.

In 1992, the Intergovernmental Negotiating Committee working on the draft of the United Nations Framework Convention on Climate Change (UNFCCC) went back to the word 'adaptation'. The text of the Convention as agreed in Rio de Janeiro in 1992 established two main categories of response to climate change: mitigation and adaptation. Mitigation refers to those actions designed to reduce emissions of greenhouse gases in order to achieve 'stabilization of greenhouse gas concentrations in the atmosphere at a level that would prevent dangerous anthropogenic interference with the climate system' (UNFCCC Article 2). Adaptation was not defined in the text of the Convention, but it was used in a number of articles and its meaning and interpretation has since been the source of much academic and policy debate. Despite growing scholarship and policy on the subject, however, the search continues for the development of a coherent theory of adaptation.

Although adaptation to change has a long history both in ecosystems and human societies, it is only in the last two decades that scientists and a growing number of policymakers have begun to grapple with how humanity can actually adapt in a planned and strategic way as the climate that life depends on changes. Successfully responding to climate variability is as old as humankind – sustainably responding to rapid anthropogenic climate change however presents a new challenge. Although it is conceptually futile to separate the two, climate change is pushing us beyond the limits of existing coping strategies in many places, and additional adaptation, autonomous or otherwise induced, will be necessary. While the questions are becoming more apparent about what adaptation is, how it can be stimulated, and what its limits are, the answers mostly remain unclear. Thus, while adaptation is being promoted by everyone from the development NGOs to the UN Secretary-General, designing adaptation projects or policies and their implementation remain a challenge for policymakers and practitioners worldwide.

The chapters in this Reader have been selected to give a flavour of the debates on theory and the relationship to emerging practice and policy.

Adaptation Theory

In an early paper on the subject, reproduced as Chapter 3 of this volume, Smithers and Smit trace more of the history of adaptation in an eclectic body of scholarship, which they show has created an incomplete and 'at times inconsistent understanding of human adaptation to environmental variations'. They propose a framework for the dimensions of adaptation and a classification scheme for differentiating adaptation strategies. This paper and others of similar genre represent the beginnings of an explosion of the scientific literature about the meaning of the word 'adaptation' and how it should be used and defined in the climate debates. A select sample of this largely theoretical literature is included in Part I.

Prominent among this literature is 'Adaptation to what and why?' by Barrie Pittock and Roger Jones (Chapter 4), which elaborates on the nature of the climate change threat and explains why adaptation is necessary. The chapter also suggests some priorities for adaptation (developing countries and tropical regions) and begins to map out an agenda for future research on adaptation (identify the limits of adaptation or the point beyond which adaptation becomes impractical or prohibitively expensive). While this question has a theoretical ring to it, the authors are driven by very practical considerations. As the authors suggest, the chapter is a contribution to the development of an adaptation science that can underpin and guide future policy.

Barry Smit and colleagues' paper (Chapter 5) is complementary to Pittock and Jones's contribution. It adopts a broader view of adaptation and extends the debate into considerations of the actual process of adaptation: how does adaptation occur? Where and by whom are adaptation decisions made? How are adaptation choices evaluated? And what adaptation is actually likely to take place and can this be foreseen? The paper has been hugely influential and many of its ideas reappear in the Intergovernmental Panel on Climate Change Working Group II's contribution to the 2001 Third Assessment Report, which has had an even broader sphere of influence.

These theoretical elaborations of adaptation have continued to expand. The concept is now larger and more complex than in its early formulations. On one level, this expansion of understanding is satisfying, but on another level the actual practice of adaptation has been slow to take off, and the international policy negotiations on adaptation still remain far short of a satisfactory agreement in terms of practical steps. The last chapter in Part I, by Ian Burton (Chapter 6), attempts to establish a bridge between theory and practice. It argues that the level of adaptation to current climate is in deficit. There is an immediate and urgent task to address the growing losses from atmospheric extremes. The adaptation deficit continues to grow while theory expands and negotiations on the development of a coherent adaptation regime with adequate funding under the UNFCCC proceed at a distressingly slow pace.

Adaptation, Vulnerability and Resilience

As the concept of adaptation has grown in richness and complexity it has come to be closely associated with the ideas of vulnerability and resilience. Hence, any discussion about adaptation theory must also include exploration of the related concepts, vulnerability and resilience, included in Part II: Adaptation, Vulnerability and Resilience. Each of these concepts has its own unique community of practice and research, which have all contributed to the development of an adaptation science. The selected papers have important perspectives for adaptation scientists, each describing the related concepts in relation to adaptation.

Susanna Davies's 1993 paper (Chapter 7) still carries important messages: coping strategies are not the same as adaptation; too much coping implies that livelihoods are not sustainable; and short-term responses can ultimately lead to depletion of assets, which can lead to increased vulnerability to hazards. If people are forced to continuously cope, then they are dealing with chronic problems. Davies says this should be a warning that there needs to be a radical reappraisal of the requirements of people's livelihoods in marginal areas. This message is important for those seeking to build adaptation onto existing coping responses in marginal areas, where the limits to adaptation may instead be met.

Chapter 8, by Jesse Ribot, Adil Najam and Gabrielle Watson, dates from 1996, and is excerpted from a book based on contributions to the International Conference on Impacts of Climate Variability and Sustainable Development in Semi-Arid Regions held in Brazil in 1992. The chapter introduces the concept of vulnerability and places it in a context of climate variability, marginal livelihoods and development. The authors unpack vulnerability, noting that acting to reduce vulnerability now will be valuable regardless of how climate changes in the future. In this regard, they point out the importance of understanding and addressing the socio-economic and political factors that determine vulnerability, and underscore the need to address these factors, rather than just their symptoms. The chapter is also useful in discussing the distinction between climate variability and change, the important conceptual differences, and builds on the discussion from Chapter 7 regarding responses to normal variability vis-à-vis responses to changed variability (i.e. climate change).

Following on this discussion, Mick Kelly and Neil Adger's 2000 paper (Chapter 9) highlights a number of the same issues, but emphasizes more explicitly the relationship between vulnerability and adaptation. They underline the important point that 'adaptation is facilitated by reducing vulnerability', which is frequently, and detrimentally, inverted in modern discourse. In the reversed view that 'adaptation reduces vulnerability' is the implication that vulnerability is something superficial that is related only to the impacts of climate variability or change. However, this shows that the terms of the relationship continue to be of relevance, and thus Kelly and Adger's paper remains apt. Further, contrary to other papers which seek solutions through international agreements and help to poor countries through their national governments, Kelly and Adger's paper targets people faced with climate events that threaten their daily lives and livelihoods.

In their 1996 paper on resilience, John Handmer and Stephen Dovers (Chapter 10) contribute not only a solid discussion about the concept, but also set out a three-class typology of resilience. While they do not specifically apply their analysis to climate change it is clear that from the perspectives of ecology and risk, institutional change is needed to facilitate the required flexibility to cope with uncertainties and unanticipated situations that are common to climate change and other environmental threats. Their typology demonstrates a spectrum of possible responses to hazards and shifts in states: resist change; change marginally; or adapt. They argue that the range of responses is necessary, but suggest that institutions often do not look beyond one type. A discussion about the role that resilience plays in ecological risk highlights the historical development of the concept, which has been so important to the adaptation discourse. Further, the paper discusses the role of risk research and risk management, two elements that have also been important in shaping adaptation science.

Adaptation and Disaster Risk

One of the reasons that climate change is a concern is its role in increasing disaster risk. Disasters are far more visible than incremental changes in climate, which may develop so slowly that they are scarcely detectible within one generation. Thus, disasters have played an important role in bringing climate change to the general public. From a practitioner and policy perspective, it has been argued that adaptation to climate change should include adaptation to climate variability and extremes. This has generated a recognition of a commonality of interests among those specialists and those agencies concerned with adaptation to climate change and those charged with the reduction of disaster risk. However, there are a number of challenges facing the building of such a bridge.

Part III: Adaptation and Disaster Risk captures aspects of the linkages between adaptation science, and scholarship and practice on disaster risk reduction. The dialogue between the two has been limited but is growing, with a number of dedicated researchers and practitioners who are driving enhanced communication, collaboration and conceptual synergies. A meeting organized in 2002 by the United Nations Development Programme (UNDP) on 'Integrating Disaster Reduction and Adaptation to Climate Change' also attempted to bridge the gap between adaptation and disaster risk reduction. Numerous constructive papers were contributed, and more interest was raised. But the growing number of voices has not been able to offset the slow movement from talk to action on creating stronger linkages. Further efforts are under way, and the next years should see further elaborations on ways to operationalize the relationship. Identifying papers for this section was less intuitive than for the other sections, and reflects the dearth of literature specific to these linkages.

In Chapter 11 John Handmer makes the point that the field of natural hazards has much to offer the emerging adaptation science in terms of policy experience and research output. Hazards policy has previously put the predominant emphasis on the hazard as the cause of risk, rather than on vulnerability as the main driver of risk. Handmer suggests that this attitude has been echoed in adaptation efforts, where emphasis needs to be placed on addressing the factors that determine vulnerability to climate change, rather than putting blame on climate change and avoiding responsibility for our lifestyles, political choices and poor governance. Although the political importance of climate change has grown significantly since the publication of the chapter in 2003, the discussion about the relative (un)importance of both climate change and disaster risk in developing countries serves as an important reminder that other priorities lie before adaptation and mitigation of greenhouse gas emissions in most of the world.

The summary of the 2002 UNDP meeting (Chapter 12) provides a good overview of the areas for possible integration of adaptation and disaster risk reduction and some explanation as to why integration has not been successful to date. The meeting brought together some of the most influential thinkers on hazards who had also worked on adaptation, and resulted in a powerful statement about the needs for greater linkages between the two approaches to risk management. This document is reproduced here in part because we feel as editors that the messages are extremely relevant and did not get sufficient attention.

Marcus Moench (Chapter 13) provides us with another perspective on the linkages between adaptation and disaster risk reduction in his rich chapter on how to move from concepts to action on adaptation and hazards. This practical piece focuses on points of entry to 'respond to the underlying systemic factors limiting adaptive capacity or causing vulnerability'. Rather than looking at the differences between disaster risk reduction and adaptation climate change, Moench suggests a pathway for integrating adaptation and disaster risk reduction under one common approach.

Adaptation and Development

There is a wide range of views about where action on adaptation should be situated for management purposes. One view is that adaptation should be addressed exclusively within the context of the climate change issue, and managed and supported through the processes of the UNFCCC. An alternative view is that adaptation requires a much broader approach. This is couched in the conviction that adapting to climate change and other environmental, social and economic threats is or should be an integral part of the development process. In policy terms this translates into a debate between those who favour a focus on the impacts of climate change as a responsibility of those countries who have historically contributed most to the present concentrations of greenhouse gases in the atmosphere, as opposed to those who are less concerned with the matter of responsibility and would prefer to focus on human development, the support for development and the mainstreaming of adaptation into development planning. Part IV: Adaptation and Development, brings together some thoughts on the implications of adaptation for developing countries.

Adaptation will in all likelihood continue to be addressed both through the provision of finance and technology, as set out in the Convention process, and the usual channels of bilateral and multilateral development assistance. The effectiveness of such programmes depends upon the capacity of donors and national governments and others to reach the places and communities where adaptive capacity is low and help is most needed. In a broad assessment of experience of rural development in response to extreme weather, drought and the Green Revolution, Robert Kates (Chapter 14) offers some cautionary tales about the processes of adaptation, adaptation to adaptation, and failure to adapt. He argues that adaptation is often beneficial for some but can introduce new inequities. It is commonly the poor who are adversely affected or least helped by development, suffering displacement, division of their resources and degradation of their environments. Kates concludes that if the global poor are to adapt to global change it is critical to focus on poor people and not on poor countries.

This argument is taken a step further by Neil Adger and colleagues (Chapter 15), who focus on the need to develop and strengthen adaptive capacity. Enhanced capacity is needed to cope with climate change both at the local scale of natural resource management and at the scale of international agreements, and both have to compete with other priorities and other sustainable development objectives. This highlights an important aspect of adaptation, namely the trade-offs and choices that society and individuals will have to confront in preparing for a changing climate. Changing crops now in anticipation of a changing climate may help adapt for a drier climate, but it may also reduce short-term productivity, income and food security. This is a reality that adaptation policies, projects and strategies have to face.

An answer to this problem, according to Saleemul Huq and Hannah Reid (Chapter 16), is to mainstream climate change adaptation into all aspects of development. An important requirement to facilitate this is additional financial resources. The several international funds under the Convention and Kyoto Protocol are described together with suggestions for their more effective deployment. As this paper is from 2004, it does not benefit from the developments regarding the Adaptation Fund, which is now nearly operational, with the Global Environment Facility serving as the secretariat and the World Bank as a trustee of the Fund on an interim basis, through an overseeing operational body, the Adaptation Fund Board, composed of members from developing and developed countries. However, the chapter provides useful reflections on the important dynamics of funding for developing countries to respond to climate change.

The debate about the role of climate change impacts in development is also addressed by Karen O'Brien and Robin Leichenko (Chapter 17). They argue that the rapid increase in the processes of globalization in the 1990s contemporaneously with the recognition of the impacts of climate change have created a situation of 'double exposure'. Their examination of the effects of this double exposure across regions, by sectors, and from the perspective of social groups and ecosystems shows that the distribution of 'winners' and 'losers' can be substantially different from that which might be expected from a consideration climate change impacts alone.

Adaptation and Climate Change Policy

Throughout the assembled texts in this book one theme persistently appears and reappears, namely the tension between adaptation and mitigation as the focus of response to climate change. In the early years of the UNFCCC, interest in adaptation was overwhelmed by concern about the need to reduce greenhouse gas emissions and stabilize atmospheric greenhouse gas concentrations. Proponents of adaptation faced two obstacles that were attributed to adaptation: reducing the apparent need for mitigation; and playing down the urgency for action. For one, 'adaptationists' were distrusted because their proposals seemed to undermine the need for mitigation. Critics felt that belief in the potential value of adaptation would soften the resolve of governments to grasp the nettle of mitigation and thus play into the hands of the fossils fuel interests and the climate change sceptics. In addition, because climate change was popularly perceived as a gradual process, adaptation was not considered urgent as there would be time to adapt when climate change and its impacts became manifest. These views dominated in the mid and late 1990s. They have now changed in large part because science has established more firmly that climate change is happening and is accelerating. In the latest round of political negotiations initiated by the Bali Roadmap and Action Plan of December 2007, adaptation is identified as one of the four main pillars on which the new agreement will rest, together with mitigation, technology and finance.

Some of the consequences of the early misplaced emphasis on mitigation were examined by Roger Pielke Jr. (Chapter 18). It has been analysis like this that has slowly turned the tables so that now, in 2009, adaptation is getting the attention that circumstances necessitate. This paper is particularly useful as it documents the attitudes and perceptions about adaptation prevalent in the 1990s. He underlines that on their own, mitigation responses will not be effective in reducing the expected adverse effects of climate change.

Continuing the mitigation–adaptation theme, Lisa Schipper (Chapter 19) provides an overview of the conceptual history of adaptation in the UNFCCC process. The paper responds to calls that adaptation had been the 'forgotten' element of climate change policy, as described by Pielke, and digs to the roots of the adaptation–mitigation dichotomy. Even with new developments, including the UNFCCC Nairobi Work Programme and the Bali Roadmap, the chapter's point stands relevant: the framework set out by the existing climate change treaty does not enable vulnerability reduction, but rather only targets the impacts of climate change and reducing greenhouse gas emissions, and will thus never be able to adequately support a process of effective and long-term adaptation.

One path towards such adaptation policy is described by Ian Burton and colleagues (Chapter 20). This chapter provides a stocktaking of past approaches and research, so-called 'first-generation'. The chapter discusses how information on impacts and adaptation was initially sought to help inform the calculation and the debate about the required amount and rate of mitigation. In other words, adaptation was seen in the climate context and not in the development context. The chapter describes the emergence of the development perspective and presents a framework for the development of climate adaptation policy.

Funding for adaptation has been another recurring theme throughout both scholarship and policy discussions on adaptation. Recently, there has been recognition of the need for much more information about the exact costs of adaptation. Previous assumptions that adaptation could come into play slowly and as needed have now been replaced by a greater sense of urgency and by recognition that anticipatory adaptation can be more efficient, not only in terms of cost. In 2007 the Secretariat of the UNFCCC commissioned a team of consultants to examine and estimate the future costs on both mitigation and adaptation. An extract from the report (Chapter 21) presents estimates of the future costs of adaptation to 2030 in five sectors (agriculture, forestry and fisheries; water supply; human health; coastal zones; and infrastructure). While a number of issues are omitted (adaptation to extreme events and disasters) and estimates for the included sectors are admittedly incomplete, the report provides a sense of the magnitude of costs associated with adaptation, and outlines some of the limitations of estimating adaptation costs. It is concluded that in the year 2030, several tens of billions of dollars of additional investment will be needed for adaptation to the adverse impacts of climate change. This information provides policymakers with a sense of the urgency of the problem posed by climate change, and underlines the importance of integrating climate change concerns into all planning, whether it be infrastructure, education or health care.

Reference

White, G. F. (1945) *Human Adjustment to Floods*, Department of Geography Research Paper no 29, University of Chicago, Chicago, IL

Part I

Adaptation Theory

2

Deconstructing Adaptation ...
and Reconstructing

Ian Burton

A is for Aardvark and Adaptation

In the space of the past five years or so 'adaptation' has been taken out of the epistemological waste basket where it has lain as an unacceptable, even politically incorrect idea. The concept now seems well on its way to becoming fashionable and in danger of being overused. It will be most useful if it is defined in a precise enough way (like 'inflation' or 'productivity'), without a pedantic insistence on too restricted a use. The best hope is that it can gain an acceptable and permanent place in the lexicon, and be deployed in support of some important components of global change research. The downside is that it may be overwhelmed by its own popularity and all meaning slowly leak out of it.

Deconstruction

The *Shorter Oxford* gives two examples of the use of the word *adapt*: 'The structure of the outer ear is adapted to collect and concentrate the vibrations' and 'A comedy adapted from the French'. The word can be applied both to biological and to socio-cultural processes: historically this has been the source of much trouble. The intellectual baggage from the word's use in evolutionary biology that it brings into the social realm has hitherto undermined its value. The phrase 'social Darwinism' springs quickly to mind, and shades of Herbert Spencer suggest a return to a social philosophy of survival of the fittest and a laissez-faire approach to social ills. It also carries a deterministic inevitability encouraging passive acceptance, to the extent of fatalism. The dodo bird was doomed by its inability to adapt.

Such considerations have helped to keep adaptation out of circulation in polite society. When climate change rose briefly to the top of the environmental agenda in 1988 the 'A' word could no longer be kept in the closet. It quickly became clear that the reduction of greenhouse gas emissions on a fast enough track to prevent all climate change was a most difficult, if not impossible task. The technological obstacles to moving away from fossil fuels, and the economic and political costs of trying to do so rapidly could not be wished away. Not could the insistence of developing countries on their rights to develop without the imposition of additional constraints imposed by the North.

At the negotiations for the United Nations Framework Convention on Climate Change and the scientific meetings that preceded it 'adaptation' was cautiously taken out of the box, examined, and inserted apologetically into the text in five places. The evident weakness of the concept of adaptation (passive, resigned, accepting) contrasted sharply with the strength of the word limitation (active, combative, controlling).

Nevertheless adaptation was to be feared for at least two reasons. Talk of adapting to global warming could make a speaker or a country sound soft on limitation. While there was a growing sentiment in the negotiations in favour of going slowly on the establishment of targets and schedules for the reduction of greenhouse gas emissions, it was dangerous to talk too enthusiastically of adaptation.

There was also another reason for caution. It was not clear how effectively some of the developing countries would be able to use adaptation as a bargaining tool (as it turns out so far, not very effectively). The Framework Convention does promise some financial assistance. 'The developed country Parties ... shall also assist the developing country Parties that are particularly vulnerable to the adverse effects of climate change in meeting costs of adaptation to those adverse effects.' (Article 4, Section 4).

Reconstructing Adaptation

The Framework Convention on Climate Change was an important route through which adaptation began to find its way back into use. It was not enthusiastically welcomed but it could no longer be ignored. In Canada two other events followed in quick succession. A Climate Adaptation Branch was established in the Canadian Climate Centre of the Atmospheric Environment Service, and a Task Force on Adaptation to Climate Change and Variability was established under the Canadian Climate Program.

The resulting report (Smit, 1993) made a number of recommendations for the strengthening of adaptation research, and an enhanced capacity is now being created in the Environmental Adaptation Research Group. At the same time other countries. Including the US, have moved to build their own capacity for adaptation research, and new efforts are under way in Canada, the US and the United Nations Environment Programme to support climate impact and adaptation studies in developing countries.

Further insight into the way in which adaptation is now going to be deployed can be gained from an appreciation of the wider context, beyond the realm of climate change. These are social, environmental and intellectual.

Many people, not only in Canada, realized that the capacity of governments to provide care from cradle to grave is overstretched and in some instances close to exhaustion. The growth of social security programmes has helped to create major debts while at the same time encouraging a sense of dependency. Over a few decades community-mindedness, social resilience, spontaneous and innovative caring, self-help and self-reliance have all been diminished and undervalued. Now governments are realizing this and are preparing to make major changes in direction. This does not represent a return to social Darwinism, but it does require the revival and strengthening of social adaptive capacity.

This recognition of the limited power of government to ward off all social ills is paralleled by a similar admission of inability to control the environment. This is most readily seen in the rising scale of natural disasters. It is also seen in the high cost of environmental regulations, and in their relative ineffectiveness despite costly efforts at policing and enforcement. The command-and-control approach often went hand in hand with a hubris that allowed environmental degradation to occur in the belief that it could always be corrected afterwards, as in the react-and-cure approach so much criticized in the Brundtland Report.

The new environmental policy of sustainable development is much more demanding. It prescribes an anticipate-and-prevent approach in which society adapts to environment in such a way as to prevent rather than cure. Hence the moves against clear-cutting, against emissions (zero tolerance), and in support of biodiversity.

Similarly adaptation to climate change is not advocated as an excuse to avoid or delay limitation of greenhouse gas emissions. It is a much more profound recognition that human beings can protect themselves from damage by living harmoniously with their atmospheric environment. Over past centuries, with much less powerful technology at their disposal, people have adapted well to climate. The very fact that people have been able to settle, make a livelihood and develop culture and high social orders in climatically extreme environments, from the arctic to the hot deserts, speaks volumes about the capacity for adaptation.

Climate varies much more rapidly over space than over time, and the capacity for adaptation has been well demonstrated. With modern technology this capacity can be greatly enhanced. Surely this is why research into the identification, development and assessment of environmental adaptation is increasingly valued? The use of natural resources and environment in a sustainable way requires an adaptive mindset and requires research.

In an intellectual context new interest in adaptation has been quietly developing in those pioneers that have led the way from catastrophe theory into non-linear and self-organizing systems and notions of complexity. Part of this intellectual ferment, especially that associated with the Santa Fe Institute in New Mexico, is focusing attention on the adaptive behaviour of systems 'at the edge of chaos'. These thought experiments (usually aided by large-scale computers!) involve mathematical economists, physicists and evolutionary biologists, as well as a wide range of other disciplines.

There is hope for the development of new understanding of both biological and social evolution. This would come from research that rejects the assumption that adaptation is an unfortunate necessity for survival in a hostile and variable environment. Rather, it posits that adaptation is an inherent and positive element in biological and social systems which is both responsive and creative.

In a keynote speech delivered on 25 November 1993 the Honourable Sheila Copps said, 'we face the need to adapt to new circumstances. Because the world itself is changing.' In the *Liberal Plan for Canada, Creating Opportunity* (The Red Book), the Right Honourable Jean Chretien writes, 'The key to our success as a nation has been our ability to face change, adapt to it, and prevail.' Clearly adaptation is on the political agenda. It also warrants a central place in global change research.

Reference

Smit, B. (ed) (1993). 'Adaptation to Climatic variability and change: Report of the Task Force on Climate Adaptation', Canadian Climate Program, Environment Canada and University of Guelph, Ottawa

3

Human Adaptation to Climatic Variability and Change

John Smithers and Barry Smit

Introduction

Among the various manifestations of global environmental change the issue of climatic changes, particularly those related to atmospheric accumulation of 'greenhouse gases', has attracted the attention of the research community, decision-makers and the public. It is now widely accepted that human-induced changes in climate are likely in the 21st century if not apparent already, and that they will have or are having significant implications for societies and economies (Houghton et al, 1996; Watson et al, 1996; Bruce et al, 1996). International concerns over global climatic change and its consequences are reflected in the 1992 United Nations Conference on Environment and Development (UNCED) which developed the Framework Convention on Climate Change (UNFCCC) signed by 154 countries, many of whom now have national plans to address the 'problem' of climate change.

Yet there still exist widely differing views, both among and within countries, about the nature and severity of the climate change problem and what, if anything, should be done about it. In some industrialized countries there is a strong lobby for limitation of greenhouse gases; but there are also those who argue that the problem is not sufficiently serious or certain to warrant the costs such policies would entail, and that human activities will adapt in any event (differing views on the adaptability of human systems to climatic changes are discussed in: Lave and Vickland, 1989; Nordhaus, 1991; Chen and Kates, 1994). This latter view reflects an abiding confidence in human ingenuity and adaptability. In recent years the notion of human response or 'adaptation' has been more widely incorporated in the climate change debate (Rosenberg et al, 1989; Stern et al, 1992; Goklany, 1995).

Notwithstanding this growing recognition of the role of human agency, relatively few impacts studies have considered the actual processes of adaptation to climate in detail. Most often, it is simply assumed that systems will either adjust or not adjust to the scenarios specified (Kaiser et al, 1993; Rosenberg et al, 1993; Rosenzweig and Parry, 1994; Delcourt and van Kooten, 1995). Some empirical studies have focused more directly on adaptation (e.g. Glantz and Ausubel, 1988; Liverman and O'Brien, 1991; Smit et al, 1996), but there has been little explicit examination of how, when, why and under what conditions adaptations actually occur in economic and social systems. Such information is now sought by decision-makers and planners attempting to assess the significance of future climatic change, and to prepare for it.

One reason for the assumption-based treatment of adaptation in climate impact assessment is that both the concept and appropriate analytic approaches are still evolving. Although adaptation is frequently referred to in scholarly work and policy discussions related to climate, there is no common understanding of what is meant by the term, let alone how the prospects for adaptation might best be analysed. This chapter summarizes the policy relevance of adaptation to climatic variability and change, synthesizes concepts of human adaptation from existing literature, and develops a general framework for classifying and understanding adaptation to climatic stresses.

Climatic variability and change

Climate is inherently variable, and these variations exist at many spatial and temporal scales. Some of this variability, such as from season to season, is well understood. But much of it, including variations over years, decades, centuries and millennia, is poorly understood and largely unpredictable (Hare, 1991). Thus decisions in sectors or activities sensitive to climatic conditions are usually taken under uncertainty or risk, sometimes employing statistical probability, but more often on the basis of heuristics.

Uncertainty is compounded by the fact that human activities in the past and present are causing the Earth's climate to change. While there is growing acceptance that the Earth's climate, particularly mean temperature, is changing, there are differing views on the rate and ultimate magnitude of these changes. Also uncertain are the potential variations about these new mean conditions (Hare, 1985; Katz and Brown, 1992). Regardless of changes in variability, the difference in the anticipated timeframe of global climate change and the planning horizon of most human activities means that any longer-term changes will be felt via differences in the frequency and magnitude of extreme events.

The perceived importance of these changes, and the impetus they provide for human response, depends to a large extent upon the forecast rate and magnitude of change and the assessed degree to which human activities will be disrupted (Parry et al, 1996). However, it also depends on the availability and attainability of response options. In some countries, especially in the developing world, longer-term global climate change is simply not a priority issue given its long time horizon and inherent uncertainty. In those regions where droughts, floods, cyclones and other perturbations associated with the current climate regime bring on massive loss of life, human dislocation and suffering, the challenges of coping with today's climatic variations do not allow the luxury of contemplating possible climate changes several decades hence (Glantz, 1992; Chen and Kates, 1994). Thus in many instances, those regions where response is most urgently needed may also be where it is most constrained (Meredith et al, 1991; Parry et al, 1996). Societies and economies function and evolve within this capriciously fluctuating climatic environment, and examples of adaptation to climate are all around us. They are embedded in building construction, transportation systems, agriculture, leisure activities and many other elements of daily life which are somehow structured or designed to take account of prevailing climatic conditions. Thus the concept of adaptation relates as much to current climatic variability as it does to long-term climatic change.

Adaptation to climate does not occur in isolation from the influence of other forces, but instead occurs amid a complex set of economic (micro and macro), social and institutional circumstances which establish a location-specific context for human–environment interactions. In effect, there are many 'non-environmental' factors which impede or mediate change in human systems (e.g. Lewandrowski and Brazee, 1993; Shackley and Wynne, 1995), and consequently there are also examples of 'maladaptation' to climate such as the construction of dwellings in flood plains or the planting of moisture–sensitive crops in drought-prone areas. Such maladaptations are driven largely by non-climatic forces and serve short-term human goals, but often with attendant costs on individuals, communities and society. In the developed world such costs are often treated as simply 'the cost of business' whereas in the developing world the human and ecological consequences of such maladaptations are often more severe (e.g. Haque, 1995).

Adaptation to climate is relevant to both long-term global climate change and to current variability in climatic conditions. In the case of global climate change, adaptation is important as an essential ingredient of any estimate of impacts and as one of the possible response options. For current variability, an improved understanding of individual and societal adaptation not only provides insights for estimating future adjustment, but also helps address current problems of sustainable development in light of variable and uncertain environments.

Adaptation, impacts and policy responses

The main elements of the climate change issue are summarized in Figure 3.1. Changes in climate are expected to have ecological and socio-economic impacts. Concern about these results in consideration of two broad families of response: limitation or mitigation of greenhouse gas emissions so that climate does not change so much or as fast, and adaptation to the changes and their impacts. This structure, which distinguishes impacts, mitigation and adaptation, is reflected in the activities of the Intergovernmental Panel on Climate Change, the Framework Convention on Climate Change, and in the national programmes of many countries including Canada.

While adaptation to climate is most commonly thought of as one of the public policy response options to the concerns about climate change, it is also an integral part of the impacts component because impacted sections or regions will adapt spontaneously (quite apart from policy) to changes in environmental conditions. Estimates of impacts of changing climate are sought for two related reasons: (a) to provide, with information on climate change itself, a basis for assessing the overall severity of the problem, and (b) to provide a benchmark (the 'do nothing' option) for evaluating the pros and cons of potential response strategies. The science of assessing human impacts of climate change is still developing (Carter et al, 1994). For the most

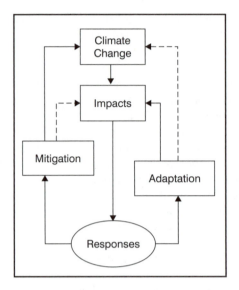

Figure 3.1 *Responses to climate change and impacts*

Source: Smit, 1993

part, studies have focused on particular scenarios of future climate, essentially representing instantaneous changes in average conditions. Typically, the studies have not considered transient effects or variability and have assumed little or no adaptation to the changed conditions (IPCC, 1996; Smit et al, 1996). However, it is extremely unlikely that social and economic systems would simply collapse in light of climatic changes. Instead, some analysts have assumed that systems will simply adapt spontaneously to a changed environment (Tobey, 1992; Bruce et al, 1996). Unfortunately, we have little basis to support or refute either the 'no adaptation' or the 'full adaptation' assumption. Without a better appreciation of the adaptations which would occur as a matter of course, we will not have credible assessments of impacts. Thus, an understanding of the spontaneous or autonomous processes of adaptation (CAST, 1992; Carter et al, 1994) is necessary for the evaluation of both the climate change problem and the merits of alternative response options.

It is increasingly accepted that the basic decision facing governments and society is not whether to pursue limitation or adaptation strategies, but rather how to combine these approaches to minimize future change and to adapt to the changes which are now under way (Burton, 1994). Concern that the accelerated rate of human-induced changes in climate may outpace the adaptive mechanisms in natural and socio-economic activities is prompting efforts to plan for possible changes and to promote adaptation (Bruce et al, 1996). Similarly, there is growing interest in identifying public policies and institutional arrangements which currently impede adaptation to environmental conditions, with a view to removing such impediments to adaptation.

Quite apart from the longer-term climatic change issue, there is also merit in policy consideration of adaptation to existing climatic variation and uncertainty. Limits to our current levels of adaptation are demonstrated by losses and damages associated with extreme events such as droughts, floods and unseasonal frosts (Burton, 1994; Niederman, 1996). Such events continue to result in economic losses, and in extreme cases, human suffering, in spite of a growing arsenal of technological and managerial response options. In some cases, social and economic systems may actually be becoming so thoroughly adapted to political, cultural and economic stimuli that they are effectively decoupled from the natural environments in which they operate. As a consequence they are increasingly vulnerable to climatic extremes regardless of the future climate scenario (Dovers and Handmer, 1991; Downing, 1992; Blain et al, 1995). The costs of these damages are borne, at least in part, by society at large. Payouts by governments for drought, hurricane and flood relief alone amount to billions of dollars over recent decades (Wheaton and Arthur, 1990; Smit, 1994; Chagnon, 1996). Thus, there is already a public policy rationale for attention to adaptation as part of a comprehensive response to climatic change and variability.

Conceptual Foundations of Adaptation

While the concept of adaptation to environment is an increasingly important component of the global climate change question, its origins and development lie elsewhere. According to Winterhalder (1980) its roots are in the natural sciences, namely population biology and evolutionary ecology. Here adaptation refers to genetic characteristics which allow individual organisms to survive and reproduce in the environment they inhabit. Successful adaptation leads to the continued viability of a species or ecosystem, but not necessarily the survival of individuals within a population (Slobodkin and Rappaport, 1974). Ecological concepts such as tolerance, stability and resilience have been used to describe the propensity of biological systems to adapt to changed conditions, and the processes by which these changes occur (Holling, 1973; Marten, 1988).

The adaptation paradigm has also found wide application in the social sciences, where these ecological principles have been applied in the context of human–environment interaction (e.g. Timmerman, 1981; Hawley, 1986; Clark, 1989; Dovers and Handmer, 1991; Stern et al, 1992). Social and economic systems, and individuals within them, can and do adapt to changing environmental circumstances. An important distinction, however, is that humans possess the ability to plan and 'manage' adaptation. Thus, while the responses of biological systems to perturbations are entirely reactive, the responses of human systems are both reactive and proactive, incorporating environmental perception and risk evaluation as important elements of adaptation strategies. Additionally, human systems may adjust in pursuit of goals other than mere species survival, for example, to enhance quality of life or to exploit perceived opportunities.

Social science applications and extensions of the adaptation paradigm are visible in many scholarly fields including human and cultural ecology, natural hazards research, ecological anthropology, cultural geography, ecological economics and, more recently, climate impact research. Applications in these various fields of enquiry have led to some distinct interpretations of the concept of adaptation. For example, some models of cultural adaptation focus on the collective behaviour of systems, while others emphasize the role of individuals as decision-makers (Hardesty, 1983). Denevan (1983) argues that there are two levels of cultural-ecological behaviour, a cultural or institutional level which is shared, and an individual level which may differ from the broader collective condition. Thus adaptation, and our understanding of it, is sensitive to scale.

Researchers have considered the capacity of human systems to adapt to global climate change using notions of vulnerability and resilience to understand the potential for damage or loss (Kasperson et al, 1991; Burton, 1991). Drawing on concepts from ecology, it is argued that the nature of response to environmental perturbation is influenced by the degree to which systems are affected, which in turn is described by various properties of the system itself. Some analysts, working from the perspectives of political economy, have examined these characteristics in the context of social, economic and institutional forces that cause some regional variations in exposure to risk (Watts, 1983; Palm, 1990; Chiotti and Johnston, 1995).

Another approach evident in adaptation research focuses on characteristics or properties of the environmental perturbation. These are believed to affect both the degree of impact and the nature of responses. These event characteristics relate primarily to the severity or magnitude of an occurrence, and to its temporal properties such as probability of occurrence (Kates, 1985; Burton et al, 1993). Consideration of such properties of climate is largely absent in most climate impact analyses where the focus is on average conditions for climatic parameters which are assumed to be of key importance for the activity system in question.

Finally, several approaches draw distinctions on the basis of certain characteristics of the action which is undertaken in response to an environmental stimulus. For example, distinctions are made on the basis of whether responses are structural (i.e. technological) or behavioural, whether they are undertaken before or after extreme events occur, and whether they are intended to buffer and sustain current activities or facilitate change to new types and patterns of activity (Meyer-Abich, 1980; Timmerman, 1992; Burton et al, 1993). Some commentators have even drawn distinctions between adaptation strategies on the basis of their availability and ease of implementation. This view contrasts actions which are readily available and implemented within existing structures and institutions with major technological innovations and transformations of institutions, economies and policy regimes (Clark, 1985; Crosson and Rosenberg, 1991).

Do all human responses to environmental change qualify as adaptations? Some definitions distinguish adaptations from other forms of response. For example, Glantz (1992) differentiates adaptation from other responses according to the time of response relative to the time of a perturbation: adaptation refers to the unplanned reactive response to an event or condition which has already been experienced, as distinct from what is termed 'mitigative' actions which seek to avoid negative impacts through anticipatory actions. Burton et al (1993) distinguish adaptations from adjustments according to the persistence of the response, where short-term measures are not deemed to be adaptations. Bryant (1994) has applied concepts from the adoption of innovations paradigm and the field of strategic planning to draw a similar distinction between actions of a managerial nature, which are short lived and consistent with existing management practices, and strategic or entrepreneurial actions which result in a fundamental change in the nature or structure of an activity system. The latter type of change is deemed to be adaptive.

Adaptation has even been cast as one of the emergent properties of human systems. In this interpretation, adaptation or adaptability is not something which is determined by various ecological properties of systems, it is itself regarded as an ecological property of a system. For example, Riebsame (1991) contrasts adaptation with resilience, where the former is equated with change and the latter with entrenchment.

These distinctions demonstrate the wide usage of the concept of adaptation by researchers interested in global environmental change, but they also paint a somewhat confused picture. The notion of human or societal adaptation to the natural environment is not just a product of our current interest in global environmental change. It has been widely, if not uniformly, applied in many scholarly fields with interest in society–environment interactions. Rather than attempting to invent yet another interpretation of adaptation we propose to synthesize several of these existing concepts into a framework to categorize the many different types and forms of human responses to environmental conditions. Our intent is not to judge whether given actions are definitively adaptive or otherwise, but to clarify and make explicit the dimensions of the adaptation issue via a framework or 'anatomy' of adaptation and a model of human responses to climatic variations.

A Framework for Understanding Climate Adaptation

Adaptation involves change in a system in response to some force or perturbation, in our case related to climate. Analyses of adaptation can begin by addressing the attributes of the perturbation, the characteristics of the impacted system, or the nature of the response. These foci represent the major dimensions of adaptation and together serve as a framework for adaptation research (Figure 3.2). Drawing on the various interpretations and distinctions noted earlier, we develop each of these dimensions in turn and, in the case of responses, offer a schema by which adaptation strategies can be classified and described.

Climatic Disturbances

Previous work has identified several characteristics of events, or environmental parameters, which influence the impact of environmental disturbances on society, and hence the pace and the nature of adaptation. Much scholarly effort has been devoted to assessing effects of sudden shocks (e.g. floods, tornados). The use of the term 'event' in the context of climate change includes not only short-term extremes, but also a number of other conditions. Climate change may involve gradual changes in long-term average conditions, greater variability within the range of 'normal conditions', changes in the types of extreme events which are possible or probable, changes in the frequency, magnitude, and distribution of extreme events, or most likely some combination of all

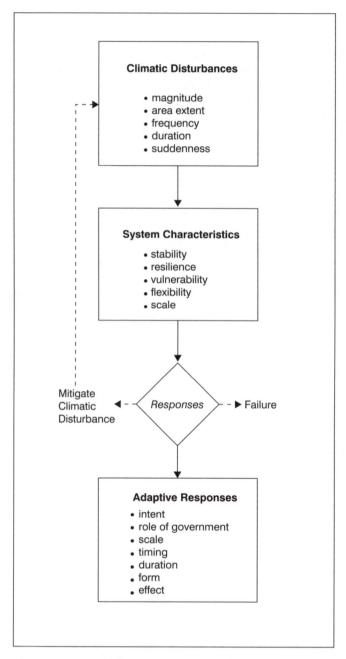

Figure 3.2 *Dimensions of adaptation*

Source: Smit, 1993

of these (Hare, 1991). Consequently, climate change may be regarded as an event in its own right, or as a broader phenomenon within which particular climatic conditions will occur at some changed frequency and/or magnitude. The latter interpretation is most relevant to the following characteristics of disturbances, which are drawn largely from the work of hazards researchers.

The scale of events, both in terms of magnitude and areal extent, is relevant in any consideration of environmental impact and adaptation. Events of greater *magnitude*, especially those which exceed a system's 'absorptive capacity', are expected to have a greater impact on human systems, and thus would be expected to necessitate and accelerate adaptation. A related consideration is the spatial scale or *areal extent* over which climatic events or changes are experienced. While some disturbances may be highly localized, others may occur over large areas. The types of responses selected for localized or concentrated events may differ greatly from strategies which might be directed toward conditions that are more widespread across regions.

The temporal properties (frequency, duration and suddenness) of climatic events have significant potential to influence adaptation. The *frequency* of occurrence of climatic events of a given type and magnitude is a potentially influential factor in the human adaptation process. Here we recognize the importance of cumulative impacts and their role in adaptation. Increased frequency of harmful climate events will also heighten decision-makers' awareness of climate and perception of risk (Schweger and Hooey, 1991). In an agricultural region, for instance, single-year dry spells may evoke a very different type of response than a series of repeated dry years (Blain et al, 1995). The combined influence of frequency and magnitude affect the time needed for system recovery after perturbation and the time available before another stress is added to the system.

Similarly, the *duration* of the stress is noteworthy. Climate events which extend over a comparatively lengthy period of time should, *ceteris paribus*, be expected to inflict greater damage or disruption to human activities than will like conditions of shorter duration. Events of longer duration may also permit greater opportunity for adaptation during the occurrence than do events of shorter duration. For example, the curtailment of municipal water use during problematic dry spells represents an adjustment during a climatic stress.

A third temporal attribute, *suddenness*, describes the speed of onset of particular climate conditions (or of climate change itself). For example, some climate-related perturbations such as flooding may vary in their rate of onset. While a steady rise in water levels as a result of seasonal rains or snow melt usually provides some opportunities for 'preventive' forms of adaptation, a flash flood necessitates a different set of responses. In contrast, global climate change is a slow and incremental process and provides a different context for adaptation altogether.

A final point on sources of disturbance. Human systems respond not only to environmental conditions but also to economic, technological, institutional, political and social conditions – and changes in any of these domains are capable of perturbing human systems. The relative importance and role of these potential influences on adaptation and their synergistic effects with climate are not well understood (Smit et al, 1996). Estimations of both impacts and human responses would be improved through a better accounting of this issue.

System Characteristics

Several system characteristics have been identified, especially in ecology and general systems theory, as affecting the ability of environmental systems to sustain shocks or stresses. More recently, the fields of thermodynamics and chaos theory have contributed to a growing understanding of the behaviour of complex systems in the face of largely unpredictable environmental stresses (Kay and Schneider, 1994; Funtowicz and Ravetz, 1994). While much of this research is oriented toward natural systems, these concepts are well suited to work on human systems. Understanding the prospects for adaptation to environmental change requires some qualitative understanding of the sensitivity of the impacted region or system (IPCC, 1996). The following properties or characteristics of human activity systems (see Figure 3.2) seem especially relevant to this task.

The *stability* of a system refers to its ability to remain fixed and unchanged in the face of disturbance; the less the fluctuation in response to climatic events, the more stable the system. Thus the notion of stability pertains to the steadfastness of systems and the lack of fluctuation about an equilibrium state (Holling, 1973; Kay, 1991). The related notion of *resilience* refers to the 'elasticity' or recuperative power of a system, its ability to recover or rebound, or the degree of impact that can be experienced without moving the system away from a previous equilibrium and onto what Kay and Schneider have termed a new attractor (Kay and Schneider, 1994). For example, a farming system which produces a consistent yield over time through resistance to impact or quick recuperative power is stable, while an agricultural system which can sustain itself despite large fluctuations in yields or prices etc. is resilient. Both attributes prompt thinking about thresholds of tolerance in human systems. Indeed, one of the most important and most difficult research challenges lies in identifying these impact thresholds.

The notion of *vulnerability* refers to the degree to which a system or 'exposure unit' may be adversely affected by a hazardous event (Timmerman, 1992; Carter et al, 1994). In the context of climate change, vulnerability relates to the susceptibility of a human or economic system to the disruption, wound or damage resulting from environmental change. At present there are efforts to identify regions of the Earth that are inherently and acutely vulnerable to environmental perturbation, and thus at greater risk of disruption (Kasperson et al, 1991; Meredith et al, 1994). It is noteworthy that efforts to reduce vulnerability have often been pursued via attempts to increase the stability of socio-economic systems. While most would agree that a stable system is appealing, at least on intuitive grounds, it is held by some that past efforts to buffer and entrench human systems, while making them more resistant to damage from small to medium scale (i.e. routine) perturbations, have also had the effect of increasing their vulnerability and loss potential in the event of major environmental perturbations (Bowden et al, 1981; Riebsame, 1990). The IPCC (1996) concluded that vulnerability depends upon economic circumstances and institutional infrastructure, and that systems are typically more vulnerable in developing countries where economic conditions and institutional arrangements are less favourable.

Flexibility refers to the degree of manoeuvrability which exists within systems or activities. It has been suggested that, in responding to current environmental stress and uncertain future conditions, the preservation of future options is as important as the immediate response (Goldberg, 1986; Waggoner, 1992). Some socio-economic activities, sectors or regions are more flexible, and therefore more adaptable, than others. For example, it might be argued that specialized monoculture farming systems, found in many parts of Canada today, are less flexible, and therefore less adaptable, than were the smaller-scale diversified systems which preceded them because of their dependence on technology, capital and marketing structures.

Finally, the issue of system *scale* is fundamental to understanding human adaptation to environmental change. Human–environment interactions can be considered at the level of an individual (Smit et al, 1996), a community (Izac and Swift, 1994), a sector (Rosenberg, 1992), a region (Koshida et al, 1993) and so on. Yet, depending upon the scale at which a system is defined, a change may or may not represent an adaptation. For example, actions designed to sustain the viability of individuals in a system may actually retard the long-term adaptation of the system itself (consider the adaptation of a farmer versus a regional farming system). Such actions are sometimes referred to as maladaptations (Smit, 1993; Carter et al, 1994). Similarly, the losses to individuals may be regarded, at the more aggregate scale of regional economy of community, as an adaptation of the system generally.

Adaptive Responses

The characteristics of human systems and the nature of climatic events together establish conditions which stimulate and influence responsive adjustments. The third dimension of our framework focuses on the characteristics of adaptive responses themselves. One set of possible responses addresses the environmental change itself, with activities to prevent or mitigate climatic disturbances (Figure 3.2). Although (as noted as the outset) these actions are important in the climate change issue, they are beyond the scope of this chapter. Another type of change or response in the human system is the outright collapse or failure of some activity (Figure 3.2). While we have not attempted to rigidly specify conditions that represent adaptation, we suggest that this type of change cannot be considered an adaptation – at least at the scale where the collapse has occurred. For our purposes, adaptation involves change, in response to environmental conditions, which maintains, preserves or enhances viability of the system of interest.

Previous research and commentary has highlighted several distinctions among the varied components of the environmental adaptation issue. This scholarship forms the basis for a schema to describe, differentiate and understand adaptation strategies. Human adaptive responses can be summarized according to seven broad attributes (Figure 3.2).

Adaptations can be distinguished according to their *intent*, i.e. whether they occur incidentally or are the result of purposeful decisions (e.g. Waggoner, 1992; Smit, 1993; Carter et al, 1994). Adaptation is often regarded as being the outcome of a conscious and deliberate response to stress, with a commonly understood (though often not stated) goal. However, it is sometimes the case that actions taken for some other purpose have the unintended or incidental effect of reducing the impact of climatic events. For example, a policy decision to discourage housing developments close to shorelines in order to preserve access and aesthetics may also incidentally make those developments less vulnerable to climate-induced changes in water levels and storms.

The question of intent often becomes less clear when attention shifts from adaptations by individuals to system-wide adaptations. A regional agricultural system subjected to a series of droughts may experience changes with a reduction in the number of operators and an increase in the debt load of farmers generally. This system-wide adaptation results not so much from a conscious decision or goal to reduce operators and increase debt, but rather this is what transpired over time given the prevailing climatic conditions and the economic and policy situation. However, it is more often the case that adaptation is the result of a deliberate attempt to avoid, or respond to, the impacts of an environmental change. Purposeful adaptation to climate implies an assessment of climatic conditions and a decision to act, i.e. something done with the intent of responding directly to climate. The resulting plan of attack represents an adaptation strategy.

The second broad basis for distinguishing responses concerns the *role of government.* Adaptation strategies may be distinguished according to whether they are undertaken privately, via public agency, or through a combination of both (Tobey, 1992). In support of private sector adaptation, there are those who possess an abiding faith in the ability of individuals and societies to adapt to environmental change on their own from a suite of existing options and emerging or anticipated technological developments. Agriculture is one sector in which it is often assumed that many of the necessary adaptations, especially in the industrialized world, will occur privately or autonomously (Waggoner, 1992) (and given the impressive track record of industrialized agriculture in the area of crop productivity over the past 50 years this is not an altogether unwarranted assumption). Nevertheless, the role of government is an important one, both in an anticipatory planning sense and in a post hoc manner following environmental perturbations.

The potential roles of government in stimulating, imposing, and/or underwriting adaptation initiatives may be direct or indirect. In some cases governments directly implement the adaptive actions, for example, modifying port facilities or water control structures, building standards, Coast Guard practices, emergency responses, land-use controls, disaster relief, and so on. Direct actions of governments may be proactive or reactive, and may be undertaken over the short term or long term. In addition, governments may also adopt an indirect supporting function via research, information dissemination, public education, or the provision of financial or other incentives. We might even question the true autonomy of private sector adaptations, especially those that derive from publicly funded research and development.

For many situations, the distinction between public and private adaptation is not clear. A very common case is where the adaptive behaviour is undertaken by private individuals or companies, but there exist government policies or programmes which influence the nature or prospect of adaptation. Thus, the degree to which farmers will take risks with climatic variations depends in part upon government policies and programmes in crop insurance, price supports, drought relief, and international trade agreements which promote certain types of production (Smit, 1994; Burton, 1994; Reilly et al, 1994). In some cases government programmes can impede adaptation; for example, subsidies to produce specific crops may discourage changes to other crops which are less vulnerable to climatic variability (Smit, 1994).

Adaptation to climate can range from local to national levels, and it is possible to distinguish both the type of adaptation and various adaptation strategies on the basis of both spatial and social *scale*. Some forms of climate adaptation may be in response to localized risks from particular types of perturbation and thus are site-specific in nature (e.g. the threat to certain vulnerable coastal communities from increased sea levels or storms). Other types of adaptation may occur at broader scales because of changes in regional climatic conditions and their effects on economic sectors such as tourism, forestry or agriculture. Still other adaptations, and the strategies developed to achieve them, may occur at a national scale; for example, the potential modification of national building code standards to reflect the increased (or reduced) stresses posed to buildings and infrastructure from an altered climate. Of course, there is also the prospect of international adaptation, such as agreements to accommodate 'environmental refugees' or to address climate-induced food shortages or distribution problems.

It is also important to consider the social scale of adaptation. At one extreme is adaptation to climate change on the part of individual decision-makers. In agriculture, for example, such individual adaptation might involve farm-level changes such as the modification of tillage practices under a new soil climate regime. In cases where sufficient numbers of individuals within a system have adapted to an existing or anticipated perturbation to have fundamentally changed the character of the system, adaptation may be described at the aggregate, or societal/community, scale as well.

A further distinguishing feature concerns the *timing* of adaptive responses. Adaptations may be classified according to their time of initiation relative to the time of the climatic perturbation. Incidental adaptation, by its nature, usually occurs either during or after a climatic event. In contrast, purposeful adaptations vary in their timing. Strategies designed to compensate loss or alleviate suffering caused by a climatic event may be conceived and initiated before, during or after the occurrence (e.g. disaster relief funding). Some forms of adaptation will require considerable lead time, especially where major institutional changes or innovations are required. These would need to be devised and implemented well in advance of the expected event.

Adaptations may also be distinguished according to their *duration*. Some adaptations may be very short-term responses to climatic conditions, while others may remain for many years, and essentially become parts of modified or transformed human systems. Elsewhere this has been the basis of a distinction between short-term 'adjustment' and more permanent 'adaptations' (Parry, 1986; Burton et al, 1993). The notion of duration also relates to the common distinction between tactical and strategic adjustments in an activity system. Tactical actions comprise the daily or weekly management decisions made in response to an immediate stimulus. Strategic actions represent more enduring, often anticipatory, actions which are made with a view to the longer term and which alter the nature of the activity in some way. To illustrate, in agriculture a tactical adaptation may be a change in the rate of fertilizer application in one growing season whereas a strategic decision could involve change to a different type of farming entirely.

The final two attributes proposed in the framework are those related most closely to the nature of adaptations themselves, namely the form that they take, and their intended effect. While some changes are quintessentially technological or 'engineered' in *form*, others are more behavioural and/or institutional. This distinction is apparent in many of the adaptation strategies already noted in this section. Technological responses to climate change and variability involve attempts to 'manage' the impact of environment on humans, whether it be in the construction of new coastal infrastructure, the design of energy-efficient housing, or the development of drought-resistant cultivars. In these types of approaches technology is used both to buffer against climate's effects and to facilitate a change in society's practices under an altered climate.

Behavioural adaptation strategies include those activities which are undertaken through modification of the practices of individuals, groups or institutions. It is likely that many adaptations to climate change will not involve the use of a 'technological fix', but will instead be achieved through adoption of new practices, shifts to different types of activities or locations, and the restructuring of institutional arrangements. While some of these adaptations may take the form of tactical 'fine tuning' responses at a micro-scale (e.g. changing the time of planting for field crops, amending zoning by-laws etc.), behavioural adaptations may also be evident and important in more dramatic ways, such as broad-scale shifts to new types of regional economic activity or changed patterns of human habitation. Indeed, such adaptations are the basis of many assumed responses in analyses of climate impacts.

Adaptation strategies, regardless of their type, may also differ according to their intended outcome or *effect*. A fundamental distinction exists between strategies or actions which seek to buffer a system from an environmental perturbation, and those which attempt to facilitate a shift or evolution to a new state. The former aims to protect current activity in the face of environmental change (enhancing stability), while the latter might be described as changing to meet altered conditions (enhancing resilience or flexibility). An example of buffering strategies in agriculture might be the development of irrigation systems to sustain existing types of production in the face of possible climate-related water shortages. A non-structural example of buffering is the use of various insurance or compensation packages to spread the financial costs of climate-related losses. While the 'first order' impacts of the event are experienced, those most directly affected are protected or buffered against its economic consequences. Hence, the impetus for other types of adaptation is reduced or removed altogether. In contrast, change-oriented adaptation strategies are directed toward a deliberate transformation of the status quo. Such strategies attempt to alter the nature of human activity in order to achieve a desired or better 'match' with environmental conditions. Consider, for example, a programme of land-use planning which freezes development in areas likely to be adversely affected by climate change, or which protects areas which are likely to become important in the migration of ecosystems, or which encourages changes in land-use practices to reduce vulnerability to certain conditions.

Thus the framework outlined in Figure 3.2 identifies dimensions and attributes by which adaptation to climatic change and variability can be systematically described and analysed.

Conclusion

Human adaptation to environmental change has been addressed in several disciplines, some of which are not well represented in climate impacts research to date. The resulting variety of terms, interpretations and assumptions is somewhat confusing, especially for those attempting to integrate across disciplines. This chapter has attempted to synthesize these concepts, and organize them in a comprehensive framework which identifies dimensions and attributes by which adaptation to climatic change and variability can be systematically described and analysed.

The framework accommodates three dimensions of adaptation to climate or other environmental stimuli: the nature of the disturbance stimulus, or force of change; the properties of the system which may influence its sensitivity; and the type of adaptation which is undertaken. Of course, there are feedbacks within and between the dimensions. For example, efforts to buffer an agricultural system from the effects of climatic variations, thus increasing its stability, may also affect other properties of the system such as its resilience, flexibility, and ultimately its vulnerability. Such adjustments also influence the nature of sensitivity to future variations in climate, and thus the type of adaptation taken.

The conceptual framework provides an organizing tool for continuing research on climate adaptation. Further research on adaptation would provide substance to the rather generic 'anatomy' of adaptation outlined in this chapter. Key gaps and information needs exist with respect to the forms which adaptations take, the conditions (or triggers) for adaptive action, and on the situations which influence the success or failure of adaptation strategies – including the institutional and economic forces which directly or indirectly promote or impede adaptation. Not only is such information essential for the development and promotion of adaptation strategies, it also provides direction for climate modelling, monitoring and impact assessment. Those attributes of climatic regimes to which human activities are sensitive are the ones for which data needs to be available for both research and decision-making.

Acknowledgements

This chapter draws upon material prepared for the Canadian Task Force on Climate Adaptation, sponsored by the Canadian Climate Program. The authors also acknowledge the support of the Environmental Adaptation Research Group of Environment Canada, the Social Sciences and Humanities Research Council of Canada, the Ontario Ministry of Agriculture, Food, and Rural Affairs, the Eco-Research Program of the Tri-Council Secretariat via the University of Guelph Agroecosystem Health Project and the Chair Program in Ecosystem Health.

References

Blain, R., Keddie, P. and Smit, B. (1995) *Corn Hybrid Selection Under Variable Climatic Conditions: A Case Study in Southern Ontario.* Department of Geography, University of Guelph, Guelph.

Bowden, M. J., Kates, R. W., Kay, P. A., Riebsame, W. E., Warrick, R. A., Johnson, D. L., Gould, H. A. and Weiner, D. (1981) The effect of climate fluctuations on human populations: two hypotheses. In *Climate and History. Studies in Past Climates and Their Impact on Man,* eds

T. Wigley, M. Ingram and G. Farmer, pp. 497–513. Cambridge University Press, Cambridge.

Bruce, J. P., Lee, H. and Haites, E. F. (1996) *Climate Change 1995: Economic and Social Dimensions of Climate Change.* Cambridge University Press, Cambridge.

Bryant, C. R. (1994) Approaches to the study of agricultural adaptation to climatic change at the farm level. In *Agricultural Adaptation to Climate Change: Workshop Proceedings,* eds M. Brklacich, D. McNabb and J. Dumanski. Department of Geography, Carleton University, Ottawa.

Burton, I. (1991) Regions of resilience: an essay on global warming. In *Defining and Mapping Critical Environmental Zones for Policy Formulation and Awareness,* eds T. C. Meredith, C. Marley and W. Smith, pp. 95–120. McGill University Department of Geography, Montreal.

Burton, I. (1994) Costs of atmospheric hazards. In *Proceedings of a Workshop on Improving Responses to Atmospheric Extremes: The Role of Insurance and Compensation.* ed. D. Etkin, pp. 1–11. Theme papers. Environment Canada, Toronto.

Burton, I., Kates, R. and White, G. (1993) *The Environment as Hazard.* Guilford Publications, New York.

Carter, T. R., Parry. M. L., Harasawa, H. and Nishioka, S. (1994) *IPCC Technical Guidelines for Assessing Climate Change Impacts and Adaptations.* World Meteorological Organization/ United Nations Environment Programme. University College London.

CAST (Council for Agricultural Science and Technology) (1992) *Preparing U.S. Agriculture for Global Climate Change.* CAST, Ames.

Chagnon, S. A. (ed.) (1996) *The Great Flood of 1993: Causes, Impacts and Responses.* Westview Press, Boulder.

Chen, R. S. and Kates, R. W. (eds) (1994) Global environmental change. Special issue. *World and Food Security* 4(1).

Chiotti, P. and Johnston, T. (1995) Extending the boundaries of climate change research: a discussion on agriculture. *Journal of Rural Studies* 11(3), 335–350.

Clark, W. C. (1985) Scales of climate impacts. *Climatic Change* 7, 5–27.

Clark, W. C. (1989) The human ecology of global change. *International Social Science Journal* 41, 316–345.

Crosson, P. R. and Rosenberg, N. J. (1991) Adapting to climate change. *Resources* 103, 17–20.

Delcourt, G. and van Kooten, G. C. (1995) How resilient is grain production to climatic change?: sustainable agriculture in a dryland cropping region of Western Canada. *Journal of Sustainable Agriculture* 53(3), 37–48.

Denevan, W. (1983) Adaptation, variation and cultural geography. *Professional Geographer* 35, 399–406.

Dovers, S. R. and Handmer, J. W. (1991) Uncertainty, sustainability and change. *Global Environmental Change* 2, 262–276.

Downing, T. E. (1992) *Climate Change and Vulnerable Places: Global Food Security and Country Studies in Zimbabwe, Kenya, Senegal and Chile.* Environmental Change Unit, University of Oxford, Oxford.

Funtowicz, S. and Ravetz, J. (1994) Emergent complex systems. *Futures* 26, 568–582.

Glantz, M. (1992) Global warming and environmental change in sub-Saharan Africa. *Global Environmental Change* 2, 183–204.

Glantz, M. H. and Ausubel, J. H. (1988) Impact assessment by analogy: comparing the impacts of the Ogallala aquifer depletion and CO_2-induced climate change. In *Societal Responses to Regional Climatic Change: Forecasting by Analogy,* ed. M. H. Glantz, pp. 113–142. Westview Press, Boulder.

Goklany, M. (1995) Strategies to enhance adaptability: technological change sustainable growth and free trade. *Climatic Change* 30, 427–449.

Goldberg, M. A. (1986) Flexibility and adaptation: some cues for social systems from nature. *Geoforum* **2**, 179–190.

Haque, C. E. (1995) Climatic hazards warning process in Bangladesh: experience of and lessons from the 1991 April cyclone. *Environmental Management* **19**, 719–734.

Hardesty, D. L. (1983) Rethinking cultural adaptation. *Professional Geographer* **35**, 399–406.

Hare, F. K. (1985) Climatic variability and change. In *Climatic Impact Assessment: Studies of the Interaction of Climate and Society*, ed. R. W. Kates. Wiley, New York.

Hare, F. K. (1991) Contemporary climatic change: the problem of uncertainty. In *Resource Management and Development: Addressing Conflicts and Uncertainty*, ed. B. Mitchell, pp. 8–27. Oxford University Press, Don Mills.

Hawley, A. H. (1986) *Human Ecology: A Theoretical Essay.* University of Chicago Press, Chicago.

Holling, C. S. (1973) Resilience and stability in ecological systems. *Annual Review of Ecology and Systematics* **4**, 1–22.

Houghton, J. T., Meira Filho, L. G., Callander, B. A., Harris, N., Kattenberg, A. and Maskell, K. (eds) (1996) *Climate Change 1995: The Science of Climate Change.* Cambridge University Press, Cambridge.

IPCC (Intergovernmental Panel on Climate Change) (1996) *IPCC Second Assessment: Climate Change 1995.* Cambridge University Press, Cambridge.

Izac, A.-M. N. and Swift, M. J. (1994) On agricultural sustainability and its measurement in small-scale farming in sub-Saharan Africa. *Ecological Economics* **11**, 105–125.

Kaiser, H. M., Riha, S. J., Wilks, D. S. and Sampath, R. (1993) Adaptation to global climate change at the farm level. In *Agricultural Dimensions of Global Climate Change,* eds H. M. Kaiser and T. E. Drennen. St Lucie Press, Delray Beach.

Kasperson, R. E., Turner, B. L., Kasperson, J. X., Mitchell, R. C. and Ratick, S. J. (1991) A preliminary working paper on critical zones in global environmental change. In *Defining and Mapping Critical Environmental Zones for Policy Formulation and Public Awareness,* eds T. C. Meredith, C. Marley and W. Smith. Department of Geography, McGill University, Montreal.

Kates, R. W. (1985) The interaction of climate and society. In *Climate Impact Assessment: Studies in the Interaction of Climate and Society,* eds K. W. Kates, J. H. Ausubel and M. Berberian, pp. 3–36. Wiley, Chichester.

Katz, R. W. and Brown, B. G. (1992) Extreme events in a changing climate: variability is more important than averages. *Climatic Change* **21**, 289–302.

Kay, J. (1991) A nonequilibrium thermodynamic framework for discussing ecosystem integrity. *Environmental Management* **15**, 483–495.

Kay, J. and Schneider, E. (1994) Embracing complexity: the challenge of the ecosystem approach. *Alternatives* **20**(3).

Koshida, G., Mills, B. N., Mortsch, L. D. and McGillivray, D. (1993) *Climate Sensitivity, Variability, and Adaptation Issues in the Great Lakes–St Lawrence Basin: A Reference Document,* Climate Adaptation Branch Bulletin No. 93-06. Atmospheric Environment Service. Environment Canada, Downsview, Ontario.

Lave, L. B. and Vickland, K. H. (1989) Adjusting to greenhouse effects: the demise of traditional cultures and the cost to the U.S.A. *Risk Assessment* **9**, 283–291.

Lewandrowski, J. K. and Brazee, R. J. (1993) Farm programs and climate change. *Climatic Change* **23**, 289–302.

Liverman, D. M. and O'Brien, K. L. (1991) Global warming and climate change in Mexico. *Global Environmental Change* **1**, 351–364.

Marten, G. (1988) Productivity, stability, sustainability, equitability and anatomy as properties for agroecosystem assessment. *Agricultural Systems* **26**, 291–316.

Meredith, T. C., Marley, M. C. and Smith, W. (eds) (1991) *Defining and Mapping Critical Environmental Zones for Policy Formulation and Public Awareness.* Department of Geography, McGill University, Montreal.

Meredith, T. C., Moore, C., Gartner, L. and Smith, W. (1994) *Canadian Critical Environmental Zones: Concepts, Goals and Resources.* Canadian Global Change Program Technical Report Series No. 94-1. The Royal Society of Canada, Ottawa.

Meyer-Abich, K. M. (1980) Chalk on the white wall: on the transformation of climatological facts into political facts. In *Climatic Constraints and Human Activities,* eds J. Ausubel and A. K. Biswas, pp. 61–92. Pergamon Press, Oxford.

Niederman, D. (1996) Storm warnings. *Report on Business Magazine,* pp. 84–94.

Nordhaus, W. (1991) To slow or not to slow: the economics of the greenhouse effect. *Economic Journal* 101, 920–937.

Palm. R. I. (1990) *Natural Hazards: An Integrative Framework for Research and Planning.* The Johns Hopkins University Press, Baltimore.

Parry, M. L. (1986) Some implications of climatic change for human development. In *Sustainable Development of the Biosphere,* eds W. Clark and R. Munn, pp. 378–407. Cambridge University Press, Cambridge.

Parry, M. L., Carter, T. R. and Hulme, M. (1996) What is a dangerous climate change? *Global Environmental Change* 6, 1–6.

Reilly, J. Hohmann, N. and Kane, S. (1994) Climate change and agricultural trade: who benefits, who loses?. *Global Environmental Change* 14(1), 24–36.

Riebsame, W. E. (1990) The United States Great Plains. In *The Earth as Transformed by Human Action,* eds B. L. Turner, W. C. Clark, R. W. Kates, J. F. Richards, J. F. Mathews and W. B. Myers, pp. 561–576. Cambridge University Press, Cambridge.

Riebsame, W. E. (1991) Sustainability of the Great Plains in an uncertain climate. *Great Plains Research* 1(1), 133–151.

Rosenberg, N. J. (1992) Adaptation of agriculture to climate change. *Climatic Change* 21, 385–405.

Rosenberg, N. J., Easterling, W. E., Crosson, P. R. and Darmstadter, D. J. (eds) (1989) *Greenhouse Warming: Abatement and Adaptation.* Resources for the Future, Washington.

Rosenberg, N. J. Crosson, P. R. Frederick, K. D. Easterling, W. E. McKenney, M. S. Bowes, M. D. Sedjo. R. A. Darmstadter, J. Katz, L. A. and Lemon, K. M. (1993) Paper 1. The mink methodology: Background and baseline. *Climatic Change* 24 (1–2), 7–22.

Rosenzweig, C. and Parry, M. L. (1994) Potential impact of climate change on world food supply. *Nature* 367, 133–138.

Schweger, C. and C. Hooey (1991) Climate change and the future of prairie agriculture. In *Alternative Futures for Prairie Agricultural Communities,* ed. J. Martin, pp. 1–36. University of Alberta, Edmonton.

Shackley, S. and Wynne, B. (1995) Integrating knowledges for climate change: pyramids, nets and uncertainties. *Global Environmental Change* 5, 113–126.

Slobodkin, L. A. and Rappaport, A. (1974) An optimal strategy of evolution. *The Quarterly Review of Biology* 49, 181–200.

Smit, B. (ed.) (1993) *Adaptation to Climatic Variability and Change: Report of the Task Force on Climate Adaptation.* Prepared for the Canadian Climate Program, Department of Geography Occasional Paper No. 19, University of Guelph, Guelph.

Smit, B. (1994) Climate, compensation and agriculture. In *Proceedings of a Workshop on Improving Responses to Atmospheric Extremes: The Role of Insurance and Compensation,* pp. 29–37, Theme papers. Environment Canada, Toronto.

Smit, B. McNabb, D. and Smithers, J. (1996) Agricultural adaptation to climatic variation. *Climate Change* 33, 7–29.

Stern, P. C., Young, O. R. and Druckman, D. (eds) (1992) *Global Environmental Change: Understanding the Human Dimensions*, National Academy Press, Washington, DC.

Timmerman, P. (1981) *Vulnerability, Resilience, and the Collapse of Society*, Monograph 1. Institute of Environmental Studies, University of Toronto, Toronto.

Timmerman, P. (1992) Why adaptation: a background paper prepared for the Canadian task force on climate adaptation. Unpublished manuscript.

Tobey, J. A. (1992) Economic issues in global climate change. *Global Environmental Change* **2**, 215–228.

Waggoner, P. E. (ed.) (1992) *Preparing U.S. Agriculture for Global Climate Change*. Council for Agricultural Science and Technology, Ames.

Watson, R. T., Zinyowera, M. C. and Moss, R. H. (eds) (1996) *Climate Change 1995: Impacts, Adaptations and Mitigation of Climate Change: Scientific-Technical Analysis*. Cambridge University Press, Cambridge.

Watts, M. (1983) On the poverty of theme: natural hazards research in context. In *Interpretations of Calamity*, ed. K. Hewitt, pp. 231–262. Allen & Unwin, Boston.

Wheaton, E. and Arthur, L. (eds) (1990) *Environmental and Economic Impacts of the 1988 Drought: With Emphasis on Saskatchewan and Manitoba*. Saskatchewan Research Council, Saskatoon.

Winterhalder, B. (1980) Environmental analysis in human evolution and adaptation research. *Human Ecology* **8**, 135–170.

4

Adaptation to What and Why?

A. Barrie Pittock and Roger N. Jones

Introduction

Adaptation to climate variability and change has been necessary for the continued existence of human and other species ever since life began. Climate varies on interannual, interdecadal and longer timescales, so that even within a supposedly 'constant' climate, spatial and temporal variations in the weather create conditions to which we must adapt or perish.

Natural ecosystems, and many species, survived throughout the Pleistocene (the last 2.5 million years), despite large amplitude fluctuations in climate and sea level over the glacial–interglacial cycles (Solomon and Cramer, 1993; Kinzie and Buddemeier, 1996). Nevertheless, ecosystem composition has changed, species have changed location, and some have evolved. In other words, while a limited numbers of species have become extinct, most have adapted.

Warming at the end of the last glaciation averaged about 1°C per thousand years (although there were much more rapid warmings over short periods in some localities such as the North Atlantic). Over the last hundred years warming has been about 0.5°C. Projected anthropogenic warming over the next 100 years is in the range of 0.8 to 4.5°C (including estimates for assumed constant sulphate aerosols) (IPCC, 1996, Chapter 6). Sea level rose, for thousands of years during the last deglaciation, by about 1m per century, but for short periods at 2 to 4m per century (Fairbanks, 1989). Estimates from tide gauge records suggest a rise of 10 to 25cm over the last 100 years, while projections suggest greenhouse warming may lead to a rise in the next 100 years of about 15 to 110cm (IPCC, 1996, Chapter 7).

Expected rates of temperature and sea-level rise in the 21st century are thus not in themselves unprecedented, but they will occur in a very different context, coming on top of a warm, high sea-level interglacial period, and accompanied by much higher atmospheric CO_2 concentrations which will affect the physiology of plant growth (Cure and Acock, 1986; Bazzaz, 1990; Gifford et al, 1996), and ocean chemistry (Buddemeier, 1994; Buddemeier and Fautin, 1996; Gattuso et al, 1999). Moreover, unprecedented numbers of humans have greatly modified 'natural' ecosystems and land cover, and placed many non-climatic stresses and limitations on nature and its capacity to adapt. In addition, humans value particular species and ecosystems as sources of food and fibre, for other ecosystem services, and for cultural and aesthetic reasons, so changes now have special human significance.

Impacts of such changes on both natural and socio-economic systems are bound to be extremely complex, with multiple stresses acting in concert. Extreme events play a major role, with both absolute levels of key variables and rates of change being critical. From a climatological viewpoint, it is relatively easy to create a long list of relevant variables (e.g. global change, air and sea temperatures, rainfall, magnitude and frequency of floods and drought, damaging wind speeds, groundwater and ocean salinity, photosynthetically active and ultraviolet radiation levels, sea level, tropical cyclone intensity and frequency, storm surge heights, turbidity of water, nutrient levels, etc.). However, at present it is difficult to quantify many of these variables in terms of either future absolute levels or rates of change. Moreover, many such changes will vary spatially and produce highly location-specific impacts. Thus single 'predictions' of global change impacts at some future date should not be expected, although much of the uncertainty may be manageable by undertaking sensitivity studies and risk analyses.

Why Adaptation?

The potential impacts of climate change need to be assessed through sensitivity and risk analyses to:

1 identify critical thresholds and risks, in a global assessment, to develop a greenhouse gas emission reduction policy under the terms of the United Nations Framework Convention on Climate Change (UNFCCC); and
2 identify and quantify risks and threats which may require a management or policy response at the local or regional level; i.e., to provide a guide to the need for and ability to adapt.

One purpose of impact assessment, therefore, is the global one of helping to decide the level of greenhouse gas concentrations which would lead to 'dangerous interference in the climate system' (UNFCCC, Article 2). While this is a global purpose, it can only be achieved scientifically by collating numerous local assessments, as critical thresholds are usually location-specific. A highly subjective value judgement must then be made as to whether the sum of these local impacts constitutes a 'dangerous' impact in some global sense. Our goal in such an exercise must therefore be to try to identify climate-related critical thresholds of absolute amounts (e.g. a maximum temperature for survival of a species, or minimum water flow in a river), or rates of change (e.g. a maximum rate at which coral might grow to keep up with sea-level rise), which give rise to unacceptable or 'dangerous' local situations and/or to a need for adaptation. This involves not only some assessment of the value of particular affected species, ecosystems or infrastructure per se, but of their function in relation to people; for example, as food or fibre sources, as tourist attractions, or as shelter, economic bases, or healthy environments. Impacts must, therefore, be assessed not only for affected elements in isolation, but in their context as part of a wider socio-economic system. *Adaptation is an essential part of this assessment, because adaptation will help to minimize adverse impacts, and maximize benefits. Any impact assessment which omits these processes will give misleading results, because thresholds for damaging climate change impacts will in fact be raised by adaptation.*

The second purpose of impact assessment, that of guiding local or regional management or policy, requires a similar type of local assessment, although perhaps less concerned with thresholds, and more with continuous adjustment or adaptation to enable better outcomes of unavoidable climate change in particular situations. *The aim of this type of local assessment thus becomes one of avoiding 'dangerous' local situations by identifying adaptation options and assessing them in order to determine which are most viable on the basis of least cost or greatest benefit.*

The adoption of protocols to reduce greenhouse gas emissions, under the terms of the UNFCCC, might be expected to reduce CO_2 concentrations, future warmings and sea-level rise, relative to those resulting from uncontrolled emissions (Bolin, 1998). Wigley (1998) has calculated the effect of the Kyoto Protocol with three assumptions for the post 2010 emissions from developed countries (Annex B countries in the Protocol), which are the only countries for which reductions are required under the terms of the Protocol. Relative to the baseline of the mid case IS92a emissions scenario, if the developed countries reduce their emissions by 5 per cent by 2010, as required by the Protocol, and then maintain constant emissions to 2100, the reduction in projected CO_2 concentration by 2100 is from about 710 parts per million by volume (ppmv) to about 665ppmv. The corresponding reduction in projected warming is about 0.15°C, or 7.5 per cent of the total warming, and that in projected sea-level rise is about 2.5cm or some 5% of the total. These results are for a 'best estimate' of the global climate sensitivity (discussed below).

The smallness of the effect of the Protocol is due to several factors:

1   Total emissions would have to be reduced by some 60–80 per cent to achieve a stabilization of greenhouse gas concentrations in the atmosphere (depending on the stabilized concentration level) because greenhouse gases have long lifetimes in the atmosphere (IPCC, 1996, p25).
2   Emissions from developing countries are still allowed to grow, and are likely to dominate the total emissions by the middle of the 21st century (Wigley, 1998).
3   There is a lag built into the climate system, largely due to the large heat capacity of the oceans, so the oceans will continue to warm long after stabilization of greenhouse gas concentrations (IPCC, 1996, p45).

Thus, even though the current policy response is primarily one of reducing greenhouse gas emissions, the reality is that this has not yet achieved major reductions in potential impacts over the 21st century. Therefore some significant impacts are to be expected, and adaptation to make the best of a changing climate is an essential response. If, in the process of assessing the options, some hard limits to adaptation are found, this would help identify 'dangerous levels' of greenhouse gases. This would contribute to the first of the purposes identified above as well as the second.

There are two types of adaptation to consider: 'autonomous' and 'planned'. Autonomous adaptation is what unmanaged ecosystems, or naive human systems (unaware of climate change predictions), would do by themselves, based on their experience of recent and current conditions (which might be changing). Planned adaptation is based on an awareness of anticipated climate change, and involves conscious human intervention in a system to protect or enhance its 'desirable' traits. (Such natural or engineered adaptations raise questions as to what is 'adaptation' and what is fundamental change.) In this context, impact assessments would explore the possibilities to see what management (planned adaptation) might accomplish, and what level of climatic change is unacceptable because it is impossible or too costly to adapt to. This requires, however, a better understanding of the likely environmental changes. Since firm predictions are not possible, this means quantification of the possibilities and risks. This chapter discusses the possibilities and suggests how the risks may be quantified.

Adaptation to What?

Actual and equivalent carbon dioxide changes

It has been recognized for over 100 years that the burning of fossil fuels and deforestation, are leading to increasing concentrations of carbon dioxide (CO_2) in the atmosphere. More recently, measurements of CO_2 concentrations of air sealed in bubbles in ice cores from Greenland and Antarctica have shown that during the previous two glaciations atmospheric concentrations were around 160ppmv, compared to about 270ppmv in pre-industrial times since the last glaciation, and some 360ppmv in 1995.

The Intergovernmental Panel on Climate Change (IPCC, 1992 and 1996) identified a broad range of possible future greenhouse gas and sulphur emissions (the latter lead to small sulphate particles in the lower atmosphere) in the absence of emission policies. Figure 4.1 shows the consequent range of scenarios for actual CO_2 concentrations, from the highest (IS92e) through a mid-range (IS92a) to the lowest (IS92c). For other greenhouse gases and sulphur, the IPCC scenarios contain a similar range of emissions, assuming a strong link between CO_2 and sulphur emissions because the burning of fossil fuels is the major cause of both. Thus most scenarios include increasing emissions and concentrations of both CO_2 and sulphur. However, with the

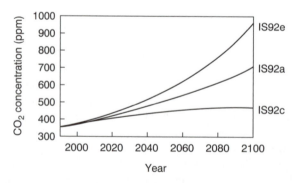

Figure 4.1 *The range of projected atmospheric concentrations (ppmv) of actual CO_2 based on the IPCC emissions scenarios, from 1990 to 2100*

increasing use of sulphur emission reduction technology, the future strength of this link is uncertain and sulphate concentrations may level out or decline. As greenhouse gases lead to a global surface warming, while sulphate particles lead to some regional cooling, a decline in sulphate concentrations would increase global warming.

Plant growth is stimulated by higher atmospheric CO_2 concentrations. This is well known from laboratory experiments, but less well determined in the field due to numerous complications (Cure and Acock, 1986; Bazzaz, 1990). CO_2 concentrations also affect ocean chemistry, and thus coral reefs (Buddemeier and Fautin, 1996; Gattuso et al, 1999). For these reasons it is important to clearly distinguish between the concentration of actual CO_2 and that of 'equivalent CO_2', which is often quoted. 'Equivalent CO_2' concentration is the CO_2 concentration which would have the same radiative forcing effect in the atmosphere as the sum of the radiative forcings from all the greenhouse gases apart from water vapour. As shown in Figure 4.1, actual CO_2 concentration may well double pre-industrial values by about 2060. Equivalent CO_2 concentration is likely to double several decades earlier.

Global average warming: An ongoing process

Global average warming is a response to the increased radiative forcing due to increases in all greenhouse gases, including CO_2, methane, nitrous oxide and water vapour (this last depending on surface temperature, thus providing a reinforcing or positive feedback effect). Warming will be reduced, mainly in the northern hemisphere, by the direct and indirect effects of the shorter-lived sulphate particles (which vary regionally), scenarios for which are at least as uncertain as (and different from) those for CO_2.

All global climate models (GCMs) show warming in response to increased greenhouse gas concentrations, but the sensitivity varies considerably between models. Where the atmospheric CO_2 concentration is doubled and a new equilibrium climate is simulated, IPCC has recognized a range of global mean warmings from GCMs of between 1.5 and 4.5°C. This so-called 'climate sensitivity' is for a highly idealized situation used to compare models. In reality, CO_2 and other greenhouse gases are increasing gradually, leading to a 'transient' response of the climate system, with lags due to the large heat capacity of the oceans.

Figure 4.2 shows the upper, mid-range and lower limit scenarios for global warming up to 2100, based on the IPCC 1995 scenarios. The solid curves show the range of warmings predicted on the basis of the IS92e (high case), IS92a (mid case) and IS92c (low case) greenhouse emission scenarios, with assumed sulphur emissions varying in proportion to CO_2 emissions out to 2050 and then held constant. The dashed curves have the same greenhouse gas scenarios, but with sulphur emissions assumed constant at 1990 levels. With varying sulphur emissions, the lower limit at 2100 is about 0.8°C warming, and the upper limit 3.5°C. Constant sulphur emissions leads to a upper limit warming of 4.5°C, but no change in the lower limit. The IS92a greenhouse gas emission scenario, with the varying sulphur emissions and the 'best estimate' climate sensitivity, leads to a global average warming by 2100 of about 2.0°C.

When considering impacts and adaptation it is most important not to become fixated on any one time in the future, such as when pre-industrial CO_2 doubles (about 2060), or say 2100. Global average temperatures will continue to rise (as in Figure 4.2),

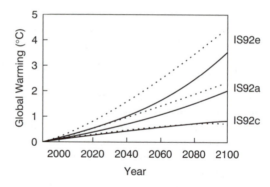

Figure 4.2 *Global warming scenarios from 1990 to 2100, in °C*

Note: Full curves are for scenarios with varying (i.e., increasing) sulphate aerosols, while dotted curves are for constant sulphate aerosols at 1990 levels. The upper pair of curves are for the IS92e greenhouse gas emission scenario assuming a climate sensitivity of 4.5°C, the middle pair are for IS92a with a climate sensitivity of 2.5°C, while the lower pair of curves are for IS92c with a climate sensitivity of 1.5°C.

associated patterns of climate change will continue to vary, and sea levels will continue to go up, as long as greenhouse gas concentrations continue to increase in the atmosphere. Indeed, temperatures and sea level may continue to rise for centuries after stabilization of greenhouse gas concentrations, due to long lags from the large heat capacity of the oceans (IPCC, 1996, p45). Thus adaptation that is adequate for the climate change or sea-level rise at 2030 or 2050 may not be adequate by 2070 or beyond. It is therefore necessary to consider evolving strategies of adaptation and to accept that investment in adaptation will not be a once-only necessity, but will need to be renewed as further change occurs. The world is entering a period of rapid (in geological terms) transient climate change, which will require not a one-off set of adaptations, but an ongoing adaptation process.

Hydrological cycle, rainfall intensity, floods and droughts

One consequence of global warming will be an enhancement of the hydrological cycle, due to higher temperatures leading to more evaporation. Rainfall must increase to maintain the global moisture balance, but this will not be uniform. GCMs tend to show that rainfall (or snowfall) will increase on average at high latitudes, but may increase or decrease in lower latitude regions (Whetton et al, 1996a), with fairly general increases in rainfall intensities; i.e., there will be proportionately more heavy falls (Fowler and Hennessy, 1995; Hennessy et al, 1997). This is illustrated in Figure 4.3, which shows simulated summer daily rainfall intensities over tropical Australia, under present ($1 \times CO_2$) conditions, and doubled CO_2 conditions (from Suppiah et al, 1998). While not occurring everywhere in the model simulations, this phenomenon is likely to lead to widespread increases in flood flows, particularly in small and urban catchments, and to increased soil erosion, turbidity and pollutant concentrations in runoff, and temporary reductions in salinity in estuarine situations (Larcombe et al, 1996).

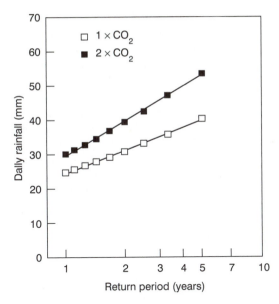

Figure 4.3 *Simulated summer daily rainfall intensities over tropical Australia*

Note: Simulated intensities of daily rainfall (mm per day of given return periods under 1 x CO_2 (open squares) and 2 x CO_2 (full squares) conditions, averaged over all 225 grid points in tropical Australia in simulations with the CSIRO regional climate model at 125km resolution, nested in the CSIRO slab-ocean GCM (from Suppiah et al, 1998). Data are for Dec.–Jan.–Feb. in a full 10-year simulation in each case.

Higher temperatures will also tend to reduce soil moisture and runoff due to increased evaporation, particularly during dry spells, and in regions where rainfall does not increase. It is therefore likely that in low and middle latitudes there will be increases in the frequency and/or severity of droughts. This will not be universal, however, and any changes in large-scale circulation features such as location of the Intertropical Convergence Zone (ITCZ), the South Pacific Convergence Zone (SPCZ), and the El Niño-Southern Oscillation (ENSO) will cause regional variations in the frequency and intensity of wet and dry periods.

Visible and ultraviolet radiation

Photosynthetically active radiation (PAR) is essential for the growth of terrestrial and marine plants. However, for corals, excess radiation (often associated with subaerial exposure and high temperatures) can lead to bleaching (Glynn, 1997), while ultraviolet radiation (UVR) may be deleterious to both terrestrial and marine plants (Teramura, 1983; Tevini, 1993; Shick et al, 1997). Levels of PAR and UVR exposure will be strongly affected by any change in cloud amount and optical depth, and air pollution. PAR reaching shallow water organisms in the ocean (Kleypas, 1997) could be reduced by rising sea level unless growth keeps up with sea level, and would be affected by changes in turbidity due to changes in wave action or in sediment or nutrient loading from terrestrial runoff.

UVR at the surface increases by about 1 to 2 per cent per 1 per cent decrease in column ozone amount in the atmosphere, depending on wavelength and the sloping path through the atmosphere (Lubin and Jensen, 1995). Stratospheric ozone is depleted by chemical reactions due to certain substances of recent human origin, principally chlorofluorocarbons, which are now regulated under the terms of the Montreal Protocol. These substances have already, or soon will peak in concentration, if the Protocol continues to be observed. Measurements indicate that in recent decades total column ozone amounts have decreased by 4 to 5 per cent per decade in mid-latitudes, and by more in polar regions, particularly over the Antarctic in spring. However, in the tropics (20°N to 20°S) no significant trends have been observed from 1979 to 1992 (Herman et al 1996), and none are expected (WMO, 1995).

Significant local changes could occur in both PAR and UVR due to systematic changes in cloud cover brought about by climate change. While cloud cover is simulated in climate models, large uncertainties remain about future changes in cloud amount and optical properties. At present we are not in a position to predict such changes, but they would certainly accompany any shifts in the position of the ITCZ and the SPCZ, or changes in ENSO.

Regional performance of climate models

IPCC (1996) statements suggest that agreement between GCMs on changes in precipitation at the regional (i.e., subcontinental) scale is poor. However, a comparison of regional simulations with five recent GCMs with surface mixed-layer-only oceans ('slab-ocean' models) and five GCMs with full deep ocean representation ('coupled-ocean' GCMs), reveals moderate agreement on the sign of change, except for parts of the southern hemisphere (Whetton et al, 1996a). Regional comparisons and validations of these models were made for their simulation of the present climate over the southern continents and the South Pacific by Whetton et al (1996b). The major differences in the southern hemisphere occur principally over Australia in summer between slab-ocean and coupled-ocean GCM results. These appear to be due to a simulated lag in warming of the Southern Ocean in the coupled-ocean models. Figure 4.4 shows the range of warmings, per degree warming at the Equator, for the five slab-ocean and five coupled-ocean models. The slab-ocean models show more warming in the Southern Ocean than at the Equator, but the coupled-ocean models show less. Recent analyses by Whetton and Long (CSIRO, unpublished) suggest that coupled model results tend toward the slab-ocean model patterns over hundreds of years after greenhouse gas concentrations are stabilized, due to the continuing warming of the Southern Ocean. Thus the patterns of climate change alter through time, not just the magnitude of change.

Even if the large-scale picture from the global climate model simulations was perfect, it would still be necessary to obtain more regional and local detail by 'downscaling' to the spatial resolution appropriate to local topography, coastlines and smaller-scale weather phenomena such as tropical cyclones, topographically forced rainfall, and sea breezes. This can be done by using regional climate models (RCMs), driven at their boundaries by global climate model output (a process called 'nesting'; McGregor et al, 1993). It can also be done by statistical downscaling, which relies on statistical

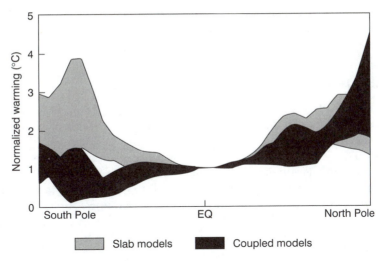

Figure 4.4 *North–south variations in simulated warming per degree warming at the Equator*

Note: The graph illustrates the difference between the slab-ocean GCM 'equilibrium' warmings and the transient warmings from coupled-ocean GCMs. This difference is largely due to the lag in warming of the Southern Ocean.

relationships between local weather or climate and the larger-scale climate features which the GCMs can simulate (Karl et al, 1990; Wilby and Wigley, 1997). There are, however, limitations on the use of statistical downscaling, as the method generally relies on long records of local climatic data to establish the statistical relationships. In many locations such records do not exist, and even where they do, they may not include variations as large as may occur under climatic change. Moreover, year-to-year variations in climate may be a poor analogue of climatic change, since the two are driven by different mechanisms.

The bottom line for studies of global change impacts is that for many locations, especially in developing countries, local simulations using nested modelling or other downscaling are not available. Nested modelling is available for North America, Europe, Australia, New Zealand and some parts of Asia, but not over most of the developing world. This is largely because many small developing countries do not have the resources to do it, and some key international agencies, with their understandable focus on 'capacity building', have been reluctant to fund relevant but non-indigenous 'scientific research'. Nevertheless, knowledge of the potential local impacts of global change, and the adaptations which may be necessary, are an essential part of the capacity of developing countries to cope with climatic change.

It should also be noted that GCMs will only provide a good basis for regional climate change scenarios in much of the developing world when they can model the ITCZ, the SPCZ and ENSO reliably. Many GCMs at present do a poor job with these major climatic features (Pittock et al, 1995). There is also a need to incorporate the direct and indirect cooling effects of sulphate aerosols (Meehl et al, 1996; Schimel et al,

1996) especially as they will have regionally varying effects. Here the problem is not only uncertainty about the modelling of these effects, but also large uncertainty about future scenarios of sulfur emissions, which will vary regionally.

Regional temperature and rainfall changes

The pattern of surface warming at 2070 relative to that at 1880, as simulated by the CSIRO coupled-ocean GCM (Mark 2 with Gent and McWilliams (GM) ocean mixing scheme – see McDougall et al, 1996, and Gordon and O'Farrell, 1997), is shown in Figure 4.5. This shows maximum warmings occurring at high latitudes in the North Atlantic and North Pacific near the southern limit of sea ice, and over the northern continents. In the tropical Pacific, warmings are a little greater in the presently relatively cool eastern section than in the west, although warmings are in excess of 2°C throughout. Warmings are least in the Southern Ocean due to the large thermal lag. This result is typical of coupled model results, as can be seen from Figure 4.4.

These results suggest that significant changes might be expected in conditions affecting many temperature-limited phenomena, with a greater likelihood of reaching critical high-temperature thresholds in low latitudes, and of exceeding low-temperature thresholds in higher latitudes. In general, this may benefit crop production in higher latitudes, but have detrimental effects at low latitudes (Pittock, 1995; Watson et al, 1998). However, all the caveats mentioned above regarding uncertainties and

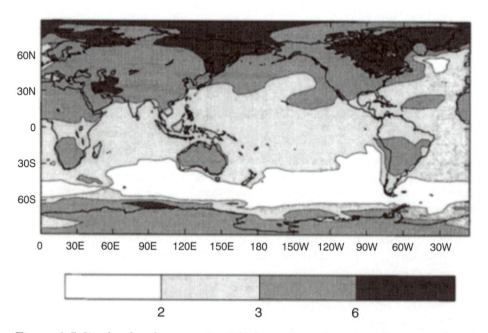

Figure 4.5 *Simulated surface warming (°C) from 1880 to 2070 derived from the CSIRO coupled-ocean GCM with the Gent and McWilliams mixing scheme, using the IPCC IS92a emissions scenario*

differences between GCMs (especially at the subcontinental scale) must be taken into account. Indeed, to understand effects on particular sub-regions, where impacts can be assessed, will generally require downscaling.

Changes in regional and local rainfall are even more uncertain and complex than for temperature. Not only will critical larger-scale features like the changes in the locations of the ITCZ and SPCZ, and their seasonality and year-to-year variations, and in ENSO, need to be determined, but changes in smaller-scale features such as tropical cyclones and orographic effects will also need to be assessed. Ideally, RCMs will be used, perhaps with double-nesting, to go to spatial scales of 10km or less, but it will be some time before this can be done for many locations, and it will be an expensive process. Rainfall changes will then need to be fed into simulations of changes in soil moisture, runoff, flood frequency etc., in order to assess impacts on various sectors and activities.

Sea-level rise

Global average sea-level rise is due to a combination of several effects (IPCC, 1996, Chapter 7):

- tectonic effects associated with land–sea movements and the shape of the oceans;
- thermal expansion of the ocean water;
- changes in water volume from melting or growing mountain glaciers;
- changes in the volumes of the grounded ice sheets of Greenland and Antarctica; and
- minor contributions from water storage in dams and changes to groundwater volume due to human activities.

Local sea-level rise is a combination of global mean sea-level rise, local effects due to subsidence and land–sea movement, and local mean variations of sea level from the global average (which are a function of currents, atmospheric pressure and other effects). For many impacts, even more important are local extremes of sea level due to time-varying effects such as ENSO, seasonally varying currents, inputs of less-dense fresh water from rainfall and runoff, and storm surges due especially to tropical cyclones.

Best IPCC (1996) estimates for global mean sea-level rise due to global warming are about 1 to 10mm per year, leading to rises of 5 to 25cm by 2030, 10 to 60cm by 2070, and 15 to 95cm by 2100 (see Figure 4.6) for varying sulphate aerosol scenarios, with upper limits a bit higher (110cm by 2100) if aerosols are assumed to remain constant. About half of the estimated rises are due to thermal expansion, with most of the rest due to melting of the mid- and low-latitude mountain glaciers. Antarctica was expected to have a small negative effect on sea-level rise, due to increased snow accumulation, but more recent results by O'Farrell et al (1997) suggest that the net effect of Antarctica in the 21st century may be close to zero. Greenland, which is warmer, may contribute a small amount to sea-level rise by some additional melting (Smith, 1999).

Estimates of each of the terms in the global sea-level rise equation are rather uncertain, with the thermal expansion component being particularly susceptible to downwards revision with improved modelling of the deep ocean circulation (England,

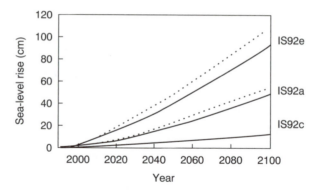

Figure 4.6 *Projected global mean sea-level rise from 1990 to 2100*

Note: The highest scenario assumes the IS92e emissions scenario, a climate sensitivity of 4.5°C, and high ice melt parameters; the lowest the IS92c emission scenario, a climate sensitivity of 1.5°C, and low ice melt parameters; and the middle scenario is for IS92a, a climate sensitivity of 2.5°C, and mid-value ice melt parameters. Full curves are for varying sulfate aerosols, while dotted curves are for constant aerosols at 1990 levels.

1995; McDougall et al, 1996). This is illustrated by recent estimates of the thermal expansion term by McDougall (CSIRO Marine Research) and colleagues, assuming the IS92a greenhouse gas emissions scenario for global warming, using the CSIRO coupled ocean-atmosphere model with two different mixing schemes in the ocean (the older iso-pycnal scheme, and the newer Gent and McWilliams scheme). The latter, which gives more realistic ocean features, reduces the thermal expansion term by about one third (Jackett et al, 2000). But as this is only about half of the total sea-level rise, this correction only reduces the best estimate total sea-level rise for 2100 by about one sixth, from 50 to about 42cm.

Sea level will not rise uniformly around the globe. This is due to different rates of warming in different parts of the global ocean, variations in atmospheric pressure on the ocean surface, and the effects of ocean circulations and varying wind stress changes (see for example, Gregory, 1993; Cubasch et al, 1994). Regional variations are typically up to ±50 per cent of the global average. More work is needed to verify the robustness of the spatial patterns, but they suggest that impact and adaptation assessments should not assume global uniformity.

In addition to mean sea-level rise, variations in time at particular locations are important. One major cause of interannual variability, especially in the tropical Pacific, is the ENSO cycle. During El Niño years sea level in the eastern tropical Pacific can be up to 50cm above that in La Niña years, and vice versa in the western tropical Pacific (Wyrtki, 1985). Smaller amplitude variations associated with ENSO also occur at places far removed from the tropics. As ENSO behaviour may change with global warming (see below), this may contribute to changes in the extended periods of local sea levels above or below normal, which can be important for aspects of coral reef biology including coral bleaching.

The other major contributor to variations in local sea level is the storm surge, especially due to tropical cyclones (Anthes, 1982; Konishi, 1995; Hubbert and McInnes, 1999). Depending on bottom topography and storm characteristics, such surges can add up to several metres to local sea level for periods of hours or days, and in addition these are associated with large and powerful waves which can damage reefs and transport debris across reef flats and lagoons. A temporary lowering of sea level is also possible with tropical storms, if they generate strong offshore winds. Thus changes in the climatology of storm surges may have major effects.

Tropical cyclones

Tropical cyclones, the generic term for non-frontal tropical low pressure systems, are variously called 'typhoons' (NW Pacific), 'hurricanes' (N Atlantic and NE Pacific) and 'severe tropical cyclones' (SW Pacific and SE Indian Ocean), when they reach wind speeds in excess of 33ms^{-1}. Such storms derive their energy from evaporation from the ocean and associated condensation in convective clouds near their centre (Holland, 1993).

Gray (1968, 1975) found that the frequency of tropical cyclone formation ('genesis') is related not simply to sea surface temperature, but to six environmental factors:

1   large values of low-level rotation ('relative vorticity') in the broad vicinity;
2   the Coriolis parameter (which is related to the rotation of the Earth, and requires that the location be several degrees of latitude from the Equator);
3   weak vertical shear of the horizontal winds (i.e., wind differences at different levels should not be large enough to disperse the storm);
4   high sea surface temperatures (generally above about 26–27°C) and a deep surface warm layer in the ocean;
5   a deep layer of relatively unstable air; and
6   lots of moisture in the lower and middle troposphere.

So warming of the sea surface, however suggestive it may be of more intense or more frequent tropical cyclones, is far from the whole story. Attempts to apply Gray's six variables to predict tropical cyclone genesis under different climatic regimes are so far inconclusive (Watterson et al, 1995), and an improved version is needed to account for climatic change.

There is controversy about the ability of GCMs and even RCMs, at relatively coarse horizontal resolution, to simulate reliably tropical cyclone genesis, paths and intensities (Lighthill et al, 1994; Broccoli et al, 1995; Henderson-Sellers et al, 1998) due to the complexity of tropical cyclones. Generally it is conceded that realistic intensities will only be approximated by simulations at resolutions of about 30km or finer. However, at coarser resolutions climate models do seem to be able to realistically simulate average tropical cyclone genesis regions and tracks (not that of individual storms in an operational sense) (Walsh and Watterson, 1997).

Genesis regions around Australia under $1 \times$ and $2 \times CO_2$ conditions as simulated by the CSIRO RCM at a resolution of 125km, nested in the CSIRO slab-ocean GCM show fairly realistic locations of cyclone genesis in the control case, and that the locations do not change significantly under the simulated $2 \times CO_2$ conditions. However, the same simulations show cyclone tracks extending further polewards (see Figure 4.7) in the $2 \times CO_2$ case. This is at least partly related to higher sea surface temperatures, which sustain the cyclone intensities longer (Walsh and Katzfey, 2000).

a

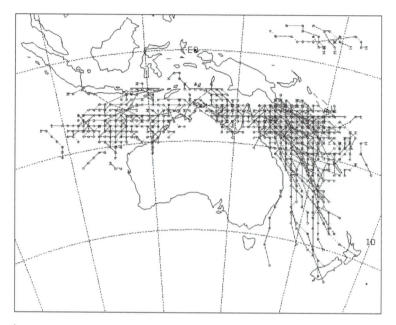

b

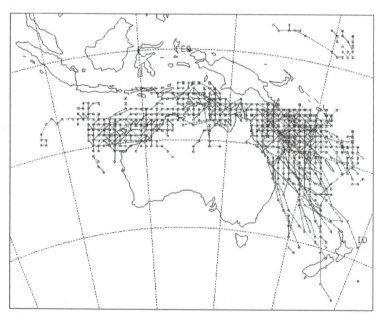

Figure 4.7 *Simulated tropical cyclone tracks under (a) $1 \times CO_2$ and (b) $2 \times CO_2$ conditions*

Note: Formation locations are marked with a cross, while circles indicate subsequent daily locations. Results were obtained using the CSIRO regional climate model at 125km resolution nested in the CSIRO slab-ocean GCM for 20 years in each case.

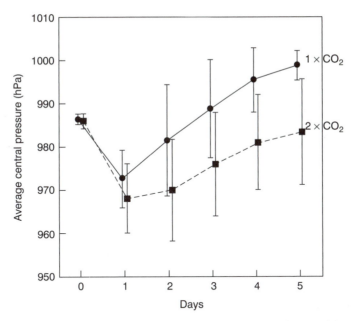

Figure 4.8 *Mean intensities of 'bogused' cyclone simulations, for 1 × CO₂ conditions (solid line, dots) and 2 × CO₂ conditions (dashed line, squares)*

Note: Standard deviations for each set of simulations are indicated by error bars. Units are hPa. Bogusing is the insertion of standard artificial vortices into modelled climate fields at points where cyclones appear to be forming. From Walsh in Suppiah et al (1998).

Henderson-Sellers et al (1998) give some credence to results using a thermodynamic estimate of maximum potential intensity (MPI) of tropical cyclones due to Holland (1997), which indicates that under doubled CO_2 conditions MPI may increase by 10–20 per cent. This result is supported by simulations of some 51 storms under lx and $2 \times CO_2$ conditions using a high-resolution (18km) hurricane prediction system, effectively nested in a GCM (Knutson et al, 1998), and by analyses done in CSIRO at 30 km resolution, shown in Figure 4.8 (from Walsh in Suppiah et al, 1998). The last two experiments both suggest that it is not only the maximum potential intensity that increases, but also the average intensity. While Holland (1997) points out that this small increase is against a large background of year-to-year variability, any general increase would result in a shift towards a greater frequency of extreme events, which would dominate the damage impacts.

Another complication arises in that tropical cyclone occurrence, especially in the Pacific, has been shown to be highly correlated with the state of the ENSO variations (Revell and Goulter, 1986; Evans and Allan, 1992). This means that reliable estimates of tropical cyclone behaviour under enhanced greenhouse conditions must await reliable simulations of the behaviour of ENSO, as discussed below.

The El Niño-Southern Oscillation (ENSO)

As discussed in part already, the state of the ENSO phenomenon under enhanced greenhouse conditions is important to climate change impacts because it affects major regional anomalies of rainfall (and thus flood and drought occurrences), cloud cover, local sea level, ocean currents and the occurrence of tropical cyclones.

Recent behaviour of ENSO, with a long sequence of El Niño events in the 1990s, has led to controversy as to whether this is part of normal ENSO interdecadal variability (e.g. Harrison and Larkin, 1997; Rajagopalan et al, 1997), or due in part to global warming (Trenberth and Hoar, 1996, 1997). Trenberth and Hoar argue that the evidence suggests that ENSO is moving more into an El Niño-dominated mode as global warming takes place, but others disagree as to the statistical evidence of any real change, given the relatively short record of ENSO variability on these timescales.

Modelling evidence is also confusing, mainly because coarse-resolution GCMs poorly simulate detailed ENSO behaviour, while most finer-resolution models of ENSO have limited domains and may be questioned regarding assumptions made as to the deep ocean temperatures and currents at their boundaries, particularly under climate change conditions.

What seems critical to this question is how the temperature contrast between the eastern and western tropical Pacific changes with global warming. This is what drives (with some feedbacks to the ocean) the so-called 'Walker Circulation', an east–west circulation in the tropical Pacific atmosphere, which is the atmospheric component of ENSO. In CSIRO we have started to look at this in simulations with our coarse-resolution coupled-ocean GCM, and with a global model which has a high-resolution ocean in the tropics only (Wilson and Hunt, 1997). The latter simulation suggests a small increase in the strength of the Walker Circulation, while the former has it substantially weakening. At present it is not certain which is more correct, but it is hoped to resolve this question when a new version of the CSIRO coupled-ocean GCM is run at finer spatial resolution globally.

Ocean currents

Ocean currents are poorly simulated in GCMs due to inadequate horizontal resolution. This applies especially to coastal boundary currents and those flowing around islands. Very broad-scale features, such as the strength of the ocean gyres may be better captured, and conceivably these could change if there are changes in the strength of the trade winds and the mid-latitude westerlies.

A simple measure of the potential change in the strength of the southern hemisphere mid-latitude westerlies, which drive the South Pacific Gyre, is the pressure difference between 45 and 55°S. Results of long simulations with the CSIRO coupled-ocean GCM with the GM mixing scheme show only a minor difference between the transient and control runs, with changes in the pressure difference at about $3 \times CO_2$ of only 10 per cent. This is not a dramatic change, and would probably be swamped by local changes which will only be captured by much finer-scale models.

Non-climatic changes

For much of the world's population, rapid economic, social, demographic, technological and political changes are far more important and immediate than climate change which occurs on a timescale of many decades. In such a rapidly changing world, environmental issues generally, and climate change in particular, seldom rate highly on the political agenda (Rayner and Malone, 1997). This may be valid where climate change is marginal, but is less valid where critical thresholds are exceeded, such as during local extreme events such as floods, drought or storm surges.

Climate change effects must therefore be considered in the context of other global changes and the stresses these impose on local ecosystems and human society. Demographic or other changes may well contribute to increased stress on food or water supplies, or to increased exposure to extreme events such as tropical cyclones on exposed coastlines. Other socio-economic and technological changes may serve, either incidentally or by intent, to reduce vulnerability to climate change. Sometimes and in some places, therefore, non-climatic developments may serve to reduce vulnerability to climate change, while in others they may make matters worse. Where socio-economic change is adding to societal and environmental stress, for instance, through increased soil erosion, increased competition for scarce water resources, or increased pollution, it will also tend to increase vulnerability to climate change effects.

What is needed, therefore, in climate change impact and adaptation assessments is to factor in other stresses and capacities to adapt, and how these might change. Such factors will alter the critical thresholds at which adaptation to climate change becomes necessary, in some cases delaying or obviating the need for planned adaptation, but in others making such adaptation far more urgent. Climate change may be slow on the timescale of the political process, but it is inexorable and global, and may over large regions impose simultaneous stresses on many people through widespread floods, droughts, disease outbreaks, or excessive temperatures. Perhaps the best analogy is the near global extent of the stresses created by the 1997/1998 El Niño event, with winter heat waves in the north-central US, ice storms in Canada, storms in Florida, heavy rains in California, drought in Brazil, floods in Peru and Ecuador, drought and fires in Indonesia, drought and starvation in Papua New Guinea, and floods in Kenya (Nash, 1998). How El Niño might change under global warming is not yet known, but unless there are dramatic reductions in greenhouse gas emissions, it is possible that climate change 50–100 years from now could be as pervasive as the recent El Niño in its effects, not just once, but year after year. Adaptation to such change would be a challenging and costly, if not impossible, task.

Towards Risk Assessment

Quantifying uncertainty

Attempts to quantify the impacts of climate change have been plagued by large uncertainties at each step in the process. Many of these, pertaining to regional and local climate changes, have been discussed above. If one adds to these the uncertainties regarding the biophysical consequences of a given climate change on complex systems, and of the response mechanisms and adaptations possible, one is easily led to the concept of an 'explosion of uncertainty' (Henderson-Sellers, 1993). This large range of uncertainty (especially where it includes changes of either sign) sometimes makes scientific advice appear unhelpful to decision-makers.

One point to remember here is that much of the uncertainty regarding climate change is due to the uncertainty of future human activities, as represented in the range of greenhouse gas emission scenarios and consequent CO_2 concentrations, global warmings and sea-level rises (Figures 4.1, 4.2 and 4.6 above). Here one can look separately at the consequences of each emission scenario, to gain an idea of the differing effects of human behaviour which decision-makers may be able to alter.

Beyond that, the wide range of possible outcomes obtained by considering the products of several ranges of uncertainty, without considering the likelihood of each combination, can be very misleading. When several ranges of uncertainty are multiplied together, the resulting range will have a non-uniform distribution favouring the median at the expense of the extremes. An example of how this may affect a regional scenario for temperature change on the north coast of Australia is shown in Figure 4.9. Here, two ranges of uncertainty, global mean warming in 2030 (based on the IPCC estimates in Figure 4.2 above), and regional changes in temperature per degree global warming (based on five GCMs), are assumed to be independent and are randomly sampled using the Monte Carlo method. While the extreme range of local warmings is 0.36 to 1.04°C (CSIRO, 1996), the 10th and 90th percentiles are 0.47 and 0.86, respectively, with a most probable (median) value of 0.66°C. This is a 43 per cent reduction in range for only a 20 per cent chance of missing extreme values.

A more complex example is shown in Figure 4.10, for a location in northern Victoria, Australia. This shows probability density plots of a two-variable change in average

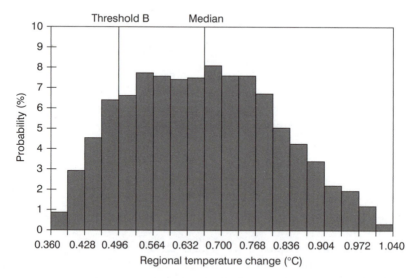

Figure 4.9 *Probability distribution of regional temperature increases by 2030 for the north Australian coast (relevant to the Great Barrier Reef)*

Note: Showing the probability of occurrence for 5 per cent increments within the total range of 0.36 to 1.04°C (CSIRO, 1996), based on Monte Carlo sampling. The component ranges are 0.4–0.8°C (global warming) and 0.9–1.3°C (local warming per degree global warming), sampled randomly and multiplied 5000 times. From Jones (1999). Threshold B is a hypothetical critical temperature (see Figure 4.11 and the section on identifying thresholds).

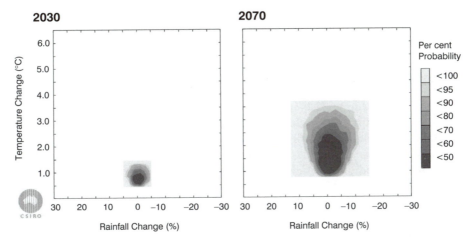

Figure 4.10 *Probability density plots of climate change for 2030 and 2070 in northern Victoria, Australia, based on CSIRO (1996) scenarios*

Note: Temperature was sampled randomly within both the global warming range of Figure 4.2, and the local warming per degree global warming (based on regional patterns from five GCMs), and the results multiplied together. A similar sampling procedure was followed for regional rainfall changes.

temperature and rainfall, based on the scenarios issued by CSIRO (1996), for 2030 and 2070 (Jones, 1999). The temperature probabilities are obtained as in Figure 4.9. The rainfall probabilities were obtained by multiplying the same random sample of global warming used for Figure 4.9 by random samples of the local range of summer and winter rainfall change per degree global warming. The outer limits represent the full ranges of temperature and rainfall changes, while the contoured areas represent the areas in the two-dimensional temperature–rainfall space within which a given percentage of cumulative probability occurs. Thus, in this assessment, the climate change is almost certain to fall within the outer shaded box, but has a 50 per cent chance of falling within the innermost shaded area, which occupies only about one sixth of the space.

This approach does not eliminate uncertainty but does manage it in a more realistic manner than assuming composite ranges of uncertainty have a uniform distribution. When combined with impact thresholds, probabilistic scenarios offer the potential to provide more focused assessments of risk.

However, to apply the method appropriately, the following conditions must be met:

- Scenarios must be independent if random sampling is used. If factors show dependence, this must be correctly applied within the sampling method.
- The full range of possibilities within a single variable must be allowed for, as a truncated range will underestimate risk.
- The major climatic variables influencing the impact under analysis should be incorporated into the scenario wherever possible.

Figures 4.9 and 4.10 are intended as illustrative examples of the method. The interdependence of variables under climate change needs to be tested more fully before this methodology can be applied in a wide range of assessments.

Identifying thresholds

To assess risk, climate impacts must be explored to determine appropriate criteria or 'thresholds'. An impact threshold is any degree of change that can link the onset of a given (and often value-laden) critical ecological or socio-economic impact to a particular climatic state or states. Biophysical or environmental thresholds represent a distinct change in the conditions or level of performance or function of an ecosystem, for instance, minimal river flow leading to algal blooms, flood levels overtopping levees, or conditions leading to insect outbreaks, crop failures or coral bleaching. Socio-economic or behavioural thresholds might relate, for example, to farm output levels leading to farmer insolvency, or failure of an urban water supply to meet demand.

Some of these thresholds will be absolute values of one or more variables which singly or in combination must not be exceeded if undesirable consequences are to be avoided, while others will involve rates of change (Parry et al, 1996; Jones and Pittock, 1997). These two kinds of thresholds are illustrated in Figure 4.11. Threshold A is a rate-of-change threshold, superimposed on the upper and lower bound estimates for scenarios of global warming. This could represent, for example, a biological threshold such as the rate of colonization of new reefs by coral species as the temperature warms, or, if the curves are imagined to be for sea-level rise, the rate of sea-level rise that corals can keep up with by upward growth (Hopley and Kinsey, 1988; Pittock, 1999). In the latter case, the value of this threshold may vary with coral species or location, and with ocean chemistry (Buddemeier and Fautin, 1996).

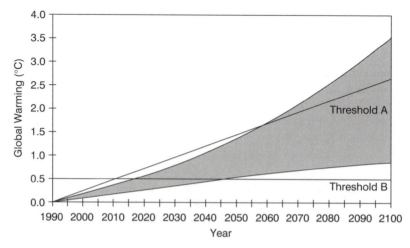

Figure 4.11 *Hypothetical examples of rate of change (A) and absolute (B) thresholds related to global warming, superimposed on the IPCC global warming projections of Figure 4.2 (variable aerosol cases only)*

Threshold B, on the other hand, is an absolute threshold. This might represent, for example, an absolute temperature above which coral bleaching is likely to occur. Again, this may be too simple, with other variables such as salinity or solar radiation playing a role (Glynn, 1997).

Such diagrams can be used to identify dates at which the thresholds might be exceeded, and if probability distributions for the critical variables (temperature or sea level), or combinations of variables, have been established, to look at the risk of exceedence of the thresholds at any date. Thus from Figure 4.11, the risk of reaching threshold B (hypothetically the onset of coral bleaching) is negligible before 2015, but becomes increasingly likely from 2015 to 2045, at which stage bleaching would be almost certain to occur. Superimposing the same threshold on a probability distribution for warming at 2030, such as that in Figure 4.9 for the north Australian coast, would enable the risk of bleaching at 2030 to be established.

Jones (1999) has used this approach to look at the time-varying probability of exceedence of present mandatory limits on irrigation water supply (known as a 'cap' on irrigation) by irrigation demand in farms in Australia as the climate changes. Above this cap some loss of production, or farm-level adaptation, is necessary. Thus, Figure 4.12 shows the probability of exceedence of a cap of 12MLha^{-1}, for an irrigated pasture in northern Victoria, as a function of temperature and rainfall changes. The statistical uncertainty here is due to year-to-year variability of rainfall and temperature about the mean climate. The critical threshold for the farmer, in relation to climate change, occurs when the irrigation supply cap is exceeded more frequently than the

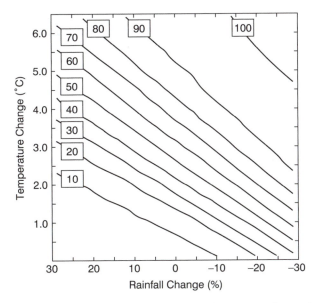

Figure 4.12 *Sensitivity matrix showing the probability of irrigation demand exceeding the present annual irrigation supply limit or 'cap' of 12MLha^{-1} for an irrigated pasture in northern Victoria, Australia, relative to average changes in temperature and rainfall*

Note: The probability comes about from the year-to-year variability within the climate.

farmer can cope with economically by farm-level adaptation. The critical threshold, for purposes of example, is set at an exceedence of the cap in 50 per cent of years.

Assessing risk of climate change impacts

Once a critical level of performance for an activity or sector has been defined in climatic terms, its probability of exceedence (taking short-term variability into account) can be expressed as a function of mean climatic variables, as in Figure 4.12. The probability of certain future climatic states can then be established by looking at the best available estimates of climate change, as in Figure 4.10. Superimposing one on the other then enables us to estimate the probability, at some time in the future, of the climate leading to some higher frequency of exceedence of the critical level of performance, as is illustrated in Figure 4.13. For example, in this largely hypothetical case, if the farmer can cope well with a frequency of exceedence of the irrigation supply cap by irrigation demand of up to one year in two, it is apparent that by 2030 there is still no problem, but by 2070 there is about a 23 per cent chance that the new climate will lead to exceedences more often than one in two years. This suggests that by 2070 the farmer will face what may well be an unacceptable risk of the climate having changed beyond his or her ability to cope via normal farm management practices: some new form of adaptation would then be necessary.

Of course, there are other complicating factors in the example shown in Figures 4.10, 4.12 and 4.13, such as the impact of climate change on irrigation water supply, and of increasing CO_2 concentrations on plant water-use efficiency, but with suitable elaboration of the models used, these can be taken into consideration. What is intended here is to illustrate the approach, and in particular to illustrate how it can make use of probability distributions of future climate changes to alert the stakeholder to the need for adaptation, and the time available.

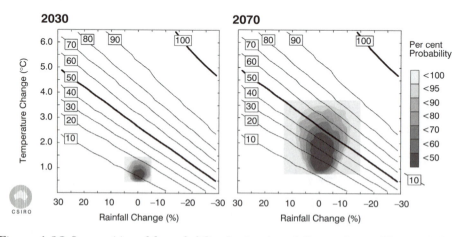

Figure 4.13 *Superposition of the probability density plots of climate change (Figure 4.10) on the sensitivity matrix for the probability of exceeding the irrigation supply cap (Figure 4.12)*

Note: Integrating the probabilities in the shaded area above the 50 per cent exceedence line gives the risk of exceeding the irrigation cap one year in two.

Integrated assessments of impacts and adaptation

In order to address the purposes of sensitivity or risk analyses identified in the introduction, it is clear that much effort needs to be put into establishing multivariate thresholds for a range of impacts, and to attach some measure of importance or value to the impacts both locally and globally. This in itself will be a complex multidisciplinary task. Nevertheless, some significant progress has been made, some of the main issues are already well addressed, and some critical parameters have been identified (Watson et al, 1998).

Another crucial need is to estimate better the time- and space-varying probability of reaching these thresholds. This requires a departure from the ideas of precise predictions, on the one hand, and of arbitrary scenarios (used in sensitivity studies) on the other, to one of estimating probabilities which can be used in risk assessments. This will lead to less focus on extreme ranges of uncertainty, and more on the most probable outcomes, while paying due heed to less probable circumstances which in some cases might have more disastrous consequences.

The role of autonomous and planned adaptation in either changing the thresholds, or in mitigating the costs and preserving the existing values, needs to be explored. This will require a lot more research: adaptation measures, along with other non-climatic changes, will have to be built into impact models to evaluate their effects. The time between identification of the need for adaptation and the time when failure to adapt would lead to unacceptable exceedence of critical thresholds represents the window of opportunity to implement adaptation. During this time the stakeholder can gather information, engage in research as to adaptation options, and invest in an adaptation strategy.

Conclusions

An important start has been made in our effort to understand how human society might be affected by and adapt to climate change, and, in general terms what it may need to adapt to (IPCC, 1996; Watson et al, 1998). However, there is a desperate need for a greater focus on regional climate change simulation, with a realistic quantification of uncertainty. Useful information on potential changes in many factors critical to impacts, such as the frequency and magnitude of extremes of temperature and rainfall, ocean chemistry, ENSO, tropical cyclones, regional variations in sea-level rise, location of the ITCZ and SPCZ, soil moisture and runoff, and cloud cover, at appropriate spatial scales, is necessary before impacts and the need for adaptation in particular situations can be understood.

The past reluctance of some international agencies to fund 'research' has been very short-sighted and damaging, in view of the inability of many small developing countries to mount effective climate change research programmes by themselves. Funds for 'capacity building' and 'adaptation measures' may well be wasted, or even used for inappropriate and counterproductive measures unless guided by a good understanding of the underpinning science. Good answers can only come by addressing the right questions. Too often these are not being asked because of the lack of a fundamental understanding of the issues and their local complexities.

The focus must move beyond prediction of extreme ranges of uncertainty, and focus instead on probability and risk assessment. Quantitative descriptions are needed of the more likely future climatic states, and of how these relate to the risk of critical or undesirable outcomes. Implicit in this is a set of values which will be used to define critical thresholds. This will include aesthetic and ecosystem values, but also some attempt to attach monetary values to impacted systems and their human and ecosystem services. Risk assessment must therefore involve both stakeholders and the social sciences: it is not a job just for climatologists and biophysical scientists (see also Beer and Ziolkowski, 1995).

Finally, adaptation researchers must address the related questions as to whether autonomous adaptation can realistically meet the UNFCCC objective to 'allow ecosystems to adapt naturally to climate change', given the present climate change projections. Will planned adaptation be essential for the continued functioning of particular impacted local ecosystems (which often have great human value), or even for their survival in general? The answers to these questions will not come from 'capacity building', unless that includes well-focused research regarding risk at the regional and local levels.

In summary:

- Climate change in the foreseeable future will not be to some new stable 'equilibrium' climate, but rather an ongoing 'transient' process.
- Climate change predictions relevant to impacts on most sectors and ecosystems are still highly uncertain.
- There is a need for a greater focus on developing countries and tropical regions, and on relevant key variables, including the magnitude and frequency of extreme events.
- The focus should shift from single predictions, or extreme ranges of uncertainty, to risk assessment.
- Thresholds critical to impacted sectors and ecosystems should be identified through consultation with stakeholders, and expressed as functions of climatic variables.
- Planned adaptations will be necessary to cope with multiple stresses, including those due to non-climatic changes.
- Given anticipated climate and other changes, there is still great uncertainty as to whether adaptation will be enough for the continued functioning or survival of individual sectors, ecosystems or activities.
- A major task of adaptation science is to identify the limits of adaptation, i.e., to identify 'dangerous levels of greenhouse gases' beyond which adaptation becomes impractical or prohibitively expensive.
- 'Capacity building' requires real knowledge of risk at regional and local levels.

Acknowledgements

We are greatly indebted to the other members of the Climate Impact Group in CSIRO Atmospheric Research (Drs R. J. Allan, K. J. Walsh, K. L. McInnes, R. Suppiah, P. H. Whetton, Mr K. J. Hennessy and Ms C. Page) for their work on many aspects of this chapter. Other members of the Climate Modelling Program in CAR (including Drs M. R. Dix, H. A. Gordon, A. C. Hirst, J. L. McGregor, S. O'Farrell, I. Smith and S. G. Wilson) also contributed through modelling development and advice. Drs T. Beer and W. J. Bouma provided helpful comments on the draft paper. A. B. P. is also grateful to the SCOR WG-104 members, and particularly Dr R. Buddemeier, for involving him in some exciting and challenging science in regard to coral reefs, and to colleagues involved in the preparation of the IPCC Special Report on *The Regional Impacts of Climate Change: An Assessment of Vulnerability,* and others who are on the Secretariat of this Workshop. This work was partly supported by funds from the National Greenhouse Research Program, Australia (notably the funding of the Climate Impact Liaison Project), the State Governments of Victoria, New South Wales, Western Australia, the Northern Territory and Queensland, and the Rural Industries Research and Development Corporation. It contributes to the CSIRO Climate Change Research Program.

References

Anthes, R.A.: 1982, 'Tropical cyclones: their evolution, structure, and effects.' *Amer. Meteorological Soc. Monographs,* no. 41, Boston, MA.

Bazzaz, F.A.: 1990, 'The response of natural ecosystems to the rising global CO_2 levels.' *Annual Review of Ecology and Systematics,* 21, 167–196.

Beer, T. and Ziolkowski, F.: 1995, 'Environmental risk assessment: an Australian perspective', Supervising Scientist Report 102, Commonwealth of Australia, Canberra, 125 pp.

Bolin, B.: 1998, 'The Kyoto negotiations on climate change: a science perspective.' *Science,* 279, 330–331.

Broccoli, A.J., Manabe, S., Mitchell, J.F.B. and Bengtsson, L.: 1995, 'Comments on "Global climate change and tropical cyclones"', Part 2, *Bulletin American Meteorological Soc.,* 76, 2243–2245.

Buddemeier, R.W.: 1994, 'Symbiosis, calcification, and environmental interactions.' *Bull. Institut Océanographique,* Monaco, no special 13, 119–131.

Buddemeier, R.W. and Fautin, D.G.: 1996, 'Saturation state and the evolution and biogeography of symbiotic calcification.' *Bull. Institut Océanographique,* Monaco, no special 14 (4), 23–32.

CSIRO.: 1996, *Climate Change Scenarios for the Australian Region.* Climate Impact Group, CSIRO Division of Atmospheric Research, Aspendale, issued November 1996, 8 pp.

Cubasch, U., Santer, B.D., Hellbach, A., Hegerl, G., Hock, H., Maier-Reimer, E., Mikolajewicz, U., Stossel, A. and Voss, R.: 1994, 'Monte Carlo climate change forecasts with a global coupled ocean-atmosphere model.' *Climate Dynamics,* 10, 1–20.

Cure, J.D. and Acock, B.: 1986, 'Crop responses to carbon dioxide doubling: a literature survey.' *Agric. and Forest Meteorology,* 38, 127–145.

England, M.H.: 1995, 'Using chlorofluorocarbons to assess ocean models.' *Geophysical Research Letters,* 22, 3051–3054.

Evans, J.L. and Allan, R.J.: 1992, 'El Niño/Southern Oscillation modification to the structure of the monsoon and tropical cyclone activity in the Australian region.' *Internal. J. of Climatology,* 12, 611–623.

Fairbanks, R.G.: 1989, 'A 17,000-year glacio-eustatic sea level record: influence of glacial melting rates on the Younger Dryas event and deep-ocean circulation.' *Nature,* 342, 637–642.

Fowler, A.M. and Hennessy, K.J.: 1995, 'Potential impacts of global warming on the frequency and magnitude of heavy precipitation.' *Natural Hazards,* 11, 283–303.

Gattuso, J.-P., Allemand, D. and Frankignoulle, M.: 1999, 'Interactions between the carbon and carbonate cycles at organism and community levels in coral reefs.' *American Zoologist,* 39(1), 160–183.

Gifford, R.M., Barrett, D.J., Lutze, J.L. and Samarakoon, A.B.: 1996, 'Agriculture and global change: scaling direct carbon dioxide impacts and feedbacks through time', in B. Walker and W. Steffen (eds.) *Global change and Terrestrial Ecosystems.* Cambridge Uni. Press, Cambridge, UK, pp. 399–416.

Glynn, P.W.: 1997, 'Coral reef bleaching: facts, hypotheses and implications.' *Global Change Biology*, 2, 495–509.

Gordon, H.A. and O'Farrell, S.P.: 1997, 'Transient climate change in the CSIRO coupled model with dynamic sea ice.' *Monthly Weather Review*, 125, 875–907.

Gray, W.M.: 1968, 'Global view of the origin of tropical disturbances and storms.' *Monthly Weather Rev.*, 96, 669–700.

Gray, W.M.: 1975, *Tropical cyclone genesis.* Dept. of Atmospheric Sci. Paper No. 234, Colorado State Uni., Fort Collins, CO, 121 pp.

Gregory, J.M.: 1993, 'Sea level changes under increasing atmospheric CO_2 in a transient coupled ocean-atmosphere GCM experiment.' *J. Climate*, 6, 2247–2262.

Harrison, D.E. and Larkin, N.K., 1997. 'Darwin sea level pressure, 1876–1996: evidence for climate change?' *Geophysical Research Letters*, 24, 1779–1782.

Henderson-Sellers, A., 1993. 'An Antipodean climate of uncertainty.' *Climatic Change*, 25, 203–224.

Henderson-Sellers, A., Zhang, H., Berz, G., Emanuel, K., Gray, W., Landsea, C., Holland, G., Lighthill, J., Shieh, S.L., Webster, P. and McGuffie, K., 1998. 'Tropical cyclones and global climate change: a post-IPCC assessment.' *Bulletin American Meteorological Soc.*, 79, 19–38.

Hennessy, K.J., Gregory, J.M. and Mitchell, J.F.B., 1997. 'Changes in daily precipitation under enhanced greenhouse conditions.' *Climate Dynamics*, 13, 667–680.

Herman, J.R., Bhartia, P.K., Ziemke, J., Ahmad, Z. and Larko, D., 1996. 'UV-B increases (1979–1992) from decreases in total ozone.' *Geophys. Research Letters*, 23, 2117–2120.

Holland, G.J., 1993. *The Global Guide to Tropical Cyclone Forecasting.* WMO/TD-560, World Meteorological Organization, Geneva, 337 pp.

Holland, G.J., 1997. 'The maximum potential intensity of tropical cyclones.' *J. Atmospheric Sciences* 54, 2519–2541.

Hopley, D. and Kinsey, D.W.: 1988, 'The effects of a rapid short-term sea-level rise on the Great Barrier Reef.' In: *Greenhouse: Planning for Climate Change*, ed. Pearman, G.I., CSIRO Pub., pp. 189–201.

Hubbert, G.D. and McInnes, K.L.: 1999, 'A storm surge inundation model for coastal planning and impact studies.' *J. Coastal Research*, 15(1), 168–185.

IPCC: 1992, *Climate Change 1992: The Supplementary Report to the IPCC Scientific Assessment*, Houghton, J.T., Callander, B.A. and Varney, S.K. (eds.), Cambridge Uni. Press, Cambridge, 365 pp.

IPCC: 1996, *Climate Change 1995: The Science of Climate Change*, Houghton, J.T., Meira Filho, L.G., Callandar, B.A., Harris, N., Kattenberg, A. and Maskell, K. (eds.), Contribution of Working Group 1 to the Second Assessment Report of IPCC, Cambridge Uni. Press, Cambridge, 572 pp.

Jackett, D.R., McDougall, T.J., England, M.H, and Hirst, A.C.: 2000. 'Thermal expansion in ocean and coupled general circulation models.' *J. Climate*, 13, 1384–1405.

Jones, R.N.: 1999, 'Climate change scenarios, impact thresholds and risk.' *Proc. Workshop on Impacts of Global Change on Australian Temperate Forests, 25–27 Feb., 1998*, Gorman, J. and Howden, S.M. (eds.), CSIRO Wildlife and Ecology, Canberra.

Jones, R.N. and Pittock. A.B.: 1997, 'Assessing the impacts of climate change: the challenge for ecology.' In: *Frontiers in Ecology: Building the Links*, Klomp, N, and Lunt, I. (eds.), Elsevier Science, Oxford, pp. 311–322.

Karl, T.R., Wang, W-C., Schlesinger, M.E., Knight, R.W. and Portman, D.: 1990, 'A method of relating general circulation model simulated climate to the observed climate, Part I: seasonal statistics.' *J. Climate*, 3, 1053–1079.

Kinzie, R.A. and Buddemeier, R.W.: 1996, 'Reefs happen.' *Global Change Biology*, 2, 479–494.

Kleypas, J.A.: 1997, 'Modeled estimates of global reef habitat and carbonate production since the last glacial maximum.' *Paleoceanography,* 12, 533–545.

Konishi, T.: 1995, 'An experimental storm surge prediction for the western part of the Inland Sea with application to Typhoon 9119.' *Papers Meteorology Geophys.,* 46, 9–17.

Knutson, T.R., Tuleya, R.E. and Kurihara, Y.: 1998, 'Simulated increase of hurricane intensities in a CO_2-warmed climate.' *Science,* 279, 1018–1020.

Larcombe, P., Woolfe, K. and Purdon, R., (eds.): 1996, *Great Barrier Reef: Terrigenous Sediment Flux and Human Impacts,* Second Ed., Nov. 1996. James Cook Uni., Townsville, 174 pp.

Lighthill, J., Holland, G.J., Gray, W.M., Landsea, C., Craig, G., Evans, J., Kurihara, Y. and Guard, C.P.: 1994, 'Global climate change and tropical cyclones.' *Bulletin American Meteorological Soc.,* 75, 2147–2157.

Lubin, D. and Jensen, E.H.: 1995, 'Effects of clouds and stratospheric ozone depletion on ultraviolet radiation trends.' *Nature,* 377, 710–713.

McDougall, T.M., Hirst, A.C., England, M.H. and McIntosh, P.C.: 1996, 'Implications of a new eddy parameterization for ocean models.' *Geophysical Research Letters,* 23, 2085–2088.

McGregor, J.J., Walsh, K.J. and Katzfey, J.J.: 1993, 'Nested modelling for regional climate studies.' In: *Modelling Change in Environmental Systems,* Jakeman, A.J., Beck, M.B and McAleer, M.J, (eds.), John Wiley and Sons, Chichester, pp. 367–386.

Meehl, G.A., Washington, W.M., Erickson, D.J. III, Briegleb, B.P. and Jaumann, P.J.: 1996, 'Climate change from increased CO_2 and direct and indirect effects of sulfate aerosols.' *Geophysical Research Letters,* 23, 3755–3758.

Nash, J.M.: 1998, 'The fury of El Nino.' *Time,* March 2, 44–51.

O'Farrell, S.P., McGregor, J.L., Rotstayn, L.D., Budd, W.F., Zweck, C. and Warner, R.: 1997, 'Impact of transient increases in atmospheric CO_2 on the accumulation and mass balance of the Antarctic ice sheet.' *Annals of Glaciology,* 25, 137–144.

Parry, M.L., Carter, T.R. and Hulme, M.: 1996, 'What is dangerous climate change?' *Global Environmental Change,* 6, 1–6.

Pittock, A.B.: 1995, 'Climate change and world food supply', and special issues of *Global Environmental Change* and *Food Policy.* Reviews in: *Environment,* 37 (9), 25–30.

Pittock, A.B.: 1999, 'Coral reefs and environmental change: adaptation to what?', *American Zoologist,* 39(1), 10–29.

Pittock, A.B., Dix, M.R., Hennessy, K.J., Katzfey, J.J., McInnes, K.L., O'Farrell, S.P., Smith, I.N., Suppiah, R., Walsh, K.J., Whetton, P.H., Wilson, S.G., Jackett, D.R. and McDougall, T.J.: 1995, 'Progress towards climate change scenarios for the Southwest Pacific.' *Weather and Climate,* 15, 21–46.

Rajagopalan, B., Lall, U. and Cane, M.A.: 1997, 'Anomalous ENSO occurrences: an alternative view.' *J. Climate,* 10, 2351–2357.

Rayner, S. and Malone, E.L.: 1997, *Ten Suggestions for Policymakers: Guidelines from an International Social Science Assessment of Human Choice and Climate Change,* Battelle Press, 39 pp.

Revell, C.G. and Goulter, S.W.: 1986, 'South Pacific tropical cyclones and the Southern Oscillation.' *Monthly Weather Review,* 114, 1138–1145.

Schimel, D., Alves, D., Enting, I., and 24 others: 1996, 'Radiative Forcing of Climate Change.' Chapter 2 in: IPCC, 1996, op. cit.

Shick, J.M., Lesser, M.P. and Jokiel, P.L.: 1997, 'Effects of ultraviolet radiation on corals and other coral reef organisms.' *Global Change Biology,* 6, 527–545.

Smith, I.: in press, *Estimating mass balance components of the Greenland ice sheet from a long-term GCM simulation.* Global and Planetary Change.

Solomon, A.M. and Cramer, W.: 1993, 'Biospheric implications of global environmental change.' In: *Vegetation Dynamics and Global Change,* Solomon, A.M. and Shugart, H.H. (eds.), Chapman and Hall, New York, pp. 25–52.

Suppiah, R., Hennessy, K., Hirst, T., Jones, R., Katzfey, J., Pittock, B., Walsh, K., Whetton, P. and Wilson, S.: 1998, 'Climate Change Under Enhanced Greenhouse Conditions in Northern Australia.' Final Report 1994–1997. CSIRO Division of Atmospheric Research, Aspendale, 49 pp.

Teramura, A.H.: 1983, 'Effects of ultraviolet-B radiation on the growth and yield of crop plants.' *Physiol. Plant.,* 58, 415–427.

Tevini, M. (ed.): 1993, *UV-B Radiation and Ozone Depletion. Effects on Humans, Animals, Plants, Microorganisms and Materials.* Lewis Pub., Boca Raton, Florida, 248 pp.

Trenberth, K.E. and Hoar, T.J.: 1996, 'The 1990–1995 El Niño-Southern Oscillation Event: Longest on Record.' *Geophysical Research Letters,* 23, 57–60.

Trenberth, K.E. and Hoar, T.J.: 1997, 'El Niño and climate change.' *Geophysical Research Letters,* 24, 3057–3060.

Walsh, K.J.E. and Katzfey, J.J.: 2000, 'The impact of climate change on the poleward movement of tropical cyclone-like vortices in the regional climate model.' *J. Climate,* 13(6), 1116–1132.

Walsh, K. and Watterson, I.G., 1997, 'Tropical cyclone-like vortices in a limited area model: comparison with climatology.' *J. Climate,* 10, 2240–2259.

Watson, R.T., Zinyowera, M.C., Moss, R.H. and Dokken, D.J.: 1998, *The Regional Impacts of Climate Change: An Assessment of Vulnerability.* A special report of IPCC Working Group II, Cambridge Uni. Press, Cambridge UK, 517 pp.

Watterson, I.G., Evans, J.L. and Ryan, B.F.: 1995, 'Seasonal and interannual variability of tropical cyclogenesis: diagnostics from large-scale fields.' *J. Climate,* 8, 3052–3066.

Whetton, P.H., England, M.H., O'Farrell, S.P., Watterson, I.G. and Pittock, A.B.: 1996a, 'Global intercomparison of the regional rainfall results of enhanced greenhouse coupled and mixed layer ocean experiments: implications for climate change scenario development.' *Climatic Change,* 33, 497–519.

Whetton, P., Pittock, A.B., Labraga, J.C., Mullan, A.B. and Joubert, A.: 1996b, 'Southern Hemisphere climate: comparing models with reality.' Chapt. 4 in: *Climate Change: Developing Southern Hemisphere Perspectives,* Giambelluca, T.W. and Henderson-Sellers, A. (eds.), John Wiley and Sons, Chichester, pp. 89–130.

Wigley, T.M.L.: 1998, 'The Kyoto Protocol: CO_2, CH_4 and climate implications.' *Geophysical Research Letters,* 25, 2285–2289.

Wilby, R.L. and Wigley, T.M.L.: 1997, 'Downscaling general circulation model output: a review of methods and limitations.' *Progress in Physical Geography,* 21, 530–548.

Wilson, S.G. and Hunt, B.G.: 1997, *Impact of Greenhouse Warming on El Niño/Southern Oscillation Behaviour in a High Resolution Coupled Global Climatic Model,* Report to Department of Environment, Sport and Territories, CSIRO Atmospheric Research, Aspendale, pp. 19–33 figures.

WMO: 1995, *Scientific Assessment of Ozone Depletion: 1994.* World Meteorological Organization Global Ozone Research and Monitoring Project – Report No. 37, Geneva, 1995, various paginations.

Wyrtki, K.: 1985, 'Sea level fluctuations in the Pacific during the 1982–83 El Niño.' *Geophysical Research Letters,* 12, 125–128.

5

An Anatomy of Adaptation
to Climate Change and Variability

**Barry Smit, Ian Burton, Richard J. T. Klein and
Johanna Wandel**

Introduction

The role of adaptation to climate change and variability is increasingly considered in academic research, and its significance is being recognized in national and international policy debates on climate change. There are two distinct, but not independent, reasons why adaptation is important when considering climate change and variability. First, the impacts of climate change, and hence its seriousness or dangerousness, can be modified by adaptations of various kinds (e.g. Smit, 1993; Tol et al, 1997). Most impact studies now make assumptions about expected adaptations in the system of interest. Thus, the key question about adaptation is: what adaptations are *likely*? This is mainly a *predictive* exercise, which requires information on how and under what conditions adaptations are expected to occur. Second, adaptation is considered as an important policy option or response strategy to concerns about climate change (e.g. Fankhauser, 1996; Smith, J., 1996). Adaptation to climate change and its impacts is receiving increasing attention as an alternative or complementary response strategy to reducing net emissions of greenhouse gases (termed 'mitigation' in the climate change community). For this policy application, the key question is: what adaptations are advocated or *recommended*? This is ultimately an advisory or *prescriptive* exercise, which requires information on possible adaptation strategies or measures, as well as principles to evaluate their merit.

As adaptation to climate change and variability has been subjected to more intensive enquiry, analysts have seen the need to distinguish types, to characterize attributes, and to specify applications of adaptation. For example, adaptation can refer to natural or socio-economic systems and be targeted at different climatic variables or weather events. Based on their timing, adaptations can be reactive or anticipatory; and depending on the degree of spontaneity, they can be autonomous or planned. Further, adaptations can take technological, economic, legal and institutional forms.

While the subject of adaptation has been approached from a variety of perspectives, there are some broad consistencies in the use of terms. This chapter aims to synthesize and clarify the treatment of climate adaptation in the existing literature. It builds on generally agreed-upon concepts and terms to establish a comprehensive 'anatomy' of adaptation. It seeks to facilitate analysis and policy development of adaptation by proposing a conceptual framework within which particular analyses and applications can be set, and a terminology to promote communication and to assist comparisons of findings in the field.

The chapter spells out what is meant by 'adaptation', and how it has been characterized and classified. The chapter begins by summarizing the role of adaptation in relation to climate change and variability. The central theme of 'what is adaptation?' is addressed by reviewing definitions, then considering in turn three questions:

1 Adapt to what?
2 Who or what adapts?
3 How does adaptation occur?

This is followed by a brief critique of approaches to improving our ability to estimate future adaptations. The final section reviews methods to evaluate adaptation options, particularly for prescriptive analyses.

This chapter adopts the convention in the Intergovernmental Panel on Climate Change (IPCC) and elsewhere that distinguishes adaptation from mitigation. Both represent responses to climate change and variability. 'Mitigation', which means abate, moderate or alleviate, could be (and sometimes is, especially in the environmental hazards, engineering and insurance fields) applied to impacts, as in 'mitigate vulnerabilities and effects by adjusting practices or structures'. In this chapter, mitigation is considered to be a response to the broad issue of climate change and involves reducing or stabilizing greenhouse gas emissions or levels, in order to mitigate changes in climate. 'Adaptation' could be (and sometimes is) applied to altering activities related to greenhouse gases (here called 'mitigation'). 'Adaptation' is also sometimes used to refer to adjustments, particularly by businesses, to changes in the political-economic environment associated with the climate change issue (notably policies promoting measures to mitigate). In this chapter, adaptation refers to adjustments in ecological-social-economic systems in response to actual or expected climatic stimuli, their effects or impacts. These differing applications of the term 'adaptation' reinforce the need for users of the term to specify adaptation in what, and to what.

Adaptation, Climate Change, Variations and Extremes

A critical document on climate change for both scientists and policymakers is the United Nations Framework Convention on Climate Change (UNFCCC), which was one of the products of the United Nations Conference on Environment and Development (UNCED), held in Rio de Janeiro in 1992. The ultimate objective of the UNFCCC, as expressed in Article 2 is:

> ... stabilization of greenhouse gas concentrations in the atmosphere at a level that would prevent dangerous anthropogenic interference with the climate system. Such a level should be achieved within a time-frame sufficient to allow ecosystems to adapt naturally to climate change, to ensure that food

production is not threatened and to enable economic development to proceed in a sustainable manner.

The challenges presented to scientists and policymakers alike include the determination of what might be regarded as 'dangerous', an essential element of which relates to adaptation. The extent to which natural ecosystems, global food supplies and sustainable development are at risk depends in part upon the magnitude, rate and nature of climate change, but also upon the ability of the impacted systems to adapt. Thus, in order to judge the seriousness of climate change as outlined in Article 2 of the UNFCCC, impact assessments of ecosystems, food production and sustainable development (including systems such as forestry, fisheries, water resources, human settlements and human health) need to address explicitly the capacity for, and the likelihood of, adaptation to potential climatic conditions. Such adaptations are what distinguish 'initial impacts' from 'residual impacts'. Therefore, for *impact assessment,* the main interest is in understanding adaptations, estimating the circumstances under which they can be expected, and forecasting their implications for the systems or regions of interest.

With regard to the *implementation* of adaptation measures as part of a response strategy, the UNFCCC commits parties to:

> Formulate, implement ... national and, where appropriate, regional programmes containing measures to mitigate climate change ... and measures to facilitate adequate adaptation to climate change (Article 4.1(b)).

More specifically, parties are committed to:

> Cooperate in preparing for adaptation to the impacts of climate change; develop and elaborate appropriate and integrated plans for coastal zone management, water resources and agriculture, and, for the protection and rehabilitation of areas, particularly in Africa, affected by drought and desertification, as well as floods (Article 4.1 (e)).

The formulation and implementation of adaptation policies and measures involves one additional analytical step as compared to the analysis of adaptation as part of impact assessment. For both implementation and assessment purposes it is important to know, for example, the forms of adaptation and the conditions under which they are expected to occur. However, analysis for implementation also requires an *evaluation* of measures, strategies or options. It is not sufficient for this implementation role to specify an adaptation and its likelihood; it also requires some judgement as to how appropriate or good it is, such that adaptations be recommended in accordance with the goals of public policy.

Considerable attention has been given to evaluating the need for, and merit of, adaptation measures in the climate change context. The IPCC Technical Guidelines (Carter et al, 1994) outline steps for the evaluation of adaptation strategies, and several other approaches to identifying recommended adaptations have been developed. These methods for advisory applications of adaptation are considered in more detail later in this chapter.

The interest in adaptation to climate change, both as an element of impact assessment and as a policy response, is not limited to changes in long-term mean climate variables. Climatic conditions are inherently variable from year to year, decade to decade, century to century and beyond. Hence, variability goes along with, and is an integral part of, climate change: a change in mean climatic conditions is actually experienced through changes in the nature and frequency of particular yearly conditions, including extremes; and it is to this variability that adaptations are made. Thus, adaptation to climate change necessarily includes adaptation to variability.

In addition, and quite apart from the climate change issue, there is an ongoing interest in adaptation to climatic *variations* in their own right. Communities frequently have to deal with extremes or anomalies such as floods, droughts and storms, both individual weather events and patterns of occurrence which may be significant over periods of days, seasons, years, decades, or more. This work on analysing the processes by which communities or regions cope with such hazards or manage such risks is all about adaptation, and it is an essential element in sustainable development initiatives (Alabala-Bertrand, 1993; Blaikie et al, 1994; Hewitt, 1997. Variability (including extremes) associated with El Niño-Southern Oscillation (ENSO) phenomena represents a particular example. Analysts and policymakers are exploring the ways in which systems have adapted to past ENSO events and the ways in which improved adaptations might be encouraged, particularly given the degree of predictability associated with ENSO conditions (Lagos and Buizer, 1992). Analyses of adaptations to climate variations and extremes have involved scholars both within and beyond the climate change community, and have employed some distinctive terms and interpretations dealing with adaptations. Yet the basic concepts are broadly consistent, and are synthesized in the following development of an anatomy of adaptation to climate change and variability.

Definitions and Gross Anatomy of Adaptation

According to dictionaries, 'adapt' means to make more suitable (or to fit some purpose) by altering (or modifying). 'Adaptation' refers to both the process of adapting and the condition of being adapted. The terms have more specific interpretations in particular disciplines (See Chapter 3). In ecology, for example, adaptation frequently refers to the changes by which an organism or species becomes fitted to its environment (Abercrombie et al, 1977; Lawrence, 1995). In the social sciences, cultural adaptation has referred to adjustments by individuals and to the collective behaviour of socio-economic systems (Denevan, 1983; Hardesty, 1983).

In the climate change literature, numerous definitions have been proposed, some of which refer only to societal adaptation; for example:

> Adaptation to climate is the process through which people reduce the adverse effects of climate on their health and well-being, and take advantage of the opportunities that their climatic environment provides. (Burton, 1992)

Adaptation involves adjustments to enhance the viability of social and economic activities and to reduce their vulnerability to climate, including its current variability and extreme events as well as longer term climate change. (Smit, 1993)

The term adaptation means any adjustment, whether passive, reactive or anticipatory, that is proposed as a means for ameliorating the anticipated adverse consequences associated with climate change. (Stakhiv, 1993)

Adaptation to climate change includes all adjustments in behaviour or economic structure that reduce the vulnerability of society to changes in the climate system. (Smith et al, 1996)

Adaptability refers to the degree to which adjustments are possible in practices, processes, or structures of systems to projected or actual changes of climate. Adaptation can be spontaneous or planned, and can be carried out in response to or in anticipation of change in conditions. (Watson et al, 1996)

These definitions have much in common. They all refer to adjustments in a system in response to (or in light of) climatic stimuli, but they also indicate differences in scope, application and interpretation of the term adaptation. For example, the question '*adaptation to what?* is answered in different ways. It can refer to climate change, to change and variability, or just to climate. It can be in response to adverse effects or vulnerabilities, but it can also be in response to opportunities. It can be in response to past, actual or anticipated conditions, changes or opportunities.

There are also differences in how the definitions relate to the question '*who or what adapts?*'. It can be people, social and economic sectors and activities, managed or unmanaged natural or ecological systems, or practices, processes or structures of systems. The nature of adaptation and its effects will vary not only according to whether the object is natural or socio-economic, small or large scale, single sector/species or complex system, but also according to properties that relate to adaptation propensity such as adaptability, vulnerability, viability, sensitivity, susceptibility, resilience and flexibility.

The definitions also hint at the ways in which forms or types of adaptation can be distinguished; in other words, '*how does adaptation occur?*'. Adaptation refers both to the process of adapting and to the resulting outcome or condition. Most definitions imply a change 'to better suit' the new conditions. Adaptations can be passive, reactive or anticipatory; they can be spontaneous or planned; and other typologies and distinctions appear in the literature. For some types of adaptation, there are insights into actual processes by which adaptive measures are adopted or implemented.

As summarized graphically in Figure 5.1, these three elements together circumscribe the overall question 'what is adaptation?'. A thorough description of adaptation would specify the system of interest (who or what adapts), the climate-related stimulus (adaptation to what), and the processes and forms involved (how adaptation occurs).

The exercise of identifying recommended adaptation options or measures as part of a response strategy involves the additional step of evaluation, in order to judge the merit of potential adaptations (*how good is the adaptation?*) (Figure 5.1). Evaluations of adaptations can be based on criteria such as costs, benefits, equity, efficiency, urgency and implementability.

The elements of a gross anatomy are distinguished to clarify the concepts and treatments of adaptation; it is not suggested that the elements are independent of each other. For example, certain systems are more adaptable to a given climate stimulus than others. Non-climate forces also affect adaptation types and evaluations. The adaptation process itself can modify systems to alter their sensitivity to climate stimuli. One of the important features of adaptations as part of impact assessment is the estimation of costs and benefits, which is also a common ingredient in the evaluations to recommend adaptations. Development of adaptation policies requires adaptations to be specified – according to the three components of 'what is adaptation?' – before they can be evaluated. Not all links are shown in the simplified Figure 5.1. Notwithstanding their interconnectedness, the main components of the anatomy, as shown in Figure 5.1, can be examined separately, and this is done in subsequent sections.

Adaptation to What?

Adaptations can be considered in the context of the various manifestations of climatic stimuli. These have been called 'doses', 'stresses', 'disturbances', 'events', 'hazards', and 'perturbations' (Burton, 1997; Downing et al, 1996). Sometimes the stimuli for adaptations are expressed as climate or weather conditions (*e.g.* annual average precipitation or experienced hourly or daily precipitation), sometimes as the ecological effects or human impacts of the climatic conditions (*e.g.* drought, crop failure or income loss), and increasingly as the risks and perceptions of risks associated with climatic stimuli or the opportunities created by changing conditions. Thus, the phenomena to which adaptations are – or might be – made need to be specified according to the climate characteristics which are relevant (e.g. temperature, precipitation, or some combination such as moisture, over the pertinent time period) *and* their connection to the system which adapts. For example, an adaptation in agriculture may be in response to a sequence such as temperature and precipitation conditions, which result in drought (magnitude and/or frequency) which influences crop yield which has consequences for income. Such distinctions among climate-related stimuli have been suggested elsewhere: direct versus indirect, proximate versus distant, effects versus impacts, and various 'levels' of impact (Parry, 1986).

One of the noteworthy developments in recent investigations of adaptation is the search for system-relevant climate-related stimuli, by examining the sensitivity of systems, rather than by considering only the limited array of climate variables provided in scenarios generated by global climate models (Kates, 1985; Kane et al, 1992; Yohe et al, 1996; Rayner and Malone, 1998).

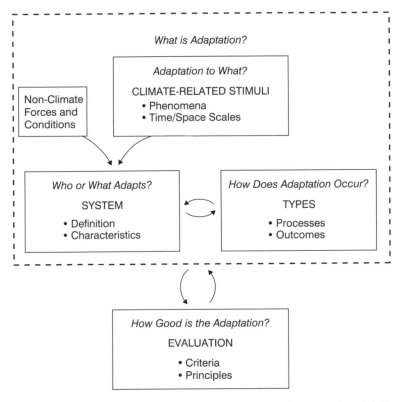

Figure 5.1 *Gross anatomy of adaptation to climate change and variability*

The climatic conditions to which adaptations have been considered (either directly or indirectly) generally fall into three broad *temporal* categories:

- global climate change, as reflected in long-term trends in, or scenarios pertaining to, mean temperatures and related climate 'norms';
- variability about norms over periods ranging from a few years to several decades – this may include shifts or changes in the shape of frequency/ probability distributions of climate variables, as well as variations or recurring anomalies associated ENSO or other forces such as volcanic eruptions and sun spots; and
- isolated extreme events or catastrophic weather conditions, such as floods, droughts or storms.

In reality, these types of climatic stimuli are not separate or independent. Extreme events are part of variability, which in turn is an inherent feature of climate, including changing climate. The mean conditions which have been the focus of the climate change studies are the summary (central tendencies) of a distribution of (variable) conditions. However, it is useful to distinguish stimuli because adaptations may be (and perhaps should be) quite different when viewed as response to, for example, an isolated extreme event as compared to a recurring anomalous condition or a gradual (or even sudden) change in an overall climate regime as reflected in changes in long-term mean conditions. Furthermore, improved understanding of adaptation to variability may provide insights into adaptation to changes (which will be experienced via variable conditions).

The relationships among extreme events, variability and climate change have been well developed in fields such as natural hazards (Hewitt and Burton, 1971; Kates, 1971), and are illustrated in Figure 5.2, with clear implications for adaptation. Do systems adapt to a slowly changing mean condition, the cumulative effect of conditions beyond some 'coping range' ('critical value', 'vulnerability threshold', 'band of tolerance' or 'damage threshold'), or to a particular extreme event? It is likely that many systems adapt in different ways to all of these timescales of stimuli – and may do so simultaneously. The coping range (Figure 5.2) may itself change (up, down, expand or contract) reflecting system adaptations (see de Vries, 1985; de Freitas, 1989). In the climate change context, the importance of means, variabilities and extremes is recognized for ecosystems (Sprengers et al, 1994) and for human systems (Parry, 1986; Downing et al, 1996).

Adaptation to climate-related stimuli in each of these timeframes is important in its own right. For example, regardless of climate change, there is considerable interest in reducing the vulnerabilities and damages associated with isolated extreme events such as storms, and with variability as reflected in recurring droughts or floods (Smith, K., 1996; Burton, 1996).

When variability and extremes are considered together with climate change, two circumstances are worth distinguishing. An increasingly debated issue is whether climate change will bring with it (or is already bringing) a change in the variability of

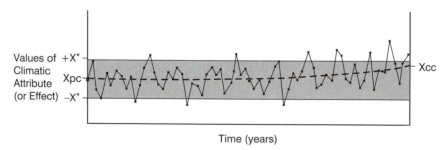

Xpc = mean value of the climatic attribute (X) at the start of the time-series (pre-climate change)

Xcc = mean value of the climatic attribute (X) at the end of the time-series (climate change)

+X* = upper critical value of X for the system of interest: values >+X* are problematic and considered 'extreme' or beyond 'damage threshold'

– X* = lower critical value of X for the system of interest: values <–X* are problematic and considered 'extreme' or beyond 'damage threshold'

━ ━   trend in mean value of X (20 years running mean)

    coping range or zone of minimal hazard potential for system of interest

Figure 5.2 *Climate time-series (hypothetical) showing sources of stimuli*

Source: after Hewitt and Burton, 1971; and others

conditions, i.e., a change in the shape or variance of the frequency distribution. One possibility is that variability increases with climate change, but there is little or no consensus on changing variability (Houghton et al, 1996).

However, even with no change in variability (i.e., no change in shape or variance of the distribution), a shift in the mean (i.e., climate change) will necessarily shift the location of the distribution, as illustrated in Figure 5.3a. The frequency of occurrence of extreme events can be extremely sensitive to small changes in the mean (Mearns et al, 1984; Wigley, 1985). The implications for impacts and adaptation are fundamental (Heathcote, 1985; Warrick et al, 1986; Parry, 1986). To demonstrate, a condition which is considered extreme or problematic for the system (e.g. values of X $>+X^*$ in Figure 5.3a) which currently occurs only once every 30 years may, under the changed climate, occur once every 4 or 5 years. Such reduced recovery time would alter the feasibility and effectiveness of adaptation options. If there are changes in the mean and the variance of the distribution of a climatic attribute (Figure 5.3b), then the frequency of extremes can be further increased (or reduced). For adaptation and impact assessment purposes, even without changes in variability, assessments of climate stimuli must consider means, and variations and extremes. Climate change is not just about average temperatures; it is also about such sector-relevant conditions as the frequency of droughts or wet years, changes in diurnal temperature differences, or the intensity of 24-hour precipitation events (Karl and Knight, 1998). The distinction between weather and climate is insufficient to capture the array of climate stimuli and temporal scales pertinent for the analysis of impacts and adaptations.

Other temporal characteristics of climate stimuli have significant implications for adaptation. The speed of onset (or rate of change) is important for adaptations in ecosystems and socio-economic systems, and the duration of a condition may also influence the nature of adaptations (Sonka, 1992; see Chapter 3, this volume).

For managed systems, where the opportunity exists for implementing adaptive measures in advance of a stimulus, the degree of certainty or predictability – and the timescale of predictions – is an essential part of understanding and undertaking adaptation. Adaptations may be in response to the anticipation or expectation of a climate-related effect as much as, or in addition to, the climate-related stimulus itself. Most climate stimuli are 'predictable' in some sense. There is some confidence about climate change expectations over several decades. Particular extreme events are largely unpredictable (i.e., a storm of certain severity next year), but they are 'predictable' in probabilistic terms (i.e., a certain chance next year), and they are 'predictable' in an early warning sense (e.g., the storm will arrive in so many hours). The degree of predictability, and the prediction period, is different again for ENSO-related phenomena, for which, upon onset, the probabilistic predictive capability is often quite high and can extend over several months (Hastenrath, 1995).

Just as climate-related stimuli for adaptation can be differentiated according to their temporal characteristics, so too can they be distinguished according to their spatial characteristics (Smit, 1993; Tol, 1996). Whether a stimulus is experienced locally or over a wide area will influence both the type of adaptation which is likely to occur autonomously and the adaptation measures which might be recommended.

Adaptations vary not only with respect to their climatic stimuli but also with respect to other, non-climate conditions, sometimes called intervening conditions, which serve

(a) Climate change with unchanged variability

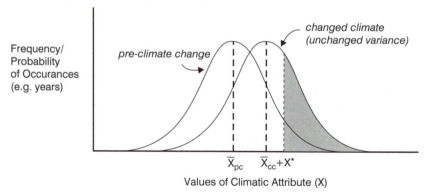

(b) Climate change with changed variability

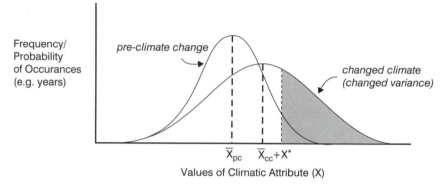

$\overline{X}_{pc}$ = mean value of the climatic attribute (X) pre-climate change
$\overline{X}_{cc}$ = mean value of the climatic attribute (X) under climate change
$+X^*$ = upper critical value of climatic attribute (X) for system of interest: values $> +X^*$ are problematic and considered 'extreme'
▨ = probability of 'extreme' events, ie. climatic attribute values $> +X^*$

Figure 5.3 *Climate change, variability and extreme events*

Source: after Fukui, 1979; and others

to influence the sensitivity of systems and the nature of their adjustments. For example, a series of droughts may have similar impacts on crop yields in two regions, but differing economic and institutional arrangements in the two regions may well result in quite different impacts on farmers and hence in quite different adaptive responses, both in the short and long terms. As indicated in Figure 5.1, systems adapt to a suite of stimuli (climate and other), with climatic effects (either direct or via environmental, social or economic manifestations, and including both risks and opportunities) sometimes being dampened and other times being exacerbated or heightened (Lewandrowski and Brazee,

1992; Sonka, 1992; Smit et al, 1997). Thus, to understand (and predict) adaptations, we need to differentiate and specify what the adaptation is to.

Who or What Adapts?

Adaptations represent adjustments in something, sometimes called the 'unit of analysis', 'exposure unit', 'activity of interest', or 'sensitive system' (Carter et al, 1994). A necessary step in any analysis or debate on adaptation (whether for impact assessment or for policy evaluation) is to define the system to which the adaptations pertain; this is the point of Figure 5.1. Are we talking about an individual or a community, a region or a nation, or are we talking about the entire globe? These questions focus attention clearly on the spatial scale of the system, but there is more to it than that. Are we considering adaptation in a species, or in an ecosystem, or in an economic sector, or across a social structure, or across a political entity? This relates to the nature or scope of the system. Are we dealing with instantaneous properties of a system or a system defined to include its variability over years or decades? This relates to the temporal scale of the system.

System definition

Any consideration of adaptation requires system definition, or delineation of the system's subject and boundaries. Thus, adaptation at the level of a farmer's field might involve planting a new hybrid; at the farm level it might involve diversification or taking out insurance; at the regional or national scales adaptation may relate to changes in the number of farms or modifications to a compensation programme; and at a global level, it may involve a shift in patterns of international food trade.

In the ecological field the conventional view is that organisms and species adapt (e.g., by altering genetic structure or moving) but ecosystems do not (Rose and Hurst, 1991; Peters and Lovejoy, 1992; Markham and Malcolm, 1996). However, ecosystems, which include communities and assemblages of species, can and do change (in structure, function, and extent) as a consequence of adaptations by species. Hence, the 'ecosystems adapt ... naturally' statement in the UNFCCC would refer to adaptations manifest in ecosystem changes. In the ecological field, 'adaptation of ecosystems' usually refers to human management practices which influence ecosystem changes. These interpretations are not universal; for example, Krankina et al (1997) discuss 'natural adaptation of long-lived, complex boreal forests', which are complexes of species or ecosystems. They also refer to management and utilization strategies as means 'to assist boreal forests in adaptation to a changing global environment' (p197). Pimm (1984) also refers to ecosystem adaptation in reference to reactive adjustments in natural systems to external stresses, including climatic variability and change.

Note that 'who' and 'what' are not necessarily synonymous. For example, actions by forest managers (who) may result in adaptations in a forest (what). In another forest system, adaptation may occur via a change in species' distribution (what) without any identifiable 'who'. Adaptations in a coastal zone (what) may reflect actions by authorities (who) which influence actions by individuals (who). Some of these situations can be clarified by distinguishing adaptation as a process from adaptation as a condition. Nonetheless, any systematic treatment of adaptation requires definition of the system of interest.

System characteristics

Considerable attention has been given to the characteristics of systems (suitably defined, of course) which influence their propensity to adapt (as part of impact assessment) and/or their priority for adaptation measures (as part of policy development). These characteristics have been called 'determinants' of adaptation. Terms such as 'sensitivity', 'vulnerability', 'susceptibility', 'coping range', 'critical levels', 'adaptive capacity', 'stability', 'robustness', 'resilience', and 'flexibility' have been used to differentiate systems according to their likelihood of adapting or need for adaptation (Sprengers et al, 1994; Klein and Tol, 1997; see Chapter 3, this volume). These characteristics influence (promote, inhibit, stimulate, dampen or exaggerate) the occurrence and nature of adaptations. In the hazards literature, these characteristics are reflected in 'socially constructed' or 'endogenous' risks (Blaikie et al, 1994; Hewitt, 1997). Together (in whole or part) they represent the 'adaptability' of a system.

Table 5.1 lists terms commonly used to characterize the adaptive propensity of systems to climate stimuli. Clearly, there is considerable overlap in the basic concepts captured in these terms. Particular terms have been employed to distinguish natural from socio-economic systems, or to differentiate between the pre- and post-adaptation conditions of a system (Klein and Nicholls, 1999). These distinctions are important, but can be captured without narrowing the meaning of widely used terms. Hence, 'sensitivity of an ecosystem' is different from 'sensitivity of a socio-economic system', and 'pre-adaptation vulnerability' is different from 'post-adaptation vulnerability'.

The terms sensitivity, vulnerability and adaptability capture the broad concepts. To illustrate the distinctions and connections among these central terms, consider a coastal community which is known to be *sensitive* to storms (a recurring climate stimulus, part of variability) in that they significantly change the local environment with effects on living conditions, structures and so on. The community is also expected to be *sensitive* to climate change (a different climate stimulus) in that any change in sea level will alter local land–water relationships, water salinity, and the magnitude of impacts associated with the aforementioned storms (now superimposed on a changed water level).

Many of these *sensitivities* (to storms and climate change) represent detrimental or harmful impacts for the coastal community. Thus, the community is *vulnerable* to storms in that it is susceptible to water contamination, property damage, temporary displacement and loss of life in the event of storms. The reasons for this *vulnerability* relate to the nature of settlement, reflecting population pressure on land resources, benefits of coastal locations in periods without storms, a socio-political system which facilitates settlement in storm-vulnerable sites, together with the relatively infrequent occurrence of severe storms, such that community members perceive little risk, and so on.

In this hypothetical case, the community has some, but limited, *adaptability* to storms. There is knowledge of the risks; there is awareness of structural designs with ability to accommodate storms; there is some preparation for evacuation in time of danger, etc.

Table 5.1 *Terms to describe characteristics of systems pertinent to adaptation**

Sensitivity	Degree to which a system is affected by, or responsive to, climate stimuli
Susceptibility	Degree to which a system is open, liable or sensitive to climate stimuli (similar to sensitivity, with some connotations toward damage)
Vulnerability	Degree to which a system is susceptible to injury, damage, or harm (one part – detrimental – of sensitivity)
Impact Potential	Degree to which a system is sensitive or susceptible to climate stimuli
Stability	Degree to which a system is not easily moved or modified
Robustness	Strength; degree to which a system is not given to influence
Resilience	Degree to which a system rebounds, recoups or recovers from a stimulus
Resistance	Degree to which a system opposes or prevents an effect of a stimulus
Flexibility	Degree to which a system is pliable or compliant (similar to adaptability, but more absolute than relative)
Coping Ability	Degree to which a system can successfully grapple with a stimulus (similar to adaptability, but includes more than adaptive means of 'grappling')
Responsiveness	Degree to which a system reacts to stimuli (broader than coping ability because responses need not be 'successful')
Adaptive Capacity	The potential or capability of a system to adapt to (to alter to better suit) climatic stimuli
Adaptability	The ability, competency or capacity of a system to adapt to (to alter to better suit) climatic stimuli

Note: *These definitions of systems' characteristics are based on widely (but not unanimously) held conventions. They focus on the distinguishing generic properties, and do not include factors which might influence the state of a property or the forms it might take. The terms 'climate stimulus' and 'system' are used as established earlier.

However, *adaptability* is limited in this hypothetical case in that risks tend to be underestimated, the storm-adaptive structures are rarely built, and early warning systems are poor at best, so evacuation cannot be initiated early. Again, the reasons underlying this limited level of *adaptability* could be documented, probably relating to similar socio-cultural, political-economic forces underlying sensitivity and vulnerability.

There is a growing literature on the conditions of regions and societies which influence their vulnerability and adaptability (Bohle et al, 1994; Ribot et al, 1996; Burton, 1997; Adger, 1999; Adger and Kelly, 1999; O'Riordan and Jordon, 1999). Drawing from the fields of natural hazards and sustainable development, researchers are attempting to better understand the nature and types of vulnerability, 'the capacity to be wounded' (Kates et al, 1985), or the amplification or amelioration of risks (Downing, 1991; Kasperson and Dow, 1991).

Perception of risks are known (e.g. from the natural hazards literature) to be important in influencing communities' actions relating to vulnerabilites. In the case of climate-related risks, such perceptions, and the role of information of various kinds in changing perceptions, are problematic because of the difficulty of separating climate change signals (including extremes) from the 'normal pulse' of systems. Some of the complexities underlying adaptability of systems, particularly related to uncertainty about climatic risks, are explored in Reilly and Schimmelpfennig (2000).

The concepts of sensitivity, vulnerability and adaptability, and the relationships among them are increasingly invoked in both impact assessments and policy recommendations. IPCC (1996) Second Assessment Report (SAR) 'Summary for policymakers' (p4) notes: 'the most vulnerable systems are those with the greatest sensitivity to climate change and the least adaptability', yet the SAR refers to very little substantive research on vulnerability, sensitivity and adaptability.

How Does Adaptation Occur?

Adaptive responses of systems to climate stimuli can occur via a variety of processes and can take many forms. Several useful distinctions and typologies have been proposed. For example, Carter et al (1994) note the widely (but not universally) acknowledged distinction between 'autonomous' (automatic, spontaneous, passive or natural) adaptations which occur in systems as a matter of course, and those that require or result from deliberate 'policy decisions', and are called 'planned' (strategic or active) adaptations. It is widely accepted that (unmanaged) biophysical systems are limited to autonomous adaptations. In socio-economic systems, autonomous adaptations can be grouped according to their degree of spontaneity (inbuilt, routine and tactical); and planned adaptations may be distinguished by the intent and timing of the initiative and/or by the actors involved (private individual or governments).

There is also the recognition that modifications (adaptations) to systems in response to non-climatic stimuli may unintentionally or 'incidentally' serve as an adaptation to climatic change or variability. For example, wetlands preservation – undertaken for the purpose of preserving wetlands – may also reduce vulnerability to sea-level rise and/or storms.

Most analysts distinguish adaptations according to when they occur relative to the stimulus: anticipatory versus reactive. Burton et al (1993) apply categories from the environmental hazards field to distinguish adaptation behaviours: prevent loss, tolerate loss, spread loss, change use or activity, change location, restoration. Stakhiv (1993) groups adaptive strategies according to the timeframe of the stimulus: long range, tactical, contingency, and/or analytical. Carter et al (1994) provide a list of adaptive management measures: structural or infrastructural, legal and legislative, institutional, administrative, organizational, regulatory, educational, financial (incentives and/or subsidies on the one hand and taxes, tariffs or user fees on the other), research and development, market mechanisms, and technological change. Bijlsma et al (1996) classify adaptations by their function: retreat, accommodate or protect. In Chapter 3, Smithers and Smit differentiate adaptations on the basis of intent or purposefulness, the role of government, the spatial and social scale, duration, form and effect.

Clearly, the question 'how does adaptation occur?' (Figure 5.1) can be answered on the basis of numerous attributes relating to processes and to outcomes, and is closely connected to the questions 'who or what adapts?' and 'adaptation to what?'. Condensing attributes into comprehensive, mutually exclusive categories yields rather non-specific classes like 'major, minor' or 'Level I, II, III'. The approach employed here is to specify the central attributes by which adaptations can be described and differentiated, either discretely or in combination. The following attributes are common elements of typologies of adaptation:

- Based on intent or purposefulness with respect to a climate stimulus, *autonomous* or spontaneous adaptations can be distinguished from consciously *planned* or deliberate intentional adaptive responses to a stimulus (actual or anticipated). Adaptations in unmanaged natural systems are considered to be autonomous. Adaptations initiated by public agencies are usually conscious strategies, but adaptations by private individuals or communities may be autonomous or planned, or some combination of the two, especially when adaptations are considered at different spatial and temporal scales (see Smithers and Smit, 1997). Impact assessments focus largely, but not exclusively, on autonomous adaptations, whereas adaptation evaluation and prescription necessarily deal with intentionally planned adaptive measures and policies.
- Based on timing of the action relative to the climate stimulus, adaptations may be *reactive* (or responsive or *ex post*), *concurrent* (during), or *anticipatory* (proactive or *ex ante*). In unmanaged natural systems adaptations are invariably reactive, and autonomous adaptations in socio-economic systems are usually concurrent or reactive. The greatest interest in planned adaptations, whether in the public or private sectors, is with anticipatory initiatives, in order to avoid or reduce harmful impacts and/or benefit from opportunities.
- Based on the temporal scope, adaptations can be short term or longer term. This distinction is often considered to be synonymous with tactical versus strategic adjustments (Stakhiv, 1993; Smit et al, 1996); in the natural hazards field it is adjustment versus adaptation (Burton et al, 1993) and is associated with instantaneous versus cumulative and autonomous versus policy (Riebsame, 1991; Easterling, 1996).
- Based on their spatial scope or institutional extent, adaptations can be localized or widespread. Based on their intent, adaptations may decrease vulnerability or modify effects (Jepma et al, 1996). Based on the form they take, adaptations can be distinguished according to whether they are primarily technological, behavioural, financial, institutional or informational.

While many types of adaptation have been distinguished, there is less scholarship on actual adaptation processes. Models of how adaptation options (particularly planned ones) should be identified and implemented are now quite common (Jodha, 1989; Smith, J., 1996; Klein, 1998; and see 'Evaluation of Adaptations', page 79). Knowledge of the processes by which individuals, communities, sectors or regions adapt, in practice, tends to come mostly from empirical analogue studies (Downing et al, 1989;

Glantz, 1996; Meyer et al, 1998; see Chapter 3, this volume). These studies suggest that adaptation tends to be incremental and ad hoc, to assume multiple forms, to be in response to multiple stimuli (usually involving a particular catalyst) and to be constrained by economic, technological and socio-economic conditions.

Numerous other distinctions exist, based on the type of process or outcome (Burton et al, 1993; Carter et al, 1994; Darwin et al, 1995; Klein and Tol, 1997; Smithers and Smit, 1997a). It is also possible to categorize adaptations according to their costliness, effectiveness, and implementability. These attributes are important differentiators, and are often considered in analyses of adaptations for impact assessment. For example, the costs of an adaptation and its reduction of impact damages (or enhancement of benefits) need to be calculated to estimate residual impacts. However, these attributes are also central features of evaluation and prescriptions of adaptations, and are addressed in more detail in 'Evaluation of Adaptations', opposite page. The term 'maladaptation' is often considered (Smit, 1993; Burton, 1997). Assuming adaptation implies an adjustment to make more suitable, effectiveness or success can range from large improvement in suitability to no improvement in suitability. In this sense, 'maladaptation' is really 'no adaptation' where, in addition to there being no improvement in suitability, there is a deterioration in suitability.

The various attributes which permit specifying types of adaptation are often related to each other and to the characteristics of climatic stimuli and the systems of interest (Figure 5.1). Several models of the interconnectedness among types of stimuli, characteristics of symptoms, and attributes of adaptations provide insights into the process of adaptation, and are considered in the following section.

Analysis and Prediction of Adaptation

An understanding of 'what is adaptation' – including who or what does it, how it occurs, and in response to what – is necessary for both the estimation of likely adaptations in impact assessment and the evaluation of adaptations in policy development. Analytical approaches to understanding and predicting adaptations – sometimes called the science of adaptation – are numerous, and are not reviewed here in detail. However, within the climate change community especially, the approaches tend to fall into one of three broad and overlapping categories: conceptual models of adaptation processes, numerical models of impacts, and empirical analyses of adaptations.

Conceptual models of the adaptation process specify sequential relationships and feedbacks, such as climatic (and non-climatic) stimuli, sensitivity and vulnerability of systems, short-term or autonomous adaptations, initial impacts, longer-term or strategic adaptations, and net or residual impacts. Such models have been developed both for adaptation processes generally (e.g. Feenstra et al, 1998) and for particular sectors or applications (e.g. Sonka and Lamb, 1987; Smit et al, 1996; Klein and Nicholls, 1999). These conceptualizations of the processes, sequences, and interconnections commonly provide the framework or structure for empirical analyses and for numerical impact assessment modelling (e.g. Easterling et al, 1993; Rosenzweig and Parry, 1994).

Numerical impact assessment models, whether of particular ecosystems or sectors, or of integrated regional or global systems, now invariably include adaptations via assumptions

(Tol et al, 1997). These assumptions about when, how and to what adaptations occur are based on theoretical principles (as in Adams et al, 1993; Yohe et al, 1996; Hurd et al, 1997; and most economic models), inference from observed associations (as in Leemans, 1992 and many ecological models), and arbitrary selection, speculation or hypothesis (as in many models assuming technological and behavioural adaptations). Comprehensive integrated assessment models (which specify connections among emission, atmosphere, climate, effects, impacts and responses) also include assumptions about adaptation (e.g. Hulme et al, 1995). The common distinguishing feature of these numerical modelling analyses of impacts is that they use information on adaptations to estimate future impacts of climate stimuli, after the effects of adaptation have been factored in.

The focus of the *empirical adaptation studies* is to better understand the nature and processes of adaptations themselves by observing, documenting and reconstructing current and past adaptations to climate (and other) stimuli. Some ecological and palaeoecological studies reconstruct species or community dynamics over hundreds and thousands of years (e.g. MacDonald et al, 1993). Analogue studies (e.g., Glantz, 1988; Olsthoorn et al, 1996), document adaptive responses to climatic stimuli in resource-based economic sectors and communities over periods of several decades. Other empirical analyses have examined the actual adaptive behaviour in key sectors such as agriculture in light of climatic variability and extremes over even shorter time periods (e.g. Smithers and Smit, 1997; Smit et al, 1997). Analyses of adaptation processes tend to start with the system of interest, then assess its sensitivity and adaptability to climate and other stimuli. This analytical strategy is consistent with the 'adjoint approach' (Parry, 1986), and the 'shift-in-risk' perspectives (Warrick et al, 1986). These empirical studies have yielded insights – particularly with regard to the relevant climate stimuli and the role of non-climate forces – which provide a basis for modifying some of the assumptions commonly made in modelling exercises.

Clearly, the empirical, conceptual, and numerical modelling analyses are complementary. Impact assessment requires improved specification of adaptations, especially the endogenous, inter-temporal, cumulative adaptation of societies and economies to variable and changing climatic stimuli. There is a recognized need in the impact assessment field for more systematic treatment of behavioural and decision-making responses to climatic stresses (e.g. Sonka, 1992) and of the inherent uncertainties (e.g. Viscusi, 1992).

The three broad approaches to the analysis of adaptation contribute primarily to the predictive objective (i.e., 'what adaptations are likely?'), which in turn contributes to answering 'what impacts are likely?' and hence 'how dangerous?'. Approaches to evaluative and prescriptive analyses address the question 'how good are adaptations?' and hence 'what adaptations should be implemented?'.

Evaluation of Adaptations

Considerable attention has recently been given to the systematic evaluation of climate-related adaptations. Two broad categories of evaluation are apparent, each with distinctive applications.

One body of work, well summarized by Tol et al (1997), deals with estimating the costs of autonomous, mainly (but not exclusively) reactive, adaptations, undertaken privately (i.e., not adaptation policies of government). As assessments of climate impacts (commonly measured as 'costs', which include both damages and benefits) have increasingly incorporated adaptations, and particularly as impact models and 'integrated assessment models' have shown the potential of adaptation to offset initial impact costs, interest has grown in calculating the costs of autonomous adaptations. Whether or not climate change or another climate stimulus is expected to have problematic or 'dangerous' impacts depends on the adaptations and their costs. A common basis for evaluating impact costs is to sum adaptation costs and residual damage costs (Fankhauser, 1996). Procedures for defining and calculating such adaptation costs are subject to ongoing debate. Tol et al (1997) note that most approaches consider equilibrium adaptation costs but ignore transition costs. Hurd et al (1997) include both market and non-market adaptation in their assessment of impact costs. Any comprehensive assessment of adaptation costs (including benefits) would consider not only economic criteria but also social welfare and equity. This cost estimation for autonomous adaptations is not only important for impact assessment, it is also a necessary ingredient in the 'base case', 'reference scenario' or 'do nothing option' for evaluations of policy initiatives, with respect to both adaptation and mitigation.

The second category of adaptation evaluations deals with planned, mainly (but not exclusively) anticipatory adaptations, undertaken or directly influenced by governments as a policy initiative. In this case, the evaluations are essentially of potential policy measures or strategies; the basic questions being asked are: 'what are good adaptations?' and 'is it worth undertaking these adaptations?'. Some very general steps to addressing these questions are offered in Carter et al (1994), including the selection and weighting of evaluation criteria. Somewhat more detailed procedures for evaluating these 'anticipatory adaptation policies' in the climate change context are outlined in Smith and Lenhart (1996). This approach addresses the management of institutional processes and players, and proposes net benefits and implementability as central evaluative criteria. Numerous other considerations are noted, including flexibility, benefits independent of climate change ('no regrets'), local priorities, levels of risk, and timeframes of decisions. Stakhiv (1996) and Frederick (1997) consider the need for adaptations to climate change in the US water resources sector, and conclude that existing institutions and planning processes can deal with climate stimuli (i.e., they represent 'adaptive management'), but there should be some adaptation in the evaluation criteria. From a disaster management perspective, Tol (1996) argues that policies need to be evaluated with respect to economic viability, environmental sustainability, public acceptability and behavioural flexibility. Klein and Tol (1997) describe methodologies for evaluation, including cost–benefit, cost effectiveness, risk–benefit, and multi-criteria methods.

Fankhauser (1996; 1997) provides an economic efficiency framework in which adaptation actions are considered justified as long as the additional costs of the adaptation are lower than the additional benefits from the associated reduced damages. 'Optimal' levels of adaptation (in an economic efficiency sense) are based on minimizing the sum of adaptation costs and residual damage costs. Such studies require the definition of a base case which involves analysis of autonomous adaptations. These, and other normative studies (e.g. Titus, 1990; Goklany, 1995) illustrate the range of principles and methods which have been proposed for identifying, evaluating and recommending adaptation measures.

Conclusions

This chapter treats adaptation separately from mitigation – as a matter of focus – yet the two main types of policy response to the climate change issue are not independent. They are driven by the same problematique. There is the question of trade-offs or complementarity between the two as policy options (Ausubel, 1991; Fankhauser, 1996). Some adaptations may also have implications for mitigation, such as those that relate to energy use. These interactions and feedbacks are developed elsewhere (e.g. Jepma et al, 1996). The contribution of this anatomy paper is to enhance the understanding of the adaptation component.

Adaptation is an essential ingredient both in assessments of climate impacts and in the development of adaptation policies. The anatomy of adaptation, drawn from a broad consistency in the use of terms across the field, distinguishes three core elements: adaptation to what, who or what adapts, and how does adaptation occur. The evaluation of adaptations addresses the question: how good is the adaptation?

Adaptation to climate stimuli includes adaptive responses to extremes, to variability from year to year, and to changes in long-term mean conditions, both independently and as they relate to each other. Yet the sensitivity and vulnerability of systems and their adaptations are not just to climate, nor do these systems occur in discrete states. Rather, social, economic and ecological systems evolve in a piecemeal, ongoing fashion in response to stimuli of all kinds. Recognition of this milieu is important for analyses of adaptation. It does not mean that adaptation studies necessarily require predictions for sectors and environments. Instead, the comparative-static approaches to adaptation and impact assessment, which begin with specified futures for climate and socio-economic systems, need to be supplemented by sensitivity analyses and investigations of the dynamics of adaptation processes – a transient adaptation approach.

Hence, there is considerable need and opportunity for improving the science of adaptation and its application to policy. The rather ad hoc treatment of adaptation in impact assessments (which still tend to rely on assumptions and focus on technological and structural measures) can be improved by specifying adaptations – including those involving institutions and behaviour – which better match observation and theory of system dynamics in response to stresses, including both risks and opportunities.

The identification and evaluation of adaptation policies can also learn from the successes and failures of the past. For example, Magalhaes (1996) shows how the experience in northwest Brazil over several decades illustrates the need for adaptation to be part of regional development planning in order to increase overall societal capacity to handle a suite of stresses.

Adaptation is not just a climate change issue. Improved adaptation to current conditions is likely to enhance prospects for reducing costs of climate change (Burton, 1996; Smith et al, 1996). However, in many parts of the world, more urgent problems are posed by current variability and extreme events in their own right. This is definitely the case in developing countries subject to recurring extremes such as droughts, floods and tropical storms. However, huge losses associated with extreme climate or weather events have been recently experienced in North America and Europe as well, highlighting the utility of adapting in order to manage risks and benefit from opportunities.

Acknowledgements

This chapter benefited from suggestions by anonymous reviewers, Sally Kane, Gary Yohe, and participants at IPCC Workshops on Adaptation. The work on which this chapter is based was supported by Environment Canada, the US National Oceanic and Atmospheric Administration, and the Social Sciences and Humanities Research Council of Canada.

References

Abercrombie, M., Hickman, C. J., and Johnson, M. L.: 1977, *A Dictionary of Biology,* Penguin Books, Harmondsworth.

Adams, R. M., Fleming, R. A. McCarl, B., and Rosenzweig, C.: 1993, 'A Reassessment of the Economic Effects of Global Climate Change on U.S. Agriculture', *Climatic Change* **30**, 147–167.

Adger, W. N.: 1999, 'Social Vulnerability to Climate Change and Extremes in Coastal Vietnam', *World Development* **27**(2), 249–269.

Adger, W. N., and Kelly, P. M.: 1999, 'Social Vulnerability to Climate Change and the Architecture of Entitlements', *Mitigation and Adaptation Strategies for Global Change* **4**, 253–256.

Alabala-Bertrand, J. M.: 1993, *Political Economy of Large Natural Disasters: With Special Reference to Developing Countries,* Clarendon Press, Oxford.

Ausubel, J. H.: 1991, 'Does Climate Still Matter?', *Nature* **350**, 649–652.

Bijlsma, L., Ehler, C. N., Klein, R. J. T., Kulshrestha, S. M., McLean, R. F., Mimura, N., Nicholls, R. J., Nurse, L. A. Pérez Nicto, II., Stakhiv, E. Z., Turner, R. K., and Warrick, R. A.: 1996, 'Coastal Zones and Small Islands', in Watson, R. T., Zinyowera, M. C., and Moss, R. H. (eds.), *Climate Change 1995. Impacts, Adaptations and Mitigation of Climate Change: Scientific-Technical Analyses.* Contribution of Working Group II to the Second Assessment Report of the Intergovernmental Panel on Climate Change. Cambridge University Press, Cambridge, pp. 289–324.

Blaikie, P., Cannon, T., Davis, I., and Wisner, B.: 1994, *At Risk: Natural Hazards, People's Vulnerability, and Disasters,* Routledge, London.

Bohle, H. G., Downing, T. E., and Watts, M. J.: 1994, 'Climate Change and Social Vulnerability: Toward a Sociology and Geography of Food Insecurity', *Global Environmental Change – Human and Policy Dimensions* **4**(1), 37–48.

Burton, I.: 1992. *Adapt and Thrive.* Canadian Climate Centre unpublished manuscript, Downsview, Ontario.

Burton, I., Kates, R. W., and White, G. F.: 1993, *The Environment as Hazard,* Guildford Press, New York.

Burton, I.: 1996, 'The Growth of Adaptation Capacity: Practice and Policy', in Smith, J. B., Bhatti, N., Menzhulin, G., Benioff, R., Budyko, M., Campos, M., Jallow, B., and Rijsberman, F. (eds.), *Adapting to Climate Change: An International Perspective,* Springer, New York, pp. 55–67.

Burton, I.: 1997, 'Vulnerability and Adaptive Response in the Context of Climate and Climate Change', *Climatic Change* **36**, 185–196.

Carter, T. P., Parry, M. L., Harasawa, H., and Nishioka, N.: 1994, *IPCC Technical Guidelines for Assessing Climate Change Impacts and Adaptations,* University College London, London.

Darwin, R., Tsigas, M., Lewandrowski, J., and Raneses, A.: 1995, *World Agriculture and Climate Change: Economic Adaptations,* United States Department of Agriculture Economic Research Service, Washington.

De Freitas, C. R.: 1989, 'The Hazard Potential of Drought for the Population of the Sahel', in Clarke, J. I., Curson, P., Kayastha, S.L., and Nag, P. (eds.), *Population and Disaster,* Basil Blackwell, Oxford.

De Vries, J.: 1985, 'Analysis of Historical Climate-society Interaction', in Kates, R. W., Ausubel, J. H., and Berbcrian, M. (eds.). *Climate Impact Assessment,* John Wiley and Sons, New York, pp. 273–291.

Denevan, W.: 1983, 'Adaptation, Variation and Cultural Geography', *Professional Geographer* **35**, 406–412.

Downing, T. E.: 1991, 'Vulnerability to Hunger in Africa: A Climate Change Perspective', *Global Environmental Change* **1**, 365–380.

Downing, T. E., Gitu, K. W., and Kaman, C. M. (eds.): 1989, *Coping with Drought in Kenya: National and Local Strategies,* Lynne Rienner, Boulder CO.

Downing, T. E., Olsthoorn, A. A., and Tol, R. S. J.: 1996, *Climate Change and Extreme Events: Altered Risks, Socio-Economic Impacts and Policy Responses,* Vrije Universiteit, Amsterdam.

Easterling, W. E.: 1996, 'Adapting North American Agriculture to Climate Change in Review', *Agricultural and Forest Meteorology* **80(1)**, 1–54.

Easterling, W. E., Crosson, P. R., Rosenberg, N. J., McKenney, M. S., Katz, L. A., and Lemon, K. M.: 1993, 'Agricultural Impacts of and Responses to Climate Change in the Missouri-Iowa-Nebraska-Kansas Region, *Climatic Change* **24(1–2)**, 23–62.

Fankhauser. S.: 1997. *The Costs of Adapting to Climate,* Working Paper No. 13, Global Environmental Facility, Washington.

Fankhauser, S. 1996.: 'The Potential Costs of Climate Change Adaptation', in Smith, J. B., Bhatti, N., Menzhulin, G., Benioff, R., Budyko, M., Campos, M., Jallow, B., and Rijsberman, F. (eds.), *Adapting to Climate Change: An International Perspective,* Springer, New York, pp. 80–96.

Feenstra, J. F., Burton, I., Smith, J., and Tol, R. S. J. (eds.): 1998, *Handbook on Methods for Climate Change Impact Assessment and Adaptation Strategies,* UNEP/ Vrije Universiteit Institute for Environmental Studies, Amsterdam.

Frederick, K. D.: 1997, 'Adapting to Climate Impacts on the Supply and Demand for Water', *Climatic Change* **37**, 141–156.

Fukui, H.: 1979, 'Climatic Variability and Agriculture in Tropical Moist Regions', in *Proceedings of the World Climate Conference,* World Meteorological Association Report No. 537, Geneva, pp. 426–479.

Glantz, M. H.: 1996, 'Forecasting by Analogy: Local Responses to Global climate Change', in Smith, J. B., Bhatti, N., Menzhulin, G., Benioff, R., Budyko, M., Campos, M., Jallow, B., and Rijsberman, F. (eds.). *Adapting to Climate Change: An International Perspective,* Springer, New York, pp. 407–426.

Glantz, M. (ed.): 1988, *Societal Responses to Climate Change: Forecasting by Analogy,* Westview Press, Boulder, CO.

Goklany, I. M.: 1995, 'Strategies to Enhance Adaptability: Technological Change, Sustainable Growth and Free Trade', *Climatic Change* 30, 427–449.

Hardesty, D. L.: 1983, 'Rethinking Cultural Adaptation', *Professional Geographer* 35, 399–406.

Hastenrath, S.: 1995, 'Recent Advances in Tropical Climate Prediction', *Journal of Climate,* 8, 1519–1531.

Heathcote, R. L.: 1985. 'Extreme Event Analysis', in Kates, R. W., Ausuabel. J. H., and Berberian, M. (eds.). *Climate Impact Assessment,* John Wiley and Sons, New York, pp. 369–401.

Hewitt, K.: 1997, *Regions of Risk: A Geographical Introduction to Disasters,* Addison Wesley Longman, Harlow, Essex.

Hewitt, K., and Burton, I.: 1971, *The Hazardousness of a Place: A Regional Ecology of Damaging Events,* University of Toronto, Toronto.

Houghton, J. T., Filho, L. G. M., Callander, B. A., Harris, N., Kattenberg, A., and Maskell, K.: 1996, *Climate Change 1995: The Science of Climate Change,* Contribution of Working Group I to the Second Assessment Report of the Intergovernmental Panel on Climate Change, Cambridge University Press, Cambridge.

Hulme, M, Raper, S. C. B., and Wigley, T. M. L.: 1995, 'An Integrated Framework to Address Climate Change (ESCAPE) and Further Developments of the Global and Regional Climate Modules (MAGICC)', *Energy Policy* 23(4/5), 347–355.

Hurd, B., Callaway, J., Kirshen, P., and Smith, J.: 1997, 'Economic Effects of Climate Change on U.S. Water Resources', in Mendelsohn, R. and Newmann, J. (eds.), *The Impacts of Climate Change on the U.S. Economy,* Cambridge University Press, Cambridge.

IPCC: 1996, 'Summary for Policymakers: Scientific-Technical Analyses of Impacts, Adaptations, and Mitigation of Climate Change', in Watson, R. T., Zinyowera, M. C., and Moss, R. H. (eds.), *Climate Change 1995. Impacts, Adaptations and Mitigation of Climate Change: Scientific-Technical Analyses,* Contribution of Working Group II to the Second Assessment Report of the Intergovernmental Panel on Climate Change, Cambridge University Press, Cambridge, pp. 1–18.

Jepma C. J., Asaduzzaman, M., Mintzer, I., Maya, R. S., and Al-Monef, M.: 1996, 'A Generic Assessment of Response Options', in Bruce, J. T. et al (eds.). *Climate Change 1995: Economic and Social Dimensions,* Contribution of Working Group II to the Second Assessment Report of the Intergovernmental Panel on Climate Change, Cambridge University Press, Cambridge, pp. 225–262.

Jodha, N. S.: 1989, 'Potential Strategies for Adapting to Greenhouse Warming: Perspectives from the Developing World', in Rosenberg, N. J., Easterling III, W. E., and Crosson, P. R. (eds.). *Greenhouse Warming: Abatement and Adaptation,* Resources for the Future, Washington DC.

Kane, S., Reilly, J., and Tobey, J.: 1992, 'A Sensitivity Analysis of the Implications of Climate Change for World Agriculture', in Reilly, J. M., and Anderson, M. (eds.). *Economic Issues in Global Climate Change,* Westview Press, Boulder, pp. 117–131.

Karl, T. R., and Knight, R. W.: 1998, 'Secular Trends of Precipitation Amount, Frequency, and Intensity in the United States', *Bulletin of the American Meteorological society* 79(2), 231–241.

Kasperson, R. E., and Dow, K.: 1991, 'Developmental and Geographical Equity in Global Environmental Change: a Framework for Analysis', *Evaluation Review* 15, 149–171.

Kates, R. W.: 1971, 'Natural Hazard in Human Ecological Perspective: Hypotheses and Models', *Economic Geography* 47, 438–451.

Kates, R. W.: 1985, 'The Interaction of Climate and Society', in Kates, R. W., Ausubel, J. H., and Berberian, M. (eds.), *Climate Impact Assessment,* John Wiley and Sons, New York, pp. 3–36.

Kates, R. W., Hohenemser, C., and Kasperson, J. X.: 1985, *Perilous Progress: Managing the Hazards of Technology,* Westview Press, Boulder, Colo.

Klein, R. J. T.: 1998, 'Towards Better Understanding, Assessment and Funding of Climate adaptation', *Climatic Change* 44, 15–19.

Klein, R. J. T., and Nicholls, R. J.: 1999, 'Assessment of Coastal Vulnerability to Climate Change', *Ambio* 28(2): 182–187.

Klein, R. J. T. and Tol, R. S. J.: 1997, *Adaptation to Climate Change: Options and Technologies,* Institute of Environmental Sciences, Vrije Universiteit, Amsterdam.

Krankina. O. N., Dixon, R. K., Kirilenko, A. P., and Kobak, K. I.: 1997, 'Global Climate Change Adaptation: Examples from Russian Boreal Forests', *Climatic Change* 36, 197–215.

Lagos, P. and Buizer, J.: 1992. 'El Niño and Peru: A Nation's Response to Interannual Climate Variability', in Majumdar, S. K., Fothes, G. S., Millet, E. W., and Schmalz, R. F. (eds.). *Natural and Technological Disasters: Causes, Effects and Preventive Measures,* The Pennsylvania Academy of Science.

Lawrence, E.: 1995, *Henderson's Dictionary of Biological Terms,* Longman Scientific and Technical, Harlow.

Leemans, R.: 1992, 'Modelling Ecological and Agricultural Impacts of Global Change on a Global Scale', *Journal of Sci & Ind. Res* 51, 709–724.

Lewandrowski, J. and Brazee, R.: 1992, 'Government Farm Programs and Climate Change: A First Look', in Reilly, J. M. and Anderson, M. (eds.), *Economic Issues in Global Climate Change,* Westview Press, Boulder, pp 132–147.

MacDonald, G. M., Edwards, T. W. D., Moser, K. A., Pienitz, R., and Smol, J. P.: 1993, 'Rapid Response of Treeline Vegetation and Lakes to Past Climate Warming', *Nature* 361, 243–246.

Magalhaes, A. R.: 1996. 'Adapting to Climate Variations in Developing Regions: A Planning Framework', in Smith, J. B., Bhatti, N., Menzhulin, G., Benioff, R., Budyko, M., Campos, M., Jallow, B., and Rijsberman, F. (eds.), *Adapting to Climate Change: An International Perspective,* Springer, New York, pp. 44–54.

Markham, A., and Malcolm, J.: 1996, 'Biodiversity and Wildlife: Adaptation to Climate Change', in Smith, J. B., Bhatti, N., Menzhulin, G., Benioff, R., Budyko, M., Campos, M., Jallow, B., and Rijsberman, F. (eds.), *Adapting to Climate Change: An International Perspective,* Springer, New York, pp. 384–401.

Mearns, L. O., Katz, R. W., and Schneider, S. H.: 1984, 'Extreme High Temperature Events: Changes in their Probabilities with Changes in Mean Temperature', *Journal of Climate and Applied Meteorology,* 23, 1601–1613.

Meyer, W. B., Butzer, K. W., Downing, T. E., Turner II, B. L., Wenzel, G. W., and Wescoat, J. L.: 1998, 'Reasoning by Analogy', in Rayner, S., and Malone, E. L. (eds), *Human Choice and Climate Change, Volume 3: Tools for Policy Analysis,* Battelle Press, Columbus, Ohio, pp. 217–289.

Olsthoorn, A. A., Maunder, W. J., and Tol, R. S. J.: .1996, 'Tropical Cyclones in the Southwest Pacific: Impacts on Pacific Island Countries with Particular Reference to Fiji', in Downing, T. E. et al (eds.), *Climate Change and Extreme Events: Altered Risks, Socio-Economic Impacts and Policy Responses,* Institute for Environmental Management, Vrije Universiteit, Amsterdam, pp. 185–208.

O'Riordan, T., and Jordan, A.: 1999, 'Institutions, Climate change and Cultural Theory: Towards a Common Analytical Framework', *Global Environmental Change,* 9, 81–93.

Parry, M. L.: 1986, 'Some Implications of Climate Change for Human Development', in Clark, W. C., and Munn, R. E. (eds.), *Sustainable Development of the Biosphere,* Cambridge University Press, Cambridge, pp. 378–07.

Peters, R. L., and Lovejoy, T. E. (eds): 1992, *Global Warming and Biological Diversity,* Yale University Press, New Haven, Connecticut.

Pimm, S. L.: 1984, 'The Complexity and Stability of Ecosystems', *Nature,* 307(5949), 321–325.

Rayner, S., and Malone, E. L. (eds): 1998, *Human Choice and Climate Change, Volume 3: Tools for Policy Analysis,* Battelle Press. Columbus, Ohio.

Reilly, J., and Schimmelpfennig, D.: 2000, 'Irreversibility, Uncertainty, and Learning Portraits of Adaptation to Long-Term Climate Change', *Climatic Change,* **45**, 253–278.

Ribot, J. C., Magalhaes, A. R., and Panagides, S. S.: 1996, *Climate Variability, Climate Change, and Social Vulnerability in the Semi-arid Tropics,* Cambridge University Press, Cambridge.

Riebsame, W. E.: 1991, 'Sustainability of the Great Plains in an Uncertain Climate', *Great Plains Research* **1 (1)**, 133–151.

Rose, C., and Hurst, P.: 1991, *Can Nature Survive Global Warming,* World Wildlife Fund International, Gland, Switzerland.

Rosenzweig, C. and Parry, M. L.: 1994, 'Potential Impact of Climate Change on World Food Supply', *Nature* **367**, 133–138.

Smit., B. (ed.): 1993, *Adaptation to Climatic Variability and Change,* Environment Canada, Guelph.

Smit, B., McNabb, D., and Smithers, J.: 1996, 'Agricultural Adaptation to Climate Change', *Climatic Change* **33**, 7–29.

Smit B., Blain, R., and Keddie, P.: 1997, 'Corn Hybrid Selection and Climatic Variability: Gambling with Nature?', *The Canadian Geographer* **41**(4), 429–438.

Smith, J. B., Ragland, S. F., and Pitts, G. J.: 1996, 'A Process for Evaluating Anticipatory Adaptation Measures for Climate Change', *Water, Air, and Soil Pollution* **92**, 229–238.

Smith, J. B.: 1996, 'Using a Decision Matrix to Assess Climate Change Adaptation', in Smith, J. B. et al (eds.). *Adapting to Climate Change: An International Perspective,* Springer, New York, pp. 68–79.

Smith, K.: 1996, *Environmental Hazards: Assessing Risk and Reducing Disaster,* Routledge, London.

Smith, J., and Lenhart, S.S.: 1996, 'Climate Change Adaptation Policy Options', *Climate Research* **6**, 193–201.

Smithers, J., and Smit, B.: 1997, 'Agricultural System Response to Environmental Stress', in Ilberry, B., Chiotti, Q., and Rickard, T. (eds.). *Agricultural Restructuring and Sustainability,* CAB International, Wallingford, pp. 167–183.

Sonka, S. T., and Lamb, P. J.: 1987, 'On Climate Change and Economic Analysis', *Climatic Change* **11**(3), 291–312.

Sonka, ST.: 1992, 'Evaluating Socioeconomic Assessments of the Effect of Climate Change on Agriculture', in Reilly, J. M., and Anderson, M. (eds.), *Economic Issues in Global Climate Change,* Westview Press, Boulder, pp. 402–413.

Sprengers, S. A., Slager, L. K., and Aiking, H.: 1994, *Biodiversity and Climate Change Part 1: Establishment of Ecological Goals for the Climate Convention,* Institute for Environmental Studies, Vrije Universiteit, Amsterdam.

Stakhiv, E. Z.: 1996, 'Managing Water Resources for Climate Change Adaptation', in Smith, J. B. et al (eds.). *Adapting to Climate Change: An International Perspective,* Springer, New York, pp. 243–264.

Stakhiv, E.: 1993, *Evaluation of IPCC Adaptation Strategies,* Institute for Water Resources, U.S. Army Corps of Engineers, Fort Belvoir, VA, draft report.

Titus, J. G.: 1990, 'Strategies for Adapting to the Greenhouse Effect', *Journal of the American Planning Association* **56**(3), 311–323.

Tol, R. S. J., Fankhauser, S., and Smith, J. B.: 1997, *The Scope for Adaptation to Climate Change: What Can We Learn from the Literature?,* Institute for Environmental Studies, Vrije Universiteit, Amsterdam.

Tol. R. S. J.: 1996, 'A Systems View of Weather Disasters', in Downing, T. E. et al (eds.), *Climate Change and Extreme Events: Altered Risks, Socio-Economic Impacts and Policy Responses,* Institute for Environmental Studies, Vrijc Universiteit, Amsterdam, pp. 17–33.

United Nations Framework Convention on Climate Change (UNFCCC): 1992, *United Nations Framework Convention on Climate Change: Text,* UNEP/WMO, Geneva.

Viscusi, W. K.: 1992, 'Implications of Global-change Uncertainties: Agricultural and Natural Resource Policies', in Reilly, J. M., and Anderson, M. (eds.), *Economic Issues in Global Climate Change,* Westview Press, Boulder, pp. 414–424.

Warrick, R. A., Gifford, R. M., and Parry, M. L.: 1986, 'CO$_2$, Climatic Change and Agriculture', in Bolin, B., Döös, B. R., Jäger, J., and Warrick, R. A. (eds.), *The Greenhouse Effect, Climatic Change, and Ecosystems,* New York, John Wiley and Sons, pp. 393–473.

Watson, R. T., Zinyowera, M. C., and Moss, R. H.: 1996, *Climate Change 1995: Impacts, Adaptations and Mitigation of Climate Change: Scientific-Technical Analysis.* Contribution of Working Group II to the Second Assessment Report of the Intergovernmental Panel on Climate Change, Cambridge University Press, Cambridge.

Wigley, T. M.: 1985, 'Impact of Extreme Events', *Nature* **316**: 106–107.

Yohe, G. W., Neumann, J. E., Marshall, P. B., and Ameden, H.: 1996, 'The Economic Cost of Greenhouse Induced Sea Level Rise for Developed Property in the United States', *Climatic Change* **32**(4), 387–410.

6

Climate Change
and the Adaptation Deficit

Ian Burton

Two Perspectives on Adaptation

Adaptation is by no means a new concept or practice. Adaptation, including adaptation to climate, is as old as our species. Human beings have adapted successfully to all except the most extreme climates on the planet. People make a living and a livelihood in the subarctic tundra of Canada, and in the steppes of Mongolia as well as in tropical rainforests, in small islands, and in mountain regions, and the Sahel. On this planet, climate varies as much or more over space than in time. Now, however, we are concerned with something different from the age-old human practice of human adjustment to environmental circumstances, including adaptation to a climate that for practical purposes can be considered as stationary. We are concerned with adaptation to a climate which is changing at a fast rate due to anthropogenic interference.

The United Nations Framework Convention on Climate Change (UNFCCC) was negotiated and agreed to deal with the new threat of anthropogenic climate change. The ultimate objective of the Convention as stated in Article 2 is the 'stabilization of greenhouse gas concentrations in the atmosphere at a level that would prevent dangerous anthropogenic interference with the climate system'. Adaptation comes into this equation because the more that adaptation can be used to reduce impacts that might be considered dangerous, the higher the threshold of concentrations that can be accepted. Thus adaptation is important in the decision about how much and how rapidly greenhouse gas emissions need to be reduced. I call this the 'pollutionist' view of adaptation, because it is important in deciding what level of greenhouse gas pollution can be tolerated in the atmosphere. It seems that the 'pollutionist' view was what was uppermost in the minds of those who drafted the UNFCCC.

There is, however, a second view of adaptation that I will call the development view. This view recognizes that climate variability and extremes, even without climate change, can inflict significant damage on human lives and activities, and that this damage can be a significant impediment to development. Climate-related extreme weather events and climate variability help to cause poverty, and to keep poor and vulnerable people, poor and vulnerable. If we are to reduce climate-related disasters, eliminate extreme poverty, and attain the Millennium Development Goals we must incorporate adaptation to climate into development planning and implementation. We must begin adapting to climate change now. You might wish to argue that the two views are really the same. In both cases adaptation is needed. One difference, however, is that the development perspective clearly implies adaptation now regardless of climate change, whereas the pollutionist view requires adaptation to be factored into decisions according to a schedule that involves the projection and observation of climate change and efforts at mitigation.

Two Categories of Adaptation

We can therefore think of two categories of adaptation. They might be called Type I and Type II Adaptation. Adaptation Type I refers to past current adaptation strategy, policy, and measures without considering climate change. Most of the adaptation that we do is still Type I. Type II Adaptation is adaptation to climate change. Because climate change risks have still not been factored into many development decisions, and because awareness of the need for adaptation has still not been well incorporated into the work of development agencies, or ministries of finance and development, not much Type II adaptation has taken place. This may also be partly explained by uncertainty about the amount and rate of future climate change, and to the lack of development assistance specifically earmarked for climate change adaptation. There is also a limited capacity to deal with adaptation in many countries in the face of a host of other urgent problems. It is also due to the adoption of short-term perspectives. Climate change is often seen as a slow process and the idea that adaptation can be left to a later date is commonplace. Type II Adaptation is therefore seen as not urgent, and also is often related to climate averages rather than variability or extremes. This is the case not only in developing countries, but even more so in the most highly developed and richest countries.

There is nevertheless a demand for attention to adaptation at the meetings of the UNFCCC, especially from those developing countries considered to be most vulnerable such as the least developed countries (LDCs), and the Alliance of Small Island States (AOSIS). Article 4.4 of the Convention states, 'the developed country Parties and other developed Parties included in Annex II shall also assist the developing country Parties that are particularly vulnerable to the adverse effects of climate change in meeting costs of adaptation to those adverse effects'. A number of funds which can be used to support adaptation have been established including the Least Developed Countries Fund (LDCF), the Special Climate Change Fund (SCCF), and the Adaptation Fund established under the Kyoto Protocol. The Global Environment Facility (GEF) is now proposing a Strategic Programme on Adaptation (SPA) that will be a pilot exercise in the implementation of adaptation. The strategic priority was adopted by the GEF council meeting in November 2003, as part of the 2005–2007 GEF business plan, which allocates US$50 million to it.

How are these funds for adaptation to be used? It is proposed that their use be limited to the incremental costs of adaptation, that is the adaptation that is necessary because of climate change (Type II Adaptation) and not the costs of adapting to current climate or Type I Adaptation. From a development perspective it makes sense to graft adaptation to climate change onto existing adaptation strategies, policies and measures. Adaptation to climate change makes no sense unless it starts from present-day adaptation. In other words Type II Adaptation should be built upon and strengthen Type I Adaptation. Type II Adaptation is what we need to do differently, both more and better, if we are to adapt to climate change. Unfortunately the science of climate change does not allow the theoretical distinction between climate and climate change to be measured. It is impossible to state how much of a tropical cyclone, or a heat wave or a flood can be attributed to climate change. Type I and Type II Adaptation therefore have to be considered as part of a seamless process of adaptation. There are, however, two important differences between Type I and Type II Adaptation. Type I Adaptation has always been the responsibility of sovereign states. Type II Adaptation involves anthropogenic climate change, and therefore some degree of globally shared responsibilities. Further Type I Adaptation has been and is to a climate considered as stationary. Type II Adaptation recognizes that the assumption of a stationary climate is no longer valid.

The Adaptation Deficit

What is the status of Type I Adaptation and how successful is it? Unfortunately the story is not encouraging. An examination of losses from extreme weather events, or what might be called climate-related disasters, shows that they have been rising (Figure 6.1). Data from the Munich Reinsurance Company show that both insured and economic (non-insured) losses have been rising at what looks like an exponential rate. Those curves if extended on the same trajectory look very ominous indeed. The losses do not yet reflect much climate change. If we add some of the projected rates of climate change into this graph the levels of loss are likely to become catastrophically high.

The high level of current losses results form what I will call the adaptation deficit. Why are weather-related losses growing so rapidly? There are a number of possible explanations (White et al, 2001). Could it be that we have insufficient knowledge of the behaviour of the climate system and that the management of weather hazards continues to be flawed by significant areas of ignorance? Scientific understanding of the processes generating natural extremes has expanded considerably in recent decades, and in many cases of atmospheric hazards, forecasting and warning capacity has improved dramatically. This accounts in large part for the reduction in the level of mortality from extreme climate-related events. Knowledge of the probability and potential magnitude of hazard events has also increased. White and his colleagues conclude that lack of scientific knowledge is not a major cause for the rise in losses.

Perhaps then the available knowledge is not used or not used effectively? There is more evidence to support this explanation. In developing countries especially, weather-related disasters continue to take people by surprise. Emergency responses are apparently improving, but longer-term programmes to reduce vulnerability through poverty reduction and related measures are slow to take off. There also might be a time lag. The initial expectations of the UN International Decade for Natural Disaster Reduction (1990–1999) were that damage could be reduced by 50 per cent by the effective use of knowledge and forecasting. Unfortunately these predictions proved to be far too optimistic. There is no doubt that more scientific knowledge would be

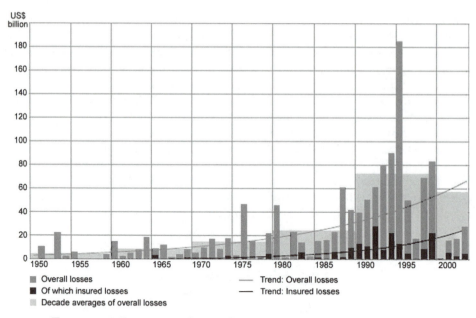

Figure 6.1 *Economic and insured losses during 1950–2003 with trends*

Source: Munich Re, 2004

Note: The chart presents the economic losses and insured losses – adjusted to the present values. The increases verify the increase in catastrophe losses since 1950.

helpful, especially the designation of hazards zones as a basis for the deployment of adaptation measures. There is no doubt that the knowledge that exists could be used more effectively, and that more timely action could bring more rapid results. While more and better knowledge, more effectively used could help, it has not so far proved sufficient to offset the growth in vulnerability and damage potential resulting from the growth of population, the increase of material wealth in some places, and the persistence of poverty elsewhere, and the expansion of human settlements and populations into high hazard zones. The adaptation deficit is increasing and is set to get larger with climate change. What seems to be needed is a much more effective process of adaptation (both Type I and Type II) that uses both structural and non-structural measures, and includes land-use planning, building codes are standards, insurance and where necessary policy innovations to bring losses under control.

The Role of the Climate Convention (UNFCCC)

Can the Climate Convention bring success where the UN Decade for Natural Disaster Reduction, and the efforts of many governments, development assistance agencies and humanitarian relief organizations have so far failed? If the Climate Convention is to help, the concentration on the 'pollutionst' perspective and on Type II Adaptation will have to be augmented by the development view and take into consideration the need for Type I adaptation to address the current adaptation deficit.

There are indeed indications that this process is already under way, for example, as noted previously, in the creation of funds to assist in meeting the costs of adaptation. While these funds are directed at anthropogenic climate change or Type II Adaptation and not specifically at the current adaptation deficit, the operational guidelines being developed for the funds make it clear that their use is to be country driven, and 'mainstreamed' or integrated into the national development process. Clearly Type I and Type II Adaptation need to be brought together. But as we have seen, Type I Adaptation is not working very well. This is leading some to suggest that adaptation promoted and supported through the Convention must be something new, and stronger, and better. Perhaps this could be facilitated by the development of a new legal instrument for adaptation which might become an Adaptation Protocol? My view of this is that before serious discussions or negotiations on such a topic are started it would be good to hear from the science and expert communities about the potential role of such a Protocol in promoting the adaptation that is needed. At the moment we have little idea of how the objective of an Adaptation Protocol might be specified, and what it might contain.

How might the international science and expert communities be asked to contribute? Some appropriate process has to be developed and put into operation. It is easier to suggest what is not likely to work. The organization of workshops under the Convention process has been one much-used method of getting expert input. In my view this rarely works well because the time is too short and the workshop syntheses and reports have rarely produced truly helpful results. Another route is to use the Intergovernmental Panel on Climate Change (IPCC), either the periodic Assessments or in the preparation of a Special Report. The deficiencies of this approach include the great length of time between IPCC Assessments, (the Fourth Assessment is not due till 2007), and the restriction that the IPCC limits its Assessments to the peer-reviewed scientific literature, perhaps extended to include some informal folk or traditional knowledge. Whereas what is needed is creativity to develop new ideas and new options for the way in which adaptation might be facilitated. In the final section of the chapter I have a few questions that could be directed to a group of scientists and experts especially selected to work for the necessary period of time on the idea of the potential contents of an Adaptation Protocol. Only when we have a better sense of what a Protocol might achieve does it make sense to start serious discussions within the established institutions of the Convention process.

Mitigation and Adaptation Compared

The reduction of greenhouse gas emissions has been the focus of attention in the Convention process, and a coherent regime has been created for mitigation. There is a clear objective in Article 2 which calls for the stabilization of greenhouse gas concentrations. There is no similar stated objective for adaptation. What is meant by mitigation is clearly understood. By contrast adaptation means too many unclear things. There is no formal definition of adaptation in the Convention. There is a mitigation baseline.The year 1990 has been chosen as the point in time against which to measure changes. There is no adaptation baseline or discussion on what it might be and how it might be measured. There are agreed targets and schedules for emission reductions. There are no targets and schedules for adaptation. Mitigation has a clear funding regime in the Clean Development Mechanism. Adaptation can be supported from several funds in principle, but these are funds based on voluntary contributions, and are not linked to any measure of progress on adaptation. Mitigation has a legal instrument in the form of the Kyoto Protocol which clearly establishes a mitigation regime and points the way forward. We are far from having a clear adaptation regime.

Towards an Adaptation Regime

It is not yet clear that an Adaptation Protocol could deliver the more effective adaptation that is required. (After all the Kyoto Protocol is not yet delivering mitigation). But it is clear that more needs to be done to create a more coherent and effective adaptation regime. Perhaps the need that is most recognized now is captured in the word 'mainstreaming'. This means that ways must be found to integrate climate change risks into development activities. National governments, planning and development agencies, ministries charged with management tasks in agriculture, water, forests, environment, physical planning, coastal development, health and others, should begin to consider how climate change risks will affect their policies, plans, projects and programmes. Bilateral and multilateral development assistance agencies and banks should be prepared to help in this process. Whatever is done under the Convention should be integrated into present efforts, or in other words Type I and Type II adaptation need to be brought together. The ideas under development at the World Bank for the application of a climate change screening tool and climate risk assessment are examples of what might be done (Burton and van Aalst, 2004).

As part of the 'mainstreaming' process, some serious thought should be given to the development of a more practical and operational view of adaptation. How is it to be defined and measured? Can the objectives of adaptation be specified in such a way that progress can be assessed? Does it make sense to formulate targets for adaptation? The International Decade for Natural Disaster Reduction (1990–1999) wanted to reduce the costs of natural disasters by 50 per cent. But they have continued to increase. Can linking climate change risks and the Climate Convention process with disaster mitigation help development and reduce poverty?

Most climate-related losses are not insured. People and nations suffer the losses and have to rely on their own resources and humanitarian assistance to attempt to recover. They can also borrow money for reconstruction. The private insurance industry is generally not expanding its services in this area and reinsurance companies are concerned about increased exposure to catastrophic losses. Could some new provision be made for insurance under the Climate Convention that would help to spread losses, ensure a safer economic climate for investment, and at the same time promote effective adaptation policies? Could such a plan, organized at an international level, and involving public–private partnerships be an attractive way of addressing the need for more adaptation? Some experiments that are being tried in the areas of earthquake insurance and weather derivatives show that some people and agencies at least are awake to the possibilities.

Let us determine that the work of this conference[1], and the messages we send out from Yunnan, will say clearly to people at least four things:

1   That there is an unacceptably large and growing adaptation deficit.
2   That we can get on the right track and begin to address the deficit more effectively by combining the Climate Convention work with the development process and mainstreaming climate risk.
3   That by developing a more coherent and operational adaptation regime we can have more confidence that the efforts we collectively make will be rewarded with success.
4   That future work on adaptation should be done in the context of applications, which include climate risk assessment. This experience should be monitored and evaluated so that a library of knowledge base of best or good practice can be built up.

Note

1   This paper was presented to the International Conference on Adaptation Science, Management and Policy Options, Lijiang, Yunnan, China, 17–19 May 2004.

References

Burton, I. and van Aalst, M., 2004. *Look Before You Leap: A Risk Management Approach for Incorporating Climate Change Adaptation in World Bank Operations*, World Bank, Washington, DC.
Munich Re, 2004. *Topics geo-Annual Review: Natural Catastrophes 2003*, Munich Re, Germany.
White, G.F., Kates, R.W. and Burton, I., 2001. Knowing Better and Losing Even More: The Use of Knowledge in Hazards Management, *Environmental Hazards*, 3 (3–4), 81–92.

Part II

Adaptation, Vulnerability and Resilience

7

Are Coping Strategies a Cop-Out?

Susanna Davies

Introduction

Coping strategies are the bundle of poor people's responses to declining food availability and entitlements in abnormal seasons or years, Households do not respond arbitrarily to variability in food supply and, as a result, people living in conditions where their main sources of income (and food) are under recurrent threat develop strategies to minimize risk to immediate food security and to longer-term livelihood security (Frankenberger and Goldstein, 1990). This chapter explores the nature of coping and adaptation in vulnerable livelihood systems, in order to see whether monitoring coping strategies can be useful in predicting food stress.

As coping strategies become an increasingly popular tool in food and livelihood security analysis and policymaking, so has the idea become more befuddled, as researchers and policymakers confound the two. The central confusion is between coping strategies as fall-back mechanisms during periods when habitual food entitlements are disrupted; and coping strategies as outcomes of fundamental and irreversible changes in local livelihood systems. Clarification is required if coping strategies are to remain a useful conceptual tool, both for monitoring declining food availability and for identifying appropriate interventions. Coping is thus defined as a short-term response to an immediate and unusual decline in access to food. Adapting, in contrast, means a permanent change in the mix of ways in which food is acquired, irrespective of the year in question. As Gore (1992, p16) has correctly argued '"coping" essentially means acting to survive within the prevailing rule systems'. When adaptation occurs, such rule systems (or the moral economy) themselves change, as do the livelihood systems in which these rules operate. Indicators which seek to track coping strategies have to be able to differentiate between coping within existing rules and adapting the rules themselves to meet livelihood needs.

Although the importance and proliferation of coping strategies have long been recognized by anthropologists (D'Souza, 1985; Campbell, 1990), it is only recently that their significance for food security monitoring has been acknowledged. Interest in coping strategies arose particularly in the aftermath of famines in the Sahel and Horn of Africa in the mid-1980s, as a means of understanding why it was that some people survived periods of dearth, while others did not. Coping strategies are concerned with livelihood system success rather than failure. This success was explained in part by the reinterpretation of food entitlements, to include a wider range of sources of and calls on entitlements than was habitually associated with food-insecure households (Swift, 1989). Among others, Watts (1983, 1988) and Longhurst (1986) have identified patterns of coping behaviour, based on a widely defined entitlement base, which have been successful in mitigating the threat of famine. In addition, the ability of the rural poor to manage risk and to adapt to longer-term changes in their livelihood systems has been accorded greater importance than in the past (Mortimore, 1989). Finally, it has been shown that populations in more marginal environments are probably much better equipped to cope with periods of food stress than those accustomed to more secure conditions (Reardon and Matlon, 1989).

The enthusiasm for coping strategies has been further fuelled by redefinitions of household food security in the light of a sustainable livelihood security approach to understanding rural communities. Contrary to conventional wisdom, there is little evidence to show that, apart from conditions of extreme food stress (when livelihood systems have collapsed and death from starvation is imminent), people will always meet food security needs first, irrespective of the consequences of so doing for other aspects of their livelihood security. De Waal (1989) found in the 1984/1985 famine in Darfur, Sudan, that people chose to go hungry in order to preserve their assets and future livelihoods. Equally, in comparing the sequential uptake of coping strategies employed in periods of food stress in a number of African and Asian cases, Corbett (1988) found that preservation of assets takes priority over meeting immediate food needs until the point of destitution, when all options have been exhausted.

How Useful is the Concept of Coping Strategies?

Increasingly, coping strategies are regarded as being an inherently good thing, but there is a tendency for them to become shorthand for a complex web of processes at work. This can add to confusion about what coping strategies indicate is happening in famine-prone communities; and what policy options are inferred. Lack of clarity about what 'coping strategies' really are makes for little dynamism in their analysis. Four areas of concern require clarification. First, 'coping strategies' is often used as a catch-all term to describe everything that rural producers do over and above primary productive activities. While it is perhaps justifiable to argue that for food-poor households, all decisions are influenced by and have some bearing on food poverty, it is not analytically helpful to think of everything as a coping strategy. It simply becomes synonymous with the socio-economy of the household or, more recently, with livelihood security.

Second, focusing on coping strategies in situations of food stress can imply that people do cope and thus that food insecurity is a transitory phenomenon. This conflicts with the distinction habitually made between transitory and chronic food insecurity (World Bank, 1986). If people also 'cope' with chronic food insecurity, then the distinction between their normal behaviour and their coping behaviour is far from clear. At the extreme, all behaviour becomes a coping strategy when, for example, pastoralists have lost their animals and hence their means of primary production. Such groups who have fallen out of the bottom of livelihood systems are uniquely vulnerable and indeed have to cope to survive. But it is conceptually confusing to lump the means of subsistence eked out by such people (the ultra-poor and destitute) with pre-planned strategies used by people within a livelihood system to overcome an exceptionally severe episode of food insecurity. Further, searching for and monitoring coping strategies can mask the collapse of livelihood systems by presupposing that people cope even in subsistence economies which are no longer viable from the point of view of either food or livelihood security. Duffield (1990), drawing on evidence from Sudan, argues that there are parts of the country where the combination of agro-climatic conditions, civil war and impoverishment from repeated famine has rendered some groups incapable of surviving, irrespective of current conditions. These are precisely the circumstances in which famine risks becoming endemic and where rural producers will need to radically alter their livelihood strategies to survive. An emphasis on 'coping' may blind policy-makers and researchers to the need for a radical reappraisal of the requirements of people's livelihoods in marginal areas.

Third, while coping strategies may be useful in the short term (and indeed, those who employ them have little option), they may be bad for longer-term development; both from the point of view of those who practise them and of those who seek to intervene to facilitate the development process. Implicit in coping strategies is that the entire working life of subsistence producers is taken up in acquiring food; enabling people to stand still, but preventing them from moving ahead. A focus on coping strategies also hides the (increasing) need of rural producers to develop livelihood strategies which will provide for greater numbers of people in the future. Growth linkages are thus central to the process of adaptation, but rarely included in analyses of coping behaviour. This assertion is, to some extent, contradicted by the sustainable livelihood security approach, insofar as meeting food needs may be pushed into second place behind securing future livelihoods. But this holds only to the point where such choices make those livelihoods more secure in the future than in the present. All too often, future livelihoods are no more secure as a result of these choices, implying that there is no saving in the household; and that livelihoods are dominated by the need to avoid risk, including the risk of investing in production.

Fourth, and linked to this, is the fact that coping strategies are not necessarily economically or environmentally sustainable. De Waal (1989) distinguishes between 'non-erosive' and 'erosive' coping, in order to differentiate those strategies which use extra sources of income and do not erode the subsistence base of the household (thereby compromising future livelihood security), from those which do not entail such costs. There is as yet little evidence to show how the trade-off between subsistence and economic sustainability works in meeting immediate food needs and longer-term livelihood ones. A study of coping strategy use over four years in Mali has shown that the overwhelming characteristic of strategies pursued is that they offer – without exception – uncertain, piecemeal and poorly remunerated means of filling the annual food gap (Davies, 1993). To find out more about the subsistence/economic sustainability trade-off, the ability of these strategies to reduce vulnerability over much longer periods than a simple cycle of famine and rehabilitation would have to be assessed. On the environmental side, quick correlations between 'abusive' coping strategies (e.g. cutting down trees to sell wood) and environmental degradation are often made. Recent evidence indicates that marginal semi-arid zones are probably much more resilient to degradation than is generally assumed (Behnke et al, 1993). Insofar as coping strategies are concerned, this suggests that much more careful analyses of the environmental consequences of poor people's actions in response to livelihood risk need to be carried out.

These last two criticisms of coping strategies have implications for the often-advocated (albeit rarely implemented) reinforcement of indigenous coping strategies as a more appropriate and effective method of famine mitigation (and promotion of livelihood sustainability) than distributing emergency food aid once livelihoods have been eroded (e.g. WFP, 1989). Reinforcing coping strategies may lock people into a vicious circle of subsistence and coping. If, on the other hand, food insurance for the very poor is provided, it enables them to be economically active (to take risks, to save). Thus, whereas there is an economic efficiency argument for guaranteeing food security, over and above the purely humanitarian one, reinforcing coping strategies may be economically inefficient because it will reinforce the risk-averse survival-orientation of poor people. Indeed, it might be argued that the focus on short-term alleviation and the allied notion of 'coping' create the very conditions of dependency rural producers are often blamed for having.

Coping with Security, Adapting to Vulnerability

Coping (in)capacity cannot be separated from the nature and intensity of vulnerability. The reasons why households pursue a particular mix of coping strategies and their timing for so doing depend on a complex range of criteria which are intimately linked to different dimensions of vulnerability, two of the most important of which are resilience and sensitivity (see Bayliss-Smith, 1991).[1] Highly resilient systems have the capacity to bounce back to a normal state after food crises, which is contingent upon having coping strategies which are reserved for periods of unusual stress. The sensitivity of a livelihood system refers to the intensity with which the shock is experienced: in highly sensitive systems, coping strategies are not available to cushion the shock. Further, the greater the sensitivity, the further the system will need to bounce back; consequently, there is a vicious circle between increasing sensitivity, declining resilience and an inability to bounce back.

Coping strategies are the means by which resilient systems weather the bottom of the drought/recovery curve shown in Figure 7.1 and, if they are to be good indicators of unusual stress, are used only at the point in the curve indicated, and abandoned once recovery is under way. Genuine coping strategies must therefore be distinguished from insurance strategies (undertaken to minimize the risk of production failure) and recovery strategies (designed to facilitate bounce-back).

If, on the other hand, coping strategies are part of a low-resilience and highly sensitive livelihood system, they will be used every year in some seasons to bridge the food gap (Figure 7.2). In this instance, their use can only indicate an anticipated hungry season and not deviations in the norm. If low-resilience systems are characterized by fundamental adaptations after each period of severe drought (because they no longer have coping strategies reserved for such periods to facilitate bounce-back), then any

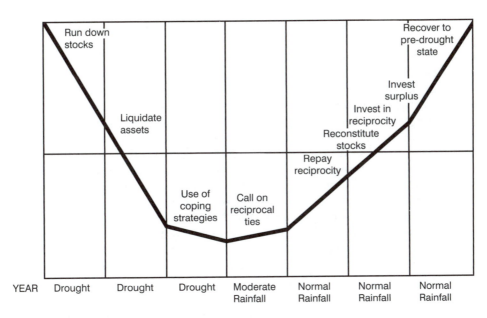

Figure 7.1 *Coping strategy use in drought/recovery cycle in secure livelihood systems*

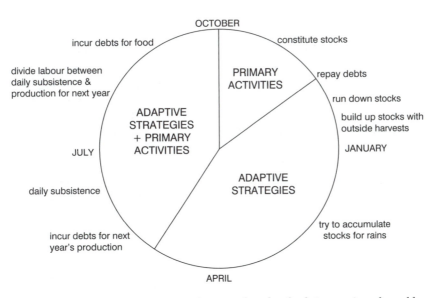

Figure 7.2 *Adaptive strategy use in annual cycle of subsistence in vulnurable cultivating livelihood system*

sequence of coping in subsequent periods of drought will be very different from what went before.

Vulnerable livelihood systems, characterized by properties of low resilience and high sensitivity, thus find it hard to cope. People in secure (resilient and insensitive) livelihood systems practise *coping* strategies only when necessary, as part of a wider portfolio of risk management. In contrast, people in vulnerable systems are more likely to pursue adaptive strategies, seeking to use all available options at all times to maximize the trade-off between increasing resilience and reducing sensitivity. In so doing, adaptive livelihood systems are moving towards a new equilibrium, part of which is the trade-off between sustainability and subsistence, or seeking to preserve assets for future production, often at the cost of current consumption. The intensity of vulnerability is greatest when proximate and structural vulnerability coincide.[2] 'Vulnerability is thus a composite of the states of past and current events' (Borton and Shoham, 1991),[3] and structurally vulnerable livelihood systems hit by drought will be less able to cope than secure systems. Within these systems there are, of course, differentially vulnerable households and individuals, further compounding livelihood system vulnerability. Thus Longhurst (1986), for example, notes that in communities with landholding and income inequalities, household responses will differ. Watts (1988) also describes how wealthier households can benefit from the distress sales (of livestock, assets or labour) at depressed prices by poorer members of the community. The most vulnerable people are those who struggle to survive in vulnerable households and vulnerable livelihood systems. It is they who have the most constrained capacity to cope with shocks such as drought; and hence who are most vulnerable to famine. The ability to mitigate this vulnerability is contingent upon their capacity to adapt.

Coping Strategies and Famine Early Warning

In line with the recognition of coping strategies as a means of explaining how poor households deal with food stress, there has been a call for monitoring their progress within famine early warning systems (EWS), particularly local information systems concerned with early detection of food insecurity, not simply of famine. Finding out what producers do to help themselves to overcome chronic and transitory food shortages – or monitoring their coping strategies – is crucial: to interpret standard indicators of food stress (e.g., does a particular pattern of migration signify a normal or abnormal activity?); to assess the intensity of food insecurity (e.g., if the harvest fails, are there sufficient fall-back options to meet food needs?); and to identify appropriate responses (e.g., do people need food to eat or help in retaining their productive assets?).

There is an appealing symmetry in a coping strategy-based approach to early warning: it can simultaneously predict, and inform how to prevent, famine. Implicit in much (but by no means all) of this call for monitoring coping strategies is a belief that they will not only assist in predicting food crises, but also indicate appropriate and sustainable interventions to mitigate that crisis. Indigenous coping strategies can be reinforced, in preference to imposing external, often late, inappropriate and unsustainable solutions to food crises, epitomized by emergency food aid distributions. Whereas food aid invariably assists producers only once they have lost the means to feed themselves, monitoring coping strategies has the potential to identify ways of protecting and reinforcing system success and adaptation before collapse. If successful, such interventions would warn earlier of the destitution implicit in famine and possibly even prevent it. In so doing, the long-term effects of structural livelihood system vulnerability to food shortages which persist once the crisis is over could be reduced.

Clearly, it is not possible to monitor all the different criteria which determine coping strategy use. Structural factors which determine coping choices are insensitive to short-term changes in the overall food situation, and tracking proximate factors at household level is beyond the scope of even local EWS, let alone those operating over larger areas. Any monitoring system, to be sustainable, has to derive indicators which can be tracked over time and sensibly interpreted without too much difficulty. It is by no means clear that coping strategy indicators of food stress can do this, certainly they cannot by implicitly assuming homogeneity of motive and livelihood status. Even when livelihoods are differentiated, differences between communities and households within the same broad livelihood system can be as great as those between livelihood systems. Further differentiation by individual or household determinants of vulnerability could assist the process; but practically, the spread of combinations of strategy use and of sequences of uptake would be so great as to make monitoring (let alone interpretation) highly complex.

Indicator Development Using Coping Strategies

The use of coping strategies to develop more appropriate indicators of food stress has been characterized by two – often conflicting – trends. On the one hand, at a conceptual level, outsiders' perceptions of the complexity of vulnerable people's responses to drought have improved significantly in the last ten years or so. On the other hand, attempts to operationalize these conceptual advances have been both limited and often unsuccessful. The iteration between conceptual advances and their practical application has often been to the detriment of the latter. Although increasingly advocated, examples of the use of coping strategies to monitor food insecurity are rare. A handful of local-level systems in the Sahel and Horn of Africa which incorporate them to some degree have been identified by Buchanan-Smith et al (1991). Eele (1987), among others, has demonstrated how possible sources of information about coping strategies could be grafted on to existing EWS relatively easily. Broadly speaking, there were three phases in the evolution of indicator development based on coping strategies:

1   1970s: during this time coping strategies were ignored by most famous EWS, reflecting the preoccupation with supply of food (but not access to it) and with aggregate indices of supply and demand (epitomized by national food balance sheets).
2   1980s: models of sequential uptake predominated in the 1980s, especially in the aftermath of the famines in the Sahel and Horn of Africa in the middle of the decade.
3   1990s: a new realism now characterizes the potential for indicator-based coping strategies, based on the realization that earlier models were oversimplified and were often operationally impractical. Whether or not the new realism at a conceptual level can be translated into functioning EWS remains to be seen.

The 1980s: Nice Idea, Shame About the Practice

The ability to monitor coping strategies to predict food crises is predicated upon the assumption that they follow a discernible and repeatable sequence. Evidence from Africa and Asia supports the idea that the range of coping strategies available to rural producers is similar across very different food systems (Longhurst, 1986; Downing, 1988). Watts (1983), drawing on evidence from northern Nigeria in 1973/1974, identified the ten most commonly observed responses to food crisis as follows: collect famine foods; borrow grain from kin; sell labour power (migration); engage in dry season farming (migration); sell small livestock; borrow grain or money from merchants/moneylenders; sell domestic assets; pledge farmland; sell farmland; and migrate out permanently. Corbett (1988), reviewing this and other empirical evidence[4] for the sequential uptake of coping strategies, identifies the sequence in Table 7.1 which

Table 7.1 *The sequential use of insurance and coping strategies*

Sequential use of strategies	Examples of strategies	Characteristics of strategies
STAGE 1 Insurance mechanisms	– changes in cropping and planting practices – sale of smallstock – reduction of current consumption levels – collection of wild foods – use of inter-household transfers and loans – increased petty commodity production – migration in search of employment – sale of possessions (e.g. jewellery)	– risk-minimizing – loss-management – low commitment of domestic resources
STAGE 2 Disposal of productive assets (coping)	– sale of livestock (e.g. oxen) – sale of agricultural tools – sale or mortgaging of land – credit from merchants and moneylenders – reduction of current consumption levels	– high commitment of domestic resources
STAGE 3 Destitution	– distress migration	– failure to cope

Source: adapted from Corbett, 1988 and Frankenberger, 1992

'provides a useful tool for analyzing the economic behaviour of households prior to and during famines' (Corbett, 1988, p1107).

The idea of sequential uptake has been refined to distinguish between insurance strategies and coping strategies. Insurance strategies are those activities undertaken to reduce the likelihood of failure of primary production (e.g. changes in cropping and planting patterns, or in levels and types of investment in primary production such as a shift from cattle to goats by pastoralists). Coping strategies are employed once the principal source of production has failed to meet expected levels, when insurance strategies have failed or are failing, and producers have to literally 'cope' until the next harvest. Thus, Frankenberger and Goldstein (1990) distinguish between various types of risk management and patterns of coping behaviour (e.g. asset depletion, breakdown of community reciprocity, non-farm coping strategies), as well as between types of household assets which will play different roles in the process of coping. On this basis they argue that 'the dilemma facing small-farm households involves ... a trade-off between immediate subsistence and long-term sustainability' (Frankenberger and Goldstein, 1990, p22). Equally, the World Food Programme (WFP, 1989) differentiates between accumulation and diversification (or insurance) strategies. The former aim to increase a household's resource base, and the latter to promote a variety of sources of income with different patterns of risk, to avoid the exposure associated with a single income source (WFP, 1989, p3). Accumulation strategies include food stocking, credit schemes, productive investment and investment in education and training. Diversification strategies include agricultural diversification, migration and remittances, and diversification of employment opportunities. A further distinction is made between hungry-season strategies used for part of most years and strategies to survive particularly bad years.

Within the framework of models of sequential uptake, three sets of indicators have been developed to monitor changing coping responses. Building on the work of the World Food Programme, Frankenberger and Hutchinson (1991) summarize these as follows:

1   Early (or leading) indicators, that is, changes in conditions and responses prior to the onset of reduced food access. They include: signs of crop failure; lack of pasture (leading to animal deaths, unusual migration patterns, unusual sales of animals); and changes in exchange relationships (e.g. unseasonal price rises of grains, falling casual labour rates);

2   Stress (or concurrent) indicators are those which occur simultaneously with reduced access to food. They include: unusual numbers of migrants in search of work; unusual sales of assets on local markets; unusual sales of land or mortgages; unusually high demand for credit, increased dependence on wild food; reduced food intake (number of meals);

3   Late outcome (or trailing) indicators occur once food access has declined. They include: increased prevalence of undernutrition and morbidity; increased land degradation; land sales; and permanent outmigration.

Refinements in the categorization of coping strategies are informed by a desire to simplify complex patterns of decision-making and response. As models of coping strategy use have been refined, so has much justified caution in their application been cast aside. Such warnings include Corbett's (1988, p1109) point that 'variations in observed strategies also suggest that there are few universal indicators of impending famine and famine warning systems need to be locally specific'. Further, as Frankenberger (1992, p84) argues, 'models that ignore the locational specificity of ecological and economic aspects are likely to select proxy indicators which are inappropriate or misinterpreted'. Even if at a conceptual level, the necessity to proceed with care is well recognized, in the practical implementation of information systems which incorporate indicators of coping strategy use, there has been a tendency to look for universal truths. If coping strategies are to be employed as predictive indicators of food stress, it is essential that their use by food insecure groups follows discernible patterns capable of being monitored. Otherwise, coping strategies are little more than random responses to food insecurity which can play no role in prediction. It is at this point that the use of coping strategies to monitor changing levels in food security runs into difficulties. Despite the apparent simplicity of models of sequential uptake, operationally they pose a number of difficulties.

The major drawback to such models is that households juggle between different activities simultaneously and in response to the seasonal options available to them. In the case of sales of assets, for example, rural people are highly conversant with the seasonal terms of trade between goods (e.g. livestock and cereals) and will seek to maximize their revenue over a year by playing the market. Although the literature identifies the grey area between strategies as responses to unusual changes in access to food, and strategies as more permanent reactions to fundamentally altered conditions, once coping strategy uptake becomes an indicator of transitory food stress, this grey area must of necessity be ignored. Either use of a particular strategy signals stress or it does not. Attempts to differentiate between why different people pursue a particular strategy at a given moment make for highly complex monitoring requirements.

Second, a coping strategy-based approach to monitoring access to food is criticized, and rejected by most EWS, because its information needs are too complex, expensive and time consuming. In recent years, the thrust of much early warning thinking, and views about information needs for rural development more generally, has been to minimize information requirements or to opt for what advocates of rapid rural appraisal (RRA) term 'optimal ignorance' (McCracken et al, 1988). A coping strategy-based approach contradicts this trend, although methodologies can be developed which simplify information collection (see Davies, 1993). Further, the raw data used as indicators can be misleading, necessitating the validation of data quality which can further add to the burden of the information system (Frankenberger, 1992).

The third obstacle is the capacity to analyse data and to interpret them quickly enough to permit timely response. Almost all concurrent indicators, for example, are prefaced by the word 'unusual', implicit in which is some baseline by which deviations from the norm can be measured. Without such a baseline, indicators are hard to interpret sensibly; and further, what is normal in one context, may be very different from another neighbouring area (Frankenberger, 1992). Unusual migration is a frequent casualty in this respect: empty villages after the harvest are used to indicate migration driven by poor harvests, whereas in fact they can be due to habitual reciprocal labour exchanges between neighbouring agro-ecological zones with differing harvest times (part of the moral economy, not of a collapsing food economy). Furthermore, such migration patterns are a function of the usual variability of production in the same agro-ecological zone, or between neighbouring agro-ecological ones.

Fourth, such models can easily disguise intra-community variation, by failing to account for the fact that one person's coping strategy is another's livelihood. Mortimore (1989), for example, shows how adaptive behaviour to drought over a 13-year period in northern Nigeria varies between households, in the same village. Differences in options and choices occur at individual, household, community and livelihood system levels. If a particular activity is identified as being a coping strategy for the purposes of food security monitoring, the assumption is that all people who take up that activity do so in order to cope with food stress. Yet, there is no easy way, for example, of distinguishing between someone who is choosing to go hungry to preserve assets and someone who is hungry and who has no choice, having previously liquidated all assets. Thus, whereas the stress indicator of increased dependence on wild foods appears to be a robust indication of local food entitlements, in fact in many marginal Sahelian communities, there are groups who now habitually depend on wild foods for subsistence in part of every year. If early response is at the heart of monitoring coping strategies, it would be necessary to disaggregate food security profiles for all groups in a given area in a normal year.

Finally, the models fail to account for changes over time. Coping strategies are not cast in stone and with each cycle of drought and partial rehabilitation, the range of options will change and the rate of take-up of particular coping strategies will vary. Riely (1991), for example, found that in Kordofan, Sudan, asset redistribution and changes in markets meant that the experience of drought itself changes the scope for coping with the next food crisis. So, even if one cycle has been successfully monitored and understood, there is no guarantee that next time around, the same pattern will repeat itself for the same groups of people, in roughly the same proportions.

The 1990s: The *Realpolitik* of Coping Strategies

Many of those populations living in the Sahel and Horn of Africa, who have been identified as potential beneficiaries of monitoring systems which are based on coping strategies, subsist in low-resilience/high-sensitivity livelihood systems which, in turn, are often found in areas of low resilience and high sensitivity in natural resource terms. The difficulty in using these strategies as the basis for developing indicators of food stress may add grist to the mill of those early warners who argue that systems should remain minimalist and deal only at a high level of aggregation, because they can never collect sufficient information or make sense of it. This is despite the fact that local people already have and make use of such information, and have their own information systems. Broad indicators of output and estimates of projected consumption, perhaps with some proxy indicators of demand such as market prices must suffice: a return to the fashion of the 1970s. Yet, these systems too have real drawbacks, not least their inability to understand how people feed themselves (rather than how they fail to do so), and what kind of interventions would reinforce this process early on in the cycle of drought and destitution, and before livelihood systems become unsustainable. The challenge is to retain the essence of coping strategy-based monitoring, which can fulfil these functions, while recognizing that '1980s models' for so doing are either too sweeping in their definition of coping strategies and too simplistic in their assumptions about when and why people use them; or alternatively, that more comprehensive '1990s models' present formidable operational drawbacks.

Conceptually, the problem is where to draw the line between behaviour that is principally driven by food stress (coping); and that which is motivated by the need to fundamentally alter the mix of activities required for subsistence (adapting). The policy options for each are very different. Coping strategies indicate that if livelihood systems are given a little one-off support, they can continue to provide security for those who depend on them. Adaptive strategies imply that livelihood systems are moving towards a new equilibrium (or not), necessitating that external support respond to the much more basic constraints encountered in such processes. This, in turn, is central to the identification and fruitful monitoring of coping strategies as indicators of unusual food stress. In structurally vulnerable livelihood systems, people combine coping and adapting by optimizing the trade-off between reducing sensitivity and increasing resilience. The implication of this distinction for evolving livelihood systems in marginal areas is that what were once coping strategies increasingly determine the level of food availability within households, irrespective of the year in question, and have hence become part of a process of adaptation. If strategies are used as part of a process of adaptation, rather than as short-term responses to isolated periods of food stress, there are a number of implications for their use as indicators of food stress and for policy. Above all, the notion of repeatable sequential uptake is untenable for the following reasons:

- The mere fact of using a particular strategy, or sequence of strategies, can indicate nothing about food stress, because some people use them all the time and others do so for part of every year. It is very hard to know in advance what the sequence of use will be and who will use which strategies, unless some historical perspective is incorporated into monitoring.
- The timing of use will change depending on how evolved the process of adaptation is for a given household or community. What may signal an alarm at a given point in one year or drought cycle will not necessarily indicate the same thing the next time around.
- The reasons for uptake will depend on the mix of adaptive strategies available to particular livelihood systems and households within them. This mix is determined by: the characteristics of the strategy in question; where the household is in the process of adaptation; and other constraints and opportunities offered by the overall livelihood system. It is very difficult to monitor the motivation for coping strategy use.
- The effectiveness of particular strategies in mitigating food insecurity is even more difficult to discern predictively, particularly if the reasons for pursuing a given strategy are themselves uncertain. Generally, the effectiveness of coping strategies is explained retrospectively to elucidate why famines did not occur, or why some people survived.

Whereas it is possible to monitor strategies, it is not clear what they tell you, unless a distinction is made between coping and adaptive behaviour. Coping strategies are most useful as contextual information which informs about how people are making trade-offs; and not as clear indicators of something going wrong. Multiple indicators are essential to help minimize drawbacks identified above (Frankenberger, 1992). In addition, if coping strategies are to be useful indicators of food stress, it is the intensity of their use (how dependent households are on such strategies in a given season year, compared to 'normal'); their sustainability when this intensity increases (in both an economic and an environmental sense); the motivation for their use (coping or adapting); and their effectiveness in meeting food and livelihood needs (or their costs and benefits), which must be assessed. This will define the threshold between fundamental and long-term changes in livelihoods, and the ability of people to bounce back to how they lived before. How then can indicators be developed to encapsulate the complexity of vulnerable livelihood systems without being unduly complex and infeasible? The first step is to grade coping or adaptive strategies according to local conditions and at livelihood system level, on the basis of these four criteria:

1   Motivation/intensity: a high score for intensity would indicate that the strategy is already pursued by many people and is thus perceived by them to be the best option available. Scoring motivation hinges on whether the strategy is abandoned once recovery is under way. The difference between motivation for and intensity of use could only be made once strategies had been monitored over a number of years. In systems undergoing a process of adaptation, motivation and intensity are part of the process of moving towards a new equilibrium. In systems which are coping, they are to facilitate bounce-back.
2   Effectiveness: a high score would mean that returns to pursuing a particular strategy were more likely than others to assist in filling the food gap, with the least cost to future livelihood security, thereby maximizing the trade-off between reducing sensitivity and increasing resilience.
3   Economic and/or environmental sustainability: high economic sustainability would mean that these strategies could be pursued over time; and high environmental sustainability, that they did not have deleterious effects on the natural resource base. As indicated above, whether or not strategies are environmentally sustainable is a much more complex issue than much of the desertification of semi-arid lands literature suggests. Certainly, it should not be assumed that apparently 'abusive' strategies always have deleterious and irreversible consequences for the environment.

In a study of coping options in Mali, it was found – not surprisingly – that very few strategies score highly in all, or most, respects, as Table 7.2 shows (Davies, 1993). It is, however, possible to infer which strategies are likely to promote immediate food security without decimating future livelihood security, and which have the potential for reinforcement.

Unpacking strategies in this way is a first step towards meeting the requirements for monitoring adaptation, by identifying the kinds of factors which will influence the intensity of, motivation for and effectiveness of coping/adaptive strategies, as well as

Table 7.2 *Grading of coping/adaptive strategies according to use*

Source of strategy	Example of strategy	Use of strategy		
		Motivation/ intensity	Effectiveness	Sustainability
Production-based	Artisan work	Medium	Medium/low	Econ. low
Common property resource-based	Collection of wild foods	High	Medium/high	Econ. high/ Env. high
Reciprocally based	Internal credit mechanisms	Medium	Medium	Econ. medium
Asset-based	Sale of animals	High	Medium	Econ. low/medium
Labour-based	Redivision of household labour	High	Medium/high	Econ. high
Exchange-based	Very small-scale retailing	Medium	Medium/low	Econ. medium
Migration-based	Work in nearby livelihood system	High/medium	Medium	Econ. medium Env. low/medium
Consumption-based	Reduce intake	High	Low/medium	Econ. medium/low

their economic and environmental sustainability. Ideally, strategies would be assessed at household level; but realistically, only system-level assessment is likely to be feasible for a local monitoring system, although household-level constraints must be borne in mind, especially when considering who will benefit from the reinforcement of a given strategy. It must be stressed that the overall assessment of coping/adaptive strategies would need to be updated regularly, to reflect the changing opportunities afforded by different strategies over time.

The next step is to derive indicators from Table 7.2, as shown in Table 7.3. Conventionally, the mere fact of pursuing a particular strategy is taken to indicate stress. This may be refined according to the timing of uptake, in both a seasonal sense and in relation to other activities. But the implicit assumption is that it is a coping strategy. Thus, collection of wild foods signals food stress, and especially so if this occurs early in the hungry season. If, on the other hand, a more dynamic multiple-indicator of strategy use model is employed, it is possible to differentiate between coping and adaptive strategies (motivation); whether or not a strategy is being unusually depended upon by many people (intensity); how effective that strategy is likely to be in filling the food gap and/or preserving assets (effectiveness); and whether it is likely to be effective in the future and capable of (or worth) reinforcing (sustainability). In the case of wild foods, the indicators suggested in Table 7.3. measure

Table 7.3 *Examples of indicators to monitor the use of coping/adaptive strategies*

Source of strategy	Example of strategy	Indicator of strategy use			
		Motivation	Intensity	Effectiveness	Sustainability
Production-based	Artisan work	Carried out every year or unusually?	Apperance of goods on market	Terms of trade goods/millet	Demand for goods
Common property resource-based	Collection of wild food	Carried out every year or unusually?	Timing of collection Pressure on foods Availability on market	No. of weeks of food supply	Stability of supply over time
Reciprocally based	Internal credit mechanisms	To buy food or invest in production?	Price and availability of credit	Price of credit (compared to formal channels)	Availability of credit
Asset-based	Sale of animals	Distress sales or habitual disposals?	Price of livestock	Terms of trade livestock/millet	Type of animals sold (seed of herd?)
Labour-based	Redivision of household labour	To subsist or to protect livelihood?	Who is doing what compared to habitual seasonal activites?	No. of weeks of food supply from unusual activites	
Exchange-based	Very small-scale retailing	To subsist or protect livelihood?	No. of traders on markets	Margins on trade	Saturation of market for small-scale trade?
Migration-based	Work in nearby livelihood system	Habitual or unusual migration?	No. of people looking for work in productive zones	Rates and type of remuneration	
Comsumption-based	Reduce intake	To protect assets of last resort?	Timing of reduction (relative to hungry season)		Health of population

a combination of: changes over time; the seasonality of uptake; production (or availability) levels; current market signals; and predictions of future supply and demand. Taken together, these indicators provide a far clearer picture of the likely meaning of wild food collection, its potential contribution to mitigating food insecurity, and whether or not this strategy should be reinforced, than would a simple recording of the fact that such foods were being collected.

Conclusions: Are Coping Strategies a Cop-Out?

Few would dispute the legitimacy of putting indigenous coping strategies firmly on the food security and famine mitigation agenda. Recognition of the central importance of vulnerable people's own responses to the threat of food and livelihood insecurity by planners and policymakers was long overdue. The reservations raised here about coping strategies – both generally and specifically in the context of their utility as indicators of food stress – are not intended to suggest a return to top–down, impositionist approaches, implicit in which is the assumption that vulnerable people are passive victims of insecurity, sitting still when faced with drought until the rains return.

On the contrary: a focus on indigenous capacity to respond is by far the most effective starting point for policies which will combat insecurity in a sustainable manner, by helping to optimize the subsistence/sustainability trade-off. Yet the danger that coping strategies become a cop-out is clear: not because they are unimportant; but rather because of the tendency for them to become shorthand for complexities which need to be understood before they can be simplified for policymaking and implementation. If not fully understood, coping strategies justify – and indeed legitimate – short-term response, even though this is often inappropriate. In the quest to use coping strategies in policymaking and planning, hard choices have to be made between operational feasibility and confronting the complexity of – and limitations to – indigenous response, close to where the action is. This includes appropriate responses to long-term changes in people's livelihoods.

People living in marginal environments have always lived with risk and a portfolio of options, and are well aware of the pathways that follow if their efforts to mitigate proximate stress are unsuccessful. They are fairly clear about how their livelihoods have changed over a two- to three-generation timeframe. To some extent, the conceptual confusion arising from researchers' and policymakers' failure to grasp the complexities of adaptation is of our own making. It implies that the immense amount of thinking about these issues in the developed world and in capital cities in the South needs to be supported by much more information about how poor people themselves see coping and adaptation and what this entails for policy and practice: greater complexity; greater innovation and risk-taking; more time and money spent closer to where the action is. But this is only worth doing – and the approach to EWS suggested only relevant – if monitoring and reinforcing indigenous coping strategies is part of a wider livelihood monitoring and reinforcing system based on the recognition that people's lives are changing irrevocably. Such a system needs to be designed to detect collapsing livelihoods, with a view to saving livelihoods not only lives.

Notes

1 Bayliss-Smith draws on Blaikie and Brookfield's (1987) analysis of the sustainability of agricultural ecosystems in distinguishing between these characteristics.
2 Downing (1990, cited in Frankenberger 1992, p82) similarly distinguishes between baseline and current vulnerability. Future vulnerability refers to the trends associated with long-term food security risks.
3 Cited in Frankenberger (1992, p82).
4 Corbett considers inter alia Cutler's sequence from Red Sea Province Sudan in 1984 (Cutler, 1986); Rahmato's (1987) sequence from Wollo Province, Ethiopia in 1984/1985; and De Waal's (1989) sequence from Darfur, Sudan in 1984/1985.

References

Bayliss-Smith, T., 1991, 'Food security and agricultural sustainability in the New Guinea Highlands: vulnerable people, vulnerable places', *IDS Bulletin*, Vol 22 No 3: 5–11

Behnke, R., Schoones, I., and Kerven C., (eds), 1993, *Range Ecology at Disequilibrium: New Models of Natural Variability and Pastoral Adaptation in African Savannas*, London: Overseas Development Institute, London

Blaikie, P., and H. Brookfield, 1987, *Land Degradation and Society*, London and New York: Methuen

Borton, J. and Shoham, J., 1991, 'Mapping vulnerability to food insecurity: tentative guidelines for WFP Offices', mimeo, Study commissioned by the World Food Programme, Relief and Development Institute, London

Buchanan-Smith, M., Davies, S., and Lambert, R., 1991, 'Guide to famine early warning systems in the Sahel and Horn of Africa: a review of the literature. Volume 2', IDS Research Report, No. 21, Brighton: IDS

Campbell, D.J., 1990, 'Strategies for coping with severe food deficits in rural Africa: review of the literature', *Food and Foodways*, Vol 4 No 2: 143–162

Corbett, J.E.M., 1988, 'Famine and household coping strategies', *World Development*, Vol 16 No 9: 1009–1112

Cutler, P., 1986, 'The response to drought of Beja famine refugees in Sudan', *Disasters*, Vol 10 No 3: 181–88

Davies, S., 1993, 'Versatile livelihoods: strategic adaptation to food insecurity in the Malian Sahel', Report to ESCOR Overseas Development Administration, IDS, Brighton

De Waal, A., 1989, *Famine that Kills: Darfur, Sudan, 1984–1985*, Oxford: Clarendon Press, Oxford

Downing, T.E., 1988, 'Climatic variability, food security and smallholder agriculturalists in six districts of Central and Eastern Kenya', unpublished PhD Dissertation, Clark University

——, 1990. 'Assessing socio-economic vulnerability to famine: frameworks, concepts and applications', FEWS Working Paper No. 2.1, USAJD Famine Early Warning System project, Washington DC

D'Souza, F., 1985, 'Anthropology and disasters', *Anthropology Today*, Vol 1 No 1: 18–19

Duffield, M., 1990, 'Sudan at the cross-roads: from emergency procedures to social security', IDS Discussion Paper, No 275, Brighton: IDS

Eele, G. 1987, 'Data sources for timely warning in nutritional surveillance', in 'Figures for food in Africa', Proceedings of the Workshop on Statistics in Support of African Food Policies and Strategies, Brussels, 13–16 May, 1986, *Eurostat News*, Special Edition

Frankenberger, T.R., 1992, 'Indicators and data collection methods for assessing household food security', in S. Maxwell and T.R. Frankenberger (eds), *Household Food Security: Concepts, Indicators, Measurements – A Technical Review*, New York: UNICEF and Rome: IFAD: 73–134

——, and Goldstein, D.M., 1990, 'Food security, coping strategies and environmental degradation', *Arid Lands Newsletter*, Vol 30, Tucson: Office of Arid Lands Studies, University of Arizona: 21–27

——, and Hutchinson C.F., 1991, 'Sustainable resource management based on a decentralised food security monitoring system', Discussion Paper, mimeo, Tucson: Office of Arid Lands Studies, College of Agriculture, University of Arizona, April

Gore, C., 1992, 'Entitlement relations and 'unruly' social politics: a comment on the work of Amartya Sen', mimeo, Brighton: IDS

Longhurst, R., 1986, 'Household food strategies in response to seasonality and famine', *IDS Bulletin*, Vol 17 No 3: 27–35

McCracken, J., Pretty, J., and Conway, G., 1988, *An Introduction to Rapid Rural Appraisal for Agricultural Development*, London: IIED

Mortimore, M.J., 1989, *Adapting to Drought: Farmers, Famines and Desertification in West Africa*, Cambridge: Cambridge University Press

Rahmato, D., 1987, 'Famine and survival strategies: a case study from North East Ethiopia', Food and Famine Monograph Series, No 1, Addis Ababa: Institute of Development Research, Addis Ababa University, May

Reardon, T., and Matlon, P., 1989, 'Seasonal food insecurity and vulnerability in drought-affected regions of Burkina Faso', in D.E. Sahn (ed.), *Seasonal Variability in Third World Agriculture: The Consequences for Food Security*, Baltimore and London: Johns Hopkins University Press

Riely, F., 1991, 'Household responses to recurrent drought: a case study of the Kababish pastoralists in Northern Kordofan, Sudan', in *Famine and Food Policy Discussion Papers*, No 6, Washington D.C.: International Food Policy Research Institute

Swift, J., 1989, 'Why are poor people vulnerable to famine?', *IDS Bulletin*, Vol 20 No 2: 8–15

Watts, M., 1983, *Silent Violence, Food, Famine and Peasantry in Northern Nigeria*, Berkeley: University of California Press

——, 1988, 'Coping with the market: uncertainty and food security among Hausa peasants', in I. De Garine and G.A. Harrison, (eds), *Coping with Uncertainty in Food Supply*, Oxford: Clarendon Press: 260–290

WFP, 1989, 'Review of food aid policies and programmes: anti-hunger strategies of poor households and communities: roles of food aid, Report No WFP/CFA:27/P/INF/1 Add.1, WFP, Rome

World Bank, 1986, *Poverty and Hunger: Issues and Options for Food Security in Developing Countries*, World Bank Policy Study, Washington DC

Climate Variation, Vulnerability and Sustainable Development in the Semi-Arid Tropics

Jesse C. Ribot, Adil Najam and Gabrielle Watson

Introduction

This chapter aims to capture the central issues that emerged from the papers, presentations and discussions at the International Conference on the Impacts of Climatic Variations and Sustainable Development in Semi-Arid Regions (ICID), held in Fortaleza-Ceará, Brazil from 27 January to 1 February 1992. But, given the breadth and depth of the 76 papers and the wide-ranging discussions during the conference, this chapter could cover only a small subset of the issues that arose. We chose to focus on the plight of socially, politically, economically and spatially marginal populations in semi-arid lands, and the urgent need for environmentally sound and equitable development efforts. These themes recurred throughout the papers, presentations and discussions at the conference.

This chapter draws from the materials and information presented at the conference, as well as the broader literature where relevant. While the themes within this chapter are derived largely from the conference, the arguments are shaped – as could not have been otherwise – by the experiences and perspectives of the authors. We did not try to represent the scope nor the depth of the issues covered at the conference, but rather, to characterize the problems and opportunities, and to explore what we felt were the most pressing concerns within the semi-arid regions of the world.

Climate variability, natural resources and development in semi-arid regions

Vulnerability to dislocation, hunger and famine are the most critical problems facing the inhabitants of semi-arid lands. These regions are subject to extreme variations in their relatively scant seasonal and interannual precipitation, resulting in recurrent droughts and floods. Natural resources of semi-arid zones, such as timely water supplies, fertile soils, vegetation and wildlife, tend to be scarce, and the existing resources are easily damaged by changes in precipitation patterns and by human action. Many of the semi-arid regions of the world, particularly the semi-arid tropics, are also characterized by subsistence vulnerability and insecurity for the large majority of their rural populations in the face of land degradation and climate variation. Vulnerability, social and geographic marginality, environmental change and dryland degradation are central, interlinked and chronic problems.

Semi-arid regions cover between 13 per cent and 16 per cent of the Earth's land area, and are home to approximately 10 per cent of the global population (Heathcote, 1996).[1] They exist in tropical, subtropical and temperate zones and fall within or encompass both developed and underdeveloped nations (see Figure 8.1). In developed areas, the southwestern United States, and parts of the western plains of Canada and the periphery of the Australian desert are semi-arid (see, for example, Cohen et al, 1992; Rosenberg and Crosson, 1992; Schmandt and Ward, 1992; Heathcote, 1996). The semi-arid tropics encompass large portions of the least developed regions on Earth. Of the 22 countries of Africa's Sudano-Sahelian region, 18 are among the world's least developed nations (Wang'ati, 1996). Brazil's semi-arid northeast is its most economically deprived region (Magalhães and Glantz, 1992). Semi-arid tropics also include Mexico's central plateau, parts of Argentina, Chile and Uruguay, central and south India, western China (22 per cent of the country), and northern Mongolia (Sen, 1987; Drèze and Sen, 1989; Tie Sheng et al, 1992; Zhao, 1996). Many of these regions are highly prone to anthropogenic and climatically related environmental deterioration, while their populations are prone to hunger and famine. Indeed, it is at this conjunction of climatic variability and underdevelopment that human vulnerability and calamitous social dislocations are most likely to occur.

While rainfall, droughts and floods are physical phenomena, associated socio-economic consequences (economic failure, food shortages and outmigration) are linked

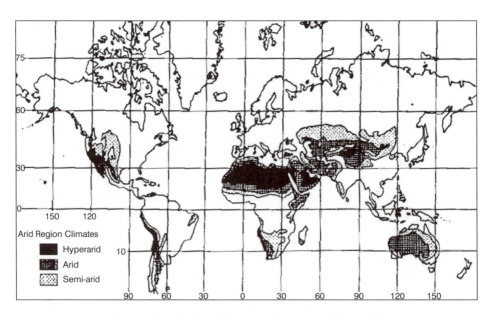

Figure 8.1 *Arid and semi-arid regions of the world*

Source: Campos-Lopez and Anderson, 1983, p54

to the ability of affected populations to anticipate, prepare for and respond to these events. The most striking characteristic of the vast majority of the populations inhabiting the semi-arid tropics is their lack of adequate human and financial resources to cope with expected – even at times (with early warning systems) predictable – variability in their climatic regimes (on early warning systems, see Nobre et al, 1992; Servain et al, 1992; Wang'ati, 1996). Because of poor human, natural resource and infrastructural development in these regions, large portions of the population of semi-arid tropics are vulnerable to hunger, famine, dislocation and the loss of both property and livelihood in the face of climatic, social, political or economic shocks. For the most part, their lives are shaped by chronic job and food insecurity; inadequate, and in many cases non-existent, health care; low wages; unemployment; under-employment and illiteracy, all of which tend to amplify the social consequences of natural phenomena.

Marginality and a low level of economic development both exacerbate and are exacerbated by environmental changes such as dryland degradation and deforestation.[2] Exploited or marginalized populations are often excluded from or bypassed by benefits of the development process, and are pushed against their resource base, further eroding its productive capacity. Mining the land (e.g. using land resources in a manner that reduces productivity in the long run) often becomes a necessity for those whose immediate survival depends on these lands (Bernstein, 1979; de Janvry, 1981; Blaikie, 1985; Blaikie and Brookfield, 1987). Those who are marginalized by the economic process onto the most economically and ecologically marginal lands are the most vulnerable populations. Under some conditions their marginality intensifies as they, and the marginal lands on which they subsist, are exploited beyond their productive capacity. The important question with respect to vulnerability in the face of climate variability and change is why and how these populations are marginalized and, hence, vulnerable. It is this question that guides our attention to the social determinants of vulnerability.

Antonio Rocha Magalhães (1992, p1) brings into focus both who is vulnerable and why, when he characterizes the critical nature of society's relation to the natural environment in Northeast Brazil:

> Over the course of history the economic, social and environmental impacts of adverse climatic events, especially droughts, have been calamitous, It is, however, the social dimension that accentuates the climatic problem in Northeast Brazil, as in many other developing regions. Here it represents a menace for the survival of a major part of the population because, unlike developed regions, the social agents are not equipped to face the consequences of adverse climatic events.

This chapter examines problems of the less-developed semi-arid regions, because these regions are in most urgent need of attention. Likewise, we focus on development as the path toward an environmentally secure and productive future.

Climate change

The regional consequences of anthropogenically enhanced global warming cannot yet be predicted with confidence. But some impacts are probable. Increases in temperature will result in an increase in evapotranspiration. This increase will be particularly significant in places where the climate is hot under current conditions. Whether rainfall in these regions will increase or decrease remains highly uncertain. But, the Intergovernmental Panel on Climate Change (IPCC, 1990, ppiii, 12–13, 20ff.) indicates that semi-arid regions are among those areas most likely to experience increased climatic stress. Further, climatic change will have as yet unpredictable and perhaps unexpectedly extreme consequences with respect to frequency and intensity of precipitation and temperature variability for semi-arid regions.

Several regional climate change scenarios designed to identify possible implications of global warming for semi-arid lands were generated by climatologists and scientists and presented at the ICID conference. The tremendous uncertainty involved in projecting regional climate change is compounded by uncertainties in future productive capacities, demographic changes and socio-economic development in these regions (see under Climate Variability and Change, below, for a discussion of these factors). There are nonetheless lessons that can be derived from climate change simulations and scenarios. For Mexico, O'Brien and Liverman (1996) found decreasing soil moisture predicted by all climate change models applied to Mexico. If soil moisture decreases in semi-arid regions, as can be derived from some general circulation models (GCMs) and is assumed in most of these scenarios, then productivity in these regions will most certainly decrease in the absence of considerable development efforts (Magalhães, 1992; Downing, 1992; El-Shahawy, 1992; Schmandt and Ward, 1992, Santibáñez, 1992; Selvarajan and Sinha, 1992; Cohen et al, 1992; O'Brien and Liverman, 1996). Most of the scenarios project worsening climatic conditions, in the form of more frequent droughts and shorter growing seasons. Some point to the possibility of a higher degree of interannual climate variability and of unexpected extreme meteorological events such as cool periods or more frequent floods (Izrael, 1992, pp2–5). For these regions in which planning productive activities is already difficult due to the high climatic variability, climate change introduces even greater uncertainties and, thus, greater risks. A better regional understanding of climate change will help in planning for its consequences. But this is an insufficient policy response to the needs of semi-arid regions. To help cope with future regional uncertainties generated by climate warming, policymakers must also address issues associated with current climate variability. Policies to address problems of populations living under current variability will be an invaluable basis for coping and adapting should climate change increase variability or drought.

Even assuming continued current climatic conditions, semi-arid regions may well be worse off in 10, 20 or 30 years due to the declining productivity of the land and increasing populations without access to alternative income-generating options (see, for example, Wang'ati, this volume). Indeed, the magnitude of natural hazard losses has increased in the past even where meteorological records do not show increasing severity of weather events (see Glantz, 1996; O'Brien and Liverman, 1996; Heathcote, 1996). Simply projecting dryland degradation, for example, highlights the need for long-term strategies to stop or reverse these trends in order to improve the productive capacity and security of populations in semi-arid regions. Each year large areas are being at least temporarily worked to the point of declining productivity (Ocana, 1991, p3; WRI, 1991, 1992).

Today, in the semi-arid regions, vulnerability to the consequences of existing climate variation is already a major problem. Dryland degradation is widespread and progressive, while semi-arid populations are growing. These trends only compound the vulnerability of people and of social systems. Without addressing current problems, future vulnerability can only get worse, exacerbated or not by climate change, making the magnitude of future crises even greater. By addressing today's vulnerability we can increase the ability of semi-arid regions to adapt to and cope with the as yet unknown characteristics of a future climate change. Actions taken today to reduce vulnerability – actions which have been justified for a long time – will increase resilience and security by providing a buffer against vulnerability to future consequences of climate change. These are called 'no-regrets policies,' since they are valuable actions regardless of climate change probabilities.

From impacts to vulnerability and beyond

Climate *impact* assessment addresses the magnitude and distribution of the consequences of climate variability and change. *Vulnerability* assessment extends impact assessment by highlighting *who* (as in what geographic or socio-economic groups) is susceptible, *how* susceptible they are, and *why*. Clearly these assessments are overlapping and interlinked. For informed policymaking purposes, both are necessary and neither is sufficient. Vulnerability analysis ensures that the assessment of impacts will be extended into the realm of social, political and economic causality that shapes susceptibility to impacts. Understanding causality, facilitates appropriate policy design.

Climate impact analysis often focuses on the range of consequences of a given climate event. Examining impacts is a way of looking at the range of consequences of a given stimulus. For instance, drought is associated with a number of outcomes including reduced crop yield, reservoir depletion, hydroelectric interruptions, dryland degradation, and some second-order effects such as economic loss, hunger, famine or dislocation. This type of analysis helps to focus attention on the range of outcomes associated with climate variability or change. But it is somewhat misleading to designate these as *climate* impacts, since they are usually the result of a *multitude* of causal agents. These may include level of development, market organization and prices, entitlement structures, access to productive resources, distribution, state policies, and local or regional conflicts (Blaikie, 1985; Watts, 1987a; Drèze and Sen, 1989; Downing, 1991, 1992; Schmink, 1992). It is some combination of these factors, not the singular result of drought, that makes a family, household, enterprise, nation or region vulnerable. Vulnerability occurs at a conjuncture of physical, social and political-economic processes and events. Hence, complete climate impact analyses must include this multi-causal perspective, placing climate as one causal agent among many.

Downing (1992) presents a method for analysing vulnerability in which he lays the groundwork for examining this conjuncture in a systematic way. In Downing's framework, vulnerability focuses on *consequences* such as dislocation, that is, vulnerability to having to migrate to the city or to some other frontier. Drought might be considered a cause, even a trigger of outmigration. But, outmigration is also, examined as a function of such factors as exploitation, the lack of local alternative income opportunities or high food prices. So, this analysis aims to reveal the range of causes of this outcome – which is of particular social concern – rather than focusing on the impacts of one of many causes or triggering events.

Analysis of vulnerability focuses on the *relative* likelihood of different socio-economic groups of geographic regions to experiencing each outcome. Hence, relative levels of vulnerability to hunger can be mapped out spatially, temporally and socially. Spatial factors might include location on the rainfall gradient or on a geopolitical map, location with respect to transport or marketing systems, or vis-à-vis soil types and other geoclimatological factors. Temporal factors might include coincidence with an economic recession or depression, or perhaps the particular moment in political or development history of a region or country. And socio-economic factors would include the level of economic development, type of livelihood, level of education, political party or socio-economic group (gender, class, ethnic group, caste or religion).

By understanding socio-economic and political factors associated with vulnerability, one can begin to trace out the chains of causal forces and relations that impinge on a given instance of environmentally related vulnerability, chronic deprivation or crisis. In the same way that human vulnerability is shaped by a multitude of causal agents, land degradation, deforestation and other forms of resource degradation are also located within a nested set of causal agents. They too can be evaluated in a similar way (see Blaikie, 1985; Blaikie and Brookfield, 1987; Schmink, 1992). With an understanding of causality, appropriate policy responses can be developed to redress the causes of vulnerability, rather than just responding to its symptoms.

To address each of the causes of vulnerability or environmental decline might require policy interventions at different levels. Political-economic and geographical analysis of vulnerability's causes can be specific enough to allow policies to be tailored for a specific population, place and problem. And finally, since causality can be traced to international, national, household and individual levels, policies can be targeted at the appropriate level if the causes are understood.

In short, the object of vulnerability analysis is to link impact analysis to an understanding of the causes of vulnerability in order to facilitate a meaningful policy process. But, in carrying out such an analysis, one must be extremely careful not to mix correlation with causality. To map out the proximate vulnerability factors, such as location, livelihood, education and income level, tells only part of the story. Without looking at structural causes, such as the way in which the farm economy is embedded within a larger extractive economy, it is difficult to target extractive mechanisms, such as rent structures, share-cropping contracts, usurious credit arrangements, terms of trade and tax structures as causes of vulnerability and environmental decline (de Janvry and Kramer, 1979; Decre and de Janvry, 1984; Bitoun et al, 1996). Hence, to reduce vulnerability, policy analysts must go beyond identifying its proximate causes to evaluating the multiple causal structures and processes at the individual, household, national and international levels.

We highlight this aspect of climate impact analysis since it (1) allows for a multi-level, multi-sectoral policy analysis, and (2) facilitates the analysis of both proximate causal factors and the broader political-economic forces that shape vulnerability.

Toward ecologically sound development

Access to education, employment, credit, licences, markets, a healthy environment, land and labour are integral for development. Those on the social and geographical margins need to be able to diversify their income-generating activities in order to reduce their vulnerability. They need an income sufficient to invest in the maintenance of their land and in the stocking of buffers against adverse climatic events, as well as in non-climate-dependent production and survival strategies. The inability of peasant farmers to save and obtain necessary productive resources is a primary structural constraint on their ability to maintain and improve marginal agricultural land. Hence, poor access to infrastructure, inputs, markets, land and credit must be redressed in order to reduce or reverse the rural ecological decline currently under way in much of the semi-arid tropics around the globe. But, given that the processes of differentiation and marginalization that produce the current distribution of assets and patterns of access are ongoing, changes in access must be accompanied by political access to assure that resource access is maintained. They must be accompanied by enfranchisement and inclusion in the political processes (see Drèze and Sen, 1989; Watts and Bohle, 1993).

An important strategy for relieving a population's pressures on the land and raising rural and urban incomes is to support the development of diverse income-generating opportunities. Diversification of local economies also buffers against severe climatic events. In some regions this may mean fostering existing local productive activities or small-scale enterprises, and in others, encouraging regional pockets of industrialization. Such development is aimed at relieving the local pressures on the resource base and building a buffer against the inherent climatic variability of these regions. But diversification and development will accomplish little if the profits they generate are extracted from the regions and/or concentrated in the hands of a few.

International assistance may be needed for some types of development programmes, as well as for avoiding potential ecological problems stemming from development in these regions. In addition, rising greenhouse gas emissions in these regions may need to be offset by reduced emissions or by forest-augmented sequestering elsewhere, such as in the industrial nations of the world. Given the severity of the existing problems the inhabitants and governments of these regions face, they will only be able to address these secondary, less-immediate problems of industrial pollution and the emission of greenhouse gases by developing industries with outside assistance. With increased levels of development, the capacity to treat and prevent environmental problems and social vulnerability will increase, and these regions may then move in the direction of more environmentally sound economic-development strategies.

Conclusion

It is important to reduce the emission of gases that are projected to change the world's climate. It is also important to evaluate how that climate change will affect future populations and the future sustainability of the productive natural-resource base. But it is equally, if not more important to examine the current environmental degradation and the livelihood insecurity of the vast majority of people living in the world's semi-arid lands. For today's environmental decline will increase tomorrow's vulnerability. Today's vulnerability will reduce tomorrow's resilience. Today's underdevelopment will undermine the potential for increasing future resilience, productivity and development.

There is an old solution to the problems these regions face, and that is development. But this new development effort must occur within the ecological constraints. These

Table 8.1 *Land area within arid and semi-arid zones in developing regions (%)*

	Africa	Central America	South America	SE Asia	SW Asia, Middle East
Arid and semi-arid lands	66	60	31	33	80
Semi-arid lands	16	22	17	21	12

Source: adapted from WRI, 1990, p287

constraints are integrally linked to the well-being of the most marginal people in these lands. There are numerous technical and institutional measures that can be taken to ameliorate current problems, most of which are worthwhile even without the spectre of global warming – these are the 'no-regrets' strategies. But ultimately, addressing the struggles of the most vulnerable populations in semi-arid areas is what will help them move beyond 'no-regrets' to more far-reaching environment and development policies.

The remainder of this chapter is organized into three sections. The first is Climate Variability and Change, which outlines the models and their limitations. The second is Responses, in which some approaches and options for development in semi-arid lands are discussed. A brief conclusion follows.

Climate Variability and Change

Introduction

Climate has always been a dynamic entity. It varies across all terrestrial scales of time and space. Large areas of the Earth experience wide uncertainty as part of normal climate. This is especially true of the arid and semi-arid areas, where precipitation varies greatly. Change over longer periods of time is also a 'normal' climatic phenomenon (Riebsame, 1989, p6).

What makes the current concern for climatic change different from past interest in its perturbations and anomalies is the unprecedented pace and magnitude of the predicted change and the attendant dangers to human and environmental systems. While the global mean surface air temperature has increased by 0.3–0.6°C over the last 100 years, its average rate of increase during the 21st century is predicted at 0.3°C per decade (IPCC, 1990, pp2–3).[3]

This dramatic change is the projected result of increasing atmospheric concentrations of carbon dioxide (CO_2) and other greenhouse gases such as methane, nitrous oxide and chlorofluorocarbons (CFCs). The greenhouse effect is an established physical principle that has enabled life on this planet. It is the accelerated accumulation of these anthropogenic greenhouse gases, however, that threatens to cause rapid climate change (IPCC, 1990).

The findings of the Intergovernmental Panel on Climate Change (IPCC, 1990, p3) mark an emerging, but unsure, consensus among experts about the effects of such a greenhouse gas build-up. Attempting to model for the radiative equivalent of a doubling of CO_2 concentration, the major global climate models predict a global average warming of between 1 and 5°C (Downing, 1992, p1). This is not much different from the first such estimate made nearly a century ago, in 1896, by the Swedish scientist Arrhenius. While the apparent similarity of these estimates makes the possibility of global warming appear more likely, the inherent uncertainties of climate-modelling science and inadequacies of the modelling tools leave all predictions open to challenge (Stone, 1992, p34).

In this section we begin by outlining the concept of climate variability and change in semi-arid lands. We then proceed to discuss the limitations of the tools now available for projecting climate change and its consequences. Finally we highlight the urgency of acting within, and despite, the uncertainty of climate change predictions.

Climate variability

There are two aspects of climate variability that are of concern: its effects on the present populations of semi-arid lands, and the projection of its magnitude and consequences into the future.

Hare (1985, p41) defines climatic 'variability' as the observed year-to-year differences in values of specific climatic variables *within* an averaging period (typically 30 years), and climatic change as longer-term changes *between* averaging periods, either in the mean values of climatic variables or in their variability.[4] The distinction between short-term climatic *variability* and long-term climatic *change* is critical. 'One affects the range and frequency of shocks that society absorbs or to which it adjusts, the other alters the resource base' (Parry and Carter, 1985, p95).

Drought is the most common consequence of current climate variability in semi-arid lands (Wilhite, 1996). And the most vulnerable to its effects are the most marginalized populations; those deprived of the mechanisms and/or resources to prepare for and adapt to climate variation, let alone to climate change (Nobre et al, 1992). Ironically, while many recent models and analyses (including the majority presented at ICID) are focusing on the impacts of future climate *change*, the problems of climate *variability*, which may indeed get worse under conditions of climate change, are here today. The consequences are not hypothetical, but are already real and known.

Scientific investigations of global climate change have focused on projecting net or average change, rather than the changed variabilities within it. This focus is due to limitations of the available forecasting tools. Projecting variability is, nonetheless, a major concern in its own right. As an intrinsic characteristic of climate regimes in semi-arid regions, variability defines the many decisions made by those who inhabit these areas (Burton and Cohen, 1992). Traditional practices of crop and income diversification, as well as spatial mobility, are a few examples (see Wisner, 1976; Parry and Carter, 1988; Huss-Ashmore, 1989; Watts, 1987a). This is an area of research that deserves considerable attention.

Projecting climate change and impacts

Projecting climate change is an important first step in evaluating the consequences associated with global warming. Modelling climate change is inherently difficult. It involves simulating the behaviour of intricately linked and complex oceanic and atmospheric processes, some of which are not fully understood. In fact, major scientific uncertainties and knowledge gaps persist at every level from predicting just how fast greenhouse gases might build up to forecasting even the simplest climatic variable of temperature (Stone, 1992, pp34–7).[1]

> Any effort to predict climate changes assumes that climate is predictable – but this is not guaranteed. Forecasts of the effects of a rise in greenhouse gases are really just predictions of what will happen in the absence of the unpredictable. (Stone, 1992, p37)

Working within these uncertainties, and acknowledging them, climate change projections by the IPCC and others have used various methods to arrive at best estimates within the available scientific knowledge and tools. Among them is the use of historical and palaeoclimatic data (IPCC, 1990), spatial and temporal analogues (Burton and Cohen, 1992) and use of the convenient increment approach (Riebsame, 1989). While these have their specific strengths and uses, the most highly developed tool to project climate change is the general circulation model or GCM (IPCC, 1990).

Working according to the laws of physics, GCMs simulate possible change by using simplified equations (or 'parameterizations') based in part on current climate conditions and in part on approximations of future factors (IPCC, 1990). The projections are, therefore, only as good as the parameterizations. The strength of a parameterization, however, is restricted by two factors: (1) the major gaps in our knowledge and understanding of complex climatic process and systems, and (2) the capacity and speed inadequacies of even the most modern computers that force all climate models to make trade-offs between the number of locations they simulate, the number of climate processes they calculate, and the accuracy of the results (Stone, 1992, p37).

These general limitations translate into a number of major problems associated with relying too heavily on GCM climate change projections. The more important include the following:

- Different models produce similar trends but differ sufficiently that impact projections can vary with choice of model (Riebsame, 1989, p66).
- Variations in grid sizes[5] and low spatial representation make for coarse resolution of GCMs, and hence local specificity is difficult to obtain (Cohen et al, 1992, p11).
- Complex topographical features are represented differently in different models with high uncertainty as to how to handle these factors (Cohen et al, 1992; O'Brien and Liverman, 1996).
- Sub-grid-scale weather patterns, which can be important determinants of precipitation, are ignored (O'Brien and Liverman, 1996).
- Inadequate understanding of and assumptions about cloud formation could result in major errors in GCM results (Stone, 1992).
- Lack of coupling of GCMs with dynamic ocean and biosphere models reduces accuracy (Downing, 1992, pp2–3).

These problems highlight the dangers of interpolating global projections from GCMs to arrive at regional forecasts. In general, the confidence in regional estimates of critical climatic factors, especially precipitation and soil moisture, is low (see Cohen, 1990; IPCC, 1990, p4; Downing, 1992, p2; Yair, 1992, p2; Schmandt and Ward, 1992, p3; Wang'ati, 1996; O'Brien and Liverman, 1996).

Long-term regional precipitation estimates are even more uncertain than regional temperature projections. This is particularly disturbing in semi-arid areas, where rainfall amounts and patterns are the key variable (Parry and Carter, 1988, p11). For example, using five major GCMs for projecting climate changes in Mexico, O'Brien and Liverman (1996) found that the projected changes in annual average precipitation varied from a 23 per cent decline to a 3 per cent increase.

As summarized by Cohen (Figure 8.2), the state of understanding in climate change projections provides credible certainty in the trends in atmospheric compositions; fair certainty in the magnitude of global warming and the regional distribution of its causes; uncertain estimations of the role of global warming, large-scale shifts in precipitation and the magnitude of regional warming; and very uncertain projections on regional water resources. Furthermore, consensus among experts is that these uncertainties are not likely to narrow in the immediate future (IPCC, 1990) (see Figure 8.3 on timescale for narrowing uncertainties).

In the light of all these uncertaintics, over-reliance on initial GCM results for projecting impacts and consequences of climate change can often compound issues. This can happen by:

- imposing the climate of the future abruptly on the world of today, without allowing for adjustment and feedback;
- imposing uniform climate changes derived from GCM grid cells onto large regions, thereby eliminating the natural variability in time and space that characterizes real climates;

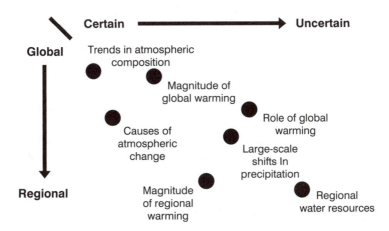

Figure 8.2 *State of understanding of global warming and its consequences*

Source: Cohen, 1992

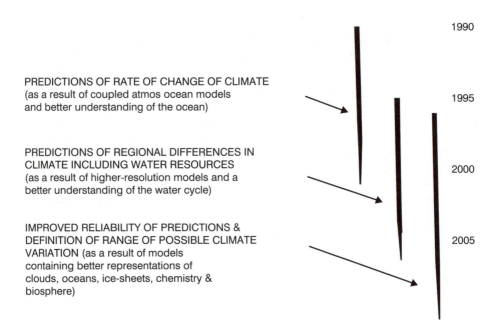

1990

PREDICTIONS OF RATE OF CHANGE OF CLIMATE
(as a result of coupled atmos ocean models
and better understanding of the ocean)

1995

PREDICTIONS OF REGIONAL DIFFERENCES IN
CLIMATE INCLUDING WATER RESOURCES
(as a result of higher-resolution models and a
better understanding of the water cycle)

2000

IMPROVED RELIABILITY OF PREDICTIONS &
DEFINITION OF RANGE OF POSSIBLE CLIMATE
VARIATION (as a result of models
containing better representations of
clouds, oceans, ice-sheets, chemistry &
biosphere)

2005

Figure 8.3 *Timescale for narrowing uncertainties*

Source: IPCC, 1990

- dealing with individual economic sectors but not addressing inter-sectoral linkages within the region and/or the linkages between the region and the rest of the world;
- failing to consider how technology and policy may facilitate adaptation to climate change;
- forecasting productivity on incomplete understanding of existing baseline and uncertain projections for changing the technical, social and economic baseline;
- opting for simplistic, and sometimes misleading, carrying capacity definitions;
- ignoring the role of the socio-economic structure in affecting vulnerability to climatic change (Rosenberg and Crosson, 1992; Downing, 1992; Cohen et al, 1992; Wang'ati, 1996).

As better computers become available, understanding of physical climatic processes is enhanced, and more developed methods become operational (e.g. fine-resolution, limited-area models), our ability to simulate climate change, and its consequences, is likely to increase, but the ingredient of uncertainty will remain important, at least in the foreseeable future (Cohen, 1990; Stone, 1992).

Acting in the face of uncertainty

Despite their limitations GCMs are valuable tools for students of climate change. Like any tool, they are most effective when used with care and with understanding of their capabilities and limitations. Climate models are only as good as our understanding of the processes which they describe, and this is far from perfect (IPCC, 1990, p19).

Despite their many problems GCMs provide basic scenarios against which to explore various climate change possibilities. Even if we had more refined tools, three crucial problems would arise in projecting future impacts:

> First, of course, no one knows how future climate might evolve; climate forecasting is an uncertain science. Second, any impact projection is only as reliable as the understanding, validity and strength of the assumed relationships between climate and the resource or human activity in question. Finally, even with a good understanding of past and current climate–society linkages, changes in technology and society may exacerbate or mitigate future impacts; and projecting social change is at least as difficult as predicting climate change. (Riebsame, 1989, p68)

While uncertainty in climate studies needs to be recognized, it must not be allowed to become an excuse for inaction. We should not allow uncertainty to obscure the very real need for policy analysis. Rather, that uncertainty should be incorporated in a credible manner into contemporary policy discussions (Riebsame, 1989, p68; Burton and Cohen, 1992, p10).

Many facets of the climate issue, like those of climate variability, are here now. They justify immediate action. The IPCC Working Group on the Formulation of Response Strategies reminds policymakers that among the most effective response strategies (especially in the short run), are the 'no-regrets' strategies – those which are beneficial even without climate change and justifiable in their own right (IPCC, 1990, p11). Riebsame (1989, p67) articulates the sentiment with much more urgency, pointing out that:

> the large uncertainty surrounding predictions of climate change may not be reduced to levels at which policy makers would be comfortable taking preventive or adaptive actions until the effects themselves become obvious. By then we may be on the verge of unpreventable and irreversible changes in the environment. Uncertainty makes planners adopt a 'wait and see' attitude to account for climate change in their decisions. It can be argued, however, that the changes which might accompany greenhouse warming are sufficiently large and sufficiently imminent (i.e., they will occur in the next few decades) that planners making decisions affecting long-term resource activities such as water development, agriculture, and settlements should consider their implications now.

This general question of action, or response, is discussed in detail in the next section below. While there may be great uncertainties in future climate projections, vulnerability in the face of current climate conditions necessitates and justifies action now.

Responses

Introduction

Current knowledge about climate change is insufficient for planners and policymakers to use models as precise predictive tools. Great uncertainty remains as to the actual mechanisms and potential effects of global warming. While enough is known to argue convincingly that greenhouse gases will result in general climate warming, the specific effects at the regional and local levels are sketchy at best. But it is not necessary to wait for tangible proof of climate change before acting. Climatic variability is currently a major problem in semi-arid regions. In conjunction with other physical, social and political-economic factors, climate variability contributes to vulnerability to economic loss, hunger, famine and dislocation. Reducing this vulnerability by increasing people's ability to cope is an immediate need. This will not only buffer them against the existing climatic variability but would increase their resilience to possible future climate change.

Adaptation is our natural response to the environment. As Burton and Cohen (1992) argue, when and what we plant, how and where we build structures, and what infrastructure we develop, are all contingent responses to environmental constraints. Adaptation is based on immediate observation of our surroundings, our knowledge of environment variation from the past, and on projections of future needs and events. Adaptation is what makes extreme events within the normal climate variation survivable, rather than catastrophic. In highly variable climates such as semi-arid regions adaptive responses mean the difference between a dry spell with some economic losses, and a deadly famine.

No regrets

Climate change introduces the possibility of climatic conditions not previously experienced in a given region. Planners and policymakers are naturally reluctant to invest in adjustments to an uncertain future scenario that may decrease productivity in the short run, or require difficult negotiation with other countries and regions. Yet much adaptation, unlike multilateral agreements about greenhouse gas reduction, is not dependent on cooperation with other nations, can be implemented locally, and can include measures that have immediate benefit, in and of themselves (Burton and Cohen, 1992). They are worth doing even if climate does not change. For example, developing drought-resistant crops for semi-arid regions can both help farmers hedge against increasingly arid conditions, and decrease water consumption needed for irrigation (O'Brien and Liverman, 1996). As semi-arid regions become dryer, water conservation will be increasingly important. Using less water is also beneficial because it reduces the likelihood of soil salinization, waterlogging of root areas, and over-draught of the water table. In regions where water is purchased from sources outside the region, using less water means less expenditure, with resources remaining for reinvestment within the region.

As Wang'ati (1996) argues, 'sustainable development is achievable provided that development policies put less emphasis on "change" in favor of "progressive improvement" on those strategies and technologies which have enabled the populations to cope in the past'. Purposeful adaptation to climate variation will save costs and 'buy time' needed to develop and implement greenhouse gas reduction strategies (Burton and Cohen, 1992).

The real opportunity in adaptive strategies, however, lies in their coincidence with long-term development aims. Sustainable development does not have to mean sacrificing increased well-being in order to preserve resources. Rather, it can mean insuring well-being through measures that conserve and improve productive capacity.

Long-term adaptation versus short-term crisis response

> as droughts come and go, left behind are ... the usual debates over the efficacy of ad hoc relief efforts and at best inadequate or incomplete plans for dealing with future droughts. With the first rains comes a new sense of security, relief efforts are dismantled, plans for the next drought forgotten, and society resumes its so-called harmony with climate until the rains fail and the cycle begins anew. (Easterling, 1987, as quoted by Farago, 1992)

Just as policymakers are reluctant to act on uncertain information about future climate change, investments to reduce vulnerability to current climate variability have been insufficient, Crisis-induced responses far outweigh preventive measures (Wilhite, 1996). Famine relief, emergency food and seed distribution during droughts, and public works projects to employ affected rural workers are all part of the crisis response mode. With the possible exception of public works projects, crisis responses tend to have immediate palliative results but no lasting effects on the resilient capacity of the population. In fact, short-term crisis-induced responses can have perverse effects on regional resilience to severe events by making governments and the population complacent in the face of repeated crisis events (Downing, 1992; Wilhite, 1996; Glantz, 1996). Rather than a strategy for change, the crisis management approach can be a recipe for maintaining, or worsening, the status quo. For example, providing food and input supports to farmers who are trying to cultivate extremely marginal lands may allow them to weather the current crisis but leaves them susceptible to future events and without incentive to buttress their defenses against vulnerability (Wilhite, 1996).

Wilhite (1996) argues that agriculturalists must either be equipped to adapt to the natural variability of the lands they are on, or should relocate to more viable areas. Glantz (1996), however, argues that all viable agricultural tracts are already under cultivation, suggesting that adaptation is the more promising policy response.

Planning for sustainable development

As will be discussed in the following section, the vulnerability of agriculturalists and pastoralists is not solely due to climatic events, but instead comes at the intersection of social, economic, political and cultural factors. Any approach to developing adaptive responses must include all of these spheres. Our discussion is necessarily incomplete, because the specific responses in any area will vary with local conditions and needs, something that would be impossible to do justice to here. Nevertheless, there are a number of general 'design criteria' to guide policymakers, engineers, local entities and the local population in their attempts to respond to the needs of people living in semi-arid regions.

First, responses to climate variability must be adaptive. By adaptive, we refer not only to the spontaneous adaptive responses of local populations, which generate a certain degree of innovation and locally appropriate responses, but also to purposefully adaptive responses on the part of population and government. Many of these responses will need to be corrective measures to increase people's access to productive resources, They will also need to include forward-looking strategies that aim to increase the availability, stability and resilience of infrastructure, markets, institutions and productive processes.

Second, adaptive responses must be integrative. Experience shows that strictly technical solutions are insufficient to address the vulnerability of people living in semi-arid regions. Economic approaches can address only part of the problem. 'Getting the prices right' cannot protect the poor against volatile prices and declining terms of trade (Bernstein, 1979; Sen, 1987). Policy measures must not only include a multi-sectoral analysis, but should be formulated through an inclusive process that involves the entire affected population, from small producers to the business community to donors. This will help assure that technologies and policies match the resources and needs of the people concerned.

Third, responses must be incremental and iterative, guiding existing institutional, technical and socio-economic structures to a more flexible and appropriate coexistence with semi-arid conditions. The comprehensive project approach can rarely encompass and project the multiple repercussions of policy interventions, not to mention unforeseen future events. An incremental, iterative approach that incorporates active feedback mechanisms to monitor and adjust to emerging events can help overcome these problems.

Finally, there must be active participation of all the parties concerned. Policy formulation, however 'comprehensive' and 'interdisciplinary,' is useless unless it responds to local needs and conditions. Policy interventions include economic and social measures which shape people's participation in economic development by effecting their access to productive resources. These policies, such as how to structure agricultural subsidies, credit systems, technical assistance, etc., have inherent distributional implications, and are therefore political decisions (Demo, 1989; Rodrigues et al, 1992: de Almeida, 1992; O'Brien and Liverman, 1996).

Demo (1989), Rodrigues et al (1992), Vallianatos (1992), Wang'ati (1996) and others argue that mechanisms to include community organizations, small-scale producers, and other marginalized populations must be developed if the effects of unequal development within semi-arid regions are to be redressed. Pressure from the affected communities, such as rural labour unions, organized community groups, producer cooperatives, etc., is a key element for trans forming unequal social and economic arrangements. Together with purposeful policies aimed at increasing producer access to productive resources, this local pressure may be capable of reducing development imbalances within semi-arid regions. Approaches that recognize these groups as legitimate stakeholders, and provide some means for including them in the decision-making process, are critical in redressing marginalization (Demo, 1989).

The following discussion provides an analysis of people's vulnerability to the consequences of climate variability, and the technical, governmental and international responses that this analysis suggests. Again, though this discussion is necessarily incomplete, the aim is to sketch out some of the more important factors that might help shape policy decisions that are compatible with the development aims of semi-arid regions.

From impacts to vulnerability and beyond

The primary problem of semi-arid regions is not climate variability, drought, soil erosion or floods, but more centrally, people's vulnerability to the effects of these events. While droughts, floods and the ecological character of the land are natural phenomena, vulnerability to the effects of environmental change or natural hazards is a social matter. It is not so much the droughts or floods that are alarming, but people's vulnerability to the consequences associated with them; hunger, famine, dislocation from land or livelihood, economic loss, and the loss of ecological assets. Vulnerability comes at the confluence of underdevelopment, social and economic marginality, and the inability to garner sufficient resources to maintain the natural resource base and to cope with the climatological and ecological instabilities of semi-arid zones.

When we write of vulnerability we are not implying that it is a thing of the future or of mere potentiality. Vulnerability to hunger does not mean that people are not hungry yet. It simply is a way of identifying the populations most likely to be hungry. The word may imply potential problems that are not yet here, but in the semi-arid regions, hunger and frequent crisis are pervasive. We therefore use this term with caution, emphasizing that many vulnerable populations suffer chronic or frequent crises.

Vulnerability is a function of a number of interlinking factors. Neither chronic nor periodic crises emerge from any single agent. Rather, they occur at the conjuncture of many. Famine, for instance, occurs at the intersection of phenomena such as drought, human need, grain prices, wars or frontier settlement policies. It is not a singular result of drought. One aim of this section is to sketch out these forces in order to help develop their policy implications and point to policy responses.

Because the purpose of this chapter is to cover the climate-related issues most pressing in the semi-arid regions of the world, we focus on those groups within these regions whose livelihoods and lives are most at risk. These include the landless and smallholder farmers, pastoralists, and small ranchers in the less-developed regions whose physical well-being is tied to the rains and the land. Risk of economic loss – which in this case is rarely life threatening – is the primary concern within more-developed semi-arid regions. We also examine the linkages between the most vulnerable populations and the population at large, because without a broad and integrated economic development of these lands, chronic underdevelopment and frequent crises will continue.

This section is devoted to defining and discussing the concept of vulnerability.

A formal definition of vulnerability

Here, we adopt Thomas E. Downing's method for evaluating vulnerability when assessing the potential consequences of climate variability and change. Downing's (1992, pp3–4) methodology consists of:

> identifying the multiple dimensions of vulnerability ... [to a specific consequence such as hunger]; determining socioeconomic groups with similar patterns of vulnerability; assessing their location and degree of vulnerability; delineating pathways by which their vulnerability may be

altered by trends in resources (including climate), population, and economy; judging the risk of future climate change, in the contest of other expected risks to sustainable agricultural development; and, finally reviewing potential responses that reduce the risk of adverse climate change and enhance the prospects of food [or for our purposes food, job or economic] security. (Downing, 1992, p3)

Focusing on food insecurity, Downing describes vulnerability as 'an aggregate measure, for a given population or region, for the underlying factors that influence exposure to food shortage and predisposition to its consequences' (Downing, 1992, p4). Below we discuss the principal characteristics of the concept of vulnerability.

Adverse, specific consequences

The concept of vulnerability is linked to *adverse* consequence. Hence, the concept has an ethical basis – in focusing on the adverse outcomes – which distinguishes it from more neutral terms such as 'sensitivity', 'consequences' or 'impacts,' Indeed, the concept is designed to help identify those groups within society most likely to experience *negative* outcomes. While crop yield may be sensitive to drought, different households may be more or less vulnerable in the face of the same low-rainfall event. For example, those who have excess grain to sell at a high price during drought-triggered food scarcity will benefit from a drought. Those who have water resources on their private property can sell access or use it to produce goods that are otherwise made scarce by drought. In addition, those with capital can buy land and equipment at low prices from those who are forced to sell out of desperation (see, for example, Demo, 1989; Magalhães, 1992; Rodrigues, et al, 1992). While these households are affected by drought, they are not as vulnerable to its consequences as are others in the same community (Downing, 1992, p5).

Vulnerability is *specific* in that it is concerned with a particular consequence, such as famine, hunger or economic loss, Vulnerability to famine, or to these consequences, can then be evaluated with respect to multiple events such as drought, access to resources, market fluctuations, state policies or regional conflicts. This is a fundamentally different formulation from previous analyses which link a single cause to an outcome, such as drought to crop yields. Rather than focusing on the consequences of a single event, vulnerability analysis traces out the multiple causes of a single consequence.

The several specific negative consequences that are discussed in the climate variability and climate change literature include vulnerability to dislocations, hunger, famine and economic loss. These can easily be extended to include the vulnerability to loss (or degradation) of assets, which in turn can be broken down into natural assets such as land, forests and water resources, and human-made capital such as farm machinery or other infrastructure. While these consequences are often discussed together, vulnerability to them must be evaluated separately, for each may have different causes.[6]

Vulnerability is relative

Vulnerability is a scale of the relative likelihood of different socio-economic groups and geographic regions experiencing negative consequences, such as hunger, famine, economic loss or the loss of productive assets. While everyone is susceptible to all of these adversities, some socio-economic groups and some areas are more susceptible than others. Clearly the semi-arid rain-fed agricultural regions at the tail end of the rainfall gradient are more likely to experience famines than are cities (see for example, Gasques et al, (1992, p38).[7] In the same regions, the poor are more likely to experience hunger than are the rich. While all are vulnerable to food shortages, some groups and regions are more vulnerable than others. And, as Downing (1992, p4) states, 'ultimately, the analysts must assign the thresholds for concern and action.[8]

Vulnerability and socio-economic status

Vulnerability is a function of the relative status of socio-economic groups. As we will see below, vulnerability is a function of income as well as class, caste, clan, religion, political party, livelihood, race, ethnicity, family, gender and age. Different socio-economic groups have differing assets as well as differing levels of access to productive resources Their asseis and access are critical aspects of their vulnerability.

Vulnerability is also a function of the degree of development. As Wilhite et al, (1987, p558) point out;

> In developed countries the proportion of commercial agricultural producers who can withstand a short-term occurrence of drought is high, in terms of both business resilience and human welfare. The impact of short-term drought is significantly reduced because of irrigation and the availability of sufficient forage (fodder) and water for livestock. Even in the case of longer-term drought, the use of irrigation coupled with sufficient grain and forage storage facilities and a fully developed infrastructure can significantly lessen the impact on society and livestock. For example, in Australia, 40per cent of the farming community is not greatly affected by a drought.

For subsistence farmers, even a short-term drought can be disastrous, especially for the peasant farmer whose only security is a small piece of land on which to grow food and some cash crops. If seasonal rains fail, no alternative supply of water is available to sustain growth. The result is critical shortages of food, inadequacy of grazing land, suffering and possibly loss of life for both human beings and livestock. The lack of adequate infrastructure (related to the lack of proactive government programmes) and the high price of grain from external markets impede governmental ability to rescue inhabitants of such distressed areas.

While China and India used to be thought of as lands of drought and famine, they appear to have reduced their vulnerability by bringing these problems under control – at least temporarily. It is now Africa that is plagued by famines. While the climate variability in India and China has not been altered, critical political, social and economic factors have changed over time. 'Although there were major droughts and climate-induced food shortages around the globe – in various parts of Africa, India, China, Indonesia, Brazil – famines occurred only in Africa' (Glantz, 1989, p46; also see Sen, 1987; Dreze and Sen, 1989). At the same time, droughts in the southwestern United States, central Canada and Australia have led primarily to economic loss (Wilhite and Glantz, 1987, pp20–3; Rosenberg and Crosson, 1992; Cohen et al, 1992, pp7–11). Here again there is a critical difference in vulnerability to hunger, famine and economic loss from place to place. Climate variability alone cannot account for vulnerability or outcomes. Both the magnitude and the type of vulnerability are different in different regions of the world, at different times, under different social and political-economic conditions, and different levels of development.

Developing countries are more vulnerable than developed ones. Not only does the level of vulnerability differ, but the type of vulnerability experienced in developing regions differs from that experienced in the industrial countries of the world. Magalhães (1992, p7) points out that 'while in developed areas the impacts are mainly of an economic and environmental nature, in developing areas they are mostly social'. Clearly, vulnerability is a strong function of the level of regional development.

Vulnerability, causality and policy

Analysis of vulnerability has several ramifications in the policy sphere. In giving a relative indication of the level of vulnerability, policies can be aimed at the most vulnerable populations. Policy priorities can be established according to need. And, since vulnerability analysis focuses on the *multiple causes* of a single consequence, it allows policies to be designed for the range of causes that make climate events into economic and social crises. In addition, given the specificity of this type of analysis, policies can be tailored for a specific population in a specific place. And lastly, since causality happens at international, national, household and individual levels, policies can be targeted at the appropriate level *if* the causes are understood.

Knowing that vulnerability to dislocation, hunger or famine is a function of geographic location and income is a first step in evaluating vulnerability. But this does not tell us why people end up on submarginal lands or how and why they are impoverished. The causes of such spatial and economic marginality, and hence vulnerability, must usually be understood historically. Such marginality could be partly a function of land concentration, as is the case in Brazil's Northeast (Demo, 1989; Magalhães and Glantz, 1992; Rodrigues et al, 1992). It could be due to state policies encouraging cultivation on marginal lands as in parts of West Africa, or as in Australia it could be a result of people moving onto these lands not knowing that they are making this move during an unusually wet period (Glantz, 1996; Wilhite, 1996). It could also be due to the inability of a farm household to accumulate sufficient capital to invest in the maintenance of the land, or to have sufficient assets to buffer against the consequences of a drought (Sen, 1981; Blaikie, 1985; Downing, 1991; Watts and Bohle, 1993). Where these vulnerabilities are a function of class or other forms of social status, they may be results of lack of access to inputs to the productive process. Alternatively, vulnerability may be due to market instabilities or to the classic case of declining producer prices with increasing input and consumption-good prices, as in a 'simple-reproduction squeeze' (Bernstein, 1979; Blaikie, 1985; Sen, 1987; Swift, 1989).

The focus on different socio-economic groups and on specific kinds of vulnerability or threats, such as famine or economic loss, facilitates the policy analysis process. First, it allows policymakers to identify those groups and regions most at risk. And second, it can illuminate the causal variables, and hence the links to appropriate policy interventions for each group vis-à-vis specific kinds of vulnerability (Downing, 1992, p4).

For example, the analysis of vulnerability to specific outcomes also often reveals different causal factors for different groups. Herders and farmers may be vulnerable to hunger for different reasons. For the pastoralist it may be a function of access to dry-season pastures, while for a farmer vulnerability may be due to a low savings rate and a lack of fall-back income opportunities or inability to diversify assets. It is in response to these types of causal factors, and the political-economic forces that shape them, that specific and appropriate policy options can be chosen and applied.

Climate variability affects rich as well as poor sectors of society. But, while hunger, famine and dislocation tend to threaten the poor, economic losses threaten the better-off. Those who are well-off may experience great material losses without ever going hungry. Thus, policies targeting both food security and economic security may be in order. But accumulation on the part of the wealthy, and policies justifying or structurally disposed to economic growth in already more economically productive regions or on larger farms, have often been part and parcel of the problem of marginalization – marginalization being a flip side of concentration. Hence, special attention must be focused on intervening in ways that do not exacerbate marginalization and vulnerability by reinforcing ongoing differentiation processes. That is, policies must acknowledge the role of accumulation and the lack of it (e.g. differentiation processes) in creating and maintaining vulnerability.

In short, the object of vulnerability analysis is to link impact analysis to the causes of vulnerability in order to facilitate the policy process. But analysts must go beyond the proximate causes of vulnerability to root causes. Correlation does not explain causality. To map out the vulnerability factors or indicators, such as location, livelihood, education and income level, is an incomplete analysis. Without addressing structural causes, such as the political economy of resource access and control – that is, the politics of accumulation and marginalization or the ongoing processes of differentiation – it is difficult to target the root causes of marginality, poverty and the resultant vulnerability to hunger and famine.

It is in response to these non-climatic causes of vulnerability that policies to reduce vulnerability can be made. Because these causes are usually multiple, interlinked and historically contingent, it is all the more important to understand their roots. It is identifying causal links that facilitates a meaningful and effective policy process, for it is in addressing the root causes of vulnerability that vulnerability can be reduced.

Levels of analysis and vulnerability

Causes of vulnerability and environmental decline, and the opportunities for their alleviation, reside at a multitude of levels within the social and political-economic context that shapes the options of individuals, enterprises and farm households. Schmink (1992) uses what she calls a 'socio-economic matrix' when evaluating the causes of deforestation, and the policy handles by which deforestation can be addressed. This matrix can be adapted to the issues of vulnerability and dryland degradation, as has been done in Table 8.2. In this schematic, the various forces that bear on vulnerability at different levels are sketched out.

In brief, access to and control over resources necessary for production and reproduction at the local level are shaped by forces at a multitude of levels. Because vulnerability is partly a function of access and control over productive resources, vulnerability itself is shaped by all of these factors. While different levels of the system will exert differing degrees of influence on the local dynamic, all of these levels are relevant. The activities and options of a resource user must be examined from all these levels if a complete understanding of that user's vulnerability is to be achieved.

Conclusion

Climate events, although they can trigger catastrophes or contribute to chronic poverty, do not cause vulnerability. Rather, vulnerability is the product of international, national, household and individual level socio-economic forces shaping people's livelihood options and choices. Catastrophe, as well as chronic underdevelopment, in

Table 8.2 *The socio-economic matrix of vulnerability*

GLOBAL CONTEXT	
Markets	*International aid policies*
Demand for natural	Development lending
resources (mineral, forest,	Structural adjustment
and agricultural goods)	Environmental conditionality
Foreign investment	
International agreements and	
cooperation	
Inter-regional cooperation	
Technology transfer	
Trade agreements	

NATIONAL CONTEXT	
Markets	*Policy*
Transportation	Roads and infrastructure
Prices	Price supports and subsidies
Financial markets	Extension services
Migration	*Land tenure*
Population pressures	Land distribution
Frontier expansion	Property regimes

REGIONAL/LOCAL CONTEXT	
Settlement patterns	*Interest groups*
Localized population	Conflicts over resources
pressures	Coalition and alliances
Resource distribution	

HOUSEHOLD/COMMUNITY CONTEXT	
Gender relations	*Family/community strategic*
Division of labour and	Access to resources
resource access control	Income sources and
Family size and composition	employment
Control over fertility	Temporary migration

Source: adapted from Schmink, 1992

the semi-arid zones comes at the intersection of nature and society. It comes at the conjunction of ecological limits, climatological events, the social organization of alternatives available to those pressed by exploitation, market prices, state policies and environmental change against falling productivity.

The most acute problems in semi-arid lands are products of a chronic lack of development, that is, a lack of the resources necessary to hedge against extreme, but expected, events: events that would surprise only a stranger to these regions, but which most local farmers know present a risk. It is not that the risk is unknown nor that the methods for coping do not exist, for people have been coping with climate variability for millennia, Rather, inability to cope is due to the lack of – or the systematic alienation from – resources needed to guard against these events.

The central issue of semi-arid regions is one of development and its distribution. Subsistence farmers need a margin of security and a level of savings sufficient to invest in maintaining, upgrading and developing their assets. They need access to infrastructure and to research commensurate with their needs and relevant to their goals. They also need access to alternative income-generating opportunities so as to increase their security in times of drought and to complement their agricultural activities.

In the final analysis, it is accumulation and concentration that marginalize, and it is marginality that makes people vulnerable in the face of environmental change. Marginality can also push people to 'mine' their natural resources, which only increases their vulnerability. But, so too do accumulation and concentration contribute directly to the ecological decline that makes marginal populations more vulnerable. Certainly, concentration and the drive for accumulation are important causes of widespread ecological insults. Pesticide and fertilizer overuse, uncontrolled effluents and speculative deforestation are all associated with concentration and wealth. These insults all increase vulnerability of marginal populations. They too must be taken into account in evaluating both environmental decline and vulnerability. Indeed, marginality of the environment, just as the marginality of the poor, results in higher vulnerability of both.

Development with a focus on equity and access is part of the solution to this set of problems. Productive security and environmental quality depend on development, access and inclusion – indeed, empowerment and enfranchisement. However, that development must be a conscientious development that accounts for the need to maintain a healthy natural-resource base and a secure population.

Governmental, institutional and policy responses

Introduction

The problems facing semi-arid regions are multiple and overlapping; so too are the opportunities. There are no purely economic strategies that will reduce regional vulnerability or increase security, just as there are no purely technical strategies that will increase production, reduce poverty and reverse dryland degradation. The papers presented at ICID were unanimous in their call for adopting a multidisciplinary approach to development in semi-arid lands. Any environmentally sound development policy requires an integrated approach that allows for iterative responses to multiple, interrelated spheres – social, economic, technological, biological, political, cultural, etc, through which policies reverberate and by which policies are reshaped.

The need to reduce and, it is hoped, reverse, the possibility of climate change cannot be over-emphasized. Although these responses tightly fall into the government (domestic and international) arena, policies that aim at reducing greenhouse gas emissions are beyond the scope of this chapter. Rather, we limit ourselves here to governmental, institutional and policy responses that may help enable the inhabitants of semi-arid regions to overcome their vulnerability in the face of current climate variations and possible future climate change. We highlight some of the important ingredients necessary for reducing vulnerability, and increasing resilience to climate variability and change.

Economic development

Environment and development are tightly linked. Unless semi-arid regions are developed, smallholders and landless peasants will continue to exert pressure on the natural resource base in their attempts to eke out a subsistence living. Due to the lack of access to resources and minimal, locally retained surplus, they often cannot buffer against the effects of drought; they are forced to 'mine' the land, simply to survive. Without the resources to invest in the maintenance and development of the land, productivity declines. As alternatives diminish, they are forced to migrate into the cities or onto increasingly marginal lands and new frontiers. Without addressing the lack of adequate farm incomes and alternative income-generating activities, preparing for drought and maintaining the resource base seem to have little chance.

A major question in development debates concerns whether to focus on large-scale and commercial agriculture and industrialization, or to support the small subsistence farmers and pastoralists. The first method has been the mode. The plight of small farmers and the landless has been seen as an inevitable cost of development, as their traditional forms of cultivation become 'outmoded.' It has often been argued that the transient inequities caused by the development process would be offset by the development to come. It would be better, the proponents of this strategy argue, to get the peasant farmers to 'modernize' or to get off the land, into the cities and the non-agricultural sector, or off to the opening of new frontiers. In short, it is better to make room for modern agriculture and industry rather than to support a 'backward' form of subsistence. While there may be truth in the notion that mechanization and modernization of agriculture is inevitable, and in many cases desirable, the dislocation of rural peasants has additional and persistent problems. Cities are overburdened with unemployed, while 'frontier' areas, typically more marginal and fragile environments than those left behind, are stressed by the influx of new migrants. In both places, the rural outmigrants often find themselves in exploitative circumstances similar to those they suffered previously.

Poverty did not disappear with agricultural mechanization. Rather, it increased during the 1960s, 1970s and the 'lost decade' of the 1980s (World Bank, 1990), leading to a call for basic needs guarantees. Later, policymakers recognized the environmental ramifications of poverty (Eckholm, 1979). Poverty leads smallholders to overuse their resource base, thus increasing their vulnerability in the face of climate variation (Blaikie, 1985; Downing, 1992). Hence it is in alleviating poverty that people's basic needs can be met, and the resource base maintained. But basic needs remain unmet and the poverty experienced by the majority of the developing world's rural populations persists.

It now seems clear that neither the modernization nor the basic needs development approach is sufficient. Development requires supporting both large commercial agriculture and small subsistence farmers. Dynamic economic regional development relies on well-integrated markets where increased production leads to increased savings, investment and consumption at the local and regional levels. Because semi-arid regions are so dependent on the primary production sector relative to other regions, the cycle of impoverishment of small rural producers and resource depletion described in the previous section signals a structural weakness in the economy (World Bank, 1990; Goldsmith and Wilson, 1991). This structural weakness is especially significant in semi-arid regions because agriculture there is highly susceptible to wide output variations with small changes in climate variability (UCAR, 1991). Unless the pattern can be reversed, it is unlikely that integrated rural development can take root (Goldsmith and Wilson, 1991: Bitoun et al, 1996).

Unfortunately, reactive famine relief has long been the only form of policy attention the semi-arid areas have received. These short-term relief measures cannot, however, solve these regions' chronic problems. While responding to emergencies will always be a part of government responsibility, policymakers must focus on developing long-term strategies that reduce semi-arid regions' vulnerability to the consequences of climatic events (Wilhite, 1996). Resilient and dynamic economic development, unlike emergency, stop-gap measures, holds more hope for semi-arid regions' economies, their ecosystems, and the people in them.

Regional development strategies for semi-arid regions often focus on diversifying regional production, particularly through industrialization (Goldsmith and Wilson, 1991; Magalhães and Glantz, 1992). The hope is that a dynamic economic process will set in, where local businesses and firms will develop to meet industrial input needs, generating an integrated and thriving economy. This strategy is particularly attractive in areas where agriculture is susceptible to wide output variations associated with periodic droughts. Focusing on industries, manufacturing, and product-processing industries that are not directly dependent on rain or agricultural inputs can buffer the economy from the vagaries of weather. This strategy, however, is frustrated by the structural limitations of semi-arid regions. The relative dominance of agricultural production, and the dominance of subsistence agriculture in terms of the economically active population, lead to demand structures in semi-arid regions which are highly variable, coinciding with drought events. As a consequence, the expected local multiplier effect of industrial development is hampered, local marketing and repair shop networks do not develop, and it becomes easier for industries and manufacturers to obtain inputs and market products outside the region from more stable sources in more developed areas (Goldsmith and Wilson, 1991). The result is well-developed economic linkages with industrial areas and markets outside the semi-arid region, and a disarticulated and stagnant economy within. For the countries of the Sahel, where the entire national territory is often within the semi-arid region, reliance on outside markets for non-agricultural development places them at the mercy of the fluctuations and generally unfavourable terms of international product markets, resulting in large deficits and continual dependence on foreign aid (Watts, 1987a; Mackintosh, 1990).

This analysis demonstrates the importance of developing a viable local demand structure within semi-arid regions. Without sufficient local demand, no amount of local product diversification will lead to an economic dynamism necessary to absorb labour from the rural sector. At best, a small sector of well-off industries will develop that are less vulnerable to climatic events than the rest of the local economy.

Development strategies must increase agricultural output and income, and absorb labour. Increasing farm output and incomes provides the basis for increased demand structure, and labour-intensive activities absorb under- and unemployed labor (Perrings, 1991; Lemos and Mera, 1992). As farm incomes increase, consumer demand at the local level increases. Increased demand for consumer products causes local businesses to expand and new ones to form. Part-time workers are employed full-time, and new workers are taken on. As the regional economy diversifies it becomes less susceptible to climatic events. Increased incomes and security allow producers to invest in improving their farm management practices such as mechanization, irrigation and use of improved seeds. These measures often increase the number of crops possible each year, thus increasing year-round agricultural employment and the need for local distributors, repair shops, etc. Hence, the multiplier effect of increased farm output and increased incomes can contribute to integrated and sustainable rural economic development (Ranis and Stewart, 1987; Storper, 1991; Timmer, 1992).

As argued in the section on technological responses in agriculture, government interventions to increase agricultural productivity must be focused on technologies, institutions and infrastructure that are compatible with producers' needs, present knowledge and adaptive capacities. Building on established coping strategies, strategies must be step-wise improvements that increase producers' resilience to climate variation while increasing their ability to produce and save (Rodrigues et al, 1992: Wang'ati, 1996). Clearly, increases in agricultural production and incomes must be accompanied by opportunities to leave the agricultural sector, income-earning alternatives such as commerce, service, and small-scale or household manufacturing at the local level provide an exit response that can reduce outmigration to major urban centres where industrial and service sectors are insufficient to absorb all the excess rural labour (Perrings, 1991; Gomes et al, 1992).

Farm income increases in a highly stratified economy tend to accrue predominantly to the already better-off because access to inputs such as credit, irrigation technologies and water, new seed varieties, etc., is shaped by socio-economic standing and politics (Demo, 1989; Lemos and Mera, 1992; O'Brien and Liverman, 1996). Larger producers tend to spend more of their increased income outside the local area, in large cities, while small producers, who are less mobile, consume more locally, contributing more to the local economy. Inputs and markets for commercial agriculture also tend to be located outside the region, particularly in a disarticulated, subsistence economy. A context of skewed landholdings, therefore, will tend to retard any multiplier effects of increased incomes in the rural sector.

These observations lead to two conclusions. The first is that land distribution is a critical issue The second is that particular emphasis must be placed on increasing smallholder output and incomes (including the creation of job opportunities in other sectors). Large agricultural production and industrial sectors already receive significant government attention and support relative to smallholdings, and generally experience dynamic growth relative to the smallholder agricultural sector. The task is not to focus on poor peasant farmers at the expense of large, and typically more dynamic agriculture and industry. Rather, it is to provide the necessary opportunities to smallholders and landless peasants so that they can enter into a process of dynamic economic growth.

Below we discuss several important factors that need to be considered when structuring policies that will foster dynamic agricultural growth.

Infrastructure

Water storage and irrigation are the first interventions that policymakers think of when trying to improve agricultural output and reduce vulnerability to the consequences of climate variation. Yet building reservoirs is not sufficient. Careful attention must be paid to the ecological ramifications of this approach, to who is going to have access to irrigation water, and to how this access will be controlled. (See the discussion of technological responses, below, for a more detailed discussion of irrigation technologies.) This is particularly important when water infrastructure projects are managed by the private sector, where market-based distribution of benefits will tend to exclude those most in need. Alternative water storage and distribution technologies may be more appropriate to local management practices and social networks (Moench, 1991; Courcier and Sabourin, 1992). Policymakers must assess the viability of multiple-scale and technology alternatives.

In general, irrigated agriculture involves a higher level of technology than subsistence agriculture. The technical 'leap' can often be a significant barrier to small producers. The cost of hybrid seeds, fertilizers and pesticides must be considered when proposing a transition to irrigated agriculture, and 'packaged' production strategies (de Almeida, 1992). Often distribution networks are inadequate to allow the entire package to be applied effectively. While large producers tend to have established relationships with distributors, small producers are often located in remote areas, and may have variable demand for inputs depending on fluctuating household incomes or access to credit, making adoption of high-input technologies difficult. Small producers are likely to apply improvements selectively, and incrementally. Risking an entire crop on what, for the producer, is an untested technology, is an irrational choice. Instead, a small section of a plot may be chosen for a new seed variety, or a small amount of fertilizer will be applied to see the effect (J. Tendler, personal communication, 1991). In general, these considerations indicate that agricultural packages requiring comprehensive application in order to achieve significant results are less appropriate for small producers. Rather, projects should involve a series of incremental improvements that build directly on producer experience, skill and financial ability.

Improved roads, communication networks, rural electrification, marketing networks, and product processing and storage are necessary for making integrated development possible (World Bank, 1990; Perrings, 1991; Gomes et al, 1992; Magalhães and Glantz, 1992; Zhao, 1996). Whether this kind of infrastructure is put in place during emergency make-work projects during a drought period, or is done gradually as a part of a regional development plan, care must be taken to design infrastructure and prioritized projects so that the distribution of benefits is as even as possible. For example, wide high-grade roads in a few areas may come at the expense of narrow lower-standard roads distributed over a larger region. Narrower roads will go further, having a more extensive positive effect on the region. These kinds of trade-offs are present in nearly every kind of infrastructure project. A policy that is directed at improving the conditions of the most vulnerable, and fostering an integrated economy, implies that the decision must benefit the greatest number of people possible.

Semi-arid zones are seen as largely lacking in resources (water, soil nutrients, etc.), but they are rich in certain resources. Developing semi-arid regions must take full advantage of these resources. Solar, wind and geothermal energy may provide viable alternatives to dependence on water-based or non-renewable resource-based electricity generation (Wang'ati, 1996; Zhao, 1996). Development of both centralized and decentralized technologies should be pursued, aiming at developing technologies that are easily implemented and not dependent on outside inputs.

Credit, marketing and inputs

Small producers tend to go from season to season with a very limited safety margin because nearly all their earnings and production are used for subsistence or extracted from the local economy. Savings are limited, or non-existent. Lack of savings limits their ability to diversify into alternative income-generating activities, or to invest in increasing the productive capacity of their farms. This does not mean that smallholders are ill equipped to adopt improved management practices and technologies, or to diversity their economic activities. On the contrary, subsistence agriculturalists are by necessity diversifies, adapters and survivors. Their lack of investment capital is a significant barrier for their adoption of more productive activities. Yet, as we argue, improving the productive capacity of smallholdings and the diversification of local economies within semi-arid regions is a basic requirement for regional development and economic growth. Credit is one possible solution to this barrier. Small producers, however, have less access to formal credit systems than better-off producers. Some have proposed alternative credit institutions that are more accessible to small producers (Caron and Da Silva, 1992). These types of flexible strategies demonstrate how government policies can be formulated to address the needs of small producers, and to structure projects that are responsive to them.

Problems of access to markets and productive inputs can constitute a more significant barrier to economic growth than lack of credit. Government interventions through 'variable' incentives, such as product and input prices, taxes, subsidies and 'user' charges are one way for governments to intervene in facilitating small-producer access to viable commercialization of their products (Perrings, 1991). Prices and financial incentives represent only part of the access equation, however. Institutional barriers also block small-producer access to productive resources. Perrings (1991) calls for user-enabling measures to correct these problems. These measures might include small grain storage facilities, small-producer product processing and marketing cooperatives, and management structures for common property resources such as grazing areas, water and forests.

Human resource development

Education, health care, safe water supplies and sanitation, and vocational training all fall within the area of human resource development. Projects and programmes of these sorts can be grouped into two categories, based on the policy intent. On the one hand, developing human resources means insuring a basic level of well-being, related to life expectancy, health, literacy, etc. On the other hand, it means creating the capacity for people to increase their own well-being through diversification into more profitable activities, or improving current techniques. The two concepts are clearly related. Without the first, the second is impossible. However, the distinction is helpful in structuring government investment policies. Training that provides skills needed in growing sectors will enable people to move readily into economically viable activities while also contributing to the dynamic growth of the region. Conversely, training for activities which are needed outside of the region can facilitate outmigration when better opportunities are available elsewhere (Wang'ati, 1996).

Agricultural extension and training play a significant role in disseminating new technologies and inputs, responding to producer emergency needs, and developing adapted technologies that reflect the specific soil, water and landholding size agriculturalists are working within. Projects and programmes dealing with agricultural research and extension must be oriented towards the needs of small producers, and be appropriate to cultivation limitations inherent in semi-arid regions. Ideally, these programmes should develop institutional links with entities at the local level to broaden the dissemination of new adaptive technologies and techniques, and to make local decision-makers aware of the need for sustainable and appropriate development policies (Rodrigues et al, 1992).

Alternative income opportunities

Much analysis of semi-arid regions focuses on the pressures of a growing population. This observation is useful only to the extent that it signals a shortage of opportunities available to people living in semi-arid regions. Rather than focusing solely on fertility controls – which are politically charged, difficult to implement, and of questionable efficacy – policies should also focus on improving the options available to people. As mentioned earlier, efforts to equip semi-arid populations with skills that are useful outside agriculture, or even outside the semi-arid regions, are one way to enable people to rise above their bare subsistence condition and to reduce pressures on the land (see, for example, Santibáñez, 1992, p41). Unless there are income-earning opportunities waiting for them elsewhere, however, there is little hope for such a strategy. It must therefore be linked to deliberate efforts to create new jobs and income-earning activities in semi-arid regions, and to foster the growth of alternative activities such as marketing, intermediary goods production and services. Directing credit for these activities, providing subsidies for start-up enterprises, and creating physical and financial infrastructure will facilitate their emergence.

Emergency responses

There will always be a need for emergency responses to climate events in semi-arid regions (see Wilhite, 1996). No matter how well adapted we are to climate variations, there will always be events which exceed adaptive structures. There are, however, ways to reduce the likelihood that we will be caught by surprise by climate events, or that when severe events occur we are completely unprepared to respond (Wang'ati, 1996). Significant advances have already been made in developing forecasting and early warning mechanisms (Downing, 1992). The task at this point is to increase the link between institutions that have forecasting capabilities and local agencies responsible for responding to emerging crises (Servain et al, 1992; Cochonneau and Sechet, 1992; Soares et al, 1992). Gomes, et al, (1992) argue, for example, that the lack of coordination and communication among institutions within the Brazilian semi-arid region leads to ineffectual responses to crisis. This situation must be addressed. While much of the large-scale early warning information is international in scope, there must be well-established links to the regional and local levels. In this way, not only will semi-arid regions be more prepared to deal with severe climatic events, but scientists and policymakers will learn more about the interrelationships between climate and environment.

Conclusion

This discussion is a cursory review of strategies and approaches that can foster adaptive strategies to the severe climate variability of semi-arid regions. It has not been an exhaustive discussion, but rather an indication of the kind of analytical orientation that is needed in order to address the multifaceted problems facing policymakers at the national, regional and local levels in semi-arid regions. Like any adaptive strategy, policy approaches will themselves evolve as we learn more about the interrelationships between climate and environment, and among the multiple spheres of society – economics, politics, technology, environment and culture. Each region and country must find those strategies that are most suited to its own particular conditions, limitations and capabilities. None of the strategies discussed here are panaceas for the triple burden of underdevelopment, marginalization and climate variation. Instead, they attempt to point to a more hopeful future for these regions, which will only come about through significant effort by policymakers, local entities and the local population.

Technological responses in agriculture

Introduction

Trying to respond to the natural fragility of semi-arid areas by applying unidimensional technical fixes without considering the socio-economic and cultural context within which they are applied can often lead to disastrous results (Glantz, 1989, p63). The challenge to policymakers is to show that they are able to develop technical responses to climate variability and change that are sensitive to the social context in which they are to be applied. Fortunately, there is ample reason to believe this can be done. In this section we investigate some of the dominant technological responses that have been applied in response to climate variability in semi-arid areas. Each has strengths as well as limitations, opportunities as well as pitfalls. The difference between understanding or ignoring these is often the difference between success and failure.

Technology has many faces. It ranges from the newest inputs and the most 'high-technology' practices, to traditional methods of cultivation. The objective of modern, high-technology systems is to maximize profit or yield, using improved crop varieties and livestock breeds, along with fertilizers, herbicides, pesticides and mechanization. The aim of many traditional systems is to minimize year-to-year variation in productivity and, especially, to minimize the risk of total loss (Scott, 1976; Popkin, 1979; Hyden, 1980). The price of this stability is often foregone potential yield. The price of modern, high-yield systems is the lack of a safety net, should the crop fail. Before any technological response can be introduced a thorough understanding of the existing systems, and their internal interactions and dynamics, is necessary. Equally, while estimation of risk levels is an essential component of agriculture analysis, the level of 'risk acceptance' and 'risk affordability' must also be taken into account (Nix, 1985, p107). Policymakers can learn from traditional coping strategies used by indigenous communities in the search for appropriate technological responses to climate variability.

Below we discuss soil and crop management, water management, high-input agriculture and pastoralism. This is neither an exhaustive list nor an exhaustive critique of the available technological options. The aim is to lay out a broad spectrum of major issues and discuss their relation to climate variability and change, particularly the latter as projected by major general circulation models. In general, any response is only as good as its compatibility with the context – physical, climatological, socio-economic and cultural – to which it is applied. Its viability depends not on the technology alone, but on how it is managed and where it is used.

Soil and crop management

Soil degradation is probably the most significant threat to sustainable agriculture. Attempts to extend agriculture by expanding agriculture onto marginal soils accelerates the process, Soil erosion, deterioration of soil structure, loss of nutrients or nutrient-holding capacity, build-up of salts and toxic elements, waterlogging, acidification, etc., remain constant threats to cultivated tracts in the semi-arid regions. Soil erosion is particularly disturbing due to its high replacement costs.

Soil degradation is largely a function of poor crop management. Yet, even on poor soils (like those often found in semi-arid areas) it can be brought under control. For example, inter-cropping, crop-pasture association, using crops with different root distribution patterns, crop rotations, alley cropping, ridging, terracing, mulching, and zero or minimum tillage check soil degradation while also promoting moisture retention (Watts, 1987b, p179; Huss-Ashmore, 1989, p27; Swindale, 1992, p7). Good soil management is the key to halting dryland degradation, or desertification.

Traditional cropping strategies have evolved sophisticated management practices to maintain soil quality (Huss-Ashmore, 1989, p28; GOP/IUCN, 1991). Increasingly, however, the ability of marginalized farmers and pastoralists to maintain traditional soil and farm management practices is being threatened. For example, the beneficial effects of soil organic matter in both improving soil quality and preventing surface degradation is well known to farmers. As access to the commons decreases or when market prices increase, competing demands for dung and crop residues can trap farmers into practices that they know are not sustainable. Dung, for example, may be burned rather than ploughed into the soil as firewood supplies grow scarce or too expensive.

Since plant cover is often sparse in semi-arid regions, evaporation from the soil surface can be a significant portion of the total evapotranspiration. With climate change some models project increased rates of evaporation due to increased temperatures (Rosenberg and Crosson, 1992; Cohen et al, 1992; Schmandt and Ward, 1992; Downing, 1992; O'Brien and Liverman, 1996). Increasing low-water-demand plant cover, either in the form of food and cash crops or in fodder crops and grasses, is an obvious and important response, especially since a simultaneous increase in net precipitation is also projected.

Salinity is a problem for semi-arid lands, especially under warmer climate regimes. But it can be turned to advantage through better management practices if the existing information and experience about saline agriculture is utilized. Headway is already being made in employing salt-tolerant crop and grass species. Fodder crops, in particular, can be grown on fairly poor soils with highly saline water to support livestock (GOP/IUCN, 1991).

Water management

Semi-arid areas are characterized by rainfall variabilities both in quantity and in spatial and temporal distribution. Wherever more regular and abundant sources of water are available nearby or where erratic or insufficient rains merit the creation of artificial water reservoirs, irrigation has historically been seen as an ideal response to climate variability. Many irrigation systems have a long record of success; from once being considered famine-prone, the dry plains of China and India are major food producers today. Mexico, Pakistan and Egypt have been equally successful in enhancing their agricultural production through intensive irrigation (GOP/IUCN, 1991).

Yet the success of many irrigation systems has not come without its economic, ecological and social price (Swindale, 1992, p12; Selvarajan and Sinha, 1992, p2). Salinity, drainage deficiencies, waterlogging, compaction and siltation are just a few of the attendant problems which, if severe enough, become the precursors of desertification. With the expansion of intensive, high-input agriculture – often on soils unprepared for the burden – the problems are compounded (see the section on High-input agriculture below). While agricultural operations can cause salinity problems even in rain-fed areas, salinity is most chronic in irrigated soils. Use of unlined canals, sinking of tube-wells into salt-bearing strata, inadequate drainage and poor water and crop management combine in irrigated tracts to reduce water and soil quality. This can substantially decrease land productivity and seriously affect the quality of drinking water (Swindale, 1992, p6).

Where irrigation systems or their management are divorced from local social realities they can increase, rather than reduce, vulnerability to the impacts of climatic variations and change (O'Brien and Liverman, 1996). Evidence shows that it is not irrigation itself, but how and where it is used, that aggravates soil degradation. Access and distributional issues of irrigation are germane to all technological interventions. The section on Governmental, institutional and policy responses above, discusses these issues in more detail.

More emphasis and attention has now turned to smaller-scale developments such as farm ponds, 'dug outs', siltation traps and small multi-purpose reservoirs (Parry and Carter, 1990, p163; Swindale, 1992, p9; Wang'ati, 1996). The aim is to retain the precious rainfall that is so often lost in semi-arid areas due to high runoffs, while improving water-use efficiency. Many of the crop management practices discussed earlier serve the same purposes.

More effective use of groundwater can reduce risk of crop failure in uncertain climates, while also circumventing the need for large and cumbersome water distribution systems (Zhao, 1996). For example, in Mali a pilot project for high-input agriculture with water pumps is already under way (Jackelen, 1992). The use of dug-wells by Indian farmers for preventing crop losses when temporary rainfall deficits occur, or to recharge soil moisture storage before planting a dry season crop, has contributed substantially to improved farm livelihoods. The use of tube-wells in irrigated plains of Pakistan has similarly given the farmer a solution to waterlogging as well as a source of demand-based water provision. In many desert areas there are vast fossil water supplies which can be exploited for agricultural use (Swindale, 1992, p9). Groundwater depletion is a risk where recharge rates are slow. Therefore, it is essential to use water as efficiently as possible, employing sprinkler or drip irrigation technologies, or other labour-intensive technologies that achieve the same level of efficiency (GOP/IUCN, 1991).

High-input agriculture

The thrust toward intensive agriculture stems not just from technological advances in irrigation systems, fertilizers, seed varieties and hybrid development, but as much, if not more, from population and government policy pressures. With projected change and uncertainty in climatic regimes compounding the already strenuous pressures on the semi-arid zones, high-input agriculture may become a necessary measure for combating vulnerability in some areas.

Improved cultivars are capable of delivering bumper crops in good years. Examples of the success of high-input agriculture in comparatively well-endowed (particularly irrigated) semi-arid lands provides optimism (Selvarajan and Sinha, 1992). Yet the need for caution must be emphasized (GOP/IUCN, 1991). High-input, mono-crop agriculture lacks the 'safety net' built into traditional systems which use multiple native varieties and rarely experience complete system failure. Further, reliable water supplies, nutrient-rich soils and high-technological investments are just a few of the prerequisites for the sustained success of intensive, high-input agriculture. On the more risk-prone rain-fed tracts, mounting pressures of production and increasing climate uncertainty could force farmers to adopt intensive agriculture with unsustainable, if not disastrous, results (GOP/IUCN, 1991; O'Brien and Liverman, 1996).

Experience points toward homogeneity and the loss of sustainability being conspicuously and directly related. Pests and diseases will always reduce crop yields to some extent, but their effects are more devastating when mixed cropping is replaced by mono-cropping and varieties are replaced by hybrids. The technological response to this technology-driven problem is chemical control (Swindale, 1992, p3). While pests quickly become immune to pesticides, the latter accumulate and contaminate food and water systems. The use of integrated pest management techniques shows significant potential in resolving this problem (Swindale, 1992). Some stability of crop production may be achieved by varying fertilizer applications to offset anomalous climatic conditions (Parry and Carter, 1990, p161). Since many semi-arid soils are deficient in organic matter and are further degraded by soil erosion, increased fertilizer application is likely to be an important response strategy.

In general, it is now being acknowledged that excessive crop specialization should be avoided, despite the short-term economic benefits it provides. Increasing environmental awareness has stimulated research into alternative agricultural practices, with particular emphasis on learning not only from past follies of intensive agriculture but also from the resilience of traditional systems. The value of crop rotation, multi-cropping, mixed farming, use of cover crops and recycling of agricultural wastes is being recognized (Richards, 1985). Most importantly, it is finally being recognized that building upon traditional wisdom and grounding strategies in the realities of specific socio-economic and natural systems can lead to increased and more stable production potentials (Huss-Ashmore, 1989, p28; Swindale, 1992).

Pastoralism

Le Houérou (1985, p155) defines pastoralism as the 'unsettled and non-commercial husbandry of domestic animals' and estimates a pastoralist population of 60 to 70 million people (in 1985), mainly in Africa and Asia. He points out that pastoralism is 'essentially – but not solely – a form of adaptation of human societies to hazards and hardships induced, and imposed on them, by climatic constraints'.

Recent famines in the Sahel and the subsequent plight of the pastoralists have focused attention on pastoralism, particularly in the context of projected climate change. The present state of crisis is often attributed to anthropogenic impacts such as overstocking, wood-cutting, bush-fires, 'wild' water development, and expansion of intensive cultivation. Le Houérou (1985, p173) and Watts (1987a, p295), however, describe how herders in Africa utilize complex social relationships as insurance against drought and point out that it is in the strangulation of these social relationships, and not just in the vagaries of climate and population pressures, that the present crisis needs to be understood.

Traditionally, pastoralists have combated the high variability in primary production of rangelands by relying on sturdy drought-resistant breeds, by the mix of livestock held, a sophisticated ethno-scientific understanding of local ranges, and by various socio-cultural relationships in addition to the basic nomadic movement (Le Houérou, 1985; Watts, 1987b). Increasingly, the options to exercise these strategies are being severely curtailed by policies that encourage farm encroachment on pastoral lands, settlement programmes and blockages in nomadic routes (Wang'ati, 1996). Even those who simplistically blame overgrazing and overpopulation as the culprits, and feel that de-stocking and resettlement of people is the most viable solution, acknowledge that issues of property rights, access to common property and efficacy of human institutions will frame the success, or failure, of any biological or physical 'fix' to these problems (Swindale, 1992, p14).

Sedentary pastoralism with particular focus on agro-pastoral systems provides one response to realizing the production potential of semi-arid areas, providing sustainable livelihoods and reducing the need for periodic drought and famine relief (Swindale, 1992, p15). Such systems would need to integrate traditional knowledge about adaptation of stocking rates, livestock mix and grazing patterns with the introduction of suitable fodder crops, trees and shrubs (including saline-tolerant varieties) and improved techniques such as ripping, subsoiling, scarifying, pitting, contour benching and water spreading (Le Houérou, 1985, p169; Swindale, 1992, p15). The viability of such programmes would, however, be dependent upon policy changes that support the development of local infrastructure and institutions, and community involvement in projects with particular focus on the displaced nomadic pastoralists.

International responses

Introduction

The global interest accorded to the Brundtland Commission (WCED, 1987) and the Intergovernmental Panel on Climate Change (IPCC, 1990) testify to the new wave of international concern for the global environment. The expectations surrounding the United Nations Conference on Environment and Development (UNCED) reflect not just the 20th anniversary of the Stockholm Conference, but more importantly the arrival of environmental issues – particularly global climate change – on the international agenda.

In this section we look briefly at the international concerns for climate change, and what expectations are being associated with the UNCED process. We then discuss why it is important to give priority to the semi-arid regions in international discussions and actions regarding global climate change. We then outline some major facets of required international responses. Finally, we discuss why restructuring international economic interventions is of concern.

International cooperation

The global nature of climate change has triggered global interest and global fears. It has even initiated some fledgling efforts toward global response initiatives, these, however, have been far from satisfactory. Whereas verbal consensus on the need for international response strategies exists, the severe distributional disparities, both in causes and in effects or climate change, have made any such effort politically charged. While the overwhelming bulk of additions to the greenhouse gas flux results from the wasteful practices in the North, the countries most vulnerable to global climate change are in the South (Agarwal and Narain, 1991). The debate is being framed by the North, for Northern interests, yet the South is more vulnerable, and the North is better able to cope with climate change impacts. Not only will the South have to bear the effects of climate change, increased climate variability and a sea-level rise, and pay part of the price of mitigating effects largely of the North's making (e.g. preserving forests, foregoing CFC use and paying higher energy prices) but there is a real danger of ignoring the North's wasteful consumption habits while placing the blame on the South's population (see Agarwal and Narain, 1991).

Global networks and institutions

Despite the pressures for action generated by UNCED, meaningful international agreements to reduce greenhouse gas emissions are still a long way off. There have, however, been a number of important international landmarks in this direction. The Montreal Protocol of 1987 to stop the production of chemicals implicated in stratospheric ozone depletion marked one such landmark – even if limited in scope and coming after a protracted, and somewhat painful, process requiring 'long and difficult negotiations and substantial compromise [on] goals' (Harris, 1991, p112).

More specifically, no major international policy initiative exists to address the problems of the semi-arid areas in the light of the projected climate change. The need for such an initiative seems obvious. But given the inherent diversity between and within semi-arid regions it must emerge from, and build upon, regional networks. Although institutions such as the United Nations Environment Programme (UNEP) or the Food and Agriculture Organization (FAO) have larger mandates, their particular interest in the semi-arid zones can be a potential asset. The Inter-governmental Committee for the Fight Against Drought in the Sahel (Comite Inter-Etal pour la Lutte contre la Sécheresse au Sahel, CILSS) and the Inter-Governmental Authority on Drought and Development

(IGADD) in the Sudano-Sahelian region and the International Crops Research Institute for the Semi-Arid Tropics (ICRISAT) are a few examples of institutions focused on issues of semi-arid lands (Swindale, 1992; Wang'ati, 1996).

Such global and regional networks can provide a forum for evaluating the vulnerability of populations in semi-arid regions facing climate variability and change, exchanging successful development strategies, and sharing information on climate trends and early warning techniques. Given the lack of funds and facilities in many semi-arid regions, such networks and institutions have a major responsibility for long-term research at the regional and local levels, with particular focus on forecasting, early warning, and control or mitigation strategies.

The need for networks also stems as much from the fact that semi-arid regions often encompass many nations – the Sahel spans 22 countries – as it does from the importance of sharing and learning from each other's experiences. At the same time, the need to communicate between the regional and local levels requires a cadre of local experts who understand local as well as regional and international issues and needs. Educating and training a cadre of experts and decision-makers may best be accomplished by regional and international networks and institutions.

International economic interventions

International trade imbalances, foreign debt constraints, international commodity markets and pricing structures, the nature of foreign loans and assistance, and the nature and level of investments by multinational corporations (MNCs) all help shape the internal policies of developing nations. Such influences can often outweigh attempts at environmental and resource management, regardless of how much 'political will' a government has (O'Brien and Liverman, 1996). The era since the Second World War has seen the internationalization of production, finance and services. This often defines policy and policy implications at local, and even village, levels (Watts, 1987a, p292). Glantz (1996) points out that international pressures can force countries to shift from food crops to export crops, sometimes causing hunger even where there is no drought.

In response to mounting public concern for the environment, some progress has been made. Efforts to restructure 'assistance' criteria, environmental impact assessments and natural resource accounting in cost–benefit analysis are a few examples (Meredith, 1992). While all these initiatives are yet too new or untried for a meaningful assessment to be made, their potential merits attention.

Balanced inclusion in the international economy is of particular relevance for the destiny of the developing world and of the semi-arid regions within them. The relative position of weakness vis-à-vis MNC investments, international terms of trade and price structures can often force developing countries into decisions to exploit resources. Passed on from the international to the local stage through national policy, such decisions (e.g. growing groundnut for export rather than food crops for domestic use) force the pace of degradation and deprivation on the semi-arid lands.

Why focus on semi-arid lands?

In addressing the threats of global climate change, international attention has, until now, been focused on the issues of coastal and island settlements and on tropical forests.

The first (such as the Maldives and Bangladesh) have received attention because they are at great risk of total inundation by rising sea level, the latter because forest management can both reduce the problem and contribute to its solution.[9] Semi-arid tropics deserve more international attention for these same reasons.

Like coastal and island settlements, the semi-arid tropics are at extreme risk in the face of projected global climate change. Rather than inundation by the sea, semi-arid lands risk inundation from increased rains, and desiccation from warming.[10] It is no mistake that the semi-arid southern edge of the Sahara desert is called the Sahel, from the Arabic word for shore or coastline, for the Sahel is the tidal zone between the desert and the humid forests to the south. Here exaggerating or shifting rainfall patterns could make these regions uninhabitable. Increasing desiccation drives the northern limit of cultivation southward, as has happened with past and current droughts, taking vast farming and pastoral regions out of cultivation and pasture, and dislocating the populations who depend on these lands.

In general, the ecosystems in semi-arid regions tend to have poor soils, problematic groundwater resources, and depend heavily on already scant and erratic rainfall; in addition, the spatial marginality of their populations is often compounded by chronic poverty and underdevelopment. This combination makes them extremely vulnerable to the negative outcomes associated with climate change. The semi-arid tropics are in real danger of severe and widespread human and environmental catastrophe (famine, desertification, etc.), and the need for action is urgent.

Degradation of the resource base not only jeopardizes the livelihoods of a region's inhabitants, but the resulting deprivation results in 'spillover' of dislocated populations onto other, often equally fragile, ecosystems. The dislocation of 'ecological refugees' is not a concept unique to Africa. A case in point is the relationship between the Brazilian Northeast and the Amazon, with more than 51 per cent of those migrating into the Amazon reported to originate from the semi-arid Northeast (Bitoun et al, 1996). The emerging pattern is clear: degradation and deprivation in one area can translate into increased pressures on others.

Semi-arid regions are among the least developed regions of the world. Consequently, they are also the most vulnerable to the current consequences of climate variability and the potential consequences of climate change. While mitigation strategies applied to the forest and energy sectors will reduce the potential for future aggravation of an already precarious situation, actions to reduce current vulnerability in semi-arid lands will do the same. Indeed, the object is to reduce or avert human suffering while upgrading productivity from the natural resource base. Balanced development in these areas has the potential to do both. Equitable development can reduce local and migration-triggered environmental deterioration, as well as vulnerability to hunger, famine and dislocation, by providing the resources necessary to invest in maintenance and improvement of the land while providing jobs to prevent migration into other fragile regions. Clearly, we do not have to look to the future to find risk or need. Development in semi-arid regions will help meet these needs and reduce both current and future vulnerability.

There are opportunities in these regions. These opportunities serve not only development aims, but environmental aims as well. Not only do they stop the exploitative 'mining' of the most marginal lands by the most exploited and marginalized populations, but they also reduce pressure on other regions by reducing outmigration or by encouraging migration into more productive (agricultural and non-agricultural) regions and activities. But most importantly, development measures in these most marginal lands increase the well-being and security of those who are chronically exposed to the risk of hunger, famine and loss.

Conclusion

It is ironic that we must look into the future, to a time distant enough to be free of commitment to immediate action or change, just to discuss the tragedy taking place before us. We project future climate change and future vulnerability to dislocation, hunger and famine, while vulnerability and crisis are already chronic and widespread. Today, future scenarios allow us to discuss these (otherwise too politically charged) development, environment and equity issues in a public forum. Indeed, they have brought these 'future' issues to the centre of international attention. But we must use this opportunity to slide back down the projection lines and point to the crisis at hand.

As illustrated in this chapter, the semi-arid regions of the world are currently experiencing the insecurity and disruptions that climate change impact analyses indicate could become more widespread. Addressing the current problems in the semi-arid tropics will diminish the future vulnerability that climate change may exacerbate. Clearly, the long-term future of these and other regions of the world depends on today's quality of life and the sustainability of current practices and social relations within these regions. While it is important to look to the future, it is much more important to act today on what we already know from direct and repeated experience. It is critical to begin investing in the future today, by investing in social changes that can support equitable and ecologically sound development.

Notes

1   Heathcote (1983, p16) cites P. Meigs' estimate that semi-arid lands make up approximately 15.8 per cent of the world's land area and the United Nations estimates that these lands cover 13.3 per cent of the world's land. The Meigs estimate is based on those areas in which the ratio of precipitation to evapotranspiration falls between –20 and –40. This corresponds, according to Meigs (published in 1953), approximately to the lands falling between the 200 and 500mm isohyets. The basis of the UN estimate (published in 1977) is not explained. It should be noted that the first estimate might be considered conservative since some definitions currently in use correspond to the lands falling between 200 and 800mm isohyets (Rasmusson, 1987). The population of semi-arid areas derived from Heathcote's (1983, pp20–21) figures is approximately 11.25 per cent of the world's total. Heathcote (1983, p21) also presents a UN figure (published in 1977) of 10.1 per cent of the world's population living in these regions. The figures for the land areas, and hence the proportion of the world's population living in these areas, are subject to uncertainty and definitional dispute. The figures presented here, given the conservative rainfall range, are probably therefore underestimated.

2   Marginality is a fact, marginalization a process. While the fact of marginality can lead to environmental decline, the process of marginalization should be identified as the cause. Marginality is the result of this process. The consequences of marginality are therefore the consequences of the marginalization process. It is this process that should be examined if marginality and its consequences are to be understood and redressed.

3   The uncertainty range is 0.2–0.5°C per decade.

4   Emphasis added.

5   The highest-resolution climate GCMs specify the state of the atmosphere at the intersections of a three-dimensional grid. Each grid is divided into sections that are approximately 250 miles on a side and about a mile thick (Stone, 1992, p37).

6   For an excellent evaluation of the multiple causes of soil erosion see Blaikie (1985) and Blaikie and Brookfield (1987). For a similar analysis of the causes of deforestation see Schmink (1992).

7   Gasques et al (1992, p38), for example, argue that in Brazil's Northeast, 'basic food production is concentrated in areas of extreme vulnerability where reduced production from climatic variations is not just an economic question of reduced output, but rather a question of survival' (translated from the Portuguese by the authors).

8   The analyst, in the authors' opinion, must be thought of as including not only the expert adviser or policymaker, but also the populations being analysed. Participation and participatory research are discussed in the introduction of the section on Responses.

9   Saving the tropical forests would reduce the release of greenhouse gases (through reduced burning and decay) as well as provide a sink for CO_2 (through forest planting and growth) from other sources, particularly energy.

10   This is not an either/or proposition, but, if rains remain unevenly distributed and drying is intensified, alternating floods and drought could be the mode.

References

Agarwal, A. and Narain, S. 1991. *Global Warming in an Unequal World*, New Delhi: Center for Science and the Environment.

Bernstein, H. 1979. African peasantries: a theoretical framework. *Journal of Peasant Studies* 6:4.

Bitoun, J., Neto, L. G. and Bacelar de Araújo, T. 1996. Amazonia and the Northeast: The Brazilian tropics and sustainable development. In *Climate Variability, Climate Change and Social Vulnerability in the Semi-arid Tropics*, ed. J. C. Ribot, A. R. Magalhães and S. Panagides, pp. 129–146. Cambridge, UK: Cambridge University Press.

Blaikie, P. 1985. *The Political Economy of Soil Erosion in Developing Countries*. London: Longman.

Blaikie, P. and Brookfield, H. C. 1987. *Land Degradation and Society*. London: Methuen.

Burton, I. and Cohen, S. S. 1992. Adapting to global warming: regional options. Presented at ICID, Fortaleza-Ceará, Brazil, 27 January to 1 February 1992.

Campos-Lopez, E. and Anderson, R. J., (eds.) 1983. *Natural Resources and Development in Arid Regions*. Boulder: Westview Press.

Caron, P. and Da Silva, P. C. G. 1992. Small production and sustained development in the semiarid tropics: the necessity of a sustainable credit system. Presented at ICID, Fortaleza-Ceará, Brazil, 27 January to 1 February 1992.

Cochonneau, G. and Sechet, P. 1992. Trying to synthesize the annual rainfall measurement of the semi-arid zone of the Brazilian Northeast Region. Presented at ICID. Fortaleza-Ceará, Brazil, 27 January to 1 February 1992.

Cohen, S. J. 1990. Bringing the global warming issue closer to home: the challenge of regional impact studies. *Bulletin of the American Meteorological Society* 71 [April]:4.

Cohen, S. S., Masterton, J. and Wheaton, E. E. 1992. Impacts of climate scenarios in the prairie provinces: a case study from Canada. Presented at ICID, Fortaleza-Ceará, Brazil, 27 January to 1 February 1992.

Courcier, R. and Sabourin, E. 1992. Handling of surface waters for the small agriculture in the semi-arid tropic of the Brazilian Northeast. Presented at ICID, Fortaleza-Ceará, Brazil, 27 January to 1 February 1992.

de Almeida, M. G. 1992. Irrigation policy: promises of prosperity in the backlands – the semiarid region of the state of Sergipe, Brazil. Presented at ICID, Fortaleza-Ceará, Brazil, 27 January to 1 February 1992.

Decre, C. D. and de Janvry, A. 1984. A conceptual framework for the empirical analysis of peasants, pp. 601–611, Giannini Foundation Paper No. 543.

de Janvry, A. 1981. *The Agrarian Question and Reformism in Latin America.* Baltimore: Johns Hopkins University Press.

de Janvry, A. and Kramer, F. 1979. The limits of unequal exchange. *Review of Radical Political Economics* 11[winter]:4.

Demo, P. 1989. Methodological contributions towards societal drought-management practices. In *Socioeconomic Impacts of Climatic Variations and Policy Responses in Brazil,* ed. A. R. Magalhães. Fortaleza-Ceará, Brazil: UNEP.

Downing, T. E, 1991. *Assessing Socioeconomic Vulnerability to Famine: Frameworks, Concepts, and Applications.* FEWS Working Paper, AID Famine Early Warning System.

Downing, T. E. 1992. Vulnerability and global environmental change in the semi-arid tropics: modelling regional and household agricultural impacts and responses. Presented at ICID, Fortaleza-Ceará, Brazil, 27 January to 1 February 1992.

Drèze. J. and Sen, A. 1989. *Hunger and Public Action.* Oxford: Clarendon Press.

Eckholm, E. P. 1979. *The Dispossessed of the Earth: Land Reform and Sustainable Development.* Washington, DC: Worldwatch Institute.

EI-Shahawy, M. A. 1992. Some impacts of regional warming. Presented at ICID, Fortaleza-Ceará, Brazil, 27 January to 1 February 1992.

Farago, T. 1992. Climatic variability, impacts and sustainability: generalization from regional climate impact studies. Presented at ICID, Fortaleza-Ceará, Brazil, 27 January to 1 February 1992.

Gasques, J. G., (coordinator), Motta Coelho, C. H., Bosco de Almeida, M., Soares, F. A., da Silva, L. A. C., Nogueira, M. J., Lins, R. C., Oliveira, J. G. B., Lins, C. J. C. and Barreto, F. 1992. A case study: overall scenario. Presented at ICID, Fortaleza-Ceará, Brazil, 27 January to 1 February 1992.

Glantz, M. H. 1987. *Drought and Hunger in Africa.* Cambridge: Cambridge University Press.

Glantz, M. H. 1989. Drought, famine, and the seasons in sub-Saharan Africa. In *African Food Systems in Crisis,* part I, ed. R. Huss-Ashmore and S. H. Kalz, pp. 45–71. New York: Gordon and Breach.

Glantz, M. H. 1996. Drought follows the plow: Cultivating marginal areas. In *Climate Variability, Climate Change and Social Vulnerability in the Semi-arid Tropics,* ed. J. C. Ribot, A. R. Magalhães and S. Panagides, pp. 125–128. Cambridge, UK: Cambridge University Press.

Goldsmith, W. W. and Wilson, R. 1991. Poverty and distorted industrialization in the Brazilian Northeast. *World Development* 19: 435–55.

Gomes, E., Da Silva, J. E. and Brandao, M. H. M. 1992. The integrated institutional aspect, basic element of sustainable development: the examples of the semi-arid of the Northeast of Brazil. Presented at ICID, Fortaleza-Ceará, Brazil, 27 January to 1 February 1992.

GOP/IUCN 1991. *Pakistan National Conservation Strategy.* Government of Pakistan/ International Union for the Conservation of Nature and Natural Resources.

Hare, F. K. 1985. Climatic variability and change. In *Climate Impact Assessment: Studies of the Interaction of Climate and Society.* ed. R. W. Kates, J. H. Ausubel and M. Berberian, pp. 37–68. Chichester: Wiley Press.

Harris, J. M. 1991. Global institutions and ecological crisis. *World Development* 19:1.

Heathcote, R. L. 1983. *The Arid Lands: Their Use and Abuse.* London: Longman.

Heathcote, R. L. 1996. Settlement advance and retreat: A century of experience on the Eyre Peninsula of South Australia. In *Climate Variability, Climate Change and Social Vulnerability in the Semi-arid Tropics,* ed. J. C. Ribot, A. R. Magalhães and S. Panagides, pp. 109–122. Cambridge, UK: Cambridge University Press.

Huss-Ashmore, R. 1989. Perspectives on the African food crisis. In *African Food Systems in Crisis,* ed. R. Huss-Ashmore and S. H. Katz, pp. 3–42. New York: Gordon and Breach.

Hyden, G. 1980. *Beyond Ujamma in Tanzania: Underdevelopment and an Uncaptured Peasantry,* Berkeley: University of California Press.

IPCC. 1990. *Report of the Intergovernmental Panel on Climate Change.* Geneva and Nairobi: WMO/UNEP.

Izrael, J. A. 1992. Climatic variability and climatic change and the related social, economic and environmental impacts. Presented at ICID, Fortaleza-Ceará, Brazil, 27 January to 1 February 1992.

Jackelen, H. R. 1992. Economic interventions in the changing environment of a semi-arid zone: introducing small-scale irrigation in the Timbuktu region of the north of Mali and assessing community participation based of financial and production indicators. Presented at ICID. Fortaleza-Ceará, Brazil, 27 January to 1 February 1992.

Khan, A. S. and Campos, R. T. 1992. Effects of drought on agricultural sector of Northeast Brazil. Presented at ICID. Fortaleza-Ceará, Brazil, 27 January to 1 February 1992.

Le Houérou, H. N. 1985. Biological impacts: pastoralism. In *Climate Impact Assessment: Studies of the Interaction of Climate and Society,* ed. R. W. Kates, J. H. Ausubel and M. Berberian, pp. 155–85. Chichester: Wiley.

Lemos, J. de J. S. and Mera, R. D. M. 1992. Rural poverty and sustainable development for the state of Ceará. Presented at ICID, Fortaleza-Ceará, Brazil, 27 January to 1 February 1992.

Mackintosh, M. 1990. Abstract markets and real needs. In *The Food Question: Profits Versus People?,* ed. H. Bernstein, B. Crow, M. Mackintosh and C. Martin, pp. 43–53. New York: Monthly Review Press.

Magalhães, A. R. 1992. Understanding the implications of global warming in developing regions: the case of Northeast Brazil. In *The Regions and Global Warming: Impacts and Response Strategies,* ed. J. Schmandt and J. Clarkson, pp. 237–56. New York: Oxford University Press.

Magalhães, A. R. and Glantz, M. H. 1992. Socioeconomic *Impacts of Climate Variations and Policy Responses in Brazil.* Brasilia: UNEP/SEPLAN/Esquel.

Meredith, T. 1992. Adjusting to environmental change impact assessment as a cultural adaptation process. Presented at ICID, Fortaleza Ceará, Brazil, 27 January to 1 February 1992.

Moench, M. 1991. *Drawing Down the Buffer: Upcoming Ground Water Management Issues in India.* Pacific Institute for Studies in Development, Environment, and Security.

Nix, H. A. 1985. Biological impacts: agriculture. In *Climate Impact Assessment: Studies of the Interaction of Climate and Society,* ed. R. W. Kates, J. H. Ausubel and M. Berberian, pp. 105–30. Chichester: Wiley.

Nobre C. A., Massambani, O. and Liu. W. T.-H. 1992. Climatic variability in the semi-arid region of Brazil and drought monitoring from satellite. Presented at ICID, Fortaleza-Ceará, Brazil, 27 January to 1 February 1992.

O'Brien, K. and Liverman, D. 1996. Climate change and variability in Mexico. In *Climate Variability, Climate Change and Social Vulnerability in the Semi-arid Tropics,* ed. J. C. Ribot, A. R. Magalhães and S. Panagides, pp. 55–70. Cambridge, UK: Cambridge University Press.

Ocana, C. L. 1991. *Assessing the Risk of Dryland Degradation: A Guide for National and Regional Planners.* World Resources Institute.

Parry, M. L. and Carter, T. R. 1985. The effect of climatic variations on agricultural risk. In *The Sensitivity of Natural Ecosystems and Agriculture to Climate Change*, ed. M. L. Parry, pp. 95–110. Dordrecht; Kluwer.

Parry, M. L. and Carter, T. R. 1988. An assessment of effects of climatic variations on agriculture. In *The Impact of Climatic Variations on Agriculture: Vol. 2: Assessments in Semi-arid Regions*, ed. M. L. Parry, T. R. Carter and N. T. Konijn. Dordrecht: Kluwer.

Parry, M. L. and Carter, T. R. 1990. Some strategies of response in agriculture to changes of climate. In *Climate and Development*, ed. H. J. Karpe, D. Otten and S. C. Trindade, pp. 152–72. Berlin: Springer-Verlag.

Perrings, C. 1991. Incentives for the ecologically sustainable use of human and natural resources in the drylands of sub-Saharan Africa: a review. Working paper presented at Technology and Employment Programme, World Employment Programme Research, International Labor Organization.

Popkin. S. L. 1979. *The Rational Peasant: The Political Economy of Rural Society in Vietnam.* Berkeley: University of California Press.

Ranis, G. and Stewart, F. 1987. Rural linkages in the Philippines and Taiwan. In *Macro-Policies far Appropriate Technology*, ed. F. Stewart, pp. 140–91. Boulder Westview Press.

Rasmusson, E. M. 1987. Global climate change and variability: effects on drought and desertification in Africa. In *Drought and Hunger in Africa*, ed. M. H. Glantz, pp. 3–22. Cambridge: Cambridge University Press.

Richards, P. 1985. *Indigenous Agricultural Revolution: Ecology and Food Production in West Africa*, Boulder: Westview Press.

Riebsame. W. E. 1989. *Assessing the Social Implications of Climate Fluctuations: A Guide to Climate Impact Studies.* Nairobi: United Nations Environment Programme.

Rodrigues, V. with H. Matallo jr., M. C. Linhares, A. L. Costa de Oliveira Galvão and A. de Souza Gorgonio. 1992. Evaluation of desertification scene in the Northeast of Brazil: diagnoses and prospects. Presented at ICID, Fortaleza-Ceará, Brazil, 27 January to 1 February 1992.

Rosenberg, N. J. and Crosson, P. R. 1992. Understanding regional scale impacts of climate change and climate variability: application to a region in North America with climates ranging from semi-arid to humid. Presented at ICID, Fortaleza-Ceará, Brazil, 27 January to 1 February 1992.

Santibáñez, F. 1992. Impact on agriculture due to climatic change and variability in South America. Presented at ICID, Fortaleza-Ceará, Brazil, 27 January to 1 February 1992.

Schmandt, J. and Ward, G. H. 1992. Climate change and water resources in Texas. Presented at ICID. Fortaleza-Ceará, Brazil, 27 January to 1 February 1992.

Schmink, M. 1992, The socioeconomic matrix of deforestation. Paper presented at the Workshop on Population and Environment, sponsored by Development Alternatives with Women for a New Era, International Social Science Council and Social Science Research Council, Hacienda Cocoyoc, Morelos, Mexico, 28 January to 1 February.

Scott, J C. 1976. *The Moral Economy of the Peasant: Rebellion and Subsistence in Southeast Asia.* New Haven: Yale University Press.

Selvarajan, S. and Sinha, S. K. 1992. Weather variability and food grains production sustainability in India. Presented at ICID, Fortaleza-Ceará, Brazil, 27 January to 1 February 1992.

Sen, A. 1981. *Poverty and Famines: An Essay on Entitlement and Deprivation.* Oxford: Oxford University Press.

Sen, A. 1987. *Hunger and Entitlements.* World Institute for Development Economics Research of the United Nations University.

Servain, J., Merle, J. and Motlière, A. 1992. The influence of the tropical Atlantic Ocean on the hydroclimates of the Sahel and the Northeast. Presented at ICID, Fortaleza-Ceará, Brazil, 27 January to 1 February 1992.

Soares, A. M. L., Leite, F. R. B., Lemos, J. de J. S., et al 1992. Degraded areas susceptible to desertification processes in the state of Ceará Brazil. Presented at ICID, Fortaleza-Ceará, Brazil, 27 January to 1 February 1992.

Stone, P. H. 1992. Forecast cloudy: the limits of global warming models. Technology Review, MIT, February/March.

Storper, M. 1991. Regional development policy 2: the global industrial economy and local industrial strategies. In *Industrialization, Economic Development and the Regional Question in the Third World: From Import Substitution to Flexible Production.* London: Pion Press.

Swift, J. 1989. Why are rural people vulnerable to famine? *IDS Bulletin,* **20**(2), 8–15.

Swindale, L. D, 1992. A research agenda for sustainable agriculture. Presented at ICID, Fortaleza-Ceará, Brazil, 27 January to 1 February 1992.

Tie Sheng, Li, Liu Zhong Lin, Xie Qinyun, Wang Shide and Ma Lanzhong. 1992. The situation, problems, countermeasures of arid, semi-arid regions in Inner Mongolia. Presented at ICID, Fortaleza-Ceará, Brazil, 27 January to 1 February 1992.

Timmer, C. P. 1992. *Agriculture and the State.* Ithaca: Cornell University Press.

UCAR 1991. *Arid Ecosystems Interactions: Recommendations for Drylands Research in the Global Research Program.* Boulder: University Corporation for Atmospheric Research.

Vallianatos, E. G. 1992. Sustainable development theory. Presented at ICID, Fortaleza-Ceará, Brazil, 27 January to 1 February 1992.

Wang'ati, F. J. 1996. The impact of climate variation and sustainable development in the Sudano-Sahelian region. In *Climate Variability, Climate Change and Social Vulnerability in the Semi-arid Tropics,* ed. J. C. Ribot, A. R. Magalhães and S. Panagides, pp. 71–91. Cambridge, UK: Cambridge University Press.

Watts, M. J. 1987a. Conjunctures and crisis: food, ecology and population, and the internationalization of capital.' *Journal of Geography* (Nov/Dec).

Watts, M. J. 1987b. Drought, environment and food security: some reflections on peasants, pastoralists and commoditization in dryland West Africa. In *Drought and Hunger in Africa,* ed. M. H. Glantz, pp. 171–211. Cambridge: Cambridge University Press.

Watts, M. J. and Bohle, H. 1993. The space of vulnerability: the causal structure of hunger and famine. *Progress in Human Geography* **17**(1), 43–68.

WCED 1987. *Our Common Future: Report of the World Commission on Environment and Development.* London: Oxford University Press.

Wilhite, D. A. 1996. Reducing the impacts of drought: Progress toward risk management. In *Climate Variability, Climate Change and Social Vulnerability in the Semi-arid Tropics,* ed. J. C. Ribot, A. R. Magalhães and S. Panagides, pp. 147–166. Cambridge, UK: Cambridge University Press.

Wilhite, D. A. and Glantz, M. H. 1987. Understanding the drought phenomenon: the role of definitions. In *Planning for Drought: Toward a Reduction of Social Vulnerability,* ed. D. A. Wilhite and W. E. Easterling with D. A. Wood. pp. 11–30. Boulder: Westview Press.

Wilhite, D. A. and Easterling, W. E. with Wood, D. A. (eds.) 1987. *Planning for Drought: Toward a Reduction of Social Vulnerability.* Boulder: Westview Press.

Wisner, B. 1976. *Man-Made Famine in Eastern Kenya: The Interrelationship of Environment and Development.* Discussion Paper No. 96. Brighton: Institute of Development Studies at the University of Sussex.

World Bank 1990. *World Development Report 1990.* Washington: World Bank.

WRI 1990. *World Resources 1990–91.* New York: Oxford University Press.

WRI 1991. *World Resources 1991–92.* New York: Oxford University Press.

WRI, 1992. *World Resources 1992–93: A Guide to the Global Environment.* A report by the World Resources Institute in collaboration with UNEP and UNDP. New York: Oxford University Press.

Yair, A. 1992. The ambiguous impact of climate change at a desert fringe: Northern Negev, Israel. Presented at ICID, Fortaleza-Ceará, Brazil, 27 January to 1 February 1992.

Zhao, Z. 1996. Climate change and sustainable development in China's semi-arid regions. In *Climate Variability, Climate Change and Social Vulnerability in the Semi-arid Tropics*, ed. J. C. Ribot, A. R. Magalhães and S. Panagides, pp. 92–108. Cambridge, UK: Cambridge University Press.

Theory and Practice in Assessing Vulnerability to Climate Change and Facilitating Adaptation

P. Mick Kelly and W. Neil Adger

Introduction

The primary aim of this chapter is to examine ways of defining vulnerability to environmental stress, specifically, climate variability and change. In the context of the global warming problem, assessing vulnerability is an important component of any attempt to define the magnitude of the threat. Moreover, analysis of vulnerability provides a starting point for the determination of effective means of promoting remedial action to limit impacts by supporting coping strategies and facilitating adaptation. We focus on the vulnerability of human individuals and communities to climate stress. A secondary aim of this chapter is to clarify the links between vulnerability and adaptation (cf. Burton, 1997). Adaptation is a topic of considerable policy relevance and concern (Smith et al, 1996) but, to date, has not been effectively assessed (Tol et al, 1998; see Chapter 3, this volume). Climate impact studies have tended to focus on direct physical, chemical or biological effects, yet a full assessment of consequences for human well-being clearly requires evaluation of the manner in which society is likely to respond through the deployment of coping strategies and measures which promote recovery and, in the longer term, adaptation.

We begin our discussion with a review of definitions of vulnerability, drawing on the food security and natural hazards literature as well as previous climate studies. From this review, a working definition of vulnerability is derived that emphasizes the social dimension neglected in previous studies and is of direct relevance to the development of policy and practice. We then draw out various implications of this definition and discuss how it might be operationalized. We argue that any analysis of vulnerability must consider the 'architecture of entitlements', the social, economic and institutional factors that influence levels of vulnerability within a community or nation and promote or constrain options for adaptation. Finally, we illustrate this largely theoretical discussion with examples drawn from field research undertaken in northern Vietnam during which the selected approach was developed, tested and refined. As a society undergoing rapid change, Vietnam provides a dynamic test bed of broad relevance illustrating how social, economic and political trends and characteristics shape patterns of vulnerability.

In the case studies, our primary concern is with vulnerability to *short-term* hazards, in particular, tropical cyclone impacts. It is short-term hazards and extreme climate events on the seasonal and interannual timescale that the bulk of any population experiences and reacts to, rather than long-term trends, and it is through the varying character of these events that any long-term change in climate will first be manifest. See the general discussion of this issue by Burton (1997) and the specific examples given by Smit et al (1996) and Palutikof et al (1997). How valid is it to extrapolate from these findings to longer timescales? We would argue that the primary linkages between social, economic and political characteristics and trends and the capacity to react to environmental stress that we identify will hold on all timescales, even if the precise response strategies alter in nature or relative significance. Glantz (1991) discusses the strengths and limitations of the use of analogies in forecasting societal responses to climate change.

Defining the Concept of Vulnerability

Definitions of vulnerability to environmental stress vary considerably. Some analysts regard assessment of vulnerability as the end point of any appraisal, others as the focal point, and yet others as the starting point. And these different views carry considerable baggage regarding, among other things, levels of certainty and uncertainty, policy relevance and disciplinary focus.

According to the Intergovernmental Panel on Climate Change (IPCC) Second Assessment Report (see the Glossary of Terms, Appendix B in Watson et al, 1996), vulnerability defines 'the extent to which climate change may damage or harm a system; it depends not only on a system's sensitivity but also on its ability to adapt to new climatic conditions'. Sensitivity, in this context, is 'the degree to which a system will respond to a change in climatic conditions'. From this perspective, the definition of vulnerability must be contingent on estimates of the potential climate change and adaptive responses. The assessment of vulnerability is the *end point* of a sequence of analyses beginning with projections of future emissions trends, moving on to the development of climate scenarios, thence to biophysical impact studies and the identification of adaptive options. At the final stage, any residual consequences define levels of vulnerability; that is, the level of vulnerability is determined by the adverse consequences that remain *after* the process of adaptation has taken place and, as such, it provides a convenient means of summarizing the net impact of the climate problem, a major goal of the IPCC process. In the context of coastal studies, Klein and Nicholls (1999) discuss a variant of the IPCC approach endorsed by the United Nations Environment Programme.

A contrasting use of the concept of vulnerability is found in the food insecurity, or famine, and natural hazards literature as well as some climate studies (e.g., Downing, 1991; Watts and Bohle, 1993; Bohle et al, 1994; Blaikie et al, 1994; Cutter, 1996; Ribot et al, 1996; as reviewed by Adger, 1996). Watts and Bohle (1993), for example, argue that the space of vulnerability to food insecurity can be defined in terms of the exposure to stress and crises, the capacity to cope with stress, and the consequences of stress and the related risk of slow recovery. Essentially, they consider vulnerability an overarching concept, *a focal point*. From a natural hazards perspective, Blaikie et al (1994) define risk as consisting of two components. The first component, equivalent to Watts and Bohle's exposure, is a measure of the natural hazard. The second, vulnerability itself, is equivalent to capacity and is, they argue, largely determined by socio-economic structure and property relations.

Blaikie et al (1994) clearly separate what we may term the biophysical and the social dimensions, defining vulnerability in terms of the human dimension alone as 'the capacity to anticipate, cope with, resist, and recover from the impact of a natural hazard'. The biophysical component, the exposure or measure of the hazard, is formally outside their definition of the concept of vulnerability. Having said that, it is intrinsic to the definition that vulnerability must always be linked to a specific hazard or set of hazards, so vulnerability and exposure remain inseparable. The concept of vulnerability, in this instance, provides a policy-relevant framework within which the value of specific interventions aimed at improving the capacity of people to respond to stress can be judged. By identifying likely sensitivities in terms of a limited capacity to respond to stress, it represents a potential *starting point* for any impact analysis. As far as the relationship between vulnerability and adaptation is concerned, vulnerability is defined in terms of the capacity to adapt, and vulnerability assessment, in this case, is not dependent on predictions of adaptive behaviour.

If we trace the linguistic roots of the word vulnerability then we find support for the conceptualisation adopted by Blaikie et al (1994). The *Collins English Dictionary* (second edition, 1986) defines vulnerability as, inter alia, the 'capacity to be physically or emotionally wounded or hurt'. The origin of this word lies in the Latin *vulnus*, meaning 'a wound', and *vulnerare*, 'to wound'. Specifically, the word vulnerable derives from the Late Latin *vulnerabilis*, and this is enlightening. *Vulnerabilis* was the term used by the Romans to describe the state of a soldier lying wounded on the battlefield, i.e., already injured therefore at risk from further attack. The relevance to the present discussion is that vulnerability, in this classic sense, is defined primarily by the prior damage (the existing wound) and not by the future stress (any further attack). By analogy, then, the vulnerability of any individual or social grouping to some particular form of natural hazard is determined primarily by their existent state, that is, by their capacity to respond to that hazard, rather than by what may or may not happen in the future.

In the research reported here, we adopt a definition closely allied to that advanced by Blaikie et al (1994). Thus, we define vulnerability in terms of the ability or inability of individuals and social groupings to respond to, in the sense of cope with, recover from or adapt to, any external stress[1] placed on their livelihoods and well-being. Implicit in this definition of vulnerability is the adoption of the 'wounded soldier' perspective in focusing attention on constraints, 'wounds', that limit the capacity to respond to stress effectively and that exist independent of the future threat. We use the term 'social vulnerability' to underline the emphasis of this approach on the human dimension, rather neglected in past studies of vulnerability and adaptation (Adger and Kelly, 1999).

The nature of the stress under consideration must, of course, be specified before tackling the question of levels of vulnerability when following this approach.

Vulnerability does not exist in isolation, only with respect to exposure to some specific impact or set of impacts. Here, the analysis of the nature of the stress, the exposure, sets the context for the study, defining the domain or scope of the research and critical issues for analysis, as illustrated in a later section. Given the focus on pre-existing constraints on the capacity to respond, it is not, however, necessary to define precisely the nature of the potential impact, nor the likely course of the adaptive process, as it would be if vulnerability were defined, as in most climate impacts studies, in terms of the residual consequences once adaptation had occurred.

We select this particular approach to the issue of vulnerability because we are concerned with identifying robust, policy-relevant recommendations and conclusions regarding vulnerability to long-term climate change that are also relevant to immediate needs and, hence, consistent with a precautionary approach to the climate problem (Kelly et al, 1994; Kelly, 2000). The 'wounded soldier' approach concentrates attention on the socio-economic and political context within which the impact process takes place, a context that may well determine vulnerability not only to climate stress but also to other forms of environmental and societal pressure. Study of vulnerability to climate stress in this fashion should, then, throw light on the broader issue of sustainability, an immediate and lasting concern. Robustness stems from the shift of focus away from the speculative future. Consider the pyramid of uncertainty that we build whenever we attempt to predict the future. Our definition of vulnerability rests the superstructure of the pyramid, implications for policy, on the relatively sound foundation of the analysis of processes that limit or favour the ability to respond to stress and means by which they can be offset or reinforced (Glantz, 1991), rather than on less certain projections of impacts and adaptive responses.

It would be foolish to suggest that any particular approach to the concept of vulnerability is more or less appropriate in the context of climate impact studies. The purpose of the analysis must guide the selection of the most effective definition or conceptualization. We wish to define the social construction of vulnerability – how different socio-economic and political characteristics, processes or trends influence levels of vulnerability – and, hence, develop policy practice that might improve future prospects. The IPCC is more concerned, at this stage of the climate debate, with assessing the overall scale of the global warming problem and providing comparative estimates. The critical point is that the result of that selection should be made explicit, as must the basis of the decision-making (cf. Schneider, 1997, with regard to the related area of integrated assessment modelling). Transparency in defining terms is important not only because, in its absence, confusion can arise in comparing the conclusions of different studies but, in dealing with vulnerability from a societal perspective, the issue of values comes to the fore. Aspirations for the future, for example, can affect perceptions of vulnerability, and the subjectivity, the values, of the analyst may skew recommendations regarding priorities for intervention. As discussed later, the inherently political nature of issues such as property rights that affect levels of vulnerability cannot be ignored. Arguably, it has been the impossibility of engaging with the more political aspects of the issue of vulnerability that has led the Intergovernmental Panel on Climate Change, operating as it must within a framework of consensus decision-making, to focus on biophysical aspects of the subject. Analysing biophysical impacts is not, of course, a value-free activity, but problematic areas may not be as obvious.

Operationalizing the Definition of Vulnerability

We base our examination of social vulnerability to climate variability on an understanding of the human use of resources. Following Sen (1981, 1990), the extent to which individuals, groups or communities are 'entitled' to make use of resources determines the ability of that particular population to cope with or adapt to stress. The concept of entitlements, which extends beyond income and other material measures of well-being, has been used in a variety of contexts (cf. Sen, 1990; Watts and Bohle, 1993; Bohle et al, 1994; Cutter, 1996; Hewitt, 1997). Determining levels of vulnerability to climate stress involves defining what we term the 'architecture of entitlements' (Adger and Kelly, 1999), the myriad factors that shape the availability of entitlements, their evolution over time, and the broader political economy of the formation and distribution of entitlements. In considering the factors that shape vulnerability, it is convenient to distinguish between individual vulnerability and collective vulnerability (Adger, 1999a), though these aspects are, of course, intrinsically linked through the political economy of markets and institutions.

Table 9.1 illustrates how particular characteristics of an individual, household or community affect entitlements and, hence, vulnerability. These are, of course, not the only factors that influence levels of vulnerability but they are central to the processes we have observed in our case studies in Vietnam. Poverty is related directly to access to resources and the process of marginalization, though wealth is not in itself a guarantor of security as resources are mediated through property rights and so on. We consider

Table 9.1 *Selected characteristics of vulnerability and their assessment*

Vulnerability indicatory	Proxy for:	Mechanism for translation into vulnerability
Poverty	Marginalization	Narrowing of coping and resistance strategies; less diversified and restricted entitlements; lack of empowerment
Inequality	Degree of collective responsibility, informal and formal insurance and underlying social welfare function	*Direct*: concentration of available resources in smaller population affecting collective entitlements *Indirect*: inequality to poverty links as a cause of entitlement concentration
Institutional adaptation	Architecture of entitlements determines resilience; institutions as conduits for collective perceptions of vulnerability; endogenous political institutions constrain or enable adaptation	Responsiveness, evolution and adaptability of all institutional structures

Source: Adger and Kelly, 1999

that increasing inequality within a population can heighten collective vulnerability, all other things being equal. Greater inequality may be associated with a reduction in communal resource allocation and in the pooling of risk and other social phenomena associated with the so-called moral economy (Scott, 1976). In addition, there are strong links between inequality and a lack of diversification of income sources as well as with poverty, placing further constraints on response options (Reardon and Taylor, 1996). The final indicator of vulnerability is what we might term the institutional context. Here, the term 'institutions' covers not only formal political structures but also the more diffuse 'rules of the game' and social and cultural norms. Poverty, the use of resources, and the distribution of wealth and income within a population, factors that shape vulnerability, are all in turn institutionally determined. Formal political institutions devise and implement the legal enforcement of property rights, for example, and all economic structures can be viewed as dependent on the institutional structure that frames them. O'Riordan and Jordan (1999) argue that, alongside holding society together, a primary role of institutions is, in fact, to enable society to adapt. Assessment of vulnerability, then, requires analysis of the political economy and examination of the structures of institutions, constraints on institutional adaptation and evolution and the constraints institutions exert on individuals (Sanderson, 1994).

While we can quantify, more or less accurately, many of the factors that influence levels of vulnerability, such as poverty and inequality, we do not consider it appropriate to take this analysis a stage further and attempt to devise a composite index of vulnerability itself. First, we cannot be confident that all the processes that determine vulnerability can be reliably identified on the basis of current understanding. Second, there is a danger that those factors that can be easily incorporated in a composite index, such as poverty, will be over-emphasized as factors such as institutional adaptation that, although no less important, cannot be as readily quantified are neglected. Finally, the links between the factors that may influence vulnerability and the overall level of vulnerability in a community are not well established, making it difficult to weight the various factors and, indeed, as we shall see, to determine the sign of the net effect in some cases. This is not to say that the quantification of vulnerability to draw, for example, contrasts between nations should not be attempted, but that other approaches to defining vulnerability may be more appropriate if comparison is the goal of the exercise.

Analysing Social Vulnerability

Introduction

To illustrate the operationalization of the concept of vulnerability developed here and to draw out key conclusions regarding factors which influence levels of vulnerability and the adaptive process, we present selected results from case study research in northern Vietnam. This work was largely conducted through household-level surveys and interviews with key informants, allied to analysis of present and potential climate regimes to define exposure. The focus was vulnerability to tropical storm impacts in coastal areas of the Red River Delta and the adjacent region. We begin this account with a summary of the physical dimension of the risk faced by the population of these areas: the exposure to present-day and future cyclone landings. This assessment provides a context for the ensuing analysis of social vulnerability, revealing which people are at risk, defining the key characteristics of the threat and identifying geophysical constraints on response options.

Exposure to cyclone impacts

The landing of a tropical cyclone or typhoon presents one of the major physical threats to the well-being of the inhabitants of the 3000km coastline of Vietnam (Kelly et al, 2001). Despite a well-developed, albeit under-resourced, storm protection system (Benson, 1997), a single storm can have devastating consequences with most damage occurring as a result of the associated surge, heavy rainfall and wind.

Southern Vietnam was, for example, hit by Severe Tropical Storm Linda during the first two days of November 1997. The rapid development of the storm in the East Sea (South China Sea) not far from the Vietnamese coast meant that little warning could be given to the thousands of fishermen who were at sea as the storm approached. The fishing fleets are made up of boats powered by small 15 to 20hp engines. Very few of the fishermen have radios and even less carry life preservers. Many had, it is said, set out to sea to take advantage of the abundant fishing as the storm's leading edge brought nutrients closer to the surface. Following the typhoon's passing, helicopters and navy cutters were used in a massive search and rescue operation with the result that around 5000 fishermen were rescued, after clinging to buoys or boat planks, even empty plastic bottles, some for days. Meanwhile, on land, entire communities were flattened, tens of thousands of people were left homeless, 22,000 hectares (ha) of rice-fields were destroyed, and roads, dykes and bridges were smashed and washed away. The overall cost of the damage approached US$600 million. Known fatalities stand at 778 people as of July 2000, but 2132 individuals remain unaccounted for.

Tropical Storm Linda was unusual, reportedly the most powerful storm to strike the extreme south since 1904. But the risk of storm landing is considerable throughout Vietnam. The nation lies at the end of one of the most vigorous cyclone tracks in the world, with the storm season lasting from May through to December (though storms can strike throughout the year). No sector of the coastline can be considered 'cyclone-free', and this represents a geographical constraint on response options. Figure 9.1 shows the record of storm incidence over the period 1900 to 1995. The year-to-year variability is great, with typhoon approaches ranging from one a year to as many as twelve a year in recent decades. These figures mask the geographical variation that also occurs, with any particular stretch of coastline experiencing a far greater variability from year to year in strike rates. The storm season of 1992 provides a graphic example of the exposure of one of our case study sites in Quang Ninh Province in northern Vietnam, with two storms passing over in just over two weeks (Figure 9.2). Recurrent strikes, of course, seriously limit the capacity to recover from each individual event, with consequences accumulating in a non-linear fashion. We are concerned, then, not only with individual events but also with the cumulative impacts occurring during seasons when cyclone numbers are high.

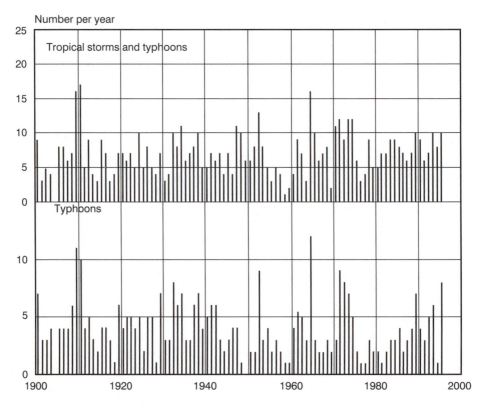

Figure 9.1 *The number of tropical storms (wind speed greater than 16 ms⁻¹) and typhoons (wind speed greater than 33 ms⁻¹) approaching the coastline of Vietnam (specifically, entering the latitude/longitude box 7.5–22.5°N and 105.0–115.0°E)*

Source: The cyclone data depicted in Figures 9.1–9.3 are drawn from the *CD-ROM, Global Tropical/Extratropical Cyclone Climatic Atlas Version 2.0* (US Navy–Department of Commerce, Washington, DC, 1996).

The El Niño-Southern Oscillation (ENSO) phenomenon is a major cause of this year-to-year variability in the number of cyclones approaching the Vietnamese coastline (Li, 1987; Chongyin, 1988; Nishimori and Yoshino, 1990; Lander, 1994; McGregor, 1994; Saunders et al, 2000; Kelly et al, 2001). Numbers are higher during La Niña events, during cold episodes, particularly late in the season over southern Vietnam (Figure 9.3). The Vietnamese Hydrometeorological Service is exploring the development of a predictive capability based on the ENSO phenomenon (Tran Viet Lien, personal communication, 7 November 1999). This is a good example of a win–win strategy, strengthening current capacity to resist short-term climate extremes and the ability to respond to any longer-term trend. There is no firm evidence, though, of any long-term trend at present. The drop in frequency from the mid-1970s to the mid-1980s is considered to be largely a result of a reduction in the number of relatively short-lived storms in the East Sea (South China Sea) and reflects the adverse effect on reporting of

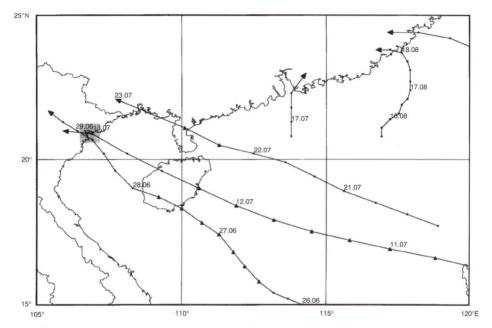

Figure 9.2 *Tracks of tropical storms approaching northern Vietnam during 1992*

Note: Position is indicated every six hours. The triangles indicate points at which the storms were classified as typhoon force. Date is given as day.month (at 00Z). The box shows the location of the case study area in Quang Ninh Province, over which two storms passed two weeks apart.

the end of the Vietnam war and the subsequent embargo. Apparent trends in earlier periods are also quite likely to be the result of variable reporting rates.

What of the future? There is concern that global warming might affect tropical cyclone characteristics, number or intensity, because sea surface temperature plays an important role in determining whether or not tropical disturbances form and intensify. See Bengtsson et al (1996), Sugi et al (1996) and Knutson et al (1998) for recent modelling studies of the possible effect of global warming on tropical storms in the western Pacific sector and Nakagawa et al (1998) and Walsh and Pittock (1998) for current overviews.

How much confidence can we have in these projections? The IPCC First Assessment Report concluded that 'there is some evidence from model simulations and empirical considerations that the frequency per year, intensity and area of occurrence of tropical disturbances may increase ...' but qualified this rather tentative statement with the rider that the evidence is 'not yet compelling' (Houghton et al, 1990). Reviewing current understanding some years later, Lighthill et al (1994) concluded that there is no reason to expect any overall change in global tropical cyclone frequencies though substantial regional changes may occur. They considered that climate models were not yet capable of predicting the nature of any regional shifts. Bengtsson et al (1996) underlined the importance of the atmospheric circulation in modifying any effect of rising ocean

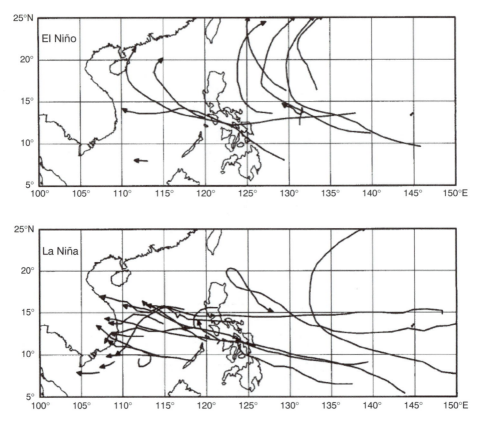

Figure 9.3 *Tropical storm tracks for November during five years during which La Niña occurred (1964, 1970, 1973, 1984, 1988) and five years when El Niño occurred (1969, 1972, 1976, 1982, 1986)*

temperature. These authors found, for example, that tropical cyclone frequencies in the southern hemisphere decreased as a result of global warming as weaker winds, reduced evaporation and changing vertical stability offset any tendency towards increased numbers caused by higher sea surface temperature.

The IPCC Second Assessment Report (Houghton et al, 1996) was even more cautious than the earlier report: 'Knowledge is currently insufficient to say whether there will be any changes in the occurrence or geographical distribution of severe storms, e.g., tropical cyclones.'

The key reasons for uncertainty in the projections remain that:

- global climate models cannot adequately simulate tropical cyclones because, inter alia, their spatial resolution is limited; and
- changes in the atmospheric circulation which may negate or modify the effects of rising temperature cannot be forecast with confidence for similar reasons.

At the local level, it is particularly important to predict shifts in the atmospheric circulation as these determine the regional distribution of storm tracks and, therefore, the risk along a particular stretch of coastline, regardless of any trend in total number over a sector as a whole.

Lack of understanding does not, of course, mean that a threat is not genuine, that an adverse change in cyclone characteristics will not occur. The fact that cyclone numbers vary greatly from year to year indicates that there is no immediate physical restraint on any long-term trend. And lack of knowledge, as interviews with Vietnamese informants suggest, does, in itself, heighten the perceived threat. Of course, the year-to-year variability also suggests that any global warming signal will not rise above the interannual noise for some time and, indeed, may not be significant from the point of view of its overall impact for many years.

The main conclusions of this assessment of the physical risk posed by present-day and future cyclone impacts are:

• The present distribution of risk associated with cyclone landings presents a serious threat to human welfare; hence, reducing vulnerability to cyclone impacts is a major priority for the Vietnamese government (and has been for centuries for the Vietnamese people), providing an indisputable precautionary response to the longer-term, albeit uncertain, threat of long-term trends in storm characteristics.
• Given the marked variability from year-to-year in storm characteristics and the centuries-long development of the storm protection system (Kelly et al, 2001), study of present-day (and historic) responses to the threat of cyclone landings should reveal abundant information of relevance to the related issues of vulnerability, coping and adaptation.
• Given the uncertainty in the storm forecasts for a global warming future, it would be unwise to base assessment of vulnerability and response strategies on these estimates directly.

The social dimension

We now consider the results of the case studies undertaken in coastal areas at risk from cyclone impacts and draw conclusions regarding the pattern of social vulnerability and trends therein. The strategy for the collection of social science data during the fieldwork at the case study locations is outlined in Table 9.2. Assessing vulnerability in the manner we have chosen does, inevitably, involve a considerable degree of data collection, reflecting the complexity of the processes being analysed.

The first major case study site is Xuan Thuy District in Nam Dinh Province (Figure 9.4). This is an agricultural district on the fringe of the Red River Delta in northern Vietnam, protected by artificial dykes and, in part, mangrove forest. In this area, the greatest number of typhoons and associated storm surges occurs, on average, in September and October, the so-called 'months of the shifting season' when the monsoonal current changes direction from southwest to northeast. Storm surges and sea-level rise, as well as high waves and strong winds, may cause extensive damage to economic assets such as agriculture and aquaculture. Observing the proxy indicators for vulnerability in this

Table 9.2 *Summary of social survey and data collection strategy*

Vulnerability issue	Social data collection strategy
Xuan Thuy, Nam Dinh Province	
Social vulnerability indicators	65 household quantitative survey. 30 household qualitative survey. Semi-structured interviews with 20 commune and agricultural cooperative officials. Discussions with other key informants.
Mangrove rehabilitation as a risk minimization strategy	Mangrove utilization survey (3 districts). Local biophysical data on coastal geomorphology collated for quantitative model.
Hoanh Bo and Yen Hung Districts, Quang Ninh Province	
Mangrove property rights and migration issues under the transition.	150 household quantitative survey. 15 semi-structured interviews with province, district and commune officials.
Short-term storm warning and vulnerability	Participatory Rural Appraisal and semi-structured interviews with officials at province and district level and focused interviews with National Hydrometeorological Service. Visualization of storm track for various typhoon seasons.

case study involved fieldwork in 1995 and 1996, investigating indicators in 11 communes (village-level administrative units) through household survey, based on a stratified area sample, and semi-structured interviewing of key informants (Adger, 1998, 1999a, b, 2000). Data for analysis of institutional adaptation and of institutional inertia in the treatment of present climate extremes in Xuan Thuy District were collected through semi-structured interviews of commune-level officials and from households within these communes, as well as discussions at the district level (Adger, 1998, 2000). A study of the costs and benefits of mangrove rehabilitation, a means of reducing vulnerability to storm impacts by increasing natural coastal protection, was also undertaken in Nam Dinh Province, based on data from the three coastal districts in the province: Xuan Thuy, Hai Hau and Nghia Hung.

The two other major case study locations lie just north of the Red River Delta in Quang Ninh Province (Figure 9.4). Ha Nam island is located in Yen Hung District on the southern border of the province. This island, forming by the accretion of sediments over recent millennia, was first settled some 700 years ago by 19 families (whose names are still known). It is now home to over 55,000 people, growing rice and vegetables irrigated by water that comes by canal from a reservoir 15km distant. Much of the island is below sea level – as much as 3m below in some places – and it is only made

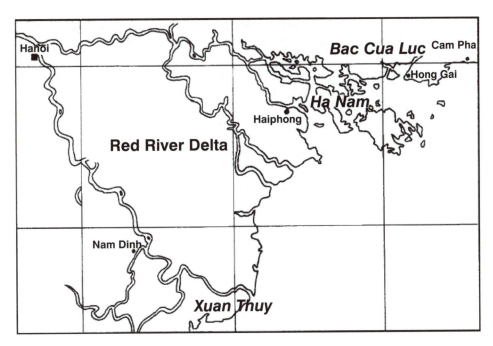

Figure 9.4 *Location of the case study sites in northern Vietnam*

Note: The bulk of Xuan Thuy District has been renamed Giao Thuy District.

habitable by the 40km of dyke, up to 5.5m high, that encircle it. It is known as the 'floating boat'. The dyke has been designed to withstand a Force 9 storm. Whether or not it will provide protection against the more powerful cyclones that cross this area is critically dependent on the direction of storm passage and the timing of the storm surge with respect to the rise and fall of the tides. Local informants consider that a key dyke within the 7km stretch of coast particularly at risk came within an hour of being breached in 1992; the tide turned just in time. Emergency provisions include a rescue boat for each household and progressive evacuation if any dyke is breached.

The central point for study at this site was the effectiveness of the storm protection system (Kelly et al, 2001). The device used was to follow the track of one storm and the response of the warning system all the way from Hanoi to Ha Nam island, providing insights into institutional processes under central planning and communist government structures as they ultimately affect the local capacity to respond, as well as more direct influences on the local response. This research involved focused interviews with staff of the Vietnamese Hydrometeorological Service and relevant national and international agencies in Hanoi, province-, district- and commune-level officials in Quang Ninh, and individual householders on Ha Nam island. The need to improve communications emerged as a key theme in this case study. Lack of contact with fishermen in small boats as a storm approaches heightens the vulnerability of this section of the community; above-ground telephone links are often lost as a storm passes over, seriously affecting command and control; and communication between the various institutional players is critical at and between all administrative levels. Communication constraints increase collective vulnerability.

The third site investigated was further north in Quang Ninh Province, an area known as the Bac Cua Luc wetland lying in Hoanh Bo District. In this province, as elsewhere, there has been a trend towards privatization of assets which were previously either managed by the state through cooperatives or were traditionally under common property rights, particularly in lowland and coastal Vietnam (Adger et al, 1997a, 2001). Mangroves are one of the coastal resources which have been privatized to a large extent. In Hoang Bo District, an area of about 1200 ha of mangrove is being converted for agriculture and aquaculture as part of a two-stage plan involving the loss of about 1900ha of mangrove in total. The research was undertaken though household interviews in the neighbouring communes of Le Loi and Thong Nhat and interviews with informants at the local, regional and national level. The conversion is being undertaken through state subsidy and the land reclaimed will be used to resettle households from densely populated parts of the Red River Delta. One third of the area allocated to aquaculture will be retained, as payment, by the construction agents to whom it is currently leased or sold off to private individuals on a ten-year lease. The aim of this case study was to examine the potential impact of mangrove conversion on the social vulnerability of the local inhabitants. The key issue is the consequences for the livelihoods of the local people when their property rights, to the mangrove in this instance, are overturned by state decree with support by state subsidy. Again, a chain of institutional processes was considered, from the national to the local level.

The context for these studies is the process of *doi moi*, under way since the late 1980s. *Doi moi*, literally 'new change', can be interpreted as 'renovation'. The process, resulting in marked economic growth sustained even through the crisis in Asian economies beginning in 1997, has involved privatization of the state-owned industries and of major product and marketing organizations, price reform, and major changes in property rights in the agricultural sector. At the same time, political control has been retained by the Communist Party. *Doi moi* is having a profound effect on the capacity of the agrarian communities to respond to environmental stress, particularly with regard to the rapidly changing institutional structure of collective action.

In the following sections, we explore particular themes emerging from these studies that throw light on the factors which influence social vulnerability and on the process of adaptation. What emerges is a perspective on vulnerability as a state that continually evolves, not only because the technological and institutional factors that shape vulnerability are themselves in a state of constant flux but also because humanity constantly experiments with new ways of responding to change.

The architecture of entitlements in practice

Analysis of the household-level data from the Xuan Thuy study, reported in Adger (1999a, b), reveals the complex mesh of factors which shape the vulnerability of a community as social and economic trends reinforce, transform or weaken existing patterns of risk:

- Overall, Xuan Thuy is, in rural Vietnamese terms, a relatively wealthy and productive district with a low incidence of absolute poverty and might be considered, from this isolated perspective, less vulnerable in the context of rural Vietnam as a whole. Based on household survey data from the case study area and the World Bank (1995) living standards survey for the other regions, 18 per cent of households in Xuan Thuy District fall below the basic needs poverty line compared to 49 per cent in the Red River Delta as a whole and 57 per cent throughout rural Vietnam (Adger, 1999a).
- Poorer households are dependent on a narrower range of resources and income sources and are thus more vulnerable, in the context of the local population, as they have reduced access to resources for coping with extreme events, such as credit sources, and are more reliant on activities such as salt-making which could potentially experience a significant impact in the face of coastal flooding (and other climate shifts such as an increase in cloudiness). The survey results show not only that poorer households tend to have fewer sources of income (lacking, in particular, income from aquaculture, wage labour and remittances) and less land for rice production, but that income from salt-making is *negatively* correlated with overall household income (Adger, 1999a).
- The distribution of resources within the district is relatively even compared to many agrarian societies, but is less even than in other parts of rural Vietnam, and underlying inequality (both between individual households and between the coastal and inland communes) is increasing due to the emergence of capital-intensive commercial activities, principally aquaculture, in the period since market liberalization. The value of the aquaculture industry rose from zero in 1988 to about three times that of agricultural production by 1993 (Adger, 1999b).

The increasing dependence on aquaculture is having complex effects on levels of vulnerability. On the one hand, it should increase the overall wealth of the district with trickle-down effects benefiting the population as a whole but, on the other hand, it is heightening levels of inequality, as noted, and tying up capital in an inherently risky venture as shrimp farms are seriously exposed to storm impacts.

The parallel analysis of institutional issues reveals how access to decision-making is a critical factor in this instance (Adger, 1998, 2000). The government institutions of the district have taken advantage of increased autonomy as a result of *doi moi*, but have become less directly influential in resource use since agricultural land has been allocated to private individuals and private enterprise encouraged. There has been a reduction in the resources available for sea dyke maintenance as monetarization of the previous labour-based system has permitted the diversion of finances away from dyke maintenance and into, for example, road building in the coastal communes, i.e., the development of infrastructure to support economic growth. The inland communes are not aware of this shift in investment in collective security; they are persuaded by the coastal communes that the maintenance programme is being maintained at former levels and gives sufficient protection. In this way, formal institutions are seeking to maintain their resources, powers, and their authority in a time of rapid change at the expense of collective security. The research also shows that informal institutions have offset some of the negative consequences of market liberalization and the reduction of the role of government by evolving collective security from below, for example, through risk spreading in credit unions, particularly in fishing communities.

The Xuan Thuy study demonstrates the difficulties in generalizing about levels of vulnerability even in a relatively small community. We do not consider it wise to attempt to determine the overall impact on levels of vulnerability of the socio-political trends currently under way. It is, however, possible to identify causal linkages and to identify measures which might compensate for adverse effects and reinforce beneficial consequences. The dynamic nature of vulnerability in this community underlines the difficulties in projecting vulnerability estimates, and the underlying social, economic and political processes, decades into the future.

Spontaneous adaptation: Win–win in action

The mangrove ecosystem plays an important role in the lives of the inhabitants of the coastal zone, providing a range of goods and services, including storm protection, staple food plants, fertile grazing land, protected nurseries for coastal and offshore fisheries, pollution control, breeding grounds for numerous birds, and fuel from peat among other marketable products. The functions and services provided by mangroves do have positive economic value, but this is often ignored and mangrove forests are frequently damaged or destroyed (Barbier, 1993; Ewel et al, 1998; Naylor and Drew, 1998). The rehabilitation of mangrove areas can provide a dual benefit in improving the livelihood of local users as well as enhancing sea defences (Field, 1998), providing a precautionary, win–win approach to climate impact mitigation.

In order to quantify the economic benefits of mangrove rehabilitation, we assessed the particular costs and benefits of rehabilitation in three coastal districts of Nam Dinh Province (Adger et al, 1997b; Tri et al, 1998). The analysis contrasted the costs of mangrove rehabilitation, that is, purchase of seeds, planting and maintenance, with the resulting benefits in terms of improved local livelihoods (increased income from wood production, fishing and bee-keeping) and the reduction in dyke maintenance. (Benefits in terms of any wider reduction in storm impacts on agriculture, infrastructure and so on were not considered.) Rehabilitation costs and livelihood benefits were derived from estimates of labour requirements, observations in local markets and other survey data. The savings in terms of dyke maintenance costs were calculated using an empirical model.

The planting of mangroves seaward of a sea dyke system reduces the cost of maintaining these defences. Mangrove stands provide protection from wave action by creating a physical barrier, stabilizing the sea floor and affecting the angle of slope of the sea bottom. Studies in southern China have resulted in an empirical relationship through which the benefit, in terms of avoided cost, can be expressed as a function of the width of the mangrove stand (as a proportion of the average wavelength of the ocean waves that the stand is exposed to) and various parameters related to the age of stand (mangrove size and density) expressed as a buffer factor; the relationship has been tested and modified for mangrove stands in Vietnam (Vinh, 1995) and was used in this study (see Tri et al, 1998, for further details). Dyke maintenance takes place in coastal Vietnam through the obligatory labour of district inhabitants each year. These commitments can prove a serious imposition on labour-scarce households and the inter-district allocation of labour contracts has proved a source of conflict (Adger, 1996). The system is now evolving under the influence of *doi moi*; individuals may, for example, be permitted to buy themselves out of the labour obligation.

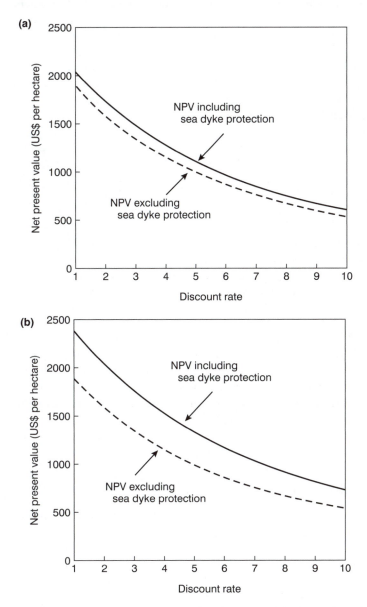

Figure 9.5 *Net present value of mangrove rehabilitation, including value of sea dyke protection, for two cases: a) stand width = 100m, incident wavelength = 75m; b) stand width = 33.3m, incident wavelength = 25m*

Source: Tri et al, 1998

The economic analysis of costs and benefits shows that rehabilitation is desirable from an economic perspective based *solely* on the direct benefits of use by local communities, that is, without consideration of benefits related to dyke maintenance (Figure 9.5). The rehabilitation schemes obviously have even higher benefit–cost ratios when the indirect benefits of the avoided maintenance cost of the sea dyke system are taken into account. The results show a benefit to cost ratio in the range of between four and five to one, relatively insensitive to discount rate as most of the costs, as well as the benefits, occur within a relatively short timeframe. Though this analysis is subject to various limitations (see Tri et al, 1998, for further discussion), the results strongly suggest that mangrove rehabilitation should be an important component of a sustainable coastal management strategy.

Through examination of the reverse process of mangrove loss, the case study of the Bac Cua Luc wetland in Quang Ninh Province demonstrates which element of the local population is most affected by mangrove conversion and, as a corollary, would benefit most from mangrove rehabilitation. Traditionally, mangrove areas were commonly owned and managed, and because their value was collectively appreciated, they were cared for, as has been shown, for example, in Indonesia and throughout Southeast Asia (Adger and Luttrell, 1998). Analysis of household-level data from the communes neighbouring the converted and remaining areas of wetland shows that the poorer households rely on the mangrove more for their livelihood than the wealthy, who are more interested in the private commercial activity utilizing of the coastal resources. The ability of the community to maintain sustainable common property management of the remaining mangrove and fishing areas is undermined by changes in the property rights and changes in inequality brought about by externally driven enclosure and conversion. At the household level, the poor, dependent, families suffer disproportionately with the loss of the habitat functions. But at the community level, there is also a loss of resilience as families compete for the remaining resources, leading to non-cooperation in use of the ecosystem. As some families gain in the new commercialism, others disproportionately lose since they have no fall-back when the formerly commonly managed resource is denied them. By this means, in the absence of compensatory action, vulnerability is exaggerated, resilience is undermined and adaptive options are lost (Adger et al, 1997a, 2001).

Opportunities for intervention

The process of *doi moi* provides a valuable chance to observe how rapid socio-political change might affect levels of vulnerability and adaptive possibilities. This understanding can also lead to recommendations regarding macro-level policies which might reduce vulnerability and facilitate adaptation.

It is clear that the economic changes accompanying *doi moi* have increased the opportunities for income generation in the coastal communities that we have studied while increasing differentiation within these communities (see also Hirsch and Thinh, 1996, for example). As far as the richer section of the community is concerned, economic reform is perceived as having a positive effect in terms of reducing the risk associated with present-day hazards. Indeed, it may be considered to have reduced the vulnerability of the community as a whole. As we have shown, though, assessing overall effects on a community is not a simple matter. Even a single socio-political shift can generate a complex set of consequences across a population. Moreover, there may be substantial divergence in consequences within a community. So, in the coastal communities we have studied, economic growth has been accompanied by substantial investment in an inherently risky venture, aquaculture, which, the risk of storm impacts apart, has been shown to be unsustainable in many parts of world (Folke and Kautsky, 1992). And levels of inequality within these communities have clearly been heightened. In related developments, the rights to common resources such as the mangrove forest have been lost and institutional changes have reduced the efficacy of various forms of collective action and investment. These trends have their major impact on the poorer members of the community, who rely on the mangrove ecosystem to supplement their livelihood and on collective action to provide protection against stress and support in times of hardship.

Other changes affect the community as a whole. For example, evidence from the Ha Nam island case study suggests that the local-level storm warning system is under greater pressure, embedded as it is in the agricultural cooperative and hierarchical government structures that are presently being 'rolled back' (Kelly et al, 2001). This can be seen in the charging for certain meteorological forecasts previously provided free and in the possibility of opting out of the requirement to provide labour for dyke maintenance, on payment of a tax, that has left some districts unable to cover the costs of hiring replacement labour. There is concern that the development of regional centres within the Vietnamese Hydrometeorological Service structure, aimed at improving efficiency, may reduce the role of the local meteorologists on whose expertise there is heavy dependence at the district and provincial level. Study of developments at the national level with regard to the storm warning system revealed other institutional processes affecting the efficiency of the system and hence vulnerability: for example, inter-agency conflict, particularly between national and international institutions, and cultural difficulties in the adoption of foreign technology and methods as well as a perceived lack of respect for established practice on the part of foreign consultants (Kelly et al, 2001). In compensation, of course, greater wealth in the local community should eventually support more effective coastal protection and the technological infrastructure of the storm warning system has improved notably in recent years.

Other trends have reduced levels of vulnerability by increasing access to resources. Diversification of income sources is an effective means of reducing vulnerability by spreading risk and *doi moi* has promoted income diversification in a number of ways. First, it has created the opportunity for private investment as well as new employment options. Second, labour mobility is now permitted, opening up possibilities for migration on a seasonal or permanent basis. Remittances from relatives working away from home provide an important means, the Xuan Thuy case study suggests, of improving access to resources. The accumulation of capital in private hands has resulted in the return of private credit as a coping strategy and informal community-based institutions, street committees and so on, have also returned replacing some of the risk-pooling functionality of more formal structures which are losing their effectiveness and influence.

What lessons can be learned from this research regarding policies that might reduce vulnerability and facilitate adaptation? Some conclusions are specific to the circumstances of these particular case studies. There are, however, a number of strands that are of wider applicability concerning the promotion of measures that might improve the situation of the poorer members of these and other communities, the people we fear are increasingly at risk as a result of recent socio-political trends:

- poverty reduction clearly must be a priority, though that alone may not be sufficient to ensure the wider access to resources necessary to reduce vulnerability;
- risk-spreading through income diversification can be promoted in a number of ways and, again, will assist mostly the poorer members of the community;
- the loss of common property management rights represents a serious erosion of the ability to resist stress and, where it cannot be avoided, compensatory measures should be implemented; and
- the reduced efficiency, or loss, of forms of collective action or investment affects the community as a whole and this process warrants careful monitoring with efforts to promote the development or resuscitation of other, perhaps traditional, forms of community security.

At a deeper level, the underlying causes of vulnerability must be tackled if we are to develop a sustainable response to extreme events and climate change. It will be necessary, for example, to address directly the maldistribution of resources. This is a widespread issue. Wisner (1978) argues that the insecure land tenure regime and the resulting perceived insecurity has been the major cause of large-scale flood impacts and mortality on the low-lying delta areas of the Ganges-Brahmaputra-Meghna (see also Brammer, 1993; Blaikie et al, 1994). Given the political nature of resource distribution and the role of institutions within such processes, institutions which themselves must evolve to support more effectively the response to stress, is it realistic to propose wealth redistribution and land reform, for example, as policy recommendations? On the one hand, social hierarchies and resource and entitlement inequalities are rarely overturned in the course of adaptation, and external changes such as climatic extremes and other natural hazards tend to reinforce those inequalities (Cannon, 1994). On the other hand, radical policy alternatives do sometimes coincide with the requirements of elites (Bardhan, 1996). For example, the political necessity to retain rural support for the present government in Vietnam has ensured a relatively equitable privatization of agricultural land, particularly in the intensive agricultural lowlands, compared to many other former centrally planned economies and other agricultural areas at risk from climatic hazards. Under particular circumstances, land reform and equitable redistribution can offer a viable policy option for tackling the underlying causes of social vulnerability – but they represent a substantial challenge, nevertheless.

Conclusions

We have defined social vulnerability in terms of the capacity of individuals and social groupings to respond to – that is, to cope with, recover from or adapt to – any external stress placed on their livelihoods and well-being, focusing on socio-economic and institutional constraints that limit the ability to respond effectively. Vulnerability is intrinsically linked to the process of adaptation through this definition; adaptation is facilitated by reducing vulnerability. We have demonstrated that this conceptualization of vulnerability can be operationalized through analysis of the architecture of entitlements, that is, access to resources, providing an effective framework for analysis and leading to policy-relevant conclusions and recommendations. Case studies in northern Vietnam have revealed a wide range of factors that influence levels of vulnerability, ranging from poverty and inequality to communication difficulties and cultural barriers. They have also revealed the complexity of the processes that shape vulnerability, suggesting that we are far from the level of understanding that would permit a detailed model of how vulnerability is constructed to be advanced.

The value of diverse approaches to a threat as complex as global warming means that it would be foolish to argue that any one framework for analysing vulnerability should become the dominant discourse. The approach that we have adopted may not be the most appropriate, for example, if a composite index of vulnerability is required for comparative purposes. Nevertheless, we do see distinct advantages to the conceptualization of vulnerability developed in this chapter from a policy point of view, both in terms of the robustness of the conclusions and the manner in which the framework reconciles the demands of immediate aspirations and long-term environmental security, providing recommendations for action of immediate relevance. The fact that this approach deals with processes at the level of the household and community, while mitigating against aggregation to larger scales (Adger and Kelly, 1999), highlights the great differences in levels of vulnerability that can occur within a nation. We strongly endorse Kates' conclusion (Chapter 14, this volume) that 'if the global poor are to adapt to global change, it will be critical to focus on poor people, and not on poor countries as does the prevailing North-South dialog. The interests of the poor are not always the same as the interests of poor countries, since in the interest of "development", the poor may grow poorer' (Kates, 2000).

The case studies illustrate the many and varied opportunities for intervention. The most effective and sustainable form of intervention, we suggest, would be to detect, then cautiously reinforce, modify or offset, trends in the factors that limit or enhance vulnerability as they emerge. Given that we are working within a framework based on analysis of entitlements, the net effect of this kind of intervention should be to empower directly those likely to be affected by climate stress, a very desirable result. We have highlighted four measures, of broad relevance, that could be taken now to improve the situation of the most vulnerable: poverty reduction; risk-spreading through income diversification; the preservation of common property management rights; and the promotion of collective security. Finally, we raise the challenge of addressing the fundamental causes of the maldistribution of resources.

Acknowledgements

Funding by the UK Economic and Social Research Council, Global Environmental Change Programme, under the project *Socio-Economic and Physical Approaches to Vulnerability to Climate*

Change in Vietnam (Award No. L320253240) is gratefully acknowledged. We thank our colleagues at the University of East Anglia for their comments on this work and acknowledge the invaluable contribution of our collaborators at the Center for Environment Research Education and Development and the National University of Vietnam in Hanoi, particularly Drs Nguyen Huu Ninh, Nguyen Hoang Tri, Hoang Minh Hien and Tran Viet Lien and Professor Duong Duc Tien, and our Vietnamese interpreters and research assistants.

Note

1   The phrase 'external stress' is used to refer to stress that it is not within the power of the individual or social grouping to avert completely at source (by, for example, substantially reducing global greenhouse gas emissions in the case of climate change). The word 'stress', with its connotation of adverse impacts, is used deliberately. Some consequences of climate change may well prove beneficial in the long run but, without a considerable degree of prescience so that adaptive strategies can be deployed in anticipation of trends, the initial impact of any change in the environment will inevitably be stressful as existing practices are rendered less effective.

References

Adger, W. N.: 1996, *Approaches to Vulnerability to Climate Change*, CSERGE Working Paper GEC 96-05, Centre for Social and Economic Research on the Global Environment, University of East Anglia, Norwich, and University College London.

Adger, W. N.: 1998, *Observing Institutional Adaptation to Global Environmental Change: Theory and Case Study from Vietnam*, Working Paper GEC 98-21, Centre for Social and Economic Research on the Global Environment, University of East Anglia, Norwich, and University College London.

Adger, W. N.: 1999a, 'Social Vulnerability to Climate Change and Extremes in Coastal Vietnam', *World Develop.* **27**, 249–269.

Adger, W. N.: 1999b, 'Exploring Income Inequality in Rural, Coastal Vietnam', *J. Develop. Studies* **35**, 96–119.

Adger, W. N.: 2000, 'Institutional Adaptation to Environmental Risk under the Transition in Vietnam', *Ann. Assoc. Amer. Geogr.* **90**, 738–758.

Adger, W. N. and Kelly, P. M.: 1999, 'Social Vulnerability to Climate Change and the Architecture of Entitlements', *Mitigation Adaptation Strategies Global Change* **4**, 253–256.

Adger, W. N. and Luttrell, C.: 1998, 'Property Rights and the Utilisation of Wetlands', in Soderqvist, T. (ed.), *Wetlands: Landscape and Institutional Perspectives*, Beijer International Institute of Ecological Economics, Stockholm, pp. 167–186.

Adger, W. N., Kelly, P. M., Ninh, N. H., and Thanh, N. C.: 2001, 'Property Rights, Institutions and Coastal Management – Coastal Resources under Doi Moi', in Adger, W. N., Kelly, P. M., and Ninh, N. H. (eds.), *Living with Environmental Change: Social Vulnerability, Adaptation and Resilience in Vietnam*, Routledge, London.

Adger, W. N., Kelly, P. M., Ninh, N. H., and Thanh, N. C.: 1997a, *Property Rights and the Social Incidence of Mangrove Conversion in Vietnam*, Working Paper GEC 97-21, Centre for Social and Economic Research on the Global Environment, University of East Anglia, Norwich, and University College London.

Adger, W. N., Kelly, P. M., and Tri, N. H.: 1997b, 'Valuing the Products and Services of Mangrove Restoration', *Commonwealth Forestry Rev.* **76**, 198–202.

Barbier, E.: 1993, 'Sustainable Use of Wetlands Valuing Tropical Wetland Benefits: Economic Methodologies and Applications', *Geog. J.* **159**, 22–32.

Bardhan, P.: 1996, 'Efficiency, Equity and Poverty Alleviation: Policy Issues in Less Developed Countries', *Econ. J.* **106**, 1344–1356.

Bengtsson, L., Botzet, M., and Esch, M.: 1996, 'Will Greenhouse Gas-Induced Warming over the Next 50 Years Lead to Higher Frequencies and Greater Intensity of Hurricanes', *Tellus* **48A**, 57–73.

Benson, C.: 1997, *The Economic Impact of Natural Disasters in Vietnam*, Working Paper 98, Overseas Development Institute, London.

Blaikie, P., Cannon, T., Davis, I., and Wisner, B.: 1994, *At Risk: Natural Hazards, Peoples Vulnerability and Disasters*, Routledge, London.

Bohle, H. G., Downing, T. E., and Watts, M. J.: 1994, 'Climate Change and Social Vulnerability: Toward a Sociology and Geography of Food Insecurity', *Global Environ. Change* **4**, 37–48.

Brammer, H.: 1993, 'Geographical Complexities of Detailed Impacts Assessment for the Ganges-Brahmaputra-Meghna Delta of Bangladesh', in Warrick, R. A., Barrow, E. M., and Wigley, T. M. L. (eds.), *Climate and Sea Level Change: Observations, Projections and Implications*, Cambridge University Press, Cambridge, pp. 246–262.

Burton, I.: 1997, 'Vulnerability and Adaptive Response in the Context of Climate and Climate Change', *Clim. Change* **36**, 185–196.

Cannon, T.: 1994, 'Vulnerability Analysis and the Explanation of Natural Disasters, in Varley, A. (ed.), *Disasters Development and Environment*, John Wiley, Chichester, pp. 13–30.

Chongyin, L.: 1988, 'Actions of Typhoons over the Western Pacific (Including the South China Sea) and El Niño', *Adv. Atmos. Sci.* **5**, 107–115.

Cutter, S. L.: 1996, 'Vulnerability to Environmental Hazards', *Prog. Human Geog.* **20**, 529–539.

Downing, T. E.: 1991, 'Vulnerability to Hunger in Africa: A Climate Change Perspective', *Global Environ. Change* **1**, 365–380.

Ewel, K. C., Twilley, R. R., and Ong, J. E.: 1998, 'Different Kinds of Mangrove Forests Provide Different Goods and Services', *Global Ecol. and Biogeog. Lett.* **7**, 83–94.

Field, C. D.: 1998, 'Rehabilitation of Mangrove Ecosystems: An Overview', *Marine Pollution Bull.* **37**, 383–392.

Folke, C. and Kautsky, N.: 1992, 'Aquaculture with its Environment: Prospects for Sustainability', *Ocean Coastal Manage.* **17**, 5–24.

Glantz, M. H.: 1991, 'The Use of Analogies in Forecasting Societal Responses to Global Warming', *Environment* **33**, 10–15, 27–33.

Hewitt, K.: 1997, *Regions of Risk: A Geographical Introduction to Disasters*, Longman, Harlow.

Hirsch, P. and Thinh, N. V.: 1996, 'Implications of Economic Reform in Vietnam: Agrarian and Environmental Change in Hien Luong', *Aust. Geog.* **27**, 165–183.

Houghton, J. T., Jenkins, G. J., and Ephraums, J. J. (eds.): 1990, *Climate Change. The IPCC Scientific Assessment*, Cambridge University Press, Cambridge.

Houghton, J. T., Meiro Filho, L. G., Callander, B. A., Harris, N., Kattenberg, A., and Maskell, K. (eds.): 1996, *Climate Change 1995. The Science of Climate Change*, Cambridge University Press, Cambridge.

Kelly, P. M.: 2000, 'Towards a Sustainable Response to Climate Change', in Huxham, M. and Sumner, D. (eds.), *Science and Environmental Decision-Making*, Pearson Education, Harlow, pp. 118–141.

Kelly, P. M., Granich, S. L. V., and Secrett, C. M.: 1994, 'Global Warming: Responding to an Uncertain Future', *Asia Pacific J. Environ. Develop.* **1**, 28–45.

Kelly, P. M., Hoang Minh Hien, and Tran Viet Lien: 2001, 'Responding to El Niño and La Niña – Averting Tropical Cyclone Impacts', in Adger, W. N., Kelly, P. M., and Nguyen Huu Ninh (eds.), *Living with Environmental Change: Social Vulnerability, Adaptation and Resilience in Vietnam* , Routledge, London, pp. 154–181.

Klein, R. J. T. and Nicholls, R. J.: 1999, 'Assessment of Coastal Vulnerability to Climate Change', *Ambio* **28**, 182–187.

Knutson, T. R., Tuleya, R. E., and Kurihara, Y.: 1998, 'Simulated Increase of Hurricane Intensities in a CO_2-Warmed Climate', *Science* **279**, 1018–1020.

Lander, M.: 1994, 'An Exploratory Analysis of the Relationship between Tropical Storm Formation in the Western North Pacific and ENSO', *Mon. Wea. Rev.* **122**, 636–651.

Li, C.: 1987, 'A Study of the Influence of El Niño upon Typhoon Action over the Western Pacific', *Acta Meteorologica Sinica* **45**, 229–236.

Lighthill, J., Holland, G. J., Gray, W. M., Landsea, C., Craig, G., Evans, J., Kuhihara, Y., and Guard, C. P.: 1994, 'Global Climate Change and Tropical Cyclones', *Bull. Amer. Meteorol. Soc.* **75**, 2147–2157.

McGregor, G. R.: 1994, 'The Tropical Cyclone Hazard over the South China Sea 1970–1989', *Appl. Geog.* **15**, 35–52.

Nakagawa, S., Sugi, M., Motoi, T., and Yukimoto, S.: 1998, 'Climate Change Projections', in Nish-ioka, S. and Harasawa, H. (eds.), *Global Warming: The Potential Impact on Japan*, Springer, Tokyo, pp. 1–33.

Naylor, R. and Drew, M.: 1998, 'Valuing Mangrove Resources in Kosrae, Micronesia', *Environ. Develop. Econ.* **3**, 471–490.

Nishimori, M. and Yoshino, M.: 1990, 'The Relationship between ENSO Events and the Generation, Development and Movement of Typhoons', *Geog. Rev. Japan* **63A-8**, 530–540 (in Japanese).

O'Riordan, T. and Jordan, A.: 1999, 'Institutions, Climate Change and Cultural Theory: Towards a Common Framework', *Global Environ. Change* **9**, 81–94.

Palutikof, J. P., Subak, S., and Agnew, M. D. (eds.): 1997, *Economic Impacts of the Hot Summer and Unusually Warm Year of 1995*, University of East Anglia, Norwich.

Reardon, T. and Taylor, J. E.: 1996, 'Agroclimatic Shocks, Income Inequality and Poverty: Evidence from Burkina Faso', *World Develop.* **24**, 901–914.

Ribot, J. C., Magalhães, A. R., and Panagides, S. S. (eds.): 1996, *Climate Variability, Climate Change and Social Vulnerability in the Semi-Arid Tropics*, Cambridge University Press, Cambridge.

Sanderson, S.: 1994, 'Political-Economic Institutions', in Meyer, W. B. and Turner, B. L. (eds.), *Changes in Land Use and Land Cover: A Global Perspective*, Cambridge University Press, Cambridge, pp. 329–355.

Saunders, M. A., Chandler, R. E., Merchent, C. J., and Roberts, F. P.: 2000, 'Atlantic Hurricanes and NW Pacific Typhoons: ENSO Spatial Impacts on Occurrence and Landfall', *Geophys. Res. Lett.* **27**, 1147–1150.

Schneider, S. H.: 1997, 'Integrated Assessment Modeling of Global Climate Change: Transparent Rational Tool for Policy Making or Opaque Screen Hiding Value-Laden Assumptions', *Environ. Model. Assess.* **2**, 229–249.

Scott, J. C.: 1976, *The Moral Economy of the Peasant: Rebellion and Subsistence in Southeast Asia*, Yale University Press, New Haven.

Sen, A. K.: 1981, *Poverty and Famines: An Essay on Entitlement and Deprivation*, Clarendon, Oxford.

Sen, A. K.: 1990, 'Food, Economics and Entitlements', in Drèze, J. and Sen, A. K. (eds.), *The Political Economy of Hunger*, Volume 1, Clarendon, Oxford, pp. 34–50.

Smit, B., McNabb, D., and Smithers, J.: 1996, 'Agricultural Adaptation to Climatic Variations', *Clim. Change* **33**, 7–29.

Smith, J. B., Bhatti, N., and Menzhulin, G. V. (eds.): 1996, *Adapting to Climate Change: An International Perspective*, Springer, New York.

Sugi, M., Noda, A., and Sato, N.: 1996, 'Will the Number of Tropical Cyclones be Reduced by Global Warming? – Implication from a Numerical Modelling Experiment with the JMA Global Model', *Proceedings of the 1996 Spring Meeting of the Japanese Meteorological Society*, p. 37 (in Japanese).

Tol, R. S. J., Fankhauser, S., and Smith, J. B.: 1998, 'The Scope for Adaptation to Climate Change: What Can We Learn from the Impacts Literature', *Global Environ. Change* **8**, 109–123.

Tri, N. H., Adger, W. N., and Kelly, P. M.: 1998, 'Natural Resource Management in Mitigating Climate Impacts: Mangrove Restoration in Vietnam', *Global Environ. Change* **8**, 49–61.

Vinh, T. T.: 1995, *Tree Planting Measures to Protect Sea Dyke Systems in the Central Provinces of Vietnam*, Paper presented at the Workshop on Mangrove Plantation for Sea Dyke Protection, Hatinh, Vietnam, 24–25 December 1995.

Walsh, K. and Pittock, A. B.: 1998, 'Potential Changes in Tropical Storms, Hurricanes, and Extreme Rainfall Events as a Result of Climate Change', *Clim. Change* **39**, 199–213.

Watson, R. T., Zinyowera, M. C., and Moss, R. H. (eds.): 1996, 'Climate Change 1995', in *Impacts, Adaptations and Mitigation of Climate Change: Scientific-Technical Analyses*, Cambridge University Press, Cambridge.

Watts, M. J. and Bohle, H. G.: 1993, 'The Space of Vulnerability: The Causal Structure of Hunger and Famine', *Prog. Human Geog.* **17**, 43–67.

Wisner, B. G.: 1978, 'An Appeal for a Significantly Comparative Method in Disaster Research', *Disasters* **2**, 80–82.

World Bank: 1995, *Vietnam Poverty Assessment and Strategy*, Operations Division, World Bank East Asia and Pacific Region, Hanoi.

A Typology of Resilience: Rethinking Institutions for Sustainable Development

John Handmer and Stephen Dovers

The most basic aim of any human society is to ensure the provision of the health and well-being of its members over time. However needs are defined, a stable flow of the goods, services and experiences that fulfil them is sought. But in hazardous environments characterized by change and unpredictability, this is a difficult task. Mostly, we seek simply to maintain the present overall political and economic structure, as if this pattern of production and consumption and related institutional arrangements was a desirable end in itself. It is not; it is merely the means for achieving the basic aim. Stability is sought, but change constantly redraws the playing field and demands redefinition of the rules. As well as stability, we need a system that can cope well with change in a proactive as well as reactive sense. These are the concepts central to this chapter, and they are important at both local and global spatial scales, and at the nearest and furthest ends of temporal scales.

First, we address the concept of sustainability and identify the critical notion of *resilience*. This notion is explored from the disciplinary perspectives of ecology and *risk*. Drawing on the results of our exploration and other material, we construct a three-tiered typology of resilience to provide a theoretical basis for thinking about the full range of potential responses to the challenge of sustainability.

Sustainability

Under the general rubric of *sustainability* (variously termed sustainable development or ecologically sustainable development), societies are now struggling with the reconciliation of the demands of human systems and the health and continuation of the biosphere that supports them. Following a long evolution (see Cleveland, 1987; Martinez-Alier, 1987; Dovers, 1990), this notion has emerged as an umbrella concept that subsumes many concerns of environment and development. The realization of interdependency has demanded such an integrative framework. It is not only an intellectual reconciliation but a challenge in the face of what are now widely accepted as potentially disastrous changes in the global system resulting from human activities (see, e.g., NCED, 1987; Davis and Bernstam, 1991; Meadows et al, 1992; Myers, 1993; Population Summit, 1993). The approach to the natural (non-human) environment has been to seek dominance, or control, mostly through technical means such as engineering approaches. But the environmental problems are now acknowledged to threaten the global environment and are less amenable to technological solutions. In fact, it is our addiction to technology that is largely responsible for much of the current crisis – the principle of techno-addiction (Boyden, 1987). There appears to be no alternative to major social, political and economic change: we must change the way we interact with the natural systems that support us.

Sustainability is commonly termed *sustainable development* and is defined by most, following the World Commission on Environment and Development (WCED, 1987), which popularized the notion, as an expression of the moral principle of *inter*generational equity: ensuring that the natural environment is maintained in a form that can continue to meet future human needs. Matched to the twin challenge of ensuring equity in the present (*intra*generational equity), the enormity of the task becomes apparent, both in a physical and intellectual sense. In sum, the task is to satisfy present and future human needs within the limits of the biosphere and in a manner that can cope with the certainty of change – though details of the change are unknowable. Uncertainty pervades the sustainability debate (Funtowicz and Ravetz, 1991; Common and Perrings, 1992; Dovers and Handmer, 1992; Faber et al, 1992): the issues of biodiversity and climatic change provide good examples. Here, the general scientific consensus as to the broad parameters at the global level are uncertain enough, but at the local-regional scale, it appears that we do not in many cases have a firm grasp on even the direction of change, let alone its magnitude. Yet this is the level where planning and land-use decisions are made. These biophysical uncertainties are compounded by uncertainties in the political system, by institutional and technological change, by evolving societal values, by economic fluctuations, and so on.

The key policy response to uncertainty and the threat of environmental change at present is the 'precautionary principle' (Cameron and Abouchar, 1991; O'Riordan, 1992; Wynne, 1992). This principle is now part of many major sustainability policies at the international and national levels and is appearing in statutory law. The 1992 Rio Declaration (United Nations, 1992) defines the principle as follows (Principle 15): 'Where there are threats of serious or irreversible damage, lack of full scientific certainty shall not be used as a reason for postponing cost-effective measures to prevent environmental degradation' (p10). Other official definitions go further, stressing 'preventive' and 'anticipatory' approaches. Some of the associated literature claims that the principle shifts the burden of proof away from the environment and its defenders to the proponents of development. Whereas the precautionary principle is an official recognition of pervasive uncertainty, it is vague, inoperative by itself, and open to wide interpretation. In addition, the tools available to support operationalization of the principle are of limited value in that, among other problems, they are applicable only with respect to spatially and temporally discrete problems with measurable factors and processes (Dovers and Handmer, 1995). Items in this tool kit include environmental risk assessment, safe minimum standards, and quantitative risk assessment. Whereas the principle is a useful reminder for decision-makers, it makes little operational advance into the realm of sustainability where 'facts are uncertain, values in dispute, stakes high and decisions urgent' (Funtowicz and Ravetz, 1991, p138).

Recognizing these issues, Dovers and Handmer (1992) define sustainability and sustainable development in terms of *systems* and *responses to change,* thus approaching the terms differently from the standard moral principle approach. They draw a distinction between the two terms that are often confused in the debate:

> *Sustainability* is the ability of a human, natural or mixed system to withstand or adapt to endogenous or exogenous change indefinitely. *Sustainable development* is therefore a pathway of deliberate change and improvement which maintains or enhances this attribute of the system, while answering the needs of the present population. (p275)

Whatever the terminology, the sustainability agenda demands the integration of a wide suite of issues concerning virtually all aspects of both natural and human systems: population and human development, pollution, resource use, biodiversit and security.

In searching for clues to ways in which to meet the challenge, it would make sense to look for areas of human experience where change and the interaction of human and natural systems have been addressed before. We examine two such areas. Ecology, broadly defined, is one. It is a discipline that has done much of the informing of the sustainability debate. The other area of research encompasses risk, hazards and disasters. Here, attention has been paid to responses to both the threat and occurrence of rapid-onset change in human and natural environments. It is proposed as axiomatic that managing ecological change (pursuing sustainability) and coping with hazards and disasters should share some common problems and features. Fundamental to both is the need to cope with pervasive risk and uncertainty. We require the creation of decision-making and management approaches that possess an ability to operate in the face of this uncertainty: an ability that can be termed the attribute of resilience.

Resilience is an important concept in both ecology and risk research. Central to both is the attention paid to systems approaches to the problems. Defining a system as a complex set of elements existing in interrelationship and interdependency, it is apparent that attempting to manage both natural environments and human societies requires the recognition of such dynamic interdependency. This is even more the case when the concern is with the *interactions between* human and natural systems, which is where environmental issues arise (Dovers and Handmer, 1992). Narrow single-issue or sectoral approaches that are not cognizant of this underlie much of the global ecological crisis. Systems and component subsystems can describe many things, and thus a systems approach can be applied at many levels – cell, organ, organism, community, institution, firm, society, nation, global biophysical processes, and so on (Lazslo, 1972, pp14–15). But recognition that any defined system will also be a subsystem is fundamental: that it is embedded in and related to a broader whole, and that a systems approach should not lapse into renewed reductionism (von Bertalanffy, 1968) – although clearly both a broad overview and detail are required. Such approaches are most often thought of as applying to the so-called 'hard' systems – biophysical, geochemical and ecological – in a quantitative fashion. They can also be applied to 'soft' systems: human systems with their innate malleability and vagueness (see Checkland and Scholes, 1990).

Against this general background, our aim is to identify and explore a serious impediment to real progress toward a sustainable society. This relates to the different kinds and levels of resilience displayed by human institutional arrangements in facing uncertainty and change. In an operational sense, this is the coal-face of sustainability: the ability of institutional arrangements to make judgements about the sort of society needed for human and ecological survival, and for the policy-formulation, decision-making and management arrangements to comprehend and implement this vision in an operating environment characterized by ignorance and uncertainty.

The Notion of Resilience

The *Oxford English Dictionary* defines resilience as '1. The (or an) act of rebounding or springing back; ... 2. Elasticity.' The term can be conceptualized in many ways. Here, it is about how a system copes with major perturbations to its operating environment. System has been defined above.

Any statement attempting to compare perspectives of resilience immediately confronts problems of spatial and temporal scale. Nevertheless, at a general level, comparison is possible. Essentially, resilience in ecology is concerned with the longer-term survival and functioning of populations, species and ecosystems in changing or fluctuating operating environments. Resilience in risk management in human systems is concerned with the preservation of the day-to-day and other activities of communities and societies within the human species. It is also concerned with the welfare of individuals.

Vulnerability, defined generally as susceptibility to injury, may be seen as inversely related to resilience: the more resilient, the less vulnerable. The scale issues are similar to those identified above for resilience.

The Perspective of Ecology

The notion of resilience in ecology and agro-ecology relates to the nature of change in ecosystems or populations over time. Holling (1973) noted the difference between resilience and stability, defining the former as follows: 'Resilience determines the persistence of relationships within a system and is a measure of the ability of these systems to absorb changes of state variables, driving variables, and parameters, and still persist' (p17). Holling defines stability, on the other hand, as the ability of a system to return to a state of equilibrium after a temporary disturbance. Thus a very stable system would not fluctuate greatly and would return to normal quickly. Conversely, a highly resilient system may be quite unstable, in that it may undergo significant fluctuation. In a mild and non-extreme environment, the attribute of stability may be more desirable and thus dominate, whereas the attribute of resilience would enable a species or population to survive in a supporting environment characterized by extremes. Terminologies differ in this area, but the principles are often the same. For example,

Begon et al (1990) talk of *local* stability (returning to original state following small disturbances) and *global* stability (returning after relatively large disturbances or impact). This is a complicated area, in keeping with the enormous spatial and temporal complexity of natural systems. Populations or species may optimize prevailing conditions and resources but be incapable of tolerating new conditions outside their evolutionary experience (e.g. the extinction of the dinosaurs, mammoths, or Australian megafauna). Alternatively, some species may find that environmental change suits them. This is the story of evolution, and a key factor is the rate of change in the surrounding environment, and thus the scope for adaptation. In the case of humans, the timing of change, of course, is such that biological evolution is not an option – sustainability must be achieved through rapid behavioural evolution. The focus now is much sharper, as human-induced environmental change occurs rapidly and is affecting species and populations already reduced and stressed. A specific example is the variable fate of vertebrate fauna in arid Australia following 200 years of European settlement (see Newsome, 1975; Morton, 1990; Stafford-Smith and Morton, 1990): against a backdrop of a harsh and unreliable biophysical environment, mammals often sought out rare refuges during drought. With the added pressure of introduced livestock, rabbits and predators, some species have disappeared, their precarious but previously adequate strategy not resilient enough in the new circumstances. Conversely, some other species – reptiles in particular – have been less affected, and some, such as the larger kangaroo species, have increased in numbers.

Resilience and sustainability have been equated in various ways, for example by Holling (1986). In the context of agricultural systems, Conway (1987) recognizes four properties of agroecosysterms, which are summarized below:

1. *Productivity* is the amount of desired output from the system per input of resource.
2. *Stability* is the constancy of output of the system under normal conditions.
3. *Sustainability* is the ability of the system to maintain productivity following large disturbances.
4. *Equitability* is the evenness of the distribution of the system output among the population (pp100–102).

Agroecosysterns are classic examples of mixed human–natural systems, and these properties can be applied to other human and/or natural systems. Conway's sustainability is clearly Holling's resilience. In the face of potential global ecological upheaval, environmental problems at national and subnational scales, and the ever-present uncertainty that attends these, explicit recognition is demanded of the different system properties. Stability of natural systems and the human systems that depend upon them is still the common goal, but resilience/sustainability is an imperative for survival.

The key contribution of the ecological view of resilience is to provide a focus on the systemic nature of the problems and on the longer-term demands on policy and management. Twenty years on, Holling's (1973) summary of an environmental management approach based on resilience is even more apposite: the need to keep options open, while appreciating heterogeneity and keeping a broader than local view. We would argue that this approach should apply to much more than just ecosystem management. Such an approach is at odds with management approaches more typical in the present, which are concerned with compartmentalizing issues, acceptance of the status quo, limiting change to the margins, and a short-term view.

The Perspective of Risk Research

The scholarly field of risk covers an immense range of activity. Most authors in the risk literature have not written on the issue of sustain-ability, although the connection has been made by O'Riordan and Rayner (1991), Dovers and Handmer (1992), and others. Nevertheless, some of the literature's themes provide valuable insights for our typo-logy of resilience and, therefore, for sustainability. It is these we concentrate on.

Acknowledgement of risk

The concept of social amplification (and attenuation) of risk (Kasperson et al, 1988; also see Hood et al, 1992) provides a possible theoretical explanation for the way in which threats to the global environment have been perceived – although this may not have been in the minds of its creators. Over the last few decades, there has been no shortage of people pointing to the threats facing Earth's ecosystem. Yet it seemed that globally, the powerful institutions of science, commerce, government and mass media (with notable exceptions) worked to attenuate the threats, in a way that would be familiar to many disaster researchers. These groups did nothing about the cause, and little about the symptoms, of the problem. Instead attenuation was achieved by simply ignoring the warnings, by active denial, by producing evidence to counter the claims, by attacking the credibility of those issuing the warnings, and so on. Such 'anti-reform' efforts should be an expected part of any process of 'cultural adaptation' (Boyden, 1987, pp32–31; Boyden et al, 1990, pp81–88). However, during the last decade, attenuation has become amplification or intensification: the same bodies that were ambivalent about or were discounting the threat now recognize its importance and in some cases are arguing for urgent action. Undoubtedly, media advocacy has helped, but there are also new players. The issues are being 'internationalized'; national governments are finding they have less effective power while the United Nations and non-government environmental organizations now occupy centre stage (Camilleri and Falk, 1992).

A standard argument of those seeking to play down, as well as by those wanting to increase concern about a hazard – whether it is of local or global significance – is to draw attention to the inevitable scientific uncertainty or ignorance. *Uncertainty* in this context is defined following the work of Smithson (1989), in which it is only a small subset in a taxonomy of the much broader concept of *ignorance*. In addition to uncertainty, the taxonomy includes socially enforced ignorance, as in *taboos,* and deliberate attempts to maintain ignorance, as in *distortion.* Current policymaking processes are not good at recognizing and coping with ignorance. We have generally handled ignorance by ignoring or denying it, or by trying to reduce it through scientific enquiry. At the 1992 Rio Earth Summit, the key areas of population growth in the developing world and per capita consumption in the developed world were effectively excluded from the main discussion – they were treated as irrelevant or taboo.

It is quite clear that as none of us are, or ever will be, omniscient, decisions about the future will be made in ignorance (Green, 1991) – Wildavsky's (1988) 'principle of uncertainty'. For a culture underpinned by the certainty and resolving power of science and technology, this is a disturbing situation (Ravetz, 1986). It is important that we do not pretend that ignorance does not exist: we need the humility to acknowledge it. However, at the same time, we must have the arrogance to make decisions (Green, 1991). Curiously, at present, we seem to have humility only in the face of the status quo and arrogance only in terms of defending it.

An important reason for the perpetuation of this apparently unsatisfactory state of affairs is that, despite much rhetoric about community and stakeholder involvement, hazard management is increasingly a professional activity closely linked to existing bureaucratic and political power bases. Again, the emphasis here is strongly on reducing uncertainty by tackling the physical source, rather than having institutional arrangements that allow adaptability. Hewett (1983) argues that much hazards research serves primarily to confirm and maintain the power of major institutions, and that technology and science are 'a creature of the most powerful, wealthy and centralised institutions' (p9). Wynne (1982) and Rayner (1992) agree and put the case forward that much risk assessment by the bureaucracies responsible for regulating hazardous technology is no more than 'legitimatory ritual'. Risk is dealt with by technocratic institutions as a discrete entity, quite separate from the social and political factors that underlie it.

A serious implication is that the risk profession may function to reassure the public and decision-makers that society as it is currently structured has the capacity to deal with threats. Certainly, much material used for public risk information is designed simply to reassure those at risk, to persuade them that the hazard is being well managed and is not worth worrying about (see, for example, de Vanssay, 1992). Organizations that feel under threat, such as the chemical or nuclear industries, may look to the risk profession to legitimize their activities. At a broader level, Webler et al (1992) argue that the use of science in the whole process of risk management plays an important role in 'managing the state's legitimacy problem', and Gilbert (1992) observes that hazards provide an opportunity for the state to parade its power and authority.

Not surprisingly, some scholars see risk as a reflection of the distribution of power in society (O'Riordan, 1990). In terms of susceptibility to damage, risk is distributed very unevenly. Certain groups are more vulnerable, or in other words, less resilient. These are generally those who are poorer or less powerful. There are different models of vulnerability, but most are based on the relationships within society. For example, Cannon's (1993) model is based on class, ethnicity, and gender, whereas Winchester (1992) asserts that the explanation for vulnerability may be found in the 'junction between the political economy and the cycle of production, exchange and consumption' (p19).

The institutional structure described above is not one that will adapt readily to a changing environment. However, its strength and ability to perpetuate itself may make it relatively invulnerable or resilient at least over the short term: in the sense that it shields us from the worst effects of environmental change. It achieves this through minor adjustments or by simply resisting change.

Risk management

Given that, generally, we must make decisions about the future in ignorance, we need decision-making and management strategies that can cope with, and readily adapt to, new or unexpected circumstances. For example, at the individual level, denial, rationalization, and various other psychological mechanisms are widely used to deal with risk (Marks, 1990). It is interesting to observe some of these mechanisms operating at the societal level – in particular, denial. But denial is a very limited approach as it prohibits adaptation to new circumstances. Another view is articulated by Wildavsky (1985, 1988), who distinguishes two ways of coping with uncertainty: 'anticipation' and 'resilience'. Anticipation relies on detecting problems and trying to avoid them. Implicit in this approach is the belief that a very low level of ignorance is achievable: ignorance can be identified, then reduced or eliminated. Wildavsky (1988) argues that this is 'trial without error' (p57) and is characteristic of much of current government. Unfortunately, the approach is fundamentally risk averse and frightened of change and is therefore most unlikely to prove capable of dealing with sustainability issues. Despite its shortcomings, the anticipatory approach has its supporters; see, for example, Short (1990).

Wildavsky's resilience is quite different, involving decentralized institutions and a rapidly moving trial-and-error approach. It 'refers to learning how to bounce back by utilizing change to cope with the unknown, and it entails dealing with dangers as they arise' – an approach often referred to as crisis management (Smithson, 1991, p47). In conventional hazard and disaster management, emphasis is often placed on having the 'flexibility' to adjust human, organizational, and material resources to rapidly changing or even completely unexpected circumstances: an ability to improvise and to adapt (Kreps, 1992). It is important to recognize, however, that the emphasis is on very short-term adaptability to deal with a threat – so that the community, the economic system, and individual households can continue as before. The resilience is to enhance the ability of the system to perpetuate itself unchanged, with minimum disruption even to day-to-day activities: It is about *institutional stability* and thus is more suited to rare, rapid-onset disasters than to those that are slow onset but that inexorably lead to major ecological change.

In assessing resilience, we would argue that the extent and type of immediate disaster losses themselves are not necessarily the critical factor – just as important is the ability to recover from those losses. The burden of recovery can be spread over space or through time. Resources are typically transferred to disaster areas through aid and insurance. Through this mechanism, the whole 'insures' parts of the world at any one time. But costs can also be transferred to the future through debt, environmental degradation, or deficient infrastructure. In this way, the whole can be insured by mortgaging the future. These are issues of intra- and intergenerational equity and are central to the management of hazards and to sustainability.

One way of increasing our ability to cope with, or to resist, sudden environmental change (i.e., decreasing our vulnerability) is to have some redundancy or spare capacity in the system. However, increasing demands for short-term economic efficiency are likely to eliminate spare capacity, as are already overexploited natural resource bases in many countries. Another route is to increase system flexibility, that is, the ease with which resources can be reallocated. However, such reallocative ability does not sit well with a system that seeks to optimize resource use in the short term through large fixed capital assets. There is confusion between ends and means. The end is seen as the perpetuation of the political and economic entity, perhaps more so than the needs of the people who inhabit the locale. Following from this, a central issue concerning the utility of the notion of resilience is the need to clearly identify the nature of the system in question. The confusing of ends and means often leads to an implicit assumption as to what it is we want to preserve. An example is the debt crisis of the 1980s, a major disturbance to many national economies. Perceptions differ: George (1988) concentrates on the negative impacts (still happening) on people, local economies and the environment -- these are the ends and the global economic arrangements are the (failed) means. In sharp contrast, a leading, involved banker provided a retrospective view of the debt crisis, painting it as a past event and a 'disaster that didn't happen' (Rhodes, 1992). His concern was solely with the international financial and economic structures involved; people, local economies and the environment were not considered.

The end, both for sustainability and hazard management, should be the health and well-being of humans within the constraints of natural systems. System resilience is targeted at these ends, and then the available means can be assessed.

Sustainability and hazard management

Our approach to hazards, in particular those involving natural phenomena, has been devoted to ensuring sustainability – but it is the sustainability of specific settlements and activities even if this involves massive transfer of resources. Often, heroic efforts will be made to 'get things back to normal'. Relevant here is the fact that decision-making processes in our political and commercial frameworks generally operate over very short time horizons (such as annual financial reports or the next election) and thus are only cognizant of currently visible, near-term costs and benefits. Of course, this generally militates against more substantial changes with their longer pay-off times, although it may encourage minor adjustments and incremental change.

A pattern emerges of very deep-seated resistance to change. However, sometimes minor changes are made and very occasionally major behavioural change will occur incrementally. But such change has not been enough to challenge the underlying assumptions and structure of the industrialized societies. The emphasis has been on *protecting or shielding from change* rather than on the ability to *adapt to change*. This may be a serious shortcoming in the face of great uncertainty. At issue is whether this emphasis – here drawn from hazard management but visible throughout much of the industrialized West – increases our vulnerability to major environmental change.

A Typology of Resilience

Much of the discussion so far points to two ends of a continuum of responses to ignorance/uncertainty and risk within the framework offered by the notion of resilience. Dovers and Handmer (1992) term these *reactive* and *proactive* resilience. The first approaches the future by strengthening the status quo and making the present system resistant to change. This is a quest for constancy or stability. Stability is seen as the end in itself, rather than as a means of achieving the goal of human well-being. Proactive resilience, on the other hand, accepts the inevitability of change and tries to create a system that is capable of adapting to new conditions and imperatives. Such a proactive strategy is similar to the resilience advocated by Holling (1973) and Wildavsky (1988), and to Conway's (1987) sustainability. Timmerman (1981) writes of modern society following 'a strategy of reliability [stability] rather than a strategy of resilience', and provides the following explanation:

> If we are vulnerable ... then there are, at least, two strategies. ... We can rely on being able to shield ourselves from the blow; or we can rely on being able to absorb the blow. The first, shielding, concentrates on a continuous, reliable defence – reliability. The second, much less popular (for obvious reasons), relies on being able to bounce back from being battered or wounded – resilience. (p32)

These two approaches are best seen as extremes; in a complex society there is likely to be – and should be – a mixture of the two in any given situation and across institutions. Any classification will oversimplify, but a typology is useful for structuring the arguments and may help to identify the limitations in the current sustainability debate and in some approaches to hazard management.

We suggest the following three-way classification of resilience, defined in terms of the response to threats of disturbance:

Type 1: Resistance and maintenance;
Type 2: Change at the margins; and
Type 3: Openness and adaptability.

Here, the discussion is at the generic level, and the responses of 'resistance', 'change at the margin' and 'adaptability' are in terms of the assumptions underlying the society or institution under study. Further work would be required for the detailed fit in the typology of any particular practical context. The key features of the typology are summarized in Table 10.1.

The typology is presented to capture the range of potential approaches from which more issue-specific responses can be framed. Optimal policy responses are context defined and demand sensitivity to variations in the nature and scale of the constituent issues of sustain-ability. Dovers (1995a) offers a basis for this, using a set of policy problem attributes and a general taxonomy of micro-, meso- and macroproblems. Insensitivity to the differences, and thus to the policy responses demanded, has serious implications. Skjaerseth (1992), comparing the relatively tractable ozone depletion problem with the climate change issue, states that 'different problems need different cures. ... Leaving problem characteristics unchecked may result in quite misleading conclusions concerning the applicability to other problems of the lessons drawn' (p30). We argue that whereas our typology represents the full menu of responses, most institutions choose from only a small part of it.

Type 1 Resilience: Resistance and Maintenance

This is characterized by resistance to change. A human system of this type would do its utmost to avoid change and would typically deny that a problem exists: the risk is socially attenuated. Enormous resources will be expended maintaining the status quo. The approach is frequently favoured by those in authority as it maintains their power.

Where threats are identified, anticipatory mechanisms will be put in place. Where proper reaction would threaten the status quo, appeals to ignorance are common. These are often expressed through calls for more information, and insistence on *inaction because of uncertainty* (Smithson, 1991). The initial stage of many major environmental debates is often characterized by appeals to ignorance: examples include the countering of concern over pesticides following the early work of Carson (1962) and pleas over the past decade and a half to await absolute proof before implementing action to address ozone depletion and potential climate change (see 'US row', 1976; Skjaerseth, 1992). Whereas uncertainty may be generally thought of as something to avoid, in some cases and for some groups, it is an attractive state of affairs – uncertainty may be exciting and may indicate opportunity. An institution may benefit from uncertainty (Smithson, 1991), as this can obscure its activities from public view. A cynical view is that uncertainty may be an essential operating input for obdurate bureaucracies, allowing the bothersome imperatives of policy reform to be diffused or deflected. A discussion of such responses in the broader context of *cultural adaptation* is given by Boyden (1987, pp23–31) and Boyden et al (1990, pp81–88).

The Type 1 approach is not sustainable at the global or continental level (Boyden, 1987; WCED, 1987; Meadows et al, 1992; Myers, 1993). Of course, it can be sustained in some areas by importing the necessary resources and by exporting waste. We have mentioned earlier the aid and insurance that may flow into a disaster-affected area in the industrialized Western world. Other examples include countries permanently dependent on food aid, and the transfer of wealth from poor to rich countries through trade and interest payments on debt, very low prices for natural resources, or the out-migration of skilled people. Occasionally, military force is used to ensure the security of resource flows. Much waste is exported from its point of origin by discharge into the atmosphere, rivers or seas. There is also the high-profile 'trade' in toxic wastes, much of it dumped in developing countries (see WCED, 1987, pp227–228).

The costs of current consumption can be, and frequently are, transferred in time as well as space – the discounting of the future by governments and other power groups is one of the interesting characteristics of modern societies. Hiskes (1992) argues that our 'liberal democracies' find it difficult to deal with the future because the only moral theory they embrace is that of 'individual rights'. At the global scale, shifting the costs to the future is the only way that help is available from outside. Future generations will find themselves responsible for past unwise patterns of consumption through outstanding financial debt, deficient infrastructure, conflicts over resources, and a degraded environment. Environmental degradation would include reduced biodiversity, declining biological productivity, poisoned land and water, and possibly changed climates. We are not suggesting that all major global resource flows are undesirable, only that they should be examined for their impact on the achievement of sustainability.

Table 10.1 *A typology of resilience*

Resilience	Key Characteristics	Sustainability		Elements	
		Implications	Approach	Positive	Negative
Type 1	Resistance or inability to change.	1. Not sustainable. 2. Possible that system will become so strained that it may collapse and change completely.	Denial of need for change.	1. Apparent stability and certainty. 2. Will not make a maladaptive change. 3. Maintenance of status quo and of optimizing capacity.	1. Lack of flexibility. 2. Inability to adjust to new circumstances. 3. Situation likely to get worse. 4. Options will narrow. 5. Irreversible damage.
Type 2	Change at the margins.	1. Acknowledge that present system is not sustainable. 2. Minor change may delay essential major changes.	Treat symptoms.	1. Admission of problem. 2. Some essential change may occur. 3. Change is incremental rather than sudden.	1. Gives impression of significant change and may lull people into a false sense of security. 2. Unlikely to force sufficient change.
Type 3	Open to radical change to social structure and institutional arrangements.	1. Major change toward a sustainable society. 2. Ability to manage uncertainty and unanticipated outcomes. 3. Chance of maladaptive change.	Treat causes.	1. Tackles underlying causes. 2. Flexible/ adaptive system.	1. May go down wrong track. 2. Loss of optimizing capacity in present and near term.

Table 10.1 *A typology of resilience* (cont'd)

Resilience	Typical Generic Arguments	Approach to Hazard	Impact on power (Political Economic) Structure	Emphasis
Type 1	1. Denial. 2. If problem is admitted, then appeals to ignorance (especially scientific) to defer action. 3. Costs of tampering with status quo emphasized.	1. Identify and plan for obvious threats, 'anticipatory planning'. 2. Substantial resources may be committed to maintaining the status quo in the face of a threat.	Maintains or enhances existing power structure.	1. On individual sovereignty. 2. Hazard management by small professional group. 3. Control of public agenda and information.
Type 2	1. Recognition that a problem may exist. 2. Enquiries, delaying tactics.. 3. Acknowledge that change is necessary and make minor adjustments.	1. Less emphasis on anticipatory planning. 2. Tinkering with hazard adjustments.	Maintains existing structure but may lead to slight shift, for example, toward environmental Interests – but these are likely to become part of existing power structure.	1. The right rhetoric. 2. Some attempts to have people take responsibility for some hazard management. 3. Control of public agenda and information, with some participative mechanisms.
Type 3	I. Change is essential. 2. Appeals to ignorance: 'We don't know, so we must change.' 3. Longer-term view.	1. Maximum flexibility to cope with unexpected threats.	More likely to lead to major changes in power distribution.	1. On humanity and the biosphere. 2. Hazard management by all – individual freedom balanced by responsibility. 3. Information systems participatory but highly variable.

It seems quite likely that much of the present flow runs counter to the objectives of both inter- and intragenerational equity.

Because Type 1 resilience lacks flexibility, it is incapable of adjustment to new circumstances. However, it has advantages. It appears to ensure a stable, if inequitable, social system through preserving the status quo and existing power structures; it maintains optimizing patterns of resource use in the short term; and it will not make maladaptive changes (as it makes no changes). In modern democracies, freedom and choice of the individual are emphasized. However, this will be constrained through information control (Herman and Chomsky, 1988; Handmer and Parker, 1992) and economic power, and will be fully enjoyed in reality only by a subset of the population. Long adherence to a chosen policy path in the face of increasing resistance may attract admiration and political benefit. Generally, these advantages will be greatest for those in power, because their position is maintained: they are likely, therefore, to advocate this approach.

At this point, it is appropriate to comment on the modern period. This is often viewed as a period of very rapid change, perhaps unique in history. Yet history is replete with periods of upheaval; and the modern Western-style democracies of the industrialized world have provided a high level of security for their populations. In contrast, the long-lasting feudal societies of Europe, for example, were often quite stable at the institutional level, but life was very uncertain for individuals. Even the middle classes frequently faced the prospect of death through starvation or disease (Tuan, 1979).

Interestingly, total resistance to change has served some communities outstandingly well. Intensely religious communities such as the Arnish of North America have succeeded in surviving unchanged for a few hundred years. Many monastic religious orders in both the Christian and non-Christian worlds go back largely unchanged for many centuries. Some, like the Carthusians, have changed little in 900 years (Lockhart, 1985). By the standards of the industrialized world, these communities have low resource consumption, an austere lifestyle, are relatively small and self-sufficient, and generally do not threaten the status quo. But these characteristics do not describe major religious institutions like the Roman Catholic church, nor do they describe many long-lived military institutions. Both are also examples of organizations that have survived with little change over the centuries. These persistent groups illustrate a subdivision of Type 1: that is, between groups that remove themselves from the broader society (*hermetic* Type 1) and those engaged politically with broader society (*open* Type 1). Such organizations and communities constitute typical institutional expressions of history. Pertinent questions here concern why these groups have persisted and whether they carry lessons for sustainable development.

It might be argued that Type 1 resilience presents a viable path to global sustainability. This is because this type of system would continue despite massive strain; it may appear to have little vulnerability, but when collapse would come it would be sudden and relatively complete, possibly paving the way for a completely different order. Recent examples would include the collapse of European communist states, the reunification of Germany, and the peaceful overthrow of the Iberian dictatorships. History provides many other examples, such as Japan in the Meiji period. Unfortunately, by the time this collapse happens, the global environment probably will be more degraded than at present, further irreversible damage will have occurred, and options will have narrowed. Perhaps a more plausible, though pessimistic, scenario is provided by the great 'hydraulic civilizations' that failed to adapt to environmental change and perished (Wittfogel, 1967). Like modern industrial societies, they were characterized by massive investment in fixed infrastructure and strong social control. That such processes continue today is well evidenced by the permanent degradation of land through desertification (Mannion, 1991, pp224–229).

Type 2 Resilience: Change at the Margins

Outright denial of global environmental strain and its implications for humanity (Type 1 resilience) is today less common than our second type of resilience, which also typifies the standard approach to risk. This is characterized by acknowledgement of the problem, discussion of the implications, and promulgation of reforms that do not challenge the basis of our societies but that may lead to changes in emphasis at the margins. There may be clear acknowledgement that the present system is not sustainable and that change is needed. The rhetoric will be there, but only minor changes occur, largely directed at alleviating symptoms. The difference between addressing symptoms and addressing causes – *antidotal* versus *corrective* cultural adaptation (Boyden, 1987, p24) – is often ignored by those enamoured of more reactive responses.

Type 2 resilience, as the dominant approach in the Western industrialized world, is not without advantages. A critical first step in conscious problem solving is acknowledgement that a problem exists and clear identification of what that problem is. With respect to environmental change, this is occurring and is an important achievement. Some attitude changes are also occurring. It is possible that, through incremental change, this approach will get us on the pathway of sustainable development. Certainly, this is the fervent hope of most politicians, senior administrators, business people and community leaders who do not advocate a Type 1 response. However attractive and reassuring this view is, it is unlikely to move us far toward a sustainable state. It is conceivable that some essential change will take place incrementally. However, the minor changes that are occurring appear unlikely to have any impact on the underlying cause: the steady escalation of total and per capita resource use and waste generation.

This can be illustrated by extrapolation of world energy use (the data here are from various sources: see Dovers and Norton, 1994; Dovers, 1995b). Energy consumption can be used as a rough proxy for the environmental load of a population. Global primary energy use in 1990 was about 340 exajoules (EJ, 10^{18}), with a world population of 5.3 billion. The global mean per capita use was 64 gigajoules (GJ, 10^9), similar to current (1990) per capita consumption in South Korea or slightly higher than Portugal. On average, in industrialized countries, consumption was 205 GJ (e.g., Japan 134, Australia 216, the United States 325 GJ). In developing countries, it was 22 GJ, a little less than the level of China or Papua New Guinea. If today, everyone used the industrial world's average, global energy use would be almost 1100 EJ – a threefold increase in environmental load. With a plausible global population of 10 billion by the year 2040, if all were to use the average per capita energy consumption of a 1990 industrialized country, the load would increase sixfold. Present policy measures designed to encourage efficiency gains at the margins contrast with such scenarios: the implications for achieving global equity through catch-up development are serious.

There is a danger that the minor changes now in train may delay essential major changes, giving the impression that the necessary changes are being, or will be, made by the current social institutions. A false sense of security may thereby be encouraged. It is comforting to argue that gradual non-disruptive change is the only realistic option. Perhaps it is currently the only politically realistic option in our democratic system with constituencies that probably place greater value on near-term stability (and current consumption) than on the needs of future generations. Human systems operate within the parameters set by previous experience and short-term expectations – the so-called 'prison of experience'. This argues in favour of incremental change.

Where substantial change does occur, it usually serves the interests of the powerful elite, not necessarily the interests of the general population or of the biosphere. At the least, changes will not disbenefit elites. This occurs, for example, when groups pushing for major change are absorbed into the mainstream political structure, where they influence the rhetoric but have little impact on the underlying structure and assumptions of society. This has been the fate of the bulk of the environmental movement (Bennett and Dahlberg, 1990) and is seen by some as the fate of the idea of sustainable development now that it has been embraced by the political mainstream (e.g. Rees, 1990).

The policy recommendations emerging from the sustainability debate in developed nations have in general been typical of a Type 2 response. In Australia, for example, the recommendations coming from the federal government's 'Ecologically Sustainable Development process', although worthy and welcome, have been described as being not really about long-term sustainability but rather about non-disruptive reforms at the margins of major resource and industry sectors (Dovers et al, 1992). The current debate around the 'Toronto' target of a phased 20 per cent cut in greenhouse gas emissions can be questioned as marginal given the Intergovernmental Panel on Climate Change's (IPCC, 1990) conclusion that stabilization of changes in atmospheric composition would require an immediate reduction of 60 per cent or more.

This typifies Type 2 resilience, the most common response to both environmental change and to hazards and risk. Many responses to environmental change, and much else besides, are shaped by what is perceived to be politically and economically palatable in the near term rather than by the nature and scale of the threat itself. The approach is often described – by those who display it – as practical, realistic, balanced or pragmatic. It certainly has its advantages, but will an approach dedicated to individual choice and market mechanisms, and preoccupied with management rather than vision, get us onto the road to sustainability? Our vulnerability as a society is being reduced in the short term, but perhaps this is just putting off the need for major change, which is likely to become increasingly urgent.

Type 3 Resilience: Openness and Adaptability

Our third type of resilience is more likely to deal directly with the underlying causes of environmental problems. This approach reduces vulnerability by having a high degree of flexibility. Its key characteristic is a preparedness to adopt new basic operating assumptions and institutional structures. An adaptable society would be prepared to move in a fundamentally new direction quickly. It would adapt to the consequences of change and uncertainty rather than resist them. Of course, this has happened through history, but usually in a slow and painful way. Paradoxically, some of the examples mentioned in the discussion of Type 1 resilience illustrate sudden dramatic change, but these changes have been enforced by circumstance rather than embraced voluntarily.

An open and adaptable system should enhance the potential for the major changes necessary for global sustainability. The underlying structural causes of the problems would be identified, the options explored, and changes put in train. This seems straightforward, so we might ask why it has not happened. We would have to abandon or at least dramatically modify many of our basic operating assumptions. For example:

- we would have to abandon our preoccupation with the present and with instant gratification and adopt longer timescales of planning and management, and work from a deeper sense of history;
- we would have to move away from intense individualism toward collective responsibility; and
- society may have to become much less risk averse in terms of different institutional design.

One powerful constraint is vested interests, in that major change is likely to alter the power structure substantially (see also the section 'The Perspective of Risk Research', above). Abandonment of the dominant ideology would disadvantage the associated institutions and key individuals. Typically, vested interests are defined as comprising agencies of the state and the major interests of capital, labour, religion and science. There is a clear paradox here, in that the state is the institution generally expected to override vested interests for the common good, yet the state is, more often than not, entwined closely and sometimes indistinguishable from these same interests. This is especially the case where 'corporatist' styles of government exist, in both democracies and dictatorships. In these circumstances, major changes in direction may be very difficult without revolution.

However, the definition of vested interests given above is too static and simplistic. Depending on the issue at hand, vested interests frequently comprise opportunistic coalitions of commerce, consumer and community groups, sections of the bureaucracy, trade unions, and so on; and the members of a coalition may be at a variety of scales, from local to international. The media can be enormously influential in sealing the fate of propositions for change, as can the environmental movement. As discussed above under Type 2 resilience, the environmental movement is frequently anti-Type 3, at least publicly to maintain legitimacy. The broader public – to the extent that it exists – is frequently reluctant to embrace change, even when such recalcitrance threatens their long-term interests. Another inhibitor of real change is that even when institutions, or even whole political systems, are abolished and reformed, typically the same people and the same organizational culture run the new creation. There is a strong devotion to protecting the status quo.

Some traditional societies showed an ability to adapt to environmental change as part of their normal functioning. But these did not have large fixed investments, and generally had well-developed safety nets, for example, through the maintenance of traditional hosts as described by Waddell (1983). Large fixed capital investments make change a costly prospect, even when, as now, the investments might be put in place precisely to shield us against the variability of our environment. A further and critical factor differentiating the responses of traditional versus industrial societies is the time available to adapt and learn relative to the pace and scale of change. In Australia, for example, Aboriginal society slowly adapted to and changed its environment and created an ecologically sustainable economy over 50,000 or more years (see Dingle, 1988). Not only was the rate of change slow, but the scale was well within the ability of the environment to assimilate. In contrast, modern industrial Australia has wrought rapid and accelerating ecological changes in the space of two centuries (Boyden et al, 1990). There is not much time for reflection and for the lessons of trial and error in the environment in the modern era; again, the adaptation now can only be via rapid behavioural change.

Great flexibility and adaptability carry dangers as well as the obvious benefits just mentioned. There might also be running costs associated with this type of resilience: For example, the system is likely to be characterized by a certain degree of instability in the manner of the resilient ecosystems described by Holling (1973), it may be economically inefficient, and it may even appear chaotic. Overreaction to symptoms, and hasty decisions, may occur, but the approach should be able to recognize this and make the necessary corrections. It is likely that some chaos is desirable, perhaps necessary, for an adaptable system: a certain amount of chaos may help ensure that there is always a choice of directions.

Another important caveat must be applied. Not all change is positive, and flexibility may also make easier changes that are maladaptive for both the environment and human welfare. It is quite possible to go down the wrong track; this might be with respect to some single issue entailing human and environmental costs, or it might even be at the macro scale of following some earlier human societies into an evolutionary dead end.

Conclusion: Stability and Adaptability

The sustainability debate centres on the question of whether marginal adjustments to the present system will suffice or whether more profound changes are demanded. So does the consideration of appropriate responses to environmental and technological hazards. Our typology offers a framework for considering the rigidity and inadequacy of present institutional responses to global environmental change.

Clearly, modern industrialized societies and their institutions are particularly good at resisting fundamental change. The most successful tactic has probably been change at the margins, or fine tuning – our Type 2 resilience. Very rarely is an opportunity taken to implement major change – Type 3. In fact the whole ethos of public management is to limit the debate to Types 1 and 2 (denial and the management of symptoms) and to avoid even discussing Type 3 (tackling the underlying causes). The strength of such societies lies in the maintenance of their basic assumptions and institutional structures: they are successful in their search for stability and fulfil their desire to perpetuate themselves. Unfortunately, reliance on Types 1 and 2 may make essential change difficult. The rapid changes apparent all around us in our societies rarely challenge the basis of our institutions. From the perspective of global survival, the thrust of these changes – as distinct from the rhetoric – may be further entrenching unsustainable practice. Yet the minor adjustments and policy statements may give the appearance that the problem is being addressed properly. When the need for fundamental shifts in society's operating assumptions can no longer be denied, the necessary change is likely to be difficult and painful to institutions that have spent most of their existence actively resisting it.

Type 3 responses are most typically advocated by more radical elements within a society, and/or ones who are disadvantaged by the current situation. Many radical change agents, such as Margaret Thatcher or the Russian Bolsheviks, engineered rapid change and then fell into a conservative pattern favouring Type 1 reactions: they did not maintain or implement a Type 3 capability to manage change. This points to an important phenomenon. Linear rates of change are rare in either human or natural systems: normality is a series of fits and starts – Lewis's (1979) 'corollary of historic lumpiness'. Similarly, Type 1 and 2 responses tend to come in lumps: over a longer period, they attempt to create evenness and stability, but they often must accelerate to answer endogenous or exogenous pressures for change. Intense phases of bureaucratic activity in the face of pressure on environmental issues (committees, enquiries, commissioning reports, etc.) typify this, as does similar activity in the wake of a natural disaster. Note that such activity is unlikely to advocate substantial change or to question the overall direction of society.

One aspect of this bureaucratic activity is often to push for an opening of policy-making institutions to a wider range of inputs and views, such as through public participation or advisory groups. Unfortunately, many apparently sensible suggestions for interdisciplinary or inter-sectoral groups to advise on appropriate futures may achieve little – even if they had any real power. Such panels may exhibit more interdisciplinary awareness and produce good advice, but they run the risk of losing sight of the goal of sustainability and of advocating, at best, Type 2 responses through consensus and compromise, that is, the level of the lowest common denominator. This is the most we usually achieve, even when the situation is one of life or death – as in hazard and disaster management. As we have observed, Type 2 responses are likely to simply put off the needed changes to a time when options will have narrowed. Such consensus groups are typically initiated and controlled by organizations with a vested interest in avoiding real solutions, and who may well be responsible for much of the problem. That this is likely is reinforced by the reality that 'many disciplines have developed direct linkages with particular industry or government sectors (like the military) and have come to share their vested interests' (Bennett and Dahlberg, 1990, p74). Hewett (1983, p9) puts forth a similar view.

Apparent institutional and scientific diversity frequently disguises a unity of purpose: maintenance of the status quo. The collective and consensus approach to resolving environmental issues favoured in Australia in the last decade has exhibited this tendency, although it has moved the debate forward (see, e.g., the products of the *National Conservation Strategy for Australia*, Australian Department of Home Affairs and Environment, 1984; and the *National Strategy for Ecologically Sustainable Development*, The Commonwealth, 1992). What is typically missing is a clear political initiative for major change aimed at longer-term goals, with a vision and sense of purpose that is not lost in a maze of diverse views, endless debate, and compromise between sectors. Those proposing change are co-opted and institutionalized along with those opposing any change, allowing Type 2 incrementalism, delay and 'balance' to set the agenda of possible outcomes. In this sense, Type 2 resilience is possibly the most dangerous path: a relief valve that gives the appearance of change and alleviates symptoms for a time. Types 1 and 3 at least imply the existence of a longer-term vision.

The precautionary principle is currently a key policy response to the sustainability challenge. It is an official recognition of pervasive uncertainty, and a statement that awaiting positive proof that an activity is harmful may no longer be tenable. Nevertheless, in implementation, the principle seems unlikely to take us beyond Type 2 responses – although a complete reversal in the burden of proof would move action strongly toward Type 3. As observed earlier, the principle is vague, inoperative by itself, and open to wide interpretation.

Within a society, institutions will generally exhibit a complex mix of types of resilience. This mix will be manifested through the range of contemporary bodies and activities, and also through the survival of apparently anachronistic practices and institutions. Ideally, a society would not only exhibit all three types of responses across its various parts but also *within* all parts. Any one institution should be prepared to choose the most appropriate response from the continuum characterized by the typology in any one situation. The degree of change from the present that this represents would be greater for the more mainstream and powerful parts of societies that currently favour Type 1 and Type 2 responses.

As a species, humanity is immensely adaptable – a 'weed' species. We are also capable of considerable adaptability as individuals, and also as households (variously defined) – the latter being the perennial and universal human social unit. At these levels, we are potentially Type 3. However, will our creaking institutions, and our preoccupation with individual rights while rejecting collective responsibility, prevent the necessary changes – whatever they may be? In recent history, we can find examples where strict maintenance of the status quo in the face of increasing pressure led to sudden and near complete collapse – paving the way for a new order. But this is not a comfortable way to entertain change. There are good lessons in history. As Ponting notes (1991):

> Many societies in the past believed that they had a sustainable way of life only to find some time later that it was not so and that they were unable to make the social, economic and political changes necessary for survival. (p407)

Homo sapiens faces a dilemma. The bulk of humanity is very vulnerable to change. This may be slow-onset change (the issue of sustainability), rapid-onset change (the issues of hazards and disasters), or the increasingly obvious interplay of the two. Intragenerational equity is needed to reduce vulnerability and is demanded morally.

Achieving this by increasing the load on the biosphere through resource-intensive development is not sustainable. Equity goals will only be achieved by reduction in resource consumption and waste generation, especially in the developed world, and through redistribution. This will require massive political and social change, led by vision and informed by science. We need the ability to entertain Type 3 approaches to change: flexibility and, above all, a preparedness to cope with uncertainties and unanticipated situations and directions. But there are huge risks that change could turn out to be maladaptive. So some Type 1 and 2 resilience is essential to give stability, in particular to people's personal lives. The mix is now there, but the emphasis is wrong. The imperative of adaptation rather than resistance to change will increase inexorably.

Acknowledgements

We thank John Salter of the Australian Emergency Management Institute and two anonymous referees for their comments on a draft of this chapter.

References

Australian Department of Home Affairs and Environment. (1984). *A national conservation strategy for Australia.* Canberra: Australian Government Publishing Service.

Begon, M., Harper, J. L., & Townsend, C. R. (1990). *Ecology: Individuals, populations and communities.* London: Blackwell Scientific.

Bennett, J. W., & Dahlberg, K. A. (1990). Institutions, social organisation, and cultural values. In B. L. Turner II, W. C. Clark, R. W. Kates, J. F. Richards, J. T. Mathews, & W. B. Meyer (Eds.), *The earth as transformed by human action* (pp. 69–86). New York: Cambridge University Press.

Boyden, S. (1987). *Western civilization in biological perspective: Patterns in biohistory.* Oxford, UK: Clarendon.

Boyden, S., Dovers, S., & Shirlow, M. (1990). *Our biosphere under threat: Ecological realities and Australia's opportunities.* Melbourne, Australia: Oxford University Press.

Cameron, J., & Abouchar, J. (1991). The precautionary principle: A fundamental principle of law and policy for the protection of the global environment. *Boston College International and Comparative Law Review, 14,* 1–27.

Camilleri, J. A., & Falk, J. (1992). *End of sovereignty? The politics of a shrinking and fragmenting world.* Aldershot, UK: Elgar.

Cannon, T. (1993). A hazard need not a disaster make: Vulnerability and the causes of 'natural' disasters. In P. A. Merriman & C. W. A. Browitt (Eds.), *Natural disasters: Protecting vulnerable communities* (pp. 92–105). London: Thomas Telford.

Carson, R. (1962). *Silent spring.* Boston, MA: Houghton Mifflin.

Checkland, P., & Scholes, J. (1990). *Soft systems methodology in action.* Chichester, UK: Wiley.

Cleveland, C. J. (1987). Biophysical economics; Historical perspectives and current research trends. *Ecological Modelling, 38,* 47–73.

Common, M., & Perrings, C. (1992). Toward an ecological economics of sustainability. *Ecological Economics, 6,* 7–34.

The Commonwealth. (1992). *National strategy for ecologically sustainable development, December 1992.* Canberra: Australian Government Publishing Service.

Conway, G. R. (1987). The properties of agroecosystems. *Agricultural Systems,* 24, 95–117.

Davis, K., & Bernstam, M. S. (Eds.). (1991). *Resources, environment and population: Present knowledge and future options.* New York: Oxford University Press.

de Vanssay, B. (1992, April). *The Sandoz pollution disaster.* Paper presented at Environmental Emergencies: An International Workshop, London.

Dingle, A. E. (1988). *Aboriginal economy: Patterns of experience.* Melbourne, Australia: McPhee Gribble Penguin.

Dovers, S. (1990). Sustainability in context: An Australian perspective. *Environmental Management,* 14, 297–305.

Dovers, S. (1995a). A framework for scaling and framing policy problems in sustainability. *Ecological Economics,* 12(2), 93–106.

Dovers, S. (Ed.), (1995b). *Sustainable energy systems: Pathways for Australian energy reform.* Melbourne, Australia: Cambridge University Press.

Dovers, S., & Handmer, J. (1992). Uncertainty, sustainability and change. *Global Environmental Change,* 2(4), 262–276.

Dovers, S., & Handmer, J. (1995). Ignorance, the precautionary principle, and sustainability. *Ambio,* 24(2), 92–97.

Dovers, S., & Norton, T. W. (1994), Population, environment and sustainability: Reconstructing the debate. *Sustainable Development: People, Economy, Environment,* 2, 1–7.

Dovers, S., Norton, T. W., Hughes, I., & Day, L. (1992). *Population growth and Australian regional environments.* Canberra: Australian Government Publishing Service.

Faber, M., Manstetten, R., & Proops, J. (1992). Toward an open future: Ignorance, novelty and evolution. In R. Costanza, B. G. Norton, & B. D. Haskell (Eds.), *Ecosystem health: New goals for environmental management* (pp. 72–96). Washington, DC: Island Press.

Funtowitz, S. O., & Ravetz, J. R. (1991). A new scientific methodology for global environmental issues. In R. Costanza (Ed.), *Ecological economics: The science and management of sustainability* (pp. 136–152). New York: Columbia University Press.

George, S. (1988). *A fate worse than debt.* London: Penguin.

Gilbert, C. (1992). *Le pouvoir en situation extreme: Catastrophes et politique* [Power in an extreme situation: Catastrophes and politics]. Paris: L'Harmattan.

Green, C. H. (1991). *Ignorance, arrogance and morality: The necessary components of decision making.* Enfield, UK: Middlesex University, Flood Hazard Research Centre.

Handmer, J. W., & Parker, D. J. (1992). Hazard management in Britain: Another disastrous decade? *Area,* 24(2), 113–122.

Herman, E. S., & Chomsky, N. (1988). *Manufacturing consent: The political economy of the mass media.* New York: Pantheon.

Hewett, K. (Ed.). (1983). *Interpretations of calamity.* Winchester, UK: Allen & Unwin.

Hiskes, R. P. (1992). The democracy of risk. *Industrial Crisis Quarterly,* 6(4), 259–278.

Holling, C. S. (1973). Resilience and stability of ecological systems. *Annual Review of Ecology and Systematics,* 4, 1–24.

Holling, C. S. (1986). The resilience of terrestrial ecosystems: Local surprise and global change. In W. C. Clark & R. E. Munn (Eds.), *Sustainable development of the biosphere* (pp. 292–317). Cambridge, UK: Cambridge University Press.

Hood, C., Pidgeon, N., Jones, D., Turner, B., & Gibson, R. (1992). Risk perception. In The Royal Society (Eds.), *Risk assessment, perception and management* (chap. 5, pp. 135–201). London: The Royal Society.

IPCC (Intergovernmental Panel on Climate Change). (1990). *Climate change: The IPCC scientific assessment.* Cambridge, UK: Cambridge University Press.

Kasperson, R. E., Renn, O., Slovic, P., Brown, H. S., Emel, J., Goble, R., Kasperson, J. X., & Ratick, S. (1988). The social amplification of risk. *Risk Analysis*, 8, 177–187.

Kreps, G. (1992). Foundations and principles of emergency planning and management. In D. J. Parker & J. Handmer (Eds.), *Hazard management and emergency planning* (pp. 159–174). London: James & James.

Lazslo, E. (1972). *The systems view of the world: The natural philosophy of the new development in the sciences.* New York: Braziller.

Lewis, P. (1979). Axioms for reading the landscape: Some guides for the American scene. In D. Meinig (Ed.), *The interpretation of ordinary landscapes: Geographical essays* (pp. 11–32). New York: Oxford University Press.

Lockhart, R. B. (1985). *Halfway to heaven: The hidden life of the sublime Carthusians.* London: Thames Methuen.

Mannion, A. M. (1991). *Global environmental change: A natural and cultural environmental history.* Harlow, UK: Longman.

Marks, D. (1990). Imagery, information and risk. In J. Handmer & E. C. Penning-Rowsell (Eds.), *Hazards and the communication of risk* (pp. 19–30). Aldershot, UK: Gower.

Martinez-Alier, J. (1987). *Ecological economics: Energy, environment and society.* Oxford, UK: Basil Blackwell.

Meadows, D. H., Meadows, D. L., & Randers, J. (1992). *Beyond the limits: Global collapse or sustainable future.* London: Earthscan.

Morton, S. (1990). The impact of European settlement on the vertebrate animals of arid Australia: A conceptual model. *Proceedings of the Ecological Society of Australia*, 16, 201–213.

Myers, N. (1993). Population, environment and development. *Environmental Conservation*, 20, 205–216.

Newsome, A. (1975). An ecological comparison of the two arid zone kangaroos of Australia, and their anomalous prosperity since the introduction of ruminant stock to their environment. *Quarterly Review of Biology*, 50, 389–424.

O'Riordan, T. (1990). Hazard and risk in the modern world: Political models for program design. In J. Handmer & E. C. Penning-Rowsell (Eds.), *Hazards and the communication of risk* (pp. 293–302). Aldershot, UK: Gower.

O'Riordan, T. (1992). *The precautionary principle in environmental management* (CSERGE GEC Working Paper 92–03). Norwich, UK: Centre for Social and Economic Research on the Global Environment.

O'Riordan, T., & Rayner, S. (1991). Risk management for global environmental change. *Global Environmental Change*, 1, 91–108.

Ponting, C. (1991). *A green history of the world.* New York: Penguin.

Population Summit of the World's Scientific Academies. (1993). *A joint statement by fifty-eight of the world's scientific academies.* Washington, DC: National Academy Press.

Ravetz, J. R. (1986). Usable knowledge, usable ignorance: Incomplete science with policy implications. In W. C. Clark & R. E. Munn (Eds.), *Sustainable development of the biosphere* (pp. 415–432). Cambridge, UK: Cambridge University Press.

Rayner, S. (1992). Cultural theory and risk analysis. In S. Krimsky & D. Golding (Eds.), *Social theories of risk* (pp. 83–115). Westport, CT: Praeger.

Rees, W. E. (1990). The ecology of sustainable development. *The Ecologist*, 20(1), 18–23.

Rhodes, C. (1992). Third-world debt: The disaster that didn't happen. *The Economist*, 324(7776), 19–25.

Short, J. F. (1990). Hazards, risk and enterprise: Approaches to science, law and social policy. *Law and Society Review*, 24(1), 179–198.

Skjaerseth J. B. (1992). The 'successful' ozone-layer negotiations: Are there any lessons to be learned? *Global Environmental Change*, 2, 292–300.

Smithson, M. (1989). *Ignorance and uncertainty; Emerging paradigms*. New York: Springer Verlag.

Smithson, M. (1991). Managing in an age of ignorance. In J. Handmer, B. Dutton, B. Guerin, & M. Smithson (Eds.), *New perspectives on uncertainty and risk* (pp. 39–65). Canberra: Australian National University and Australian Emergency Management Institute, Centre for Resource and Environmental Studies.

Stafford Smith, D. M., & Morton, S. R. (1990). A framework for the ecology of arid Australia. *Journal of Arid Environments*, 18, 255–278.

Timmerman, P. (1981). *Vulnerability, resilience and the collapse of society* (Environmental Monograph 1). Toronto, Canada: University of Toronto, Institute for Environmental Studies.

Tuan, Y-F. (1979). *Landscapes of fear*. New York: Pantheon.

United Nations. (1992). *Agenda 12: The United Nations programme of action from Rio*. New York: Author.

US row over aerosol ban. (1976, 4 November). *New Scientist*, p. 262.

von Bertalanffy, L. (1968). *General systems theory: Foundations, development, applications*. New York: Braziller.

Waddell, E. (1983). Coping with frosts, government and disaster experts: Some reflections based on a New Guinea experience and a perusal of the relevant literature. In K, Hewett (Ed.), *Interpretations of calamity* (pp, 33–63). Winchester, Australia: Allen & Unwin.

WCED (World Commission on Environment and Development). (1987). *Our common future*. Oxford, UK: Oxford University Press.

Webler, T., Rakel, H., & Ross, R. J. S. (1992). A critical look at technical risk analysis. *Industrial Crisis Quarterly*, 6, 23–38.

Wildavsky, A. (1985). Trial without error: Anticipation versus resilience as strategies for risk reduction. In M. Maxey & R. Kuhn (Eds.), *Regulatory reform: New vision or old curse* (pp. 200–201). New York: Praeger.

Wildavsky, A. (1988). *Searching for safety*. New Brunswick, NJ: Transaction Books.

Winchester, P. (1992). *Power, choice and vulnerability: A case study in disaster mismanagement*. London: James & James.

Wittfogel, K. A. (1967). *Oriental despotism: A comparative study of total power*. New Haven, CT: Yale University Press.

Wynne, B. (1982). *Rationality and ritual: The Windscale inquiry and nuclear decisions in Britain*. Chalfont St. Giles, UK: British Society for the History of Science.

Wynne, B. (1992). Uncertainty and environmental learning: Reconceiving science in the preventive paradigm. *Global Environmental Change*, 2(2), 111–127.

Part III

Adaptation and Disaster Risk

Adaptive Capacity: What Does It Mean in the Context of Natural Hazards?

John Handmer

Is Climate Change Important?

I would like to start with an assertion: that unfortunately, in terms of action, climate change is not seen as particularly important, nor is it viewed as a high priority in most countries. Even where it is allegedly a high priority, this is often because it serves other purposes – or because it is of interest to the groups developing the policy agendas.

Following the UK floods of autumn 2000 reaction by the media and government officials focused largely on climate change. John Prescott, Deputy British Prime Minister, announced at the UN climate conference in The Hague:

> This was a wake-up call that struck home. When people see and experience these ferocious storms, long summer droughts, torrential rains – more extreme and more frequent – they know something is wrong and that climate change now affects them. (BBC News Online, 21 November 2000, 'UK floods, a climate alarm call'.)

This is a strong statement, but with the blame primarily directed at climate change the pressures to learn and adapt were largely oriented toward global environmental change rather than long-standing inadequacies in the government's approach to climate hazard management. It seems likely that the severe flooding of autumn 2000 may be blamed on climate change as a way of shifting responsibility, rather than as a signal to rethink policy. To the extent that this is the case, acknowledging the importance of climate change may actually inhibit adaptation to change by enabling government to escape responsibility for adaptation to climatic hazards. Elsewhere, such as the United States (under George W. Bush) and Australia (under John Howard), governments simply deny that climate change is a significant problem.

The chapter starts by examining this assertion about the unimportance, or perhaps more accurately the low priority, of climate change for developing countries. After showing that climate change may be very important in certain contexts and arguing that adaptation to climate change would be beneficial and useful – regardless of the extent or direction of change – I examine trends in research on climatic disasters. The research is examined for what it has to say about the 'generic' and 'specific' approaches to adaptation to climate change. In brief, generic, or macro-scale, adaptive activity includes increasing wealth and education, income distribution, institutions and health care so as to improve countries' ability to cope with climate and other changes. Specific, or micro-scale, adaptive activity is sector-specific, for example planning for sea-level rise, increased heat or drought or flood-plain management. Before concluding, a third way is suggested for those situations where neither generic nor specific approaches show promise.

Coping with Day-to-Day Uncertainties in Developing Countries

People in developing countries are likely to be much more vulnerable to natural hazards, and are certainly more directly impacted by climatic hazards. The poorer the country, the worst the impacts appear to be. Yet even more than industrialized countries, they have immediate priorities often related to basic survival. The figures concerning health problems, including AIDS, access to potable water, illiteracy and absence of livelihoods, are well known (for example, see the various UN *Human Development Reports*). Some of the general global statistics are even more daunting:

- About half of humanity survives on less than 2 dollars a day–and about half of these exist on less than 1 US dollar a day (UNDP 2001).
- Some 56 countries are currently directly affected by warfare.

Clearly, people and communities in these circumstances are likely to find it challenging coping with their day-to-day existence in ways that most of us cannot begin to imagine, and will be preoccupied with coping with daily uncertainties. How concerned should they be about climate change – which is after all someone else's priority? Their priorities for the future are likely to focus on improving livelihood security, ending war and violence and rebuilding lives. This is not restricted to developing countries; most countries contain substantial groups whose social and economic status forces day-to-day survival priorities.

Of more general importance is simply that political, business and community leaders will almost always have priorities that are a long way from any concern with climate change. This is the case even if their priorities are visionary rather than preoccupied with immediate concerns. Their priorities will concern security, re-election, commercial viability and trade, health, education, infrastructure, environmental management and so on. It is not necessarily that climate issues are seen as unimportant, but they are not as important as other priorities. The relative lack of interest in the UN International Decade for Natural Disaster Reduction (IDNDR) in terms of profile, resources and political support illustrates the point.

Given the legitimate priorities of many poorer people and countries, and the relative lack of interest among the industrialized nations, it should come as no surprise that few countries are as well adapted as they could be to the present regime of climatic hazards. Adaptation has come about gradually through improvements to building standards, access to insurance and welfare and, importantly in many countries, decreased reliance on agriculture with its acute sensitivity to climate and global markets. This is not so much a criticism as an observation that the best adapted might fall a long way short of the ideal in practice. Good policy on paper needs to go through the process and pitfalls of implementation where it competes continuously for attention, resources and expertise.

Making Climate Change Important

Despite these serious problems of poverty, war and lack of development affecting so many countries and communities worldwide, climate change is certainly being noticed. It is being noticed through climatic disasters that are drawing attention to change and variability, making climate important and forcing the issue up the political and media priority list.

It is not simply the occurrence of disasters that is important in this context, but rather the apparent increase in their frequency.

The global reinsurer Munich Re (2001) observes that since the 1950s there has been a threefold increase in major natural disasters, an eightfold increase in losses from such events, and a fifteenfold increase in the losses carried by insurers. The peak year was 1995, at US$190 billion or 0.7 per cent of global gross domestic product (GDP). This is probably not a reflection of climate change as much as a reflection of the social changes set out below and the global spread of insurance. During the 1990s disasters resulted in a global average each year of 75,250 deaths and 211 million people affected (Walter, 2001).

These figures apply to all disasters other than warfare. From the perspective of our interest in climate change, it is important to note that overwhelmingly these figures refer to climatic hazards, with 90 per cent of the deaths from that source. By way of contrast, conflict claimed 2.3 million lives over the same period – or 230,000 per year (Walter, 2001).

Disasters and Development

Disasters and the developing world

If we are going to tackle climate disasters we need to consider their underlying causes carefully. In doing so it is worth reminding ourselves that disasters interest us only because of their impacts on humanity or things we value. An extreme storm or heat wave is of little concern to us unless it impacts on humanity – apart of course from scientific interest in the natural phenomena. We also need to be aware of where the burden of loss falls, since this may provide additional insights into the causes of disaster and therefore potential avenues for improving the situation.

Most of the human impact of natural disasters is in the developing world. The following figures come from the International Federation of Red Cross and Red Crescent Societies (IFRC, 2001) and draw on their database of 2557 disasters from 1991 to 2000. They show the dramatic difference between rich and poor countries:

- HDCs (highly developed countries): 22.5 deaths per disaster;
- MDCs (countries with a medium level of development): 145 deaths per disaster (includes China and India);
- LDCs (least developed countries): 1052 deaths per disaster.

It has been conventional wisdom that while developing countries bear the brunt of human losses from natural disasters, developed countries suffered more economically. However, it appears that the poorer the country the greater the impact on the economy and on development progress:

- Honduras (Hurricane Mitch, 1998) = 75 per cent of GDP;
- Turkey (earthquake in 1999) = 7–9 per cent of GDP;
- United States (Hurricane Andrew, 1992) = < 1 per cent of GDP.

Hazards are clearly a vitally important issue for poor countries – even if they are not reflected in budgetary or public sector arrangements. It is to be expected that small countries would be much more affected by a single hazard event than a large country. However, this explains only part of the variation in impact set out above. Many developing countries find that their hopes for development are severely constrained by natural hazards. In some cases, the countries may also be constrained by internal conflict, weak institutions or other social or economic problems.

Why are 'natural' disasters increasing?

There is a widely held perception that there are now more climatic disasters because of the increasing number of climate extremes or severe events. For example, this appears to be the perception in Europe following a series of severe storms, floods and heat waves through the late 1980s and 1990s.

However, as mentioned above this is only part of the story. In fact, the evidence set out above concerning the global distribution of disaster losses suggests that even if there were now fewer climatic extremes we might be seeing increasing disaster losses. This is because social, economic and political factors – factors other than climate – are key to vulnerability and to ability to adapt. The factors that appear to be important explanations of why climatic disasters are increasing are listed here. This list ignores issues surrounding the information on disasters itself. Improved reporting of losses and awareness of all parts of the globe may be contributing to the apparent increase in disaster occurrence.

- *Increasing frequency of climatic extremes.* The evidence is ambiguous, but even if this is the case more climatic extremes do not by themselves result in disaster: climate events must interact with human activity or assets for a disaster to occur.
  But in addition our exposure and vulnerability are increasing because of the rest of the factors in this list.
- *Increase in world population.* Any given event affects more people. The evidence for increased population is incontrovertible.

- *Larger increase in poorer areas.* Most population increase is in poor countries that are disproportionately affected by climatic hazards. In addition, many newly occupied areas were previously vacant because they are hazardous. The disproportionate population increases in poor areas, in many cases with a strong increase in areas dependent on agriculture, exacerbate existing wealth inequities and may also increase susceptibility to climatic hazards. The evidence is strong.
- *Dispossession by war or civil strife.* Refugees and those driven into marginal areas are often the most dramatic examples of people vulnerable to the negative effects of natural events – people often completely cut off from their coping mechanisms and support networks. Of the world's (approximately) 191 countries, 96 are directly linked to uprooted populations, with people being forced to flee in some 60 countries (US Committee for Refugees, 2000).

  The key linkage with climate change here is the increase in vulnerability usually brought on by warfare. Reasons for this increase include an exodus of trained people, an absence of inward investment, disruption of social networks, destruction or abandonment of shelter, redirection of resources from social to military purposes, collapse of trade and commerce, lawlessness, and abandonment of subsistence farmlands due to fighting or landmines (see, for example, Levy and Sidel, 2000). In the recent wars in Bougainville and the Solomon Islands, major businesses and the education and health sectors were the first casualties, closely followed by the collapse of livelihoods for many of those driven out of the affected areas. The proliferation of weapons and minefields and the absence of basic health and education can ensure that the effects of war on vulnerability are long lasting. This is particularly the case where the affected area is off the global media radar.
- *Economic and social factors and rapid change.* Chronic corruption, aspects of economic 'structural adjustment programmes' and the changes accompanying the collapse of communism in Eastern Europe are examples of social factors that undermine people's capacity to cope with hazards. Many countries have serious corruption problems – that is corruption that inhibits development and people improving their lives and prospects. Corruption is by no means restricted to developing countries, but its impacts seem to be far worse in poorer countries.
- *The growth of urbanization.* Much of the hazards literature argues that large contemporary cities are incubators for disasters because of the concentration of people and activities in a confined space and the generation of new hazards (e.g. Mitchell, 1999). However, in many parts of the world – but less so in the world's poorer countries – this situation is balanced by the fact that cities contain massive resources to cope with hazards. In addition, the growth of cities may also be an adaptation against other forms of hazard, including lawlessness and climatic hazards such as drought. The overall situation is unclear, but cities are growing very rapidly and now contain about half of humanity. They are an important focus for future work on adaptation.
- *Economic globalization and gradual environmental degradation.* Again, both these trends may act to undermine the coping abilities of many people. These issues are put together here because of evidence that the factors are often linked. Economic globalization is seen as an unqualified good by almost all political leaders in the industrialized world. The essence of the argument is that through free trade, the

whole world will become much richer. However, many poorer countries and those working with poorer sections of society the world over reject this claim. Focusing on distributional issues, they cite as evidence the growing gulf between nations and between rich and poorer people in all countries. The implication is that the capacity of these poorer groups and countries to adapt to change is declining.

Evidence on these issues is complicated by the strong ideological commitment of both the supporters and detractors. The economies of the major trading nations appear to be benefiting, but much of the world's population is not. Even where per capita incomes in developing countries are rising there is little evidence that this is a direct result of contemporary economic globalization. EU development ministers, the World Bank and other organizations have recently pledged to address the increasing marginalization of least developed countries and the debt issue (Kabissa-Fahamu-Sangonet Newsletter, 2001). One argument is that the process of globalization as managed by the World Trade Organization (WTO), the World Bank, etc., will not benefit poorer countries because it was not designed to. The original proposal at the Bretton Woods meeting – which established the post-war global financial system – was to create a trade body with much broader powers intended to promote the development of poor areas and restrict corporate power, along the lines of the initial European Economic Community agreement. However, the result was the narrowly focused agencies we have today.

The linkages made with environmental degradation are various; for example, the use of environmentally damaging farming techniques for survival in both rural and urban areas (CEPAL and BID, 2000). The 2002 World Summit on Sustainable Development will focus on 'poverty, development and the environment', including trade and the environment, according to South Africa's Minister of Environmental Affairs. He cites the linkages between poverty, environmental degradation, water-borne diseases and the burden on women who bear the burden of daily scavenging for water and energy resources (Moosa, 2001). These are people for whom survival is an effort. Any further environmental degradation, or slight decrease in rainfall, would seriously increase their vulnerability to climatic hazards.

Adaptive Capacity Does Not Occur in Isolation

It should be clear that concentrating solely on specific measures to alleviate the impacts of climatic hazards or climate change is unlikely to address the causes of disaster – even though many such measures save lives. Adaptive capacity exists in most communities, but it is unlikely to have been developed solely for climate change. As we can see, promoting adaptive capacity to climate change may require attention to many areas of society, including areas normally seen as well outside the ambit of climate and hazards research and policy. We need to consider what is undermining adaptive capacity or making people more vulnerable. Without doing this we may be attempting to provide a solution to the wrong problem.

If it is thought that capacity to adapt to climate change should be promoted as a special programme separate from other areas of society, where should the necessary resources come from? Climate change is invisible, intangible and to many rather esoteric – except of course when it manifests or appears to manifest itself in extreme events that trigger disasters. Why should it receive priority over the many tangible, visible, immediate and urgent needs of the countries concerned, needs like national security, clean water, housing and employment?

Even when the question of priorities is set aside and external funds are available, success is not guaranteed – the measures must be seen as desirable and supported by those at risk or adaptive capacity may not increase. There is an important difference between having measures in place and success. Implementation of policy can be plagued with individual and organizational deviance, unintended consequences, legal problems, conflict with other social goals and expectations and changing political or administrative priorities. The same comments can be made about the actual process of measurement of success (Handmer, 2000).

How Can Natural Hazard Research and Policy Experience Support Adaptation?

Natural hazards research brings over 50 years of effort dedicated to working out how to deal best with the problem of climatic and other hazards. And most of this effort has been devoted to what is termed 'adaptation' in the climate change literature: much effort has focused on humans rather than on the geophysical phenomena. The field started as a branch of American geography in the human ecology tradition. One of its initial concerns was that despite very substantial investment in engineered structures flood losses were continuing to grow (White et al, 1975). Some might say that it was a reaction against a dominant type of 'specific' strategy, that of major flood control works.

Hazards research and policy recommendations in geography initially emphasized the need to consider all options, especially planning approaches, as well as individual choice in location. The evolution of the field's dominant view since the early 1950s is set out in Table 11.1. More detail on the evolution of thinking by the themes of main emphasis

Table 11.1 *Stages in the evolution of dominant thinking in hazards research*

1.	Individuals are economically rational. Hazards come from nature.
2.	Individuals act rationally given the limits of their knowledge and perception. Early 1960s on.
3.	Individuals act within constraints set by social and economic structures. Late 1970s on.
4.	Social groups organize to share and manage vulnerability to hazards. Hazards are from humans. From the early/mid-1980s.
5.	Vulnerability reduction and sustainable development are interlocking aims. From 1990 onward – set out in the IDNDR declaration.

of the research, construction of the problem, and the types of solutions recommended, are set out in Table 11.2. However, it is important to appreciate that the field is now very diverse, and attempts to capture its main themes will inevitably be inadequate. Please note that here I have followed convention within the hazards research field in which 'hazard' refers to the overall problem, in contrast to the emerging international agreement on the use of 'hazard' as simply the geophysical phenomenon and 'risk' as the whole problem (see, for example, EMA, 2000).

The five stages shown in Table 11.1 represent dominant thinking at the time indicated. As a general observation, each successive stage shows increased understanding of human and societal behaviour, and recognizes that humans have more control over disaster creation than previously acknowledged. Note that different strategies are pursued simultaneously by different groups, and today all five are used in policy.

What does the experience of 50 years of hazards research tell us? Tables 11.1 and 11.2 suggest a trend from specific adaptation toward generic-type measures – and this is certainly an important trend. In part this reflects recognition by many hazard researchers of the need to engage with the root causes of vulnerability and disaster. It also shows a realization that specific strategies require appropriate contexts (the 'generic' level) for success. The trends in approach to hazard research and management reflect a range of interests and concerns, some of them common to other public policy areas:

- seeking to put hazards research and practice in the mainstream (with sustainable development) and away from a marginal activity;
- seeking to deal with causes rather than the symptoms;
- looking for long-term solutions;
- recognizing the limits of individual choice and action; and
- balancing a long-standing emphasis on specific approaches that appear to have achieved only limited success in many circumstances.

Table 11.2 *Trends in hazards research*

From	To
Emphasis:	
Individual decision-making	Community vulnerability
Local	Local–global
Choice	Constraints/social structures
The hazard:	
Hazards as 'other'	Hazards are generated by us
Event driven	Situational and less visible creeping hazards included
Solutions:	
Reduce losses	Manage vulnerability or increase resilience
Solutions as separate	Solutions found in organization of society and the development process

As a general statement we can say that among hazards researchers in the social and policy sciences, adaptation to hazards and sustainable development are now seen as interlocking aims (Mileti, 1999). The 10-year follow-up on the first UN conference on Environment and Development, planned for late 2002 in Johannesburg, has made disaster reduction one of its central themes. In summary, today natural hazards management is largely about being resilient in the face of uncertainty – a description that might well apply to the concept of adaptive capacity for climate change.

Now I would like to briefly examine generic and specific approaches to adaptation in the context of hazards research, taking the generic approach first.

Generic approaches in hazards research

Much of the recent hazards research and advocacy – that is, literature advocating that efforts be devoted to dealing with hazards – promote the generic approach. Generic approaches generate the wealth, expertise and other conditions needed for implementation of specific strategies such as building regulations. They generally assume effective government and can be expensive. But whatever the difficulties, an overwhelming advantage of generic approaches is that they serve other and often multiple social goals. They are not limited to serving the goal of reduction or management of a specific hazard – important though this might be to those in the field it is rarely a high priority in poor countries. Even when climate is not part of the rationale for generic approaches, they may still reduce the risk by diversifying economies and improving livelihood security by reducing dependence on agriculture or fisheries, and by increasing wealth, so climate change and climatic hazards impact directly on a declining percentage of GDP. Agriculture by definition is highly susceptible to climatic conditions and hazards. In most wealthy countries it is either highly subsidized or compensation and welfare provisions exist – in contrast to poorer countries. Generic measures may also increase resilience to all climatic hazards through improved building, planning and infrastructure, and by increasing or establishing access to resources in a crisis.

A brief overview of some key statements and literature on hazards management in developing countries reinforces the assertion above about the dominance of generic approaches. The development literature on hazards and disasters overwhelmingly supports a generic approach with the emphasis on vulnerability reduction through the development process. For example, the Inter-American Development Bank (CEPAL and BID, 2000) states that 'disasters are clearly a development problem'. The arrangements for the IDNDR specified that by the end of the 1990s all countries would have disaster reduction plans and activities in place as part of their plans for sustainable development. The follow-up to the IDNDR, the International Strategy for Disaster Reduction (ISDR), makes the link between disasters and sustainable development in its 1999 Declaration of Intent. It emphasizes the need to reduce vulnerability, to safeguard 'natural and economic resources, and ... social wellbeing and livelihoods' (UN/ISDR, 1999). This theme will be taken up at the 2002 World Summit on Sustainable Development where disasters will be on the agenda. In its *World Disasters Report 2001,* the IFRC takes a similar line: '... disasters become ever more frequent, aid dollars and development gains are being washed away. ... disaster is no longer a brief dip on the curve of development but a danger to the [development] process itself' (IFRC, 2001, p1).

The academic literature on the topic generally takes as its reference point the late Fred Cuny's *Disasters and Development* (1983), with its emphasis on broad development issues.

The links between disasters and development, particularly sustainable development, are not confined to developing countries. The theme of the summary report of the US second assessment (Mileti, 1999) of natural hazards emphasizes generic issues and in particular the integration of hazard management with sustainable development.

Specific approaches in hazards research

To turn to specific approaches – hazards research traditionally has focused on these strategies, although there have always been other voices. They have saved many lives and inestimable amounts of property damage. Some success stories include shelters designed to provide safe havens from sea flooding have saved thousands in Orissa, India (Sparrow, 2001); cyclone warning systems in the Pacific provide timely warnings to poor small island countries; and thousands of flood-resistant houses provide protection in Vietnam (Jaquemet, 2001) and many other rich and poor countries. Major levee or dyke systems protect the populations of many countries against sea and river flooding. The Netherlands may present the extreme case, where dykes keep the sea out and allow the nation to flourish. However, the situation is not simple because appropriate institutional arrangements and governance are needed for large-scale specific measures.

Opportunities for specific approaches present themselves:

- immediately following a disaster when these measures have high priority;
- where there are climate and hazards organizations whose mission includes the use of specific tools;
- when local people demand action in the face of perceived risks; and
- when the institutional context would enable and support low-cost measures such as minor changes to building techniques that can often result in large improvements, and locally based warning systems, which are an underused, low-cost measure.

Important constraints are that:

- the measures are often given low priority by governments – and by the people themselves, so those at risk must be involved and must support the measure;
- they divert scarce resources from other urgent priorities;
- the measures may not be dealing with underlying causes; and
- occasionally they may make the situation worse.

What Do the People Think?

The material set out so far reviews the experience of senior policymakers and the conclusions of the bulk of published researchers. This material is typical in that most of the international literature on development is produced by aid donors, their consultants or academics, mostly from Europe or North America. But what about the opinions of those at risk – the people that all this work and effort is dedicated to helping? They are rarely consulted in a way in which their views might have some influence over the shape of work to reduce vulnerability. (A report by the IIED (2001b) provides some insight into this issue and the views of the urban poor in developing countries.)

Katrina Allen, a PhD student at Middlesex University, undertook a major village-level study in the Philippines on vulnerability to flooding (2000, 'Vulnerability to flooding in the Philippines', unpublished paper, Flood Hazard Research Centre, Middlesex University, London). To put it simply, she enquired into the approaches to vulnerability reduction preferred by a major non-governmental organization (NGO) and government agencies on one hand, and the preferences of those at risk on the other.

The NGO and government agencies adopted the specific approaches of building sea walls and sponsoring counter-disaster training. But those at risk saw the generic or macro issue of livelihood security as key to their resilience. Interestingly, livelihood security was often related to household structure and to having household members sending money gained from employment in a metropolitan area or overseas. Such external income sources continue to flow regardless of local climate disasters and in this way enhance resilience and adaptive capacity. Active kinship networks appear to be more important than community networks in this context.

But is the difference between the NGOs and local people as large as it seems? In general, the two approaches are probably intertwined, with many specific approaches depending on the right generic or macro conditions for their success.

Is There a Third Way?

Sometimes neither generic nor specific approaches appear to improve adaptation capacity or local resilience.

In some Pacific island countries disaster management has had limited success with institutional strengthening, generic approaches, the application of geospatial information or more specific measures. Reasons for failure vary across the region. They include violence, weak and ineffective governments, corruption, illiteracy, inappropriate technologies and failure to appreciate cultural issues. Cultural issues mitigating against change include the enormous influence of 'tradition', as interpreted by those in positions of power, the importance of village power structures and the general absence of women from formal power structures in many countries even though they may be responsible for the domestic economy, including food production and associated specific enterprises such as selling produce. Strong reciprocal obligations among people from the same areas – the *wantok* system of Papua New Guinea, the Solomon Islands and elsewhere – help people cope with climatic and other disasters. However, the rigidity of the system and its imperative of sharing wealth and resources can also inhibit social and economic change as defined by aid donors and the expectations of a capitalist system (see also Chapter 3 of Robertson and Sutherland, 2001).

Under such circumstances a focus on achieving improved resilience by working through governments typically fails regardless of whether generic or specific measures are involved. An appealing solution may be to work on correcting the obvious shortcomings of government. But, this has proved difficult in the circumstances outlined at the beginning of this section. In addition, governments may have different priorities for legitimate reasons – as outlined earlier in this chapter.

Is there another way? A focus on the village or community level may be the only possibility in such cases.

The Australian Landcare programme provides an interesting example of this approach. I am not suggesting that the programme could be directly transferred to other countries – simply that it is an interesting approach. The official websites (e.g. www.landcareaustralia.com.au) state that Landcare is a high-profile movement or network of people in Australia who are committed to sustainable management and use of natural resources. Landcare has been about social change, a change in the ideas and practices of people who work on and care about the land. The driving logic is that the other approaches tried by government did not deliver the desired sustainable outcomes. Today there are almost 5000 Landcare groups working in communities throughout Australia. Groups consist of local landowners and others with an interest in the land or a local problem. The groups are generally supported by facilitators and coordinators funded by government and may apply for project grants. Many groups attract commercial sponsorship. Despite its apparent success, Landcare has attracted intense debate and criticism (see, for example, Curtis et al, 2000).

Whatever is said about the national framework and about the degree of inclusiveness, governments abrogating their responsibilities and tangible achievements on the ground, the Landcare programme is also about a process for local people to identify their problems and develop locally appropriate solutions. The programme recognizes that valuable local resources and expertise exist which with support can deal with many local problems. It is the recognition of the value of local resources and process elements, in addition to the approach's ability to harness informal networks, that may be relevant for some developing countries. The Landcare programme is coordinated and supported by government, but other groups could be substituted for government where appropriate.

Where adaptation is concerned, a community- or village-based approach is where those at risk are helped through a deliberative process to decide what (adaptation) actions are appropriate. This help would generally take the form of assistance with the decision process including any necessary technical advice. The local groups would then receive support so that they can implement their decisions. Ultimately, the process would build local support and capacity for adaptation. Possibilities include local warning systems and emergency preparedness, improved building practices and livelihood strategies. Another approach, based on similar principles of local organization and action, is set out in a briefing paper by the International Institute for Environment and Development (IIED, 2001a).

Conclusions

Disasters frequently demonstrate the importance of climate events. This is the case particularly for the least developed countries, which bear the brunt of human losses and are also most likely to see economic progress reversed by climatic disasters. Governments and communities around the world face many challenges of which climate change is only one, and rarely one that rates a high priority in a context of a daily struggle for survival by half the world's population, and the imperatives of trade, security, health and so on.

It is hardly surprising therefore that most countries could be much better adapted to the *existing* natural hazards regime – and fall far short of dealing seriously with future climate change. There are many individual examples where future climate has been incorporated into design and policy, but these are of an ad hoc nature and rarely extend to poorer countries.

The low priority and status of climate change in policy means that most specific or micro adaptation is likely to be an extension of existing natural hazard management. It is unlikely that new programmes for climate change would be implemented successfully unless they ran in parallel with other high-priority issues. But generic programmes with their multiple aims might be possible.

The research and policy experience of the natural hazards field has much to offer the search for adaptation to climate change as the problems are very similar. Research suggestions are set out in Table 11.3.

Table 11.3 *Research suggestions*

- Spend time defining the problem – to avoid providing the right answer to the wrong problem. If the real problem is weak governance, war or corruption, then that needs to be considered and addressed – or a way found to avoid these impediments.
- Ways of ensuring synergism between specific and generic approaches are needed.
- Related to both of the above issues is the issue of how to improve the management capacity of households, communities and governments so that they are better able to cope with climatic hazards.
- Climate change concerns need to be mainstreamed, e.g. with sustainable development issues.
- Indicators of adaptation and of resilience need to be developed.
- What to do where both generic and specific approaches fail? Should a village-level approach be developed?
- Processes are needed to ensure that the informal, the traditional and local are part of adaptation strategies. (I appreciate that 'traditional' is always the subject of debate and often invented for commercial or political reasons.)
- The role of rapidly expanding cities in adaptation should be examined and opportunities harnessed.
- What should the role of the private sector be?

Much of the hazards and development literature, and development and humanitarian aid groups now emphasize approaches to hazards management which focus on causes rather than symptomatic treatment of the problem. However, there appears to be a near symbiotic relationship between these generic development strategies and specific approaches aimed at alleviating identified hazards, suggesting that both are needed to reduce vulnerability to climatic hazards. Despite their costs and other problems, generic approaches can be seen as 'no-regrets' strategies. In other words, they are generally worth putting in place even if their effectiveness against hazards is uncertain, provided they have other potential benefits. These benefits normally take the form of improvements in, for example, health, education, housing quality or livelihood security.

However, sometimes neither generic nor specific approaches seem effective, often because of the inability to create an adequate institutional framework. In such circumstances, a 'village'-level approach should be developed because this may be the only effective way forward.

An important outstanding issue concerns the assessment of progress in adaptation. We need to be able to say with some authority whether or not adaptation is occurring, and how effective it is. The basis of these assessments needs to be clear. The best way to proceed may be through the development of indicators of adaptation.

Acknowledgements

My appreciation goes to Richard Klein and Joel Smith for organizing the Potsdam Workshop and for inviting me to participate. Thanks also to Cassia Read for research assistance during the preparation of this chapter.

References

CEPAL and BID (Economic Commission for Latin America and the Caribbean and Inter-American Development Bank) (2000), *A Matter of Development: How to Reduce Vulnerability in the Face of Natural Disasters*. CEPAL, Mexico.

Cuny, F. C. (1983), *Disasters and Development*. Oxford University Press, New York.

Curtis, A., van Nouhuys, M., Robinson, W. and Mackay, J. (2000), Exploring landcare effectiveness using organizational theory. *Australian Geographer* 31, 349–366.

EMA (2000), *Emergency Risk Management Applications Guide*, Emergency Management in Australia, Canberra.

Handmer, J. (2000), Are flood warnings futile? *Australasian Journal of Disaster and Trauma Studies*, www.massey.ac.nz/~trauma/ (Journal issue: 2000-2).

IFRC (2001), *World Disasters Report 2001*. International Federation of Red Cross and Red Crescent Societies, Geneva.

IIED (2001a), Deep Democracy: Transforming Opportunities for the Urban Poor. Environment and Urbanisation Brief 4. International Institute for Environment and Development, London.

IIED (2001b), Rethinking Aid to Urban Poverty Reduction: Lessons for Donors. Environment and Urbanisation Brief 3. International Institute for Environment and Development, London.

Jaquemet, I. (2001), Post-flood recovery in Viet Nam. Chapter 5 in *World Disasters Report 2001.* International Federation of Red Cross and Red Crescent Societies, Geneva.

Kabissa-Fahamu-Sangonet Newsletter (2001), Pambazuka News. 43, 22/11/01. www.pambazuka.org/en/issue/43

Levy, B. S. and Sidel, V. W. (2000), *War and Public Health.* American Public Health Association, Washington, DC.

Mileti, D. (1999), *Disasters by Design: A Reassessment of Natural Hazards in the United States.* Joseph Henry Press, Washington, DC.

Mitchell, J. K., ed. (1999), *Crucibles of Hazards: Megacities and Disasters in Transition.* UN University Press, Tokyo.

Moosa, M. V. (2001), Johannesburg 2002 must be about people, planet and prosperity. In *Environment Matters at the World Bank.* The World Bank, Washington, DC, 4–5.

Munich Re (2001), www.munichre.com/index.html.

Robertson, R. and Sutherland, W. (2001), *Government by the Gun: The Unfinished Business of Fiji's 2000 Coup.* Pluto Press, Annandale, Australia.

Sparrow J, (2001), Relief, recovery and root causes. Chapter 1 in *World Disasters Report 2001.* International Federation of Red Cross and Red Crescent Societies, Geneva.

UNDP (2001), Human development: past, present and future. Chapter 1 in *Human Development Report 2001.* UN Development Programme, New York.

UN/ISDR (1999), International Strategy for Disaster Reduction, 1998 Declaration of Intent. www.unisdr.org/eng/about_isdr/bd-geneva-mandate-eng.htm

US Committee for Refugees (2000), *World Refugee Survey 2000.* US Committee for Refugees, Washington, DC.

Walter, J. (2001), Disaster data: key trends and statistics. Chapter 8 in *IFRC World Disasters Report 2001.* International Federation of Red Cross and Red Crescent Societies. www.ifrc.org/publicat/wdr2001/chapter8.asp

White, G. F. (1975), *Flood Hazard in the United States: A Research Assessment.* Institute of Behavioral Science, University of Colorado, Boulder, USA.

A Climate Risk Management Approach to Disaster Reduction and Adaptation to Climate Change

United Nations Development Programme

Risk Management and Adaptation to Climate Change

In 2000, the United Nations convened the Millennium Summit, where the heads of state of more than 100 countries agreed on the broad development goals for the next 15 years. The Millennium Development Goals define eight major objectives that the world community should strive to attain by 2015. These goals have a direct relationship with improving overall human welfare, health, education and environmental sustainability, particularly in the world's poorest countries. As such, the Millennium Development Goals seek to reduce the vulnerability of the worlds poor by improving their income, education, health and environment.

Achievement of these goals is difficult, if not impossible, if integral human security and sustainability are not enhanced and guaranteed. Disaster risk levels and losses in society have shown such progressive growth over the last 40 years that they now comprise a serious threat to sustainability and development. A very significant part of this loss is associated with hydrometeorological events, and this is so both in developed and developing world contexts. Current trends and the constant introduction of new risk factors suggest ever-increasing losses in the future if deliberate, coordinated and conscientious action is not taken in the short and medium terms.

Disaster risk, or the probability of future loss and damage associated with the impact of external physical events, is socially constructed in contexts where hazards interact with exposed and vulnerable communities or societies. The very notion of hazard remits to the socially induced transformation of physical elements and resources into dangerous or potentially dangerous phenomena. This transformation is achieved when population, infrastructure and production are located in hazard-prone areas and live or exist under vulnerable conditions. Vulnerability is a socially constructed condition implying lack of resilience and fortitude when faced with environmental extremes. This lack of resilience may be manifested at the structural, physical, economic, social, and political and institutional levels.

Determined levels of risk associated with extreme physical phenomena are inherent to human existence on planet Earth. The history of human endeavour and societal advance is in many ways the history of adaptation to our physical environment. The positive utilization of the natural resource base has always been accompanied by periodic loss associated with the natural flux of nature from benign to extreme conditions. Resources and hazards are in fact part of the same equation and continuum. Managing this continuum has guaranteed, during long periods of time, that the balance of gain and loss has essentially been positive.

However, during the last 200 years in particular this 'natural' equilibrium has been rapidly lost or eroded. The inherent risk associated with life on an unstable and still evolving planet has been compounded with what could be called 'excess' or 'surplus' risk. That is to say, potential loss associated with the creation or generation of new socially induced and spurious risk factors, whether on the hazard or vulnerability side of the equation. Many of these new factors derive from inadequate development practices, the inadequate location of human endeavour, the accelerating processes of environmental degradation, the introduction of potentially dangerous new technologies and the impacts and consequences of poverty and destitution.

Environmental insecurity and the threat of extreme disaster loss or damage increasingly add to the human insecurity associated with the disadvantaged social condition and position of billions of people, particularly in the developing world. The rapid increase in risk factors that followed the advent of the Industrial Revolution now promises to enter into a new progressive if not, abrupt phase. Global climatic change associated with the emission of greenhouse gases promises to introduce new risk factors that build on existing risks associated with normal climatic variability and extremes. The magnitude of these risk factors, their social and territorial distribution and impact, their temporality and overall consequences are as yet subject to speculation.

Global climate change is caused by an intricate chain of micro and macro processes, forcing us to distinguish truly global transformations in atmospheric, biosphere and human systems with what are pervasive worldwide environmental problems and hazards. Meshed with the problems of scale (what to include) are the problems of complexity (how to account for it), which pose formidable challenges for modelling, predicting and monitoring environmental change. Uncertainty is a dominant concern, but few now deny that the rate of advent of new climatic patterns and the hazards (and benefits) associated with these will be unprecedented in human history. Concatenation and synergy will increase the problems associated with hazards leading to new and as yet unexperienced types and levels of loss.

Managing risk will inevitably become a major societal concern going way beyond past and existing preoccupations associated with inherent and excess risk. Current trends and forecasts would suggest that the social distribution of risk and loss could become one of the dominating concerns of humanity in the future. Now is the time to begin to redress the current situation in which insufficient concern is paid to such matters and existing management and societal schemes are extremely unarticulated, dispersed and inefficient when faced with the magnitude and importance of the problem of risk and disaster. Short-term attention to existing and recurrent problems must be complemented with, and seen in the light of medium- and long-term changes and impacts. Temporal, spatial and institutional integration must be promoted in order to take due account of the challenges associated with the management of societal risk in general, and disaster and climate change risk in particular.

Risk and risk management must be placed squarely in the centre of the equation, and notions of disaster displaced from the still dominant concern and action in favour of preparedness and response in favour of proactive and prospective risk reduction and control. This must be achieved guaranteeing a close, synergic and interactive relationship between existing risk management, climate adaptation and sustainable development practitioners.

Climate-Related Disaster Loss and Unsustainable Development

Although disasters are associated with a wide range of hazard types, hydrometeorological phenomena account for a very significant part of disaster loss each year. Hurricanes, flooding, drought, hail storms and storm-driven wave action account for over 70 per cent of economic loss, again with a far higher relative incidence in the developing countries. By far the most damaging of natural hazards are floods, which account for 40 per cent of all deaths in disaster events. It is estimated that half of humanity (3 billion) now lives in coastal areas or near rivers.

With regard to climate change, it is estimated that 14 of the 20 hottest years on record during the 20th century occurred between 1980 and 2000, and the hottest year to date was 1998. This same year also broke records in the cost of destruction and disruption caused by disaster, with some US$98 billion in damages and 32,000 casualties due to climatic phenomena, a 50 per cent difference as compared to the previous year.

Overall, disaster occurrences and losses associated with extreme and increasingly not so extreme climatic events have increased dramatically in recent years and particularly

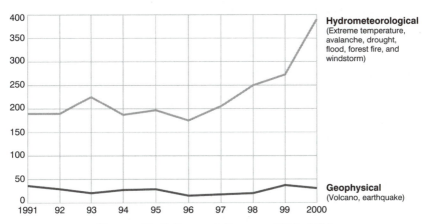

Figure 12.1 *Reported disasters, 1991–2000*

Source: Center for Research on the Epidemology of Disasters
Note: Includes all natural disasters declared by national authorities in OECD and non-OECD countries, regardless of their severity.

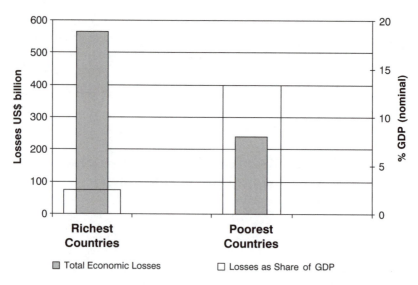

Figure 12.2 *Disaster losses, total and as share of GDP, 1985–1999*

since 1996. While the number of reported disasters associated with geophysical events such as volcanic eruptions and earthquakes remained remarkably constant, those associated with hydrometeorological events such as floods, drought, forest fires and storms have demonstrated a curve of exponential growth. The number of reported hydrometeorological disasters in 2001 was approximately double the figure reported in 1996. Hypothesis and speculation are inevitable with regard to the possible links between increased disaster loss, temperature rises and climate change.

Seen from the perspective of economic impact, in constant monetary terms, the losses during disasters throughout the world during the 1990s were *nine times* superior to those sustained during the 1960s and *six* times superior to those during the 1970s. This can be explained in terms of the increased exposure of population, infrastructure and production, increases in the value of assets and increases in human vulnerability to hazard events.

Although economic losses tend to be higher in absolute terms in the developed countries, the overall impact of disaster events is far higher in developing countries where over 90 per cent of human losses occur in any one year. The small island developing states of the Pacific, Indian Ocean and Caribbean are particularly hard hit due to the very small size of their economies and the highly vulnerable nature of their economic base.

However, even developed countries have over the last decade suffered increased impacts from disasters, with enormous losses to national economies and the insurance and reinsurance business. Speculation now exists as to changing patterns of risk with greater threats to these countries in the future.

The levels of loss are now so great that some see the development process as a 'loss factory' where gains are constantly drained off at the bottom. The burgeoning levels of loss are beginning to outweigh development gains in a number of countries and as such are fast becoming unsustainable. This is particularly the case in the small island developing states (SIDS). On the other side of the equation, it is now very clear that flawed development and environmental practices are at the root of much new disaster risk.

Risk and Disaster: The Basic Causes

Disasters actualize existing risk conditions. Hazards serve as detonators of pre-existing risk conditions revealing errors in the location of human activities and existing levels of social, economic and ecological vulnerability. Today, faced with the inevitability of many natural phenomena, the major bent in terms of explaining disasters and disaster loss favours the analysis of social vulnerability. Thus, although natural phenomena must be understood in terms of their physical attributes, magnitude and recurrence in order to provide information for risk managers and the population in general, it is human vulnerability, location and lack of resilience that are at the centre of the explanation of many large-scale disasters. And, it is these factors that must be considered and modified in order to decrease disaster risk and incidence in the future.

Despite the dominance of large-scale or extreme natural phenomena as detonators of current-day disasters, no disaster is in a scientific and real sense, 'natural'. Moreover, many hazards associated with increasing levels of loss are also not natural. Thus, whereas natural phenomena are transformed into hazards by human actions that expose population to their effects (they are socially constructed) and lead to social vulnerability, human intervention and action also creates new hazards.

Much has been written and is known as regards what are called technological, social or anthropogenic hazards. Conflagrations, explosions, oil spills, nuclear accidents and even terrorist activities are some of the many expressions of inadequately managed technology, human activity and social dissent. Natural hazards interfacing or interacting with technological or anthropogenic hazards many times lead to concatenation and synergy and new types, forms and extent of disaster loss.

Between the natural and anthropogenic hazards there exists a third major category of hazard type which as yet has received little attention, but which effectively establishes one point of convergence between the risk and disaster and the adaptation to climate problematic. Here we refer to what have been called socio or pseudo natural hazards. This notion refers to hazards that are created at the interface between human activity and natural or modified ecosystems. Examples may be found in the increased threat and potential for flooding, drought and landslides associated with river basin degradation and deforestation, the potential for coastal erosion associated with the wide-scale destruction of mangrove swamps and with urban flooding patterns that relate to the lack of adequate pluvial drainage systems in cities. Many other examples may be found including the threats for downstream populations and economic activity associated with large dams and reservoirs. This type of human intervention is also increasing the hazardous character of truly natural hazards and extending their impact to new areas.

Socio-natural hazards are ever on the increase and associated with much small- and medium-scale loss and damage that is rarely registered in the disaster loss databases maintained by the international organizations. Increasing evidence exists to suggest that the accumulated impact of small- and medium-scale disasters is equivalent to or exceeds large-scale disaster impacts. These types of event are recurrent and their impacts are mostly felt at the local or community levels. With the scaling up of their multiple and diverse effects, the sum of many local impacts may be transformed into regional or even national impacts.

Whatever the types of hazards that help explain disasters, mainstream thought now places the risk and disaster problematic firmly in the development debate and concern. Sustainability of development in developing countries, in particular, is increasingly seen to be impossible without increased and sustained levels of security for humans and their endeavours and natural ecosystems.

Risk is seen as a product of differing processes of social and economic transformation that many times are euphemistically referred to as 'development'. Therefore, any major move in favour of risk reduction and control must be conceived within the framework of the development and project planning processes. Risk and disaster do not exist as separate and autonomous conditions but are intimately related to ongoing social processes and must be dealt with in this context if any major advances are to be achieved. Skewed processes of social and territorial development are generating increasingly complex and intractable patterns of disaster risk, particularly in developing countries.

Although vulnerability, lack of social resilience and reduced levels of adaptation to environment are not defining characteristics of poverty per se, there can be no doubt that poverty is a major factor in explaining these, and their particular social and territorial distribution. Disaster risk is but one component of the risk faced by society. But, disaster risk is many times constructed on the basis of everyday or life-style risk typified by conditions of malnutrition, ill health, unemployment, lack of income, social and family violence, drug addiction and alcoholism, lack of education and opportunity etc. Dealing with existing disaster risk inevitably requires dealing with everyday risk. Social, community and human resilience in general are indispensable for reduction and control of disaster risk in the future. Reducing vulnerability means enhancing resilience and adaptation. Reduction of vulnerability requires development and increased resilience and sustainability cannot be achieved without this.

Global Change, Complexity and Uncertainty

Processes of global change are adding new and even more intractable dimensions to the problems of risk accumulation and disaster occurrence and loss, associated with climatic events. Global change encompasses both socio-economic and environmental processes, and the links between them.

The globalization of local, national, sub-regional and regional economies over recent decades has increased the complexity of risk in spatial, temporal and semantic terms, continuously forging and reproducing new and as yet unpredictable patterns of risk at the social and territorial levels.

Due to global change, rapid and turbulent changes in risk patterns in a given region are rarely autonomously generated and may, in numerous cases, be caused by economic decisions taken on the other side of the globe. This territorial complexity and concatenation of causal factors extends down to include the impacts of national sectoral and territorial development policies on regions and localities.

The impacts of globalization are being felt in both rural and urban areas. Urban areas often concentrate a complex interplay of multiple hazards and vulnerabilities with synergic effects and a very heterogeneous social and locational distribution. Rural areas in the developing world suffer diverse processes of incorporation and exclusion with differential impacts in terms of vulnerability and risk.

The accumulation of greenhouse gases in the atmosphere and resulting changes in the world's climate is a second global process that is increasing the complexity of risk. The scientific evidence that climate is changing due to greenhouse gas emissions is now incontestable. At the same time, it is equally well accepted that climate change will alter the severity, frequency and spatial distribution of climate-related hazards. However, even while modelling of the linkages between global climate change and particular climate events becomes increasingly sophisticated, it is still not possible to predict with any degree of confidence how particular climate events, in specific locations will behave in the future. Even with regular climatic variability associated with phenomenon like the El Niño-Southern Oscillation (ENSO), important changes in types and areas of impact occur from event to event leading to imprecision in alert systems and preventive actions.

The notion of socio-natural hazards discussed above has generally been limited to the consideration of lower-scale phenomena and local impacts. However, the notion establishes a natural bridge between current-day disaster concerns and the problem of global climatic change. The hazards now being experienced, or to be expected in the future with global climatic change are essentially socio-natural in origin, product of the relationship between human activities and the natural atmospheric system. Scale determinations and considerations may differ between the normal range of socio-natural hazards and those associated with global climatic change, ranging from local to global, but the two types of concern have more in common than differences. Reversion or control of the hazard construction process is possible in both cases. And, despite the global nature of climate change, its impacts will in the end be felt locally or regionally, and interaction will occur with existing hazard patterns, the product of more localized socio-natural processes.

Humans have been adapting to changing climatic conditions and to the impact of extreme climate events ever since their appearance on the planet. Much of this adaptation occurred gradually and spontaneously, and the economies of many traditional societies to this day still depend on sophisticated production and social systems adapted to manage climate risk and variability. Much natural-resource-based development over centuries has depended on constant adaptation to changing environmental conditions.

The rapid accumulation of climate-related risk in recent decades and the resulting patterns of loss, however, point to a loss of effectiveness and even breakdown in spontaneous adaptation and coping. As the range of hazards and vulnerabilities faced by any given community increases, it often becomes possible only to play one kind of risk off against another in search of a 'less bad' scenario. Many highly vulnerable communities may deliberately choose to inhabit a hazard-prone environment if this reduces other risks, related to income generation for example. Or, should they find themselves in hazard-prone zones due to exclusion from formal land markets or for other reasons, they will many times opt to stay in order to maintain those conditions that provide them with the means to reduce daily-life risk and vulnerability. On the other hand, factors such as poverty, limits to migration, land tenure systems, migration between ecologically distinct areas and a continuous reduction in terms of knowledge of ecosystems, inevitably place barriers to spontaneous adaptation.

The processes of global change mentioned above have stacked the odds even higher against successful adaptation. As the causal processes of risk become increasingly global, the options available to local communities and other local stakeholders to influence risk generation processes becomes restricted, or non-existent. At the same time, the growing complexity of risk, due to both economic globalization as well as to global climate change, greatly reduces the predictability and increases the uncertainty surrounding the occurrence of particular climate-related disaster events: be they the rapid impact of floods, landslides, forest fires or hurricanes in given locations or the obsolescence of productive systems through changing climatic or market conditions.

In other words, the evidence from patterns of disaster occurrence and loss shows that climate-related risks are rapidly increasing, which in turn indicates the growing failure of and breakdown of adaptation at all levels. The growing complexity and globalization of climate-related risk translates at the national and local levels into impotence to affect the causal processes of risk, and increasing uncertainty regarding the nature of risk itself and what could be viable strategies to manage and reduce it. Moreover, disaster risk becomes for the poor an unheeded notion when faced with more pervasive everyday risk conditions associated with ill health, malnutrition, illiteracy, unemployment, drug addiction, and family and social violence.

Risk Management: Differing Entrances, the Same Problem

Faced with the bleak scenario of increasing disaster risk and loss, different approaches to manage and reduce climate-related risks have been sought or attempted by the humanitarian or disaster response, development, environmental and climate change communities.

Disaster response, development and environmental institutional approaches

Since the 1970s the national and international organizations responsible for responding to disaster events and for providing humanitarian assistance, have been gradually expanding their approach to address first hazards, then vulnerabilities, and eventually risks themselves. From their beginnings in response, many disaster-related organizations have moved on to strengthen capacities in preparedness and early warning (enabling the conjunctural mitigation of losses associated with extreme climate events); reduce hazard levels, through structural measures such as flood control embankments, soil conservation measures and others; reduce vulnerabilities through strengthening community- and national-level capacities and resilience, and eventually to address integrated disaster risk management, in which a range of measures are designed to address the full range of hazards and vulnerabilities present in a given location.

However, despite the UN International Decade for Natural Disaster Reduction (IDNDR) in the 1990s, in which member states with the support of international organizations were supposed to make a concerted effort to reduce disaster risk, risks have continued to accumulate and increase, while most national and international efforts directed by humanitarian and response-oriented institutions continue to be fundamentally preparedness and response focused. A large number of successful experiences, however, in Asia, Latin America, the Caribbean and Africa, in which different risk management approaches were piloted, have built up a substantial body of knowledge on the theory and practice of risk management. These successful pilot approaches provide a glimpse into the future of risk management, if they were to be mainstreamed and applied as part of a concerted and integrated programme.

For its part, the risk-conscious development community has attempted to promote more integrated schemes where risk considerations are factored into development planning and projects. Despite the fundamental importance of such approaches, they are not as yet a common or regular practice. At the same time few deny the fact that it is with a greater involvement of development-based institutions that risk reduction can become more effective. Attempts to add risk reduction concerns on to existing traditional response-oriented organizations faces enormous difficulties and limitations and a need exists to break out of traditional schemes and construct risk reduction endeavours on the basis of development-oriented organizations and institutions.

Finally, the environmental community has increasingly seen the relevance of environmental management and good resource use for hazard control and reduction. This has been particularly apparent over the last five years and has been stimulated by the impacts of large-scale events during this period, which clearly revealed the relationship between environmental degradation and hazard occurrence. This is the case with large-scale disasters in Central America, the Caribbean, Venezuela, Mozambique, China and Indonesia between 1998 and the present, particularly associated with flooding and landslides. The discussion on win–win and no-regret policies now much in vogue are part of this packet. Equilibrium and resilience of ecosystems offers natural protection from natural hazards and reduces the likelihood of new hazards generated by processes of environmental degradation.

The climate change adaptation approach

Scientists and organizations examining the problem of global climate change have gradually expanded their approach from an initial concern with the causes of climate change, through a concern with modelling its potential effects, for example in terms of sea-level rise and desertification, towards a concern with how societies and economies can adapt to changing climatic conditions.

Greenhouse gas emissions and their potential effect on world climate has been the subject of research and debate for over 20 years. Major movements forward in the search to limit this phenomenon date primarily from the Earth Summit in Rio in 1992, with the signing of the UN Framework Convention on Climate Change (UNFCCC). In programme terms, this led to international efforts, through the UNFCCC, to mitigate climate change through international agreements to reduce green house gas emissions. The Kyoto Protocol in 1997 and the establishment of stipulated reduction levels over the next decade was the most important of these agreements and recent negotiations have centred essentially on the debate of common but differentiated responsibilities for climate change, and intractable discussions surrounding the Clean Development Mechanism.

On the other hand, the climate change arena – broadly speaking, the UNFCCC and the Intergovernmental Panel on Climate Change (IPCC) frameworks, and the array of research and advocacy entities that interact with these – has tended to identify increased human vulnerability to climate extremes as a likely outcome of climate change. As such, it has advised and undertaken research on vulnerability, produced an array of vulnerability assessments and to a lesser extent, advised and undertaken assessments of climate change adaptation.

Despite the search to limit the rate of climatic change and, in consequence, the hazards it will suppose for different regions and population groups, the inevitability of change has increasingly been recognized. Already accumulated emissions will guarantee this change and this is now unavoidable. Reductions in emissions over the next years cannot be achieved at a rate that is sufficient to greatly ameliorate change. In recognition of this fact, increasing attention has been given over the last five years in particular to the need to foment and support initiatives that promote or enhance the adaptation capacities of the population in affected regions and areas. By and large, however, actors in this arena have yet to make concrete and specific recommendations for *how* adaptation ought to be undertaken, nor to engage in actual responses to the specific instances of human vulnerability, although the issue of adaptation to the effects of climate change was first contemplated by the first Conference of the Parties (COP-1) in 1995 in the following three stage process:

Stage I: Inventory and planning, including studies on the possible impact of climate change, the identification of countries or regions particularly vulnerable and defining the policy options to guide adaptation measures and increase capacity building.

Stage II: Measures, which include continuing capacity building to lead the adaptation process in those countries most vulnerable to climate change, as defined in Article 4.1 (e) of the Framework Convention.

Stage III: Measures to facilitate the adequate adaptation of other countries, including insurance and other measures contemplated in Articles 4.1 (b) and 4.4 of the Framework Convention.

In its last COP-7 in Marrakesh, the Climate Change Convention parties agreed on guidelines to orient adaptation strategies to climate change in those regions and countries most likely to be affected. This movement was consolidated with the results of the meeting where commitment to expanded funding for the development of adaptation strategies was agreed through the Global Environment Facility (GEF) and other financial sources.

Box 12.1 *Vulnerability and climate change*

Adaptations to current climate and climate-related risks (e.g., recurring droughts, storms, floods and other extremes) generally are consistent with adaptation to changing and changed climatic conditions. Adaptation measures are likely to be implemented only if they are consistent with or integrated with decisions or programs that address non-climatic stresses. Vulnerabilities associated with climate change are rarely experienced independently of non-climatic conditions.

IPCC Working Group II (2001) *Third Assessment Report*

With this gradual turn to adaptation considerations and an increase in its salience, the climate change adaptation community has clearly commenced to take up on a topic that is very close and complementary to the traditional preoccupations of the risk and disaster community. How to live with and adapt to climatic extremes and how to promote more resilient and secure communities are questions that are in the centre of concerns for both communities.

However, in the same way as the risk and disaster community has failed in practice to substantially move beyond response to extreme disaster events, the climate change community has not yet been able to move beyond fairly theoretical formulations of vulnerability and adaptation, towards concrete plans and programmes of action. Such notions as planned and spontaneous adaptation, and even the concepts of vulnerability and risk, are far more easily used and talked about than understood in practical and applied terms. The problems of uncertainty surrounding the modelling of the impact of climate change in particular locations, together with the difficulties of mobilizing political will and support to adapt to uncertain future events are factors which conspire against the development and implementation of adaptation strategies.

The challenge of integrating the concerns of different practitioner communities

The clear coincidence that exists as regards a good part of the subject matter and concerns embodied in the climate risk management and adaptation to climate change problems has not as yet been reflected in wide-scale collaboration, consensus and integration of the scientific and practitioner communities that espouse them. This is even truer when it comes to civil society and government in general where, in addition to misunderstandings as regards the problematic and the relationships that exist, consciousness levels as regards the seriousness of the problem and commitment to action are as yet ephemeral. Despite changes over the last decade, the disaster problematic is still essentially seen as being almost inevitable and the subject of preparedness and response planning. And the global climatic change scenario is mostly seen as distant in the future, unspecified in terms of possible impacts and so unpredictable that planned action is not seen to be really feasible. Laissez-faire notions exist and short-term responses are still the predominant answer given.

Important discrepancies exist as regards fundamental notions and concepts, and common misunderstandings exist as regards the approach and subject matter considered under these two non-discrete subject areas. Many of the differences in understanding, concept and approach probably derive from the different scientific origins of the two problems, the far more recent development of the climate change and adaptation problematic and a lack of communication between the different communities which is reflected in the lack of a common literature and the different institutional and organizational structures for the promotion of advances and change.

Despite this there can be little doubt that the two problems are essentially linked and represent a continuum where risk, human security and sustainable development are in the centre of analysis and concern.

Unlike the patterns of hazard occurrence and disaster incidence related to normal climatic variability where certainty, if not very high levels of certainty, exists as to potentially affected areas and populations and patterns of hazard intensity over time, global climatic change is plagued with the problem of uncertainty. When and how climate changes will impact on populations and ecosystems, and the attendant risks are as yet very obscure. Modelling procedures as developed to date do not permit a sufficient degree of spatial and social accuracy. Moreover, how these changes will interact with current hazard patterns and risk scenarios is also unknown. The difficulties of projection and prediction can be appreciated when examining the tentative nature with which current science can predict impacts from a recurrent phenomenon such as El Niño. Evidence shows that different Niños have different spatial and social impacts.

Uncertainty as to trends and patterns, concatenation and synergy, are paralleled, however, with the certainty that new macro- and micro-scale hazards will be created with major impacts on population and environment. Given that climate is an integral part of the global environment, climate changes will not only affect socio-economic systems but also ecosystems, water resources and biodiversity, disrupting the natural resource base and threatening long-term sustainability. Traditional disaster-related problems associated with hurricanes, flooding, drought, landslides and coastal erosion will be compounded with the impacts of climate change, with the risk of ever-increasing damage and loss to society, particularly in the more vulnerable countries and population groups where resilience is lower and adaptation more difficult. This will be particularly apparent in rural areas where to date a still dominant portion of the world's poor population lives, and natural resources are the basis of sustenance and livelihoods. However, this will also be a severe problem for the urban poor and other population groups. This is particularly true in the short and medium term in Latin America where today over 75 per cent of the population is urban and the trend is ever upwards.

Any possible long-term benefits of climate change notwithstanding, dis-synchronization of climatic and terrestrial systems will probably involve numerous incidences of loss, both large and small, including disasters, impoverishment stemming from losses of assets and opportunities of the poor, disease outbreaks, water resource shortages, loss of viability of particular agricultural systems and ecosystem decline.

In effect, the potential changes associated with global climatic change and the new patterns of risk and disaster that will develop, constitute a 'natural' follow-on to and outcome of the current risk and disaster problematic. Risk is constantly evolving as new or modified risk factors are introduced by societal action. Historically, the risk scenario has been moulded and modified with all major societal advances, changes and innovations. The Industrial Revolution led to the introduction of technological hazards and rapid changes in land use and environmental practices that have had severe consequences as regards the generation of risk. The advent of nuclear energy added new risk factors. And, the present trend with global climatic change, incited by human intervention in the environment, comprehends a further step in the constant evolution of risk in society, with the added problem of the rapid speed of change, the probable magnitude of the possible effects and the new challenges this signifies in terms of human adaptation.

As regards the different understandings that exist as to practice, there is a tendency for external viewers to see disaster and risk management practice as being dominated by preparedness and response concerns when faced with current and repetitive problems. And to see practice as being directed essentially to already existing and more or less predictable risk contexts related to normal climatic variability. Moreover, risk management specialists and practice have done very little to date to incorporate climate change variables and contexts in their action frameworks. These still show a tendency in favour of short-term actions and solutions based on historical patterns of hazard incidence. This is compounded by the still dominant approach oriented in favour of single hazard approaches as opposed to the use of multi-hazard analysis and action frameworks.

Despite this general context, reality shows that the risk and disaster management communities are not monolithic blocs. Efforts and movement that attempt to change the status quo, promoting more integral visions as regards risk management, and pushing practice more in favour of risk reduction and risk control areas (as opposed to traditional and dominant response concerns) have been prevalent over the last decade. Nowadays, risk management tends to be progressively seen as a cross-cutting, integrative and cross-sectoral practice covering concerns that go from disaster prevention and mitigation through response to reconstruction. Decentralization and community and local participation are seen as essential components of this practice. Moreover, the dominant tendency to see disaster prevention and mitigation as something that attempts to reduce existing risk levels in society and thus 'prevent disasters' has been gradually eroded giving way to a vision that also incorporates prospective considerations. Corrective or compensatory risk reduction operating on existing levels of risk has been complemented with a move in favour of prospective risk management that attempts to foresee and control future risk. This can be seen with the insistence that risk management should be an integral component of development and project planning cycles. New developments must be analysed and considered in the light of potential new risk factors.

For its part, the adaptation to climate change community is also not a monolithic bloc as regards thought and practice, despite the relatively youthful nature of these concerns. This community may have commenced development of ideas thinking in terms of adaptation under conditions of uncertainty and in long time periods using the complementary notions of 'spontaneous' and 'planned' or 'independent' or 'formally planned' adaptation to climate change. And this may have been done basically ignoring present hazard scenarios associated with normal climatic variability. However, today this is not always the case, and some current thought favours more incremental approaches, building on current patterns of risk, introducing incentives to increased resilience and adaptation under current conditions as a basis for longer-term adaptation.

The notions of no-regret and win–win policies and practice reflect this current train of thought. That is to say, many adaptation strategies are consistent with sound environmental practice and wise resource use today, and are appropriate responses to natural hazards and climate variability and to the threat of creation of new socio-natural hazards. No-regret adaptation strategies are seen to be beneficial and cost-effective even in the absence of climate change. Win–win strategies have their rationale in ecosystem maintenance, improved resilience and enhanced livelihoods. Finally, current thought also tends to support the idea that long-term planned adaptation will not really be feasible in many instances, although government incentives and support for adaptation must exist. Spontaneous or independent adaptation is already happening in many hundreds of diffuse, incremental actions by many stakeholders.

In sum, it is clear that despite the still de-linked nature of the two scientific and practitioner communities the points of convergence between them far outweigh the differences in emphasis and approach. A common problem related to risk in society and uncertainty as to future impacts and the social and territorial distribution of these, a concern for the relations between society and environment, and a flux between short- and long-term considerations typifies both. Moreover, it is also very clear that the basic point of departure for both communities is the notion of sustainable development and livelihoods.

Despite the similarities in the climate risk management and adaptation problematic, the evidence shows that present national and international efforts to design strategies to adapt societies and their economies to the effects of climate change, and national and international efforts to manage the disaster risks associated with extreme climate events, remain fundamentally divorced. In many, if not most, developing countries totally separate and parallel institutional systems and programming mechanisms exist for promoting adaptation to climate change on the one hand and disaster risk management on the other hand. On another related front, it is only recently that a search for synergy between objectives and institutional frameworks has been sought with regard to the UN Environmental Conventions on wetlands, biodiversity, global climatic change and desertification. These are all clearly related one to the other but have been dealt with until recently as if they were separate and discrete problems.

Retrospective analysis will show that an important problem during the International Decade for Natural Disaster Reduction was that insufficient gains were made in integrating diverse specialist groups and caucuses all with a clear importance for risk reduction and related to sectoral and territorial development, environmental management, poverty reduction etc. The tendency was still for these groups to work apart and not as an articulated whole. We are now faced with a similar problem on the expanded basis given by current concerns for climate change adaptation.

This divorce between the adaptation to global climate change and the disaster risk management communities is unproductive and even absurd if it is accepted that both are addressing the same issue of climate-related risks, but from apparently different viewpoints. This includes supposed differences related to the time period under consideration. Risk managers are seen to deal with current and short-term risk, and climate adaptation specialists with longer-term changes and risk. But this is essentially a false separation. Risk, by definition, refers to the probability of certain events occurring in the future. The uncertainty surrounding the specific impacts of future climate change in particular space–time coordinates is therefore an intrinsic characteristic of existing risk and which has to be dealt with by risk management in the here and now.

The lack of capacity to manage and adapt to climate-related risks is already a central development issue in many developing countries, particularly in SIDS. From this perspective the lack of capacity to manage the risks associated with current climate variability and with already occurring extreme climate events is the same lack of capacity that will inhibit countries from addressing the future increases in the complexity and uncertainty of risk due to global climate change. In the sense that the entire potential of the future already exists like a seed in the present moment, strengthening national and local capacities to manage climate-related risks, as they can currently be assessed, is the best strategy to be able manage more complex climate risk in the future. At the same time, it is more feasible to mobilize national and international political and financial resources to manage an existing risk scenario than to address a hypothetical future scenario. Medium- and long-term adaptation must begin today with efforts to improve current risk management and adaptation initiatives and contexts. And lessons from current practices along with the notion that learning comes from doing are of critical importance.

Despite the prevalent divergence between the two communities, some convergence can now be witnessed, however, in various areas where risk management and climate change adaptation communities have come together, and these with the development community. This is the case in the Caribbean, Central American and South Pacific areas for example where attempts at methodological and strategy integration are occurring. However, this is still not the case in general and a relatively deep divide still exists in conceptual, methodological and practical terms. This must be overcome and integration achieved in the interest of promoting more coherent and efficient approaches. Each community has much to learn from the others as regards concepts, methods, strategies and instruments of common use in the promotion of short-, medium- and long-term risk reduction, control and management in general.

There is an urgent need, therefore, to build on the successful approaches piloted by the disaster risk management community over recent decades, while using increasingly accurate modelling of the impact of global climate change in specific locations, to develop integrated or total climate risk management plans and programmes.

Integrated Climate Risk Management

Whether dealing with actual potential disaster contexts, or future impacts associated with climate variability and change, the essential challenge is risk reduction, risk control, the increase in human resilience and increased capacities to adapt continually and prospectively to possible environmental extremes and conditions. In view of this, it is imperative that we develop an *integrated risk management focus* that brings together current risk and disaster and adaptation to climate change concerns and communities, relating these closely to sectoral and territorial sustainable development caucuses and agencies. This synthesis should be articulated and operationalized into one of total risk management for a wide range of elements at risk, ranging from communities to ecosystems, at long and short timescales and across spatial scales.

Integrated climate risk management, as a concept, would address both the hazards and vulnerabilities which configure particular risk scenarios and would range in scale from actions to manage the local manifestations of global climate risk, through to global measures to reduce hazard (for example, by reducing greenhouse gas emissions) and to reduce vulnerability (by increasing the social and economic resilience of vulnerable countries such as SIDS, for example). Integrated climate risk management would need to include elements of anticipatory risk management (ensuring that future development reduces rather than increases risk), compensatory risk management (actions to mitigate the losses associated with existing risk) and reactive risk management (ensuring that risk is not reconstructed after disaster events). Moreover, it will have to take into account potential impacts on both socio-economic and environmental systems.

Integrated climate risk management could provide a framework to allow the disaster community to move beyond the still dominant focus on preparedness and response, and for the adaptation to climate change community to move beyond the design of hypothetical future adaptation strategies. In some regions, such as the Caribbean and the South Pacific, synergy such as this is already being achieved. However, urgent actions must be taken at the international, national and local levels if integrated climate risk management is to move from a concept to practice and serve to reduce risks and protect development.

At the international level, if it were recognized that most disaster risk is now climate related and that adaptation must refer to the management of existing climate-related risks, the United Nations should promote an integrated international framework and partnership for risk management, which incorporates elements of and builds on existing frameworks for addressing climate change, disaster reduction, desertification and others. Such a framework needs to start from a clear concept that climate-related risk is one of the central development issues of our time and that, as stated in the first part of this summary, the achievement of the UN Millennium Goals will not be possible unless climate-related risks are significantly managed and reduced. The current proliferation of parallel international frameworks and programming mechanisms for addressing what is a holistic development issue is counterproductive if the objective is to strengthen national capacities to manage and reduce climate-related risks.

At the national level, integrated climate risk management strategies, plans and programmes need to be built on the dispersed institutional and administrative mechanisms, projects, human and financial resources currently applied to disaster risk management as well as adaptation to climate change and other related areas such as desertification. The United Nations should develop new programming mechanisms and tools to promote integrated national climate risk management programmes as well as resource mobilization strategies to ensure that such programmes can be adequately funded.

Ultimately, integrated climate risk management needs to take root at the local level. Most climate-related disaster events are small to medium scale and have spatially delimited local impacts. Even large-scale events can really be interpreted as the sum of a large number of local impacts. Ultimately, risk is manifested and losses occur at the local level and it is at this level that national and international support to integrated climate risk management has to be realized and capacities strengthened. Differential levels of loss at the local levels when faced with similar hazard conditions can only be explained by the differential levels of vulnerability that exist.

Some Parameters and Indicators for Integrated Climate Risk Management

The raising of consciousness among critical political decision-makers and the public in general as regards the needs and challenges associated with integrated risk management may be achieved concentrating first on the present disaster problematic and more adequately dimensioning its real impacts on development, and then linking in climate change considerations. Short-term, existing problems are probably more convincing elements for decision-makers than long-term uncertainty. On the other hand, seeking to manage impacts associated with such phenomenon as El Niño and other sources of interannual timescale climatic variability gets political actors, sectoral experts and the public involved in managing climatic risks. Therefore, learning to prevent negative impacts from such phenomena presents a strategic opportunity for building resilience to climate change and for increasing social consciousness as regards the need for increased attention to future possible climate impacts.

Applications of an integrated risk management framework in decision-making should take into consideration that:

- The current development situation and needs in a particular location are the most appropriate starting point for additional risk reduction and control efforts of an adaptive nature.
- Adaptation strategies currently being pursued in local, regional and national settings are often extensions of ongoing efforts to reduce climate-related disaster risks.
- While past climate is not a good guide as to the future climate, past experiences and lessons learned from efforts to improve management of climate variability are valuable for adapting to climate change. In addition, spatial and temporal trends in past disaster events reveal current vulnerabilities and risks.
- Adaptive learning comes from doing, and lessons must be learned from successful and best practices already implemented. It is highly unlikely that adaptation will come from a priori planning.
- Adaptation will require continual adjustment of risk management practices to account for changing climate hazard and vulnerability conditions.

People will, out of their resourcefulness or out of necessity, adapt to climate change. This constitutes independent or autonomous adaptation. This contrasts with formally planned adaptation that involves deliberate policy decisions, plans and implementation by external parties. In many cases, independent adaptations will be adequate, satisfactory and effective. However, under some circumstances independent adaptation may not be satisfactory or successful due to erroneous or limited understanding of climate change, limited knowledge of possible adaptation options, the negative impact of group adaptation on others, the ignoring of the needs of future generations, cultural constraints to adaptation, lack of resources, or the greater cost effectiveness and efficiency of collective responses, as opposed to individual or community schemes. In such cases, the role of external agents should be to facilitate the adaptation process in order to ensure that the stated obstacles, barriers and inefficiencies are addressed in an appropriate manner. This will require provision of reliable information, financial, technical, legal and other assistance, and the direct implementation of adaptation options where the scale of response is most appropriately at the national level, provisions to guarantee that adaptation options do not have adverse environmental, social, economic or cultural effects, and the ensuring of equity in the adaptation process.

Information and access to reliable data will be a critical factor in adequate decision-making from the government through the community levels, and in the reduction of uncertainty associated with medium- and long-term climate change. In addition to the generation of more temporally and spatially specific information, more will need to be done to translate climate information into decision support tools for sector- and region-specific applications. Information on both climate variability and long-term trends needs to be translated into risk information for decision-making. Reduction of uncertainty will be facilitated through the exchange of information up and down spatial and social scales, from scientists to policymakers and between specialists. But uncertainty about risks and impacts of disasters and climate change needs to be explicitly recognized in the decision-making process for all development decisions. This could be achieved by creating 'headroom' for environmental considerations in all development planning decisions.

Uncertainty is a major factor as regards future changes. New information will in many cases change the nature and appropriateness of decisions that have been made. Flexible institutional arrangements should be promoted that have the capacity to incorporate new information on environmental risk into development planning, as it becomes available. Flexibility within the institutions to adapt to the new information is necessary to avoid inappropriate path dependency and maladaptation.

The integrated climate risk management approach should draw on frameworks that have been developed to date for disaster risk identification, reduction and transfer, as well as others developed in such contexts as farming systems research and commodity, food security and financial risk management. And, in order to assess and address risks across a wide spectrum, and develop improved management decisions relating to short- and long-term risks, there is a need for cross-cutting coherence in such areas as assessment methodologies, assessment studies, recommendations based on sound analysis and risk/related terms and concepts. A more coherent approach to risk assessment and reduction will assist in identifying risk management alternatives in both the structural and non-structural domains such that both the short-term objectives of disaster risk reduction and the longer-term objectives of adaptation to climate change will be more fully achieved.

Any approach to risk management and adaptation should be essentially prospective or anticipatory, and promoted in the very short term. This will:

- Widen the range of possible response options, decrease costs in the medium and long terms, limit the possible levels of social disruption and prove to be more environmentally sustainable than with reactive approaches.
- Gain immediate advantages through the promotion of *win–win* and *no-regret* policies that build on current conditions, strengthening ecosystems and providing immediate and future benefits as regards social protection for vulnerable communities, sectors and critical systems.
- Provide increased levels of protection for many development plans and projects now under consideration, which are likely to be subject to impacts by future climate change and sea-level rises.
- Provide for the immediate enhancement of institutional capacity, developing expertise and building knowledge. These are factors of critical importance for adaptation and take time to develop.

On the other hand, the complexity of risk-generating processes, the range of socio-economic and environmental considerations that come into play, and the diverse and complex nature of the social intervention required, requires the search for coherence and coordination across the following:

- Geographical scales: community, local, regional, national and global.
- Timescales: seasonal, interannual, decadal and centennial.
- Climate-affected sectors: water resources, health, agriculture, food security, ecosystems, etc.
- Development concerns: poverty reduction, coastal zone management, rural development, urbanization, economic growth etc.
- Stakeholder groups: scientists, experts, politicians, nation states, non-governmental organizations, regional and international organizations, financial institutions and civil society in general.

The primordial emphasis in risk reduction, risk control and adaptation schemes should be on increases in the resilience of the poor in particular, favouring the most vulnerable. To date there has been an over-emphasis on adaptation and mitigation, and insufficient attention paid to resilience, livelihood strengthening and risk management in general.

The integration of the risk and disaster, and adaptation approaches in a single risk management approach must be supported with a strengthening of the ongoing process favouring synergies between existing UN environmental conventions relating to global climatic change, biodiversity, wetlands and drought. The complexity of risk contexts demands increased integration, harmonization and cooperation between until now separate concerns, caucuses and interest groups. This will also require institutional reform and reorganization permitting more flexible and agile relationships between complementary areas of concern. The modification of intergovernmental frameworks and policies will be required in order to dissolve barriers separating the issues of climate change adaptation, disaster risk management and sustainable development. And concrete actions must be taken to support local, national, and regional efforts to manage climate-related risks, beginning in the present and building on current initiatives.

A starting point for more committed and integrated action relates to the UN system as such, where even greater efforts must be made to assure that risk considerations are incorporated in existing planning and programming mechanisms such as the Common Country Assessment (CCA) and United Nations Development Assistance Framework (UNDAF). The UN should serve as a promoter, advocate, and stimulation to innovative behaviour and change.

Conclusion

To conclude, climate-related risk, aggravated by processes of global economic and climatic change poses central unresolved development issues for many countries, particularly but not exclusively for SIDS. Unless such risks can be managed and reduced the achievement of the UN Millennium Goals will be a mirage.

Current approaches towards managing disaster risk and adaptation to climate change fail for different reasons to address the issue. The first is still predominantly focused on response to disaster events and fails to address the configuration of hazards, vulnerabilities and risks. Moreover, mono-hazard approaches still prevail in contexts more and more typified by concatenation, synergy and complexity and there is still a great deal to do in order to bring risk management and sustainable development concerns and practices together. The second focuses on the impact of future climate change on risk but fails to make the connection with currently existing climate-related risk events and patterns. At the same time, both approaches are divorced both in concept and in terms of the institutional arrangements and programming mechanisms at the national and international levels.

If development is to be protected and advanced in countries affected by climate risks, an integrated approach to climate risk management needs to be promoted, building on successful approaches piloted by the disaster risk management community but mainstreamed into national strategies and programmes. Addressing and managing climate risk as it is manifested in extreme events and impacts in the here and now is the most appropriate way of strengthening capacities to deal with changing climate in the future.

13

Adapting to Climate Change and the Risks Associated with Other Natural Hazards: Methods for Moving from Concepts to Action

Marcus Moench

The Challenge

Climate change is increasingly recognized as among the greatest challenges human society will face over the 21st century. While it will affect everything from basic ecosystem processes to the spread of disease, some of the greatest impacts are anticipated to occur due to increases in the frequency and intensity of extreme climate events, i.e. storms, floods and droughts. In total, between 1974 and 2003, preliminary data from 6384 events show that windstorms, droughts, extreme temperatures, floods and wave surges accounted for 75 per cent of natural disasters (Hoyois and Guha-Sapir, 2004). Extreme weather events already account for over 70 per cent of recorded disasters and are known to have a disproportionate impact on poor communities. If one adds in landslides and wildfires – both of which could be affected, though less directly, by climate change, the percentage of climate-related disaster deaths increases to nearly 85 per cent (EM-DAT data cited in Dilley et al, 2005). The recurrent losses due to such extreme events have, in fact, been identified as a major factor contributing to endemic poverty (Benson and Clay, 2002; ISDR, 2004; Wisner et al, 2004; IRIN, 2005). Furthermore, the incidence and economic impact of climate-related disasters has been increasing over recent decades (World Meteorological Organization, Co-operative Programme on Water and Climate et al, 2006). As the Hyogo framework for disaster risk reduction highlights, disaster risk reduction is essential if the world is to succeed in reaching the Millennium Development Goals (ISDR, 2005). In many cases, risk reduction cannot be achieved only through structural measures, and societies need to develop social systems and adaptive capacities that enable populations to live with risk. This involves, in essence, largely similar sets of capacities as those required for adapting to climatic variability and change. Strategies for responding to climate change, reducing disaster risk and alleviating poverty are, as a result, inherently intertwined.

At a global level some of the consequences of climate change – increases in average temperature, changes in the frequency and intensity of extreme weather events, changes in sea level, etc. – are relatively well understood. What such changes actually mean for local areas is, however, far less so. At this level, a myriad of factors come into play. Economic and livelihood systems, transport, communications, land-use patterns, formal and informal mechanisms for risk sharing, cultural values, etc. all play a major role in shaping *who* will be affected by climate change and *how* they will be affected. The impacts, although heavily shaped by global systems, are thus inherently local. As with impacts, options for adapting to climate change – or indeed the risks posed by any natural hazard – are inherently location specific but are shaped by economic, climatic, water resource and other systems that operate at regional to global levels.

The fact that climate and other risks are location specific, but that the options for responding to them depend heavily on regional to global systems, presents a methodological challenge for entities seeking to understand and support risk mitigation or adaptation. In most situations, local knowledge, the foundation of community-based risk reduction strategies, only partially reflects the opportunities and constraints emerging at higher levels. The case of early warning systems illustrates this well. A decade ago, in the mid-1990s, cell phone technology was accessible only to wealthy urban households in countries of South Asia. Now it is ubiquitous even in distant rural areas and, in addition to its core communication function, is being tested as a mechanism to disseminate disaster warnings. Access to this type of communication and early warning system – to say nothing of the behavioural changes it could enable – was until recently unthinkable for individuals in rural communities. Now it is a central feature in attempts to reduce risk and support adaptation. Similar fundamental shifts in economic systems, demographics, transport, environmental conditions, government policies, and so on are contributing to the reshaping of livelihood systems and climate/hazard vulnerability across South Asia. Communities experience the local effects of such shifts but are often too embedded in their context to envision the opportunities and constraints the shifts will create over time. As a result, strategies for disaster risk reduction and adaptation require the integration of local, community-based, knowledge with knowledge of higher-level changes in policies, economic systems, technologies, environmental systems and a myriad of other factors. Achieving this integration represents a major challenge.

The challenge is further complicated by the cross-sectoral nature of risk and adaptation issues and the 'pulsed' nature of change processes (Gunderson and Holling, 2002). Where the cross-sectoral aspect is concerned, adaptation and disaster risk reduction do not map neatly onto sector-based organizations, such as those that exist in most countries for water management or urban planning. Instead, risk reduction and adaptation are inherently interdisciplinary topics and will require changes or action across multiple sectors. As a result, they are not 'natural' focal points for projects or other types of action. Furthermore, many of the most effective avenues for supporting adaptation and risk reduction are only tangentially linked to the specific impacts associated with climate change or natural hazards. Recent research in India and Nepal, for example, highlights the role that income diversification plays in reducing climate risks, particularly in areas that are heavily dependent on agriculture (Moench and Dixit, 2004). Over the long term, educational levels are a central factor influencing the ability of populations to diversify. It is difficult, however, to argue that general education programmes should form a central element in strategies for climate adaptation and disaster risk reduction – the link with exposure to extreme climatic events is, at best, tangential. This said, when viewed from a systemic perspective support for general education as the foundation for diversification may, in actuality, be central to any strategy for climate adaptation and disaster risk reduction.

Finally, the pulsed nature of change processes is a major complicating factor. Socially and politically, pressure for change often rises during and immediately following crises. This window of opportunity, however, dissipates rapidly as time passes and other issues take centre stage. Most development planners and other actors focus on incremental processes of change – the gradual development of infrastructure, social capital, institutions and policy frameworks. Pressures for fundamental change, however, often emerge suddenly and then dissipate. This disjuncture between societal approaches and the nature of change processes is of particular relevance in the case of natural hazards and climate change. Events that are now classified as 'extreme' may become the norm. Reducing risk may, as a result, depend on societies' ability to recognize longer-term change processes and take advantage of the brief windows of opportunity for bringing about fundamental change following crises. The case of Hurricane Katrina illustrates the issue well. The US Gulf Coast is extremely vulnerable to sea-level rise, particularly if that is accompanied by increases in the frequency or intensity of hurricanes. Ideally, the process of reconstruction following Katrina would take this vulnerability into account through fundamental changes in, for example, land-use and water management systems (Moench and Stapleton, 2007). Unfortunately, although more radical changes have been discussed, most reconstruction activities emphasize replacement of pre-existing infrastructure and livelihood systems. Rather than moving settlements to higher ground away from the coast, for example, most investments are going into strengthening or raising existing levees. However unsustainable current conditions may be, post-disaster reconstruction efforts generally focus on replacement of pre-disaster infrastructure, livelihoods, organizations and procedures rather than replacing these with more sustainable systems.

Adaptation to climate risk, particularly the hazards associated with extreme events, will require basic changes in approaches to disaster risk reduction. Effective mechanisms will need to be found for implementing courses of action across sectors and between communities and higher levels of organization. Perhaps more importantly, effective strategies will need to be developed that shape local and regional development pathways in ways that reduce or avoid climate risks. In many regions this may need to 'go beyond' the incorporation of risk reduction measures in standard development programmes. Little long-term benefit may, for example, be achieved by improving coastal storm defences as part of a regional development programme if sea-level rise threatens the entire coastal region. In this case, alternative development pathways that either focus on the construction of major assets on higher lands or change the design of assets in ways that accommodate sea-level rise (scientists in the Netherlands are, for example, proposing the development of 'hydrometropols' – modern Venices) will be essential (Kabat et al, 2005). Radical changes of this sort may, in some cases, only be possible when existing infrastructure in vulnerable regions has been disrupted and there is widespread acceptance of fundamental change. Such conditions are perhaps most likely when extreme storms or other similar events create windows of political and social opportunity for change. As a result, mechanisms for anticipating and working with the windows of opportunity for fundamental change that exist following crises will also be essential. However complicated it may be – and existing experience documented by ProVention (www.proventionconsortium.org) with attempts to incorporate risk reduction in reconstruction programmes does highlight the constraints faced – we argue here that the post-disaster period does represent a critical window of opportunity for interventions to reduce risk over the longer term. Just as incorporation of risk reduction in development programmes is increasingly recognized as a major challenge for the development community, we argue that incorporation of risk reduction in reconstruction is an equally important challenge for the communities of actors involved in reconstruction.

Conceptual Foundations

Philosophically, the starting point for all our work on adaptation is founded on systems theory. We view the challenges of responding to climate risk as being shaped by the complex interaction between dynamic natural, social, economic, cultural and political systems. These dynamics are, due to their complexity, dependence on initial conditions and non-linearity, inherently chaotic and difficult to predict. Surprise is, as a result, inevitable. Consequently, attempts to develop 'integrated' approaches that respond to all the potential consequences and dynamic changes in human and natural systems will be ineffective and are inherently inappropriate (Holling and Meffe, 1996). Instead, as a growing body of literature now recognizes, approaches need to be founded on an understanding of systems – broad perspectives that recognize the complex interplay between diverse human and natural systems (Gunderson 1999; Holling, 2001; Gunderson and Holling, 2002).[1] Solutions to emerging problems will be clumsy, constructed on the basis of partial measures that are targeted toward key factors that constrain or enable humans to adapt to conditions as they emerge within the continuous process of change. It is this focus on the factors that *enable* or *constrain* people to respond to the challenges faced in a particular situation that creates a practical linkage between the concepts discussed below and what can practically be done. This is important to keep in mind as basic conceptual elements are discussed below.

Adaptation

At a conceptual level, adaptation in human systems can be thought of as driven by two core processes: *selective pressures* (the equivalent of natural selection in ecosystems) and what might be termed *agency-driven innovation* (that is, proactive forms of innovation or action in response to perceived constraints and opportunities). These two processes are not separate; they interact as agents experience selective pressures or perceive opportunities and most commonly act proactively or 'adapt' within the limits of their capacities, perceptions and priorities.

The role of selective pressures has been a central pillar in evolutionary theories and has served as a cornerstone of modern biology since Charles Darwin published *The Origin of Species*. In biology it has been defined as: 'the process whereby organisms better adapted to their environment tend to survive and produce more offspring.'[2] Organisms having characteristics that are favourable or give them comparative advantages in relation to other organisms (whether of the same species or different species) survive and reproduce better than organisms lacking such characteristics or having other characteristics that place them at a competitive disadvantage. When such characteristics can be 'inherited' (whether genetically or through education across generations), over time advantageous features are propagated and negative features 'sifted out.' As a result, population characteristics evolve in ways that are increasingly adapted to their context.

Concepts of selection apply equally well with regard to many aspects of human systems as they do with regard to biological systems. Basic economic theory, for example, views the selective pressures generated by competitive markets as the major force driving efficiency and innovation. Efficient business models and technologies tend to have a competitive advantage over less efficient ones and thus tend to survive and proliferate. Better educated workers have a comparative advantage over others in competitive job markets, a factor that provides a strong selective pressure supporting education and the gradual evolution of social capital at a societal level.

As in ecosystems, the nature of selective pressures in social systems and the ability of different entities (individuals, households, businesses, etc.) to adapt to them vary greatly. Entities that exist in contexts where key resources (such as financial and intellectual capital) or key inputs (such as labour, energy or water) evolve in ways that maximize their ability to capture, minimize dependency on, or make efficient use of scarce inputs. Often this evolution involves proactive (agency-driven) courses of action undertaken by individual agents in response to the opportunities and constraints emerging from the selective pressures encountered. When conditions are highly variable, as they are for example in volatile currency markets, specialized mechanisms are developed for managing that variability. In this case, entities (firms) often diversify assets, set prices based on baskets of currency or take other steps that minimize the impact of variability on their core activities. Major challenges emerge when variability exceeds the range commonly encountered in recent history. Just, however, as ecosystems can be drastically reshaped by sudden extreme events (such as intense, extended droughts) so economic and social systems can be reshaped by periods of intense economic or social disruption (such as a war or extended economic downturn). In this case the characteristics that made an entity 'well adapted' to the pre-existing context may contribute to its demise under the new conditions. Firms, for example, that have adapted to operating in protected markets often lack the characteristics necessary for survival when protective barriers are removed. This is also the case in agricultural and natural systems. If, for example, exposure to drought is eliminated, people have little incentive to plan for it by implementing efficient water technologies, purchasing insurance or diversifying crops. When this occurs, the 'shock' to an agricultural economic system is likely to be far higher when droughts eventually do occur. Similarly, in the western US, decades of effort to reduce forest fires have led to high levels of fuel loading in the forests. Now, when fires occur, they tend to be far larger, far hotter and far more destructive than ever before. Removal or reduction of selective pressures often limits perceptions regarding the underlying risks – and thus limits the ability of agents to take proactive action.

Selective pressures also can contribute to the maintenance of resilience. Regular exposure to variability and risk forces entities to develop and maintain the adaptive mechanisms necessary to adjust when events occur (Gunderson and Holling, 2002). When households or businesses are continuously exposed to the selective pressures generated by variability and risk, they are subject to strong immediate incentives for diversification, strategy shifting and learning. These contribute to their flexibility, adaptive capacity and resilience. Such dynamics occur in relation to virtually all risks.

Overall, selective pressures within societies are often seen as one, if not the, major force underlying the continuous adaptation of skills, technologies, institutions, relationships and other forms of social capital to ever-evolving contexts. Such adaptive processes are, it is important to recognize, not always positive in relation to many social objectives – such as poverty alleviation or social equity. Comparative advantages (whether from education, wealth, location or other sources) in competitive contexts often persist across generations and sections of society giving rise to deeply entrenched social, ethnic, class and caste divisions.

Although selective pressures are a major factor, adaptation in human systems is not driven only by them. Unlike natural systems, actors within human systems strategize and take action in response to aspirations and perceived opportunities. As a result, the concept of *agency* can be seen as a major difference between adaptation processes in human and natural systems. Agency, in the philosophical sense, is the capacity of an individual, group or organization (an 'agent') to act. Agency can operate at any level from the individual to the societal. At the individual level, courses of action to improve skills or acquire resources that enable people to take advantage of the opportunities or to respond to the constraints they perceive represent a form of proactive adaptation. Planning, strategizing and the proactive innovation and development of capacities and institutions in response to perceived opportunities and constraints also occurs within organizations such as households, firms and governments. This type of 'agency-driven innovation' underlies courses of action ranging from investments in education, livelihood diversification and migration at the individual and household level (the so-called 'autonomous forms of adaptation') up to programmes and adaptation plans implemented by governments or international organizations (so-called 'planned adaptation'). It also underlies the responses agents (individuals, households, organizations, etc.) make in relation to sudden pressures encountered during disasters.

As with adaptation in response to selective pressures, *agency-driven* forms of adaptation depend heavily on exposure to and familiarity with sources of risk or opportunity. Perceptions catalyse responses to both opportunities and risks. If people have never been exposed to specific conditions, their ability to perceive and respond to a potential opportunity or threat is likely to be limited. When the threat or opportunity is obvious, responses are much more likely to follow. As a result, as with selective pressures, the frequency of events and the degree to which people are exposed to them has a major influence on proactive adaptation. When changes or fluctuations are infrequent and sudden, then the ability to perceive (and take seriously) both the opportunities and risks associated with them is limited and thus so is the ability to take proactive steps to adapt. In this situation, a prime 'window of opportunity' for reducing future risks may exist in the immediate aftermath of disasters when awareness is high and existing entrenched systems are disrupted. In nature, adaptive processes often operate in pulses of rapid change followed by slower periods of more linear growth and refinement. This is also the case in social systems. It is a major point where adaptation processes link with our next topic – disaster risk reduction.

Disaster risk reduction

Conceptually, reducing the risk of disasters is closely associated to adaptation processes. The Swiss disaster preparation cycle, a fairly conventional approach to disaster risk reduction (DRR), characterizes preparation as part of a continuous cycle of activities which move from disaster events through recovery (damage limitation) and risk reduction (preparation) phases until the next event occurs. Many of the elements identified in this cycle – strengthening of resilience, land-use and other planning, insurance and the development of early warning information – should reduce vulnerability to the next event and thus, in essence, assist regions in 'adapting to' the types of events that can cause disaster.

The contribution DRR measures of the type envisioned in the Swiss disaster preparation cycle can make to adaptation is, however, partial. In most disaster preparation contexts, resilience is largely discussed in relation to strengthening of physical structures, not in relation to the underlying systems and sets of capacities that enable societies to adapt to variable and changing conditions. Other measures such as land-use planning, insurance, warning and information are also only partial steps toward adaptation.

Wider approaches to the conceptualization of disaster vulnerability, such as those developed by Ben Wisner and others in their classic book *At Risk* are, however, much more closely linked to concepts of adaptation (Wisner et al, 2004). In specific, the disaster pressure and release (PAR) model focuses on the connections between the progression of vulnerability, disaster and hazards. It defines the progression of vulnerability in relation to *root causes* (limited access to power, structures and resources and ideologies – political and economic systems), *dynamic pressures* (lack of institutions, training, skills, etc. and macro-forces such as urbanization, population growth, etc.) and *unsafe conditions* (physical environment, local economy, social relations, and public actions and institutions). Hazards are physical events such as earthquakes, floods and so on. They analyse the links between hazards and the progression of vulnerability – that is the 'disaster' component of the PAR model – using a separate dynamic framework which they term the 'access' model. The access model 'focuses on the way unsafe conditions arise in relation to the economic and political processes that allocate assets, income and other resources in a society (Wisner et al, 2004, p92). Access is further defined as involving 'the ability of an individual, family, group, class or community to use resources which are directly required to secure a livelihood in normal, pre-disaster times, and their ability to adapt to new and threatening conditions' (Wisner et al, 2004, p94). Individuals and other entities which have access to key resources are seen as much better positioned to cope with the range of hazards that can cause disaster – with 'coping' defined as 'the manner in which people act within the limits of existing resources and range of expectations to achieve various ends' (Wisner et al, 2004, p113).

This wider conceptualization of vulnerability and the links between social conditions and hazards is used as a basis for identifying a very wide range of potential points of leverage or courses of action that could be used to reduce disaster risk. These points of leverage include many that focus on addressing root causes, dynamic pressures and unsafe conditions – that is reversing the factors in the PAR model that create vulnerability as part of post-disaster recovery and sustainable development programmes. This is, in essence, very similar conceptually to the types of activity that are involved in adaptation. Individuals, households, organizations and other entities are seen as 'adapting' by responding to the opportunities and constraints in their environment.

Fragility

In the disaster risk reduction community, the concept of fragility is used to define the relationship between damage and hazard intensity. As fragility increases, damage for a given intensity hazard event increases. Fragility functions are used to identify changes in direct and indirect losses to different classes of assets or activities in relation to flood depth, earthquake intensity and so on (Mechler, 2005).

Disaster risk reduction interventions, particularly those focused on physical infrastructure and assets such as buildings, often focus on reducing fragility. This is, for example, the case with incorporating earthquake strengthening into building codes or raising river levees to contain higher flood levels. In many cases the goal is to ensure structures or the assets they protect suffer minimal or no damage in events with a specific magnitude. When design events are exceeded, such as when levees or dams fail, the result is often catastrophic. In other cases, however, structures are designed to allow controlled failure and partial protection as the magnitude of events increases. This would be the case, for example, when low-level levees are used to protect agricultural lands with higher levees for urban areas. Often in such cases, lower-level levees breach during large flood events and reduce pressure on levees protecting more valuable assets. Under these conditions, asset losses are often step functions with distinct breaks at different event magnitudes.

Resilience: Hard and soft concepts

Concepts of resilience take two broad forms:

1   the direct strength of structures or institutions when placed under pressure – an attribute we refer to as hard resilience; and
2   the ability of systems to absorb and recover from the impact of disruptive events without fundamental changes in function or structure – an attribute we refer to as soft resilience.

In the disaster context, resilience is often treated as the simple inverse of fragility. Engineers, for example, often refer to increasing the resilience of a structure through specific strengthening measures to reduce their probability of collapse with respect, for example, to earthquake intensities, wind loading or other physical stresses. As resilience increases, the degree of damage for a given intensity hazard decreases. Such approaches fall largely under what we term strengthening the hard resilience. More nuanced concepts of what we would call *soft resilience* are, however, well established in scientific communities working on systems dynamics. The *Resilience Alliance,* one of the main forums for discussion within these communities, defines resilience in the following manner:

> Ecosystem resilience is the capacity of an ecosystem to tolerate disturbance without collapsing into a qualitatively different state that is controlled by a different set of processes. A resilient ecosystem can withstand shocks and rebuild itself when necessary. Resilience in social systems has the added capacity of humans to anticipate and plan for the future. Humans are part of the natural world. We depend on ecological systems for our survival and we continuously impact the ecosystems in which we live from the local to global scale. Resilience is a property of these linked social-ecological systems (SES). 'Resilience' as applied to ecosystems, or to integrated systems of people and the natural environment, has three defining characteristics:
>
> - The amount of change the system can undergo and still retain the same controls on function and structure
> - The degree to which the system is capable of self-organisation.
> - The ability to build and increase the capacity for learning and adaptation.[3]

Under the above concept, rather than simply strengthening structures or institutions in relation to specific stresses (adding cement, etc.), soft resilience attributes depend on the flexibility and adaptive capacity of the system as a whole. Practically, our prior research in South Asia (Moench and Dixit, 2004) indicates that resilience and adaptive capacity in communities depends on:

- flexibility (within livelihood systems, economic systems, water management systems, institutional systems);
- diversification (multiple independent income flows to livelihood systems);
- the ability to learn from events (at both individual and institutional levels);
- education (the knowledge base required to develop new systems when existing ones are disrupted);
- mobility (an attribute of flexibility);
- risk pooling and spreading (institutional arrangements or other mechanisms for spreading and pooling the impacts of disruptions on the system as a whole);
- operational techniques for risk reduction before and following disruptions (techniques for directing the reorganization process so that growth and conservation phases do not increase rigidity and ultimate vulnerability); and
- convertible assets (the ability to convert assets accumulated during periods of growth into other forms when disruptions occur).

All of the above contribute to system resilience – that is the ability to adjust to shocks and variability without fundamental changes in overall system structure.

Investing in Change: What do Concepts Mean for Strategy?

The conceptual foundations for understanding adaptation, disaster risk reduction, fragility and resilience have a wide variety of implications for organizations of any type that are seeking to develop a sound basis for investments to reduce risks and encourage adaptation. While full discussion of this is beyond the scope of this chapter – and is indeed an evolving field where many elements remain to be developed – some basic principles can be identified at this point. Here we'll address two major areas: (1) the factors influencing the costs and benefits of risk reduction and adaptation strategies; and (2) determining strategic points of entry for change.

Costs and benefits of investing in DRR and adaptation

There is an emerging body of work that documents the financial benefits and frequently large benefit/cost ratios associated with disaster risk reduction (FEMA, 1997; Uddin, 2002; Benson and Twigg, 2004; Department for International Development, 2005; Donga and Mechler, 2005; Mechler, 2005; MMC, 2005; Bouwer and Aerts, 2006; Messner et al, 2006; Benson, 2007). This literature does not, however, generally emphasize differences between strategies for risk reduction. Instead it focuses on evaluation of specific individual investments in specific locations. On a more generic level, we believe investments in risk reduction and adaptation are likely to have high benefits in relation to costs when:

- *They address multiple hazards and serve multiple purposes* (rather than being tied to one specific hazard or use). Early warning systems, for example, are much more likely to be economically viable when they are part of multi-function communication systems and can provide warning of any hazard.
- *They are embedded in development activities and are supported by sustainable public or private sector business models.* When cyclone shelters are built as multi-function public buildings such as schools, for example, the sustaining business model is education (with taxes or fees supporting services and the maintenance of facilities to meet specific day-to-day demands).
- *They have low sensitivity to core assumptions and uncertainties.* Physical structures that are designed to operate within very specific hydrological tolerance ranges (flows, sediment loads, etc.) are, for example, very sensitive if changes in climate are likely to exceed those ranges. Similarly, institutional arrangements that depend on very specific assumptions (such as insurance programmes that are designed on the basis of historical weather losses) may be highly sensitive if assumptions are violated. This point is elaborated on further below.
- *They do not involve major distributional issues.* In many cases, actions that reduce exposure to climate risks for one group or set of assets, increase risks for other groups. This is, for example, the classic case with flood embankment systems. Those outside the embankments largely benefit while those inside are subject to much

more intense flooding. Furthermore, each time an embankment is strengthened in one location, the potential for breaching in other (now comparatively weaker) locations increases. Issues of fairness and the operational difficulties of compensating losers aside, when major distributional issues exist, the costs of compensating losers are often underestimated.

- *They do not create new patterns of vulnerability while alleviating existing risks.* Again, the case of levees and embankments provides a classic example. Levees around New Orleans encouraged settlement of low-lying and highly flood-prone areas. When Hurricane Katrina occurred, the resulting damages were far higher than would have been the case if development had not been enabled in these low-lying areas. This type of issue is inherent in many conventional DRR and climate protection strategies. Providing irrigation as a buffer against drought, for example, is only as reliable as the source of water. Many farmers in Gujarat (India) were impoverished when their wells went dry during the 2000–2002 drought because they had developed an intensive, high-investment, form of agriculture based on the assumption that groundwater was an absolutely secure source (Moench and Dixit, 2004).

The factors influencing the economics of investing in risk reduction as part of climate adaptation are illustrated further below.

Conceptually, in natural situations the damage due to climate events and other natural hazards almost always follow a rough logistic curve (Figure 13.1). Losses are low (and there may even be benefits) with low intensity events. These losses increase at inflection points as various system thresholds are crossed and then probably level off past the point where most of the system assets or attributes have been damaged, disrupted or destroyed.

Risk reduction and adaptation interventions are designed to shift the logistic curve downward and to the right. For a given magnitude event, they are designed to reduce

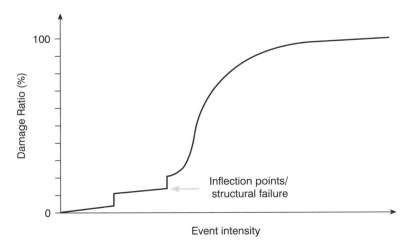

Figure 13.1 *Fragility function for direct and indirect flood damages*

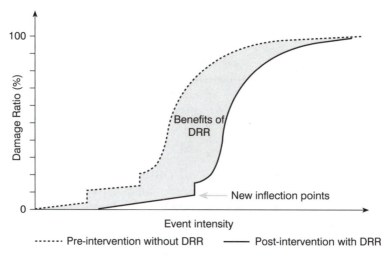

Figure 13.2 *Fragility function with and without DRR*

damages (costs) and, if possible, increase benefits. The economic returns from investments in such interventions are represented by the space between the pre-intervention and post-intervention curves (Figure 13.2).

Elements influencing the costs and benefits of hard resilience

While the above is true in a generic sense, the nature of disaster risk reduction and adaptation strategies have fundamental implications for the shape of the cost and benefit curves and the nature of curves in areas that are not protected. As previously noted, approaches to risk reduction that depend on hard resiliency tend to provide full protection until they fail – and when they fail it can be catastrophic. This is, for example, the case with protective embankments. Either they keep flood water completely out of an area or they breach and allow flooding (Figure 13.3).

The curve in Figure 13.3 illustrates the absolutely critical issue of threshold levels that is inherent in most hard resiliency measures. In order to design a dam or a levee, some knowledge of the magnitude of flood and storm flows is essential. This is also the case for low flows. If thresholds are exceeded, then structures fail, whereas below the thresholds protection tends to be complete. Strengthening structures to meet 'any' threshold is often unaffordable. As a result, to determine design thresholds architects and engineers need to have information on the recurrence intervals of specific magnitude events – the '100-year flood' or 'Category 5' hurricane. Obtaining such information and determining its reliability is a particular challenge in the context of climate change.

A more nuanced version of gains and losses from hard resiliency measures, such as embankments, is shown in Figure 13.4 In the 'natural' situation without embankments, low levels of exposure to hazards such as flooding actually create benefits (shaded area 'A'). Such benefits from low-intensity short-duration floods include groundwater recharge, drainage and the distribution of nutrients and soil. They are eliminated in both

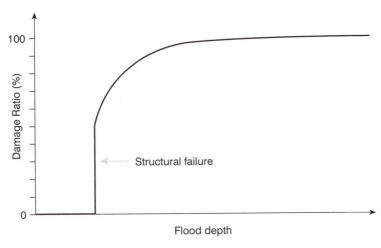

Figure 13.3 *Fragility function, hard resilience (e.g. embankments or dams)*

protected zones and those where water is concentrated when hard resiliency measures are implemented. This loss of benefits essentially shifts the benefit/damage curve upward in the section shown as 'A' in Figure 13.4 relative to natural baseline conditions. In some cases, for example when levees cause waterlogging, new damages in addition to those in the baseline case are also part of the costs. Losses may also be increased during high-magnitude events when protective structures fail. This essentially shifts the upper portion of the damage curve upward and to the left causing the additional losses shown in the 'C' section of Figure 13.4. The actual benefits generated by the protective measures are shown as the 'B' section in figure 13.4. The net benefits from hard protective measures are, as a result, the 'B' section minus the 'A' and 'C' sections of the damage curve.

Figure 13.5 illustrates the distributional issue that is often present with this type of hard resiliency measure. For areas that are between embankments (as large areas are in some locations such as the Gangetic plains), damages can be increased because flood waters are concentrated in much smaller areas. Populations living between levees lose the amount shown by the shaded area between the 'natural baseline' damage curve and the increased damage curve in Figure 13.5. This amount would need to be transferred from the economic benefits shown in Figure 13.4 (again the area marked 'B' between the natural baseline damage curve and the new reduced damage curve) as compensation for losses. In addition to the practical difficulties in effecting such a transfer, it represents a reduction in the overall benefits from the DRR or adaptation intervention.

A second feature to note about Figures 13.4 is the change in the percentages of total asset value at risk for events that exceed the critical threshold that represents levee failure in relation to baseline conditions (area 'C'). When hard resiliency measures encourage the concentration of assets in protected areas, then a much larger percentage of assets is at risk if the measures fail. The additional amount at risk is illustrated by the upper

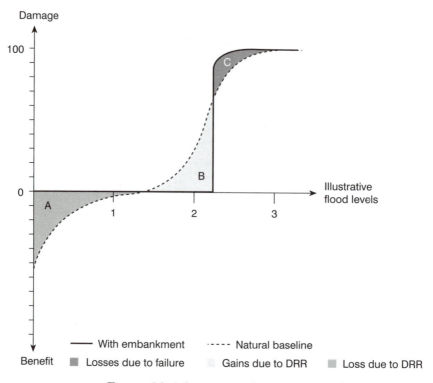

Figure 13.4 *Impact area damage curve*

shaded area below the 'reduced damage' curve and above the natural baseline after the critical damage inflection point.

Moving beyond the simplified case of river levees, it is important to recognize that most hard resilience interventions are part of systems that *as a whole* can be designed to fail incrementally rather than catastrophically when critical thresholds are reached. Dams, for example, are designed in ways that allow flood waters to be released rapidly (often resulting in some flooding) when storage capacities are full. Similarly, levees are generally constructed as systems where failure in one section does not result in flooding of an entire protected area. This doesn't reduce the importance of threshold values – but, it changes the nature of the damage curve into a step function with multiple thresholds.

Elements influencing the costs and benefits of soft resilience

In contrast to hard resilience measures, soft resilience measures alter damage curves relative to natural baselines in ways that do not tend to depend heavily on sharp threshold values. Instead, they tend to attenuate the damage curve, moving it down and to the right, as illustrated in Figure 13.6. They also do not tend to create major 'losers' (such as the individuals owning assets in areas 'between levees') and thus greatly reduce compensation issues. In some cases, soft resiliency measures can create benefits that are in addition to those specifically related to the risk reduction or adaptation objectives.

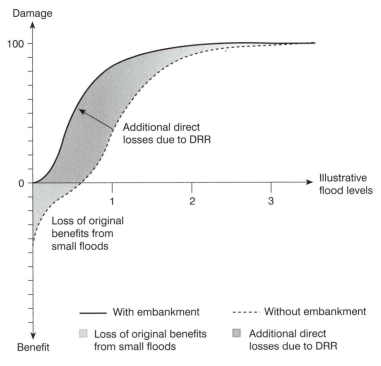

Figure 13.5 *Loss of benefits (areas between embankments)*

These new benefits add to the value of the intervention as a whole. The examples below involving weather information and the construction of multi-purpose flood buffer ponds illustrate these features.

Improvements in weather forecasting and communication are often seen as major inputs for reducing the vulnerability of individuals and households to extreme events, such as those anticipated as a consequence of climate change. In this case, the benefits of forecasting accrue through the changes in behaviour catalysed by new information. When storm warnings are provided, the individuals who receive and respond to the information move themselves and their assets out of harm's way or take other protective measures to reduce losses. Individuals who don't receive or don't respond to the information don't gain but, relative to their prior vulnerability levels, neither do they lose. Losses associated with the early warning element of weather information do, however, occur. These primarily take the form of costs incurred when individuals take avoidance behaviour – and then the predicted events don't occur. This is, for example, the case when regions are evacuated in advance of projected storms, but storm paths change and the evacuation ends up being unnecessary. These gains and losses are illustrated in Figure 13.7, the damage curve is shifted downward (arrow 1) to a new level by the soft measures but the net gains are reduced when people take avoidance measures against events that don't occur (illustrated by arrow 2 shifting the damage curve back up part of the way to the original baseline).

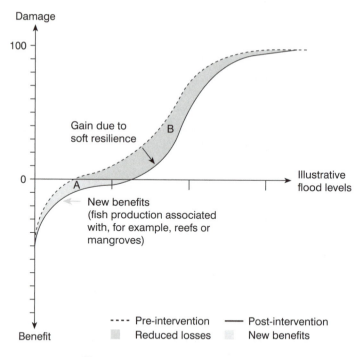

Figure 13.6 *Gains to soft resilience*

Loss reductions associated with early warning aren't, however, the only benefit from a good weather information system. Provision of high-quality weather information enables individuals and many businesses to 'fine tune' their activities in ways that increase productivity. Farmers, for example, often schedule irrigation based on weather projections. This is often critical to increasing yields and reducing pumping or other production costs. Weather forecasts are equally important in other industries such as construction and tourism. These benefits should be accounted as part of the benefits associated with weather information. Similar benefits are also present with many other 'soft resiliency' interventions designed to support adaptation and reduce climate risks. Insurance, for example, is often part of a larger system of credit and banking facilities that generate a wide range of benefits. Economic diversification often generates new sources of income as well as reducing the risks inherent in depending on one source alone. Social networks provide support during crises – but are also major elements giving individuals access to resources, jobs and other benefits. As a result, for low-intensity events, the lower portion of the 'damage' curve shows benefits other than those achieved through loss reduction.

Soft resiliency forms of infrastructure (infrastructure that is designed to accommodate climatic variability instead of controlling it) can have similar economic attributes to the more institutional and financial measures discussed above. The case of flood retention ponds illustrates this well. Flood retention ponds reduce risk directly by

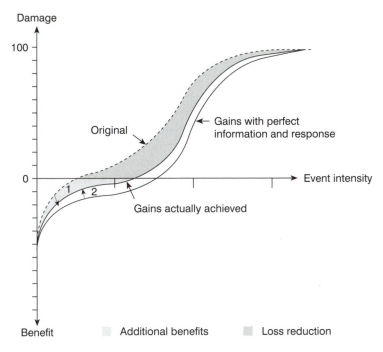

Figure 13.7 *Fragility function information example*

absorbing excess flows. Depending on how they can be operated and managed, however, they can have a number of additional direct benefits. Conceptually these include:

1   providing groundwater recharge;
2   serving as water sources for livestock, irrigation and other uses; and
3   serving as a resource for the development of aquaculture and other 'water-based' livelihood activities.

The above benefits, (illustrated in Figures 13.6 and 13.7) add to the direct risk reduction benefits associated with flood protection. They also don't reduce or disrupt existing benefits that are already present as part of the baseline context. Sediment delivery, for example, isn't blocked from areas by flood retention ponds as it is by levees. As a result, the fertility benefits associated with the natural system could be retained. This combination of created and maintained benefits represents, in many ways, the economic benefits of adapting livelihoods to flood-prone environments. Similar benefits could be identified or created in other contexts. In coastal areas which are particularly vulnerable to climate change, for example, the creation of brackish water wetlands and fisheries could accommodate increases in sea levels and buffer storm effects while also allowing the development of new sources of income.

As with hard resiliency measures, soft resiliency measures would rarely be implemented in isolation. In the Gangetic plain, for example, the development of flood retention ponds could be coupled with activities to raise villages (a traditional method of flood risk reduction in the Gangetic Plain), increase drainage, improve insurance and provide early warning. With this type of portfolio it may be possible to provide equal levels of asset protection as river regulation using dams and embankments would generate with few of the distributional issues – raising one village protects the inhabitants but doesn't adversely affect the inhabitants of other villages. Furthermore, packages that emphasize soft resiliency interventions are far less subject to thresholds. Their viability does not depend heavily on information regarding specific flows or the frequency of floods and storms to be effective and economically viable.

Overall, the economics of investing in disaster risk reduction as part of climate adaptation depend heavily on specifics and the wider network of costs and benefits in addition to those associated with specific reductions in risk. A number of key questions must be evaluated including: *Do measures reduce some benefits relative to baseline conditions? Do they depend heavily on information regarding thresholds – and, if so, is that information available? Do measures have large distributional implications – are there clear losers as well as beneficiaries? Can measures to reduce risk also serve as income generation and adaptation opportunities?* Evaluating the costs and benefits of packages of DRR interventions as part of climate adaptation requires, as a result, a broad economic analysis rather than one that focuses narrowly on damages avoided. It will also in most cases require a mix of hard and soft resiliency interventions.

Identifying points of entry

As already noted, in most contexts the projects and other interventions implemented by governments and other actors to reduce disaster risk focus directly on the proximate causes of disaster and tend to involve measures designed to increase hard resilience. As the above conceptual discussions and some of the best research on risk suggest, however, *underlying systemic factors* are often of greater fundamental importance to adaptation, disaster risk reduction and resilience (Dreze et al, 1995; Sen, 1999; ISDR, 2004; Wisner et al, 2004). Consequently, interventions designed to respond to the underlying systemic factors limiting adaptive capacity or causing vulnerability are essential. These will often involve 'soft resilience' measures that contribute in fundamental – but generally indirect – ways to adaptive capacity and risk management.

Direct risk reduction

Direct measures that appear, at least on the surface, to reduce risk or support adaptation are often relatively easy to identify. They are interventions, in the form of structures, financial mechanisms, communication systems, organizations and so on that can be seen as directly influencing the risk of disasters or supporting adaptive risk reduction. The embankment case discussed extensively in preceding sections is a case in point. The idea of building embankments to keep floods out of vulnerable regions is something most people can intuitively understand. The fact that people often move and settle in 'protected' areas and that this will compound the scale of disasters when embankments breach – as they are ultimately likely to do for a variety of much more complex reasons – is not as easily understood (or if understood, not seriously appreciated). As a result, evaluating the potential unintended indirect consequences of direct risk reduction measures is perhaps *the most important challenge in identifying effective points of entry for direct risk reduction.* The complexity is further compounded by the transitional role measures such as embankments can provide in some situations as long as measures are in place to ensure they do not compound disaster risk. In coastal regions, for example, carefully designed embankments can assist in controlling salinity. While, given projected sea-level rises, this may not be viable in the long term, in the short term protection of productive land can generate the resources necessary for transition.

While the process of identifying potential indirect consequences of direct risk reduction measures is complex and often site or case specific, the six criteria below can serve as warning flags regarding the viability of a measure:

1　**Low levels of diversification**: Any strategy that relies heavily on one form of intervention or that reduces diversification within systems has a high risk of failure if the assumptions on which that strategy is based prove unreliable.

2　**Heavy dependence on key data and technical assumptions**: If infrastructure is built to withstand a Category 3 storm, the benefits are heavily dependent on whether or not higher-intensity storms occur. If interventions are intended to provide interim protection as a basis for transition, then consequences depend heavily on assumptions regarding whether or not such interventions actually contribute to transition or instead compound future vulnerability.

3　**Reliance on narrow assumptions regarding appropriate human incentives and behaviour**: If approaches are framed based on cultural perceptions of what groups (such as rural farmers or fishermen) 'should' want and how they 'should' live, then projected benefits will not occur if actual behaviours differ in response to the opportunities and constraints such groups face in a given context. This is a particular challenge in the many rapidly urbanizing and globalizing societies where livelihoods have traditionally been based on agriculture or similar activities but incomes and opportunities are increasingly derived from other sources.

4　**Long lead times and high capital investments required**: If the measures require substantial time and investment to put in place and are intended to repay this through benefits generated over the long term, then they are heavily dependent on difficult-to-predict conditions in that future and are especially vulnerable to the impacts of climate change.

5　**Major distributional differences between groups 'benefiting' from the intervention and others who bear direct costs**: If there are major 'losers' as well as 'gainers' from an intervention (whether direct or simply in relation to perceptions of equity) then conflicts can undermine objectives.

6　**Lack of a clear business model that will ensure risk reduction measures are maintained over the long term, particularly during extended periods when extreme events do not occur**: If the source of funding or other inputs required to sustain an organization or set of infrastructure during the potentially long gaps between 'events' is unclear, then sustainability is highly questionable.

Systems level (indirect)

In addition to interventions that are directly targeted at specific risks, points of entry for reducing risk and supporting adaptation are present within systems. In previous research on responses to floods and droughts, a variety of systemic factors were identified that contribute to livelihood resilience and adaptive capacity (Moench and Dixit, 2004). Adaptive capacity and livelihood resilience depend, in essence, on:

*   *knowledge systems* – the basic education required to access multiple job and skill markets along with institutional or other forms of memory and learning;
*   *environmental systems* – the condition of basic land, water and air resources along with the productive ecosystems they support;
*   *livelihood and economic systems* – the manner in which systems spread risk through diversification combined with their ability to generate surpluses and distribute them in a manner that provides access to the assets all sections of the population require for strategy shifting as well as day-to-day survival;
*   *communication systems* – the ability of information to flow in and out of areas, both the technology itself and the institutions and rules governing that flow;
*   *Transport Systems* – the ability of goods, people and resources to flow in and out of areas;
*   *financial systems* – the ability of funds to flow in and out and for assets to be converted as required;
*   *organizational systems* – the ability to self-organize following disruption as well as during more linear and controlled phases of change processes; and
*   *adapted infrastructure systems* – the degree to which physical and institutional structures are designed to accommodate and respond flexibly to climatic variability and change including extreme events.

While interventions at this level are often difficult to relate directly to risk reduction or climate adaptation, they are often of much more fundamental importance than direct risk reduction measures. Direct measures for risk reduction are often of an interim nature – humans respond to the risks they perceive in a given context and, as the immediacy of that risk perception dissipates, the willingness to invest time or other resources in risk reduction will dissipate as well. Adaptive capacity and the ability to respond to risks as they emerge are, as a result, maintained over time more by the functioning of underlying systems than by direct measures.

Adaptive capacity depends at a basic level on the ability to self-organize, respond flexibly, convert assets and shift strategies as risks emerge or during the period following disruptive events. This, in turn, depends in an absolutely fundamental manner on the presence and functioning of underlying systems. As a result, activities that strengthen such systems and improve access to them for vulnerable groups represent a critical point of entry for supporting risk reduction and adaptive capacity.

It is important to emphasize here that care must be taken in identifying potential points of intervention to reduce risk through interventions at the level of systems. Although the list above identifies what we believe are critical factors that contribute to adaptive capacity and risk reduction in relation to floods, droughts and similar extreme climate events, little actual global experience exists regarding the impact of specific 'systems-level' interventions to manage climate or other risks. This is a major emerging area where experience, research and further conceptual development are essential. Clearly the role of specific systems in reducing – or increasing – risk depends on the nature of the hazard. Transport systems, the foundation for mobility, clearly play a major role in reducing the livelihood and food security impacts of floods and droughts. At the same time, where communicable diseases are concerned, the increased mobility of populations greatly increases the probability of major global epidemics.

Phasing

Windows of opportunity points of entry for initiating activities to reduce risk or support adaptation depend heavily on timing. In most situations, government and international programmes emphasize the gradual development of capacities as part of ongoing development activities. Such contexts, however, tend only to allow incremental change – the refinement of policies, gradual development of economic or institutional systems, the diffusion of new technologies and so on. Fundamental changes, particularly those that disrupt embedded patterns and relationships, are both difficult to envision and undertake when current systems are functioning in a normal manner. Crises precipitate other forms of change.

This dynamic was, cynically but very accurately, captured by P. Sainath in the title and content of his seminal book *Everybody Loves a Good Drought* (Sainath, 1996). Crises catalyse behavioural and other changes that would be impossible in 'normal' times. In many cases such changes are ephemeral and dissipate over time – the disaster response community often highlights the manner in which political will and the social urgency for change wither rapidly as relief transitions to reconstruction. The chaos and humanitarian urgency that characterizes relief contexts also is not conducive to the development or implementation of strategies that respond to longer-term risks.

The above said, however, crises often do catalyse basic changes in conditions and systems. Hurricane Katrina caused the largest migration in the history of the United States since the Civil War of the early 1860s.[4] In contrast to a pre-Katrina population of over 400,000 (484,674 in the 2000 United States census), according to Logan (2006), the full-time population of the city was estimated at only 150,000 in January 2006. Logan further indicates that 'if the future city were limited to the population previously living in zones undamaged by Katrina it would risk losing about 50% of its white residents but more than 80% of its black population' (Logan, 2006). Following Katrina, debates are under way regarding approaches to water and land management throughout the US Gulf region that would have been unthinkable before the inadequacy of existing levee systems was so unequivocally demonstrated. In India the famines and droughts of the 1940s and 1960s provided much of the impetus for both the Green Revolution (which represented a fundamental change in agriculture) and the development of major support programmes (such as the Public Distribution System) that continue to the present. In the Netherlands the highly sophisticated water management systems owe their establishment to disastrous floods and levee failures that occurred in the 1950s. Overall, identifying points of entry for making fundamental changes that reduce disaster risk and support adaptation requires strategies that address and bridge the gap between incremental change processes that characterize most development contexts and those that can occur during the windows of opportunity created by crisis.

In discussing the windows of opportunity for change created by disaster it is extremely important recognize the limitations of existing terminology and the conceptual frameworks different groups of actors use to frame their arenas of action. The disaster management community has developed relatively broad conceptual definitions for the relief, recovery (damage limitation) and risk reduction (preparation) phases of activity. Drawing on these definitions, humanitarian actors have developed specific types of relief, reconstruction and rehabilitation or disaster risk reduction programmes for each of these phases. These programmes are generally separate from the equally broadly conceptualized sector-focused programmes that are part of most national development strategies. When we emphasize the windows of opportunity to reduce risk during the reconstruction process that follows disasters, this does not necessarily imply that DRR activities of the type often promoted by humanitarian organizations can easily be incorporated in reconstruction programmes. Existing experience, in fact, suggests that this may face quite basic challenges – see, for example the array of recovery studies supported by ProVention (www.provention consortium.org/?pageid=18#rel) and the report of the Tsunami Evaluation Commission (Telford et al, 2006). In the case of the 2005 Pakistan Earthquake, we are sceptical that many of the activities currently being implemented in the name of risk reduction will have much impact. At the same time, changes in communications, transport and other systems following (and catalysed by) the earthquake may have fundamentally reshaped risk exposure. Similarly, the major interventions to control risk in the Netherlands and India discussed above did occur within the window of opportunity when awareness and political will were high following disasters. Learning to work with this window and identifying the points of entry for doing so effectively is, as a result, both a major opportunity and a major challenge. Doing so may require both the disaster management and development communities to move beyond the frameworks used to define programmes.

The development context

Windows of opportunity for supporting risk reduction and adaptation as part of an ongoing development process exists in the array of projects being implemented by governments, multilateral and other organizations in a multitude of fields. Identifying the openings for action in these projects is challenging. Screening tools are being developed by the World Bank, ProVention and other organizations to identify projects that have particular relevance for climate adaptation and risk reduction. These tools can be used to identify windows of opportunity, such as during project development and interim review phases, where activities can be inserted or strengthened. They also represent a critical window of opportunity for review to ensure that maladaptive activities do not occur. Finally, in addition to such tools for identifying points of entry for risk or adaptation-specific interventions, *the development context represents the primary window of opportunity for strengthening the underlying systems that enable or constrain adaptation.*

The development context presents, as previously noted, particular challenges for the implementation of approaches that require fundamental changes in livelihood, land-use or other such systems. Individuals, communities, policymakers and other actors tend to focus on problems or opportunities present in their immediate context. As a result, approaches to development, whether community-based or driven at national policy levels, are unlikely to make fundamental rather than incremental changes in response to risks or needs that are not immediate or have not been previously experienced. In most cases, as a result, the development context represents a poor window of opportunity for making rapid or large changes in basic systems. This is clearly illustrated by the National Adaptation Programmes of Action (NAPAs) that have been prepared by several countries. Most of the interventions contained in the NAPAs represent business as usual – incremental strengthening of existing programmes that address climate-related hazards but little that would fundamentally change current patterns of vulnerability (Moench and Stapleton, 2007).

Although the development context provides little opportunity for restructuring systems, it is the primary period of time when emerging problems can be identified and the analysis necessary to envision alternatives can occur. Throughout the world governments and other organizations are currently analysing the impact climate change is likely to have on hazard risks in different regions. Whether the hazards are related to cyclone paths, sea-level rise or drought, the likely distribution of climate-related hazards is increasingly well known. This knowledge and the opportunity for advanced planning that it presents could be utilized as a point of entry for bridging the gap between the incremental processes of change and the much more abrupt opportunities for change that can emerge in post-disaster contexts.

The post-disaster context

Actions to provide humanitarian relief and begin the process of re-establishing infrastructure and livelihood systems characterize, as they should, most post-disaster contexts. Such contexts are not conducive to long-term planning or the identification of avenues for restructuring systems in ways that reduce risk or enable adaptation. Yet *if planning and the building of awareness can take place in advance of disasters in vulnerable regions, they could serve as windows of opportunity.* Existing livelihood and infrastructure systems are often disrupted and local populations are often more willing – or pushed – to make basic changes than at other times. Disasters are also times when large pulses of funding become suddenly available and when political support exists for change. As a result, if strategic approaches can be developed in advance that support effective change in highly disrupted contexts, disasters could serve as windows of opportunity to address some of the long-term, root causes of vulnerability and unsustainable development.

Learning to work more effectively with the post-disaster recovery context could also contribute to better understanding of development processes in general. Virtually all development activities focus on linear processes of change. They involve interventions that are designed to build social capacity and infrastructure in an incremental planned manner. While this type of work is important, recent research on complex systems emphasizes that change is, at fundamental levels, a *pulsed* process. It often occurs in bursts or phases that are catalysed by disruption in pre-existing systems. Instability, in effect, frees resources and shatters conventional ways of doing things. This often leads to fundamental reorganization of economic, social and livelihood systems. Reorganization sets the stage for the next phase of more gradual 'linear' development. Attempting to recreate pre-existing conditions merely recreates pre-existing patterns of vulnerability.

Viewed in this way, disruptions, including the extreme forms that cause disaster, are windows for structural rebirth. As a result, learning to work with the pulses of change that accompany disaster could lead to fundamental new insights into development processes. By learning to work with pulsed change it may be possible to identify new windows of opportunity and strategic points of entry that are fundamentally different and can achieve results at a much larger scale than conventional linear 'development' processes.

Strategically, identification of vulnerable regions and the development of shared visions regarding alternative futures in such regions could be used to plan and develop awareness of the need for fundamental changes – even if such changes can only be implemented following disruptive events. Just as relief organizations pre-position supplies and other materials in regions that are known to be vulnerable to earthquakes or other natural hazards, advanced planning and dialogue with key stakeholders in regions that are vulnerable to climate risks could enable restructuring as part of post-disaster recovery processes. Processes for working with communities to identify sources of vulnerability – and much more importantly, to envision alternatives – represent we believe a key opportunity for bridging the gap between proactive development processes and reactive disaster recovery.

Moving from Concepts to Action

How can organizations working on disaster risk reduction or programmes to support climate adaptation move from the above principles to logically identifiable and justifiable courses of action in specific areas? The approach outlined below represents an initial attempt to move beyond screening of existing projects for climate risks toward the development of strategies that respond to location-specific contexts.

A systematic process

The approach has four core steps: *scoping, building common understanding, structured review of potential strategies* and finally, where necessary, *financial evaluation* of the costs and anticipated benefits interventions are likely to have. These steps are designed to enable identification of specific courses of action that contribute to climate risk reduction and adaptive capacity either *directly* or by *strengthening underlying systems.* Ideally these steps should be followed by implementation and then cycle back to a new round in which incorporation of experience and learning replace scoping but the process otherwise remains the same.

The core element required throughout all of the above steps is a clear understanding of the manner in which specific types of interventions within complex systems relate to resilience and adaptive capacity. That is to say, both conceptually and practically how they enable strategy shifting or increase resilience by addressing specific constraints or responding to specific opportunities. To make this clear it is worth reiterating the core factors prior research and our own more recent analysis suggests contribute to resilience and adaptive capacity within communities. These include:

1   *diversification* of livelihood activities, assets and financial resources particularly into non-farm and other activities that have low levels of sensitivity to climatic variability or extreme events;
2   *mobility and communication*, particularly the ability of goods, people, information and services to flow between regions in ways that enable local populations to access markets, assets, the media and other resources beyond the likely impact of specific climatic events;
3   *ecosystem maintenance*, particularly maintenance of the basic ecosystems services (such as drinking water) without which local populations cannot survive;
4   *organization*, particularly the social networks, organizations and institutional systems that enable people to organize responses as constraints or opportunities emerge;
5   *adapted infrastructure*, particularly the design of physical structures (for water, transport, communication, etc.) in ways that can maintain their basic structure and function regardless of changes in climatic systems;
6   *skills and knowledge*, in particular the ability to learn and the basic educational skills required to shift livelihood strategies as required;
7   *asset convertibility*, the development of assets or markets that enable populations to transform the nature of assets and their use as conditions evolve; and
8   *hazard-specific risk reduction*, the development of early warning, spatial planning, implementation of building codes, establishment of community DRR organizations and other systems to reduce exposure and vulnerability to known climate-related hazards.

Scoping

In virtually any situation, scoping is the first step toward identification of potential avenues for risk reduction or supporting adaptation. Because climate hazards and potential strategies for addressing them cut across scales and sectors, scoping activities need to as well. In order to identify initial points of entry for reducing climate risks, scoping processes need to achieve four objectives.

First, they need to pull together current information on the nature of the risks associated with climate change for the particular area. Translating global scientific information on climate into formats usable at the local level is a key part of this first step. It is important to recognize that this information does not need to be highly specific in order to be useful. Individuals and organizations often wish to specify, for example, the maximum magnitude of storms that may be encountered or whether or not their specific area will encounter floods of a given magnitude – but advanced information on climate change may never provide information of that specificity. Information that historical storm and flood magnitudes do not reflect those likely to be encountered in the future can, however, be extremely useful for everything from the design of structures to disaster planning.

Second, scoping processes need to assess vulnerabilities, capacities (vulnerability capacity analysis – VCA) and the factors enabling or constraining different groups or regions in responding to current and the array of potential future climate conditions. This assessment needs to be guided by factors such as the eight basic elements identified in the previous section that contribute to livelihood resilience and adaptive capacity. It also needs to be conducted using a systemic perspective that recognizes the links between constraints, opportunities and the behaviours of entities (individuals, communities, businesses, etc.) at levels ranging from the household to the region. Depending on the scale and focus of the assessment, information required will include the basic secondary 'data' (statistics, maps, policies, programmes, etc.) that many organizations already gather on natural hazards and vulnerability. It will also include the wide array of local-level participatory rural appraisal (PRA) and stakeholder processes currently used in many DRR or development activities at local levels. Finally, it will need to include key actors and activities in the private sector. The importance of this is clearly illustrated by the case of disaster risk reduction in Muzaffarabad (Pakistan) discussed by Khan and Mustafa (2007). Our analysis suggests that following the earthquake major improvements in communications, transport, financial systems and organization, most of it driven by the private sector, has contributed far more to sustainable risk reduction than the much discussed – but in reality relatively minor – attempts at incorporating DRR in government and relief programmes.

Third, the scoping process needs to generate initial insights regarding how emerging climate risks are perceived and the responses (if any) different groups of actors are already taking or believe may be appropriate. The core objective here is to generate understanding of how different actors (individuals, households, businesses, etc.) are actually responding to the constraints and opportunities they perceive or already face. *Who* is doing well and *why* is just as important for identifying constraints and opportunities as identification of the factors affecting particularly vulnerable groups. This type of understanding is a core source of insights on strategies to address risk that is generally not captured in conventional VCA processes.

Fourth, the scoping process needs to identify a preliminary set of potential strategies for risk reduction and supporting adaptation that: (1) addresses the underlying systemic factors identified in the previous section; (2) builds as far as possible on the behavioural incentives, opportunities and constraints facing different groups; and (3) responds to perceptions of climate risks at the local level and from emerging global scientific information.

Building common understanding

Building common understanding of the risks associated with climate change and the potential strategies for addressing those risks is the second basic step in moving from concepts toward courses of action that can be implemented. The immediate objective here is to move from a preliminary identification of potential strategies to a set of approaches that could actually be implemented. This is, however, only one element. The larger objective is to build a common basis for learning that can be sustained over the long time period essential to address climate-related risks. The essential element in this step is *shared learning*.

Climate change poses risks for regions that have never previously been encountered. The perceptions and activities of different communities at the local level (whether villages, businesses, governments or other actors) are, as a result, highly unlikely to represent an adequate basis for identifying or responding to the risks and vulnerabilities climate change processes will create. At the same time, the perceptions of higher-level actors (whether climate scientists, business entities or government entities), rarely reflect an understanding of local conditions or the incentives driving behaviour at local levels as households and communities respond to the opportunities and constraints they face. *Shared learning processes that are structured in relationship to the basic systemic factors known to contribute to resilience and adaptive capacity are, as a result, essential.*

The case studies outlined in Moench and Dixit (2007) illustrate the shared learning dialogue process partners in our programmes are developing and testing as a core step in moving from the preliminary understanding and strategies identified during scoping, toward a menu of practical activities. It is important to recognize that shared learning dialogue processes are not a one-time activity. Developing effective responses to climate change is inherently a long-term process that, at a global level, will continue indefinitely. Knowledge, insights, challenges and strategies will evolve substantially over time in response to dynamic climate and social contexts. As a result, continuous processes for translating new insights into practical courses of action will be required. Shared learning – that is processes for building understanding between communities of actors at all levels – will be essential throughout. At a practical level, initial scoping and shared learning activities should be used to develop a list of potential actions that relate both to the core factors contributing to resilience and adaptive capacity and have sufficient support to enable implementation among involved actors.

Structured review of identified actions

Following identification of potential courses of action during scoping and initial shared learning dialogues, structured review is important to ensure that these actually *do* address both the specific risks emerging as a consequence of climate change and the core factors contributing to resilience and adaptive capacity. This step has two core components: strategy mapping and strategy evaluation.

Strategy mapping involves locating identified activities or strategies within a matrix that clearly identifies the relationship between proposed activities and the factors that either directly or indirectly contribute to risk reduction and adaptive capacity. This mapping process is intended to force consideration of the real links between specific activities and underlying concepts. It is also intended as a mechanism to ensure that approaches are balanced (i.e. that they do not focus heavily on one element such as structural measures to promote hard resilience while ignoring other core dimensions). A sample matrix for coastal areas is included in Table 13.1 showing illustrative factors contributing to climate risk reduction and adaptation directly and at a systemic level.

Strategy evaluation involves analysis of the likely risks and effectiveness associated with each activity mapped out within the above matrix. The core goal is to ensure that each of the component activities does not itself carry a high level of uncertainty with respect to its effectiveness in supporting risk reduction and adaptive capacity. This is the critical stage for returning to and evaluating identified activities in relation to the warning flags discussed in detail in the preceding section on direct risk reduction. These flags are:

1   *low levels of diversification;*
2   *heavy dependence on key data and technical assumptions;*
3   *reliance on narrow assumptions regarding appropriate human incentives and behaviour;*
4   *long lead times and high capital investments required;*
5   *major distributional differences;* and
6   *lack of a clear business model.*

Table 13.1 *Potential arenas for intervention: A coastal example*

Livelihood and economic diversification	Ecosystem	Organization	Education and skill development	Financial and risk spreading	Communication for adaptation (climate specific)	Adapted infrastructure
Risk- and adaptation-specific interventions						
Adding livelihood activities outside coastal areas	Mangrove and reefs as storm buffers	Formation of DRR and rescue committee	Training about cyclone relief	Storm insurance	Storm warning system	Cyclone shelter
Non-farm, non-fishing livelihoods	Salinity control structures	Establishment of state DRR and relief organizations	Targeted strengthening of construction to increase resilience to storms	Catastrophe bonds	Strengthening communication towers	Breakwater
Underlying systems for risk reduction and adaptation						
Increasing ability to access global and regional labour and other markets	Developing productive brackish and saline water fishery and farming systems	Increasing the number and diversity of civil society organizations in coastal regions – the right to organize	Skills, such as global languages, that enable populations to access global labour and other markets	Strengthen banking system and improve access to it	Cell phones and other personal communication devices	Improving transport systems
General diversification within economic and livelihood systems	Controlling pollution to enable long-term productivity of coastal ecosystems as they change	Incubating new forms of business organizations that can utilize and manage coastal resources	Coastal-specific skill training (aquaculture, tourism, etc.)	Strengthen remittance flows	Increasing access to and freedom of the media	Changing approaches to infrastructure design (houses, roads, bridges, etc.) to account for uncertainty

Note: Columns can be added and activities can be targeted at specific vulnerable groups.

This step will assist in weeding out strategies that may be popular or appear appropriate at a first cut but that on more systematic evaluation have substantial flaws.

Financial evaluation

Evaluation of the costs and benefits of identified risk reduction activities can serve as a final step in moving from concepts to concrete courses of action. Methods for this have been developed and tested in a variety of situations (FEMA, 1997; Uddin, 2002; MMC, 2005; Bouwer and Aerts, 2006; Messner et al, 2006) and many of the basic principles have been outlined here previously. These methodologies are currently being refined and will be available in subsequent publications.

In the climate case, evaluations will need to be derived based on scenarios and historical data. While such scenarios and data can generate important insights, they cannot be relied on as a guide to future conditions. This said, it is important to recognize that scenario-based approaches can provide clear indications of the sensitivity of cost–benefit expectations in relation to key uncertainties or assumptions. Some strategies will have high benefit to cost ratios regardless of future conditions – that is they will be robust under uncertainty – while the benefits and costs associated with other strategies will depend heavily on conditions. Quantitative and qualitative cost–benefit analyses can highlight such sensitivities.

Governance of the process

This section has focused on outlining a relatively linear process organizations could use for moving from broad concepts of climate risk and adaptation to practical courses of action. It is important to recognize, however, that processes such as the one outlined above will be occurring in highly contested contexts. The nature of problems, viable solutions, potential courses of action, ethical and other considerations are all likely to be contested. Governance of the process will, as a result, be a critical consideration.

While a full discussion of the governance considerations is beyond the scope of this writing, one key point is essential to make here: *pluralistic strategies involving civil society, the private sector and governments in an environment where information and perspectives can be effectively communicated are essential.*

The underlying factors determining how different groups of people cope with conditions that can cause disaster are central to understanding potential responses to climate change. *We believe these factors are rooted in the dynamics of social exclusion and the relationships between technology and the democracy of institutional pluralism.* Flexibility and the ability to switch strategies are fundamental to resilience and adaptive capacity. Social, political and economic systems that deny groups access to key technologies – whether buses for evacuation, communications, insurance or credit – reduce their flexibility, increase their vulnerability and leave them disproportionately subject to loss when extreme events occur. The case of Muzaffarabad in Pakistan clearly illustrates the central role of the private sector in creating and maintaining these systems. This role, however, must be balanced by the regulatory ability of government and the voices of civil society organizations if access is to be assured for all vulnerable groups rather than just the wealthy.

In addition to access, vulnerability is also influenced by the way technological choices are made. Whether the technology in question is a physical embankment system for controlling floods or an institutional safety net, such as an insurance system, the choice and design of technologies often depends on the degree to which decision-makers in governments, organizations and the market hear and are subject to pressure from diverse voices within society. The degree to which diverse voices 'can be heard' is, we believe, heavily influenced by the balance between individualistic market structures, hierarchically organized government entities and egalitarian social organizations. This is, in turn, a critical factor determining whether or not the approaches proposed will be accessible to, and protect the interests of, different groups. This does not have so much to do with the presence of a specific form of government but with the nature of pluralistic societies and the multiple institutions, entitlements and rights systems that shape them.

What does this mean on a practical level? It implies that to be effective, approaches must involve the private sector, civil society and government actors on an equal basis. The presence of multiple voices channelled through shared learning dialogue processes and public debate are the foundation of effective governance for long-term processes such as the ones required for responding effectively to the challenges of climate change.

Conclusions

The evolution of effective strategies for reducing disaster risks and adapting to climate change represents a fundamental challenge for human society on which our common future in many ways rests. Some responses targeted at specific risks or fully documented changes in climate, are essential. There is, however, substantial uncertainty regarding how changes in climatic conditions will affect local areas. Furthermore, disasters – whether climate related or caused by other natural hazards – often occur intermittently over long timescales. As a result, it is often difficult to sustain – or even identify – narrowly targeted responses. The ability to adapt and respond effectively to surprise and change, however, depends as much on underlying systems that enable communication, transport, finance, self-organization and learning as it does on risk-specific interventions. These systems – many of which can be developed and maintained through sustainable public, private or community-based operational models – represent a largely overlooked dimension in DRR and climate adaptation debates. Courses of action to strengthen them may, however, ultimately prove far more effective than generic attempts to target first-order risks.

In addition to underlying systems, the post-disaster context represents a largely unexplored terrain for risk reduction and adaptation. There is, of course, a fundamental ethical dilemma in focusing on the post-disaster reconstruction context for reducing vulnerabilities that have already been identified as affecting large areas and large populations. When accumulating scientific and other evidence clearly indicates the high vulnerability of populations or specific groups in coastal and other regions, responses are essential. This said, the social organization of human societies – the hugely differing perspectives and political positions they encompass – often makes it impossible to respond proactively to creeping or pulsed environmental problems (Glantz, 1999).

Few societies would, for example, support major population relocations or huge investments to alter basic infrastructure in coastal regions now as a response to sea-level rise or the likelihood of increases in storm activity. Political and popular support for actions of this nature to reduce future vulnerability is far more likely when existing systems have been disrupted. On a practical basis, therefore, change will occur in pulses. Building understanding and identifying the types of changes that can be both technically effective and socially viable represents, as a result, a major potential avenue for responding to hazards and the risks associated with climate change.

Notes

1   See also www.resalliance.org.
2   The *Oxford Pocket Dictionary of Current English 2006*, originally published by Oxford University Press 2006.
3   www.resalliance.org/576.php (accessed 4 December 2007).
4   www.epodunk.com/top10/diaspora/index.html and www.csmonitor.com/2005/0912/p01s01-ussc.html.

References

Benson, C. (2007). *Economic Analysis. Tools for Mainstreaming Disaster Risk Reduction.* Geneva, ProVention Consortium: 12.

Benson, C. and E. J. Clay (2002). *Disasters, Vulnerability and the Global Economy.* Washington, DC, World Bank.

Benson, C. and J. Twigg (2004). *Measuring Mitigation: Methodologies for Assessing Natural Hazard Risks and the Net Benefits of Mitigation – A Scoping Study.* Geneva, ProVention Consortium: 36.

Bouwer, L. M. and J. C. J. H. Aerts (2006). Financing climate change adaptation. *Disasters* 30(1): 49–63.

Department for International Development, (2005). *Natural Disaster and Disaster Risk Reduction Measures: A Desk Review of Costs and Benefits.* J. Samuel. London, Department for International Development, DFID: 45.

Dilley, M., R. S. Chen, et al (2005). *Natural Disaster Hotspots: A Global Risk Analysis.* Washington, DC, The World Bank: 132.

Donga, M. and R. Mechler (2005). *Cost-Benefit Analysis – A Useful Instrument for Assessing the Efficiency of Natural Disaster Risk Management,* One World and GTZ.

Dreze, J., A. Sen, et al, Eds. (1995). *The Political Economy of Hunger.* New Delhi, Oxford University Press.

FEMA (1997). *Report on Costs and Benefits of Natural Hazard Mitigation.* Washington DC, Federal Emergency Management Agency: 57.

Glantz, M. H., Ed. (1999). *Creeping Environmental Problems and Sustainable Development in the Aral Sea Basin.* Cambridge, Cambridge University Press.

Gunderson, L. H. (1999). Resilience, flexibility and adaptive management — antidotes for spurious certitude? *Conservation Ecology* 3(1): 7.

Gunderson, L. H. and C. S. Holling, Eds. (2002). *Panarchy: Understanding Transformations in Human and Natural Systems.* Washington, DC, Island Press.

Holling, C. S. (2001). Understanding the complexity of economic, ecological and social systems. *Ecosystems* 4: 390–405.

Holling, C. S. and G. K. Meffe (1996). Command and control and the pathology of natural resource management. *Conservation Biology* 10(2): 328–337.

Hoyois, P. and D. Guha-Sapir (2004). *Disasters Caused by Flood: Preliminary Data for a 30 Year Assessment of their Occurrence and Human Impact*. Health and Flood Risk Workshop; A Strategic Assessment of Adaptation Processes and Policies, University of East Anglia, Norwich, International workshop organized by the Tyndall Centre for Climate Change Research.

IRIN (2005). Disaster Reduction and the human cost of disaster. *IRIN Web special*, United Nations Office for the Coordination of Humanitarian Affairs: 41.

ISDR (2004). *Living with Risk: A Global Review of Disaster Reduction Initiatives*. New York and Geneva, International Strategy for Disaster Reduction, United Nations.

ISDR (2005). *Hyogo Framework for Action 2005–2015: Building the Resilience of Nations and Communities to Disasters*. World Conference on Disaster Reduction, Kobe, Hyogo, Japan, International Strategy for Disaster Reduction.

Kabat, P., W. v. Vierssen, et al (2005). Climate proofing the Netherlands. *Nature* 438(17): 283–284.

Khan, F. and M. Daanish (2007). 'Navigating the contours of the Pakistani hazardscapes: Disaster experience versus policy', in M. Moench and A. Dixit (Eds) *Working with the Winds of Change*, ProVention Consortium, ISET and ISET-Nepal, Geneva, Boulder and Kathmandu.

Logan, J. R. (2006). *The Impact of Katrina: Race and Class in Storm-Damaged Neighborhoods*, Brown University: 16.

Mechler, R. (2005). *Cost-benefit Analysis of Natural Disaster Risk Management in Developing and Emerging Countries*. Manual. Working paper, GTZ, Eschborn.

Messner, F., E. Penning-Rowsell, et al (2006). Guidelines for Socio-economic Flood Damage Evaluation. *FLOODsite Project*. Wallingford, European Community Sixth Framework Programme for European Research and Technological Development: 181.

MMC (2005). *Natural Hazard Mitigation Saves: An Independent Study to Assess the Future Savings from Mitigation Activities: Volume 2 – Study Documentation*. Washington DC, National Institute of Building Sciences: 144.

Moench, M. and A. Dixit, Eds. (2004). *Adaptive Capacity and Livelihood Resilience: Adaptive Strategies for Responding to Floods and Droughts in South Asia*. Institute for Social and Environmental Transition-International, Boulder; Institute for Social and Environmental Transition-Nepal, Kathmandu.

Moench, M. and A. Dixit, Eds. (2007). Working with the Winds of Change, ProVention Consortium, ISET and ISET-Nepal, Geneva, Boulder and Kathmandu.

Moench, M. and S. Stapleton (2007). *Water, Climate, Risk and Adaptation*. Cooperative Programme on Water and Climate, The Netherlands: 88.

Sainath, S. (1996). *Everybody Loves a Good Drought: Stories from India's Poorest Districts*. New Delhi, India, Penguin Books India.

Sen, A. (1999). *Poverty and Famines*. Delhi, Oxford University Press.

Telford, J., J. Cosgrave and R. Houghton (2006). *Joint Evaluation of the International Response to the Indian Ocean Tsunami: Synthesis Report*. London, Tsunami Evaluation Coalition.

Uddin, N. (2002). Disaster Management System in Southwestern Indiana. *Natural Hazards Review* 3(1): 19–30.

Wisner, B., P. Blaikie, et al (2004). *At Risk: Natural Hazards, People's Vulnerability and Disasters*. London, Routledge.

World Meterological Organization, Co-operative Programme on Water and Climate, et al (2006). *Risk Management, Thematic Document, Framework Theme 5*. 4th World Water Forum, Mexico City, CONAGUA.

Part IV

Adaptation and Development

14

Cautionary Tales:
Adaptation and the Global Poor

Robert W. Kates

Introduction

As environments change, all life adjusts, adapts and evolves. Human life responds in conscious and unconscious ways to such environmental change and even in anticipation of that change. These actions are variously termed human responses, coping actions, mitigating actions, adjustments and adaptations. Depending on context, both substantive and disciplinary, the terms have various shades of meaning. We geographers generally employ the long-established distinctions used in hazard assessment, and distinguish between short-term purposive or incidental adjustment and long-term biological or cultural adaptation. Over time, the distinction fades as the adjustments of yesteryear become incorporated into the cultural repertoire of adaptations. In this chapter the various terms are used interchangeably because of the widespread and official use of adaptation when referring to adjustment to climate change, but also because with a long-term perspective – tomorrow's adjustments may well be 2060's adaptations.

To date, almost all efforts to address global climate change focus on preventive action to limit greenhouse gases rather than adaptation. The subtitle of volume II of the Intergovernmental Panel on Climate Change (IPCC) report: *Impacts, Adaptations, and Mitigation of Climate Change: Scientific-Technical Analyses* (Watson et al, 1996) is a misnomer, where adaptation is concerned. Of the 728 pages of substantive text, about two-thirds are devoted to impacts, one third to mitigation and only 32 pages to adaptation. That so little work is done on adaptation is a function of both 'limitationist' and 'adaptationist' biases. The 'limitationists' fear that such work may weaken the social will to undertake greenhouse gas reduction and thus play into the hands of those that argue that any action is premature. Many 'adaptationists' see no need to study adaptation in any special way, simply trusting the invisible hand of either natural selection or market forces to encourage adaptation. Many also think of adaptation as providing little or no burden and ignore, for example, the often high social costs of adaptation. Finally, both sides are rooted in studies from the industrialized world and tend to ignore the lack of capacity to both prevent and adapt in developing countries.

Where adaptation has been considered, as in modelling of agriculture, the effects of using various adjustments are simulated. In the state-of-the art regional study of a four-state area in the US: Missouri, Iowa, Nebraska, and Kansas (MINK), 'low-cost' on-farm adjustments were considered for a climate scenario that uses as a climate analogue the decade of the 1930s (Rosenberg, 1993). In this study, economic costs of adaptation were considered and where they exceeded benefits, the adjustments were assumed not to have been adopted. Adaptations were also simulated in the major global study of climate change and world food supply, Fischer et al (1994) found that on average, climate changes resulting from a doubling of CO_2, would have only a small impact overall on global agricultural productivity, assuming a modest level of adjustment and the enrichment benefits for plant growth of increased CO_2 in the atmosphere. In their modelling, they employed two levels of adaptation: adjustments to be undertaken at the farm level without major changes in the agricultural system and those requiring a transformation of the agricultural system itself. The costs of adaptation or the availability of future water supplies were not modelled.

The possibilities for adaptation as well as its impacts are surely different in rich and poor countries and for different groups and places within countries (Bohle et al, 1994; Downing et al, 1997). For example, in the world food supply study, cereal production with adaptation was reduced by less than 3 per cent on average and even increased in one of the climate scenarios with a high level of adaptation. This global average was sharply differentiated, however, between developed and developing countries, with net declines in cereal production in the developing world, and net gains in the industrialized countries. Even assuming high levels of adaptation in developing countries, losses were reduced but not eliminated.

Within countries, one of the early findings of hazard research was that the ability to adjust and people's access to adjustments reflect existing divisions between rich and poor, powerful and powerless, ethnic or gender-favoured and ethnic or gender-denied. Wisner (1977), for example, identified such differences in drought adjustment in Kenya and subsequent studies have led to a generalized model of differential resource access (Blaikie et al, 1994).

We need to understand much more about the social costs of adaptation and differential access to it because adaptation, even by the invisible hand of the market, is not cost-free and does not yield the same benefits everywhere. The costs of adaptation include not only economic and social costs of the efforts to adapt, but also the social costs of adapting to the secondary effects of the adaptations themselves, and the losses suffered by groups and the locations bypassed or marginalized by the ensuing changes. Serious study of the true costs of adaptation and the differential ability to undertake it should be a major focus in contemplating response to global climate change. However, designing good studies is difficult.

Thus, much of the reasoning as to the success (or in rare cases, failure) of adjustment is by analogy, observing how people have adjusted to instances of socio-economic or technological change or to short-term environmental change (Glantz, 1988; Easterling, 1996; Burton, 1997). These analogue studies are from industrialized countries and include the use of climate analogues as in the MINK study (Rosenberg, 1993) or changes in resource use as in the case of the declining Ogallala Aquifer in the American high plains (Glantz and Ausubel, 1988). Easterling (1996) has recently reviewed these and other North American studies, using as analogues the translocation of crops (winter wheat; maize); introduction of new crops (soybeans and canola); and substitution of resources in response to scarcity (energy; groundwater). In another North American context, using today's weather and climate as an analogue, Burton (1997) cites a Canadian study that estimates the annual costs of adapting to their cold climate are US$11.6 billion while the average annual losses from 'atmospheric disturbances' of storm, hail, tornado and flood (1983–1994) were around $110 million.

This study, initiated with Robert S. Chen, sought to use five analogues from developing countries to see what can be learned about the adjustment to global change that can be made by poor people. Two of these involved adjustments to natural hazards directly related to climate: a comparative cross-national study of flood, drought and cyclone and of the Sahelian drought. Two others considered how agriculture was adapted in response to population growth in Africa and South Asia and addresses the process and problems of adaptation, not climate per se. The fifth examines a series of case studies that incorporate interactive effects of changes in population, economy and environment including in some cases, climate events. In all of these, three types of social costs were considered: the direct costs of adjustment, the costs of adjusting to the adjustments or responding to the secondary effects, and the costs of failing to adjust. Not all situations provided information on all sets of costs, but what they did provide is instructive.

Adaptation to Extreme Weather and Climate in Developing Countries

The best-studied analogues of adapting to environmental change in developing countries come from natural hazard research which studies human adjustments to extreme weather and climate events, such as droughts, floods and tropical cyclones. The most comprehensive cross-cultural study of adjustments, *The Environment as Hazard*, is now more than 20 years old but is available in a second edition (Burton et al, 1993). Its central findings appear still relevant today.

Table 14.1 *The comparative annual social costs of associated adaptation with various hazards (≈ 1975)**

Hazard	Country	Deaths/ 10^6 pop.	Damage	Adjustment	Total costs	Costs % GNP
Drought	Tanzania	40	0.70	0.80	1.50	1.84
	Australia	0	24.00	19.00	43.00	0.10
Flood	Sri Lanka	5	13.40	1.60	15.00	2.13
	US	2	40.00	8.00	48.00	0.11
Tropical	Bangladesh	3000	3.00	0.40	3.40	0.73
Cyclone	US	2	13.30	1.20	14.50	0.04

Source: (Burton et al, 1993, pp68–74).
Note: *Total costs, damage costs, and adjustment costs are in 1970s US dollars per person at risk.

In a series of national studies, agricultural drought in Australia and Tanzania, floods in Sri Lanka and the US, and tropical cyclones in Bangladesh and the US were compared. In each case, the annual social cost of each hazard was estimated using two basic measures: the annual average number of deaths (per million at risk) due to the hazard and the estimated economic value of damages sustained and of adjustment effort expended to prevent losses. For purposes of comparison, these are shown as costs per person at risk (in 1970s dollars) and as percentages of gross national product (GNP) as of the time that the study was carried out.

To illustrate, in Tanzania deaths due to agricultural drought were low and estimated to average annually 40 per million of the then 12 million at risk. Total costs of agricultural drought was estimated as equivalent to 1.8 per cent of GNP or a $1.50 per person at risk. Adjustments at $0.80 per person at risk were slightly more costly than damages at $0.70 for farm households. A reasonable approximation for labour invested in reducing possible drought losses was 10 days per year. The balance of the costs of adjustment were government expenditures ($0.21 per person at risk) for meteorological, climatological and crop varietal research; weather modification, irrigation and rural water-supply development; famine relief, food import and storage; and provision for migrants. For historical context, the period under study (prior to 1970) was generally favoured with ample precipitation. More recent costs would be considerably higher.

The economic costs of floods in Sri Lanka were much higher than for drought in Tanzania (about the same as a percentage of GNP). Damage losses far outweigh the costs of adjustment, despite significant investment in channels, dams and levees to avert flood damage. The most important social costs of tropical cyclones in Bangladesh were the enormous death toll (average 3000 per million for the 10 million at risk), with at least 225,000 having died in the storm of 1970 and over a 100,000 in 1991.

Global warming will almost surely bring more drought to some areas, more floods to others, and possibly more and greater cyclones. Adjustments to such extreme events in developing countries are ancient, widely implemented, primarily household based, and costly in effort expended. As a proportion of GNP, the social costs of adjustment are already high in developing countries and are relatively more costly than in industrialized countries, not absolutely, but in the proportion of available resources expended. And with economic and social change, many traditional adjustments become less relevant while at the same time government-organized adjustments, characteristic of industrialized countries, are as yet poorly developed. Under conditions found in much of the developing world, vulnerability to extreme events is actually growing because reasonably successful traditional adjustments are no longer being implemented and societal-organized adjustments are not yet available. Therefore the ability of developing countries to make cost-effective adjustments to climate extremes caused by global warming is by no means assured.

Adapting to Drought: Sahel 1968–1990

The Sahelian-Sudanic Zone of Africa marks the border between the desert and the forest and crosses a dozen African countries mostly between 10 and 20 degrees latitude. Rainfall below the previous 30-year norm has been experienced in most of the years between 1968 and 1990. Adjusting to this two decade-long drought period has been extraordinarily difficult for the peoples of the region and might be a harbinger of what increased warming without compensating moisture increases might bring. While there has been extensive writing on the drought, its impacts, and some analysis of the responses to it (Dalby et al, 1977; Somerville, 1986; Downing, et al, 1987; Glantz, 1987), there has been no overall study of the cumulative impacts of the drought and of the adjustments to it. An early study of the Sahelian drought (Kates, 1980, 1981) and subsequent events since then suggest the following observations regarding adjustments.

Despite slow starts, over two decades the international community acquired an increasing capability to prevent famine, except in situations of armed conflict. This capability includes: improved early warning of potential crop and animal loss, coordinated donor and food-aid mobilization; and the logistics to move and distribute large amounts of food and to do so with some consideration of its effect on local markets. This capability is reflected in successful efforts to provide food where people live rather than in distant relief camps to which they have been forced to migrate. And in a few countries, this international capability is matched locally with improved crisis planning and governmental coordinating mechanisms.

Some attention has also been focused on adjustments to reduce vulnerability to persistent drought and its stresses on ecosystems. Proposed adjustments have been often quite contradictory, reflecting the professional and ideological differences of their advocates. One group of proposed adjustments focuses on improved production technologies, such as higher-yielding drought-resistant plants and animals, irrigation, or improved ranching and grazing schemes. Another group of proposed adjustments focuses on the human- and drought-induced stress on natural ecosystems and proposed ways of scaling down production to a more appropriate carrying capacity or of encouraging tree-planting and agroforestry. On the consumption side, there are also some efforts to improve transportation and marketing and diminish the urban bias that moves food from the hungry rural areas to relatively well-fed cities.

It is also recognized that any successful adjustment is difficult without solving the problems that make the region so vulnerable to drought impacts. The list of such problems is long, and advocates strongly differ among themselves as to which problems to emphasize, but they include: poverty, global economics, neocolonialism, ethnic conflict and rapid population growth. Recurrent droughts exacerbate the many existing problems of the region. Thus it is difficult to separate out adjustments designed to cope with these long-term problems and those responsive to the extraordinary conditions of the drought. Indeed, it might be argued that the drought, when it received popular attention, helped initiate some longer-term externally aided projects that might not otherwise have been supported, such as major dam construction in West Africa.

Thus, over time, there is an improving capability to respond to drought as an extreme event, to prevent famine and to save lives. There is little success, however, in adjusting livelihood systems to the persistent drought and the stress placed on the ecological systems supporting agriculture and pastoralism. In fact, serious differences emerged in expert views as to which adaptations to pursue. Moreover, persistent drought is but one of a set of overwhelming problems affecting some of the poorest nations in the world and in most countries there is little internal capacity to cope even with the most pressing impacts of the drought, let alone the more subtle ones.

The Green Revolution: Food Production Adaptation to Population Growth

Between 1960 and today, population in Asia more than doubled. During that same period, a Green Revolution in rice and wheat production in Asia enabled that region to become essentially self-sufficient in cereal grains despite the enormous increase in population. At the core of the revolution were internationally developed rice and wheat varieties that were able to respond to high inputs of nutrients and water and by growing grain rather than straw. An extensive system was developed for producing and distributing seeds, providing credit, fertilizer, pesticides and water, and marketing the surplus.

If the Green Revolution is viewed as a massive adjustment to rapid population growth, the immediate direct costs of that adjustment are the costs of creating and maintaining that system. Over time the value of the increased production has clearly exceeded these costs. But over the last 20 years an extensive literature (Karim, 1986) has emerged that has documented a wide range of other costs of adjustment, adjusting to the adjustments, and of failure to adjust. These studies must be cautiously interpreted, however, as they tend to be highly polemical and polarized on the one hand and dated on the other.

Early studies trumpet achievements in increasing yields and output, and improving incomes for the early innovators adopting the new technology (Borlaug, 1971). Later writings are primarily revisionist, faulting the revolution for the inequalities engendered between small and large, rich and poor farmers, between well-watered and dry regions, and even between developing and industrialized countries (Griffin, 1974). Still later writings fault the technology itself on environmental and ecological grounds, for its large and unsustainable input requirements of energy, chemicals and water; for its vulnerability to pests and less than optimal growth conditions; for its displacement through the monoculture of rice and wheat of needed dietary complements of protein- and oil-rich crops; and for related impacts on forests, soils; and waters (Glaeser, 1987; Shiva, 1991).

Most recently, revisions of the revisions, purport to demonstrate that problems identified earlier did not actually occur, or were overcome over time. They demonstrate that over time small farmers benefited from the technology equally with large farmers, that wages and employment opportunities for landless labourers actually increased, and that improvements in the seeds and accompanying technologies have coped with many of the earlier problems (Lipton, 1989; Hazell and Ramasamy, 1991).

A judicious review of this literature suggests the following important observations with respect to adaptation costs. Adjustment can be rapid and in appropriate situations very favourable – social benefits exceeding social costs. Where irrigation and fertilizers were available and affordable, over the space of two decades both large and small farmers adopted the new technologies. More food, at lower prices was made available to the much larger population. Adapting to these adaptations, however, requires considerable and sustained effort.

The extensive monoculture, has increased the numbers and varieties of pests (Jirström, 1996). New pest-resistant varieties are needed every few years as well as new pest control regimes to cope with pesticide resistance and the threats to humans and other organisms from massive pesticide use. Intensive cropping with chemical nutrients has depleted soil micronutrients requiring these to be added as well. Intensive water use has required new water works with their social and environmental problems and has led to increased waterlogging and salinity. The very bounty itself has lowered market prices for grains, squeezing farmers between decreasing real prices and increasing costs for manufactured inputs, narrowing margins of profitability and increasing indebtedness. And there is ample evidence that the productivity gains have slowed or stopped altogether and thus a new technological fix, perhaps from biotechnology, is required. There are also large, but poorly defined social costs in failing to adjust. Inequality between regions has increased, the numbers of farms and farmers has decreased, and little is known of the fate of the poor, impoverished and dispossessed.

For adaptation to climate change, many features of the Green Revolution are most encouraging. With international aid, traditional biotechnology was effectively harnessed in a relatively short space of time to address a high-profile problem – in this case the inability to feed a rapidly growing population. But success was limited to favoured regions and the adaptations themselves have created a set of secondary effects that require new remedies. The costs of adapting to the adaptations continue to be high.

Adapting to Population Pressure in African High-Density Areas

Unlike Asia, in Africa there has not been a Green Revolution. While population growth rates in Africa are the highest in the world, per capita food availability has declined since 1977. While sub-Saharan Africa overall is still sparsely populated (27 people/km²), high-density areas (>200/km²) are scattered throughout the continent. These create a 'natural experiment' for examining the relationship between population growth, increased density, agricultural intensification and the well-being of people. How did the inhabitants of these areas adapt to population growth and increased density over five decades?

Five case studies from densely settled areas of East Africa (Kenya, Rwanda, Tanzania, and Uganda) and five from West Africa (central, eastern, and northern Nigeria) were prepared by researchers with extensive knowledge of the study areas, many of whom had conducted field research in the areas over a period of decades (Turner et al, 1993). Each case study, using a common protocol, examined agricultural and other societal changes over periods ranging from 10 to 50 years as adaptations in response to increasing population.

Overall, farmers have kept pace with population growth by intensifying agricultural productivity through increased labour (rather than modern technology), by dietary changes to higher-caloric yielding crops such as cassava, by finding new and diverse sources of income, and by outmigration. These adjustments have been sufficient to sustain a much larger population, but not to make the transition to the higher levels of productivity needed for improved well-being. There were also considerable differences between study sites. In three, there was evidence of success, not merely maintaining subsistence but improving the quality of life. And in three of the ten studies, there had been a clear deterioration in the quality of life with the ability to sustain the population only through substantial outmigration. Thus, this African experience with high-density populations does not support expectations of a Malthusian collapse of food supply in the face of rapid population growth. But it also indicates that technological changes sufficient to achieve the much higher levels of agricultural productivity required for an improvement in well-being will not occur spontaneously.

In contrast to the Green Revolution analogue, the many adjustments evidenced in the case studies were unplanned, locally undertaken, and used primarily indigenous technology. As an analogue, these case studies tell us of the considerable capacity of poor people to adapt to prolonged and extended change similar to what some expect with global warming. Adjustment can be local, spontaneous, and successful in maintaining subsistence under difficult conditions. At the same time, in the absence of external inputs, markets or new technology, it is clearly limited in its capacity to move beyond subsistence. Also, the studies do not examine the social costs of some of the adjustments undertaken, for example the nutritional and gastronomic loss in dietary change to denser but less desirable foods or the impact of outmigration on cities or marginal rural areas.

Adapting to Interactive Stresses of Population, Economy and Environment

Studies of adaptation are difficult to undertake due to many simultaneous changes – for example, population growth interacts with environmental change and with economic conditions. Several such important interactions are documented in case studies that link poverty and environment in developing countries. Such case studies are rare though, for despite the widespread view that poverty and environmental degradation are strongly linked, there are actually few studies that carefully describe the actual linkages. Through surveys of colleagues and searches of 40 journals, some 30 case studies (14 from Africa, 6 from Latin America, 9 from Asia, and 1 global) were located (Kates and Haarmann, 1991, 1992).

Despite the variety of locales, methods of study and reporting, the case studies have much in common. The rural inhabitants of these case study locales found it increasingly difficult to maintain access to their natural resources for agriculture, herding or fishing in the face of growing population, increased competition for land, and 'development' itself. Common threads run through these stories of poor people's displacement from their lands, division of their resources and degradation of their environments.

Poor people were displaced by activities intended for development or commercialization that deprive them of land or traditional access to common property resources of land or water. Lands and water were divided and reduced as they shared with children or sold off pieces as needed to cope with extreme losses (crop failure, illness, death), social requirements (marriages, celebrations) or simple subsistence. Resources were also degraded by excessive or inappropriate use (clearing, overgrazing, unsuitable cropping), by failure to maintain or restore protective works (canals, check dams, drainage, terraces) and by the loss of productive capacity from natural hazards.

Driving these processes were two forces external to the case study locales: development/commercialization and natural hazard events, and two internal to the communities studied: population growth and existing poverty (Figure 14.1). These culminated in three major spirals of impoverishment and environmental decline – displacement, division and degradation – in each of which two of the driving forces dominate. Poor people were displaced from their resources by richer claimants or by competition for existing land or employment, driven by development activities, commercialization and by population growth. For these displaced people, division of the remaining resources followed, or else forced migration to other, usually more marginal, areas. Driven, by population growth and the existing poverty, meagre resources were further divided to meet the needs of generations or the exigencies of poverty. Remaining resources were then degraded by excessive use of divided lands, or inappropriate use of environments unable to sustain the requisite resource use. Driven by poverty and natural hazard events, poor families were unable to maintain protective works or to restore damaged resources affected by natural hazards of disease, drought, flood, soil erosion, landslides and pests.

The very development-commercialization activities that displace poor people are precisely those that would constitute adaptive strategies to climate change, other environmental change and to population growth – large-scale agriculture, irrigation, hydroelectric development, forestry, and wildlife preservation. While these strategies may benefit some groups and larger national or regional purposes, they frequently harm local, indigenous and poor populations. Poor households are increasingly unable to pay the costs of adaptation because they lack the labour to restore or to maintain protective works, the means to hire specialized skills or make needed inputs, or the access to public programmes of resource improvement and renewal. The studies also tell of the high cost of trying to adjust to existing natural hazards and the pauperization and enforced

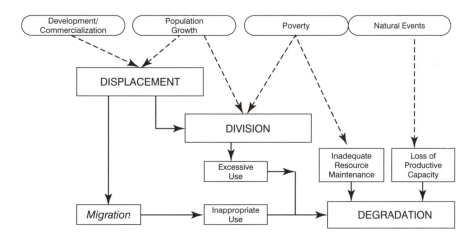

Figure 14.1 *Impoverishment–degradation spirals.*

migration that failure to adjust entails. Thus, they tell us that the social costs of adaptation includes the displacement of poor people from their lands, waters and vegetation; that poor people are hard-pressed to maintain even existing adjustments; and that the failure to adjust is extraordinarily heavy on those least able to bear additional burdens.

Can the Global Poor Adapt to Global Climate Change?

The conclusion from these five studies must surely be yes, but with great difficulty and much pain. Poor people everywhere cope with drought, flood and storm, and inhabitants of some of the poorest countries in the world have weathered two decades of severe drought. In the face of population growth unique in human history, food supplies kept up with population growth, not only in the lands favoured by the Green Revolution, but in places in Africa where it was and is still unknown. But the social costs of adaptation have been enormous: in the tolls of lives lost or diminished and in the direct costs of adaptation, the costs of adapting to the adaptations, and the costs of failing to adapt.

In developing countries, coping with the climate extremes of drought, flood and storm is the moral equivalent of war – requiring the equivalent effort in percentage of GNP that most countries expend on national defence. Despite this enormous effort, success is limited. The damage toll is very high from natural hazard or as in the case of responding to population growth, indigenous adaptation can maintain life but not much more. And the linked tales of poor people and environment tell of how one group's adaptation is another group's hazard.

Thus, if the global poor are to adapt to global change, it will be critical to focus on poor people, and not on poor countries as does the prevailing North–South dialogue. The interests of poor people are not always the same as the interests of poor countries, since in the interest of 'development', the poor may grow poorer. In adapting to global environmental change, we need to break the impoverishment–degradation spiral by addressing the underlying causes of population growth, poverty, hazards, and development and commercialization, and by interrupting the cycles of displacement, division and degradation. For it is in these cycles that the true social costs of adaptation appear.

References

Blaikie, P., Cannon, T., Davis, I., and Wisner, B.: 1994, *At Risk: Natural Hazards, People's Vulnerability and Disasters,* Routledge, London.

Bohle, H. G., Downing, T. E., and Watts, M. J.: 1994, 'Climate Change and Social Vulnerability: Towards a Sociology and Geography of Food Insecurity', *Global Environmental Change* 4(1), 37–48.

Borlaug, N. E.: 1971, *The Green Revolution, Peace and Humanity,* PRB Selection No. 35, Population Reference Bureau, Washington.

Burton, I.: 1997, 'Vulnerability and Adaptive Response in the Context of Climate and Climate Change', *Climatic Change* **20**(1), 1–12.

Burton, I., Kates, R. W., and White, G. F.: 1993, *The Environment as Hazard,* Second edition, The Guilford Press, New York.

Dalby, D., Harrison Church, R. J., and Bezzaz, F. eds.: 1977, *Drought in Africa II,* African Environment Special Report No. 6., International African Institute, London.

Downing, J., Berry, L., Downing, L., Downing, T. E., and Ford, R.: 1987, *Drought and Famine in Africa, 1981–1986: The U.S. Response,* Cooperative Agreement on Settlement and Resource Systems Analysis, Clark University, Worcester, MA.

Downing, T. E., Ringius, L., Hulme, M., and Waughray, D.: 1997, 'Adapting to Climate Change in Africa', *Mitigation and Adaptation Strategies for Global Change* **2**, 19–44.

Easterling, W. E.: 1996, 'Adapting North American Agriculture to Climate Change in Review', *Agricultural and Forest Meteorology* **80**, 1–53.

Fischer, G., Frohberg, K., Parry, M., and Rosenzweig, C.: 1994, 'Climate Change and World Food Supply, Demand, and Trade: Who Benefits, Who Loses?' *Global Environmental Change* **4**(1), 7–23.

Glaeser, B. (ed.): 1987, *The Green Revolution Revisited: Critique and Alternatives,* Allen and Unwin, London.

Glantz, M. H.: 1987, 'Drought and Economic Development in Sub-Saharan Africa', in D. A. Wilhite and W. E. Easterling eds. *Planning for Drought: Toward a Reduction of Societal Vulnerability.,* Westview Press, Boulder CO, 297–316.

Glantz, M. H. ed.: 1988, *Societal Responses to Regional Climatic Change: Forecasting by Analogy,* Westview Press, Boulder CO.

Glantz, M. H. and Ausubel, J. H.: 1988, 'Impact Assessment by Analogy: Comparing the Impacts of the Ogallala Aquifer Depletion and CO_2-Induced Climate Change', in M. H. Glantz, ed. *Societal Responses to Regional Climatic Change: Forecasting by Analogy,* Westview Press, Boulder CO, 113–142.

Griffin, K. B.: 1974, *The Political Economy of Agrarian Change: An Essay on the Green Revolution,* Macmillan, London.

Hazell, P. B. R. and Ramasamy, C.: 1991, *The Green Revolution Reconsidered: The Impact of High-Yielding Rice Varieties in South India,* Johns Hopkins University Press, Baltimore.

Jirström, M.: 1996, *In the Wake of the Green Revolution: Environmental and Socio-Economic Consequences of Intensive Rice Agriculture – The Problem of Weeds in Muda, Malaysia,* Lund University press, Lund, Sweden.

Karim, M. B.: 1986, *The Green Revolution: An International Bibliography,* Greenwood Press, New York.

Kates, R. W.: 1980, 'Drought Impact in the Sahelian-Sudanic Zone of West Africa: A Comparative Analysis of 1910–15 and 1968–74', *Office of Evaluation Working Paper* No. 32, USAID, also *Background Paper No. 2,* Center for Technology, Environment and Development, Clark University.

Kates, R. W.: 1981, 'Drought in the Sahel: Competing Views as to What Really Happened in 1910–14 and 1968–74', *Mazingira* **5**(2), 72–83.

Kates, R. W. and Haarmann, V.: 1991, *Poor People and Threatened Environments: Global Overviews, Country Comparisons, and Local Studies,* Research Report RR-91-2, Alan Shawn Feinstein World Hunger Program, Brown University, Providence RI.

Kates, R. W. and Haarmann, V.: 1992, 'Where the Poor Live: Are The Assumptions Correct?' *Environment,* **34**(4), 4–11, 25–28.

Lipton, M.: 1989, *New Seeds and Poor People,* Unwin Hyman, London.

Rosenberg, N.: 1993, *Towards an Integrated Impact Assessment of Climate Change: The MINK Study,* Kluwer Academic publishers, Dordrecht, The Netherlands.

Shiva, V.: 1991, 'The Green Revolution in the Punjab', *The Ecologist* **21**(2), 57–60.

Somerville, C. M.: 1986, *Drought and Aid in the Sahel: A Decade of Development Cooperation,* Westview, Boulder, CO.

Turner, B. L. II, Hyden, G., and Kates, R. W. eds.: 1993, *Population Growth and Agricultural Change in Africa,* University Press of Florida, Gainesville, FL.

Watson, R. T., Zinyowera, M. C., and Moss, R. H.: 1996, *Climate Change 1995: Impacts, Adaptations, and Mitigation of Climate Change: Scientific-Technical Analyses,* Cambridge University Press, Cambridge.

Wisner, B. G., jr, : 1977: *The Human Ecology of Drought in Eastern Kenya,* PhD Dissertation, Clark University, Worcester, MA.

15

Adaptation to Climate Change in the Developing World

W. Neil Adger, Saleemul Huq, Katrina Brown, Declan Conway and Mike Hulme

Introduction

Negotiators from many of the world's industrialized and developing countries meet each year in an ongoing evolution of one of the most contentious and critical international environmental agreements, the UN Framework Convention on Climate Change (UNFCCC). This convention encapsulates the major dilemmas of development, equity, marginalization and globalization within its remit and is likely to have far-reaching consequences across the world in matters as wide-ranging as energy use and settlement patterns. Climate change is arguably the most persistent threat to global stability in the 21st century. The Convention itself has learned the lessons from existing international environmental agreements in building legitimacy through a large-scale significant international scientific effort funded by governments through the UN, known as the Intergovernmental Panel on Climate Change (IPCC) (see Jäger et al, 2001). In Marrakesh in Morocco in November 2001, at the Seventh Conference of the Parties, delegates focused their minds on both adaptation to climate change and mitigation measures and, for the first time, formally recognized the dilemmas of adaptation for the developing nations. This recognition took the form of funding mechanisms to assist countries to adapt. The Delhi Declaration from the Eighth Conference of the Parties in November 2002 reinforced the importance of adaptation. The Delhi Declaration, in effect, has linked the participation of the developing world in mitigation of emissions to action and funding on adaptation to the impacts of climate change.

The IPCC proclaims that there is now little doubt that human-induced climate change is happening. All societies consequently need to learn to cope with the changes that are predicted – warmer temperatures, drier soils, changes in weather extremes and rising sea levels. Although it remains difficult to unambiguously distinguish human-induced change from natural variation in climate at small scales, evidence of long-term geophysical and biological changes is now apparent in many parts of the world, such as the retreat of mountain glaciers, the earlier arrival of spring (IPCC, 2001a) and changes in primary productivity (Lucht et al, 2002). But research in this area necessarily encompasses insights from social as well as natural sciences and from policy analysts even outside the IPCC process that, by its nature, cannot be all-encompassing. Participants at a meeting in London in October 2001, hosted by the Tyndall Centre and the International Institute for Environment and Development, including climate scientists, humanitarian relief and international development agencies,[1] argued that new priorities for research and policy in this area are required, reflecting the lived experience of resource-dependent societies in the developing world in coping with climate variability, and even with observed climate change in the recent past. And these lessons, they argued, should feed upwards into the actions of international development agencies and to the whole notion of adaptation within the processes and mechanisms of the UN Framework Convention on Climate Change.

The IPCC in its Third Assessment published in 2001 (IPCC, 2001b) has assessed the capacity of the world to cope with and adapt to the inevitable impacts that climate change will bring. While this assessment was far from comprehensive, it finds, not surprisingly, that the impacts of climate change are not evenly distributed – the people who will be exposed to the worst of the impacts are the ones least able to cope with the associated risks (e.g. Smit et al, 2001). But the meeting in London highlighted that people of developing nations are not passive victims. Indeed, in the past they have had the greatest resilience to droughts, floods and other catastrophes. Pastoralists in the West African Sahel have adapted to cope with rainfall decreases of 25–33 per cent in the 20th century, while resilience in the face of changing climate has been documented for smallholder farmers in Bangladesh and Vietnam, and indigenous hunting communities in the Canadian Arctic (e.g. Cross and Barker, 1992; Mortimore, 1998; Huq et al, 1999; Huq, 2001; Berkes and Jolly, 2001; Adger et al, 2001b; Roncoli et al, 2001).

Given this apparent paradox – the discrepancy between the conclusions of a global assessment and the past experience of societies living with environmental change – a new and agreed research agenda is clearly required. What are the parameters of risk and vulnerability in developing countries? How can people in developing countries enhance their capacity to adapt to changes in climate that are now both more persistent and more extensive?

Are Developing Countries at Risk from the Impacts of Future Climate Change?

Elements of vulnerability

Nearly all human societies and activities are sensitive to climate in some way or other. This is because in large measure where people live and how they generate a livelihood and wealth is influenced by the ambient climate. Since climate is inherently variable for quite natural reasons, human societies have always and everywhere had to develop coping strategies in the face of unwelcome variations in climate or weather extremes – for example migration and transhumance in semi-arid pastoralist societies or financial insurance mechanisms in the case of industrial societies. Some of these coping strategies are more technologically dependent, better resourced, or more robust or resilient than others – compare coastal communities in the Netherlands with those in Bangladesh – and therefore populations today are differentially vulnerable to existing variations in climate and weather based on structural factors.

The vulnerability or security of individuals and of societies is determined, not only by the likely responses of the resources on which individuals depend, but by the availability of resources and, crucially, by the entitlement of individuals and groups to call on these resources. This is well documented across a wide range of political and economic circumstances and development processes (e.g. Sen, 1981, 1999; Hewitt, 1983, 1997; Watts and Bohle, 1993; Ribot et al, 1996; Adger, 1999). Vulnerability is therefore a socially constructed phenomenon influenced by institutional and economic dynamics. The vulnerability of a system to climate change is determined by its exposure, by its physical setting and sensitivity, and by its ability and opportunity to adapt to change. To illustrate these categories, sensitivity will be high where the system in question includes, for example, settlements built on flood plains, hill slopes or low-lying coastal areas. In terms of action, adaptation may take the form of reducing dependence on vulnerable systems such as diversifying food production away from a limited number of drought-prone crops, of decreasing sensitivity by avoiding building settlements and infrastructure in high-risk locations, or by strengthening existing systems so that they are less likely to be damaged by unusual events.

These emerging conceptualizations of vulnerability and adaptation clearly draw on insights from risk and natural hazards, vulnerability to hunger and famine, and ideas of entitlement and autarky in development (e.g. Sen, 1981, 1999; Hewitt, 1983, 1997; Ribot et al, 1996). But vulnerability to climate change, as with vulnerability to hazards, is not strictly synonymous with poverty. Although poverty and marginalization are key driving forces of vulnerability and constrain individuals in their coping and long-term adaptation (see Cannon, 1994), vulnerability to future climate change is likely to have distinct characteristics and create new vulnerabilities. This is not to say that those most marginalized are not most at risk. Indeed it has been argued that both vulnerability and adaptation processes to climate change are likely to reinforce unequal economic structures (see Chapter 14, this volume).

How will the underlying vulnerability change in the future as climate changes? Or does the vulnerability 'map' of today's world simply project forward in time? Just as there is differential vulnerability to today's climate, is there differential vulnerability to future climate change? Answering these questions requires some understanding of the broad characteristics of future climate change, as well as an understanding of the sensitivity and exposure of different communities and activities to climate.

Global climate is already warming at a rate unprecedented in the past 1000 years (IPCC, 2001a) and is therefore inevitably altering the character of local and regional weather around the world. A different global climate must by definition induce different experiences of local weather. Although we cannot lay out a simple cause-and-effect chain from a severe weather episode back to human-induced climate change, we can begin to identify those parts of the world where we are already observing rather different weather characteristics from those that have been experienced in earlier decades. Thus the frequency of intense precipitation events is increasing over many northern mid-latitude regions (Easterling et al, 2000); instances of extreme summer heat, often combined with high humidity, have increased in most world regions; El Niño-Southern Oscillation

(ENSO) episodes over the last two decades have been both unprecedently large (e.g. 1997/1998) and prolonged (e.g. 1991/1994; Trenberth and Hoar, 1997); and severe hurricanes (e.g. Hurricane Mitch) and extensive riverine (e.g. Mozambique) and coastal flooding (e.g. Orissa) have led to many tens of thousands of premature deaths.

That the global climate is changing is undisputed. The trend in climate over the past century – a globally averaged change of nearly 1°C has occurred concurrently with changes in some extreme event regimes as shown in Table 15.1, based on the summaries of the IPCC (2001a). This suggests that future climate change will bring about further extension of many of these trends. Of course, some of the projections, and some of the observed historical trends, are known with more confidence than others. So although data from around the world show very evident patterns in reduced diurnal temperature ranges and higher minimum temperatures and frost-free days, there is little or no consensus on whether tropical cyclones have been becoming more damaging than in the past, let alone whether the regimes will alter significantly in the future (e.g. Diaz and Pulwarty, 1997; Henderson-Sellers et al, 1998).

Table 15.1 *Estimates of confidence in observed and projected change in extreme weather and climate events*

Changes in climate phenomenon	Confidence in observed changes (latter half of 20th century)	Confidence in projected changes (during 21st century)
Higher maximum temperatures and more hot days over nearly all land areas	Likely	Very likely
Higher minimum temperatures, fewer cold days and frost days over nearly all land areas	Very likely	Very likely
Reduced diurnal temperature range over most land areas	Very likely	Very likely
Increase of heat index over land areas	Likely over many areas	Very likely over most areas
More intense precipitation events	Likely (northern hemisphere mid–high lat. areas)	Very likely over many areas
Increased summer continental drying and associated risk of drought	Likely in a few areas	Likely over most mid-latitude continental interiors
Increase in tropical cyclone peak wind intensities	Not observed in few analyses available	Likely over some areas
Increase in tropical cyclone mean and peak precipitation intensities	Insufficient data for assessment	Likely over some areas

Source: IPCC, 2001a

None of the historically observed extreme weather events, such as the ENSO events mentioned above, on their own represent particularly convincing evidence that humans are altering global climate. Taken collectively, however, and placed in the context that at a global scale there is strong evidence of a human fingerprint on climate (Mitchell et al, 2001), a wise inference from these data is that historical statistics and experiences of local weather are *unlikely* to provide a sound basis for economic planning and resource management for the future. We can illustrate this past and future change in climate using annual average temperature at a country level as an indicator. We do this for Brazil, Tanzania and Bangladesh in Figure 15.1. All three countries have experienced a warming of their climate over the last 100 years – between 0.4 and 0.8°C – and this warming is likely to continue, if not accelerate, in the decades ahead. For this particular model calculation these countries warm by a further 1–2°C over the next 50 years, the rate of warming partly depending on the future growth in global greenhouse gas emissions. In either assumed world, however, further warming is substantial and easily exceeds natural variability within the next two decades (after 2015 vertical line in each part of Figure 15.1).

Uncertainty and its characteristics

The estimates of temperature for three developing countries in Figure 15.1 show widening ranges the further into the future we look. Quantifying this uncertainty has been the subject of the greatest efforts among climate scientists, teasing out how much is due to our inability to model precisely the physical climate system and how much is due to our inability to foresee the evolution of the human system and its production of greenhouse gases.

Part of the reason why there are diverging estimates of temperature and other variables into the future is associated with not knowing accurately how the climate system reacts to unprecedented emissions of greenhouse gases or knowing how clouds, forest, grasslands and particularly the world's oceans react to climate perturbations and how they feed back into the system. This uncertainty surrounding future climate

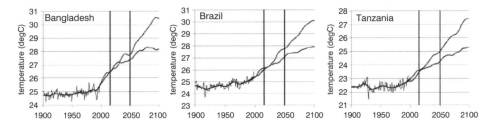

Figure 15.1 *Past and future changes in annual average temperature for Brazil, Tanzania and Bangladesh*

Notes: Figures from 1900–2000 are observed. 2000–2100 estimates are calculated using the Hadley Centre model (HadCM2) assuming two different global greenhouse gas emissions scenarios – unmitigated (upper line) and mitigated (lower line). Vertical lines mark 2015 and 2050.

projections is often manifest in ranges of estimates for particular climate parameters. Table 15.2 highlights inter-model disparities in future rainfall change in Africa (from IPCC, 2001a) for the key rainfall seasons in West Africa (June to August) and Southern Africa (December to February). In Southern Africa the rainfall change in December, January and February is inconsistent between models and in West Africa the coherence of the signal in June, July and August is affected by the level of the emissions scenario, with low emissions producing an inconsistent signal and high emissions suggesting no change in rainfall. Similar levels of uncertainty in future rainfall apply elsewhere in Africa and the developing world, although inter-climate model differences in future temperature changes are much smaller, particularly in the northern hemisphere (IPCC, 2001a). For the agricultural and water sectors, however, inter-climate model differences in rainfall change often remain a barrier to the effective use of climate change information by managers and stakeholders.

Uncertainties to do with the evolution of societies are of a different nature. The rate of growth of the world's population into the 21st century, the rate of development of low or zero carbon technologies and their global uptake, are fundamentally unknown. Yet these properties of our future world will increasingly determine the future emissions of greenhouse gases into the global atmosphere. For these parameters, the uncertainty stems less from the various methods for their estimation than from the contested and political nature of the changes implied (Carter and La Rovere, 2001; O'Neill et al, 2001).

Some recent efforts have been made to reconcile these two sets of uncertainties – physical modelling and social forecasting – or at least to characterize and distinguish between them (Schneider, 2001; Wigley and Raper, 2001). Although projections of climate change into the future remain fundamentally uncertain, and are even less clear for any specific location within a country, climate change will nevertheless present a significant challenge for developing countries. Climate change is likely to result in societal impacts through changes in water, natural resources, food systems, marine ecosystems and through the need to cope with a changing regime of weather extremes. The need to adapt to these changes remains an inescapable conclusion. Following from these observations, we argue that there are two further key research areas – understanding adaptation processes and understanding the international political economy of response to the threat.

Table 15.2 *A summary of inter-climate model consistency regarding future rainfall change for Africa caused by scientific uncertainty and future emissions rates of greenhouse gases*

Region	December to February		June to August	
	High emissions scenario	*Low emissions scenario*	*High emissions scenario*	*Low emissions scenario*
West Africa	Small increase	Small increase	No change	Inconsistent
Southern Africa	Inconsistent	Inconsistent	Small decrease	Small decrease

Source: adapted from IPCC, 2001a

Adaptation in Developing Countries: Past, Present and Future?

Given the potential risks associated with climate change, a serious effort on characterizing and understanding adaptation is therefore now under way. Analogues of adaptation in the past are complemented with policy and social science research on the present adaptive capacity of governments, civil society and markets to deal with climate perturbations. The economic costs of future adaptations are being derived by examining the differences between the economic losses associated with scenarios of technology uptake and diffusion. Among these approaches, a key issue is the identification of successful adaptations in the developing world where the greatest risk and physical vulnerability persists. But even where successful examples are identified, from indigenous strategies for resource management to large-scale infrastructure and irrigation, there will still be winners and losers.

First of all it is necessary to distinguish adaptation by who is undertaking it and the interests of the diverse stakeholders involved. It is clear that individuals and societies will adapt and have been adapting to climate change over the course of human history – climate is part of the wider environmental landscape of human habitation. Thus individuals and societies are vulnerable to climate risks and other factors and this vulnerability can act as a driver for adaptive resource management. There are various geographic scales and social agents involved in adaptation. Some adaptation by individuals is undertaken in response to climate threats, often triggered by individual extreme events (Ribot et al, 1996). Other adaptation is undertaken by governments on behalf of society, sometimes in anticipation of change, but, again, often in response to individual events.

But these levels of decision-making are not independent – they are embedded in social processes that reflect the relationship between individuals, their networks, capabilities and social capital, and the state (Adger, 2001). Sometimes a distinction is drawn between planned adaptation, assumed to be undertaken by governments on behalf of society, and autonomous adaptation by individuals (summarized in Smit et al, 2001). But this distinction obfuscates the role of the state in providing security, or in using security as a weapon of coercion when faced with an environmental risk. The nature of the relationship between individuals and agents of government in handling risk is a fraught but under-researched area (Adger, 2001). Political ecology approaches demonstrate that, for example, when faced with a flood risk, residents of marginalized but risky areas of Georgetown, Guyana, have only a limited set of adaptation options – and the state allows such risks to exist as part of the politized nature of urban planning and control (Pelling, 1999).

Realizing that action is required to enhance the adaptive capacity of the most vulnerable societies and groups, an emerging research agenda is focused on identifying generic determinants of resilience. This is being undertaken in part through learning the lessons from present and past adaptations. These determinants include the social capital of societies, the flexibility and innovation in the institutions of government and the private sector to grasp opportunities associated with climate change, and the underlying health status and well-being of individuals and groups faced with the impacts of climate change (Adger, 2001). Agricultural communities in northern Nigeria have demonstrated resilience through continued increases in per capita agricultural production and stability in the last three decades of the 20th century at a time of increasing aridity and population growth. In Bangladesh, new local government investments in shelters have helped to reduce mortality from cyclones. The key is to pick out the characteristics of the institutional and technological conditions that promote broad-based and equitable adaptation.

So the role of collective action in facilitating adaptation is an important issue where lessons can be learned from political ecology, and other theoretical insights, for present-day adaptation processes. From research on collective action (Agrawal, 2001) it is clear that the size of the group undertaking the collective action, the boundaries of the resource at risk, the homogeneity of the decision-making group, the distribution of benefits of management, and other factors are all important in determining the ultimate success of collective management. Research is required on how collective action is central to adaptive capacity at various scales of decision-making. At present, insights about responses to climate change as collective action are primarily used to examine national-level cooperative action to reduce greenhouse gas emissions under the UN Framework Convention on Climate Change (Müller, 2002), rather than on how the process of adaptation evolves.

Analogues of past climate change contrast with scenarios derived from climate model experiments in the search for adaptation insights. The analogue approach involves taking detailed case studies of past responses to climate variability and extremes (temporal analogues) or present-day behaviour in regions with climate conditions similar to those that might possibly develop in the region of interest (spatial analogues). The aim is to establish how individuals and institutions anticipate or respond to reduce the risks of different types of climate variability and how policy has influenced these actions. Understanding the present-day effects and response to climate variability at all levels of social organization is a prerequisite for studying the effects and responses to future climate change and for identifying the key determinants of successful adaptation in the future.

High levels of interannual rainfall variability and their effects on water resources in Africa can provide illustrative examples of climate–environment–society interactions. A commonly cited drawback to the analogue approach to climate change assessment is that the characteristics of future climate change are likely to be very different to past climate variability, particularly in terms of the rate and magnitude of change. Examples exist for Africa, however, where the observed rainfall variability is *greater* than changes suggested by climate models for the next 50–100 years (Hulme, 1998).

Figure 15.2 shows three patterns of rainfall variability together with examples of the high level of variability in African water resource systems primarily in response to rainfall conditions during the 20th century. The panels on the left depict catchment average rainfall series and the panels on the right depict the river discharge or lake levels of the corresponding catchments that generally exhibit similar temporal characteristics to rainfall. The three locations highlight examples of long-term *trend* (Niger river, Sahel), *periodic fluctuations* (Blue Nile, Ethiopian Highlands), and long-term *change* and short-term *extremes* (Lake Victoria, East Africa).

The most pronounced example of variability has been the multi-decade decline in rainfall over the Sahel where the 1961–1990 average is about 25 per cent drier than

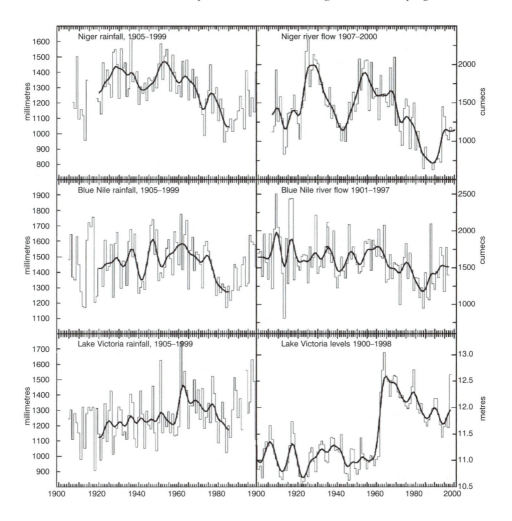

Figure 15.2 *Three examples of rainfall and river systems in Africa exhibiting high levels of temporal variability: the Niger, Sahel; the Blue Nile, Ethiopian Highlands; and lake levels in Lake Victoria, East Africa*

Source: adapted from Conway, 2002

Note: Left-hand panels: catchment average rainfall series (1905–1999), the decadel filter is not shown for the early and later parts of the rainfall series because for these periods the series are less reliable as they are based on low numbers of rain gauges. Right-hand panels: river discharge and lake levels.

earlier decades (Hulme et al, 2001) with dramatic consequences for river flows in the region (e.g., the Niger; Figure 15.2). Local long-term studies of agricultural practices and the social and economic conditions during this dry period highlight the dynamic nature of individuals' capacity to successfully adapt to change (see, for example, Mortimore and Adams, 1999) and the complex interplay of other, non-climate factors.

Benson and Clay (1998) illustrate the complexity of relating drought shocks to macroeconomic indicators in some African countries, highlighting highly differentiated, economy-wide impacts and the importance of national economic structure, resource endowments and other short-term economic factors.

The second example in Figure 15.2 shows periodic fluctuations in Blue Nile river flows that have led to significant water resource management problems in Egypt. During the past two decades conditions have moved from a prolonged period of low flows with the very real threat of water shortage in Egypt (only alleviated by a timely high flood in 1988) to a series of relatively high flows that have brought the High Aswan Dam reservoir to record levels and enabled the Egyptian government to pursue a major expansion programme of irrigated agriculture into the Western Desert and Sinai. The resultant increase in demand for water may, from a climatic perspective, be maladaptive in that it is likely to increase Egypt's vulnerability to climatically induced future changes in water supply.

The third example in Figure 2 shows long-term change and rapid fluctuations in Lake Victoria levels due to the combined effects of rainfall variability and a large hydrological system with complex and delayed response to climate events (Conway, 2002). The immediate hydrological impacts of such events include disruption and damage resulting from temporary inundation of lakeside and wetland areas and river flooding. Longer-term management implications revolve around the dynamic nature of water resources over time and the need for flexible management systems that consider the inherent uncertainty in the resource base. This undermines traditional assumptions of reliable yields for planning water supply projects, in the case of Lake Victoria, for example, fluctuating water levels have generated controversy surrounding the feasibility of two major hydropower installations (Waterbury, 2002). Fluctuating lake levels and wetland extent also present challenges and opportunities for agriculture, fishing and other lakeside activities (e.g. Sarch and Allison, 2002).

In all these cases isolating the effects of climate from other factors of change during the analogue period is an extremely complex undertaking. Nevertheless, detailed study of their impacts and responses including the influence of non-climatic factors is a prerequisite for understanding the importance of future climate change and for identifying effective adaptation strategies. Indeed, an interesting test of our ability to do this for future climate change would be to step back into the 1960s and ask: what would be the impacts of a 25 per cent reduction in rainfall sustained over the Sahel during the next 30 years? Whether this would produce answers similar to what actually happened is a moot point, but it certainly underscores the enormity of the challenge to predict the impacts of what remains highly uncertain change in future climate.

The limits to many adaptation options are already apparent in areas such as population movement and migration, in the ability to bring new agricultural land under irrigation when rainfall is threatened, or to bring about large-scale infrastructural changes to minimize the impacts of sea-level rise on coastal areas. Migration, for example, is a coping mechanism used throughout history by societies as part of their resource utilization strategies and as a means of coping with climate variability. Indeed migration, including to urban centres, continues to play an important role in livelihood resilience to the present day in many parts of the developing world. There is a substantial degree of certainty that areas of the present-day developing world will face greater incidence of extreme weather events in the future. If desirable migration is not available to those affected, it may ultimately increase the necessity of displacement migration, typically undertaken as a last resort when other coping strategies are exhausted.

There is emerging evidence from Brazil, Vietnam and the small island developing nations that, contrary to received wisdom, new migrants to frontier areas build up knowledge of the local environments and promote sustainable utilization of resources (Connell and Conway, 2000; Muchagata and Brown, 2000; Adger et al, 2002). Migration would appear to be a feasible climate adaptation strategy in particular circumstances. But the right to migration, particularly international migration, at a time when there are increasing inequities in international labour flow practice, is likely to be increasingly contested (O'Neill et al, 2001). This implies that migration may be a limited option in many parts of the world; thus other means of supporting adaptive capacity and enhancing resilience are required. These may build on existing coping strategies or may attempt to introduce innovation in terms of technology or institutional development. These new adaptation innovations are the current focus of some of the most recent international developments in climate change policy.

This review suggests that there are critical limits as to how far analogues of past and present adaptation experiences are relevant for adaptation to future climate change as a result of two interrelated phenomena. First, there may well be non-linearities, or critical thresholds, in the climate change impact or response function of natural and social systems. And, second, the magnitude and rate of the change in climate in many parts of the world may turn out to be unprecedented in human history. Taking these factors together, human societies may experience what is already hypothesized in emerging ecosystem science – that smooth change and adaptation can be interrupted by sudden and dramatic switches to another state, resulting in the inability to cope with new circumstances. These sudden shifts can be seen in forest, coral reef, grassland and other ecosystems as a result of apparently gradual climate change (e.g. Scheffer et al, 2001). There is also the reverse situation where climate change is not gradual – i.e., a sudden discontinuity in climate or more than one extreme weather event coming in close sequence which may also undermine the inability to cope. Indeed, this characteristic of the sequencing and recovery time from weather-related hazards is well understood within the hazards research area. Blaikie et al (1994) suggest that the timing of hazardous discrete events in nature constitutes a building of pressure on the vulnerability of marginalized populations. The vulnerability of populations is both event-based and a product of political and economic structural factors (Mustafa, 1998; Adger, 1999; Pelling, 1999). As with ecosystems, interventions to facilitate societal adaptation in the developing world and the developed world, require new priorities to maintain individual and social resilience.

International Institutional Policy Responses on Adaptation to Climate Change

Adaptation to climate change has increasingly become a focus of policy debates. A number of articles in the UNFCCC and the Kyoto Protocol refer to adaptation. The

IPCC recognizes different forms of adaptation, but also states that there is little evidence that efficient or effective adaptations to climate change risks will be taken autonomously (Smit et al, 2001). Thus intervention is necessary to enhance adaptive capacity or the ability to adapt to new or changing conditions without becoming more vulnerable or shifting towards maladaptation. The seventh meeting of the Climate Change Convention in Marrakesh in 2001 expanded the scope of activities eligible for funding, including in the areas of adaptation and capacity building, and established two new funds under the Convention (plus another fund, the Adaptation Fund, under the Kyoto Protocol), that will be managed by the Global Environment Fund (GEF) in addition to its climate change focal area: a Special Climate Change Fund will finance projects relating to: capacity building, adaptation; technology transfer; climate change mitigation; and economic diversification for countries highly dependent on income from fossil fuels. Also a Least Developed Countries Fund will support a special work programme to assist LDCs (least developed countries). The GEF is charged with implementing the provisions of the Marrakesh Accords in a manner that respects both procedural fairness and reflects the priorities of developing countries in seeking to adapt to both climate variability and change.

Most of the focus so far has been on assisting LDCs to develop National Adaptation Programmes of Action (NAPAs). Contributions to funds were to be voluntary and a number of developed countries pledged to make contributions at the level of over US$400 million a year that would be channelled to the developing countries through the GEF. The GEF has been supporting work in developing countries on adaptation to climate change through a staged process. Stage I was to support studies and planning, Stage II to support detailed planning and capacity building and Stage III to support actual adaptations. Most developing countries have already carried out the initial assessment (or Stage I) studies on adaptation (many of which are reported in their National Communications to the UNFCCC). A few Stage II studies (for example in the Caribbean, Pacific and Bangladesh) have also been initiated. However, there is a need for the developing countries to prepare more detailed assessments of adaptation to climate change including policies and ensuring their compatibility with action plans under other multilateral environmental agreements (such as biodiversity and desertification) as well as with other national sustainable development plans or strategies (Huq, 2002).

Within this set of international negotiations there are divergent views as to what constitutes adaptation and the role of development, particularly sustainable development, in the process. Adaptation to climate change is not a costless exercise. We have already highlighted in this paper that it is inextricably intertwined with the political economy of natural resource use. Hence investments in adaptation will inevitably have winners and losers (see Chapter 14, this volume). Equally the nature of uncertainty concerning the scope and magnitude of climate changes, as discussed above, suggests that some adaptation strategies may turn out to be redundant. In the worst scenarios, investments in adaptation may be offset by maladaptive policies in other sectors (Burton, 1997). So, within the international negotiations the view is often expressed that sustainable development is required both in terms of managing future climate change risks, as well as weather-related hazards in the present day, and indeed in seeking to promote low-emission-based industrialization. But others argue that the climate threat and the need for adaptation is a not a continuation of what has gone before and that climate change brings new and urgent dimensions to sustainable development. Further, the Kyoto Protocol, and related mechanisms around the international agreements on climate change, has authority only to focus on environmental impacts and adaptation provoked by a narrowly defined human-induced climate change. Hence there is a fundamental dilemma at the heart of international action on this issue – the need for reductionist identification of the 'climate'-related part of global social and economic trends, versus the desire to see climate change as another important dimension of global environmental threats to development.

These same issues are played out throughout the mechanisms of the international agreements. Projects implemented as part of the Clean Development Mechanism (CDM) of the Kyoto Protocol, one of the so-called flexibility mechanisms, have the dual mandate of reducing greenhouse gas emissions and contributing to sustainable development. The Protocol suggests that a 'share of the proceeds' from the CDM shall be used to assist particularly vulnerable developing countries in meeting the costs of adaptation to the adverse effects of climate change. Ambitious claims have been made about the likely benefits of CDM projects in developing countries without basis in research or observation. Developing countries are unlikely to become fully engaged in implementing the UNFCCC unless they perceive development benefits. At present there are serious risks to developing countries engaging in CDM activities, not least of which is that it may distort development priorities, and may also lead to the situation where the only domestic mitigation measures remaining are higher-cost activities (Parson and Fisher-Vanden, 1999; Karp and Liu, 2000; de Jong et al, 2000). Thus the implementation of the various mechanisms, including the CDM and associated adaptation funds do not offer the desired but elusive 'win–win' solutions to climate change and development – they always result in winners and losers, and the losers are invariably the most marginalized in terms of resources, new technologies and access to decision-making (see also Chapter 17).

Conclusions

Adaptation to climate change is the adjustment of a system to moderate the impacts of climate change, to take advantages of new opportunities or to cope with the consequences. Many participants in the meeting in London argued that because of the nature of the new challenges brought about by climate change in natural resource management and other areas of governance, adaptation will inevitably be characterized both by processes of negotiated adjustments involving individuals, civil society and state, and by renegotiation of risk-bearing and sharing between them. This is different to the dominant discourses of adaptation in international negotiations which perceive adaptation as a process that can be smoothed through international development transfers. Global managerialism dominates these policy and international institutions and discourses (Adger et al, 2001a). It creates a distortionary focus in these debates toward 'planned adaptation', either at the global scale through international institutions or at the scale of states through national governments. Of course, the role of international action is critical in this area, if only because of the interaction between planning for adaptation with an emerging scientific understanding of the risks involved as expressed by the IPCC. Yet there are serious limits as to what international actions regarding adaptation can achieve. However, a realignment to focus on how policy can support the adaptive capacity and resilience of vulnerable communities would also potentially find synergies with more conventional development policy and analysis.

This review of issues has shown that much adaptation in the developing world will rely on past experience of dealing with climate-related risks. Thus much adaptation by farmers, fishers, coastal dwellers and residents of large cities will be autonomous and facilitated by their own social capital and resources. This will not easily be identifiable among a myriad of social, demographic and economic factors impinging on development trajectories and experiences (see Chapter 17). But there is a key role for planning for adaptation in these ongoing processes. International institutions need to appropriate these latest research insights on adaptation from the developing world and build a global coalition, not only to take action to reduce damaging emissions, but to facilitate the inherent resilience of populations coping with an uncertain future.

The competing objectives of sustainable development are both highlighted and exacerbated by the dilemmas of climate change. Populations 'at risk' from climate change impacts range from owners of second-home beach-front properties in Europe and north America through to resource-dependent farmers and labourers in Africa and Asia – building adaptive capacity necessarily requires consideration of rights to development and security rather than just avoidance of pertinent risks. We would argue that the resources and space for adaptation should become a central development imperative. It is also becoming clear when considering the nature of global climate change that poverty reduction policies and goals will in themselves not address the specific climate change-related risks for the most vulnerable portions of developing societies. Nevertheless climate change and its associated risks give greater impetus for both dematerialization and empowering and institutionalizing sustainable development.

Acknowledgements

We thank the UK Research Councils – NERC, ESRC and EPSRC – for financial support for the Tyndall Centre for Climate Change Research. This chapter stems from a meeting hosted jointly by the Tyndall Centre, CSERGE and the School of Development Studies at the University of East Anglia and the International Institute for Environment and Development in London. We thank all the participants for stimulating discussions and feedback. We also thank three referees for constructive comments. We retain full responsibility for this final version.

Note

1   'Adaptation to climate change: setting the agenda for development policy and research'. Symposium hosted by the Tyndall Centre for Climate Change Research and International Institute for Environment and Development, Royal Society, London, 25 October 2001.

References

Adger, W. N. 1999: Social vulnerability to climate change and extremes in coastal Vietnam. *World Development* 27, 249–69.

Adger, W. N. 2001: *Social capital and climate change.* Working Paper 8, Tyndall Centre for Climate Change Research, University of East Anglia, Norwich.

Adger, W. N., Benjaminsen, T. A., Brown, K. and Svarstad, H. 2001a: Advancing a political ecology of global environmental discourses. *Development and Change* 32, 681–715.

Adger, W. N., Kelly, P. M. and Ninh, N. H., editors, 2001b: *Living with environmental change: social vulnerability, adaptation and resilience in Vietnam.* London: Routledge.

Adger, W. N., Kelly, P. M., Winkels, A., Huy, L. Q. and Locke, C. 2002: Migration, remittances, livelihood trajectories and social resilience. *Ambio* 31, 358–66.

Agrawal, A. 2001: Common property institutions and sustainable governance of resources. *World Development* 29, 1649–72.

Benson, C. and Clay, E. 1998: *The impact of drought on sub-Saharan African economies.* World Bank Technical Paper No. 401. Washington DC: World Bank.

Berkes, F. and Jolly, D. 2001: Adapting to climate change: social-ecological resilience in a Canadian Western Arctic community. *Conservation Ecology* 5(2), online at: www.consecol .org/Journal/vol5/iss2/ (last accessed 19 February 2003).

Blaikie, P., Cannon, T., Davis, I. and Wisner, B. 1994: *At risk: natural hazards, people's vulnerability and disasters.* London: Routledge.

Burton, I. 1997: Vulnerability and adaptive response in the context of climate and climate change. *Climatic Change* 36, 185–96.

Cannon, T. 1994: Vulnerability analysis and the explanation of natural disasters. In Varley, A., editor, *Disasters development and environment.* Chichester: John Wiley, 13–30.

Carter, T. R. and La Rovere, E. L. 2001: Developing and applying scenarios. In McCarthy, J. J., Canziani, O., Leary, N. A., Dokken, D. J. and White, K. S., editors, *Climate change 2001: impacts, adaptation and vulnerability. Intergovernmental Panel on Climate Change (IPCC) Working Group II.* Cambridge: Cambridge University Press, 877–912.

Connell, J. and Conway, D. 2000: Migration and remittances in island micro-states: a comparative perspective on the South Pacific and the Caribbean. *International Journal of Urban and Regional Research* 24, 52–78.

Conway, D. 2002: The hydrological effects of two extreme rainfall events over East Africa: 1961 and 1997. In Van Der Leden, H., editor, *Flow regimes from international network data (FRIEND) 2002 – regional hydrology: bridging the gap between research and practice.* Proceedings of the Fourth International FRIEND Conference, Cape Town, South Africa. IAHS Publication No. 274, Wallingford: IAHS, 475–82.

Cross, N. and Barker, R., editors, 1992: *At the desert's edge: oral histories from the Sahel.* London: SOS Sahel.

de Jong, B. H. J., Tipper, R. and Montoya-Gomez, G. 2000: An economic analysis of the potential for carbon sequestration by forests: evidence from southern Mexico. *Ecological Economics* 33, 313–27.

Diaz, M. F. and Pulwarty, R. S., editors, 1997: *Hurricanes, climate and socio-economic impacts.* New York: Springer Verlag.

Easterling, D. R., Karl, T. R., Gallo, K. P., Robinson, D. A., Trenberth, K. E. and Dai, A. G. 2000: Observed climate variability and change of relevance to the biosphere. *Journal of Geophysical Research* 105, 20 101–14.

Henderson-Sellers, A., Zhang, H., Berz, G., Emanuel, K., Gray, W., Landsea, C., Holland, G., Lighthill, J., Shieh, S.-L., Webster, P. and McGuffie, K. 1998: Tropical cyclones and global climate change. *Bulletin of the American Meteorological Society* 79, 19–38.

Hewitt, K., editor, 1983: *Interpretations of calamity from the viewpoint of human ecology.* Boston: Allen and Unwin.

Hewitt, K. 1997: *Regions of risk: a geographical introduction to disasters.* Harlow: Longman.

Hulme, M. 1998: The sensitivity of Sahel rainfall to global warming: implications for scenario analysis of future climate change impact. In Servat, E., Hughes, D., Fritsch, J. M. and Hulme, M., editors, *Water resources variability in Africa during the 20th century.* IAHS Publication, No. 252. Wallingford: IAHS, 429–36.

Hulme, M., Doherty, R., Ngara, T., New, M. and Lister, D. 2001: African climate change: 1900–2100. *Climate Research* 17, 145–68.

Huq, S. 2001: Climate change and Bangladesh. *Science* 294, 1617.

Huq, S. 2002: The Bonn–Marrakech agreements on funding. *Climate Policy* 2, 243–46.

Huq, S., Karim, Z., Asaduzzaman, M. and Mahtab, F., editors, 1999: *Vulnerability and adaptation to climate change in Bangladesh.* Dordrecht: Kluwer.

IPCC 2001a: *Climate change 2001: the scientific basis.* Contribution of Working Group I to The Third Assessment Report of the IPCC. Cambridge: Cambridge University Press.

IPCC 2001b: *Climate change 2001: impacts, adaptation and vulnerability.* Cambridge: Cambridge University Press.

Jäger, J., van Eijndhoven, J. and Clark, W. C. 2001: Knowledge and action: an analysis of linkages among management functions for global environmental risks. In Social Learning Group, editors, *Learning to manage global environmental risks: volume 2. A functional analysis of social responses to climate change, ozone depletion and acid rain.* Cambridge, MA: MIT Press, 165–78.

Karp, L. and Liu, X. 2000: *The clean development mechanism and its controversies.* Working Paper 903, Department of Agricultural and Resource Economics, University of California, Berkeley.

Lucht, W., Prentice, I. C., Myneni, R. B., Sitch, S., Friedlingstein, P., Cramer, W., Bousquet, P., Buermann, W. and Smith, B. 2002: Climatic control of the high-latitude vegetation greening trend and Pinatubo effect. *Science* 296, 1687–89.

Mitchell, J. F. B., Karoly, D. J., Hegerl, G. C., Zwiers, F. W., Allen, M. R. and Marengo, J. 2001: Detection of climate change and attribution of causes. In Houghton, J.D., Ding, Y., Griggs, D. J., Noguer, M., van der Linden, P. J., Dai, S., Maskell, K. and Johnson, C. A., editors, *Climate change 2001: the scientific basis.* Cambridge: Cambridge University Press, 697–738.

Mortimore, M. J. 1998: *Roots in the African dust.* Cambridge: Cambridge University Press.

Mortimore, M. J. and Adams, W.M. 1999: *Working the Sahel.* London: Routledge.

Muchagata, M. and Brown, K. 2000: Colonist farmers' perceptions of fertility and the frontier environment in eastern Amazonia. *Agriculture and Human Values* 17, 371–84.

Müller, B. 2002: The global climate change regime: taking stock and looking ahead. In Schram Stokke, O. and Thommessen, O., editors, *Yearbook of international co-operation on environment and development 2002–2003.* London: Earthscan, 27–40.

Mustafa, D. 1998: Structural causes of vulnerability to flood hazard in Pakistan. *Economic Geography* 74, 289–305.

O'Neill, B. C., MacKellar, F. L. and Lutz, W. 2001: *Population and climate change.* Cambridge: Cambridge University Press.

Parson, E. A. and Fisher-Vanden, K. 1999: Joint implementation of greenhouse gas abatement under the Kyoto Protocol's Clean Development Mechanism: its scope and limits. *Policy Sciences* 32, 207–24.

Pelling, M. 1999: The political ecology of flood hazard in urban Guyana. *Geoforum* 30, 240–61.

Ribot, J. C., Magalhães, A. R. and Panagides, S. S., editors, 1996: *Climate variability, climate change and social vulnerability in the semi-arid tropics.* Cambridge: Cambridge University Press.

Roncoli, C., Ingram, K. and Kirshen, P. 2001: The costs and risks of coping with drought: livelihood impacts and farmers' responses in Burkina Faso. *Climate Research* **19**, 119–32.

Sarch, M-T. and Allison, E. 2002: Fluctuating fisheries in Africa's inland waters: well adapted livelihoods, maladapted management. In *Microbehaviour and macroresults*. Proceedings of the tenth biennial conference of the International Institute of Fisheries, Economics and Trade, Corvallis, 2001, 2.

Scheffer, M., Carpenter, S., Foley, J. A., Folke, C. and Walker, B. 2001: Catastrophic shifts in ecosystems. *Nature* 413, 591–96.

Schneider, S. H. 2001: What is dangerous climate change? *Nature* **411**, 17–19.

Sen, A. K. 1981: *Poverty and famines: an essay on entitlement and deprivation.* Oxford: Clarendon.

Sen, A. K. 1999: *Development as freedom.* Oxford: Oxford University Press.

Smit, B. et al 2001: Adaptation to climate change in the context of sustainable development and equity. In McCarthy, J. J., Canziani, O., Leary, N. A., Dokken, D. J. and White, K. S., editors, *Climate change 2001: impacts, adaptation and vulnerability.* IPCC Working Group II. Cambridge: Cambridge University Press, 877–912.

Trenberth, K. E. and Hoar, T. J. 1997: El Niño and climate change. *Geophysical Research Letters* 24, 3057–60.

Waterbury, J. 2002: *The Nile Basin: national determinants of collective action.* London: Yale University Press.

Watts, M. J. and Bohle, H. G. 1993: The space of vulnerability: the causal structure of hunger and famine. *Progress in Human Geography* 17, 43–67.

Wigley, T. M. L. and Raper, S. C. B. 2001: Interpretation of high projections for global-mean warming. *Science* **293**, 451–54.

16

Mainstreaming Adaptation in Development

Saleemul Huq and Hannah Reid

Introduction

Adaptation to climate change is one of two principal response strategies to the problem of human-induced climate change (the other response strategy is 'mitigation', which is to reduce the emissions of greenhouse gases, or GHGs). The principle difference between these two response strategies is that mitigation attempts to prevent the climate change problem from occurring at all (or getting worse), while adaptation aims to cope with the problem of climate impacts when they occur. This chapter describes how adaptation issues have been addressed in the climate negotiations to date. Because the impacts of climate change are likely to increase in the coming years and there is growing realization that vulnerable countries and communities will be disproportionately adversely affected, much more attention is now being paid to adaptation than was previously the case, particularly by development organizations (see also Agrawala, 2004; Pachauri, 2004). This chapter describes what is meant by adaptation, before focusing in more detail on the challenges facing the international community as it tries to gear up to responding to climate change. Specific actions on how adaptation can be mainstreamed in development, including financial issues, are provided in the concluding section.

Mitigation vs. Adaptation: A Brief History

As described in more detail by Professor Rogers (2004) and by Agrawala (2004), historically, the climate change issue has been seen primarily as one which is likely to occur in a gradual fashion in the medium- to long-term future (i.e. anything from 50 to 100 years' time) and that the policy priority in the short term (i.e. the next 10 to 20 years) has been the reduction of the emission of GHGs through mitigation actions. Hence, the first decade of the negotiations under the United Nations Framework Convention on Climate Change (UNFCCC) focused largely on the elaborating mitigation commitments and related institutional and financial mechanisms, to ensure that the main emitting countries took actions to reduce their emissions. This focus, which fitted well with early understandings of climate science and was fully in accordance with the precautionary principle set out in the Convention, tended, however, to overshadow policy discussions about adaptation. Although both the UNFCCC and the Kyoto Protocol contain adaptation provisions, included largely at the insistence of vulnerable developing countries, the main emphasis of national and international climate policy has been on mitigation. This is reflected in the National Communications (reports) submitted by developed and developing country parties to the UNFCCC, which contain much less information about adaptation than about mitigation.

The publication of the Third Assessment Report of the Intergovernmental Panel on Climate Change (IPCC) in 2001 (IPCC, 2001) highlighted that emissions continue to rise and that some impacts may already be discernible. It thus emphasized the need to pay more attention to adaptation responses in addition to mitigation responses. Accordingly, negotiations under the UNFCCC since then, particularly those at the Seventh Conference of Parties (COP-7) held in November 2001 in Marrakesh, Morocco (UNFCCC, 2001), have paid much greater attention to adaptation issues, including agreement to establish new funds to assist poorer developing countries in dealing with the potential impacts of climate change. Because adaptation strategies to climate change, especially for the most vulnerable developing countries, are intimately linked to the larger development strategies in those countries, more development agencies have become active in the climate change regime. The linkages between adaptation to climate change and development, as well as the funding of adaptation in developing countries, including the role of donors and other players active the development, is explored further below and by Agrawala (2004).

What is Adaptation and Adaptive Capacity?

Adaptation is the process of coping with the potential impacts of climate change. It can be characterized in different ways:

- *Anticipatory adaptation vs. reactive adaptation:* Anticipatory adaptations are ones which are taken in anticipation of expected climate change impacts. Reactive adaptation occurs after the impacts have taken place.
- *Adaptation to climate change vs. adaptation to climate variability:* The former refers to adaptation to anticipate human-induced climate change, whereas the latter refers to adaptation to naturally occurring climate variability. In practice, there is little difference between actions that would enhance adaptation to climate change and actions that would enhance adaptation to climate variability, but the distinction is significant in the context of funding for adaptation under the UNFCCC (which is supposed to fund the former but not the latter).

Our understanding of adaptation depends on where society places its values. For example, ecologists argue that any definition of adaptation must also take into account species and communities other than humans, which must also adapt to climate change. This is important when it comes to prioritizing adaptation activities and funding, as decisions on whether it is more important to protect unique ecosystems or focus on potentially catastrophic abrupt changes, such as the collapse of the Gulf Stream, will need to be made. The question of what degree of climate change is 'dangerous' is dependent on these value-based judgements, but science and local contextualized knowledge, such as that held by local communities, can also help inform the basis for such decision-making.

Issues relating to equity and justice in the field of adaptation are also relevant and have attracted recent interest (Adger et al, 2006). Justice issues are important at several levels, such as the international legal framework, national adaptation policies and actions and everyday adaptation actions. At each level it is important to consider both distributive and procedural justice. For example, distributive justice is paramount when considering the funds for adaptation mentioned above and responsibility for climate change impacts, which in turn raise procedural issues about who decides these questions and on the basis of what information: is it donor-driven or country-led? Is it conditional on submissions of recent kinds of reports (such as National Communications due under the UNFCCC) or dependent on ensuring there is sufficient information to ensure that resources are being well utilized? Procedural justice is also important when considering what kind of public consultation is necessary and possible in developing National Adaptation Programmes of Action (NAPAs) in the least developed countries (Paavola presentation, in Reid et al, 2004).

Adaptive capacity is the ability of a community (or country) to adapt to climate change. One key distinction is the difference between generic adaptive capacity and specific adaptation: generic adaptive capacity refers to the inherent or existing capacity of a community or country as a whole to cope with climate impacts. This is a function of levels of income, education, development, etc. of the whole community or country. Specific adaptive capacity refers to the capacity of the community or country to cope with the impacts of climate change based on an understanding of the anticipated impacts of human-induced climate change.

Two approaches have been used to try to understand adaptive capacity: initially a scenario, or top–down, approach was used to help understand how dangerous climate change is, and more recently a systems, or bottom–up, approach (Figure 16.1) has been used to understand how best to adapt to climate change. This approach assesses current vulnerabilities to climate change, starting at the community level, and is therefore the most appropriate approach to use when trying to identify current and future local risks to climate change.

Adaptation and Development Linkages

Adaptation to climate change is fundamentally linked to development both for the developed as well as the developing countries (both of which will be impacted by the adverse consequences of climate change). However, it is in the context of the developing countries that potentially adverse impacts of climate change will negatively affect

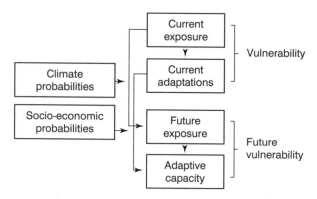

Figure 16.1 *Systems approach – vulnerabilities*

Source: Barry Smit presentation, in Reid et al, 2004

development in a number of key sectors, including water resources, floods, droughts, agriculture and costal zone management. Linkages between adaptation and development occur at several different scales or levels and many are discussed in more detail by other authors as indicated below:

- *Local level:* The most severely impacted communities in developing countries will be those communities living in geographic regions most exposed to climatic impacts (e.g. flood-prone and drought-prone areas). As these people are generally poorer than the rest of the population within the country, they need to be targeted with programmes providing support for adaptation to climate change (see Pachauri, 2004; Agrawala, 2004).
- *Sectoral level:* Within countries, the most adversely impacted sectors include agriculture, water resource management, costal zone management as well as disaster (e.g. floods, cyclones and droughts) management (for more detailed discussion of particular sectors, see Burton and May, 2004; Denton, 2004; Leach and Leach, 2004). Policymakers, planners and managers in those sectors need to anticipate the future impacts of climate change in their sectoral planning.
- *National level:* At the national level, policymakers will need to take into account potentially adverse impacts of climate change in different sectors and also take policy decisions across different sectors. One important feature of national policymaking includes the need to address existing policies (and actions), which enhance (rather than reduce) vulnerabilities to climate change, and remove 'maladaptations' to climate change.
- *Regional level:* Many climate change impacts will be felt most acutely at the regional level in areas such as West Africa, eastern Africa, southern Africa and South Asia. Regional-level actions (e.g. for river basins or major drought-prone areas such as the Sahel, see Devereux and Edwards, 2004) may therefore be most appropriate. The regional level is also the smallest scale (at least at present) at which potential climate change impacts under different scenarios can be effectively modelled.

- *Global level:* Actions implemented at the global level will require the global community of nations to act together under the UNFCCC as well as under other development-oriented efforts. For example, reaching many of the Millennium Development Goals (MDGs) may be more difficult due to the adverse impacts of climate change. International cooperation will also be required for the development of innovative financial mechanisms such as insurance (see Hamilton, 2004) and/or the more effective implementation of existing multilateral and bilateral sources of funding, discussed below.

Funding Adaptation

At present, most international funding is largely directed towards mitigation efforts, despite the clear need in many countries for concrete adaptation projects (see Greene, 2004). Increasing international interest in adaptation has not been associated with equivalent increases in quantities of funding, reflecting a broader stagnation or actual decline of official development assistance (ODA) to developing countries over the 1990s. However, several new funds dealing with adaptation were established following COP-7 (Huq, 2002):

1   *The Least Developed Countries Fund (LDCF)* to enable the least developed countries (LDCs) to conduct National Adaptation Programmes of Action (NAPAs) to identify priority adaptation actions for further funding.
2   *The Special Climate Change Fund (SCCF)* for all developing countries, to support adaptation as well as other actions (e.g. including mitigation and technology transfer).
3   *The Adaptation Fund (AF)* under the Kyoto Protocol, which is to be based on contributions from the 'Adaptation levy' placed on all transactions under the Clean Development Mechanism (CDM) of the Kyoto Protocol. This fund is meant to support 'concrete adaptation' actions.

All three funds are to support adaptation in developing countries, but differ in important ways. The LDCF and SCCF are established under the UNFCCC and based on voluntary contributions from donor countries. The LDCF has already received funding (around US$20 million) from a number of countries to enable the LDCs to carry out their respective NAPAs, whereas the SCCF has not received any contributions yet. Despite this, a number of developed countries have made a 'political commitment' to provide up to US$400 million a year for adaptation activities in general, starting from 2005. The AF does not become operational until the Kyoto Protocol enters into force, although CDM transactions are now being registered under the legal auspices of the UNFCCC and thus will start generating funding for the Fund once the Executive Board of the CDM starts issuing 'certified emissions reductions' (on the CDM see Humphrey, 2004).

In addition to these funds, the Global Environment Facility (GEF) has recently allocated US$50 million to a new pilot adaptation action programme, for use over the next few years. Guidance on how these funds should be distributed is being developed. In the past, the GEF funded a wide range of initiatives, but now it has a more strategic approach towards funding adaptation activities; critical policy and project needs will now be identified using the Adaptation Policy Framework (UNDP, 2003), UNFCCC National Communications and the NAPAs.

The respective roles of the different sources of international funding support for adaptation actions are shown schematically in Figure 16.2. It is important to note that the GEF trust funds (with the exception of its small grants programme aimed at small communities) are currently restricted to those projects that cross the barrier of funding by producing 'global environmental benefits' – thus only addressing the 'tip of the iceberg' – whereas the vast majority of the adaptation actions that will be needed will not be funded by the GEF because they generate co-benefits with both development as well as with adaptation to *climate variability* and not just adaptation to anthropogenically induced climate change alone. For example, the six case studies on adaptation to climate change undertaken under the auspices of the Organisation for Economic Co-operation and Development (OECD) (see Agrawala, 2004) define adaptation to climate change narrowly so that it refers to only those climate change impacts that are deemed to be directly attributable to human-induced climate change, rather than to adaptation to the broader range of impacts associated with 'climate variability'. A narrow definition of climate impacts would tend to then only produce a small range of adaptation responses as being necessary and hence requiring funding – in essence addressing only a very narrow set of examples of adaptation–development linkages (i.e. the 'tip of the iceberg' in Figure 16.2) and hence missing the much larger set of relevant adaptation–development linkages where there are additional co-benefits. Leaving aside such important definitional issues, it should also be noted that

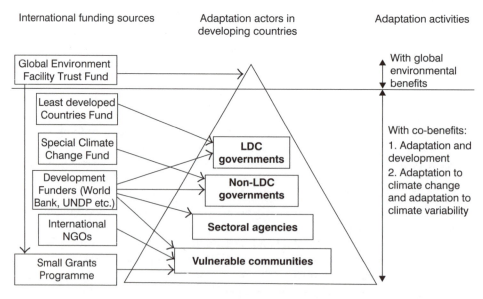

Figure 16.2 *The adaptation funding 'iceberg'*

communities that are most vulnerable to climate change (which need the assistance the most) are generally poorly served by existing mechanisms of funding (both international as well as national), because community-based projects tend to be smaller, site-specific and thus less replicable which makes them unattractive to many funding agencies.

Mainstreaming Adaptation

It is clear from the above that many of the activities that need to be undertaken to reduce vulnerability to the adverse impacts of climate change in developing countries relate closely to ongoing mainstream development activities at local, sectoral and national levels. Successful adaptation to climate change therefore requires incorporation of potential climate change impacts into ongoing strategies and plans at sectoral and national levels (Huq and Burton, 2003; Huq et al, 2003, Agrawala, 2004). This is best illustrated by taking a sector such as water resource management, where planners and managers are used to planning water management (e.g. for reservoirs) and will now have to plan for a future hydrological regime which includes potential climate change impacts (in other words they can no longer assume that the hydrological regimes of the past will be the same as future regimes – as illustrated by the example provided by Burton and May, 2004). Once the relevant planners and managers have been provided with the appropriate methodologies and tools, they are quite capable of incorporating climate change issues into their regular planning (at relatively low costs). However, the issue of 'mainstreaming' adaptation has caused some friction between stakeholders in climate change discussions to date. This is because the term 'mainstreaming adaptation' is being used in the discussions in two distinct senses, namely:

1 *Mainstreaming adaptation into development:* This requires the main actors engaged in development work – governments, international development funding agencies, non-governmental organizations (NGOs), local communities, etc. – to increase their awareness of the potentially adverse impacts of climate change and then to 'mainstream' issues relating to this into their regular activities.
2 *Mainstreaming adaptation funding:* Broadly speaking this refers to utilization of existing ODA resources to fund climate change-related adaptation.

The second sense of mainstreaming adaptation causes friction for two reasons. First, it is problematic because it blurs funding mandated by the Convention (which is supposed to be 'new and additional') with funding donors are supposed to provide through their 'regular' ODA for developmental activities generally (i.e. development activities that do not factor in climate change). Second, the use of existing ODA is being proposed because of the restricted approach to funding adopted by the GEF, which operates the Convention's financial mechanism, including the new funds outlined above. To date, the extent to which the GEF has been able to fund climate-related adaptation has been extremely limited because of its 'incremental cost' approach which allows it to only fund the component of adaptation projects that produces 'global environmental benefits'. In the case of mitigation projects, calculating global benefits is conceptually quite straightforward as one less ton of GHG emissions is a global benefit and the costs of avoiding it can be calculated relatively clearly. However, in the case of adaptation projects such a calculation is much more difficult as most of the benefits of adaptation activities accrue locally rather than globally. Additionally trying to separate and then calculate the costs of adaptation to climate change (as opposed to climate variability) is almost impossible as discussed above. Use of ODA to fund climate adaptation would avoid the procedural changes that are necessary for the GEF to ensure the existing and new Marrakesh funds are operationalized in a flexible manner to provide funding for a wide range of adaptation activity, leaving other sources of ODA to support activities that are solely (or primarily) for ongoing development goals such as education, sanitation, health and poverty reduction.

What Next?

The importance of adaptation as a response action to the problem of human-induced climate change has recently become increasingly well recognized both in the climate change discussions (e.g. the Delhi Declaration at COP-8) as well as within (at least some of) the development funding agencies, for example the ten funding agencies who prepared the report on climate change and poverty (Sperling, 2003). However, the problem has received little attention from most developing countries (with the exception of the small island states) or from the research and NGO community. Efforts therefore need to be enhanced to raise the level of awareness of climate change impacts (and hence the need for adaptation) among all relevant stakeholder groups, while simultaneously supporting adaptation actions on the ground, targeting the most vulnerable countries and communities. Specific actions that need to be taken by different stakeholder groups include the following:

- *UNFCCC:* To agree pragmatic rules and criteria for supporting adaptation actions in developing countries under the newly created adaptation funds (primarily the LDCF and SCCF).
- *Developed countries:* A number of developed countries (including the European Union, Canada and Norway) have already provided a relatively small amount of funding for the LDCF, but none have committed any funds for the SCCF yet. They need to do so (at least to the level of their 'political commitment' at COP-6 bis to provide US$400 million/year). Incorporating climate adaptation into development will require additional financial resources.
- *GEF:* The US$50 million allocated by the GEF to support adaptation activities needs to be used to support adaptation actions (rather than just studies as has occurred in the past). However, current GEF rules on incremental costs for global benefits provide a major barrier to funding adaptation projects. The GEF also favours larger projects, which do not necessarily respond to the needs and scale of the most vulnerable countries and communities. These barriers need to be overcome.

- *Other bilateral/multilateral donors:* The inherent unreplicability of adaptation projects (each will need to be site/community-specific) and the fact many are likely to be small scale (if they are to enhance local livelihoods) is a major challenge for international donors, and may require institutions to become more responsive and flexible to these realities.
- *LDCs:* They need to complete their respective NAPAs as soon as possible (and in a participatory manner with inputs from civil society and the most vulnerable communities) and determine priority actions.
- *Other developing countries:* All the other developing countries also need to conduct adaptation planning to identify key adaptation actions. This can be done under the aegis of preparing their second National Communications and could utilize tools such as the Adaptation Policy Framework (UNDP, 2003).
- *Development NGOs:* International and national NGOs working in the development sector have so far engaged little with the problem of climate change and the potentially adverse impacts it will have on their target groups (who are often the most vulnerable communities) (Reid et al, 2004).
- *Researchers:* The level of research on adaptation to climate change has been relatively poor to date, particularly when compared with the level of research effort invested in mitigation. More activists and researchers need to be persuaded to examine adaptation to climate change and to answer questions such as: what are the indicators and components of adaptive capacity and how can they best be strengthened? What are good tools for adaptation in the different sectors (e.g. agriculture, water resources management, costal zone management, etc.)? What links between adaptation and mitigation should be developed?

There are many theoretical, policy and practical challenges ahead. Ensuring there is greater awareness of climate change by the development community – and vice versa – will thus require more concerted collaborative efforts bringing together a global network of donors, policymakers, researchers and those working at the local level. Because our knowledge of climate impacts and adaptive capacity will evolve, and because surprises and shocks will occur, such networks must necessarily be of a long-term nature if continuous learning and dialogue is to take place at multiple levels on adaptation issues. Unfortunately, the funding cycles of most donors, research and policy bodies do not currently favour this kind of continuous large-scale effort, which has to bring together those engaged in theoretical, policy and implementation work from literally all corners of the globe. A first step in the right direction would be the creation of mechanisms and channels to facilitate such learning and dialogue.

References

Agrawala, S. (2004) 'Adaptation, development assistance and planning: Challenges and opportunities', *IDS Bulletin*, vol 35, no 3, 1 July, pp50–54

Adger, W. N., Huq, S., Mace, M. J. and Paavola, J. (eds) (2006) *Fairness in Adaptation to Climate Change*, MIT Press, Cambridge, MA

Burton, I. and May, E. (2004) 'The adaptation deficit in water resource management', *IDS Bulletin*, vol 35, no 3, 1 July, pp31–37

Denton, F. (2004) 'Giving the "latecomer" a head start', *IDS Bulletin*, vol 35, no 3, 1 July, pp42–49

Devereux, S. and Edwards, J. (2004) 'Climate change and food security', *IDS Bulletin*, vol 35, no 3, 1 July, pp22–30

Greene, W. (2004) 'Aid fragmentation and proliferation: Can donors improve the delivery of climate finance?', *IDS Bulletin*, vol 35, no 3, 1 July, pp66–75

Hamilton, K. (2004) Insurance and financial sector support for adaptation', *IDS Bulletin*, vol 35, no 3, 1 July, pp55–61

Humphrey, J. (2004) 'The Clean Development Mechanism: How to increase benefits for developing countries', *IDS Bulletin*, vol 35, no 3, 1 July, pp84–89

Huq, S. (2002) 'The Bonn–Marrakech agreements on funding', *Climate Policy*, vol 2, nos 2–3, pp243–246

Huq, S. and Burton, I. (2003) 'Funding adaptation to climate change: what, who and how to fund?', Sustainable Development Opinion Paper, IIED, London

Huq, S., Rahman, A., Konate, M., Sokona, Y. and Reid, H. (2003) *Mainstreaming Adaptation to Climate Change in Least Developed Countries (LDCs)*, IIED, London

IPCC (2001) 'Climate Change 2001: Impacts, adaptation, and vulnerability', a contribution of the Working Group II to the *Third Assessment Report of the Intergovernmental Panel on Climate Change* (J.J. McCarthy, O.F. Canziani, N.A. Leary, D.J. Dokken and K.S. White, eds), Cambridge University Press, Cambridge, UK

Leach, G. and Leach, M. (2004) 'Carbonising forest landscapes? Linking climate change mitigation and rural livelihoods', *IDS Bulletin*, vol 35, no 3, 1 July, pp76–83

Pachauri , R. K. (2004) 'Climate change and its implications for development: The role of IPCC assessments', *IDS Bulletin*, vol 35, no 3, 1 July, pp11–14

Reid, H., Huq, S. and Murray, L. (2004) *Adaptation Day at COP 9*, IIED, London

Rogers, P. (2004) 'Climate change and security', *IDS Bulletin*, vol 35, no 3, 1 July, pp98–101

Sperling, F. (ed.) (2003) *Poverty and Climate Change: Reducing the Vulnerability of the Poor through Adaptation*, Multi-Agency Report, The World Bank, Washington, DC

UNDP (2003) *The Adaptation Policy Framework*, UNDP-GEF, New York

UNFCCC (2001) *The Marrakech Accords and the Marrakech Declaration*, FCCC/CP/2001/13 and Addendum 1–4, United Nations Framework Convention on Climate Change

17

Double Exposure: Assessing the Impacts of Climate Change within the Context of Economic Globalization

Karen L. O'Brien and Robin M. Leichenko

Starting today, representatives of some 150 countries will meet in Kyoto, Japan, to take what they hope will be the first step in a decades-long effort to cope with the prospect of global climate change. Rarely, if ever, has humanity made an attempt like this one: to exercise deliberate, collective foresight on a risk whose full impact is unclear and will not be felt for decades. (New York Times, 1 December 1997)

Globalization is the big economic event of the 1990s. It means that investors anywhere, seated at their computers and using global instant communications, can invest their money in anything – stocks, bonds, property, factories, other countries' money – almost anywhere in the world. ... Globalization promises benefits galore – jobs and prosperity for Third World countries, global markets for American and other First World companies, cheap imports for U.S. consumers, cost-cutting pressures that will force firms everywhere to be more efficient. (Chicago Tribune, 28 October 1997)

Global Processes

Climate change is emerging as one of the most challenging problems facing the world in the 21st century. Scientists and policymakers have become embroiled in extensive debates about potential changes brought about by an increase in anthropogenic greenhouse gas emissions, along with strategies for mitigation and adaptation. Assessments of the global and regional impacts of climate change have formed the cornerstone for climate policy debates. Underlying these debates is the recognition that some areas are more vulnerable to climate change than others. Differential impacts superimposed on dissimilar vulnerabilities have resulted in a complex geography of climate change. To add further complexity to the picture, climate change is taking place within a rapidly changing world. In particular, ongoing processes of economic globalization are modifying or exacerbating existing vulnerabilities to climate change.

Although globalization and climate change are both considered important areas for contemporary research, few studies have considered the two issues together, particularly from the perspective of impacts. Much more attention has been focused on the implications of globalization, and particularly trade liberalization, for the environment (Esty, 1995; Bredahl et al, 1996; Krissoff et al, 1996; OECD, 1997a, b; Rauscher, 1997). Other key issues that these studies focus on relate to environmental governance, economic competitiveness, foreign investment, sectoral economic policies, technological change, business strategies, employment, and environmental policies. While qualitative research has been carried out on many aspects of globalization–environment relationships, OECD (1997a, p17) notes that quantitative evidence is currently lacking on virtually all components of the relationship.

A number of studies have addressed the role of global corporations in fostering climatic change. UNCTC (1992), Robbins (1996) and Mason (1997) each examine the environmental practices of transnational corporations (TNCs) and their contribution to greenhouse gas emissions. UNCTC (1992) and Robbins (1996) find that TNCs are major contributors to global emissions of greenhouse gases. Mason (1997) looks at the emissions patterns and environmental impacts of TNC activity, focusing on the aluminium industry. While each of these studies provides important insights into the causes of climatic change, they do not address the joint impacts that globalization and climatic change may have for regions, sectors, ecosystems or social groups.

In addition, several studies have examined the effects of climate change on global agricultural trade, highlighting the impacts on yields, commodity prices, and imports and exports for individual countries (Fischer et al, 1994; Reilly et al, 1994). Neither of these studies, however, considered agricultural interactions with other economic sectors, or structural economic changes that might influence agricultural production, even in the absence of climate change. Reilly et al (1994) do note, however, that economic restructuring could intensify the effects of climate change through a marginalization of production conditions. To obtain a better understanding of the future of world agriculture and other environmentally sensitive sectors, the joint impacts of globalization and climate change should be examined, with an emphasis on *how* the impacts of each process may exacerbate or offset each other.

In this chapter, we establish a framework for examining the impacts of climate change and economic globalization based on the concept of *double exposure*. By double exposure, we refer to the fact that regions, sectors, ecosystems and social groups will be confronted both by the impacts of climate change and by the consequences of globalization. Our point of departure lies in the widely recognized perception that there are 'winners' and 'losers' associated with both of these global processes. Climate change and economic globalization, occurring simultaneously, will result in new or modified sets of winners and losers. Double exposure has important policy implications, especially for those that are likely to experience the negative consequences of both globalization and climate change.

In highlighting the synergisms between the impacts of globalization and climate change, this chapter does not attempt to survey the causal linkages between globalization and climate change. In addition to the direct contributions of transnational corporations to greenhouse emissions, as mentioned above, globalization may also exacerbate climate change by fostering more rapid development and consequently higher levels of fuel consumption by consumers throughout the world. Conversely, policies intended to control greenhouse emissions may indirectly promote globalization, as industries shift location to avoid enforcement of new emissions standards in certain countries. Rather than focusing on these various causal mechanisms, we emphasize the need to consider the impacts of the two processes simultaneously.

Winners and Losers

The idea of winners and losers has been referred to frequently in discussions of both climate change impacts and the consequences of globalization. Winners are considered those countries, regions or social groups that are likely to benefit from the ongoing processes of climate change or globalization, while losers are those that are disadvantaged by the processes and likely to experience negative consequences. The notion of winners and losers is contentious in both arenas, as it undermines any consensus on climate change mitigation or economic liberalization.

In discussions of climate change, there is a strong reluctance among scientists and policymakers to recognize, address or discuss the existence and identity of winners and losers, particularly winners (Glantz, 1995). Such discussions are considered by many to be divisive and counter-effective to efforts to gain a global consensus on climate change (Schneider, 1989; Glantz, 1995). Nevertheless, climate impact assessments inevitably point to winners and losers, and the perception alone of winning or losing can significantly influence climate negotiations (UNEP, 1993).

Debates over the impacts of economic globalization are also often focused on the subject of winners and losers (e.g. Conroy and Glasmeier, 1993; Greider, 1997; Tardanico and Rosenberg, 2000). Proponents of economic globalization argue that as the result of increased economic efficiency, everyone eventually benefits from falling trade barriers and liberalized investment policies. Critics, however, are quick to point out that many regions, sectors, or social groups may be losers in the process of globalization.

Within the context of both globalization and climate change, the identification of winners and losers is not straightforward. It can be considered subjective, relative and to a large extent based on perception. Glantz (1995) identifies some important questions that should be considered when discussing winners and losers:

- What is meant by a win or a loss?
- What factors must be taken into account in labelling a region, an activity, an economic sector, or a country a winner or a loser?
- Can wins and losses be objectively and reliably identified and measured?
- Can wins and losses be aggregated?
- How do perceptions of winning or losing compare with reality?

In discussing winners and losers in climate change and economic globalization, it is important to first identify what is meant by a win or a loss (Glantz, 1995). In terms of climate change, a win might refer to any net benefit from changes in temperature, rainfall, or climate variability. Such benefits may be measured by increased productivity (e.g. agriculture), increased resource availability (e.g. water), decreased hazards (e.g. frequency of floods), or decreased climate-related expenditures (e.g. heating expenses, snow removal costs). A loss could refer to any adverse effects that result from climate change, such as decreased agricultural productivity, increased water scarcity, or increased climate-related mortality.

In terms of economic globalization, a win is often associated with an improvement in economic performance, as measured by gross domestic product (GDP), foreign direct investment (FDI), employment, trade balance and so forth. A win can also refer to improvements in social well-being, as represented by various indicators of health, education and access to services. A loss may be defined by economic hardships influenced by globalization processes, such as higher levels of unemployment, increased income inequality, and reductions in social services.

Many integrated assessments of climate change seek to determine whether the net impact of climate change is positive or negative for a given sector, such as energy, agriculture or forestry (Alcamo et al, 1998). The philosophy behind such studies is that regional dislocations and negative impacts caused by climate change may be offset by gains or surpluses elsewhere. Aggregate measures of economic growth also emphasize the net outcome, rather than the local or regional impacts. But as Glantz (1995, p51) points out, 'wins and losses cannot be meaningfully aggregated. A win is a win, and a loss is a loss'. Attempts to identify 'net' winners and losers gloss over the real impacts, and trivialize the significance for specific regions, sectors or social groups.

The scale of analysis thus makes a difference in the identification of winners and losers. For example, while globalization, as manifest through the North American Free Trade Agreement (NAFTA) between the United States, Canada and Mexico, may indeed lead to aggregate increases in total employment in all three nations, this increase will not be uniform across different regions of each country (Conroy and Glasmeier, 1993). Rather it will be unevenly distributed, with some regions and groups experiencing large gains, and others experiencing net losses. Shifting scales from groups of individuals or regions to the nation requires aggregation and generalization, such that some losers will not be identified when the country is considered a winner. Likewise, some winners will not be identified when a country is considered a loser. Capturing an overview of winners and losers consequently requires analyses at multiple scales.

It is also important to recognize that winners and losers may shift over time, particularly in the case of economic globalization. For example, a current winner may eventually become as loser. As witnessed by the recent financial crisis in Asia, many countries that have enjoyed rapid growth and increasing living standards as the result of globalization, have, at the same time, becoming increasingly vulnerable to international financial disruptions.

Climate alone is unlikely to determine winners and losers, as vulnerability differences and adaptation measures can significantly shift the outcome of any climate change. Likewise, it is often difficult to isolate the consequences of economic globalization from other social and economic changes. Because the concept of winners and losers is imprecise, it is important to consider it within the social, economic and environmental context appropriate to different regions, sectors or social groups.

Climate Change

There is a growing consensus that anthropogenic greenhouse gas emissions have contributed to a change in the climate, and that such trends will continue into the future unless dramatic mitigation measures are adopted (Houghton et al, 1996). As discussed above, there is a broad recognition that there will be both winners and losers associated with climate change. Although there is a large amount of uncertainty associated with future climate scenarios, it is quite clear that the distribution of winners and losers will be varied, reflecting the diversity of climate change impacts.

Climate change can be considered a spatially differentiated process. Although many areas could experience temperature increases in the order of 1.5–4.5°C, some areas may actually cool under 'global warming' conditions (Houghton et al, 1996). Patterns and amounts of precipitation are also likely to change, and it is projected that rainfall will increase in some areas and decrease in others (Houghton et al, 1996). Although there are difficulties associated with modelling regional and local precipitation, there is little doubt that the impacts will vary across space and time. Figure 17.1 shows projected temperature and precipitation changes based on the Hadley Centre model. According to this model, the greatest warming will occur at high latitudes during winter, whereas precipitation changes will be strongest in tropical regions. Some ocean regions will experience minimal temperature changes. However, the model projects changes in ocean circulation that can alter temperature patterns over the North Atlantic, which could, for example, contribute to changes in storminess in Europe (Met Office, 1998).

The physical and social impacts of climate change are not considered to be homogeneous for two reasons. First, global circulation models project spatial differences in the magnitude and direction of climate change. Second, even within a region experiencing the same characteristics of climate change, the impacts are likely to vary because some ecosystems, sectors or social groups are more vulnerable to climate change than others.

Vulnerability is varied across space, as well as across social groups. Each 'exposure unit' has a unique sensitivity or resilience to climate change that is dependent on an array of factors (Parry and Carter, 1998). The most vulnerable are considered those who are most exposed to perturbations, who possess a limited coping capacity, and who are least resilient to recovery (Bohle et al, 1994). Other definitions of vulnerability focus on concepts of marginality, susceptibility, adaptability, fragility and risk (Liverman, 1994). In further exploring the concept of vulnerability, Liverman (1994) distinguishes between biophysical vulnerability and social vulnerability. The former refers to the physical conditions of the landscape and how they impact humans or biological diversity. The latter, referred to as a political economy approach to vulnerability, defines vulnerability according to the political, social and economic conditions of a society. Different dimensions of vulnerability can also be considered. For example, in relation to agriculture, Reilly (1996) recognizes differences among sector vulnerability, regional economic vulnerability, and hunger vulnerability. Adger (1999) disaggregates social vulnerability into individual (or household) vulnerability and collective (i.e., national, regional or community) vulnerability.

A number of efforts have been made to map vulnerability, largely in association with food security. Many of these efforts have used geographic information systems (GIS) to

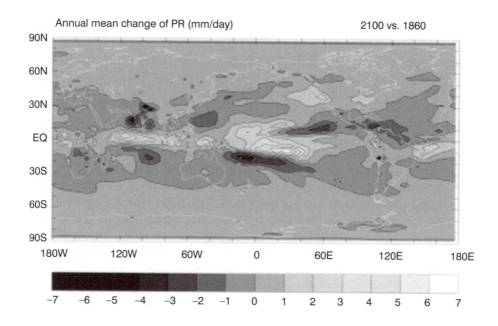

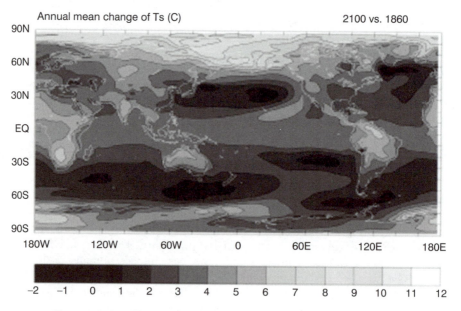

Figure 17.1 *Climate change results from the Hadley Centre model for precipitation and surface temperature*

show the spatial distribution of various indicators. The World Food Programme (1996) outlines five approaches to mapping food-related vulnerability (Table 17.1). Though each of these approaches can be used to assess vulnerability to climate change, some are more appropriate to large-scale assessments, and others to localized assessments. In a

Table 17.1 *Five approaches to vulnerability assessments*

- Use poverty as a proxy indicator of vulnerability to food insecurity, drawing on national data to identify the number and location of socio-economic groups judged to be vulnerable.
- Carry out surveys to collect information directly related to vulnerability. These surveys can incorporate the notion of coping strategies and levels of entitlements.
- Identify important determinants of vulnerability to food insecurity to create a proxy indicator based on available data. (The strength of this approach is dependent upon the selection of different indicators and knowledge about the context in which the indicators are being used.)
- Conduct a rapid rural appraisal.
- Make use of individuals with expertise related to the issues addressed, and with extensive knowledge of conditions throughout the country.

Source: The World Food Programme, 1996

study of climate vulnerability, Bohle et al (1994) use three indicators to construct a food security index that illustrates differential vulnerabilities to climate change among countries. The indicators represent national food availability or shortages, household food poverty and individual food deprivation. This vulnerability assessment serves as a point of departure for further analysis involving trends in vulnerable groups and risks associated with climate variability (Bohle et al, 1994).

Climate change: Winners and losers

Climate has been increasingly recognized as one among many processes that influence vulnerability. To determine the winners and losers in climate change, both biophysical and social vulnerability should be taken into account. As Liverman (1994, p332) emphasizes: '... the most vulnerable people may not be in the most vulnerable places – poor people can live in productive biophysical environments and be vulnerable, and wealthy people can live in fragile physical environments and live relatively well'. This suggests that assessments of vulnerability should not be limited to developing countries or countries with precarious physical environments.

In any case, vulnerability to climate change is not exclusively related to poverty. Extreme climate events can impact the wealthy and poor alike, particularly in high-risk environments. For example, all owners of coastal properties are susceptible to storm surges, whether they are wealthy or poor. Although one could argue that the wealthy are more resilient to recovery through mechanisms such as insurance, it is likely that premiums in high-risk areas will become increasingly difficult to obtain if climate variability increases with climate change (Stix, 1996). Even if an area is not considered to be high-risk, extreme climatic events can inflict serious damages and render a sector or social group vulnerable. For example, the 1998 ice storm that hit eastern Canada debilitated the maple sugar industry, and had enormous impacts on dairy farmers who lacked backup generators (Kerry et al, 1999).

Numerous country studies have been conducted to identify how climate change might play out in particular regions or sectors within the context of existing environmental and socio-economic conditions (Smith et al, 1998; O'Brien, 2000). The objective of these impact assessments is to measure the positive and negative consequences of short- or long-term climate change, and to evaluate different adaptation strategies that could be taken in response to the impacts. Within the assessment framework lies the goal of identifying climate sensitivities and vulnerabilities, with an emphasis on the regions, sectors, ecosystems and social groups within each country that are likely to be most affected by climate change (Parry and Carter, 1998).

In considering the linkages between climate change and socio-economic conditions, Parry and Carter (1998, p24) note that '... the effects of any climate change in the future will be influenced by concurrent economic and social conditions and the extent to which these create a resiliency or vulnerability to impact from climate change'. Nevertheless, most impact analyses consider only crude socio-economic scenarios, developed from baseline scenarios representing 'the present state of all the non-environmental factors that influence the exposure unit' (Parry and Carter, 1998, p75). Most socio-economic scenarios involve a simple extrapolation of present-day trends, such as population and economic growth rates. Often different trajectories are considered, including high-growth, low-growth and 'business as usual' scenarios.

Regardless of which socio-economic scenario is used, there is generally little concern for how the patterns of social and economic development will change in an increasingly globalized economy. Changes in trade and investment patterns, combined with improvements in transportation and communications networks, are contributing to profound changes in local and regional economies. Furthermore, the process of globalization, like climatic change, is ongoing and will continue over time. Over the next 20–50 years (the timeframe in which climate change impacts may be profoundly felt) the uneven spread of globalization will continue, and will probably accelerate. As a consequence, future patterns of development for many countries and regions may deviate substantially from past trends and the current development trajectory.

Economic Globalization

Economic globalization describes a set of processes whereby production and consumption activities shift from the local or national scale to the global scale. Globalization is manifest through a number of interrelated changes, including rising levels of international trade, foreign investment, and multinational firm activity. It is also manifest through falling political barriers to trade and investment, integration of global financial markets, integration of production activities across international borders, development of global communication systems, and homogenization of demand for consumer goods across countries.

Frequently cited indicators of economic globalization include the growth in international trade and foreign direct investment (FDI) relative to levels of economic output. Between 1950 and the middle 1990s, world trade grew by a factor of 14, whereas world output increased by a factor of 5 (Dicken, 1997). FDI has also grown rapidly, particularly over the past several decades. Whereas world output has approximately doubled since 1970, FDI has quadrupled during the same period (Dicken, 1997).

Rising levels of trade and investment have been accompanied by important changes in the production process. Production in many industry sectors now occurs across international borders. In most cases, multinational firms are continuing to locate their headquarters and research and development facilities in their home country, but are increasingly able to shift lower-skill, lower-wage components of the production process to other regions of the world. This proliferation of a global spatial division of labour has meant that a growing share, perhaps as much as one third, of international trade now involves trade between subsidiaries of the same firm (Dicken, 1997).

Another key change associated with economic globalization involves the integration of world financial markets. As a result, countries have less control over their own currencies and macroeconomic policies. As noted by Epstein (1996, p211):

> ... financial capital moves around the globe at such an amazing speed that national governments seem helpless in its wake. Legislatures and citizens who want to buck the trend and achieve goals of high employment, egalitarian development and sustainable growth, are paralyzed by the threat that any policy which lowers the rate of profit will cause capital to be moved to more profitable environs, thereby reducing investment and lowering the community's standard of living.

A large literature has emerged to explain what accounts for globalization (e.g. Stalk and Hout, 1990; Harrison, 1994; Boyer and Drache, 1996; Castells, 1996; Dicken, 1997; Greider, 1997). Important factors driving globalization include:

- technological changes, especially changes in communication and transportation technologies;
- changes in production processes involving both increased use of information technologies and a shift from large-scale, mass production to more flexible production methods; and
- changes in the nature and intensity of competition between firms as a result of the general slowdown in global economic growth since approximately 1970; growing international competition has pushed firms to broaden their search for new markets and cheaper production sites and has generated new types of cross-national inter-firm collaborative behaviour.

While there is continuing debate over both the extent of globalization as well as the relative contributions of various driving forces, there is general agreement that processes of globalization are ongoing and will continue well into the 21st century. For this reason, the social, economic and environmental impacts of globalization must be considered over the long term.

Winners and losers from economic globalization

Despite a widespread perception that globalization is a unifying and all-encompassing force, these processes have (heretofore) been highly uneven across all geographic scales. In fact, it has been argued that globalization accentuates, rather than erodes, national and regional differences (Mittelman, 1994).

Processes of globalization have been uneven among major regions of the world, characterized by an increasing proportion of trade and resource flows taking place both within and between between three major economic regions, including North America (US, Canada and Mexico), the European Union, and East and Southeast Asia (led by Japan). These three regions, often referred to as the Triad, accounted for 76 per cent of world output and 71 per cent of world trade in 1980 (Dicken, 1997). By 1994, the Triad accounted for 87 per cent of world merchandise output and 80 per cent of world merchandise exports (Dicken, 1997).

Increased concentration of global economic activity among the Triad has meant that large regions outside the Triad, particularly sub-Saharan Africa and South Asia, have become increasing marginalized vis-à-vis the global economy (Mittelman, 1994; Castells, 1996). Examination of the global distribution of FDI among low- and middle-income countries aptly illustrates these regional differences (Table 17.2). More than 10 per cent of the world population currently lives in sub-Saharan Africa, yet this region receives only 1 per cent of total world FDI (World Bank, 1998a). Similarly, South Asia contains 22 per cent of the world population, but receives only 1.1 per cent of world FDI (World Bank, 1998a).

Globalization processes are also uneven among regions within countries (Hirst and Thompson, 1996). Within China, for example, coastal regions have been increasingly integrated into the global economy, while more remote areas of the country remain largely untouched by globalization. As a result, globalization is exacerbating existing patterns of uneven development within China. Even within an advanced country such as the United States, the impacts of globalization have been highly uneven. Studies of international trade involvement of US cities and regions by Markusen et al (1991), Hayward and Erickson (1995) and Noponen et al (1997), for example, find substantial variability in the level of involvement in international trade and in the relative contribution of international trade to regional economic growth.

As with climate change, the uneven nature of globalization leads to the emergence of winners and losers. In addition to globalization's frequently identified winners, which include large transnational corporations, and advanced and newly industrializing countries (Fischer, 1990; Cook and Kirkpatrick, 1997; Greider, 1997), winners may also include subnational regions and social groups which benefit directly or indirectly

Table 17.2 *Regional distribution of foreign direct investment among low- and middle-income countries in 1996*

	Foreign direct investment (millions)	FDI share of world total (%)	Population (millions)	Population share of world total (%)
World total	314,696	100.0	5755	100.0
East Asia and Pacific	58,681	18.6	1732	30.1
Europe and Central Asia	14,755	4, 7	478	8.3
Latin America and Carib.	38,015	12.1	486	8.4
Middle East and N. Africa	614	0.2	277	4.9
South Asia	3439	1.1	1266	22.0
Sub-Saharan Africa	3271	1.0	596	10.3

Sources: World Bank, 1998a, b

from globalization (Tardanico and Rosenberg, 2000). Frequently identified losers in the process of globalization include countries of sub-Saharan Africa, as noted above, as well as unionized labour and small, locally oriented firms (Conroy and Glasmeier, 1993). Additional losers may include other regions and groups that are left out of globalization processes or that experience direct negative impacts.

Like climate change vulnerability assessments, the identification of winners and losers in globalization is not strictly an advanced versus developing country issue. In analysing the impacts of changing patterns of international trade for wages and employment within both advanced and developing countries, Wood (1994) identifies groups of both winners and losers within advanced ('North') and developing areas ('South'). Based on traditional theory of comparative advantage, Wood demonstrates that liberalization of trade benefits those factors of production that are relatively abundant in both the North and South, and harms factors that are relatively scarce in each region.

The example of NAFTA further illustrates how globalization results in new categories of winners and losers (Conroy and Glasmeier, 1993; Tardanico and Rosenberg, 2000). Conroy and Glasmeier (1993) identify some of the winners with NAFTA, including US workers in high-technology and service-oriented industries, especially in large urban areas, as well as Great Plains farmers producing crops such as corn, sorghum and soybeans. Within Mexico, winners are identified as workers in low-skill manufacturing industries and farmers producing speciality crops for export. Losers within the US include workers in low-wage sectors, especially those located in rural areas of the US South, such as textiles and apparel, and farmers in dairy, sugar, and speciality fruit and vegetable sectors. Within Mexico, losers include workers in previously protected manufacturing industries and grain farmers located in rural areas throughout the country (Conroy and Glasmeier, 1993).

Double Exposure

Both climate change and economic globalization are ongoing processes with uneven impacts, and both include implicit winners and losers. Nevertheless, discussions of winners and losers rarely take into account the fact that both processes are occurring simultaneously. To address this, we introduce the concept of double exposure. Double exposure refers to cases where a particular region, sector, ecosystem or social group is confronted by the impacts of both climate change and economic globalization. It recognizes that climate impacts are influenced not only by current socio-economic trends, but also by structural economic changes that are reorganizing economic activities at the global scale.

The overlays between globalization and climate change impacts can be viewed from a regional perspective, a sectoral perspective, or with an emphasis on one or more social groups or ecosystems. In some cases, the consequences of globalization may offset the impacts of climate change, or vice versa. In other cases, exposure to both globalization and climate change may result in 'double winners' or 'double losers'. The following examples illustrate the concept of double exposure, and show that different outcomes emerge when the two processes are considered together.

Regional perspectives

From a regional perspective, certain geographic areas may be strongly impacted by both globalization and climate change. As new trade and economic zones emerge, other areas become peripheral or marginalized. Border regions or rural areas that undergo similar experiences related to climate change or globalization processes can be analysed from a regional perspective. Clusters of countries that share common characteristics, such as economies in transition or semi-arid environments, can also be analysed from a regional perspective.

Africa is often cited as a region that is vulnerable to both climate change and the consequences of economic globalization. In the case of Africa, it is the lack of globalization that is considered to be significant. Relative to many other areas of the world, most of the African continent remains 'left out' of globalization processes (Mittelman, 1994; Agnew and Grant, 1997; Castells, 1998). Africa's share of world trade represents only 1.8 per cent of the total, and has been falling steadily in recent years (Dohlman and Halvorson-Quevedo, 1997). Within Africa, only a handful of countries account for almost 60 per cent of the region's imports. Of these, South Africa has the most dynamic economy, accounting for 30 per cent of the continent's imports in 1995 (Hawkins, 1997). While foreign direct investments are contributing to growth and prosperity in some regions of the world, Africa is notable for its small share of FDI (see Table 17.2). The exclusion or marginalization of Africa in terms of globalization processes suggests that it is a loser relative to other regions.

From a climate change perspective, Africa can also be considered a loser. Approximately two-thirds of the continent is comprised of drylands, and considered to be highly vulnerable to climate change. Much of the continent is currently affected by interannual climate variability, with droughts or floods recurring frequently. Widespread poverty makes the continent more vulnerable to the impacts of projected changes because of limited adaptation capabilities (Watson et al, 1997). Increased temperatures and decreased precipitation, as suggested by some computer model results for Africa, could have a strong impact on the region's agricultural sector. Agriculture accounts for 20–30 per cent of GDP in sub-Saharan Africa, and contributes 55 per cent of the total value of African exports (Watson et al, 1997). Environmental and health problems may also be exacerbated by climate change.

Although current conditions suggest that Africa is a 'double loser' in terms of climate change and globalization, in reality the situation is more heterogeneous and dynamic. Some sectors or regions may experience benefits from climate change. For example, in areas where precipitation does not change, the fertilizer effect of increased CO_2 concentrations could benefit agriculture (Hulme, 1996). The impacts of globalization are also likely to change over time. In fact, most African countries are currently seeking to globalize and open the door to foreign investment through liberalization of trade and payments regimes. Although small in comparison to other regions, foreign investment increased from US$1.7 billion in 1993 to US$5 billion in 1996 (Hawkins, 1997). These investments have differential impacts on the 53 countries in Africa, and on sub-regions and social groups within each country. For this reason, it is useful to consider multiple perspectives when assessing winners and losers associated with economic globalization and climate change.

Sectoral perspectives

Both climate change and economic globalization will have varying consequences for different sectors of the economy. Certain sectors are considered to be at the forefront of globalization activities. These include the communications and electronics industries, but also resource-based sectors, such as agriculture and forestry. Agriculture provides a vivid example of double exposure and the convergence of impacts related to climate change and economic globalization. To illustrate, we will focus on the case of agriculture in Mexico.

The opening of Mexico's economy through liberalized trade and deregulation of markets has had a number of important implications for agricultural production (Bonnis and Legg, 1997). In Mexico, agriculture is important to approximately 30 per cent of the country's population. Over the past decade, Mexican agriculture has become increasingly integrated into the global food market, especially within the North American region (Gates, 1996). Under the 'comparative advantage' argument associated with liberalized trade, Mexico is seen to have a competitive advantage in the production of horticultural crops, particularly winter vegetables for export markets in the north. With less protectionism, prices are increasingly dictated by international markets, and farmers are forced to compete with imports, particularly for basic grains (Hewitt de Alcantara, 1994; Barry, 1995).

Who are the winners and losers in terms of globalization of the agricultural sector? According to Kay (1997, p19), 'the beneficiaries are a heterogenous group, including agro-industrialists, capitalist farmers, and some capitalized peasant households. The losers are the semi- and fully proletarianized peasantry, the majority of rural labourers whose employment conditions have become temporary, precarious and "flexible"'. Although agro-industrial modernization has benefited a small part of the rural population, for the most part small farmers in Mexico have been excluded from the benefits of globalization (de Janvry et al, 1997; Cornelius and Myhre, 1998).

Mexico can also be considered very sensitive to climate variability and change. Of Mexico's 195 million hectares of land, 85 per cent is considered semi-arid, arid or very arid, with climates characterized by low, seasonal and highly variable rainfall. Only about 16 per cent of Mexico's land is considered to be suitable for crop production (Appendini and Liverman, 1994). Furthermore, the country's rainfall is disproportionately concentrated in the south. As a result, much of Mexico is affected by climate variability, especially droughts. The severe droughts, fires and floods of 1998 provide some examples of the enormous economic and social consequences of climate variability. Global climate change is likely to make some parts of the country hotter and drier than at present, and possibly increase climate variability (Liverman and O'Brien, 1992).

A greater emphasis on the production of water-intensive fruit and vegetable crops for the export markets means that this specialized sector is vulnerable not only to price fluctuations on international markets, but also to climate variability and change (Appendini and Liverman, 1994). Rural labour markets have also been transformed by the expansion of export agriculture. The transformation has been characterized by the growth of temporary and seasonal wage labour, which is dictated by the flexible needs of producers. Climate change is likely to increase the supply of wage labour, as more farmers are driven from production on marginal lands. It could also lead to a reduced demand for labour on agro-industrial farms during years with severe weather. Farmers who are trying to compete in these international markets as well as agricultural wage labourers in Mexico are thus likely to be double losers in terms of climate change and globalization.

Social group perspectives

The example cited above suggests that it is important to consider the social consequences of globalization and climate change, even within a sectoral analysis. Within Mexico's agricultural sector, farmers who cultivate marginal, rain-fed lands are more vulnerable than those with access to the most productive lands (Liverman, 1990). Adaptation measures, such as improved seeds, fertilizers and irrigation treatments, are often not options for small farmers. For instance, many adaptation measures require access to credit, which is not evenly available to all producers (Myhre, 1994).

Examples of other social groups that are double exposed to globalization and climate change include poor residents of large cities in advanced and developing countries. Within the United States, for example, processes of globalization have reduced both demand and wages for low-skilled workers, and have contributed to rising levels of urban income inequality and increased the spatial concentration of poverty within central city areas (Jargowsky, 1997; Castells, 1998).

At the same time that globalization is contributing to the economic vulnerability of disadvantaged residents of US cities, climate change may increase the physical vulnerability of these groups to weather-related events. Climate change may increase mean summer temperatures in northern cities, and may also increase the frequency and magnitude of summer heat waves, consequently increasing heat-related illnesses and deaths (Stone, 1995). Residents of poor, inner-city communities are among the most vulnerable to heat waves due to lack of resources to pay for air conditioning or to leave stifling central city areas. In the case of the Chicago heat wave of 1995, for example, most of the more than 700 deaths occurred among poor and elderly residents of inner-city areas. Other large US cities, such as New York, St Louis, and Los Angeles are also expected to experience increases in summer heat-related mortality as the result of global warming (Stone, 1995), and the impacts will probably fall disproportionately on poor, inner-city residents. Globalization and climate change thus represent a dual threat to these groups.

For poor residents of cities in the developing world, the double impacts of globalization and climate change may be even more severe. Economic globalization increases the vulnerability of the urban poor to income and employment disruptions as the result of precipitous currency movements and shifts in global financial capital. The recent devaluation of the Brazilian real, for example, had substantial impacts on livelihood of shantytown – or *favela* – residents in the Brazilian city of Belo Horizonte, many of whom have moved into the consumer economy from a subsistence one since 1994 (*Wall Street Journal*, 1999). The Brazilian currency devaluation has had the most severe impacts on the poor, who spend the bulk of their income on basic goods and who typically are unable to shield their financial assets in interest-bearing bank accounts. In the case of the recent devaluation, prices of many basic foodstuffs increased by nearly 30 per cent (*Wall Street Journal*, 1999).

In conjunction with increased financial vulnerability as the result of globalization, poor residents of developing world cities are also among the groups that are most vulnerable to climatic change. Many of the urban poor live in shantytowns and squatter settlements located in precarious areas such as on hillsides, as in the case with the *favela* residents of Belo Horizonte, or in flood plains. Such areas are especially vulnerable to mudslides or flooding as the result of severe storms, events that may increase in both frequency and magnitude as the result of climate change. In addition to direct physical hazards, the urban poor are also vulnerable to climate change-related health hazards, particularly outbreaks of diseases such as cholera and malaria, both of which increase with warm spells and heavy rains (Stone, 1995). In considering the potential impacts and adaptations to climate change and globalization, the special needs of different types social groups must be taken into account.

Ecosystem perspectives

Natural ecosystems considered vulnerable to climate change may also be affected by economic globalization, particularly as economic activity becomes more concentrated in certain areas, such as coastal zones. Economic globalization may also lead to the restructuring or demise of local industries, such as fisheries or forestry. Consequently, the biophysical impacts of climate change may be exacerbated by an expansion of economic activity, or they may be reduced by the alleviation of anthropogenic influences, brought about through local economic changes.

For example, in China, investment flows and other trends associated with economic globalization have been focused on coastal ecosystems. In contrast, the western region of the country has lagged behind in terms of exports and participation in international markets (Mittelman, 1994; Sun and Dutta, 1997). Four special economic zones (SEZs) were established in coastal areas in 1979, when the country moved from a product-based economy to a market economy. In 1984, 14 coastal cities were opened to foreign investment. The coastal region now has a much better transportation and communications infrastructure than inland regions of China, and has since then received more foreign direct investment and generated larger exports. Between 1983 and 1993, 89.7 per cent of China's FDI was directed to the coastal region, whereas only 6.9 and 3.4 per cent was located in the central inland and western inland regions, respectively (Sun and Dutta, 1997). Even though the coastal region may be considered a winner from a globalization perspective, the impacts of increased economic activity (e.g. pollution, loss of wetlands) are generally considered negative from an ecosystem perspective.

Coastal areas are also among the most vulnerable to climatic change. In addition to the possibility of inundation as a result of sea-level rise, climatic change will also increase risks of flooding and erosion due to storm surges and increased runoff (Handley, 1992; Watson et al, 1996). In the case of China, the Intergovernmental Panel on Climate Change (IPCC) estimates that approximately 70 million people living in the coastal region will be affected by climatic change (Watson et al, 1997). In addition to threats to China's population centres, sea-level rise and increased storm surges may also damage coastal fisheries and low-lying rice farms throughout the region. In light of globalization-related development trends and the increasing importance of coastal areas for the Chinese economy as whole, climatic change may have severe economic impacts. From an ecosystem perspective, coastal areas of China are thus likely to experience the negative consequences of both economic globalization and climate change.

Issues and Questions for Future Research

The examples above illustrate how the concept of 'double exposure' can be approached from various perspectives. Climate change is likely to have differential impacts among regions, sectors, social groups and ecosystems. In some cases, the changes will be beneficial, whereas in other cases, they will cause major economic, social and environmental disruptions. Likewise, as certain regions, sectors or social groups take advantage of opportunities associated with globalization, others are left out or forced to absorb the negative impacts. By superimposing the effects of globalization on the regions, sectors, social groups and ecosystems that are vulnerable to climate change (as well as on those that may benefit from climate change), a new set of winners and losers emerges.

There is clearly a need for further research related to the concept of double exposure. Most of the current studies of climate change and economic globalization have examined the two processes in isolation from each other. Although there has been a growing interest in the relationship between globalization and the environment, the majority of studies in this area focus on causal linkages, rather than double exposure. Yet as we have discussed in this chapter, there are winners and losers associated with both processes. Given potential synergisms between the different sets of winners and losers, the two processes should be considered together.

The notion of winners and losers can be used as a framework for examining the impacts of climate change and economic globalization. However, there is a need to address some of the questions posed earlier about 'winners' and 'losers' within the context of climate change and globalization research. In particular, it is necessary to elaborate how (or if) wins and losses can be objectively and reliably identified and measured. Issues surrounding the scale of analysis must also be explicitly addressed, as subsets of winners and losers are often merged in aggregated analyses.

Different perspectives can be adopted when examining globalization and climate change, including regional, sectoral, social group and ecosystem perspectives. The examples described above demonstrate that a winner from one perspective is not necessarily a winner from other perspectives. Although case studies may serve as a useful means for examining double exposure to climate change and economic globalization, the implications of different perspectives should be acknowledged.

From a policy standpoint, the regions, sectors, social groups or ecosystems that are adversely affected by both globalization and climate change should be of particular concern, as these 'double losers' are likely to emerge as challenges to both processes. In terms of climate change, adaptation strategies may be counteracted or rendered ineffective by outcomes associated with economic globalization. For example, in agriculture, attempts by small-scale farmers to adopt drought-tolerant seeds in response to drier conditions may be hindered by the more restrictive access to credit associated with economic liberalization policies. In terms of globalization, efforts to retrain labour or reorient economic activities to adjust to the global economy may be frustrated by the impacts of climate change and variability. This could be a particular problem in regions facing increasing water scarcity.

The potential for double losers raises some important research questions: to what extent are the losers in climate change also the losers when it comes to economic globalization? Is resilience to economic restructuring related to resilience to climate variability and change? What are the links between adaptations to the new global economy and adaptation of strategies to address long-term climate change? These questions can be addressed within the research framework described above.

In terms of methodology, there is a need for both qualitative and quantitative analyses of double exposure. Qualitative studies can be based on individual case studies or comparative studies that examine the impacts of climate change and economic globalization together, from one or more of the perspectives mentioned above. Quantitative studies that make use of economic and social statistics can be combined with the results generated from climate simulation models to identify regions or social groups that are vulnerable to both processes. As in vulnerability analyses, proxy indicators can be developed to highlight the differential consequences of climate change and economic globalization across regions, sectors or social groups. Geographical information systems (GIS) can serve as a useful tool for integrating climate impacts with globalization impacts, so that the outcome of the two processes can be analysed together, and at a number of spatial scales.

Processes of climate change and economic globalization are complex, uncertain, and to a large extent inevitable. Both processes will have winners and losers, which in turn will have important implications for economic development strategies in the 21st century, as well as for climate change adaptation policies in both developed and developing countries. By focusing on the concept of double exposure, this chapter has outlined an approach by which the joint impacts of these processes can be better understood.

References

Adger, W. N., 1999. Social vulnerability to climate change and extremes in coastal Vietnam. *World Development* 27, 249–269.

Agnew, J., Grant, R., 1997. Falling out of the world economy? Theorizing 'Africa' in world trade. In: Lee R., Wills, J. (Eds.), *Geographies of Economies*. Arnold, London.

Alcamo, J., Kreileman, E., Krol, M., Leemans, R., Bollen, J., van Minnen, J., Schaeffer, M., Toet, S., de Vries, B., 1998. Global modelling of environmental change: an overview of IMAGE 2.11. In: Alcamo, J., Leemans, R., Kreileman, E. (Eds.), *Global Change Scenarios of the 21st Century*. Pergamon, Oxford.

Appendini, K., Liverman, D., 1994. Agricultural policy, climate change and food security in Mexico. *Food Policy* 19 (2), 149–164.

Barry, T., 1995. *Zapata's Revenge: Free Trade and the Farm Crisis in Mexico*. South End Press, Boston.

Bohle, H. G., Downing, T. E., Watts, M. J., 1994. Climate change and social vulnerability. *Global Environmental Change* 4 (1), 37–48.

Bonnis, G., Legg, W., 1997. *The Opening of Mexican agriculture*. The OECD Observer No. 206, 35–38.

Boyer, R., Drache, D. (Eds.), 1996. *States Against Markets: The Limits of Globalization*. Routledge: London.

Bredahl, M. E., Ballenger, N., Dunmore, J. C., Roe, T. L. (Eds.), 1996. *Agriculture, Trade, and the Environment: Discovering and Measuring the Critical Linkages*. Westview Press: Boulder, CO.

Castells, M., 1996. *The Rise of the Network Society*. Blackwell, Malden, MA.

Castells, M., 1998. *End of Millenium*. Blackwell, Malden, MA.

Conroy, M. E., Glasmeier, A. K., 1993. Unprecedented disparities, unparalleled adjustment needs: winners and losers on the NAFTA 'fast track'. *Journal of InterAmerican Studies and World Affairs* 34, 1–37.

Cook, P., Kirkpatrick, C., 1997. Globalization, regionalization and third world development. *Regional Studies* 31 (1), 55–66.

Cornelius, W. A., Myhre, D. (Eds.), 1998. *The Transformation of Rural Mexico: Reforming the Ejido Sector*. Center for US–Mexican Studies, University of California, San Diego/La Jolla.

de Janvry, A., Gordillo, G., Sadoulet, E., 1997. *Mexico's Second Agrarian Reform: Household and Community Responses, 1990–1994.* Center for US–Mexican Studies, University of California, San Diego/La Jolla.

Dicken, P., 1997. *Global Shift: Transforming the World Economy,* 3rd Edition. Guilford Press, New York.

Dohlman, E., Halvorson-Quevedo, R., 1997. *Globalisation and development.* The OECD Observer No. 204, 36–39.

Epstein, G., 1996. International capital mobility and the scope for national economic management. In: Boyer, R., Drache, D. (Eds.), *States Against Markets: The Limits of Globalization.* Routledge, London.

Esty, D., 1995. *Greening the GATT: Trade, Environment, and the Future.* Institute for International Economics, Washington, DC.

Fischer, B., 1990. Developing countries in the process of economic globalisation. *Intereconomics,* March/April, 55–63.

Fischer, G., Frohberg, K., Parry, M. L., Rosenzweig, C., 1994. Climate change and world food supply, demand and trade: who benefits, who loses? *Global Environmental Change* 4 (1) 7–23.

Gates, M., 1996. The debt crisis and economic restructuring: prospects for Mexican agriculture. In: Otero, G. (Ed.), *Neoliberalism Revisited: Economic Restructuring and Mexico's Political Future.* Westview Press, Boulder, pp. 43–62.

Glantz, M. H., 1995. Assessing the impacts of climate: the issue of winners and losers in a global climate change context. In: Zwerver, S., van Rompaey, R. S. A. R., Kok, M. T. J., Berk, M. M. (Eds.), *Climate Change Research: Evaluation and Policy Implications.* Elsevier Science, Amsterdam.

Greider, W., 1997. *One World, Ready or Not: The Manic Logic of Global Capitalism.* Touchstone, New York.

Handley, P., 1992. Before the flood. *Far Eastern Economic Review* 155, 65–66.

Harrison, B., 1994. *Lean and Mean: Big Firms, Small Firms, Network Firms: Dualism and Development in the Age of Flexibility.* Basic Books, New York.

Hawkins, T., 1997. Rich in optimism and opportunity. *Financial Times,* December 11, 1997.

Hayward, D. J., Erickson, R. A., 1995. The North American trade of US states: a comparative analysis of industrial shipments, 1983–1991. *International Regional Science Review* 18, 1–31.

Hewitt de Alcantara, C. (Ed.), 1994. *Economic Restructuring and Rural Subsistence in Mexico.* Center for US–Mexican Studies, University of California, San Diego/La Jolla.

Hirst, P., Thompson, G., 1996. *Globalization in Question.* Polity Press, Cambridge, UK.

Houghton, J. J., Meiro Filho, L. G., Callander, B. A., Harris, N., Kattenberg, A., Maskell, K. (Eds.), 1996. *Climate Change 1995: The Science of Climate Change* (Contribution of Working Group I to the Second Assessment Report of the Intergovernmental Panel on Climate Change). Cambridge University Press, Cambridge.

Hulme, M. (Ed.), 1996. *Climate Change and Southern Africa: An Exploration of Some Potential Impacts and Implications in the SADC Region.* WWF International and Climate Research Unit, UEA, Norwich, UK.

Jargowsky, P. A., 1997. *Poverty and Place: Ghettos, Barrios, and the American City.* Russell Sage Foundation, New York.

Kay, C., 1997. Latin America's exclusionary rural development in a neo-liberal world. Paper presented at the 1997 Meeting of the Latin American Studies Association (LASA), Guadalajara, Mexico, 17–19 April 1997.

Kerry, M., Etkin, D., Burton, I., Kalhok, S., 1999. Glazed over: Canada copes with the ice storm of 1998. *Environment* 41 (1), 6–33.

Krissoff, B., Ballenger, N., Dunmore, J., Gray, D., 1996. Exploring linkages among agriculture, trade, and the environment: issues for the next century. Agricultural Economic Report

No. 738, Natural Resources and Environment Division, Economic Research Service, US Department of Agriculture, Washington, DC.

Liverman, D. M., 1990. Vulnerability to drought in Mexico: the cases of Sonora and Puebla in 1970. *Annals of the Association of American Geographers* 80 (1), 49–72.

Liverman, D. M., 1994. Vulnerability to global environmental change. In: Cutter, S. L. (Ed.), *Environmental Risks and Hazards*. Prentice-Hall, New Jersey.

Liverman, D. M., O'Brien, K. L., 1992. Global warming and climate change in Mexico. *Global Environmental Change* 1 (4), 351–364.

Markusen, A. R., Noponen, H., Driessen, K., 1991. International trade, productivity, and US regional job growth: a shift-share interpretation. *International Regional Science Review* 14 (1), 15–39.

Mason, M., 1997. A look behind trend data in industrialization. *Global Environmental Change* 7 (2), 113–127.

Met Office, 1998. Climate change and its impacts: some highlights from the ongoing UK research programme: a first look at results from the Hadley centre's new climate model. The Met Office, Exeter.

Mittelman, J. H., 1994. The globalization challenge: surviving at the margins. *Third World Quarterly* 15 (3), 427–443.

Myhre, D., 1994. The politics of globalization in rural Mexico: campesino initiatives to restructure the agricultural credit system. In: McMichael, P. (Ed.), *The Global Restructuring of Agro-Food Systems*. Cornell University Press, Ithaca, pp. 145–169.

Noponen, H., Markusen, A., Driessen, K., 1997. Trade and American cities: who has the comparative advantage? *Economic Development Quarterly* 11(1), 67–87.

O'Brien, K. L. (Ed.), 2000. Developing strategies for climate change: the UNEP country studies on climate change impacts and adaptations assessments. CICERO Report 2000:3. CICERO, Oslo.

OECD, 1997a. *Economic Globalisation and the Environment*. Organisation for Economic Co-operation and Development, Paris.

OECD, 1997b. *Globalisation and Environment*. Organisation for Economic Co-operation and Development: Paris.

Parry, M., Carter, T., 1998. *Climate Impact and Adaptation Assessment*. Earthscan Ltd, London.

Rauscher, M., 1997. *International Trade, Factor Movements and the Environment*. Clarendon Press, Oxford.

Reilly, J., 1996. Climate change, global agriculture and regional vulnerability. In: Bazzaz, F., Sombroek, W. (Eds.), *Global Climate Change and Agricultural Production*. Food and Agriculture Organization and Wiley, Chichester, pp. 237–267.

Reilly, J., Hohmann, N., Kane, S., 1994. Climate change and agricultural trade: who benefits, who loses? *Global Environmental Change* 4 (1) 24–36.

Robbins, P., 1996. TNCs and global environmental change. *Global Environmental Change* 6 (3), 235–244.

Schneider, S. H., 1989. *Global Warming: Are We Entering the Greenhouse Century?* Sierra Club Books, San Francisco.

Smith, J. B., Huq, S., Lenhart, S. (Eds.). 1998. *Vulnerability and Adaptation to Climate Change: Interim Results from the US Country Studies Program*. Environmental Science and Technology Library, New York.

Stalk, G. J., Hout, T. M., 1990. *Competing Against Time: How Time-based Competition Is Reshaping Global Markets*. Free Press, New York.

Stix, G., 1996. Green policies: insurers warm to climate change. *Scientific American* 274 (2), 19–20.

Stone, R., 1995. If the mercury soars, so may health hazards. *Science* 267, 957–958.

Sun, H., Dutta, D., 1997. China's economic growth 1984–93: a case of regional dualism. *Third World Quarterly* 18 (5), 843–864.

Tardanico, R., Rosenberg, M. B., 2000. Two souths in the new global order. In: Tardanico, R., Rosenberg, M. B. (Eds.), *Poverty or Development? Global Restructuring and Regional Transformation in the US South and the Mexican South.* Routledge, New York.

UNCTC, 1992. *Climate Change and Transnational Corporations.* United Nations, New York.

UNEP, 1993. The issue of winners and losers, Climate Change Fact Sheets, United Nations Environment Programme, Nairobi, Kenya.

Wall Street Journal, 1999. Real thing: central bankers come and go: radio favela delivers another Brazil, 2 February, p. A1.

Watson, R. T., Zinyowera, M. C., Moss, R. H. (Eds.), 1997. *The Regional Impacts of Climate Change: An Assessment of Vulnerability.* Cambridge University Press, Cambridge.

Watson, R. T., Zinyowera, M. C., Moss, R. H., Dokken, D. J. (Eds.), 1996. *Climate Change 1995: Impacts, Adaptations and Mitigation of Climate Change: Scientific–Technical Analyses.* Cambridge University Press, Cambridge.

Wood, A., 1994. *North–South Trade, Employment and Inequality: Changing Fortunes in a Skill-Driven World.* Oxford University Press, Oxford.

World Bank, 1998a. *World Development Report 1998–99: Knowledge for Development.* World Bank, Washington, DC.

World Bank, 1998b. *World Development Indicators 1998,* World Bank, Washington, DC

World Food Programme, 1996. *WFP Vulnerability Mapping Guidelines.* World Food Programme, Rome, Italy.

Part V

Adaptation and
Climate Change Policy

18

Rethinking the Role of Adaptation in Climate Policy

Roger A. Pielke, Jr.

In December of 1997, representatives from nations around the world met in Kyoto, Japan, to debate the establishment of international policy in response to human-caused climate change. A problem exists in that the policy cannot succeed according to its own goals.

Since the late 1980s, scientists and policymakers have devoted considerable attention and resources to the issue of global climate change.[1] For instance, from 1989 to 1997, the US Congress appropriated more than US$11 billion to study the issue, representing approximately half of worldwide expenditures over this period.[2] The international response is guided by the United Nations Framework Convention on Climate Change (UNFCCC), which, by June 1996, had been ratified by 149 countries. The development and promulgation of the Framework Convention has depended a great deal upon a series of assessments of the science, impacts and economics of the global change issue conducted by the Intergovernmental Panel on Climate Change (IPCC), widely considered to be the leading authority on climate change. The IPCC was organized in November 1988 by the World Meteorological Organization in the United Nations Environment Programme, and since that time has published a number of assessments of climate change, most recently in 1996. Together, the UNFCCC and IPCC largely comprise the international response to the issue of climate change.

Domestic and international policymakers discuss response alternatives in terms of mitigation and adaptation (IPCC, 1996a). Mitigation refers to prevention of future climate impacts on society through the limitation of greenhouse gas emissions. The Framework Convention focuses on mitigation, as does most domestic political attention around the world. Academic attention is also largely focused on issues of mitigation. Adaptation refers to adjustments in individual, group and institutional behaviour in order to reduce society's vulnerabilities to climate. In 1996, the IPCC wrote that adaptation offers a 'very powerful option' for responding to climate change and ought to be viewed as a 'complement' to mitigation efforts (IPCC, 1996b, pp187–188). Yet, the IPCC also wrote that 'little attention has been paid to any possible tradeoff between both types of options' (IPCC, 1996b, p250). This chapter presents a case for adaptation to occupy a larger and more formal role in climate policy and for greater attention by academics and policymakers to it.

As a point of departure, this paper begins with acceptance of the conclusions of the IPCC. Specifically, that:

- Greenhouse gas concentrations have continued to increase.
- Anthropogenic aerosols tend to produce negative radiative forcing.
- Climate has changed over the past century.
- The balance of evidence suggests a discernible human influence on climate.
- Climate is expected to continue to change in the future.
- There are still many uncertainties (IPCC, 1996c).

Further, the IPCC finds that changes in climate will probably have negative impacts (costs) to society in a range of areas and sectors (IPCC, 1996b, Chapter 6). In accepting the IPCC conclusions, the point of this chapter is to move beyond what has become a contentious and largely unproductive debate over the science of climate change. This is not to say that scientific research on climate is by any means complete or that there are not grounds for legitimate debate. Rather, from the perspective of policy, resolution of the ongoing scientific debate is less important than other factors. To understand those other factors we must move beyond arguing over the science of climate change.

This paper argues two related main points. First, there is a realistic possibility that mitigation efforts will not succeed according to their own goals. Thus, adaptation responses must occupy a larger and more formal role in climate policy. Second, even with complete faith that mitigation efforts will succeed, a broader justification exists for adaptation responses to occupy a more prominent role in climate policy. As Nordhaus has observed, 'mitigate we might; adapt we must' (Nordhaus, 1994, p189).

Climate Policy

Society's concern about climate originates in actual or expected climate-related impacts.[3] These impacts could be societal or environmental, and can only sometimes be effectively expressed in monetary terms (IPCC, 1996c). Generally, climate policies are focused on capitalizing on the positive aspects of climate impacts (e.g. a good growing season) and the reduction of future negative impacts (e.g. reduction in vulnerability to floods), subject to considerations of the monetary and non-monetary costs and benefits associated with alternative courses of action.

How decision-makers think about the concept of 'climate change' is an important factor in the climate policies which they adopt. Surprisingly, there is not consensus within the climate community on the meaning of the phrase 'climate change'. On the one hand, the Framework Convention defines climate change as:

> a change of climate which is attributed directly or indirectly to human activity that alters the composition of the global atmosphere and which is in addition to natural climate variability over comparable time periods.

On the other hand, the IPCC adopts a broader definition of climate change as 'any change in climate over time whether due to natural variability or as a result of human activity' (IPCC, 1996c, p3). The distinction between the definitions is critical to how the problem of climate is viewed by decision-makers: is climate a problem only to the extent that human activities change it in addition to existing variability? Or is climate a problem irrespective of the sources of change?

Mitigation and adaptation

Climate policy has focused on two categories of response: mitigation and adaptation.[4] Mitigation refers to efforts to prevent climate change, and thus prevent future climate impacts, through intentional alteration of the climate system. The IPCC states that mitigation:

> 'or 'limitation' attempts to deal with the causes of climate change. It achieves this action through actions that prevent or retard the increase of atmospheric greenhouse gas concentration by limiting current and future emissions from sources of greenhouse gases and enhancing potential sinks'. (IPCC, 1996a, p831)

It is generally accepted that humans might intentionally alter climate through one of two ways. Geo-engineering refers to attempts to alter climate by physically interfering with the climate system. Recently, there has been discussion of the possibility of seeding oceans with iron in order to alter climate (NAS, 1992; Broad, 1996). Other geo-engineering techniques that have been discussed include mirrors in space, increasing oceanic alkalinity, and placing aerosols or reflective balloons into the upper atmosphere (NAS, 1992; IPCC, 1996a). A second way that society might intentionally alter climate is through social policy. That is, policy decisions could be made to alter human behaviour in order to modulate the concentration of greenhouse gases in the atmosphere.[5] To date, policymakers have not advocated geo-engineering, relying instead on efforts to alter the composition of the atmosphere through policy actions.

Adaptation refers to efforts to reduce society's vulnerabilities to climate. According to the IPCC, adaptation:

> is concerned with responses to both the adverse and positive effects of climate change. It refers to any adjustment – whether passive, reactive, or anticipatory – that can respond to anticipated or actual consequences associated with climate change. It thus implicitly recognizes that future climate changes will occur and must be accommodated in policy. (IPCC, 1996a, p831)

For instance, in 1992 a US Government task force completed a comprehensive overview of how the United States might modify its susceptibility to flooding (FIFMTF, 1992). Actions surveyed included structural (e.g. dam building) and non-structural (e.g. insurance) measures such as regulation, forecasting and warning plans, and flood-proofing and elevation. For any potential climate impact there are a wide range of such adaptive structural and non-structural measures that might be incorporated to reduce impacts.[6]

Not surprisingly, the Framework Convention implicitly favours mitigation responses because the definition of 'climate change' it uses places emphasis on only those climate impacts attributable to human-caused changes in the composition of the atmosphere.[7] The goal of the Framework Convention is:

> to achieve ... stabilization of greenhouse gas concentrations in the atmosphere at a level that would prevent dangerous anthropogenic interference with the climate system. Such a level should be achieved within a time frame sufficient to allow ecosystems to adapt naturally to climate change, to ensure that food production is not threatened and to enable economic development to proceed in a sustainable manner.

The definition of 'dangerous anthropogenic interference' is the subject of much debate.[8] Another important aspect of the Convention's objective is that it focuses on stabilization of greenhouse gas concentrations, rather than on emissions.

Compared to mitigation, adaptation has not received the same level of attention from either policymakers or researchers. In Chapter 2 of this volume, Ian Burton remarks that adaptation became 'an unacceptable, even politically incorrect, idea'. There are at least four reasons why consideration of adaptation responses has been discouraged by the climate change community.

The first reason is a perception that discussion of adaptation 'could make a speaker or a country sound soft' on mitigation (Burton, Chapter 2). In other words, talk of adaptation could lend an impression, rightly or wrongly, that one was against mitigation activities and in a broader sense anti-environmental. A second reason is the difficulty of incorporating adaptation measures in an international negotiation process. According to Burton (Chapter 2), 'it was not clear how effectively some of the developing countries would be able to use adaptation as a bargaining tool'. Adaptation raises further complications in a negotiation process. For instance, what obligation does a country have to participate in the negotiations if it expects to be able to largely adapt to expected impacts and is not viewed as one of the more significant causes of the problem?[9]

A third reason is that adaptation has been associated with 'passive acceptance' or 'fatalism' about human effects on the environment. Then-Senator Al Gore espoused this view 'believing that we can adapt to just about anything is ultimately a kind of laziness, an arrogant faith in our ability to react in time to save our skin' (Gore, 1992). Burton (Chapter 2) finds this weak view of adaptation, i.e., 'passive, resigned, accepting' present in the Framework Convention, compared with its strong presentation of mitigation as 'active, combative, controlling'. A final reason is a perception that future climate impacts must be known with some degree of specificity before it is possible to plan adaptation responses. As a Framework Convention report notes, 'few studies have been attempted to compare the costs of adaptation strategies with the cost of greenhouse gas mitigation strategies because it is difficult to assess adaptation costs accurately when the regional impacts of climate change are highly uncertain' (UNFCCC, 1996, p16). Presently, global circulation and integrated assessment models do not have the capability to accurately predict climate impacts at regional or local scales.[10]

There is little wonder that adaptation has been out of favour: who wants to be viewed, at best, as working prematurely on adaptation studies and, at worst, as obstructionist, lazy, arrogant and anti-environmental? A close look at the logic of mitigation suggests that dismissals of adaptation are misplaced. Adaptation deserves a larger and more formal role in climate policy.

Mitigation Logic

Mitigation has the following scientific underpinnings:

(i)   human activities, particularly the use of fossil fuels, have increased greenhouse gas concentrations in the atmosphere;
(ii) these greenhouse gases are associated with changes in climate; and
(iii) these changes in climate will result in negative impacts (e.g. costs) to society.

The logic of response is as follows:

(a) mitigation activities, i.e. reduction of greenhouse gas emissions and increase of greenhouse gas sinks, will lead to a reduction in the increase of greenhouse gas concentrations (or, more optimistically, a stabilization of atmospheric concentrations);
(b) fewer greenhouse gases will lead to fewer (less) changes in climate; and thus;
(c) society and the environment will experience less adverse impacts.

Debate over climate change has focused almost exclusively on (i)–(iii). The IPCC working groups roughly map onto these three assertions, focusing on science, impacts, and economics of climate change. In contrast, very little attention has been paid to evaluation of (a)–(c).

Mitigation Responses Evaluated

Why do policymakers and scientists expect that mitigation activities can succeed? One important answer to this question is the lessons that have been distilled from the precedent of international policy responses to ozone depletion, which is often used to justify the present course of climate policy (Gore, 1992). Ozone depletion refers to the effects of human-produced chemicals on the Earth's ozone layer, which were addressed through international negotiations leading to the Montreal Protocol in 1987. There is reason to believe that the ozone precedent has been misapplied to the case of climate change. While a full elaboration of this issue goes well beyond the scope of this chapter, four important differences between the two cases are as follows: (1) the science of ozone depletion was 'simpler' (Darmstadter and Edmonds, 1989); (2) fewer political and economic actors were involved (Haas, 1991); (3) the issue was socially easier to deal with, e.g. ease of finding substitutes (Doniger, 1988); and (4) a framework for policy action appeared early on (Pielke and Betsill, 1997). The ozone precedent is widely viewed as a success story. However, its success may be less relevant to the climate issue than many have suggested. Beyond the ozone precedent, a close look at the logic of mitigation suggests that success may be difficult to achieve. (The following sections follow the discussion of mitigation logic presented in the previous section.)

Will societies be able to institute the mitigation activities needed to reduce increases in greenhouse gases?

Recent experience in seeking to limit the growth of greenhouse gas emissions provides a sobering lesson in the difficulties of that task. Political and technical obstacles to successful implementation of mitigation activities coupled with recent experience provide a reason for restrained optimism at best, and outright pessimism at worst, about the likelihood of mitigation activities actually resulting in emission reductions of the sort agreed to in Kyoto. An even more dismal outlook is warranted for proposed future actions of the Framework Convention that go beyond existing proposals.

The experience of the United States is a cautionary tale. On Earth Day 1993, President Clinton announced that:

> We must take the lead in addressing the challenge of global warming that could make our planet and its climate less hospitable and more hostile to human life. Today, I reaffirm my personal and announce our nation's commitment to reducing our emissions of greenhouse gases to 1990 levels by the year 2000. (UNFCCC, 1995)

In October 1993, the US Government released its Climate Change Action Plan (CCAP), detailing the means to be employed to reach the emission goal, which would have required a 7 per cent cut in emissions from what was expected for 2000 (Paarlberg, 1996). Within little more than a year, the United States stated that it would not meet the goal of reducing emissions to 1990 levels by the year 2000 because the economy had grown faster than expected, the price of oil fell sharply, and the Action Plan was not fully funded (UNFCCC, 1995; cf. CAR, 1994; Cushman, 1997). Another report notes that, 'regardless of whether the CCAP is successful in meeting the year 2000 target, and despite the fact that the CCAP will affect net greenhouse gas emissions well beyond that date, emissions are expected to be at least 10% above 2000 levels in 2010' (UNFCCC, 1996, p14).

At the core of the Clinton administration's plan to meet its emission reduction goal was an energy tax proposed during the President's first term. The tax was proposed primarily as a means to achieve deficit reduction and not in terms of climate policy. It focused on all energy uses, greenhouse gas producing or not, in order to mollify the band of the political spectrum that relied on coal production and use (Paarlberg, 1996; Muller, 1996). The Democratic Congress quickly rejected the proposal for a number of reasons, including a middle class who had been promised a tax cut during the election and a number of exemptions granted to certain industries and not others (Muller, 1996). In its place, the president proposed, and Congress enacted, a modest gasoline tax

(US$4.30 per gallon). The gasoline tax became an issue in the presidential election of 1996, when Republican candidate Bob Dole promised to rescind the tax if elected. Senator Dole's proposal received much popular support, including that of President Clinton (Mitchell and Rosenbaum, 1996). To place in broader global context the Clinton administration's failure to meet its reduction target, consider that had the goal been met that total global emissions of greenhouse gases would have been reduced by only 1.4 per cent (Paarlberg, 1996).

More broadly, of the nations participating in the Earth Summit in 1992 in Rio de Janeiro that voluntarily agreed to limit global greenhouse emissions by the year 2000 to 1990 levels, only two, Germany and the United Kingdom, were expected in 1996 to meet the target (White, 1996).[11] The shortfall reveals technical obstacles to meeting emissions targets:

> Meeting a target is technically tricky because future emissions and the consequences of policy actions are not perfectly predictable. Modelers and scientists are marked by different, incompatible core assumptions ... . Yet much is at stake depending upon the view adopted because different forecasts and models imply vastly different policy actions, costs, and benefits. (Victor and Salt, 1994, pp8–9)

Perhaps more importantly, the shortfall also reveals that domestic politics often limits what can be achieved:

> no single government agency – not even the head of a delegation – speaks for the full interests of the state. Translating broad international objectives into domestic plans that can be implemented requires complicated and time-consuming coordination across ministries and interests. (Victor and Salt, 1994).

Recent experience, including that of Kyoto in 1997, does not lend optimism to future efforts to limit or reduce global greenhouse gas emissions (Muller, 1996; Malakoff, 1997).

Some have suggested that future climate impacts will provide the impetus necessary to overcome such obstacles. However, Ungar (1995) is less sanguine, documenting a decrease in public and political concern about climate change during a period of extreme climate impacts around the world, 'if weather impacts of this magnitude are barely newsworthy, revitalizing global warming as a celebrity social problem may take more extreme events than one would like to countenance'.

Steps actually needed to stabilize greenhouse gas concentrations at levels lower than are present in 1997 dwarf those currently proposed. It has been estimated that stabilization of greenhouse gas concentrations in the atmosphere at *current levels* would require reductions of 60–80 per cent in greenhouse gas emissions (IPCC, 1994). One economist has estimated that reductions of that magnitude might cost $30 trillion (in 1989 US$, over 120 years) (Nordhaus, 1992). Others have proposed that reductions could be achieved with relatively modest emissions reductions in the near term and more drastic ones in the future (Wigley et al, 1996). Discussion of such steps has predictably garnered the attention of a range of economic interests.

A further point of concern in the implementation of the Framework Convention is rapid development in many countries around the world. Because many developing countries view the industrialized world as the cause of the climate change problem, they suggest that industrialized countries should bear the burden of greenhouse gas reductions while simultaneously providing energy-efficient technologies to lesser developed countries to allow continued growth and development (White, 1996). These issues complicate negotiations. They also only thinly mask a more fundamental issue for many developing countries: the relative benefits of development and increased energy use associated with higher standards of living versus the costs expected from climate change. For many countries, such a calculus may not swing in the favour of the Framework Convention.

Will a reduction in greenhouse gases mean less change in climate?

For the purposes of conducting a thought experiment, assume that implementation of the Framework Convention is successful (that is, countries stabilize concentrations of greenhouse gases in the atmosphere at levels agreed upon to prevent dangerous interference with the atmosphere). Under this 'success scenario', there are at least two reasons why the problem of climate change will not have been solved. One involves the inevitability of climate change, based on the IPCC projections, and the second is related to changes in climate independent of human causes.

Under the analysis conducted by the IPCC, concentrations of greenhouse gases in the atmosphere will not for the foreseeable future be reduced to pre-industrial levels. Thus, the IPCC (1996b, p188) notes that 'even with the most ambitious abatement policy, some climate change seems likely to occur'.[12] In short, even under a scenario of aggressive mitigation most experts expect climate change. Thus, mitigation efforts alone cannot completely deal with the problems associated with human-induced changes in climate, as projected by the IPCC.

A second scenario, mentioned by the IPCC, is the possibility that climate might change in surprising and unpredictable ways, independent of any human-induced changes (Kates and Clark, 1996). The recent historical record is full of such surprises such as changes in the frequency and intensity of El Niño-Southern Oscillation (ENSO) events and for particular locations variation in periods of drought, precipitation and extreme events.[13] Over much longer periods of centuries, millennia and eons, the climate record has shown significant variability, all of it essentially prior to the industrial age. Thus, the possibility exists that mitigation activities would succeed yet climate would still change.

Will less change in climate mean fewer (less) adverse impacts?

For purposes of extending the thought experiment, assume that mitigation activities succeed in stabilizing concentrations of greenhouse gases and also that as a result there are fewer changes in climate. Under this scenario, there remains significant cause to expect *more* rather than less adverse impacts to environment and society, as many actions taken by society are increasing vulnerabilities of people and the environment to climate impacts.[14] Such actions include development of marginal lands (e.g. Glantz, 1994), development of land at greater risk to extreme events (e.g. IRC, 1995), dependence upon highly technical, interdependent systems (e.g. Quaranelli, 1996), increased need around the world for food, clean water, health care, etc. (e.g. WRI, 1996). Most, if not all, of these trends are driven by population growth and technological change. It is certainly possible to imagine a scenario under which the frequency and magnitude of climate events remains constant, yet societal impacts (in terms of economic and other measures) increase because more people and property have put themselves (or been placed) in harm's way (cf. Pielke and Landsea, 1998). A number of measures of climate impacts exhibit such a trend (e.g. Swiss Re, 1997). In short, the problem of climate change might be successfully dealt with without positively affecting the majority of society's climate problems because societal change will continue to increase vulnerability.

It is an interesting thought experiment (and indeed an ongoing focus of research) to study various climate phenomena around the world and examine to what degree mitigation efforts would address climate-related problems. A working hypothesis is that there are *no* situations in the climate/society relation, existing or predicted, in which some type of adaptive measures do not make sense. Further, to the extent to which societies around the world are maladapted to climatic variability, these adaptive measures will almost certainly provide benefits under the entire spectrum of climate change scenarios offered by the IPCC (1996a, Chapters 1–18).

Implications and Recommendations

To summarize, there are a number of reasons to believe that mitigation responses will not or cannot succeed with respect to their own goals, including:

- political and technical obstacles in the way of cutting emissions in developed and developing countries;
- inevitable climate changes as projected by the IPCC;
- changes in climate due to factors other than human-induced climate change;
- increasing climate impacts due to the increasing vulnerability of society due to population growth and technological change.

Any one of these reasons supports the need for adaptation to occupy a larger and more formal role in climate policy. However, in spite of various observations made from time to time that adaptation has been neglected and subsequent calls for more attention, it remains to be viewed as a necessary and fundamental element of climate policy (see e.g. Meyer-Abich, 1980; FIFMTF, 1992; Carter et al, 1994; IPCC, 1996b; Smith et al, 1996; White, 1996).[15]

If one accepts the possibility that mitigation efforts might possibly fall short of the goal of preventing future climate impacts, then it is prudent and precautionary that climate policy reflect that possibility. Current climate policy is conducted under a success-oriented strategy, i.e. all eggs in one basket. It would make more sense to adopt a backup strategy that would provide complementary benefits even if mitigation efforts do succeed. Adaptation responses provide such a complementary approach. Further, even if one believes that mitigation activities are certain to succeed, adaptive measures are needed independent of concern about climate change, as society is in many respects poorly adapted to certain aspects of documented climate variability.

Acceptance of the need for adaptation as complement to mitigation to occupy a larger and more formal role in climate policy has at least four implications for conceptualization of the climate problem. First, with a greater focus on adaptation, debate over whether or not climate will change in harmful ways need not stand in the way of effective action, as most adaptation measures make sense under any climate scenario. Second, the issue of trade-offs between mitigation and adaptation cannot be avoided. Rather than being viewed as a cost of climate change (IPCC, 1996b, p411), adaptation measures should be viewed as actions that will result in benefits independent of climate change, and marginal benefits in the case of climate change. Indeed, because adaptation has been viewed as a cost of climate change, mitigation has been viewed preferentially in comparison (IPCC, 1996b, pp411–412). Third, the goals of climate policy must continue to be discussed and refined. Climate policy may have recently undergone a period of goal substitution, i.e. when means become ends. As happens often in institutions, high-order goals become largely forgotten in efforts to meet the objectives supporting attainment of the goals. The need for climate policies was at first motivated by concern above the adverse impacts of climate on society and environment. Mitigation activities were put forth as a means to meet the goal of limiting adverse impacts ('dangerous interference' in the language of the UNFCCC). Today, most discussion and debate is focused on mitigation as an end in itself, rather than as a means to a higher-order goal of reducing climate impacts. Finally, for those who wish to reduce society's vulnerabilities to weather and climate, they must be prepared to face the possibility that there does not exist a single global solution to the problem of climate change.

What might a reconsideration of adaptation look like in practice? Experience suggests three guiding principles:

1   Adaptation proceeds in a procedurally rational fashion (cf. Brunner, 1996). Adaptation is not a 'response' but instead a portfolio of responses. Within this portfolio some will make better decisions than others. This will allow for learning based on experience, as well as meaningful evaluation with respect to criteria of reduction in actual impacts and vulnerability. Mitigation cannot easily be evaluated with respect to impacts, leaving its success or failure as an open question for many years into the future.

2   Adaptation is a shared responsibility. Adaptation should not be thought of as 'every country for itself'. Rather, nations should build upon the framework of shared governance developed under the UNFCCC. A guiding principle of adaptation should be that the climate 'winners' of the world bear some responsibility to support and aid the climate 'losers' of the world (cf. Glantz, 1995). As climate changes, today's 'winners' and 'losers' might shift in such a way that the flow of support and aid changes in its intensity and direction.

3   Adaptation links the documented needs of today with the expected problems of tomorrow. One frequently involved criticism of the current response is that in focusing on future climate change, we put the needs of future generations ahead of those in today's generation who suffer climate impacts. Adaptation encourages the refinement of existing policies in response to climate variability in a manner which

will reduce future vulnerabilities to climate fluctuations, thereby serving the needs of today and tomorrow (cf. Jamieson, 1998).

Under these three guiding principles, adaptation can be thought of in a manner that is every bit as ethical, responsible, global and comprehensive as mitigation has been by its proponents (cf. Chapter 2, this volume).

For the ongoing research agenda, a greater focus on adaptation means that more systematic attention must be paid to at least three areas. First, policymakers would benefit from a more systematic understanding of the costs and benefits of adaptation, (a) compared to the costs and benefits of mitigation and (b) in the context of existing climate-related problems. As is noted by the IPCC (1996b, pp249–250), very little work has been done in this area, and some working under the auspices of the IPCC are currently working to change this situation. Second, attention must be paid to society's vulnerability to *climate* (vs. society's vulnerability to climate change), where climate refers to the entire range of society/climate interactions (e.g. variability, extreme events, etc.), not just climate change. For most decision-makers, the problem of climate change is a matter of degree, not of kind, with respect to the sorts of climate-related problems that they typically face. Conceptually, it may be possible to draw a distinction between climate impacts and climate change impacts. In practice, there is less significance and it may, in fact, be impossible to make the distinction in any meaningful scientific manner. How much sense would it make to inform a decision-maker with, say, flood-related concerns that mitigation responses will help them to deal with only those floods caused by climate change, not those resulting from other climate variabilities? Finally, with a greater commitment to adaptation, research will be needed to assess how far reducing society's vulnerabilities to climate goes toward reducing society's vulnerability to climate change. This information would allow decision-makers to better assess which sorts of mitigation responses to adopt, and could thus actually enhance the possibilities that mitigation activities would actually succeed.

Notes

1   On the history of the issue, see Hart and Victor (1993).
2   According to a 1993 report of the International Group of Funding Agencies Working Group on Resource Assessment, US funding represented about half of the worldwide total for global change research by 20 or so agencies around the world (Helmut Kuehr, personal communication, 1997).
3   The phrase 'climate-related impacts' is used to explicitly acknowledge that climate is one factor of many in the relation of society and its broader environment. Throughout the remainder of the chapter, the less cumbersome terms 'climate impacts', 'climate policies', etc., are used in recognition of the broader context.
4   For a review of various terms used to describe response to climate change, see Glantz and Ausubel (1988).
5   There are certainly other important factors in the relation of human behaviour and the atmosphere (e.g. land use). To date, however, discussion of climate change has focused almost exclusively on greenhouse gases.
6   An anonymous reviewer notes that 'a distinction should be made between what the IPCC terms "autonomous adjustment", which is (usually low cost) adaptation that takes place

automatically in response to a climate event (e.g. stomatal closure in plants during droughts) and adaptive responses requiring deliberate policy decisions. Autonomous adjustments are frequently examined and accounted for in impact assessments. It is the policy-related adaptive responses that are poorly investigated in these studies, although there is a rich literature on adaptation to climate variability based on historical case studies.' Indeed, the focus of this chapter is on deliberate policy decisions and seeks to integrate the rich literature on 'adaptation' to historical climate variability with a future-looking policy of adaptation to climate change.

7   According to Burton (Chapter 2, this volume), the UNFCCC mentions 'adaptation' in only five places.

8   For example, Moss (1995) and Parry et al (1996).

9   An anonymous reviewer notes that 'fundamentally, mitigation measures are conducted locally but affect everyone (i.e. their effect is global). In contrast, adaptation measures are conducted locally and their effect is generally local.' This is a prevailing view of adaptation as 'everyone for themselves'. This need not be so, as is argued in the conclusion to this chapter.

10 For example, Henderson-Sellers (1996). There is debate as to whether such models can *ever* accurately predict impacts. See, for example, Brunner (1996).

11 Only the 24 so-called Annex I (developed) countries agreed to emission limits. Under the UNFCCC, developed and developing countries follow different rules. It remains unclear how many European nations will meet their 1992 commitment (*Economist*, 1997).

12 On this, Kauppi (1995) concludes that 'climate will change, there will be dangerous effects, and the [Framework] Convention objective will be attainable'.

13 Some have suggested that recent changes in ENSO frequency might be attributable to climate change. See, for example, Trenberth and Hoar (1996).

14 It is often observed by proponents of mitigation that the *rate* of change is as important as the change itself, citing estimates of future rates of change greater than any in the past 10,000 years. But from the standpoint of climate impacts, a more appropriate point of reference might be the broader context of change in which climate change occurs, i.e., as compared to other human influences on society and environment.

15 The IPCC (Carter et al, 1994) does have in place means to oversee adaptation studies; however, 'to date, few studies have been performed' (Carter, 1996, p41). Smith et al (1996) is one of the few studies focusing significant attention on adaptation.

References

Broad, W. J. (1996) Debating use of iron as curb of climate: a plan to ease global warming passes an early test at sea. *New York Times.* 12 November, section B5.

Brunner, R. D. (1996) Policy and global change research: a modest proposal. *Climatic Change* 32, 121–147.

Carter, T. R. (1996) Assessing climate change adaptations: the IPCC guidelines. In *Adapting to Climate Change: An International Perspective,* ed. J. B. Smith, N. Bhatti, G. V. Menshulin, R. Benioff, M. Campos, B. Jallow, F. Rijsberman, M. I. Budyko and R. K. Dixon, Springer, Berlin.

Carter, T. R., Parry, M. L., Harasawa, H. and Nishioka, S. (1994) *IPCC Technical Guidelines for Assessing Climate Change Impacts and Adaptations.* University College, London.

Cushman, J. H. (1997) Why goal for reducing green house gases wasn't met. *The New York Times on the Web,* 20 October, www.nytimes.com.

Darmstadter, J. and Edmonds, J. (1989) Human development and carbon dioxide emissions: the current picture and associated uncertainties. In *Greenhouse Warming: Abatement and Adaptation,* ed. N. J. Rosenberg et al, Resources for the Future, pp. 35–52, Washington, DC.

Doniger, D. D. (1988) Politics of the ozone layer. *Issues in Science and Technology.* 4, 86–92.

Economist (1997) Hot air? 9 August, p. 24.

FIFMTF (Federal Interagency Floodplain Management Task Force) (1992) *Floodplain Management in the United States: An Assessment Report, Volume 2: Full Report.* L. R. Johnston Associates.

Glantz, M. H. (1995) Assessing the impacts of climate: the issue of winners and losers in a global climate change context. In *Climate Change Research: Evaluation and Policy Implications,* ed. S. Zwerver, R. S. A. R. van Rompaey, M. T. J. Kok and M. M. Berk, Elsevier, New York.

Glantz, M. H. (1994) *Drought Follows the Flow: Cultivating Marginal Areas.* Cambridge University Press, Cambridge, UK.

Glantz, M. H. and Ausubel, J. H. (1988) Impact assessment by analogy: comparing the impacts of the Ogallala Aquifer depletion and CO_2-induced climate change. In *Societal Responses to Regional Climatic Change: Forecasting by Analogy,* ed. M. H. Glantz, Westview Press, Boulder, CO.

Gore, A. (1992) *Earth in the Balance: Ecology and the Human Spirit.* Houghton Mifflin Company, New York.

Haas, P. M. (1991) Policy responses to stratospheric ozone depletion. *Global Environmental Change* 2, 224–234.

Hart, D. M. and Victor, D. G. (1993) Scientific elites and the making of US policy for climate change research. *Social Studies of Science* 23, 643–680.

Henderson-Sellers, A. (1996) Climate modelling, uncertainty and responses to predictions of change. *Mitigation and Adaptation Strategies for Global Change* 1(1), 1–21.

IPCC (Intergovernmental Panel on Climate Change) (1996a) *Climate Change 1995: Impacts, Adaptations and Mitigation of Climate Change: Scientific-Technical Analyses,* ed. R. T. Watson et al, Cambridge University Press, Cambridge, UK.

IPCC (1996b). *Climate Change 1995: Economic and Social Dimensions of Climate Change,* ed. J. P. Bruce et al, Cambridge University Press, Cambridge, UK.

IPCC (1996c) *Climate Change 1995: The Science of Climate Change,* ed. J. T. Houghton et al, Cambridge University Press, Cambridge, UK.

IPCC (1994) *Climate Change 1994: Radiative Forcing of Climate Change and An Evaluation of the IPCC IS92 Emission Scenarios,* ed. J. T. Houghton et al, Cambridge University Press, Cambridge, UK.

IRC (Insurance Research Council) (1995) *Coastal Exposure and Community Protection: Hurricane Andrew's Legacy,* IRC/IIPLR Report. Insurance Research Council, Wheaton, IL.

Jamieson, D. (1998) Global responsibilities: ethics, public health and global environmental change. *Indiana Journal of Global Legal Studies* 5, 99–119.

Kates, R. W. and Clark, W. C. (1996) Expecting the unexpected. *Environment* 38(2), 6–34.

Kauppi, P. E. (1995) The United Nations Climate Convention: unattainable or irrelevant. *Science* 270, 1454.

Malakoff, D. (1997) Thirty Kyotos needed to control global warming. *Science* 278, 2048.

Meyer-Abich, K. M. (1980) Socioeconomic impacts of CO_2-induced climatic changes and the comparative chances of alternative political responses: prevention, compensation, and adaptation. *Climatic Change* 2, 373–385.

Mitchell, A. and Rosenbaum, D. (1996) Dole and Clinton refocus on tax cuts as an option. *The New York Times,* Internet version, 9 June 1996.

Moss, R. H. (1995) Avoiding 'dangerous' interference in the climate system. *Global Environmental Change* 5(1), 3–6.

Muller, F. (1996) Mitigating climate change: the case for energy taxes. *Environment* 38(2), 13–43.

NAS (National Academy of Sciences) 1992. *Policy Implications of Greenhouse Warming: Mitigation, Adaptation, and the Science Base.* Panel on Policy Implications of Greenhouse Warming, National Academy Press, Washington, DC.

Nordhaus, W. D. (1994) *Managing the Global Commons: The Economics of Climate Change.* Massachusetts Institute of Technology, Cambridge, MA.

Nordhaus, W. D. (1992) An optimal transition path for controlling greenhouse gases. *Science* 258, 1315–1319.

Paarlberg, R. L. (1996) A domestic dispute: Clinton, Congress, and international environmental policy. *Environment* 38(8), 16–33.

Parry, M. L., Carter, T. R. and Hulme, M. (1996) What is a dangerous climate change? *Global Environmental Change* 6, 1–6.

Pielke, R. A., Jr and Betsill, M. M. (1997) Policy for science for policy: a commentary on Lambright on ozone depletion and acid rain. *Research Policy* 26, 157–168.

Pielke, R. A., Jr and C. W. Landsea (1998) Normalized hurricane damages in the United States: 1925–1995. *Weather and Forecasting* 13, 621–631.

Quaranelli, E. L. (1996) Problematical aspects of the information/communication revolution for disaster planning and research: ten non-technical issues and questions. *Disaster Prevention and Management* 6(2), 94–106.

Smith, J. B., Bhatti, N., Menzhulin, G., Benioff, R., Budyko, M. I., Campos, M., Jallow, B. and Rijsberman, F. (eds) (1996) *Adapting to Climate Change: An International Perspective.* Springer, New York.

Swiss Re (1997) Natural catastrophes and major losses in 1996: high losses from man-made disaster, but no extremely costly losses from natural catastrophes. *Sigma* 3, 1–38.

Trenberth, K. E. and Hoar, T. J. (1996) The 1990–1995 El Niño-Southern Oscillation event: longest on record. *Geophysical Research Letters* 23(1), 57–60.

UNFCCC (Framework Convention on Climate Change) (1996) *Report on the In-depth Review of the National Communication of the United States of America.* FCCC/IDR.l/USA. US GPO, Washington, DC.

UNFCCC (Framework Convention on Climate Change) (1995) *Executive Summary of the National Communication of the United States of America.* FCCC/NC/7. US GPO, Washington, DC.

Ungar, S. (1995) Social scares and global warming: beyond the Rio Convention. *Society and Natural Resources* 8, 443–456.

Victor, D. G. and Salt, J. E. (1994) Managing climate change. *Environment* 36(10), 6–32.

White, R. M. (1996) Climate science and national interests. *Issues in Science and Technology,* Fall, 33–38.

Wigley, T. M. L., Richels, R. and Edmonds, J. A. (1996) Economic and environmental choices in the stabilization of atmospheric CO_2 concentrations. *Nature* 379, 240–243.

WRI (World Resources Institute) (1996) *World Resources 1996–97: A Guide to the Global Environment.* World Resources Institute, Washington, DC.

19

Conceptual History of Adaptation in the UNFCCC Process

E. Lisa F. Schipper

While adaptation has, in the last three years, become the most fashionable item on the climate policy agenda, this was not always so. Since the early 1990s, numerous scientists and policymakers have been making the case that adaptation has been the overlooked cousin of greenhouse gas mitigation. As both are seen to be of equal importance, the lack of policy on adaptation is interpreted as a political strategy by developed countries to avoid admitting liability and the financial consequences of this admission. A tension between those in favour of mitigation over adaptation activities has strongly characterized the discourse on climate change policy. However, a closer look at the history of the concept of adaptation as applied in the United Nations Framework Convention on Climate Change (UNFCCC) process underscores the original intention that the treaty should focus on reducing the source of climate change, rather than on adapting to the changes. Adaptive capacity was considered to be an indicator of the extent to which societies could tolerate changes in climate, and was not seen as a policy objective. As a result of events that have unrolled since the inception of the UNFCCC, needs and perceptions have shifted. Today, there are strong grounds for having adaptation as a policy goal, but it must be recognized that the UNFCCC, and its Kyoto Protocol in particular, are first and foremost about abating greenhouse gas emissions. Thus, adaptation policy may find a more appropriate home beyond the existing climate change regime.

Introduction: Emergence of Adaptation as a Policy Response

Although adaptation and abatement of greenhouse gas emissions (mitigation) are both set out in the United Nations Framework Convention on Climate Change (UNFCCC)[1] as responses to anthropogenic climate change, a dichotomy between the two as policy approaches has emerged as one of the most striking features of the discussion on how to respond. A fervent debate on the merits of each approach with respect to the other has been ongoing among negotiators, policymakers and scholars since the inception of the dialogue on climate change.[2] Separation of mitigation of greenhouse gases from adaptation to climate change in thinking, practice and policy is well documented in the climate change literature,[3] and is evident, not only in relation to law setting, but also in the treatment of the two issues in scientific forums.[4] As a result, the conflict between adaptation and mitigation has become central in framing the science and policy debates on climate change. However, the flavour of the debate has shifted since the 1980s, as perceptions and political perspectives on adaptation have altered. This article explores some of the conceptual directions that thinking on adaptation to climate change has taken since the 1980s and the possible triggers for these shifts.

In order to reverse trends of changes in climate, scientists predominantly agree that anthropogenic sources of greenhouse gas emissions must be limited. In acknowledgement of this need, the international community adopted the UNFCCC in 1992 as the global legal policy framework for doing this. Not without reason therefore, policy on climate change has primarily emerged as mitigation policy, particularly focused on energy.[5] Kates remarks that the Intergovernmental Panel on Climate Change (IPCC), the scientific body supporting the UNFCCC process, reflected this prioritization in its earliest reports, which paid only scant attention to adaptation, vulnerability or equity.[6] Because of this focus on mitigation rather than adaptation in both scientific and policy forums, a number of scholars made the case in the 1990s for adaptation to 'occupy a more prominent role in climate policy'.[7] A move in this direction has now begun. Since agreement on the 2001 Marrakesh Accords[8] under the UNFCCC, focus on adaptation as a policy response to climate change flourished and adaptation projects have mushroomed. Indeed, even the UNFCCC has adopted a vital work programme on adaptation, which can certainly be considered the highest pinnacle for adaptation policy so far. However, to understand fully why this process took so long, we must appreciate the underlying reasons, which range from divergent political interest to a shift in scope of the definition of adaptation.

This article investigates the conceptual history of adaptation under the UNFCCC. It begins by exploring the dichotomy between adaptation and mitigation as it has evolved. The article looks back at the inception of political negotiations on a climate change convention, analysing past literature and discussions with key individuals. Based on this background, it discusses the conceptual evolution of adaptation. In conclusion, it looks at the current understanding and status of adaptation under the UNFCCC, suggesting that adaptation may now have reached its most important crossroads yet in terms of both discourse and policy.[9]

Adaptation and Mitigation as Responses to Climate Change

In looking at how to address climate change, some have made the case that individuals and society will be able to adapt to changes in climate just as they have since humankind's first appearance on Earth,[10] and, thus, explicit policy on adaptation is not necessary.[11] Another perspective holds that while all societies are either adapted or adapting to their climate to some extent, capacity to adapt to new variability and more rapid changes differs significantly and adaptation must be supported by policy. The former argument that adaptation could be left aside to 'happen' could be justified rather easily in the early stages of political negotiation when there was considerable hope that policy action could mitigate climate change[12] for two main reasons: there was faith in the extent to which mitigation would be possible and effective; and there was uncertainty over the extent to which climate change would occur and thereby how to adapt. In addition, there were several political and conceptual reasons why adaptation was left off the agenda. However, the most recent science confirms that climate change is not a distant prospect but a current reality. It has consequently been recognized that what can be achieved through mitigation at this stage may be insufficient for avoiding or even reducing certain features of climate change. It is consequently recognized that other responses – particularly adaptation – are necessary.[13] Thus, proponents of adaptation during the 1990s have finally had their voices heard.

Broadly, three schools of thought[14] can be discerned from the literature over time with regard to responding to climate change: the 'limitationist' view, where action to reduce greenhouse gas emissions (mitigation) is the core of efforts;[15] the 'adaptationist' view, where no explicit action is required as the 'invisible hand of either natural selection or market forces' will ensure that societies will adjust to the changes;[16] and the more recently expressed 'realist' view, where climate change is considered a fact, uncertainty of impacts acknowledged, and adaptation is considered a 'crucial and realistic response option along with mitigation'.[17] Kates notes that both the 'limitationist' and 'adaptationist' views have discouraged research on adaptation,[18] particularly as the 'limitationist' view holds that focus on adaptation would undermine incentives to reduce emissions.[19] Klein says that emerging policy responses, such as the funds created by the Marrakesh Accords to finance adaptation under the UNFCCC and Kyoto Protocol,[20] reflect that a 'realist' view has now been adopted.[21] This is also one that recognizes the vulnerability and lack of capacity of developing countries to adapt to climate change, which is seen as ignored by the other two extreme views.[22] It is also the only perspective that supports a complementary approach between adaptation and mitigation, a view that has only very recently emerged.

The dichotomy: Adaptation versus mitigation

While mitigation focuses on the source of climate change, adaptation addresses its consequences. The relationship between adaptation and mitigation is such that, in theory, the more mitigation that takes place, the less adaptation will be needed, and vice versa.[23] Nevertheless, the impacts of mitigation will not be immediately evident, just as the full effects of current greenhouse gas emissions will not be experienced for many years due to the inertia in the global climate system. Mitigation is also slow due to lags in the implementation of effective policies,[24] including the delay in the entry into force of the framework for emissions reductions under the Kyoto Protocol. On the other hand, the results of adaptation efforts will have near-term visibility because of strong links with development initiatives. Those in favour of promoting adaptation policy made the case in the 1990s that adaptation had been sidelined by the climate change negotiations through explicit emphasis on mitigation embodied by the negotiations on the instrument that became the Kyoto Protocol, urging for adaptation to be given greater prominence in the climate change debate.[25] Thus, while adaptation and mitigation are different types of responses, they have been pitted against each other.

In examining the literature, it is possible to identify a number of specific reasons why adaptation has not been granted as much attention as mitigation from the start. For one, adaptation was viewed as a 'defeatist' option, and support for it was considered an acknowledgement that climate change impacts would require adjustments beyond normal behaviour,[26] as well as an admission that mitigation would be insufficient or ineffective. In the context of building support for a mitigation framework, a focus on adaptation was therefore seen as unconstructive.[27] Further, there was a view that identifying adaptation options would be tantamount to admitting that climate change was really occurring[28] in the times of high scientific uncertainty and a distinct rift between 'believers' and 'climate sceptics'.[29] Burton claims that it was 'dangerous' for a nation to propose adaptation in the negotiations,[30] as it might also demonstrate a country's lack of discipline towards emissions limitation, and countries proposing adaptation would be seen as 'closet polluters'.[31] The adaptation approach was associated with not only a 'fatalistic and optimistic' view, similar to a 'do nothing' strategy, but also with 'faith in scientific progress', because it was considered that adaptation efforts would primarily come from technical and technological solutions.[32]

Discussing the funding of adaptation was also considered 'an implicit acceptance of responsibility for causing climate change',[33] something that touched too much on the highly politicized early debate surrounding accountability. To this end, adaptation was implicitly linked with discussions on liability and compensation, which developed countries wanted to avoid.[34] There is also an indication that some developing countries were fearful that discussions on adaptation would derail developed-country commitments to mitigation of greenhouse gas emissions.[35] As a result, the policy debate in the early 1990s was 'framed as a choice between mitigation and adaptation'.[36]

In terms of cost effectiveness and urgency, adaptation was considered secondary to mitigation because adaptation was seen as a long-term strategy that should be undertaken once the effects of climate change were more evident.[37] Another complication was that the UNFCCC only addresses anthropogenic climate change and does not extend to climate variability. Lack of scientific evidence has been a constraint to distinguishing between the two, although according to the IPCC's most recent reports, this distinction is negligible when climate change is defined as including variability.[38] Nevertheless, this too contributed to creating an additional methodological barrier to advancing adaptation work under the UNFCCC.[39]

These possible pathways, as illustrated by Figure 19.1, clearly influenced those drafting the UNFCCC. In this context, Bodansky comments on the interpretation of Article 2 of the UNFCCC,[40] which states the objective of the Convention (Box 19.1) as favouring mitigation over adaptation. The objective was specified in the Second World Climate Conference Ministerial Declaration[41] and the Noordwijk Declaration,[42] which state that 'stabilizing the atmospheric concentrations of greenhouse gases is an imperative goal'.[43] Although this phrase did not survive the negotiations on the final Convention text, Article 2 describes stabilization of greenhouse gas concentrations as the primary action.[44] It is the latter section of the article regarding food production and economic development, not adaptation of ecosystems, which is interpreted as supporting human adaptation.[45] As described above, at the time of writing the

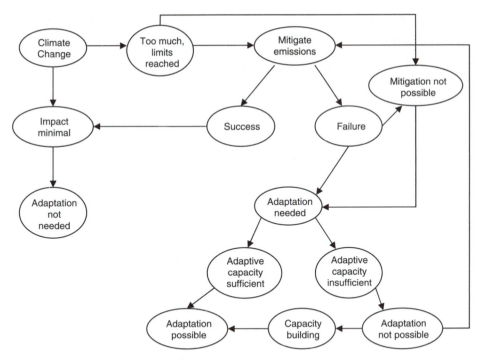

Figure 19.1 *Pathways for responding to climate change*

Convention text, it was believed that mitigation was a greater priority, because mitigation was considered the most effective method for responding to climate change. It was in this sense an 'upstream' approach, like those advocated by environmentalists for dealing with pollution problems, and the model appropriate for the previously

---

Box 19.1 *UNFCCC Objective*

UNFCCC, Article 2: Objective:

The ultimate objective of this Convention and any related legal instruments that the Conference of the Parties may adopt is to achieve, in accordance with the relevant provisions of the Convention, stabilization of greenhouse gas concentrations in the atmosphere at a level that would prevent dangerous anthropogenic interference with the climate system. Such a level should be achieved within a time-frame sufficient to allow ecosystems to adapt naturally to climate change, to ensure that food production is not threatened and to enable economic development to proceed in a sustainable manner.

Source: United Nations, 'United Nations Framework Convention on Climate Change', in *Report of the Intergovernmental Negotiating Committee for a Framework Convention on Climate Change on the Work of the Second Part of its Fifth Session, held at New York from 30 April to 9 May 1992: Addendum* (Doc. No A/AC.237/18 (Part II)/Add.1, Annex I, 16 October 1992).

negotiated Montreal Protocol[46] and action on acid rain,[47] where those countries that were the source of the problem were also responsible for taking action to mitigate and consequently had to bare the associated costs. Vellinga recalls that the predominantly Organisation for Economic Co-operation and Development (OECD)-member writing and research team were fearful of the potential costs their countries would face with respect to providing funding to developing countries to respond to the changes in climate.[48]

Thus, mitigation was the policy response of choice in the early stages of the UNFCCC because adaptation was considered only the secondary response, and a controversial one at that. This has also implied that literature and research on each of the two responses have advanced at different speeds: much more work has been carried out on mitigation,[49] creating a lack of understanding and consensus about adaptation. Because of the challenges to furthering adaptation policy, the adaptation discourse stemming from those seeking stronger policies on adaptation was strongly influenced by a need to justify equivalent treatment of adaptation and mitigation. Due to delays in the implementation of the Kyoto Protocol, however, adaptation emerged as the only viable option for furthering climate change policy. So, whereas thinking originally suggested that there could be a choice between whether to mitigate emissions or to adapt to the changes, this perspective has largely disappeared from the mainstream. On the other hand, it is still recognized that whereas mitigation comes down to following regulations and making conscious changes in production, transport and other service industries, adaptation will not be an optional action. Nordhaus makes the point regarding our choices succinctly: 'Mitigate we might; adapt we must'.[50] Thus, the question is simply whether capacity is sufficient to undertake the necessary adaptation. But this shift has happened quite unexpectedly and not quite as logically as may be expected. The conceptual understanding of adaptation to climate change has also evolved throughout the UNFCCC negotiations and has had a strong influence on the development of adaptation policy as well.

Conceptual Shift in Thinking about Adaptation

Waggoner noted in the early 1990s that 'the first obstacle to adaptation is reluctance to contemplate it',[51] reflecting the political atmosphere during the UNFCCC's infancy. This sentiment would also have resonated with many adaptation scholars 10 years after being made, although then it would not have been as accurate. A look at changes in interpretations of adaptation in the climate change science and policy provides further insight into how adaptation has been left 'behind' in climate policy. Such an examination informs us that the original understanding of what adaptation meant differs from how adaptation is currently understood. The first indication is found by looking at how adaptation was defined in the early 1980s. The subsequent conferences, workshops and research have contributed a shift in interpretation of the concept, which has now become associated with developing-country interests, as shown in Table 19.1. This section indicates how the science and negotiations that produced the UNFCCC reflected an initial application of adaptive capacity as a way to assess how much

Table 19.1 *Historical framing of climate change debate and adaptation thinking*

Timeframe	Forum	Main Questions	Strategies
Climate Change Debate			
1960s–1970s	World Meteorological Organization Climate scientists	Is climate change an issue we need to worry about? How will climate change affect the weather?	Weather modification, monitoring
Mid-1980s– early 1990s	IPCC INC UNFCCC COP	Is climate change occurring? How will climate change affect global ecosystems and humanity? Who should be responsible for reducing emissions?	Global emissions reductions regime, activities implemented jointly/joint implementation
Late 1990s– early 2000s	UNFCCC COP Regional decision-makers	What are the relative costs of mitigation and adaptation? How vulnerable are communities to variability and its consequences?	Planned adaptation strategies
Adaptation Thinking			
1970s–early 1980s	Club of Rome Academics	What are the ecological limits to human development and growth? How can we respond to climate change? What sort of impacts can systems sustain? Will systems adapt automatically?	Individual adaptation
Late 1980s	Advisory Group on Greenhouse Gases IPCC	What will the impacts be? How much adaptation are society and ecosystems capable of? How much can ability to adapt offset need to mitigate?	Ecosystem adaptation
Early 1990s	IPCC INC	Is mitigation more important than adaptation for responding to climate change? Mitigation and adaptation as alternatives to responding to climate change.	UNFCCC
Late 1990s	UNFCCC COP Research bodies	How can policy support adaptation? Who is vulnerable to climate change and why? Climate change will occur – adaptation will be necessary. Close link between adaptation and development.	Vulnerability and impact assessments Adaptation policy
Early 2000s	UN Development Programme/Global Environmental Facility World Bank and donor agencies Research bodies IPCC Third Assessment Report	What constitutes adaptive capacity? How can adaptation be integrated into existing sustainable development plans? What is needed to mainstream adaptation? How can adaptation policy be designed?	Development policy programmes and projects by multilateral and bilateral donor agencies

Source: Climate change debate information adapted from Miller et al, *Shaping Knowledge, Defining Uncertainty: The Dynamic Role of Assessments,* Background Paper to A Critical Evaluation of Global Environmental Assessments: The Climate Experience Workshop (College of the Atlantic in Bar Harbor, Maine, 22–26 June 1997) under the Global Environmental Assessment Project, Harvard University, CARE/IGES and IIASA, available at www.hks.harvard.edu/gea/index.html

mitigation was needed. This also helps to explain further why adaptation was interpreted as secondary to mitigation, and the consequent bias toward mitigation.

In the years of drafting the UNFCCC, scientists working on adaptation issues considered adaptive capacity to be a measure of the limits to responding to climate change,[52] in line with the Club of Rome's 1972 report *The Limits to Growth*.[53] More precisely, the emphasis was on the 'ecological limits or levels of tolerance'.[54] This was referred to as 'tolerable limits', building on the original work in 1975 by economist William Nordhaus to examine what these limits might be.[55] The focus was on how much a system could be stressed before it would collapse, an essentially ecological approach, although both ecosystems and human systems were considered. Climate scientists meeting in Villach, Austria, in 1987 attempted to address the question of how much climate change could be tolerated by ecosystems and society.[56] In direct response to this, the Advisory Group on Greenhouse Gases[57] (AGGG) developed climate change targets and indicators in 1990 for estimating the 'limits' of temperature and sea-level rise that could be tolerated by nature.[58] The Second World Climate Conference Ministerial Declaration in 1990 recommended that 'limitations and adaptation measures be addressed',[59] thus picking up on the concept of ecological and social limits of climate change being defined by the extent of human and ecosystem capacity to adapt to the changes. From this perspective, capacity to adapt was considered something inherent in ecosystems and society, therefore not requiring explicit policy. Bodansky highlights the view that if adaptation to climate change is possible, 'such change could be viewed as benign'.[60] Thus, the amount of mitigation necessary was dependent on these limits – societies and ecosystems could adapt to a certain amount of change, but beyond that limits would be breached.

On the policy front, adaptation appeared primarily on the agenda of small island developing states (SIDS), although the 1992 World Conference on Environment and Development[61] underscored a four-track approach for managing climate change, of which the final one mentioned strategies for adaptation:

1   improved monitoring and assessment of the evolving phenomena;
2   increased research to improve knowledge about the origins, mechanisms and effects of the phenomena;
3   the development of internationally agreed policies for the reduction of the causative gases; and
4   adoption of strategies needed to minimize damage and cope with the climate changes, and rising sea level.[62]

The UNFCCC does not define adaptation, but during the Convention's Intergovernmental Negotiating Committee (INC) process, a submission by Australia and New Zealand identified it as 'all purposeful and deliberate activity taken in response to or in anticipation of the adverse effects of rapid climate change'.[63] At the Tenth INC (INC-10), they proposed to develop a research and policy framework on adaptation that would, among other things, elaborate an agreed definition of adaptation;[64] however, this never took place. The Alliance of Small Island States (AOSIS) had early on proposed a set of tasks on adaptation for the UNFCCC, highlighting, in particular, funding related to adaptation activities.[65] AOSIS had been an advocate of greater emphasis on adaptation throughout the negotiations process, and had been granted recognition of the importance of protecting SIDS from sea-level rise in Agenda 21.[66] In its 1991 proposal to the INC, AOSIS stressed the importance of addressing sea-level rise for the survival of small islands as a consequence of the melting of ice caps.[67] In the proposal, they drew attention to the adaptation needs of poor, vulnerable countries.

After the entry into force of the UNFCCC in 1994, the next years were devoted to negotiating the Kyoto Protocol and, thus, explicitly focused on mitigation, as the Protocol is an instrument for reducing greenhouse gas emissions. Following its adoption in 1997, parties then agreed that a number of issues needed to be addressed before the Protocol could be put into operation – these were set out in the 1998 Buenos Aires Plan of Action (BAPA).[68] The negotiations were intended to culminate at the Sixth Conference of the Parties (COP-6) in 2000; however, due to failure in negotiations and high-level political dispute, it was not until COP-11 in 2005 that the set of rules, entitled the Marrakesh Accords, were adopted. During this in-between period, adaptation emerged as a policy option. However, in the lead-up to COP-6, where details on implementation of the Protocol were to be hammered out, there were still a number of barriers that continued to hinder rule development for adaptation in the UNFCCC process.[69] Concerns included scientific uncertainty, an overt focus of studies on impacts rather than on adaptation measures, and a lack of understanding of priority needs for vulnerability reduction. The concern on the part of developing countries that focus on adaptation would contribute to a 'declining focus and efforts to achieve greenhouse gas mitigation in developed countries'[70] was still relevant. Furthermore, adaptation efforts were built mostly on the substance of Decision 11/CP.1[71] (Box 19.2) that had been adopted at the first COP in 1995. This decision addresses the funding of adaptation activities but does not propose any explicit work programme on adaptation.

After the failure at COP-6, developing countries began to realize that attaining the Protocol targets presented a considerable political and practical challenge, and mechanisms would be implemented less rapidly than expected. In particular, the US's

---

Box 19.2 *UNFCCC Decision 11/CP.1*

Decision 11/CP.1 Stages for Adaptation Activities and Funding

Stage I: Planning, which includes studies of possible impacts of climate change, to identify particularly vulnerable countries or regions and policy options for adaptation and appropriate capacity building.

Stage II: Measures, including further capacity building, which may be taken to prepare for adaptation as envisaged in Article 4.1(e).

Stage III: Measures to facilitate adequate adaptation, including insurance, and other adaptation measures as envisaged by Article 4.1(b) and 4.4.

Source: UNFCCC, 'Initial Guidance on Policies, Programme Priorities and Eligibility Criteria to the Operating Entity or Entities of the Financial Mechanism', in *Report of the Conference of the Parties on its First Session, held at Berlin from 28 March–7 April 1995* (FCCC/CP/1995/7/Add.1, 6 June 1995).

repudiation of the Protocol in March 2001 may have contributed to this change in mindset. Negotiation for additional funds set out in the Marrakesh Accords, and completion of the BAPA issues, also created an opportunity for adaptation to play a larger role. Indeed, Decision 5/CP.7[72] addresses the implementation of UNFCCC articles on the adverse effects of climate change on vulnerable countries, and the adverse effects of policies and measures taken to implement the Kyoto Protocol. Shortly after the publication of the IPCC's Third Assessment Report in 2001, however, an agenda item taking up adaptation was introduced in the UNFCCC's Subsidiary Body for Scientific and Technological Advice,[73] amid a discussion on how to address the impacts of climate change, and, in 2004, a work programme on adaptation was adopted.[74] This outcome can be considered a considerable breakthrough. As the UNFCCC has no article solely on adaptation, and adaptation is mentioned only five times in the Convention text, the case had previously been made by negotiators that there were insufficient opportunities to address adaptation under the UNFCCC. This contributed to a movement for the development of an Adaptation Protocol, or some similar legal instrument on adaptation on par with the Kyoto Protocol.[75] Although no official proposal on this issue has been made, the raising of the issue is testimony to the opportunities seen in adaptation. The continued interest in a larger platform for adaptation policy indicates that the existing provisions, even with the various funds adopted through the Marrakesh Accords to support adaptation and the 2004 work programme on adaptation, are not considered sufficient.

Part of the reason that adaptation policy developed so slowly thus stems from the lack of explicit provisions within the UNFCCC, which has left policymakers and scholars struggling to identify where best to address adaptation to climate change under the UNFCCC.[76] However, a strategy – whether conscious or unconscious – has overcome this dearth to some extent. Adaptation has primarily been discussed in the context of other articles that address related issues,[77] particularly 'developing-country issues' such as capacity building and technology transfer. It has been noted that this approach is too piecemeal[78] and continues to reflect lack of consensus on the meaning of the concept. What it has done is to broaden the definition of adaptation to include the other developing-country issues currently on the agenda and provided for in the UNFCCC – thus a space has been created for it within the legal framework. However, this has implied that adaptation has been 'used' and 'abused' when necessary. Oil-exporting countries can be described as abusers in that they have continuously attempted to couple any discussion on adaptation to the impacts of climate change with a discussion on adaptation to the impacts resulting from measures taken by developed countries to mitigate emissions, such as reduced fossil-fuel consumption.

But, ultimately, adaptation discussions in the UNFCCC have been linked to discussions on funding, which is in itself a particularly contentious issue in the UNFCCC negotiations. Calls for adaptation policy have been frequently and closely accompanied by calls for adaptation funding. Bodansky notes that the inclusion of financial resources at all in the final text of the Convention was part of the bargaining package, and that one of the purposes it aimed to fulfil was 'to aid developing countries in adapting to the adverse effects of climate change if steps taken under the convention fail to abate global warning adequately'.[79] Thus, in another way, supporting adaptation became synonymous with supporting development, and adaptation was profiled as an equity issue. The most significant push for this came out as a result of negotiations at COP-6 in 2000. At that point, the COP President, Jan Pronk, divided the negotiation issues into four categories, and placed adaptation along with technology transfer, capacity building and funding – thereby explicitly branding adaptation as a developing-country issue. Adaptation then began appearing in parties' statements but was scattered in different negotiation issues, which is closely related to the conceptual confusion about its meaning. Thus, while adaptation had carved out a niche for itself among the other developing-country issues, this did not facilitate the advancement of adaptation policy – in fact the contrary was true. The lack of a specific definition of adaptation, even more confused by its association with other aspects of the UNFCCC, posed as a significant constraint to furthering policy on adaptation.[80]

This is also related to a question regarding whose interests are met by pursuing an adaptation agenda. Adaptation has been characterized as a developing-country issue; however, it is clear that developing countries have different priorities. For those who already emit large quantities of greenhouse gases, adaptation is a useful measure to take focus off mitigation discussions in the UNFCCC negotiations. However, these countries do not necessarily need assistance in identifying or driving adaptation processes, but may require financial support. SIDS may need assistance with infrastructural adaptation, but are generally more concerned with halting the rise in greenhouse gas emissions that is threatening to cause sea-level rise such that the territory of their countries will disappear. At the same time, it is thought that developed countries may be playing a role in bolstering the importance of adaptation to developing countries. The ultimate aim here would be eventually to compel high-emissions developing countries to agree to mitigation commitments as a result of provisions on adaptation. Calls for adaptation funding continue to challenge the existing funding structures in an effort to seek channels for funding adaptation efforts this way. They also recall older proposals that appeared to have been abandoned, such as for an insurance mechanism. The new funds, the Special Climate Change Fund and Adaptation Fund,[81] adopted through the Marrakesh Accords, are being put into operation, but questions about the definition of adaptation appear to be halting this process. There is evidence that scholarly discussions about adaptation are not in complete rhythm with policy debates.

More recently, mitigation has also been linked with funding for developing countries, through the 'flexible mechanisms' established by the Kyoto Protocol, particularly the Clean Development Mechanism (CDM).[82] The CDM allows a developed country to gain emissions-reduction credits for investing in sustainable-development projects in developing countries. The CDM increased the appeal of the mitigation argument also for developing countries. This was particularly the case up to and immediately after the negotiation of the Protocol. This may no longer be the case, as many recognize now that the CDM may not bring the benefits originally expected.[83] Furthermore, the delay in the entry into force of the Kyoto Protocol and the resulting uncertainty may have been a catalyst for developing countries to look beyond the CDM and the Kyoto Protocol for funding opportunities. Furthermore, beginning at COP-8 in 2002, discussions have highlighted the possibility of elaborating targets for emission reductions for developing countries after 2012, therefore souring the appeal to developing countries of discussions surrounding mitigation. Thus, adaptation appears as a convenient topic to take the focus off mitigation. The strong developing-country support for the Delhi Ministerial Declaration on Climate Change and Sustainable Development, focusing on the role of climate change in development policy, adopted at COP-8, is evidence for this specific strategy.[84]

In sum, mitigation has been given more attention since the UNFCCC was drafted, not only out of political choice, but because mitigation was considered more important even from the beginning. This is the primary reason why the UNFCCC does not reflect a great emphasis on adaptation. Table 19.1 indicates the shifts in thinking in the climate change debate, and reflects how understandings of adaptation have altered since the 1970s. It reflects how different approaches for responding to climate change were questioned by various groups over time. Figure 19.1 indicates the differing conceptual pathways to adaptation that were considered by these groups. Thus, within the policy context of negotiations and the UNFCCC, adaptation has gone from being understood as a spontaneous adjustment that would determine the limits of how much climate change could be tolerated, and hence how much mitigation was necessary, to being seen as a fundamental policy strategy to promote the attainment of sustainable development. Placement of adaptation on the development agenda has been encouraged by the linking of adaptation with other related developing-country issues under the UNFCCC.

The Way Forward for Adaptation

The discussion above identifies that adaptation is not an alternative to mitigation, but is now a necessary objective. An increasingly dominant perspective holds that this should be supported by explicit adaptation policy, linked with the UNFCCC regime, on par with mitigation policy. But the UNFCCC and, in particular, the Kyoto Protocol are focused primarily on mitigating emissions, and space is limited for action on adaptation. As described above, several additional factors have constrained widespread acceptance of adaptation as a part of the UNFCCC's tasks. This includes a lack of conceptual consensus on adaptation and political abuse of the concept, which have in turn been caused by an attempt to carve out adaptation's place in the UNFCCC. While adaptation began its life in the UNFCCC process as an ecological concept, it has more recently been used as a synonym for development. With a new work programme on adaptation and an operational Adaptation Fund, adaptation looks set to stay a part of the mainstream of UNFCCC discussions.

Since 2002, a complementary approach between adaptation and mitigation has gained support, with the acknowledgement that adaptation and mitigation are not alternatives,[85] but rather 'two sides of one coin'.[86] Adaptation has greater prominence on the political and research agendas now and there is no longer the same need to justify its importance. Interest in developing synergies between mitigation and adaptation is growing, and the IPCC's Fourth Assessment Report (AR4) will consider, as a cross-cutting issue, the linkages between the two responses.[87] This suggests more than simply recognizing the complementary roles of adaptation and mitigation, or the 'balanced portfolio of responses' suggested by Burton.[88] In the context of discussions on cost optimization of adaptation and mitigation measures, it has also been suggested that an 'optimal mix' of adaptation and mitigation could exist.[89] Work on assessing this mix has been based on cost–benefit analyses,[90] and economic approaches based on public choice theory have been attempted.[91] The goal would be to assess how a country or organization could best invest money, but also to identify individual projects that would contribute both adaptation and mitigation components. Such solutions would have an extra advantage of being eligible for funding under mechanisms for both adaptation and mitigation. Certain policy measures may already fall under the category of both, i.e. mitigation measures can also reduce impacts and vulnerability, such as certain energy-efficiency programmes.[92] Agriculture projects with a focus on adaptation that also include a component of carbon sequestration fall under both categories as well.[93] There is some resistance to an approach to consider the two together,[94] partly due to the fact that the separationist sentiment between adaptation and mitigation remains strong, but also because it is acknowledged that an approach to 'optimize' would entail trade-offs that can result in neither the adaptation nor the mitigation component being effective.

More than anything, adaptation is currently receiving much 'lip-service' and it can certainly be seen as one of the 'trendiest' topics with respect to climate change and development, as evidenced by the numerous new research agendas, programmes and projects from disparate corners of the world with a prominent emphasis on adaptation.[95] But many of the key questions about adaptation remain unanswered – including to what extent it needs to be supported by *global* policy and, if so, the more fundamental question is whether the UNFCCC is the most appropriate policy framework for adaptation. Whereas it can hardly be denied that adaptation to climate change is necessary, the reason for this need is because many societies are highly vulnerable to both climate variability and change. But addressing only options for how to adapt will not enable us to get to the crux of the problem, namely how to reduce our vulnerability. In many places, vulnerability to climate is determined by factors that are far beyond the scope of the UNFCCC or any global treaty. While this concern may seem irrelevant if actions to reduce vulnerability are also ongoing, the truth is that many of these determinants of vulnerability are very difficult to influence because they are often part of larger socio-economic and cultural building blocks of nations. The related concern is that calls for adaptation policy that would mirror mitigation policy in scope and importance in the UNFCCC process may detract from the mitigation agenda. Consequently, mitigation of greenhouse gas concentrations, through emissions reductions, sequestration or storage might be considered less urgent.

The dichotomy between adaptation and mitigation, though now less visible, continues to exist in the UNFCCC process. Adaptation now represents policy-driven adjustments to changes in climate, particularly in developing countries, and is promoted as a standard element in development agencies' work programmes. The objective of mainstreaming adaptation into development and sectoral policies[96] can be discerned on various agendas, from development agencies to research institutes and sectoral ministries in developing and developed countries. A recent development is the push by developed countries to set concrete adaptation plans and integrate adaptive management into their governance structures. What now needs to be the focus is not how to get funding for adaptation – as this has more or less been addressed – but rather how to ensure that adaptation strategies actually influence vulnerability in a successful and sustainable manner, so that existing development problems are also addressed. This would be the most effective way to optimize adaptation efforts, but still requires research and strategic thinking in the years to come.

Notes

1   United Nations Framework Convention on Climate Change (UNFCCC) (New York, 9 May 1992).
2   M. Oppenheimer and A. Petsonk, 'Global warming: Formulating long-term goals', in D. Michel, *Climate Policy for the 21st Century: Meeting the Long-Term Challenge of Global Warming*, pre-publication version (Center for Transatlantic Studies, 2004); T. J. Wilbanks et al, 'Possible responses to global climate change: Integrating mitigation and adaptation', 45:5 *Environment* (2003), 28–38; E. Boyd, et al, 'UNFCCC COP-8 highlights: Wednesday, 30 October 2002', 12:207 *Earth Negotiations Bulletin* (2002), 1–2; and R. Verheyen, 'Adaptation to the impacts of anthropogenic climate change: The international legal framework', 11:2 *RECIEL* (2002), 129–143.
3   S. Cohen, et al, 'Climate change and sustainable development: Towards dialogue', 8:2 *Global Environmental Change* (1998), 341–371.
4   S. Huq and M. Grubb, *Scientific Assessment of the Inter-relationships of Mitigation and Adaptation*, paper prepared for AR4 Scoping Meeting (8 August 2003).
5   R. J. T. Klein, E. L. Schipper and S. Dessai, 'Integrating mitigation and adaptation into climate and development policy: Three research questions', 8 *Environmental Science and Policy* (2005), 579.
6   R. W. Kates, 'Climate change 1995: Impacts, adaptations, and mitigation', 39:9 *Environment* (1997), 29.
7   Chapter 18, this volume.
8   *Report of the Conference of the Parties on its Seventh Session*, held at Marrakesh from 29 October to 10 November 2001 (FCCC/CP/2001/13/Add.1, 21 January 2001) (Marrakesh Accords).
9   The interpretation in this chapter is based on discussions with key individuals involved in formulating the UNFCCC and early work of the Intergovernmental Panel on Climate Change and the Advisory Group on Greenhouse Gases. Other relevant information is found in the United Nations General Assembly (UNGA) *Noordwijk Declaration on Atmospheric Pollution and Climatic Change* (Doc. No A/C.2/44/5, 1989), Annex, the UNGA *Ministerial Declaration of the Second World Climate Conference* (Doc. No A/45/696/Add.1, 1990), Annex III, documents of the Intergovernmental Negotiating Committee (INC) for a Framework Convention on Climate Change *Mechanism and Technical and Financial Support to Developing Country Parties, Synthesis Report on Adaptation* (Doc. No A/AC.237/68, 11 August 1994); *Report of the INC for a Framework Convention on Climate Change on the Work of its Tenth Session held at Geneva from 22 August to 2 September 1994* (Doc. No A/AC.237/76, 10 October 1994); *Submissions from Parties or Other Member States on the Specific Near-Term Priorities and Needs of Developing Countries, Adaptation and Issues Related to the Financial Mechanism* (Doc. No A/AC.237/Misc.38, 17 July 1994); *Preparation of a Framework Convention on Climate Change: Set of Informal Papers Provided by Delegations,*

related to the Preparation of a Framework Convention on Climate Change (Doc. No A/AC.237/Misc.1/Add.3, 18 June 1991); *Report of the Intergovernmental Negotiating Committee for a Framework Convention on Climate Change on the Work of its 4th session, held at Geneva from 9 to 20 December 1991* (Doc. No A/AC.237/15, 29 January 1991); 'Elements related to mechanisms', *Draft Annex Relating to Insurance Submitted by Vanuatu* (Doc. No A/AC.237/WG.II/CRP.8, 17 December 1991)) and the UNFCCC text itself, note 1 above.

10 J. H. Ausubel, 'Does climate still matter?', 350 *Nature* (1991), 649–652.

11 Cf. B. Smit, *Adaptation to Climatic Variability and Change: Report of the Task Force on Climatic Adaptation*, Occasional Paper (Department of Geography, University of Guelph Canadian Climate Program, 1993).

12 See T. J. Wilbanks et al, note 2 above.

13 M. Parry et al, 'Adapting to the inevitable', 395:6704 *Nature* (1998), 741.

14 A fourth approach has recently emerged from behind a political agenda to dismiss the integrity of the Kyoto Protocol which emphasizes adaptation as the only option; K. Okonski (ed.), *Adapt or Die: The Science, Politics and Economics of Climate Change* (Profile Books, 2003).

15 Chapter 14, this volume.

16 Ibid.

17 R. J. T. Klein, 'Adaptation to climate variability and change: What is optimal and appropriate?', in C. Giupponi and M. Schechter (eds), *Climate Change and the Mediterranean: Socio-Economic Perspectives of Impacts, Vulnerability and Adaptation* (Edward Elgar, 2003), at 2.

18 Kates originally proposed this view in a 1997 paper, where he used the term 'preventionist' instead of 'limitationist'. His observations on the lack of research on adaptation stem from this initial paper; see R. W. Kates, note 6 above, at 32.

19 See Chapter 14, this volume.

20 Kyoto Protocol (Kyoto, 11 December 1997).

21 See R. J. T. Klein, note 17 above, at 2.

22 See Chapter 14, this volume.

23 See S. Huq and M. Grubb, note 4 above.

24 S. Huq, personal communication via electronic mail (24 February 2004); I. Burton, *Mitigation and Adaptation: The Case for Separation*, Paper Presented at Mitigation and Adaptation: Towards a Mutual Agenda Workshop (Essen, 15–16 May 2003).

25 B. Apuuli et al, 'Reconciling national and global priorities in adaptation to climate change: With an illustration from Uganda', 61:1 *Environmental Monitoring and Assessment* (2000), 145–159; Chapters 2 and 18, this volume.

26 See M. Parry et al, note 13 above, at 741.

27 See Chapter 2, this volume.

28 D. Sarewitz and R. A. Pielke, Jr, 'Breaking the global warming gridlock', 286:1 *The Atlantic Monthly* (July 2000), 54–64.

29 An example of climate sceptics is the Global Climate Coalition (GCC), a lobbying group representing large businesses, primarily in the US, including Exxon, Shell Oil and other petroleum companies. The various members had been questioning the science behind the calls for the UNFCCC since the early days, and was active as a group between 1997 and 2002. In the early 2000s, several GCC members left in recognition of the need to embrace opportunities for responding to climate change, rather than ignore the reality of climate change.

30 See Chapter 2, this volume.

31 See I. Burton, note 24 above, at 3.

32 A. D. Tarlock, 'Now, think again about adaptation', 9 *Arizona Journal of International and Comparative Law* (1992), 169, at 172.

33 P. Sands, 'The United Nations Framework Convention on Climate Change', 1:3 *RECIEL* (1992), 270, at 275.

34 P. Vellinga, personal communication via telephone (October 2003).

35 O. Pilifosova, 'Where is adaptation going in the UNFCCC?', in A. C. de la Vea-Leinert, R. J. Nicholls and R. S. J. Tol (eds), *Proceedings of SURVAS Expert Workshop on European Vulnerability and Adaptation to Impacts of Accelerated Sea-Level Rise (ASLR)* (Hamburg, 19–21 June 2000), available at www.survas.mdx.ac.uk/pdfs/2volwher.pdf.

36 See A. D. Tarlock, note 32 above, at 170. This is particularly documented in US literature, where the government was encouraging the private sector to make a choice as to whether they would mitigate, prevent or adapt to climate change. As quoted in W. A. Morrissey, *Global Climate Change: A Concise History of Negotiations and Chronology of Major Activities Preceding the 1992 UN Framework Convention*, CRS Report for US Congress (1998), available at www.cnie.org/NLE/CRSreports/Climate/clim-6.cfm: 'The selection of any particular (strategy) package ... is a largely political choice of preferred means to achieve the overall policy goal'.

37 I. Burton, 'Adaptation to climate change and variability in the context of sustainable development', in L. Gómez-Echeverri (ed.), *Climate Change and Development* (Yale School of Forestry and Environmental Studies and United Nations Development Programme, 2000).

38 J. T. Houghton et al (eds), *Climate Change 2001: The Scientific Basis*, PCC WG I contribution to the TAR (Cambridge University Press, 2001).

39 See O. Pilifosova, note 35 above.

40 D. Bodansky, 'The United Nations Framework Convention on Climate Change: A commentary', 18:2 *Yale Journal of International Law* (1993), 451–558.

41 See UNGA, Ministerial Declaration of the Second World Climate Conference, note 9 above.

42 See UNGA, Noordwijk Declaration on Atmospheric Pollution and Climatic Change, note 9 above.

43 Ibid., para. 8.

44 'United Nations Framework Convention on Climate Change', in *Report of the Intergovernmental Negotiating Committee for a Framework Convention on Climate Change on the Work of the Second Part of its Fifth Session, held at New York from 30 April to 9 May 1992: Addendum* (Doc. No A/AC.237/18 (Part II)/Add.1, Annex I, 16 October 1992).

45 See S. Huq, note 24 above; P. Sands, note 33 above.

46 Protocol on Substances that deplete the Ozone Layer (Montreal, 16 September 1987).

47 An early proposal for a 'Law of the Atmosphere' to address atmospheric changes, including acid rain, ozone depletion and climate change as part of one legal instrument, rather than in separate protocols, recognized the interdependence of these issues; I. Burton, 'Human dimensions of global change: Toward a research agenda', in N. J. Rosenberg et al (eds), *Greenhouse Warming: Abatement and Adaptation* (Resources for the Future, 1989). Advocated by Canada in the late 1980s, this initiative eventually lost out to the option for a convention specifically on climate change; see D. Bodansky, note 40 above.

48 See P. Vellinga, note 34 above.

49 See T. J. Wilbanks et al, note 2 above; S. Fankhauser, *The Costs of Adapting to Climate Change*, GEF Working Paper No 16 (GEF, 1999).

50 W. D. Nordhaus, *Managing the Global Commons: The Economics of Climate Change* (Massachusetts Institute of Technology, 1994), at 189.

51 P. E. Waggoner, 'Now, think of adaptation', 9 *Arizona Journal of International and Comparative Law* (1992), 137, at 146.

52 See P. Vellinga, note 34 above.

53 D. L. Meadows et al, *The Limits to Growth* (Universe Books, 1972).

54 S. Boehmer-Christiansen, 'Global climate protection policy: The limits of scientific advice, Part 1', 4:2 *Global Environmental Change* (1994), 140, at 151.

55 See M. Oppenheimer and A. Petsonk, note 2 above.

56 W. E. Franz, *The Development of an International Agenda for Climate Change: Connecting Science to Policy*, IIASA Interim Report IR-97-034/ August (Harvard University and International Institute for Applied Systems Analysis, 1997).

57 The AGGG was established in 1986 by the World Meteorological Organization, United Nations Environment Programme (UNEP) and International Council of Scientific Unions (ICSU) as an expert group on climate change science responsible for organizing workshops and promoting studies. To some, the AGGG is seen as the precursor to the IPCC, although the purpose and agenda of the two bodies are not identical.

58 F. J. Rijsberman and R. J. Swart (eds), *Targets and Indicators of Climate Change* (Stockholm Environment Institute, 1990).

59 UNGA, Ministerial Declaration of the Second World Climate Conference, note 9 above, para. 14.

60 See D. Bodansky, note 40 above, at 500.

61 This was based on scientific findings from meetings that took place from 1980 to 1987 in Villach, Austria, and Bellagio, Italy, organized by the World Meteorological Organization, UNEP and ICSU. The conferences concluded that an enhanced greenhouse effect was evident and that negative impacts on human beings and ecosystems might be experienced; W. C. Clark et al, 'Acid rain, ozone depletion, and climate change: An historical overview', in The Social Learning Group, *Learning to Manage Global Environmental Risks*, Vol. 1 (The MIT Press, 2001).

62 UNGA, 'Note by the Secretary General: Report of the World Commission on Environment and Development' (Doc. No A/42/427, 4 August 1987).

63 See *Mechanism and Technical and Financial Support to Developing Country Parties, Synthesis Report on Adaptation*, note 9 above, para. 11.

64 See *Submissions from Parties or Other Member States on the Specific Near-Term Priorities and Needs of Developing Countries, Adaptation and Issues Related to the Financial Mechanism*, ibid.

65 See *Preparation of a Framework Convention on Climate Change*, ibid.

66 Chapter 17, para. 17.125 of Agenda 21 states: 'They are considered extremely vulnerable to global warming and sea-level rise, with certain small low-lying islands facing the increasing threat of the loss of their entire national territories. Most tropical islands are also now experiencing the more immediate impacts of increasing frequency of cyclones, storms and hurricanes associated with climate change. These are causing major set-backs to their socio-economic development'; Agenda 21 (A/CONF.151/26, 5 June 1992).

67 UN, *Preparation of a Framework Convention on Climate Change*, note 9 above.

68 See *Report of the Conference of the Parties on its Fourth Session, held at Buenos Aires from 2 to 14 November 1998* (FCCC/CP/1998/16/Add.1, 20 January 1999).

69 See O. Pilifosova, note 35 above.

70 Ibid., at 140.

71 Decision 11/CP.1 (Doc. FCCC/CP/1995/7/Add.1, 1995).

72 Decision 5/CP.7 (Doc. FCCC/CP/2001/13/Add.1, 2001).

73 See *Third Assessment Report of the Intergovernmental Panel on Climate Change: Scientific, Technical and Socio-Economic Aspects of Impacts of, and Vulnerability and Adaptation to,*

Climate Change, Scientific, Technical and Socio-Economic Aspects of Mitigation (FCCC/SBSTA/2003/L.15, 12 June 2003).

74   Decision 1/CP.10 (Doc. FCCC/CP/2004/10/Add.1).

75   B. Müller, *An FCCC Impact Response Instrument as part of a Balanced Global Climate Change Regime*, Paper presented at Tata Energy Research Institute, New Delhi (16 May 2002); CAN Equity Summit, Nusa Dua, Bali, 20 May 2002; IIED Special Event at FCCC SB16, Bonn, 11 June 2002, Brazilian Climate Change Forum, Rio de Janeiro, 26 June 2002, and International Federation of Red Cross and Red Crescent Societies' Climate Change Conference, The Hague, 27 June 2002; B. Müller, *Montreal 2005: What Happened, and What it Means* (Paper No EV 35, Oxford Institute for Energy Studies, 2006).

76   F. Yamin and J. Depledge, *The International Climate Change Regime: A Guide to Rules, Institutions and Procedures*, Draft copy (Institute of Development Studies, University of Sussex, December 2003).

77   M. J. Mace, *Adaptation Under the UN Framework Convention on Climate Change: The Legal Framework*, Paper presented at ZICER Seminar, Justice in Adaptation to Climate Change, 7–9 September 2003 (University of East Anglia, 2003).

78   E. L. Schipper and E. Boyd, 'UNFCCC COP 11 and COP/MOP 1: At last, some hope?', 15:1 *Journal of Environment and Development* (2006), 75.

79   See D. Bodansky, note 40 above, at 32.

80   See P. Vellinga, note 34 above.

81   The Adaptation Fund became operational following the entry into force of the Kyoto Protocol on 16 February 2005 and the adoption of the Marrakesh Accords at COP-11 in November 2005. The Special Climate Change Fund falls under the UNFCCC and was technically operational in 2001 but rule development has been slow.

82   Kyoto Protocol, Article 12.

83   A. Michaelowa, *Mitigation Versus Adaptation: The Political Economy of Competition Between Climate Policy Strategies and the Consequences for Developing Countries*, Discussion Paper 153 (Hamburg Institute of International Economics, 2001).

84   UNFCCC, 'Delhi Declaration on Climate Change and Sustainable Development', Decision 1/CP.8 (Doc. No FCCC/CP/2002/7/Add.1, 2002).

85   N. Brooks, *Vulnerability, Risk and Adaptation: A Conceptual Framework*, Tyndall Centre for Climate Change Research, Working Paper TWP No 38 (University of East Anglia, 2003); see also R. J. T. Klein, note 17 above and I. Burton, note 37 above.

86   See R. Verheyen, note 2 above, at 131.

87   See S. Huq and M. Grubb, note 4 above.

88   See I. Burton, note 37 above, at 155.

89   See A. Michaelowa, note 83 above.

90   S. Kane and J. F. Shogren, 'Linking adaptation and mitigation in climate change policy', 45:1 *Climatic Change* (2000), 75–102.

91   See A. Michaelowa, note 83 above.

92   See S. Cohen et al, note 3 above.

93   See R. J. T. Klein et al, note 5 above.

94   See I. Burton, note 24 above; R. J. T. Klein et al, note 5 above; R. S. J. Tol, *Adaptation and Mitigation: Trade-offs in Substance and Methods*, Working Paper (University of Hamburg, 2003); A. Michaelowa, note 83 above.

95   The new Linking Climate Adaptation database on organizations active in adaptation and the UNFCCC's similar database, mandated by COP-11, are examples.

96   See R. J. T. Klein et al, note 5 above.

From Impacts Assessment to Adaptation Priorities: The Shaping of Adaptation Policy

Ian Burton, Saleemul Huq, Bo Lim, Olga Pilifosova
and E. Lisa F. Schipper

Adaptation in the Framework Convention

The main purpose of this chapter is to assess the evolution of adaptation research from its initial place as a handmaiden to impacts research in the mitigation context, up to its present emergence in a role crucial to the development of adaptation policy. On this basis, it becomes possible to identify the requirements that the next generation of adaptation research will have to meet. This development is already under way and can be further strengthened. While the broad new directions of both research and policy can now be discerned, there remain a number of outstanding issues to be considered, and the chapter concludes with some relevant suggestions.

Adaptation is defined as 'adjustment in natural or human systems in response to actual or expected climatic stimuli or their effects, which moderates harm or exploits beneficial opportunities' (IPCC, 2001, p72). Climate adaptation policy refers to actions taken by governments including legislation, regulations and incentives to mandate or facilitate changes in socio-economic systems aimed at reducing vulnerability to climate change, including climate variability and extremes. Changes can be made in 'practices, processes, or structures of systems to projected or actual changes in climate' (Watson et al, 1996).

Adaptation to climate change is an integral part of the United Nations Framework Convention on Climate Change (UNFCCC) in two related but distinct ways that relate to different policy domains. The first is the prevention of dangerous interference with the climate system by the stabilization of greenhouse gas (GHG) concentrations in the atmosphere, commonly referred to as 'mitigation'. The second is reduction of vulnerability to climate change by the process of 'adaptation'. The relationships are illustrated diagrammatically in Figure 20.1. Both cases involve the science of impacts and their assessment. In the first case, it is crucial to assess the potential impacts of climate change because such assessments are an essential input to policy decisions about what constitutes 'dangerous interference with the climate system'. Prevention of

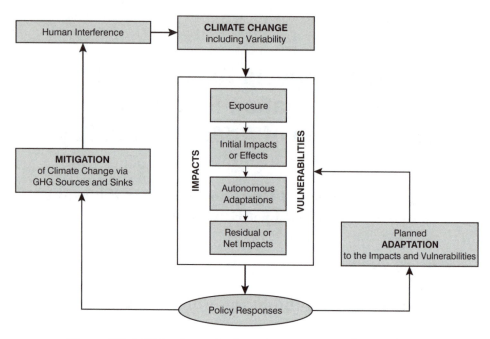

Figure 20.1 *Mitigation and adaptation responses to climate change*

Source: IPCC, 2001

dangerous interference is specified as the 'ultimate objective' of the UNFCCC (Article 2). What matters in this connection is the extent to which the gross impacts of climate change can be reduced by adaptation. The growing scientific understanding of the probable net impacts of climate change is being used to inform policymakers in their task of making choices about the level of urgency in the political climate change negotiations, and therefore, the targets and schedules that need to be adopted if 'dangerous interference' is to be avoided. Most research about adaptation as reported by the Intergovernmental Panel on Climate Change (IPCC) has been carried out in this 'impacts and mitigation' context and this is reflected strongly in the methodology employed. It is essentially directed to the 'mitigation' side of climate policy. By implication, the greater the impacts the more need for mitigation. Furthermore, the greater the effectiveness of adaptation in reducing vulnerability to climate change, the less will be the urgency to reduce emissions of greenhouse gases. Adaptation cannot prevent economic and other losses from climate change, but it can reduce and delay them (Smit and Pilifosova, 2001). Type 1 adaptation research essentially contributes to the debate about trade-offs between mitigation and adaptation.

The second way in which adaptation arises in the Framework Convention relates to development and related policy questions. The developed country parties to the UNFCCC have committed to 'assist the developing country Parties that are particularly vulnerable to the adverse effects of climate change in meeting the costs of adaptation to those adverse effects' (UNFCCC, Article 4.4).

In order to inform the policy process about adaptation in this second context, the emphasis shifts from the question of gross and net impacts to questions about vulnerability, and how and where to deploy adaptation responses. These questions are important to the developing countries both because they wish to reduce their vulnerability to climate change in the most effective ways, and because they are essentially in competition with each other for whatever international funds may become available to help them meet the costs of adaptation. It is to the advantage of each country, therefore, to be able to show how vulnerable it is to climate change; how much adaptation policies and measures will cost; where it lacks sufficient capacity to adapt without external assistance; and generally how donor funds can be effectively used. Donor countries also have an interest in these questions because they wish to be reassured that their assistance in helping to meet the costs of adaptation will be money well spent, i.e. it will allow developed countries to meet their commitments to assist. The developed countries have shown less interest in their own need for adaptation, and have generally assumed that they have the financial and technical resources to adapt as and when necessary. To this extent, adaptation will only be seriously entertained in developed countries when it becomes evidently necessary.

Thus, there are two directions and purposes in adaptation research; adaptation research for mitigation policy, and adaptation research for adaptation policy. To date, the overwhelming preponderance of adaptation research has been conducted in response to the mitigation issue. This can be explained to a considerable extent by the predominance given to mitigation over adaptation in the text of the UNFCCC itself and in the negotiations leading up to the initial signing of the Kyoto Protocol in 1997. The interest of the policymakers and the requirements of the negotiations have been largely directed to mitigation. The interest in adaptation as a response has been comparatively low and often absent, and to the extent that it was present at all, it was in the context of mitigation debates. One important reason for this is that it is widely understood that in the long term adaptation will not suffice. The atmospheric concentrations of greenhouse gases will have to be stabilized eventually at some tolerable level. More recently, however, the interest in adaptation as a legitimate policy response has increased, led by developing country negotiators. This has happened at least partly in response to a growing recognition that climate change is now occurring, impacts are being observed, and that even if fully implemented on time the Kyoto Protocol would only be a first small step towards achieving stabilization of greenhouse gases in the atmosphere. Some adaptation is now recognized as inevitable. The new challenge is to change the character of adaptation research from one that largely addresses the needs of the mitigation policy agenda, to one that also responds explicitly to the needs of adaptation policy. This requirement became manifest at the Sixth Conference of the Parties to the UNFCCC,[1] and was subsequently reinforced at the Seventh Conference of Parties (COP-7) in Marrakesh in November 2001, where more attention was given to matters of adaptation, and agreement was reached in principle to establish three different funds, each with an adaptation component. Quite suddenly the need for better understanding of the requirements of adaptation policy has assumed a prominent place on the research agenda.

The research questions that need to be addressed are implicit in earlier decisions by the COP, especially Decision 11/CP.1 taken in Berlin as long ago as 1995. Understanding this decision helps in the appreciation of the gulf between the impacts and mitigation orientation of what may be called the 'first generation' of adaptation research and the policy orientation of the 'second generation', now beginning. The first generation of studies mainly span over the 1995–2001 period and can be found in the 70 non-Annex I National Communications published to date (see UNFCCC National Communications, 2002).

From the outset of the climate change negotiations, some developing countries insisted on the need for adaptation, and the responsibility of the developed countries to help meet the costs of adaptation due to the historical record of emissions of developed countries. The small island nations at risk from sea-level rise, and the least developed countries with low capacity to meet the costs of adaptation, were prominent among those making these demands. While agreeing to accept their responsibility to provide financial help in principle, donor countries were concerned that adaptation to climate change could become a bottomless pit, or a 'black hole', absorbing a disproportionate amount of development assistance funds. Nor was it clear how adaptation funds could best be used. The COP-1 meeting in Berlin, therefore, formulated and adopted Decision 11/CP.1 in order to set in motion studies of adaptation, and laid out a broad timetable over which these studies would be conducted. These reflected, inter alia, the developed country view that adaptation was something for the future and that the immediate need was to prepare to adapt.

Adaptation was to be approached in three stages. The first stage was described as 'short term' and the second and third stages as 'medium to long term'. They were defined as follows:

Stage I: 'Planning, which includes studies of possible impacts of climate change, to identify particularly vulnerable countries or regions and policy options for adaptation and appropriate capacity building.'

Stage II: 'Measures, including further capacity building which may be taken to prepare for adaptation as envisaged in Article 4.1(e).'

Stage III: 'Measures to facilitate adequate adaptation, including insurance, and other adaptation measures as envisaged by Article 4.1(b) and 4.4.'

The precise meaning of these definitions is open to interpretation, and there has been no further formal elaboration from the COP since 1995. The definition of Stage I is the clearest: studies on impacts, the identification of vulnerability and policy options as well as capacity building, are to be carried out. Stage II refers to preparation for adaptation and Stage III to the facilitation of adaptation, but nowhere has it been explicitly agreed how adaptation policies or measures will be implemented. According to some negotiators who participated in the drafting of Decision 11/CP.1, the ambiguity was unavoidable. Negotiators were not certain what they wanted to agree upon, and in 1995 it was assumed that Stages II and III would be delayed, perhaps long delayed.

The fact that adaptation was not seen as an immediate priority is reflected in the articles of the UNFCCC cited in the definition of the stages. Also, only in Article 4.1(b) of the UNFCCC is any reference made to implementation of adaptation, and this apparently refers to measures '*to facilitate adequate adaptation*', which may not mean necessarily to actually adapt.

Although a relatively slow progress towards adaptation seems to be implied in the three stages, it is clear that the focus was to be on adaptation policy (Stage I), as well as plans, programmes, measures and capacity building. What Decision 11/CP.1 called for was adaptation studies for adaptation policy, and not adaptation studies for mitigation policy. Nevertheless the momentum of adaptation research to contribute to the impacts/mitigation debate was well established and much research continued with that aim. The international agencies including the United Nations Development Programme (UNDP), the United Nations Environment Programme (UNEP), the World Bank, as well as the research community in universities and non-governmental research centres have now begun to recognize the importance of adaptation research for adaptation policy as it was envisaged in Decision 11 of COP-1.

The Buenos Aires Plan of Action, adopted in 1998 to prepare for the future entry into force of the Kyoto Protocol, reflected increased demands of the developing countries to address climate change adaptation. It included a decision in principle to move to Stage II adaptation. The Marrakesh Accords that emerged from COP-7 went further and established two new funds (the Special Climate Change Fund and the Least Developed Countries Fund) under the UNFCCC to support, inter alia, 'the implementation of adaptation activities where sufficient information is available'. COP-7 also adopted guidance for the operation of the Fund for Least Developed Countries (LDCs) to support the preparation of National Adaptation Programmes of Action (NAPAs) which 'will serve as a simplified and direct channel of communication of information relating to the vulnerabilities and adaptation to climate needs of the least developing countries'. A third fund, the Adaptation Fund, is to be established under the Kyoto Protocol by the imposition of a levy on the Clean Development Mechanism.

Before turning to an assessment of the 'first generation' adaptation research it may be helpful to briefly report the definitions of three important concepts used in the adaptation literature.

Concepts and Definitions

The report of Working Group II in the Third Assessment of the Intergovernmental Panel on Climate Change (McCarthy et al, 2001) provides definitions of three of the more important concepts employed in the climate debate:

Sensitivity

Sensitivity is the degree to which a system is affected, either adversely or beneficially, by climate-related stimuli. Climate-related stimuli encompass all the elements of climate change, including mean climate characteristics, climate variability, and the frequency and magnitude of extremes. The effect may be direct (e.g. a change in crop yield in response to a change in the mean, range or variability of temperature) or indirect (e.g. damages caused by an increase in the frequency of coastal flooding due to sea-level rise).

Adaptive capacity

Adaptive capacity is the ability of a system to adjust to climate change, including climate variability and extremes, to moderate potential damages, to take advantage of opportunities, or to cope with the consequences.

Vulnerability

Vulnerability is the degree to which a system is susceptible to, or unable to cope with, adverse effects of climate change, including variability and extremes. Vulnerability is a function of the character, magnitude and rate of climate change and variation to which a system is exposed, its sensitivity, and its adaptive capacity.

These are 'working definitions' subject to evolution as the science and the policy context change. For the purposes of this chapter it is important to note how these concepts as currently defined lead to an enormous expansion of the factors that enter into climate adaptation policy. General adaptive capacity for example, can be seen as a function of wealth; population characteristics, such as demographic structure, education and health; organizational arrangements and institutions; and access to technology, and equity, to name only the most salient variables. More specific adaptive capacity relates to the specialized training, research and institutions that are required as inputs to climate adaptation measures and policy.

One consequence of the move towards a second generation of adaptation studies has been the emergence of vulnerability as a central concept. A useful, if simplified, formulation is that vulnerability is a function of impacts and adaptation. Impacts depend upon the exposure of a system to climate and its sensitivity. Impacts are less where the climate is more benign (adequate and reliable rainfall, less frequent and severe extremes events such as tropical cyclones, heat waves and the like), and where systems are less sensitive or more robust (drought-tolerant crops, buildings more resistant to wind damage). Adaptation depends upon the capacity of systems to adapt, and also on the will or intent to deploy adaptive capacity to reduce vulnerability. The mere existence of capacity is not itself a guarantee that it will be used (Burton and Lim, 2001).

Given the breadth of these concepts, and the need for adaptation policy, what is the record of adaptation research? What is the level and quality of adaptation science for adaptation policy? These questions are addressed in the following section.

First Generation Impacts and Adaptation Research

The need for comparability has been a persistent theme in climate change research related to the UNFCCC. This applies at all levels from measurements to data, information, knowledge and understanding. In a sense the whole of the IPCC enterprise is aimed at assuring comparability and trust in the science. This stems from the global nature of the climate change issue. It has been recognized from experience in other domains (acid precipitation and ozone layer depletion, for example) that negotiations can best be advanced if the negotiators are working from a common understanding and acceptance of the underlying science. For this reason, it has become standard practice to develop and agree upon common methodologies to guide the research. The first guide for impacts and adaptation was written under the authority of the IPCC in the early 1990s (Carter et al, 1994; Parry and Carter, 1998). These IPCC Guidelines have been expanded and elaborated in the guidelines prepared for the United States Country Studies Program (USCSP) (Smith and Lazo, 2001) and also the UNEP *Handbook on Methods for Climate Change Impact Assessment and Adaptation Strategies* (Feenstra et al, 1998). These texts contain descriptions of many useful tools, methods, and guides to the literature, especially in the areas of climate change impacts studies. Taken together these guidelines and the ways they have been applied, have become known as the 'standard approach', corresponding to what is referred to here as the 'first generation' or Type 1 adaptation studies.

The essential character of the standard approach is contained in the seven steps of the IPCC Guidelines. These are listed as:

1   Define problem (including study area, its sectors, etc.).
2   Select method of assessment most appropriate to the problems.
3   Test methods/conduct sensitivity analysis.
4   Select and apply climate change scenarios.
5   Assess biophysical and socio-economic impacts.
6   Assess autonomous adjustments.
7   Evaluate adaptation strategies.

The thinking behind these steps has its own internal logic. It is also highly condensed and omits or leaves implicit many other possible and useful 'steps'. For example, in order to assess future impacts of climate change it is not only necessary to think about future climate (climate scenarios), but also to consider the state of the systems that will be impacted, for example in socio-economic scenarios. The present and future condition of an economy (especially its vulnerability) is often a more powerful determinant of net impacts than projected climate change. Similarly Steps 6 and 7 both assume that adaptation responses are known, whereas in fact this is often not the case. Furthermore, it is important to note that the IPCC approach is impacts driven, rather than vulnerability driven, and this is reflected in the design of the steps.

A crucial feature of the standard approach is identified in Step 4, the selection and application of climate scenarios. By relying on climate change scenarios the standard approach directs attention to the impacts of future climate change and by default, away from current impacts and vulnerability. This orientation stems from a view of the issue as a pollution problem (like acid precipitation or stratospheric ozone layer depletion) that has to be addressed largely through the control of emissions. But climate change is not only a 'pollution problem' related to the energy sector. It is also a broad development issue – a problem in which the whole character and values of human society on a global level and its future sustainable development are at stake. Economic growth and development, patterns and levels of consumption and lifestyle, are drivers of climate change, not simply emissions. Development has been taken into account on the emissions side of the climate issue by the creation of emission scenarios which are dependent on assumptions about population growth, per capita energy consumption, the 'energy mix' in future supplies and changes in energy technology. The patterns and distribution of economic development has been given little consideration on the impacts and adaptation side, except as part of the global scenarios needed to project emissions.

Step 4 requires the selection of climate scenarios, or projections derived from global climate models (GCMs), which are then imposed upon biophysical and socio-economic systems usually through the use of models such as agro-meteorological crop models, or similar models for forest ecosystems or hydrological systems. Research along these lines has been very successful in producing a voluminous 'impacts literature' summarized and assessed in the successive IPCC Assessment Reports of 1990, 1995, and 2001. This literature is most impressive in the identification and assessment of biophysical impacts. It is less developed and less convincing in the case of socio-economic impacts, in part because less attention is given to socio-economic changes than to climate changes.

In applying the standard approach to many National Communications and 'country studies' a common experience is that the overwhelming part of the time and funds allocated have been devoted to the selection and application of the climate scenarios and first-order or gross impact studies. It is invariably noted that insufficient time was left to fully develop the adaptation component of the study. This has been widely reported in workshops organized under the UNDP Global Environment Facility (GEF) National Communications Support Programme (NCSP), and elsewhere in the impacts literature.

From the position of seeking to advance the understanding and analysis of adaptation policy there are other limitations in the standard approach. There are at least five important explanations why models and climate scenario-based methods have not yielded useful results for the purposes of adaptation response and policy options.

First, by the time the analysis reaches Steps 6 and 7 researchers are faced with a battery of results that show a wide range of potential impacts of future climate conditions upon economy and society. There are substantial uncertainties in both the climate scenarios and future socio-economic conditions, and these uncertainties cascade forward into the impacts assessments. It is practically impossible, therefore, to specify with sufficient precision or in any meaningful way what it is that must be adapted to. Analysis of the choice of adaptation measures at some future time to an uncertain future climate in an unknown socio-economic context is bound to be highly speculative. This fact alone has served to discourage and delay serious interest in the development of adaptation policy on the part of the research and policy communities. It certainly does not capture the interest of either policymakers or practitioners in developing countries who are concerned with more pressing immediate and short-term issues such as economic growth, productivity and sustainable development: poverty alleviation and equity; public health, education, energy supply, efficiency and security; and related significant issues.

Second, the climate model projections themselves have two important constraints. Many adaptation measures are location or site specific, whereas the best climate scenarios provide information only for the globe and large regions. GCM scenarios are not sufficiently precise in terms of spatial resolution or scale for adaptation assessment. Downscaling is a technique that can be applied to climate projections in order to give more detailed local information, but at the same time accuracy tends to diminish (Hulme, 1996). Furthermore adaptation is driven more by variability and extremes of climate than by averages. Climate scenarios have the disadvantage of specifying mostly average conditions and for a few variables only. These are not the only variables that are important for adaptation decisions that often require information about combinations of different variables and forecasts of the duration of sequences of weather conditions. Climate change may lead to small changes in means and large changes in extremes. With more time and resources better models of future climate will no doubt be produced, but it is unclear how much improvement will be achieved and how soon. In the near term at least the design of adaptation measures is not likely to be much influenced by climate scenarios. Given these limitations, however, it should be noted that GCM scenarios can be applied to usefully identify a range of uncertainties for the purpose of strategic policymaking.

Third, the impacts assessments themselves are not designed to consider a range of adaptation options, measures or strategies. For example, crop yields forecasts, which use crop growth models, can be useful in studying farm-level adaptations such as the application of fertilizer, pesticides, irrigation and other capital inputs. They do not help in considering other adaptations, especially off-farm policies such as price supports or other market interventions, or changing land ownership and tenure systems.

Fourth, where adaptation has been incorporated into climate impacts studies it has been on the basis of assumptions about the adoption of possible measures. Commonly it is assumed that all of the theoretically available adaptation options will be used and that these will be instantaneously and effectively adopted by all the decision-makers in question. In some studies (e.g. Rosenzweig and Parry, 1994), this assumption has been varied. Two possible levels of adaptation are assumed, partial adaptation (50 per cent) or full (100 per cent). The 50 per cent assumption may mean that only 50 per cent of the adaptation measures will be adopted, or that only 50 per cent of the decision-makers will adapt. The point here is that the assumptions are not based on any knowledge or understanding of the adaptation process itself. There has been little or no consideration of the social and behavioural or other obstacles in the adaptation process.

Fifth, because the standard approach has been developed for the scientific purpose of understanding impacts it pays less attention to the policy context of adaptation or to the key actors or stakeholders involved. The focus of the analysis is a top–down effort to understand impacts, rather than to find ways of reducing vulnerability by the development of policy options in association with stakeholders including those at risk.

Supporting evidence for limitations to the standard approach used in first generation impact and adaptation studies is found in research papers that have resulted from the US Country Studies Program (Smith and Lazo, 2001) and the UNEP Country Studies (O'Brien, 2000) as well as in the reviews of literature in the report of the IPCC Third Assessment Report from Working Group II (McCarthy et al, 2001); in reports of workshops held under the UNDP-GEF National Communications Support Programme (UNDP-GEF, 2000a, b, c); in reviews of the adaptation content of National Communications carried out by the UNFCCC secretariat; and in reports of the work of the Consultative Group of Experts on Initial National Communications from Parties not included in Annex I to the UNFCCC, (Earth Negotiations Bulletin, 2001).

In addition, a number of other comments and suggestions can be found in these documents:

- The content of National Communications is limited largely to discussion of biophysical impacts, and the initial identification of possible adaptation options in lists.
- Vulnerability and adaptation assessments are an optional component in National Communications.
- The guidelines for National Communications do not provide sufficient direction on vulnerability and adaptation assessments.
- The current knowledge of adaptation and adaptive capacity is insufficient for reliable prediction of adaptation, and is inadequate for rigorous evaluation of planned adaptation options, measures and policies.

This analysis of the first generation of impact and adaptation research provides a basis for the development of new guidelines and a new approach. This is not meant to suggest that the first generation of research has not been useful, nor that it should be discontinued. Scenario-driven impacts and adaptation studies in the context of mitigation policy negotiations are needed as much as ever, and must be expanded and improved. What is now needed is a second generation of studies to be conducted in parallel, and designed to meet the needs of adaptation policy development. The next section of the chapter describes the requirements that the second generation of studies should attempt to satisfy.

The Development of a Policy Framework

Adaptation research for policy is different in character from adaptation research in the impacts/mitigation context. Although both are conducted in a policy context and are being comparatively well supported for that reason, the impacts/mitigation variety of adaptation research includes more fundamental science, especially in biological and geophysical systems. This facilitates the development of policies that promote common methodologies and tools, and common standards of measurement. This is the purpose of the IPCC and other guidelines documents, already mentioned in the previous sections.

In the case of adaptation research for the reduction of vulnerability and related policies such a degree of top–down guidance is neither feasible nor desirable. Effective adaptation policy has to be responsive to a wide variety of economic, social, political and environmental circumstances. A different kind of creativity and ingenuity is required. It is, therefore, inappropriate to provide guidelines in a prescriptive style. What is required is a common framework of concepts, linked together in a flexible manner that helps in the design and organization of research for adaptation policy to reduce vulnerability. Given the experience with first generation impacts and adaptation research, and the needs of the policy process, the following framework is presented as a possible way to proceed. It draws in part upon work carried out under the UNDP-GEF National Communications Support Programme (Burton and Lim, 2001).

The lessons from the experience of the first generation of impact and adaptation studies, and the need for more policy-related results suggest many new requirements. These are best characterized in terms of a shift in emphasis from impacts to vulnerability. This leads us to ask the following questions: what is the nature of vulnerability? How is it to be measured or assessed? Is it possible to create a common yardstick for vulnerability? How can vulnerability best be reduced? What is involved in vulnerability reduction? What are the responsibilities of those considered to be most vulnerable, and those who intend to provide assistance for vulnerability reduction? A convergence of efforts is developing to address these questions (see for instance, Ribot et al, 1996; Klein and Nicholls, 1999; Clark et al, 2000; UNEP, 2001; Chapter 9, this volume).

While the current wave of interest in vulnerability is a welcome development in adaptation research, there is a certain danger that it will become an end in itself. The adaptation framework presented here, therefore, treats policy as the overarching purpose and the concept of vulnerability as subordinate to it.

The essential starting point is the present. This may seem to be self-evident. But in fact it differs from the standard impacts/mitigation research paradigm that begins with a consideration of future climate as characterized in climate scenarios. Policymaking starts with recognition of the need for policy innovations or changes in existing policy.

In order to ground adaptation in the present, the framework begins with an assessment of current policy. The standard approach in the first generation of adaptation research tends to assume that adaptation policy has to be created from scratch. This is because it is concerned with adaptation to climate change as characterized in climate scenarios. From a vulnerability and development perspective, however, it is clear that present-day climate has impacts, both positive and negative. Human societies have always adapted to their climatic environment, and adaptation policy already exists, although it is rarely recognized by that name. A national government wishing to develop a policy for adaptation to future climate change might best begin, therefore, by assessing current vulnerability to present-day climate including its variability and extremes, and the ways that existing policy and development practice serve to reduce vulnerability.

The assessment of current vulnerability requires answers to the following extensive set of questions:

- What has been the recent experience with climate variability and extremes?
- What economic damage has resulted and how has this been distributed spatially and among socio-economic groups?
- What other non-economic impacts, such as social and environmental impacts, have occurred?
- Are there any trends in climate variability and extreme events, and if so to what can they be attributed?

- Are there are trends in damages and other impacts, and if so how can they be explained?
- What adaptation policies and measures have been used to reduce vulnerability and how successful have they been?
- What is the extent of adaptation in practice and what are the barriers, obstacles or incentives to adaptation?
- How does public policy (in any and all domains) affect impacts and adaptation?
- How does public policy with respect to climatic hazards relate to the economic and sustainable development policies and strategies in place?
- How do public policies with respect to climate hazards relate to policies for other atmospheric issues such as ozone layer depletion, acid precipitation, and air quality?
- How do public policies for atmospheric hazards relate to other natural resource management and environmental policies?
- To what extent have stakeholders (including those at risk) been involved in the policy development process, and how can this be facilitated?

Answers to these and related questions can be summarized and synthesized into an assessment of current vulnerability. This diagnosis also provides the basis for the compilation of an inventory of potential adaptation policy initiatives and reforms.

The next step in the policy development process involves the design of policy initiatives and alternatives, and their assessment and prioritization. In order to conduct this exercise, account should be taken of what can be surmised about future conditions, including climate change and changes in the socio-economic environment. The questions to be asked largely mirror the questions about current vulnerability:

- In what ways is climate expected to change?
- What can be said about future climate variability and extremes compared with recent experience?
- What are the prospects for economic and sustainable development and how will this affect climate change impacts?
- What are the prospects for adaptation and how much can vulnerability be reduced?
- What are the constraints and limitations to public policy for adaptation?
- What are the costs of adaptation measures and what benefits can be anticipated?
- What will be the distribution of the benefits and costs of adaptation?
- What would happen in the absence of public policy reform and innovations?
- How does public policy for adaptation to climate change relate to other atmospheric, natural resource and environmental policies?

These questions provide the basis for the framework diagram (Figure 20.2). The answers to the questions provide input to the policy process. The purpose of the framework diagram is not to present a prescription of policy or even policy development. It serves more in the nature of a checklist of things that should be taken into consideration in policy development. The only prescriptive elements are the admonitions to ground policy analysis in an assessment of current vulnerability, to take climate variability and extremes into account as well as changes in means, and to embed adaptation measures into development policy.

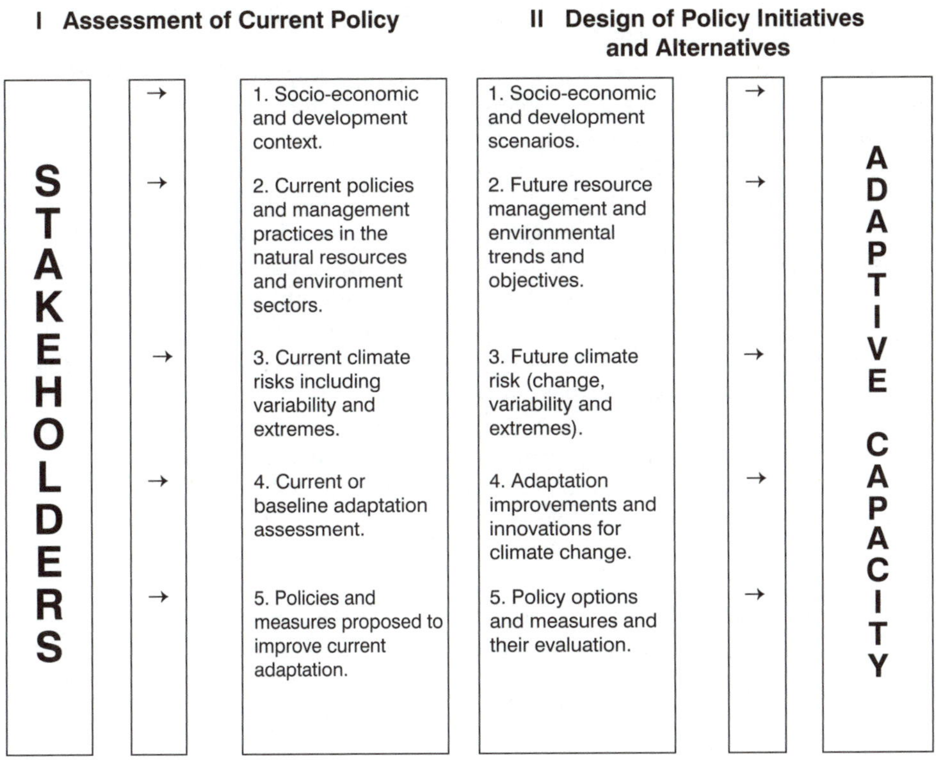

I Assessment of Current Policy   **II Design of Policy Initiatives and Alternatives**

STAKEHOLDERS		Assessment of Current Policy	Design of Policy Initiatives and Alternatives		ADAPTIVE CAPACITY
	→	1. Socio-economic and development context.	1. Socio-economic and development scenarios.	→	
	→	2. Current policies and management practices in the natural resources and environment sectors.	2. Future resource management and environmental trends and objectives.	→	
	→	3. Current climate risks including variability and extremes.	3. Future climate risk (change, variability and extremes).	→	
	→	4. Current or baseline adaptation assessment.	4. Adaptation improvements and innovations for climate change.	→	
	→	5. Policies and measures proposed to improve current adaptation.	5. Policy options and measures and their evaluation.	→	

Figure 20.2 *Adaptation policy framework*

The Shape and Content of Adaptation Policy

At the end of the day, policy decisions are made by governments which have responsibility for the success or failure of the policies they adopt. The purpose of policy-related research for adaptation to climate change, as for other policy domains, is not to decide or advocate policy, but to provide the policymakers with policy choices, an analysis of the rationale of alternative policy choices, and additional information upon which they can base their judgements. Climate change adaptation can be a component in many different policy domains (Apuuli et al, 2000). Effective climate adaptation policy cannot be made on a 'stand-alone' basis, but has to be incorporated into other policies. For example, adaptation to climate change in agriculture should be a part of a broader agricultural policy. The same applies to, inter alia, forests, water resources, coastal zone management, public health, natural ecosystems, infrastructure and human settlements. Relevant policies are not limited to such socio-economic sectors, but can also include policies for management of natural hazards and disasters (floods, droughts, tropical and extra-tropical storms, etc.). Governments may also have special policies that are directed to part of the country only, such as regional development policies, including rural and urban-centred regions, or particular river basins.

An assessment of current policy in agriculture, for example, will normally take into consideration the broad strategic objectives for agriculture in the national socio-economic and development context. Is the aim to expand commercial agriculture for export-led development? How much importance is given to local food security and the maintenance and improvement of agriculture-based livelihoods? Such policy directions inform choices throughout the agricultural sector that include matters of trade relations, duties, taxes, subsidies and insurance. They also influence choice of crops, and many agricultural practices at the farm level. Of specific interest in the case of agriculture are other policies in related areas of natural resource and environmental management such as watershed protection and rehabilitation, soil erosion, soil salinity, the use of genetically modified crops and so forth.

Current climate risks are best assessed in the light of these related policies. Measures designed to reduce vulnerability to drought, or to other direct and indirect climate risks (e.g. floods, pest invasions, diseases, unseasonable frosts), will be less effective and can be counterproductive unless they are considered in this broader context. For example the introduction of irrigation into some regions of Africa has contributed to the spread of schistosomiasis.

A crucial element in the assessment of current policy is the review and evaluation of adaptation practices now in use, and the absence of others that might be used, but which are blocked or difficult to use for whatever reason. A description of the current 'adaptation baseline' can provide a benchmark against which to measure progress in the development and adoption of adaptation policy.

From an assessment of the successes and failures of current adaptation, new ideas and proposals are certain to emerge for better adaptation in the future. In many instances, improvements in adaptation (or the elimination of policies which tend to increase vulnerability) will yield net benefits to the economy or the agricultural system even in the absence of climate change. Policy innovations are especially desirable if they bring benefits under the present climate, which can be shown to bring greater benefits as the climate changes. The assessment of current policy, therefore, leads directly to policy initiatives and alternatives for climate change. Unlike the lists of adaptation measures, which have been suggested in first generation adaptation research, these policies are grounded in empirical studies of what has worked (and not worked) in the past.

Suggested Directions

The evolution of climate adaptation research from its initial orientation towards the assessment of impacts for the purposes of mitigation policy to the emerging needs for adaptation policy, suggest some new directions and next steps. A broad approach to the development of adaptation policy has been described, and embodied in a flexible framework (Figure 20.2). This framework should now be tested in a variety of locations. Such activities will require an elaboration of the framework, especially the preparation of some specific guidance on particular components. While there is most likely no need for a new and elaborate methods manual, some formulation of generic approaches would be useful. These might include socio-economic and development scenarios; assessments of climate risk, including alternative ways of characterizing and measuring future climatic hazards in quantitative terms relevant for adaptation decisions; adaptation assessment, including baseline adaptation; and the evaluation of possible future policies and measures.

The framework may also be helpful as part of a new round of enabling activities under the UNFCCC to assist in the preparation of second National Communications by developing countries; the preparation of NAPAs, and to carry out the studies proposed in Stage II adaptation. These should be based on the knowledge and experience gained from the first generation of studies, as well as the post-first generation studies done in selected regions and countries, such as the Caribbean, and Pacific islands (World Bank, 2000b) and Bangladesh (World Bank, 2000a). Although not done under a common methodological framework, these studies have nevertheless taken the adaptation analysis forward in a more adaptation policy direction, and results need to be incorporated into any second generation of adaptation analysis and research.

A critical question to be addressed in the design of second generation studies concerns the quality and the rigour of the analysis. There is a sense of urgency especially in the most vulnerable countries, leading to demands for prompt action. In some cases the adaptation policies and measures needed may be very evident, and further delay in design and implementation while studies are carried out may not be defensible. On the other hand, the situation in many countries is that there is insufficient knowledge or information upon which to base good policy choices. For example, one concern increasingly being expressed is that it would be comparatively easy to allocate adaptation funds to 'concrete' or hard adaptations of an engineered and structural kind. It cannot be safely assumed that such adaptation policies and measures would be the most cost-effective in reducing vulnerability to climate change, and there are reasons to suppose that such measures could have counter-intuitive results, by serving to increase vulnerability. This is the challenge faced by the teams that will prepare the National Adaptation Programmes of Action, and by studies that are currently in the planning stages for Central America and Mexico, the Caribbean, the south Pacific, some regions of Africa, and elsewhere.

Climate change impacts are not yet truly severe. The consequences are likely to be incremental and cumulative. There is, therefore, a case to be made for taking the time for sufficient policy analysis and development before taking decisions that could prove to be seriously wrong. At the same time, there are many instances where present-day climate variability and extremes are now exacting a heavy toll on development. In such cases, with or without climate change, there is need for more urgent anticipatory action.

Note

1 COP-6 was held in The Hague in November 2000, and COP-6 bis in Bonn in July 2001.

References

Apuuli, B., Wright, J., Elias, C., Burton, I., 2000. Reconciling national and global priorities in adaptation to climate change with an illustration from Uganda. *Environ. Monitor. Assess.* 61, 145–159.

Burton, I., Lim, B., 2001. *Adaptation Policy Framework*, Draft Report, UNDP, New York.

Carter, T. R., Parry, M. L., Harasawa, H., Nishioka, S., 1994. *IPCC Technical Guidelines for Assessing Climate Change Impacts and Adaptations with a Summary for Policy Makers and a Technical Summary*. Department of Geography, University College London, UK and the Centre for Global environmental Research, National Institute for Environmental Studies, Japan.

Clark, W. C., Jaeger, J., Corell, R., Kasperson, R., McCarthy, J. J., Cash, D., Cohen, S. J., Desanker, P., Dickson, N. M., Epstein, P., Guston, P. H., Hall, J. M., Jaeger, C., Janetos, A., Leary, N., Levy, M. A., Luers, A., MacCracken, M., Melillo, J., Moss, R., Nigg, J. M., Parry, M. L., Parson, E. A., Ribot, J. C., Schellnhuber, H., Schrag, D. P., Seielstad, G. A., Shea, E., Vogel, C., Wilbanks, T. J., 2000. *Assessing Vulnerability to Global Environmental Risks*, Report of the Workshop on Vulnerability to Global Environmental Change: Challenges for Research, Assessment and Decision making, Airlie House, Warrenton, Virginia (December 2000), Environment and Natural Resources Program, Belfer Centre for Science and International Affairs (BCSIA), Kennedy School of Government, Harvard University, Cambridge, MA.

Earth Negotiations Bulletin (ENB), 2001. *Summary of the Inter-Regional Workshop of the Consultative Group of Experts on Initial National Communications from Parties not Included in Annex I to the UNFCCC*. International Institute for Sustainable Development, New York, 19–22 March 2001.

Feenstra, J. F., Burton, I., Smith, J. B., Tol, R. S. J. (Eds.), 1998. *Handbook on Methods for Climate Change Impact Assessment and Adaptation Strategies*, Version 2.0. UNEP/IVM, The Netherlands.

Hulme, M. (Ed.), 1996. *Climate Change and Southern Africa: An Exploration of Some Potential Impacts and Implications in the SADC Region*. A Report Commissioned by WWF International and Co-ordinated by the Climatic Research Unit, UEA.

IPCC (Intergovernmental Panel on Climate Change), 2001: *Impacts, Adaptation, and Vulnerability, Summary for Policymakers and Technical Summary of the Working Group II Report*. IPCC, Geneva.

Klein, R. J. T., Nicholls, R. J., 1999. Assessment of coastal vulnerability to climate change. *Ambio* 28, 182–187.

McCarthy, J. J., Canziani, O. F., Leary, N. A., Dokken, D. J., White, K. S., 2001. *Climate Change 2001: Impacts, Adaptation, and Vulnerability – Contribution of Working Group II to the Third Assessment Report of the Intergovernmental Panel on Climate Change*. Cambridge University Press, Cambridge.

UNDP-GEF, 2000a. *Workshop Report: Thematic Workshop on Vulnerability and Adaptation Assessment, Chisinau, Moldova*. UNDP-GEF, New York, 26–28 January 2000.

UNDP-GEF, 2000b. *Workshop Report: Thematic Workshop on Vulnerability and Adaptation Assessment, Amman, Jordan*. UNDP-GEF, New York, 7–9 March 2000.

UNDP-GEF, 2000c. *Workshop Report: Thematic and Regional Training Workshop on Vulnerability and Adaptation to Climate Change – English Speaking African Countries, Nairobi, Kenya*. UNEP, Nairobi, 4–7 July 2000.

Parry, M., Carter, T., 1998. *Climate Impact and Adaptation Assessment*. Earthscan, London.

Ribot, J. C., Magalhaes, A. R., Panagides, S. S. (Eds.), 1996. *Climate Variability, Climate Change and Social Vulnerability in the Semi-Arid Tropics*. Cambridge University Press, Cambridge, UK.

Rosenzweig, C., Parry, M. L., 1994. Potential impact of climate change on world food supply. *Nature* 367, 133–137.

Smith, J. B., Lazo, J. K., 2001. A summary of climate change impact assessments from the US Country Studies Program. *Clim. Change* 50 (1/2), 1–29.

Smit, B., Pilifosova, O., 2001. *'Adaptation in the Context of Equity and Sustainable Development, IPCC Second Assessment Report.* Cambridge University Press, Cambridge, UK, Chapter 18.

O'Brien, K. (Ed.), 2000. *Developing Strategies for Climate Change: The UNEP Country Studies on Climate Change Impacts and Adaptations Assessment,* Report 2000–02. CICERO, Oslo, Norway.

UNEP, 2001. Downing, T. E., Butterfield, R., Cohen, S., Huq, S., Moss, R., Rahman, A., Sokona, Y., Stephen, L., *Vulnerability Indices, Climate Change Impacts and Adaptation.* UNEP Division of Policy Development and Law, Nairobi.

UNFCCC National Communications, 2002. see www.UNFCCC.int.

Watson, R. T., Zinyowera, M. C., Moss, R. H.(Eds.), 1996. *Climate Change 1995: Impacts, Adaptations and Mitigation of Climate Change: Scientific-Technical Analyses Contribution of Working Group II to the Second Assessment of the Intergovernmental Panel on Climate Change.* Cambridge University Press, Cambridge, UK.

World Bank, 2000a. *Bangladesh Climate Change and Sustainable Development,* Report No. 21104-BD. Rural Development Unit, South Asia Region, World Bank, Washington, DC.

World Bank, 2000b. *Adapting to Climate Change, Cities, Seas, and Storms: Managing Change in Pacific Island Economies,* Vol. IV. World Bank, Washington, DC.

21

An Overview of Investment and Financial Flows Needed for Adaptation

United Nations Framework Convention on Climate Change

Introduction

Raising the standard of living of the poorest peoples in the world to meet the Millennium Development Goals (MDGs) will be challenging, particularly as populations in the developing world continue to increase. Climate change will make this task more challenging by increasing risks to human health, inundating low-lying areas, changing extreme weather events, altering water supplies, changing crop yields and ecosystems, and through many other impacts. The investment and financial flows needed for development in the midst of population growth and climate change will be substantial. It is important to be aware of how adaptation to climate change will affect the needs for investment and financial flows.

This analysis does not aim to provide a precise estimate of the total cost of adaptation, but assesses the order of magnitude of additional investment and financial flows that could be required in 2030 to adapt to the impacts of climate change. Although the intimate link between economic growth, population growth, human development and adaptation is acknowledged, this analysis focuses on the additional need for adaptation over and above the investment and financial flows required to address needs related to expected economic and population growth.

The investment and financial flows needed for adaptation to climate change have been estimated for five sectors identified by the Working Group II contribution to the Fourth Assessment Report (AR4) of the Intergovernmental Panel on Climate Change (IPCC):

- agriculture, forestry and fisheries;
- water supply;
- human health;
- coastal zones; and
- infrastructure.

Adaptation of natural ecosystems (terrestrial and marine) was also analysed. There is, however, very limited literature on adaptation in this sector, and it was not possible to estimate the investment needs associated with adaptation to climate change.

Instead, the need for investments to protect ecosystems from all current threats was analysed.

This chapter first presents the scenarios used to undertake the analysis and addresses limitations in estimating adaptation costs. For each sector included in this study, the chapter briefly reviews climate change impacts, the methods used for the analyses, current level of investment and financial flows in the sector, estimated future investment and financial flows needed in 2030 and a brief analysis of the adequacy of current investment and financial flows to meet the additional needs. Finally, an analysis of damages that can be avoided with mitigation measures is then presented.

Scenarios

The analysis of investment and financial flows needed for adaptation to climate change was based on emissions scenarios for which climate change impacts could be inferred and responses to the climate impacts could be projected, so that the associated investment and financial flows could be estimated. The scenarios were selected based on their suitability for the analysis, the detail they provide on estimated investment and financial flows, and how representative they are of the literature. The following scenarios have been used for different sectors:

- IPCC Special Report on Emissions Scenarios (SRES) A1B and B1 scenarios are used for the water supply and coastal zones sectors (Nakicenovic and Swart, 2000);
- For the human health sector, the scenarios used were variation from the IPCC IS92a: a scenario resulting in stabilization at 750 parts per million by volume (ppmv) CO_2 equivalent by 2210 (s750), and a scenario resulting in stabilization at 550ppmv CO_2 equivalent by 2170 (s550) (Leggett et al, 1992). These scenarios were used in the context of a World Health Organization (WHO) study on the global and regional burden of disease (GBD) (McMichael et al, 2004);
- Projected investment in physical assets for 2030 from the Organisation for Economic Co-operation and Development (OECD) ENV-Linkage model as used as the basis for estimating additional investment and financial flows needed in the agriculture, forestry and fisheries (AFF) and infrastructure sectors.[1] The projected investment in physical assets for 2030 based on the OECD ENV-Linkage model corresponds to the projection of the International Energy Agency World Energy Outlook (IEA WEO) reference scenario.

Higher greenhouse gas (GHG) emission levels than projected under these scenarios are possible.

The impacts on needs for investment and financial flows for adaptation have not been modelled based on the reference and mitigation scenarios used for the mitigation analyses. Given the lack of data, this work could not be undertaken in the context of this study, so different scenarios had to be used for the adaptation analyses.

In 2030, the year for which needs for investment and financial flows are estimated in this study, the CO_2 concentrations and projected changes in temperature and thus the associated differences in the adverse impact of climate change between any scenarios can be expected to be quite small.[2] For some sectors, it was assumed that adaptation would only be to the realized impact of climate change in 2030 so there would be little difference across scenarios in investment and financial flows needed by then. However, in the water supply and coastal zones sectors, adaptation to climate change anticipates some change in climate for, respectively, another 20 and 50 years. In those sectors, it is assumed that those adapting have perfect information on changes in global and regional climate in 2050 and 2080. In those cases differences in greenhouse gas emissions across scenarios would be significant.

Limitations in Estimating Adaptation Costs

There are many difficulties and limitations in estimating the costs of adapting under various scenarios as well as the ability of countries to self-finance adaptation. These include (1) differences in adaptive capacity; (2) the fact that most adaptations will not be solely for the purpose of adapting to climate change; (3) the uncertainties associated with any readily available methods to estimate adaptation costs; and (4) the existence of an adaptation deficit.

Adaptive capacity

One of the key limitations in estimating the costs of adaptation is the uncertainty about adaptive capacity. Adaptive capacity is essentially the ability to adapt to stresses such as climate change. It does not predict what adaptations will happen, but gives an indication of the differing capacities of societies to adapt *on their own* to climate change or other stresses. Smit et al (2001) identified six determinants of adaptive capacity:

- economic resources;
- technology;
- information and skills;
- infrastructure;
- institutions; and
- equity.

Unfortunately, all the scenarios used in this study leave many key aspects of adaptive capacity undefined. Although, in some cases, economic resources are specified and the level of technology is defined to some extent, the other four determinants of adaptive capacity are not defined. For example, institutions, which to some extent are a proxy for governance, a key factor in adaptive capacity, are not defined. It is not clear how this and other factors might differ across the scenarios.

A further limitation of the scenarios is that the socio-economic variables are defined at best, only at highly aggregated scales. Development paths are not projected for individual countries. Within any scenario, it is reasonable to expect that the development paths of individual countries will differ. Some may have economic or population rates of growth that are faster or slower than the regional averages. Thus, it is not possible to determine how adaptive capacity will change at the country level based on the selected scenario.

Adaptations are typically not solely climate change related

A second key limitation is that most adaptations to climate change will most likely not be made solely to adapt to climate change. Most activities that need to be undertaken to adapt to climate change will have benefits even if the climate does not change. For example, improvements in the management of ecosystems to reduce stresses on them or water conservation measures can typically be justified without considering climate change. Climate change provides an additional reason for making such changes because benefits of the adaptations are larger when climate change is considered. Indeed, the need for these adaptations may not depend on specific greenhouse gas concentration levels and thus climate change associated with scenarios. It may well be justified to introduce water-use efficiency or reduce harm to coral reefs no matter what scenario is assumed.

However, some adaptations would happen solely on account of climate change considerations. Such adaptations are typically marginal adjustments to infrastructure or land-use decisions. For example, flood protection infrastructure could be enlarged to account for additional risks from sea-level rise or more intense precipitation (or both). Land-use decisions such as defining flood plains, regulating and guiding land use or setbacks from the coast could be adjusted to account for future risks from climate change.

Methods for estimating adaptation costs

At least four methods for estimating global and regional adaptation costs could be used; these are briefly reviewed here. The last three have been used in this study or in other studies. A discussion of the four methods and their limitations follows.

The first method is a complete bottom–up approach. It involves estimating the costs of specific adaptations across the world. Currently, partial information can be obtained from National Adaptation Programmes of Action (NAPAs) and National Communications. Where costs have been estimated, they can be used; where they are not estimated in the NAPAs or National Communications, they can be derived. This approach has the advantage of building on adaptations identified by countries. Moreover, it is likely that different costing methods would be applied by different countries (or even within countries). The existing information on bottom–up adaptation needs is far from being comprehensive and complete. Therefore, it is impossible to assess needs entirely from the bottom within any reasonable time and resources constraints.

A second method is an extrapolation of the bottom–up method. Oxfam America (Raworth, 2007) extrapolates from estimated adaptation costs in NAPAs to the rest of the developing world using three factors: population, income and land. It estimates that adaptation costs will be more than US$50 billion per year. This method has the advantage of using official estimates of adaptation costs as the basis for the extrapolation. However, as the report notes, only 13 NAPAs have been written. It is not known if these 13 NAPAs are representative of adaptation needs across the developing world or if the identification of adaptations is comprehensive. The NAPAs target only 49 least developed country (LDC) parties to the United Nations Framework Convention on Climate Change (UNFCCC) and may not reflect needs in more developed countries. It is also important to note that the NAPAs focus on 'urgent' needs, not all adaptation needs.

A third method, used for the AFF, natural ecosystems, and infrastructure sectoral analyses in this study, is to use current global expenditures in the sectors and apply a rule of thumb to estimate additional costs for meeting development needs and climate change adaptation. For example, the World Bank (2006) assumed that development costs will increase by US$10 billion to US$40 billion per year by assuming that climate-sensitive portions of the Bank's investment portfolio will need an additional 5 to 20 per cent in resources to adapt to climate change. This approach is akin to a sensitivity analysis and can help give an order of magnitude of adaptation costs. A key uncertainty is related to the need to use assumptions about additional costs. The assumptions could be based on experience or a wide and representative sample of studies of specific adaptations; or it could be an educated guess and may not reflect actual conditions or variance of adaptation needs. Because such assumptions may be applied to a large base (the current total level of investment), even small percentage changes can yield large differences in estimates of investment and financial needs.

The fourth approach is a top–down quantitative analysis and is used in the water resources, coastal resources and human health analyses in this study. Models can be applied to estimate biophysical impacts and needs for adaptation such as infrastructure for water supply or coastal defences. Uniform cost rules (perhaps adjusted for different per capita income levels) can be applied to estimate costs. The advantage of the uniform approach is that differences across countries can reflect different conditions and needs. This approach can give a rough estimate of total costs, but typically will not capture site-specific differences. Actual investment and financial flows needed could vary quite substantially from the uniform rules. Furthermore, top–down approaches may not be comprehensive. For example, the model used to come up with estimates of needs for the water resources sector only includes water supply, not water quality, flood protection or the systems to distribute or treat the water. Models can be very expensive and time consuming. Finally, the use of different assumptions can result in quite different estimates of magnitudes. The water supply and coastal resources analysis considers the need for investment and financial flows associated with economic and population growth, while the health analysis does not consider these two factors.

The existence of an adaptation deficit

Before examining how development and climate change will affect needs for investment and financial flows, it is important to note that for all of the sectors examined herein, there is a substantial deficit in investment and financial flows. In many places property and activities are insufficiently adapted to current climate, including its variability and extremes. This has been labelled as the 'adaptation deficit' (Burton, 2004).

Evidence for the existence and size of the adaptation deficit can be seen in the mounting losses from extreme weather events such as floods, droughts, tropical cyclones and other storms. These losses have been mounting at a very rapid rate over the last 50 years. This increase is likely to be mostly due to the expansion of human populations, socio-economic activities, real property, and infrastructure of all kinds into zones of high risk. Moreover, much of this property is built at a substandard level and does not conform even to minimal building codes and standards. This widespread failure to build enough weather resistance into existing and expanding human settlements is the main reason for the existence of an adaptation deficit. Real property and socio-economic activities are just not as climate-proof as they could and arguably should be. The evidence suggests strongly that the adaptation deficit continues to increase because losses from extreme events continue to increase. In other words, societies are becoming less well adapted to current climate. Such a process of development has been called 'maladaptation'.

Analysis of Investment and Financial Flows to Address Adaptation Needs

Agriculture, forestry and fisheries

Introduction

Potential impacts of climate change on agriculture, forestry and fisheries

The effects of climate change on agriculture are different across regions and over time. Yields are projected to decline in low latitudes with any increase in temperature. In high latitudes, yields can increase with up to about 3°C of warming of local temperatures,[3] then start to decrease. For the first several degrees of increase in global mean temperature over 1990, global agricultural production could increase, driven by the increased yields in mid- and high latitudes. But, this will happen while yields in low-latitude areas decrease; thus, the potential for malnutrition in developing countries can rise. Malnutrition is projected to decline as a result of development, but the declines could be partially offset by climate change. Beyond several degrees of warming, global agricultural production is projected to decline (Easterling et al, 2007). That would involve widespread adverse economic impacts and greater levels of malnutrition.

There are many important caveats in these findings. Changes in extreme events could disrupt agricultural production with even just a few degrees of warming. Adaptive capacities will play a key role in determining vulnerability. The IPCC concluded that a 3°C regional warming would exceed the capacity of developing countries to adapt to climate change impacts on crop yields (Easterling et al, 2007). The potential for technological adaptations such as crop breeding to increase tolerance for heat and drought or taking better advantage of elevated atmospheric CO_2 concentrations has not been studied. Thus uncertainties about estimated impactsof climate change on agriculture mean that actual impacts could be more negative or more benign than projected. Whatever the climate change and its impacts, global agriculture will need to adapt by changing location and types of cropping systems. For example, increased agricultural output will require changes in locations of crops and expansion of agriculture into high-latitude areas. Such adaptations will require capital investment to be realized.

Meanwhile, Easterling et al (2007) projected that global forestry would be affected modestly by climate, but that regional impacts could be more substantial. Generally, production of forests would shift from low-latitude to high-latitude areas. There could be significant changes in distribution and productivity of fisheries, with fish species in many locations becoming extinct, but fish productivity increasing for some species in some locations. Higher temperatures could adversely affect aquaculture, as could increased extreme weather, presence of new diseases and other factors (Easterling et al, 2007).

Adaptation

Many actors, varying from individual farmers, ranchers, herders and fisherpeople to national governments, international research organizations and multinational corporations will be involved in adapting to climate change and in responding to the growing need for investment and financial flows in the agriculture, forestry and fisheries sectors. Some of the fundamental forms of adaptation are as follows:

- *Change in mix of crop, forage and tree species/varieties.* The mix of crop, forage grasses or trees species employed, for example, growing crops, grasses or trees can be changed toward varieties and species that are more heat, drought or moisture tolerant. More generally, this involves replacing some proportion of the crop, forage and tree species with alternative species better adapted to new climate regimes.
- *Change in mix of livestock and fish species/breeds.* This involves replacing some proportion of current species or breeds with alternative species or breeds that are more suitable for the altered climatic regime. For fisheries, this may mean harvesting species that have potentially migrated into the fishing grounds. In aquaculture and domestic animal raising this involves adopting livestock and fish species from areas that have had comparable climates.
- *Change in management of crops, forests and fisheries.* Crops can be planted or harvested earlier to adjust to altered soil warm-up rates, soil moisture conditions, earlier maturity dates, and altered water availability regimes. Livestock and fish management changes can include altering aquaculture facility characteristics, changing stocking rates, altering degree of confinement, among many other possibilities. Adaptation in wild fish management may involve using species that migrate to fishing grounds or travelling farther to catch the same species being harvested now.
- *Moisture management/irrigation.* Climate change can increase crop water needs, decrease water availability, decrease soil moisture-holding capacity, and increase flooding and waterlogging. Adaptation may involve using irrigation, which may require investing in irrigation facilities or equipment, changing drainage management regimes, altering tillage practices to conserve water, altering time of planting/harvesting to better match water availability, changing species to more drought-tolerant plants/trees;
- *Pest and disease management.* Climate change is likely to exacerbate pest, disease and weed management problems. Adaptation could involve wider use of integrated pest and pathogen management or preventative veterinary care, development and use of varieties and species resistant to pests and diseases, maintaining or improving

quarantine capabilities, outbreak-monitoring programmes, prescribed burning, and adjusting harvesting schedules.

- *Management of natural areas.* Some AFF production such as livestock management relies on passively managed, natural ecosystems that may require more active management under climate change to introduce new, better-adapted species or to deal with climate change-enhanced pest, disease or fire risks.
- *Fire management.* Forests, grasslands, and to some extent crop lands are vulnerable to climate change-induced increases in fire risk. Such risks may stimulate adaptive actions like salvaging dead timber, landscape planning to minimize fire damage, and adjusting fire management systems.
- *Land-use or enterprise choice change.* Climate change may make current land uses such as cropping unsustainable, and it may be desirable to adapt by changing the land use from crops to pasture or trees, or from trees to grazing land. For fisheries, it may be desirable to abandon aquaculture or discontinue pursuing certain fish species in some regions. In some cases, loss of productivity in agriculture, forestry or fisheries may lead to migration of people to areas such as cities or other countries that may offer better employment opportunities.

Governments, international organizations and non-governmental organizations (NGOs) have important roles to play in adaptation. The types of adaptation actions that can be pursued are as follows:

- *Research.* Public resources can be placed into research to provide adaptation strategies that could be adopted by the AFF producers, as discussed previously. These resources will be funding domestic government research organizations, international research organizations such as the Consultative Group for International Research, universities or research-oriented NGOs.
- *Extension and training.* Traditionally, substantial funding has gone into extension services and training to disseminate information to farmers, foresters and fisherpeople on practices and technologies. Funding would need to go into rural training and extension programmes to disseminate adaptation options, by providing information and training on practices that could be adopted by AFF producers. Extension services may need to be enhanced to cope with the demands of development and climate change.
- *Transitional assistance.* Climate change may stimulate location changes and migration. There may be scope for identifying resources for creating job opportunities, supporting incomes, developing new infrastructure/institutions, relocating industry, providing temporary food aid, improving market functions and developing insurance.
- *Trade policy.* Governments may need to revise trade policies to adapt to new climate change conditions to allow imports and exports to mitigate lost AFF production or to sell or dispose of surpluses.
- *Infrastructure development.* Public investment may be needed to adapt to climate change conditions, including development of new transport and municipal infrastructure, development of new lands, protection or improvements of existing lands, construction of irrigation and water control structures, protection of coastal resources, and incubation of new industries, among other possibilities.

Method used to estimate need for investment and financial flows

Although extensive literature exists on the impacts of climate change on agriculture production, it tends to focus on the net effects on production, not on the costs of adaptation. Indeed, many of the studies related to AFF do not specify needed adaptation measures, not to mention costing them. In the face of these realities the approach used here relies on subjective statements about the current degree to which research expenditures are directed at climate-related issues and a broad assumption about how capital formation might be affected.

The AFF sector estimated the additional investment and financial flows needed in the primary sector (e.g. the growing of crops, the farming of animals, logging and fish farms) and the secondary sector (e.g. food, wood product, and pulp and paper manufacturing industries) to cope with expected economic and population growth and the impacts of climate change.

In order to assess investment and financial flows needed to cope with expected economic and population growth in 2030 based on the relevant literature, it is expected that the level of resources spent on research will continue to grow at about 2 per cent per year in both developed and developing countries. Total resources spent on extension are assumed to rise by 20 per cent in developing countries due to their current and emerging food issues, and the current level of resources spent on extension in developed countries are assumed to be adequate and remain constant. The projected level of investment in physical assets needed in 2030 is based on the OECD ENV-Linkage model and corresponds to the projection of the IEA WEO reference scenario.

In order to meet climate change adaptation needs, the following was assumed:

- Based on a study of the implications of future agricultural research needs and subjective estimates of the amount research expenditures in the Consultative Group on International Agricultural Research (CGIAR) system related to climate, it is estimated that expenditures in research and extension to cope with expected economic growth in 2030 would need to increase by 10 per cent;
- It was assumed that there will be new capital needed to, for example, irrigate areas, adopt new practices, move fish and timber processing facilities, etc. However, in 2030 the need for additional investment will be limited by the fact that most agricultural and fisheries capital tends to have a short life (10 – 20 years) and would be replaced and adapted as climate change proceeds. As a consequence, a low 2 per cent estimate was used to reflect the additional level of investment needed in new facilities for the development of new and larger land areas to cope with regionally diminished production plus expanded irrigation and other inputs, relocation of food, wood industry, and pulp and paper manufacturing facilities. Based on this, the additional investment in gross fixed capital formation between 2005 and 2030, as estimated by the OECD ENV-Linkage model, will need to increase by 2 per cent.[4]

Overview of current investment and financial flows by source of financing

Current expenditures on AFF are presented in Table 21.1. Public expenditures on research are about two-thirds of the total, but are more than 90 per cent of the

Table 21.1 *Expenditures in agriculture, forestry and fisheries*
(millions of US dollars)

Type of expenditures	Amount
Research in developing countries[a]	15,422
Research in high income countries[a]	25,111
Extension in developing countries[a]	3083
Extension in high income countries[a]	4161
Capital formation in developing countries[b]	190,102
Capital formation in high income countries[b]	354,017
Total developing countries	208,608
Total high income countries	383,288
Total	**591,896**

[a]Estimated for 2000
[b]Estimated for 2005

expenditures in developing countries and less than half of the expenditures in developed countries.

Of the total gross fixed capital formation (GFCF) for the three AFF sub-sectors (agriculture, forestry and fisheries) in 2005 and for 2030, as projected by the OECD ENV-Linkage model about three-fifths of the investment is for agriculture, one third is forestry, and the remaining 2 per cent is for fisheries. GFCF is projected to almost double in 25 years, but the shares devoted to the sub-sectors are expected to remain about the same. Domestic investment represents 97 per cent of the investment in the primary sector, growing of crops, farming of animals, logging and operation of fish hatcheries and fish farms, and 84 per cent in the secondary sector, the food, wood product and pulp and paper manufacturing industries, while official development assistance (ODA) represents 1.2 per cent in the former sector and 0.1 per cent in the latter. In both cases, foreign direct investment (FDI) is likely to play a more significant role than ODA; however, the FDI role is likely to be significantly greater in activities related to the manufacturing industries than in the primary sector.

Total ODA to AFF reached US$6.4 billion in 2005. Total ODA in AFF rose by 8 per cent from 2000 to 2005, but expenditures in extension increased by 38 per cent and expenditures in research increased by almost 80 per cent during the same period.

Estimated investment and financial flows needed

Table 21.2 presents estimates of additional investment and financial flows needed to address expected economic growth and population growth. Table 21.2 also presents the additional investment and financial flows needed to adapt to climate change.

Overall, a substantial increase in investment and financial flows will be needed to meet the growing demand due to expected economic and population growth in 2030. It is estimated that investment and financial flows into R&D, extension activities and physical assets will need to nearly double (an increase of about US$575 billion) between 2005 and 2030. Adaptation to the adverse impacts of climate change is estimated to add about 2 per cent to this amount or about US$14 billion in 2030. About 75 per cent of this latter amount will be required for investment in physical assets (capital formation-

Table 21.2 *Investment and financial flows needed in 2030 for economic and population growth and for adaptation to the adverse impacts of climate change (millions of US dollars)*

Type of expenditures	Additional investment and financial flows needed due to economic and population growth	Additional investment and financial flows needed for adaptation to the adverse impacts of climate change
Research in developing countries	13,526	1353
Research in high income countries	20,374	2037
Extension in developing countries	617	62
Extension in high income countries	0	0
Capital formation in developing countries	291,093	5822
Capital formation in high income countries	248,001	4960
Total developing countries	305,236	7237
Total high income countries	268,375	6997
Total	**573,611**	**14,234**

related investment) and 25 per cent will be required in the form of financial flows for research and extension activities. Slightly more than half of this amount will be needed in developing countries.

Assessment of needed changes in investment, financial and policy arrangements to fill the gap in investment and financial flows

The additional investment and financial flows needed in 2030 to cope with the adverse impacts of climate change in the AFF sector is about US$14 billion. Slightly more than half of this amount will be needed for developing countries alone. It is estimated that approximately US$11 billion will be needed to purchase new capital; for example to irrigate areas, adopt new practices and to move processing facilities. The additional financial flows needed in the AFF sector for research and extension activities to facilitate adaptation would be about US$3 billion.

Most of the additional investment in physical assets needed in the AFF sector is for assets that are currently financed by domestic private agents. ODA currently accounts for less than one per cent of the resources channelled to this sector in non-Annex I parties and for about 3 per cent in LDC parties. FDI is likely to play a more significant role than ODA; however, its role is likely to be significantly greater in activities related to the manufacturing industries than in the primary sector. Consequently, it can be expected that the majority of the additional investment needed would come from private sources, such as domestic AFF producers and processing firms and multinational seed companies, chemical companies and companies in the manufacturing industries. It can be expected that additional public resources will be needed to provide the private sector with the necessary information and incentives for

---

Box 21.1 *Agriculture, Forestry and Fisheries*

Investment and financial flows needed in 2030

To address climate change impacts in this sector, an additional US$14 billion in investment and financial flows would be needed. About half of this amount is estimated to be needed in developing countries. It is estimated that approximately US$11 billion will be needed to purchase new capital; for example to irrigate areas, adopt new practices and to move processing facilities. The additional US$3 billion will be needed for research and extension activities to facilitate adaptation.

Current investment and financial flows

Total current expenditure on AFF for capital formation, research and extension is estimated to be in the order of US$591 billion. A large proportion of the investment in the AFF sector is made in privately own physical assets by AFF producers and processing firms and multinational seed companies, chemical companies and companies in the manufacturing industries. Public expenditures on research are about two-thirds of the total, but are more than 90 per cent of the expenditures in developing countries and less than half of the expenditures in developed countries. A relatively substantial level (2.9 US$billion in 2000) of external public resources are channeled into agricultural and forestry sector policies in developing countries as compared to other sectors, in particular in Africa and Latin America.

---

it to make the required additional investment to better adapt to climate change. The design of adequate and coherent national policies could play a key role and targeted support will be needed for this to happen. Substantial external public resources are already channelled into agricultural and forestry policies in developing countries, in particular in Africa and Latin America. A higher fraction of these resources might be needed for this, depending on the region.

Public sources account for two-thirds of the current funding for AFF research worldwide but for as much as 90 per cent of AFF research funding in developing countries. Thus, for the additional US$3 billion needed in investment and financial flows in 2030 for research and extension in developing countries, most of the additional funding would need to come from public sources unless adequate incentives are provided to the private sector. Assuming that public spending continues to increase by slightly more than 2 per cent per year in developing countries, an additional US$1.4 billion would need to come from new sources of external public financing in 2030 to cope with the adverse impacts of climate change.

Water supply

Introduction

Potential impacts of climate change on water resources
The IPCC reports that water resources around the world will be highly sensitive to climate change. Higher temperatures, increased melting of glaciers, salinization from

rising oceans, an increased speed of the hydrological cycle and changes in precipitation patterns will affect the supply, quality and demand for water resources around the world (Kundzewicz et al, 2007). One likely outcome from an increased hydrological cycle is precipitation falling in fewer but more intense events, thus increasing the likelihood of flooding in many regions and more days without precipitation, thus also increasing likelihood of drought (Tebaldi et al, 2006; IPCC, 2007). One recent finding from the literature is the likelihood of certain regional patterns of precipitation. For example, most climate models project that the Mediterranean Basin, Southern Africa, many parts of northern Brazil and southwestern North America are likely to see a reduction in precipitation (Milly et al, 2005; Kundzewicz et al, 2007).

Adaptation

The IPCC also notes that there are many options for adaptation related to water resources and that many water bodies in municipalities (particularly, but not exclusively, in developed countries) are already beginning to take steps to prepare for climate change. Table 21.3, from Kundzewicz et al, (2007), summarizes some options for adaptation. The IPCC identified reservoir construction and decommissioning, increased waste water re-use and desalination, more efficient waste water treatment, and application of water-saving technologies as other options for adaptation.

Method used to estimate need for investment and financial flows

Given the need to use readily available data for this analysis, estimates presented are only for changes in water supply and demand. The investment resources needed for water quality and flood control are not estimated. The supply costs also do not include

Table 21.3 *Adaptation measures in the water resource sector*

Supply side	Demand side
Prospecting and extraction of groundwater	Improvement of water-use efficiency by recycling water
Increasing storage capacity by building reservoirs and dams	Reduction in water demand for irrigation by changing the cropping calendar, crop mix, irrigation method, and area planted
Desalination of seawater	Reduction in water demand for irrigation by importing agricultural products, i.e., virtual water
Expansion of rainwater storage	Promotion of indigenous practices for sustainable water use
Removal of invasive non-native vegetation from riparian areas	Expanded use of water markets to reallocate water to highly valued uses
Water transfer	Expanded use of economic incentives, including metering and pricing to encourage water conservation

Source: Kundzewicz et al, 2007

estimates of needs for distribution systems. Consequently, the estimates in this study might be underestimating the cost of adaptation in the water resources sector.

Modelling was used to estimate changes in demand by each country for water supply for two scenarios: the SRES A1B and B1 scenarios. The estimates consider the needs of increasing populations and growing economies. Change in 2030 assumed planning for the next 20 years and perfect knowledge about climate change impacts in 2050. Estimates of demand for water supplies and estimates of change in supply (as affected by climate change) used by Kirshen (2007) were used. Uniform assumptions were used about how much water in basins could be used to meet off-stream uses such as domestic consumption and irrigation. Some use of desalinated water in coastal cities and some use of reclaimed water for irrigation in countries facing particular water shortages were assumed. The cost of unmet irrigation demands have not been considered in the analysis.

Applying uniform rules of thumb is a practical method for generating estimates of financial costs. However, it implies that country-by-country variance in costs and approaches cannot be considered. In the context of this study, uniform assumptions were applied for costs for extracting groundwater, building additional surface water storage capacity, installing desalination plants, and reclaiming water. However, the cost estimates considered differences in costs in developed and developing countries. Results for regions, and particularly countries, should be treated as preliminary.

The cost estimates for 2030 are the total costs associated with the construction of additional infrastructure (reservoirs, wells, desalination, re-use facilities) needed to meet the projected demand for water supplies because of projected population and economic growth and expected climate change under the two scenarios.

Overview of current investment and financial flows by source of financing

Briscoe (1999) estimates current annual expenditures for water-related infrastructure in developing countries to be US$15 billion for hydropower, US$25 billion for water supply and sanitation, and US$25 billion for irrigation and drainage, for a total of US$65 billion. GFCF for water is estimated at US$38.4 billion in 2005. Briscoe (1999) and Winpenny (2003) both state that the majority of present financing for all aspects of water resources use comes from public sources, with Briscoe presenting estimates that 90 per cent is from mainly public sources and 10 per cent is from external sources. In 2000, total ODA in the water sector infrastructure (US$4.2 billion) accounted for about 6 per cent of the total annual expenditures estimated by Briscoe (1999).

From 2000 to 2005, real ODA directed towards water infrastructure increased by approximately 40 per cent (from US$4.2 billion in 2000 to US$5.9 billion in 2005). The regional distribution changed markedly, with Latin America and the Caribbean receiving in 2005 only 32 per cent of the amount it received in 2000. Contributions to Asia, Africa and the Middle East increased significantly from 2000 to 2005.

Estimated investment and financial flows needed

Much has been written about the challenges of financing Target 10 of the MDGs for halving 'by 2015 the number of people without sustainable access to safe drinking water and basic sanitation' (e.g. Winpenny, 2003; Toubkiss, 2006). Eleven different estimates ranged from US$9 billion to US$100 billion per year. A commonly accepted estimate is that meeting the most basic domestic water and sanitation goals would require an annual expenditure of US$10 billion to 2015 (Winpenny, 2003). It appears that none of the reports included climate change impacts on water supply or demand. This is reasonable, as domestic water demands are only a small portion of global water demands. The estimates presented below do not include the costs of meeting Target 10 of the MDGs, rather they complement it.

The estimated investment needs for the SRES A1B and B1 scenarios by region are summarized in Table 21.4. The estimates of investment and financial flows needed represent the total flows needed for the construction of additional infrastructure required to meet the projected demand for water supply caused by population and economic growth and expected climate change by 2030.

The investment cost for meeting the A1B scenario, assuming climate change to 2050 is anticipated, is estimated to be US$797 billion; the cost of meeting the B1 scenario is estimated to be US$639 billion, some 20 per cent less. This 20 per cent reduction is mainly due to differences in socio-economic conditions between the two scenarios; there is significantly more economic growth in the A1B scenario.

The fraction of the change in investment needs attributable to climate change alone is estimated to be 25 per cent under both the SRES A1B and B1 scenarios. Thus climate change is estimated to increase total investment needs by 2030 by US$225 billion under the A1B scenario and US$180 billion under the B1 scenario.

Assuming that funding is provided through grants for a 20-year period, the additional investment and financial flows needed for adaptation would be about US$9–11 billion in 2030. About 85 per cent of the investment (US$8–9 billion) is estimated to be needed in non-Annex I (NAI) parties. Interestingly, this is of the same order of magnitude as the additional investment and financial flows needed to meet the MDG related to sustainable access to safe drinking water and basic sanitation.

Table 21.4 *Investment and financial flows needed in 2030 for economic and population growth and for adaptation to the adverse impacts of climate change for the SRES A1B and B1 scenarios (billions of US dollars)*

Region	SRES A1B	SRES B1
Africa	233	223
Developing Asia	303	230
Latin America	23	23
Middle East	151	148
OECD Europe	87	25
OECD North America	41	16
OECD Pacific	3	1
Transition economies	57	54
World total	**898**	**720**
NAI parties	720	628
Least developed countries	57	45

Box 21.2 *Water Supply*

Investment and financial flows needed in 2030

The total cost associated with the construction of additional infrastructure needed to meet the projected demand for water supply is estimated to increase investment needs in 2030 by US$11 billion. About 85 per cent of the investment is estimated to be needed in non-Annex I parties.

Current investment and financial flows

In 1999, expenditures for water-related infrastructure in developing countries were estimated at US$65 billion. Total investment in physical assets only in this sector was estimated at US$38.4 billion in 2005. Most of this investment is undertaken by governments. About 90 per cent of the cost for all aspects of water resource use is currently covered by domestic funding sources and 10 per cent by external funding sources. From 2000 to 2005, ODA directed towards water infrastructure increased by approximately 40 per cent (from US$4.2 billion in 2000 to US$5.9 billion in 2005).

Assessment of needed changes in financial and policy arrangements to fill the gap in investment and financial flows

For adaptation alone, the additional investment and financial flows needed would be about US$9–11 billion in 2030. Winpenny (2003) describes three types of obstacles to increasing the financing for water-related infrastructure and then presents many recommendations to overcome them. The major classes of obstacles include: governance; particular funding risks of the water sector such as its low rate of return, capital intensity with long payback period; and the large number of projects that cannot obtain financing from any source because of project size or the credit risk of the borrower (called the 'exposed segment'). Briscoe (1999) estimates that 90 per cent of funding for all aspects of water resources use is from domestic sources and 10 per cent is from external sources. Both sources might be inadequate to meet future challenges associated with climate change. If the increase in investment needs solely related to climate change in non-Annex I parties (US$8–9 billion) is to come entirely from ODA, which is currently US$5.9 billion per year, then ODA would need to rise by about 50 per cent to meet the additional requirements. Despite the important recent increases in ODA allocated to the water and sanitation sector, it is unlikely that this is indicative of the expected change from the present to 2030. New domestic and external public resources will be needed.

Human health

Introduction

Potential impacts of climate change on human health
Climate change is likely to have widespread, diverse, and on the whole negative impacts on human health across the world. The impacts include changes in the location and

incidence of infectious and diarrhoeal diseases, increases in air and water pollution in many locations, increase in risk of heat stress, increases in intensity and frequency of many extreme events, and increased risks of malnutrition and other consequences of poor food quality. In addition, disruption of natural ecosystems could enable the further spread of infectious diseases, and climate change-induced human migration can be injurious to mental and physical health. On the positive side, there could be reductions in some cold-related health outcomes. On the whole, the Human Health chapter of the IPCC AR4 concluded that climate change has begun to negatively affect human health, and that projected climate change will increase the risks of climate-sensitive health outcomes (Confalonieri et al, 2007).

Adaptation

The fundamental adaptation requirement for the health sector in relation to climate change is to improve the capacity of the public health system. There is tremendous disparity in health risks between the developing and developed world. The main reason is that, on average, the public health systems in the developed world function at much higher levels than do the systems in the developing world. Improving the delivery of health care in the developing world would go a long way toward helping developing countries develop and could substantially reduce vulnerability to climate change. Without substantial improvement in the public health systems, human health in developing countries will be highly vulnerable to climate change. However, even with significant improvements in health care, climate change is projected to increase the burden of climate-sensitive health determinants and outcomes.

Beyond this, there are many specific measures that can be taken to reduce vulnerability to climate change. These include, for example, improved monitoring systems to detect the arrival or presence of infectious diseases and heat-watch warning systems to warn urban populations about heat waves.

Method used to estimate need for investment and financial flows

The Global Burden of Disease (GBD) study conducted by the WHO (McMichael et al, 2004) was used to estimate the total increase in health cases in 2030. The GBD study is the most comprehensive study of the total impacts of climate change on global human health that has been conducted to date. The study used internally consistent estimates of incidence, health state prevalence, severity and duration, and mortality for more than 130 major health outcomes, and estimated change in disability adjusted life years (DALYs) lost compared with the base period 1961 to 1990. Twenty-six risk factors were assessed, including major environmental, occupational, behavioural and lifestyle risk factors. The analysis for this adaptation study focuses on three human health outcomes: diarrhoeal disease, malnutrition and malaria. Models were used to estimate risks for each outcome. The model output is reported as a mid-range estimate. As with the study of water investment needs, the advantage of this approach is that a consistent and comprehensive framework is applied across the globe.

The limitations of this approach are similar to the limitations of the water assessment. What is essentially top–down modelling typically does not account for many varying local and regional factors that affect results at these scales. Such top–down approaches, however, are useful for providing a consistent and approximate estimate of impacts.

The GBD study uses two scenarios. The first scenario is the 750ppmv stabilization scenario from the GBD analysis; this results in CO_2 concentrations in the atmosphere slightly higher than the SRES A1B scenario. The second scenario is the 550ppmv stabilization scenario from the GBD analysis. This CO_2 concentration is similar to that from the SRES B1 scenario. The GBD relied on climate change estimates from one general circulation model, the HADCM2 model (Johns et al, 2001).

A further limitation is the estimated costs for treating health outcomes. The cost estimates are low because they consider only the cost of treating one case of each health outcome, thus assuming that there is sufficient public health infrastructure to administer the treatment. The estimates do not include the costs of setting up new infrastructure (such as the ability to distribute bed nets) when a health outcome increases its geographic range. In addition, some estimated costs are low. For example, the average cost of intervention per child to combat malnutrition is estimated to be about US$20, whereas more recently published studies estimated costs of one order of magnitude higher.

Other human health impacts such as increased heat stress, exposure to air and water pollution, exposure to many other diseases such as dengue fever, and exposure to increased intensity of many extreme weather events are not examined. So the total estimated number of cases caused and the costs associated with climate change are not complete.

Based on Rosenzweig and Parry (1994), malnutrition is projected to increase. Despite its vintage, it is perhaps the most comprehensive study of climate change impacts on agriculture done to date. The study assumed global population growing to 10.8 billion by the middle of the century, whereas the SRES A1B and B1 scenarios assumed global population peaks at about 8 billion. The agriculture estimates do not account for the effect of potential increases in extreme weather on agricultural production or distribution of food. Further, the estimates are of crop yields, not food security. Micronutrient deficiencies are a major source of ill health, even in regions with sufficient crop yields. On the other hand, the study did not account for adaptations such as the development of more heat- and drought-tolerant crops, or crops that can take better advantage of higher atmospheric CO_2 levels. Finally, for malnutrition, stunting and wasting were analysed, but not all the health impacts. Stunting and wasting are a small percentage of the impacts of climate change, so this can represent a significant underestimate.

Overview of current investment and financial flows by source of financing

Health expenditures come from both the public and private sectors. In many countries, government spending is the majority of total expenditures on health, whereas in many other countries, government spending is less than half of total expenditures. External expenditures on health are typically a small share of total expenditures. However, for very poor countries, external expenditures are a large share of total expenditures and even up to 30 to 50 per cent in a few cases. Table 21.5 provides regional details on the above.

Total real ODA rose by two-thirds from 2000 to 2005, with bilateral aid doubling. Total ODA for health reached US$5.5 billion in 2005. Africa received the largest share

Table 21.5 *Selected indicators of health expenditure ratios for the year 2000*

Region	Total expenditure on health (millions of US dollars)	Government expenditure on health as a percentage of total expenditure on health	Private expenditure on health as a percentage of total expenditure on health	External resources for health as a percentage of total expenditure on health	Out-of-pocket expenditure as a percentage of private expenditure on health
Africa	34,813	43	57	5	63
Developing Asia	122,935	36	64	1	93
Latin America	119,458	50	50	1	66
Middle East	37,252	63	37	2	79
OECD Europe	862,604	75	25	0	63
OECD North America	1,572,296	45	55	0	29
OECD Pacific	477,591	78	22	0	86
Other Europe	257	70	30	0	82
Transition Economies	33,526	60	40	1	79
World Total	**3,260,733**	**58**	**42**	**0**	**45**
NAI parties	355,384	46	54	2	81
Least developed countries	8330	37	63	17	85

Source: WHO, 2006

of aid in both years, with South Asia second. Hecht and Shah (2006) estimated development assistance for health for the Disease Control Priorities in Developing Countries project (Table 21.6). Although aid in the health sector is still dominated by multilateral and bilateral sources, NGOs such as the Bill and Melinda Gates Foundation are becoming a relatively more important source of funding and research.

Estimated investment and financial flows needed

The increased health risks for the middle scenario from the 750ppmv and 550ppmv stabilization scenarios relative to 1990 are presented in Table 21.7. Regions are based on WHO classification. The groupings are not based on income level but rather on child and adult mortality rate.

Table 21.6 *Development assistance for health, selected years (millions of US dollars)*

Source	Annual average 1997 to 1999	2002
Bilateral agencies	2560	2875
Multilateral agencies	3402	4649
European Commission	304	244
Global Fund to fight AIDS, Tuberculosis and Malaria	0	962
Bill and Melinda Gates Foundation	458	600
Total	**6724**	**9330**

Source: Michaud, 2003; OECD, 2004

Table 21.7 *Projected excess incident cases (in thousands) in 2030 of diarrhoeal diseases, malnutrition and malaria for the 750ppmv and 550ppmv stabilization scenarios (middle estimates)*

Region	Diarrhoeal diseases		Malnutrition		Malaria	
	750ppmv scenario	550ppmv scenario	750ppmv scenario	550ppmv scenario	750ppmv scenario	550ppmv scenario
Africa	50,343	41,952	437	328	17,703	14,170
Americas-A	0	0	0	0	0	0
Americas-B	1465	1465	200	86	323	258
Eastern Mediterranean	5779	5779	533	335	3211	2535
Europe	785	785	0	0	0	0
Southeast Asia-A	0	0	225	113	0	0
Southeast Asia-B	73,608	63,092	3067	2165	70	0
Western Pacific-A	0	0	0	0	2	15
Western Pacific-B	0	0	211	70	478	404
Total	**131,980**	**113,073**	**4673**	**3097**	**21,787**	**17,369**

Based on model output, under the 750ppmv stabilization scenario, there would be about 132 million additional cases of diarrhoeal disease, 5 million additional cases of malnutrition, and 22 million additional cases of malaria for these three health outcomes alone. Although virtually all of the malnutrition and malaria cases would be in developing countries, 1–5 per cent of the diarrhoeal disease cases would be in developed countries.

The number of additional cases in the 550ppmv stabilization scenario is lower than in the 750ppmv stabilization scenario. For example, additional cases of diarrhoeal disease would drop from 132 million per year to 113 million. Incidences of malnutrition would drop from 4.7 million additional cases to 3.1 million additional cases per year.

The estimated total global financial flows needed to cover the cost of the additional number of cases of diseases are reported in Table 21.8.

The annual financial flows needed under the two scenarios to cover the cost of these three health outcomes arising from the adverse impacts of climate change would be US$4–5 billion. Although the additional financial flows needed could not be allocated to different regions in a meaningful way, it is assumed to be all in developing countries.

The 550ppmv stabilization scenario results in fewer cases and lower financial flows needed than the 750ppmv stabilization scenario. The needs are about US$1 billion lower, from US$5 billion down to US$4 billion.

Although an estimate of the increased financial flows needed resulting from the socio-economic changes has not being developed for this study, an estimate of current financial needs can be derived by comparing the increase in health cases from climate change with the current number of cases. This can give an indication of the magnitude of financial flows that may be needed. Table 21.9 presents the current number of cases of the three health outcomes, the projected number of cases under the two scenarios used, and the percentage increase.

Assuming the cost per case remains unchanged, under the reference scenario, the total financial flow would need to increase by 3 per cent to treat diarrheal disease, by 10 per cent to treat malnutrition and by 5 per cent to treat malaria.

Although this study did not estimate the costs of improving health to meet the development needs associated with the 750ppmv and 550ppmv stabilization scenarios, Stenberg et al (2007) estimated the costs to scale up essential child health interventions to reduce child mortality by two-thirds under the four MDGs aimed at children's health by 2015 in 75 countries; the countries chosen accounted for 94 per cent of death among children less than five years of age. The interventions focused on malnutrition, pneumonia, diarrhoea, malaria and key causes of death of newborns. Costs included programme-specific investment and financial flows needed at national and district levels. The authors estimated that an additional US$52.4 billion would be required for the period 2006–2015. This averages about US$5 billion per year. It is interesting to note that this is of the same order of magnitude as the estimated additional level of resources needed to treat additional cases of diarrhoea, malnutrition and malaria due to climate change in 2030. Projected costs in 2015 were equivalent to increasing the average total health expenditures from all financial resources in the 75 countries by 8 per cent and raising general government health expenditure by 26 per cent over 2002.

Table **21.8** *Estimated additional financial flows needed in 2030 to cover the cost of additional cases of diarrhoeal diseases, malnutrition and malaria due to the adverse impacts of climate change (millions of US dollars)*

	Diarrhoeal diseases		Malnutrition		Malaria		Total	
	750ppmv scenario	550ppmv scenario	750ppmv scenario	550ppmv scenario	750ppmv scenario	550ppmv scenario	750ppmv scenario	550ppmv scenario
Financial flows needed	2235	1923	92–122	61–81	2173–3033	1773–2418	4500–5390	3757–4422

Table **21.9** *Comparison of current diarrhoeal disease, malnutrition and malaria cases with estimated climate change impacts in 2030 for the 750ppmv and 550ppmv stabilization scenarios (thousands of cases)*

Scenario		Diarrhoeal diseases	Malnutrition	Malaria
Current		4,513,981	46,352	408,227
750ppmv scenario	Climate change impacts	131,980	4673	21,787
	Percentage increase	3	10	5
550ppmv scenario	Climate change impacts	131,073	3097	17,369
	Percentage increase	2.5	7	4

Box 21.3 *Human health*

Investment and financial flows needed in 2030

The financial flows needed in 2030 to cover the cost of treating the additional number of cases of diarrhoeal disease, malnutrition and malaria due to climate change is estimated to be US$ 4–5 billion. By assumption, all of this amount will be needed in developing countries.

Current investment and financial flows

Total expenditures on health were in the order of US$ 3.3 trillion in 2000. Government expenditure on health as a percentage of total expenditures on health varies from 36 per cent in developing Asia to 75 per cent in Europe. In several countries still, the cost of treating a particular health condition is paid for mainly by the families of those affected, with some domestic public funds covering the costs of operating health care facilities. Least developed countries are particularly reliant on external funding sources for health care. Aid in the health sector is still dominated by multilateral and bilateral sources (total real ODA rose by two-thirds from 2000 to 2005 and reached US$ 5.5 billion in 2005), NGOs are becoming a relatively more important source of funding and research.

Assessment of needed changes in financial and policy arrangements to fill the gap in investment and financial flows

The estimated additional financial flows needed for the health sector to treat the additional number of cases of diarrhoea, malnutrition and malaria due to climate change in developing countries are about US$4–5 billion, the same order of magnitude as current ODA. Based on current financing trends of health care, this amount is likely to be paid for mainly by the families of those affected, with some domestic public funds paying for the operation of health care facilities. Whether the resources available will be adequate to meet the additional needs will vary a lot from one country to another, depending on the burden the additional needs represent compared with the availability of public and private resources. In countries where private individuals cannot cope with the additional cost of treatment, new and additional public financing will be necessary. Not being able to treat these diseases will increase morbidity and mortality. Countries that are already currently highly reliant on external sources for health care, such as LDCs, may need new and additional external support to cope with climate change.

Natural ecosystems (terrestrial and marine)

Introduction

Potential impacts of climate change on natural ecosystems

Climate change has already been linked to impacts on species across the world (e.g. Parmesan and Yohe, 2003; Root et al, 2005; Cassassa et al, 2007). Migration patterns, productivity, location and other changes are being observed. In one dramatic example, the Fish and Wildlife Service of the United States of America proposed listing polar bears as a threatened species because of declining Arctic ice cover (United States Fish and Wildlife Service, 2007).

The future impacts of climate change on ecosystems are likely to be profound and dramatic. The IPCC notes that the resilience of many ecosystems is likely to be overcome by the combination of climate change and other socio-economic influences (in particular land-use change and overexploitation). A 1.5–2.5°C warming over 1990 could cause the extinction of approximately 20 to 30 per cent of plant and animal species (Thomas et al, 2004). A 3°C warming would transform about one fifth of the world's ecosystems (Fischlin et al, 2007). There also are likely to be substantial impacts on marine ecosystems with a 3°C warming.

Adaptation

The term 'adaptation' needs be applied in a relative sense to natural ecosystems. In the so-called managed sectors such as coastal and water resources, agriculture and health, adaptation has the potential to substantially maintain most of the services currently provided in these sectors, particularly in the developed countries. It is not clear, however, that human intervention can substantially offset the impacts of climate change and other socio-economic drivers on natural ecosystems. At best, based on what we know now, adaptation could reduce some of the harmful impacts of climate change.

The IPCC concluded that human intervention to assist ecosystem adaptation should consist of actions to reduce the impacts of other threats to ecosystems, such as habitat degradation, pollution and introduction of alien species. For example, diminished or lost ecosystems could be enhanced or replaced (e.g. ecosystem recreation, rapid dispersal by humans, pollinator reintroduction and use of pesticides for pest outbreaks). In addition, captive breeding and reintroduction and translocation or provenance trials in forestry could be used.

Adaptation for natural ecosystems can be put into the following categories:

- Reduce and manage stresses from other sources and activities, such as pollution, over-harvesting, habitat conversion and species invasions.
- Restore habitats.
- Increase size and/or number of reserves.
- Increase habitat heterogeneity within reserves, for example, by including gradients of latitude, altitude and soil moisture and by including different successional states.
- Maintain ecosystem structure and function as a means to ensure healthy and genetically diverse populations able to adapt to climate change.
- Increase landscape connectivity using corridors and stepping stones to link areas of habitat or reserves.
- Increase landscape permeability through reduction of unfavourable management practices and increasing area for biodiversity.
- Translocate and reintroduce species, especially those having essential functions such as pollination.
- Conserve threatened and endangered species ex situ, for example, using seed banks or collecting germplasm and zoos, including captive breeding for release into the wild.

Method used to estimate needs for investment and financial flows

There is very limited literature on adaptation of natural ecosystems to the adverse impacts of climate change. The existing literature emphasizes ideas about ways to reduce vulnerability of natural ecosystems to climate change. There is virtually no information on the effectiveness of these adaptations in reducing the damage to ecosystems from climate change, or on the costs of adaptation to climate change.

As a consequence, information on current investments and financial flows going to natural ecosystem protection and how much might be needed to protect ecosystems from current threats was used as the basis for analysis. James et al (2001) estimated the additional costs needed to protect biodiversity. The results of the analysis are discussed.

Although the method used by James et al (2001) may be the best method to estimate adaptation costs for protecting natural ecosystems, the approach is quite approximate and indirect. The James et al study is an attempt to estimate the investment and financial flows needed to protect natural ecosystems from current threats. But, as is discussed below, the authors use educated guesses as to how much additional land needs to be set aside as biodiversity protection areas. This study is not able to rely on bottom–up or top–down (e.g. modelling) estimates of natural ecosystem protection needs.

Furthermore, the James et al study does not estimate the additional protection needs that climate change might require. Given the potential for massive disruption of habitats and ecosystems, the need for many species to migrate hundreds of kilometres and the limited options for adaptation for many species, it is possible that the additional costs for addressing adaptation to climate change would be quite substantial. There is insufficient information to hazard even an educated guess as to the magnitude of the additional resources, not to mention their effectiveness in protecting natural ecosystems and biodiversity.

Overview of current investment and financial flows by source of financing

Between 1991 and 2000, the Global Environment Facility (GEF) provided about US$1.1 billion in grants and leveraged an additional US$2.5 billion in co-financing for biodiversity-related projects. Most of these grants were channelled through developing-country governments and NGOs and used to support more than 1000 protected sites covering 226 million hectares in 86 countries. OECD data show only US$198 million in biodiversity projects from the World Bank system (including the GEF) in 2000 and US$267 million in 2005.

James et al report that in the mid-1990s an average of US$6.8 billion per year was spent on global protected areas, with about 89 per cent of that amount spent in developed countries.

The private sector resources allocated to biodiversity protection have been relatively limited and focused in areas such as ecotourism, agroforestry and conservation of medicinal and herbal plants.

Estimated investment and financial flows needed

James et al examined what they called a relatively modest goal by the World Conservation Union (IUCN) to increase protected areas by 10 per cent (but noting that some scientists call for increasing protected areas by 50 per cent). They examined two options for such an expansion, one more ambitious than the other. James et al estimate that improving protection, expanding the network in line with IUCN guidelines, and meeting the opportunity costs of local communities could all be achieved with an annual increase in expenditures of US$12–22 billion. The range is based on different options for redressing the current lack of resources going to conservation. Note that this estimate does not consider the level of resources needed to reduce other threats to natural ecosystems, such as pollution. It also does not consider any additional requirements for protecting natural ecosystems from climate change. Such requirements could include developing migration corridors for species to migrate as climate zones shift.

It does not appear possible to estimate how resources needed for the protection of natural ecosystems would increase as a result of the reference or mitigation scenarios. However, it is clear that the larger the magnitude of climate change, the greater the harm to natural ecosystems. Therefore, the resources needed for protecting natural ecosystems will in all likelihood be higher for the reference scenario than for the mitigation scenario.

Assessment of needed changes in financial and policy arrangements to protect ecosystems from current threats

The James et al analysis indicates that just to meet current natural ecosystem protection needs, current levels of investment and financial flows would have to increase by a factor of three to four. This would require increasing public sources of funds and leveraging private sector funding as well.

However, so far, attempts at leveraging private sector financing for ecosystem protection have had limited success. Demonstrating that there is a business case for ecosystem protection is a difficult endeavour. ODA for ecosystem protection is currently two orders of magnitude below the identified level of investment and financial flows needed. Clearly, a substantial increase in public domestic and external funding will be needed to address not just the current lack of resources going to ecosystem protection but also the additional needs of climate change.

Box 21.4 *Natural ecosystems*

Investment and financial flows needed in 2030

Estimates in the literature indicate that improving protection, expanding the network of protected areas and compensating local communities that currently depend on resources from fragile ecosystems could be achieved for an increase in annual expenditure of US$ 12–22 billion.

Current investment and financial flows

Current annual spending to ensure natural ecosystem protection is of the order of US$ 7 billion from public domestic and external funding.

Coastal zones

Introduction

The IPCC (Nicholls et al, 2007) reports that hazards relating to human development of coastal areas are quite high. About 120 million people are exposed to hazards from tropical cyclones each year, and on average these events kill more than 12,000 people a year. Climate change will result in higher sea-levels, increased intensity of coastal storms and the destruction of many coral reefs and coastal wetlands. The combination of this and continued expansion of human settlements in coastal areas is likely to lead to an increasing need for protection from coastal hazards.

Adaptation

Nicholls et al note that, in general, the costs of adaptation to sea-level rise (e.g. through protection of threatened areas) are far less than the losses associated with not protecting coastal areas. It is not clear if it is feasible to adapt to more than a few metres of sea-level rise. Protection of natural ecosystems such as wetlands and coral reefs can increase their resilience to climate change. The three basic options for adaptation are:

- Protect – to reduce the risk of the event by decreasing the probability of its occurrence:
- Accommodate – to increase society's ability to cope with the effects of the event.
- Retreat – to reduce the risk of the event by limiting its potential effects.

Table 21.10 summarizes major adaptation options for coastal resources.

The benefits of mitigation of GHG emissions could be quite substantial over the very long term. The IPCC found that a sustained warming of 1–4°C above 1999–2000 levels could result in the deglaciation of Greenland. This would lead to many metres of sea-level rise over many centuries. Such an amount of sea-level rise appears to be beyond the capacity of societies to adapt to through coastal protection. Abandonment of coastal areas would be necessary in response to such an outcome. The costs of abandoning coastal development around the world would be a few orders of magnitude above protection costs for a metre or two of sea-level rise and entail major implications for human migration and cultural heritage.

Method used to estimate the need for investment and financial flows

The dynamic interactive vulnerability analysis (DIVA) tool was used for this analysis. DIVA is a very detailed model of the world's coasts. It divides the world's coasts into more than 12,000 segments and can account for the effect of different adaptation options. The study examined protection only from coastal flooding through the building of dykes or the use of beach nourishment. A benefit–cost test was applied to estimate whether the costs of coastal protection were less than the value of lost economic output should no protection measures be used. Although use of benefit–cost analysis could favour protection of wealthier coastal areas, coastal lands in many developing areas apparently had a high enough value to justify use of protection

Table 21.10 *Major physical impacts and potential adaptation responses to sea-level rise*

Physical impacts		Examples of adaptation responses (P – protection; A – accommodation; R – retreat)
1. Inundation, flood and storm damage	a. Surge (sea)	Dykes/surge barriers (P) Building codes/ buildings (A)
	b. Backwater effect (river)	Land-use planning/hazard delineation (A/R)
2. Wetland loss (and change)		Land-use planning (A/R) Managed realignment/ forbid hard defences (R) Nourishment/sediment management (P)
3. Erosion (direct and indirect change)		Coast defences (P) Nourishment (P) Building setbacks (R)
4. Saltwater Intrusion	a. Surface waters	Saltwater intrusion barriers (P) Change water abstraction (A)
	b. Groundwater	Freshwater injection (P) Change water abstraction (A)
5. Rising water tables and impeded drainage		Upgrade drainage systems (P) Polders (P) Change land use (A) Land-use planning/hazard delineation (A/R)

measures. The results are provided globally, for the IPCC regions, and at a finer resolution.

DIVA analyses a limited set of adaptations in a uniform manner. This has the advantage of applying a uniform method that can account for local and regional differences in conditions such as value of threatened areas. However, it has the disadvantage of not accounting for unique local circumstances or varying decision criteria that may be applied around the world. Such a top–down approach was also used in the water supply analysis and has similar limitations.

Socio-economic conditions for all scenarios were assumed to be the conditions in the SRES A1B scenario (Nakicenovic and Swart, 2000). The estimated additional investment and financial flows associated with the SRES A1B and B1 scenarios presented in this analysis are exclusively to cover the cost of adaptation measures to address sea-level rise itself, not socio-economic development. However, the value of protected economic output is based on the A1B scenario. The A1B scenario assumes the highest gross domestic product (GDP) growth of all of the SRES scenarios.

DIVA estimates investment needs without a sea-level rise. This considers the costs of adapting to subsidence and flooding. The SRES scenarios incorporate sea-level rise. The difference between the SRES scenarios and no sea-level rise is the effect of climate change alone.

DIVA estimates a number of impacts from sea-level rise including beach nourishment costs, land loss costs, number of people flooded, costs of building dykes, and losses from flooding. Of these, only the costs of beach nourishment and the costs of building dykes will be counted as adaptation costs. The other categories are damages. In reality, adaptation costs would probably be involved in responding to the damages.

Investment needs in 2030 were analysed assuming that decision-makers can project future rates of sea-level rise and plan for a 50- to 100-year timeframe. This study assumes that decision-makers plan for sea-level rise out to 2080. Planning for a shorter timeframe is likely to result in lower adaptation costs in 2030, whereas planning for a longer timeframe (such as for expected sea-level rise in 2130) would result in higher costs in 2030. Planning for 100 years rather than 50 is estimated to increase costs by about two-thirds.

Table 21.11 gives sea-level rise projections to 2130. These projections were taken from the IPCC Third Assessment Report (Houghton et al, 2001). There is virtually no difference between SRES emissions scenarios in 2030 A1B and B1. However, by 2080, there is a substantial difference between the two scenarios.

Overview of current investment and financial flows by source of financing

While there is significant interest in elaborating coastal adaptation measures and understanding their costs (e.g. Klein et al, 2001; Bosello et al, 2007), the level of investment in coastal adaptation is difficult to assess as there is never a single agency with published accounts in any country. However, there is some information on the level of investment and actions to protect vulnerable coastal areas in some countries and regions:

Table 21.11 *The range in sea-level rise by 2030 (relative to 1990) expected for each SRES scenario (cm)*

	SRES emissions scenario	
	A1B	B1
Minimum rise	3	3
Mean rise	9	9
Maximum rise (2030)	15	15
Maximum rise (2080)	53	44
Maximum rise (2100)	69	57
Maximum rise (2130)	96	75

- *European Union.* The Eurosion (2004) review reported that the total annual cost of coastal adaptation for erosion and flooding across the European Union was an estimated 3.2 billion Euros (in 2001 Euros; using current exchange rates this would be about US$4 billion). These measures mainly involved protection.
- *United Kingdom.* The Flood and Coastal Management budget increased substantially since 2000/2001 from approximately UK£300 million to more than UK£500 million per year in 2005/2006 (about US$443 million to US$910 million using current exchange rates). However, coastal investment is not directly defined and is only an element of this budget.
- *Netherlands.* This is the archetypal country threatened by sea-level rise, and it invests large sums in erosion and flood management. They amount to 0.1 to 0.2 per cent of GDP at present.
- *Bangladesh.* Bangladesh has experienced the highest death toll from coastal flooding of any country on Earth (Nicholls and Tol, 2006), and is a good example of a vulnerable deltaic country. Following the 1970 and 1991 cyclones, when at least 400,000 people died, an accommodation strategy was implemented via a system of flood warnings and the construction of more than 2500 elevated storm surge shelters. Despite recent severe storms, the death toll for people (and their animals via associated raised shelters) has fallen markedly.
- *The Maldives.* These islands are a good example of a vulnerable atoll nation where sea-level rise could literally extinguish the nation over the coming century without adaptation. However, significant adaptation is occurring on the island. After a significant Southern Ocean swell event that flooded much of the capital Male in the 1980s, a large wall was built around the city with aid from Japan (Pernetta, 1992). However, the costs are not known. More recently, after the Indian Ocean tsunami of 2004, there has been interest in developing tsunami shelters, which may also have a function against climate change.

Estimated investment and financial flows needed

The estimated investment needs for the SRES A1B and B1 scenarios are displayed in Table 21.12. Beach nourishment, land loss and flooding costs are estimated for 2030. There is no anticipation of future climate change impacts in these categories. The estimated investment required for dykes in 2030 assumes that the coastal infrastructure built in that year is sufficient to adapt to the maximum amount of sea-level rise anticipated in 2080. The cost of dykes is very sensitive to the length of the planning horizon. For instance, under the A1B scenario, if the dykes were built only for the sea-level observed in 2030, the costs would be US$11.7 billion. If, however, the dykes are built to adapt to projected sea-level rise 100 years hence (to 2130), the annual cost in 2030 would be US$16.8 billion. Since the cost of dykes represents more than half of the total costs, the selection of a planning horizon is a critical assumption affecting total costs.

Total costs including investment costs (beach nourishment and sea dykes) and losses (inundation and flooding) are estimated to be US$21–22 billion in 2030.

Table 21.13 examines the increase in investment needed by region. About half of the required investment will be in non-Annex I parties.

Table 21.12 Investment and financial flows needed in 2030 for adaptation to sea-level rise assuming anticipation to 2080 for the SRES A1B and B1 scenarios (millions of US dollars)

Impact category	Investment and financial flows needed with no sea-level rise	A1B scenario		B1 scenario	
		Investment and financial flows needed with sea-level rise	Difference in investment and financial flows needed with sea-level rise	Investment and financial flows needed with sea-level rise	Difference in investment and financial flows needed with sea-level rise
Beach nourishment costs	573	3042	2469	2888	2316
Sea dyke costs	5601	13,803	8202	12,815	7214
Total investment costs	**6174**	**16,845**	**10,681**	**15,703**	**9529**
Land loss costs	0	6	6	6	5
Sea flood costs	6385	8119	1734	7853	1467
Total loss costs	**6385**	**8125**	**1740**	**7859**	**1472**
Total cost (investment and losses)	**12,559**	**24,971**	**12,422**	**23,562**	**11,002**

Table 21.13 *Estimated additional investment needed in coastal infrastructure for the SRES A1B and B1 scenarios in 2030 by region (millions of US dollars)*

Region	A1B scenario		B1 scenario	
	Mean 2030	Maximum in 2080	Mean 2030	Maximum in 2080
Africa	612	1319	528	1197
Developing Asia	951	2181	801	1928
Latin America	680	1597	573	1414
Middle East	72	171	60	153
OECD Europe	737	1785	624	1587
OECD North America	1002	2022	882	1838
OECD Pacific	460	1080	388	958
Transition economies	189	479	158	421
Total	**4702**	**10,634**	**4014**	**9496**

The estimated investment needs for the A1B and B-1 scenarios differ by US$1 billion per year, or about 10 per cent.

Assessment of needed changes in financial and policy arrangements to fill the gap in investment and financial flows

Additional investment in worldwide coastal infrastructure of about US$10–11 billion will be required in 2030 for adaptation to sea-level rise. Adaptation of coastal resources to climate change is highly dependent on public sources of funding. Although much coastal infrastructure may be private (e.g. buildings and homes), efforts to protect coastal areas from coastal storms and sea-level rise are typically undertaken by governments. In the developed world and in parts of the developing world, the necessary financial resources are likely to be available to adapt coastal resources to climate change. However,

---

Box 21.5 *Coastal Zones*

Investment and financial flows needed in 2030

With sea-level rise, the investment needed is estimated to represent an additional US$ 11 billion in 2030. This estimate assumes that decision-makers take into account the expected sea-level rise in 2080. About half of the required investment will be needed in non-Annex I parties.

Current investment and financial flows

Although much of the infrastructure in coastal areas may be private (e.g. buildings and homes), efforts to protect coastal areas from coastal storms and sea-level rise are typically undertaken by governments.

certain settings and regions present particular challenges, as identified in the recent IPCC AR4 assessment of coastal areas (Nicholls et al, 2007). Deltaic regions, particularly the large coastal deltas in Asia and in Africa and small island states may have significant problems responding to sea-level rise and climate change. In these countries, additional sources of external public financing will be needed.

Development and integration of coastal zone management institutions and processes, while in itself not demanding large amount of resources, could increase the efficiency of adaptation to climate change and sea-level rise. GEF-funded initiatives such as the Caribbean Planning for Adaptation to Climate Change project, the Mainstreaming Adaptation to Global Change in the Caribbean project and the Pacific Islands Climate Change Assistance Programme are contributing to build the capacity in this area.

Infrastructure

Introduction

Climate change is likely to have substantial consequences for the integrity, performance, lifetime and design criteria for much of the world's infrastructure. Infrastructure for water supply, sanitation, flood control, hydropower, and coastal development and defences could be substantially affected by climate change. Changes in average climate, but also changes in extreme events, will affect infrastructure. For example, sea-level rise threatens to inundate coastal infrastructure. In addition, the potential for more intensive tropical cyclones would put more coastal infrastructure at risk. Changes in runoff patterns will affect flood control, water supply and sanitation. Changes in intense precipitation, flooding and droughts will affect and most likely have major implications for construction of water supply infrastructure. Even changes in peak high and low temperatures may require adjustments to buildings and their heating and cooling systems.

Adaptation

In general, there are two types of climate change adaptation in infrastructure. The first involves making modifications to or changes in operations of infrastructure that would be directly affected by climate change. This applies to infrastructure used to manage natural resources such as water or coastal resources infrastructure. For example, coastal defences may be raised or otherwise strengthened to adapt to higher sea-levels and the potential for more intense coastal storms. Infrastructure for water resource management applications such as flood protection, water supply, water quality treatment, hydropower production and other uses may be modified to adapt to changing runoff patterns and water quality conditions. For example, the size of reservoirs could be increased to provide more storage for water supply or flood protection. These changes will also apply to infrastructure such as heating and cooling systems directly affected by climate change.

The second type of adaptation affects infrastructure needed to support activities that cope with climate-affected sectors or resources. Provisions of public health services, agriculture extension, research and many other applications require supporting infrastructure. Hospitals, clinics, disease monitoring systems, buildings for extension services, laboratories and so on may need to be built to enhance the capability to adapt to climate change.

Method used to estimate the need for investment and financial flows

The analysis of climate change impacts on infrastructure estimates the share of infrastructure investment that is currently vulnerable to climate variability and then estimates the additional investment in infrastructure that may be necessary to adapt to climate change. It addresses only the first type of adaptation mentioned above.

The share of infrastructure vulnerable to the impacts of climate change is estimated based on losses due to extreme weather events.

Munich Re provided a data set of 'Great Weather Disasters' from 1951 to 2005, from which annual regional losses were estimated. The value of overall losses for each major event from 1951 through 2005 by region and/or country is included in the database. These were summed and averaged over the 55-year record of the database to obtain average annual losses by region. Since the Munich Re data set is only for large catastrophes and does not include damage from smaller climate events, it might underestimate total losses from weather extremes. Furthermore, the analysis in this study does not consider other infrastructure costs such as damage from inundation, erosion, melting of permafrost and other causes. On the other hand, although the vast majority of the 'Great Weather Disasters' are likely to be made more intense by climate change (e.g. cyclones, droughts and floods), some, but not all, cold weather events could be less severe with climate change. The Munich Re data were used to obtain an estimate of the minimum additional investment needed to adapt infrastructure to climate change. The Munich Re data were scaled up to cover all weather-related losses and accounts to get an estimate of the potential upper bound on the level of additional investment needed. The adjustment used is 4.3, and corresponds to the ratio of the Association of British Insurance (ABI) data on total weather-related losses for the period 2000–2006 to the Munich Re losses for the same period. The average annual loss is thus estimated at between US$21.1 billion and US$87.7 billion.

To estimate the share of infrastructure vulnerable to the impacts of climate change, the annual infrastructure investment in the middle of the period 1951–2005, that is for 1978, was used. Global GFCF data are not available for that year. The GFCF for 1980 is estimated by assuming that the growth rate projected for the period 2005–2030 by OECD (3.65 per cent per year) can be applied to period 1978–2005. That yields a global GFCF for 1978 of about US$3025 billion. Based on the average annual loss estimated above, the average annual loss is estimated to be between 0.7 per cent (based on Munich Re data) and 2.9 per cent (based on ABI data) of the estimated 1978 GFCF. Note that the World Bank estimates that 2 to 10 per cent of gross domestic investment could be sensitive to climate change, although it uses a much lower figure for the annual investment.

To estimate the potential additional costs of adapting vulnerable infrastructure to the impacts of climate change, the World Bank estimate of a 5 to 20 per cent (as cited by Noble, 2007) increase in investment was used. The infrastructure analysis implicitly assumes that the incremental cost of 5 to 20 per cent covers the cost of adapting to all climate change impacts over the life of each facility. The upper end was not adjusted, although some studies (e.g. Kirshen et al, 2006; Smith et al, 2006) indicate that some infrastructure investment needs might be 30 per cent higher.

The projected level of investment in physical assets needed in 2030 is based on the OECD ENV-Linkage model and corresponds to the projection in the IEA WEO reference scenario.

Overview of current investment and financial flows by source of financing

Total GFCF was US$7.8 trillion in 2000. It is unclear what is the fraction of private and public infrastructure that is vulnerable to climate change. Total ODA for infrastructure is estimated at more than US$15 billion in 2005; this represents a 36 per cent increase in real terms from 2000. Multilateral assistance increased by almost 60 per cent in the same period. South Asia was the largest recipient on ODA in this sector in 2005 and Africa was close behind.

Estimated investment and financial flows needed

In 2030, projected total GFCF is US$22.3 trillion. When this number is multiplied by the estimated share of infrastructure vulnerable to the impacts of climate change (0.7 and 2.9 per cent) this yields a value of between US$153 billion and US$650 billion of infrastructure investment vulnerable to climate change.

Assuming adaptation to the impacts of climate change requires a 5 to 20 per cent increase in capital costs, the adaptation costs would be US$8–31 billion per year in 2030 based on the Munich Re data and US$33–130 billion per year in 2030 based on the ABI data. Although the share of infrastructure vulnerable to climate change is higher in some developing country regions, total infrastructure investment is higher in developed countries, hence most of these adaptation costs are in developed countries. Table 21.14 presents the investment needed to adapt infrastructure to the adverse impact of climate change by region in 2030. About two-thirds (68 per cent) of the investment would be in OECD countries.

The World Bank (2006)/Stern Review (Stern et al, 2006) estimated the added costs necessary to adapt investments to climate change risks at 2000 US$40 billion, with a range of US$10–100 billion. The range estimated in this study above is very much in line with this estimate.

The costs of adapting infrastructure to cope with climate change are estimated to be in the range of US$8–130 billion, depending on the climate change scenario and assumption of sensitivity. As noted above, the additional investment needed to adapt infrastructure to climate change could be larger than the upper-end estimate used here. Two-thirds of the investment is expected to be in developed countries.

Assessment of needed changes in investment, financial and policy arrangements to fill the gap in investment and financial flows

The investment needed to adapt new infrastructure to climate change is estimated to be US$8–130 billion. This corresponds to less than 0.6 per cent of total GFCF in 2030. About a third of the investment needed will be in non-Annex I parties of which more than 80 per cent are in developing Asia. The potential sources of financing depends on the nature of the new infrastructures that are vulnerable to climate change and whether they are typically financed by the private or the public sector and whether they are

Table 21.14 *Additional investment needed to adapt infrastructure to climate change risks in 2030 (millions of US dollars)*

Region	Estimate based on Munich Re data		Estimate based on ABI data	
	5 per cent additional investment	20 per cent additional investment	5 per cent additional investment	20 per cent additional investment
Africa	22	87	92	371
Developing Asia	1901	7605	8106	32,424
Latin America	405	1620	1726	6906
Middle East	66	264	282	1127
OECD Europe	1000	3999	4262	17,050
OECD North America	3736	14,943	15,925	63,702
OECD Pacific	473	1892	2017	8067
Transition economies	24	97	102	412
World total	**7627**	**30,508**	**32,514**	**130,058**

financed with domestic or external resources. Although it is unclear what fraction of private and public infrastructure is vulnerable to climate change, the amount is likely to be financed by all types of sources: domestic and external, public and private. The additional investment is assumed to be on average a small fraction of the total cost of each new infrastructure vulnerable to climate change. Therefore the additional investment is likely to be financed in the same manner as the overall infrastructure:

Box 21.6 *Infrastructure*

Investment and financial flows needed in 2030

The additional investment needed to adapt new infrastructure vulnerable to climate change is estimated at 5 to 20 per cent of its cost. The additional investment needed is estimated at US$8–130 billion, or less than 0.5 per cent of global investment in 2030. About one third of the additional investment would be needed in non-Annex I parties, and more than 80 per cent of that in Asian developing countries.

Current investment and financial flows

Total investment in physical assets was estimated to be about US$6.8 trillion in 2000. Current sources for investment in infrastructure are private sources for infrastructure such as commercial buildings and industrial plants, and from public sources for infrastructure such as roads and public buildings. Total ODA for infrastructure is estimated at more than US$13 billion in 2005, this represents a 36 per cent increase in real terms from 2000. South Asia was the largest recipient in 2005, although Africa was close behind.

from private sources for infrastructure such as commercial buildings and industrial plants, and from public sources for infrastructure such as roads and public buildings. Public resources will also be needed to provide adequate support and incentives for new private infrastructures that are vulnerable to climate change to be adequately adapted. The latter might be necessary in order to avoid severe damages that can have important impacts on sectoral or overall economic development. The design of adequate national policies including the integration of adaptation considerations into sectoral agencies might have an important role to play in ensuring that an optimal amount of resources both domestic and private are available to cover the cost of adaptation.

The World Bank/Stern Review estimated the share of ODA and concessional finance investments sensitive to climate change to be higher (20 per cent) than the global average (2–10 per cent). They estimated the annual cost of adapting such infrastructure to the impacts of climate change at 2000 US$1–4 billion. This would be equivalent to as much as a 30 per cent increase in the ODA infrastructure spending between 2005 and 2030.

Avoided Damages

Although the adaptation costs described in the previous chapters may seem significant, it is clear that the value of the climate change impacts that these expenditures would avoid could be as large or greater. This study does not estimate the total value of impacts avoided by adaptations to climate change. However, the adaptation costs can be put in perspective by looking at the cost associated with extreme events and reviewing the literature on total damages from climate change, even though it is unlikely that the adaptations discussed in this study would avoid all of these damages.

A major component of the total impacts from climate change is likely to be losses from extreme weather events. Climate change is projected to increase the intensity of storms, cyclones, droughts, heat waves and other events. Estimating how losses from extreme events will change as a result of climate change is challenging for a number of reasons including:

- Since there is considerable variability in year-to-year damages from extreme climate (e.g. Hurricane Katrina dramatically increased weather-related losses in 2005), establishing a baseline for extreme weather damages can be difficult.
- Estimating the change in total infrastructure stock over time is challenging. For example, it is not clear whether infrastructure investments will grow proportionately with output or fixed capital investment or another set of data.
- It is very difficult to estimate how extreme climate events will change and how they will affect infrastructure.
- Clearly a lot of present infrastructure will be replaced over coming years. Whether climate change is factored into the replacement or redesign of infrastructure is not clear, nor is it clear how effective such adaptations would be in reducing risks from climate change.

In the context of this study, an attempt is made to estimate expected changes in damages due to extreme weather events. The analysis is based on different sources of data from the insurance industry on current losses. As mentioned in the infrastructure sector above, Munich Re catalogued 'great natural catastrophes' which involve the loss of thousands of lives or severe economic impacts from extreme events. Such a database can substantially underestimate damages from climate because only large events are included. Taking into account differences in various insurance industry estimates of losses, estimates of current losses to climate range from about US$160 billion to as much as US$330 billion, and most likely between US$200 and 300 billion. The estimates are in the order of 0.5 per cent of current gross world product.

The Munich Re data suggest that damages are increasing at a rate of 6 per cent per year in real terms. A paper by Risk Management Solutions (RMS) estimates that the increase in damages caused by climate change is 2 per cent per year in real terms, although it is a weak signal.[5] Accounting for the under-reporting of losses in the Munich Re 'great disaster' data and extrapolating the trend at 6 per cent per year, or at 2 per cent plus economic growth results in a range of estimates of annual climate damages in 2030 of approximately US$850–1350 billion. This corresponds to approximately 1.0–1.5 per cent of gross world product. These estimates consider climate change and make no allowance for reduced losses following new adaptation strategies. Losses are very likely to escalate non-linearly when events become more extreme. Thus, a reduction in the increase in global mean temperature through mitigation would probably have a greater proportional effect in reducing losses from extreme events.

Estimating the total damages from climate change is very difficult because all potential adverse impacts need to be not only identified but also costed. This is relatively more straightforward for impacts of climate change on sectors such as agriculture and infrastructure, but is more challenging for non-market impacts such as human health and ecosystem impacts. Indeed the term 'damages' includes financial impacts of climate change such as building sea walls, but also includes impacts on services such as those provided by ecosystems. These services are often not offered in markets and can be challenging to monetize.

In spite of these challenges, several economists have developed estimates of the total damages from climate change. The magnitude of these estimates differs quite substantially across studies. However, in spite of these differences, there are two important common findings across the studies:

- Damages increase with the magnitude of climate change. The more climate changes, with climate change typically measured as the average increase in global mean temperature, the greater the total damage. Some studies anticipate initial net benefits with up to 1 to 3°C of increase in global mean temperature, whereas others studies anticipate net damages with any increase in temperature. Even those studies estimating initial benefits find that benefits peak and become net damages at some level of climate change. Net damages keep rising with greater magnitudes of climate change.
- On average, developing countries are estimated to have larger damages as a percentage of their gross product (i.e., relative to their national incomes) than developed countries. This implies that damages and benefits are not spread evenly.

In some studies, developed countries are estimated to have benefits up to some level of warming, whereas developing countries suffer damages. Note that there will probably be variation among individual countries.

The IPCC AR4 (Yohe et al, 2007) reported findings from numerous studies, including those from Mendelsohn et al (2000), Nordhaus and Boyer (2000), and Tol (2002). It also cited in the Stern Review (Stern et al, 2006). In a comparison of damage estimates from these studies,[6] the IPCC reported the following range of possible outcomes:

- A 0.5°C increase in global mean temperature could lead to negligible damages, or a possible increase in welfare equivalent to between 0.5 and 2 per cent of world GDP.
- A 2°C increase in global mean temperature could lead to negligible damages, or damage equivalent to between a 0.5 per cent and 1.5 per cent loss in world GDP.
- A 4°C increase in global mean temperature could lead to negligible damage, or damage equivalent to between a 1 per cent and 6 per cent loss in world GDP.

Mendelsohn et al (2000) reported country-specific results according to which a 2°C global-mean warming would result in net market benefits for most OECD countries and net market damages for most non-OECD countries. The study applies response (to climate change) functions that were developed empirically for the US to all countries in the world. The two types of response functions used (reduced-form and Ricardian) yield different results.

The more recently released Stern Review (Stern et al, 2006) estimated substantial losses, particularly for large amounts of warming. Their findings suggest that the economic effects of a 5–6°C increase in global mean temperature by 2100 could reduce welfare by an amount roughly equivalent to an average reduction in GDP of 5–10 per cent.[7] Estimates in the Stern Review increase to:

- 11 per cent of GDP when non-market impacts are included (e.g., environment, human health);
- 14 per cent when evidence indicates that the climate system might be more responsive to GHG emissions than previously thought; and
- 20 per cent when using weighting that reflects the expected disproportionate share of damages that will fall on poor regions of the world.

The Stern Review has been criticized for relying on the most pessimistic literature on climate change impacts and for using very low discount rates for estimating the present value of climate change impacts (e.g. Tol, 2006; Yohe, 2006).

Although there is uncertainty about whether there will be initial net benefits or damages with a small amount of warming and about the magnitude of damage with a large amount of warming, there is agreement across the economic studies that the effects of climate change will be uneven and will on average hurt developing countries the most, and that the damages will eventually increase as warming continues.

Conclusion

The sectoral analysis demonstrates that for all sectors and regions covered, several tens of billions of dollars of additional investment and financial flows will be needed for adaptation to the adverse impacts of climate change.

In the sectors dependent on privately owned physical assets (such as the AFF sector and a portion of the infrastructure sector), private sources of funding may be adequate to meet adaptation needs, especially in developed countries. The additional spending likely to be required will be for climate-proofing physical assets or for shifting investment to infrastructure or productive activities that are less vulnerable to the adverse impacts of climate change. Policy changes, incentives and direct financial support will be needed to encourage a shift in investment patterns and additional spending of private resources.

In all sectors at least some additional external public funding will be needed. This will be particularly the case in sectors and countries that are already highly dependent on external support, such as the health sector in LDCs or for coastal infrastructure in developing countries vulnerable to sea-level rise.

National policies may play an important role in ensuring that the use of resources, both public and private, is optimized. In particular there is a need for:

- domestic policies that provide incentives for private investors to adapt new physical assets to the potential impacts of climate change;
- national policies that integrate climate change adaptation in key line ministries; and
- local government adaptation policies in key sectors.

Bilateral donors and multilateral lenders have been directing financial resources to support the design of policies in developing countries in the sectors analysed in this study. A particularly high amount of resources is allocated to support agricultural policies when compared with other sectors. It is not possible to determine how much of these financial resources address climate change issues, let alone adaptation issues. However, the current level of support channeled explicitly for adaptation purposes is likely to be suboptimal.

These estimates should be treated as indicative of adaptation needs but may represent a lower bound of the amount actually required for adaptation because some activities that are likely to need additional financial and investment flows to adapt to climate change impacts have not been included. For example, the water supply sector does not address other aspects of water resource management. The estimate for the health sector does not include many diseases that are expected to become more widespread because of climate change. The estimates for coastal zones are based on the additional costs related to investment in dykes and beach nourishment. The estimate for infrastructure includes only the cost of building new infrastructure with a design that takes climate change into account.

There are other reasons why the estimates of costs of adapting to climate change presented in this chapter should be considered preliminary and be treated with caution. One of the most important reasons is that simple assumptions were used to develop all of the specific estimates. On the ground, adaptations may vary considerably in type and their costs. In addition, cost estimates may be too high, as there might be some amount of double counting. This may be the case with the estimate for infrastructure investment, which may overlap with some of the estimates for water supply and coastal zones. Also, the estimates do not take into account the potential for learning to do adaptation better. The analysis assumes a fixed cost. With a significant need for adaptation, there will probably be lessons learned on how society will adapt more efficiently. In addition, new technologies or technological applications will probably be developed which could reduce costs. The costs of adaptation by people resulting from migration, loss of employment and switching of livelihoods, have not been estimated for this study.

Although the additional investment and financial flows needed for adaptation described above are significant, the value of the climate change impacts that those expenditures would avoid could be larger. This study does not estimate the total value of impacts avoided by adaptation to climate change and therefore does not determine whether benefits of avoided damage exceed the adaptation costs. Existing estimates of the future damage caused by climate change vary substantially; however, available studies yield three important common findings:

- Damages increase with the magnitude of climate change.
- Investment needs for adaptation would almost certainly increase substantially in the latter decades of the 21st century. They will be particularly high if no mitigation measures are implemented.
- On average, developing countries suffer more damage as a percentage of their GDP than developed countries, which implies that damages and benefits are not distributed evenly.

The global cost of adaptation to climate change is difficult to estimate, largely because adaptation measures to climate change will be widespread and heterogeneous. More analysis of the costs of adaptation at the sectoral and regional levels is required.

Notes

1   OECD. ENV-Linkages Model calibrated to the IEA WEO 2006 Reference scenario. Personal communication with Philip Bagnoli at OECD.
2   For example, in the SRES A1B and B1 scenarios by 2050, the CO_2 concentrations are almost 540ppmv and 490ppmv respectively. The global mean temperature increase differs only slightly between the two scenarios, about 1.6°C for the A1B scenario and 1.4°C for the B1 scenario. By 2100, the A1B scenario results in CO_2 concentrations of more than 700ppmv, while the B1 scenario results in concentrations of about 550ppmv. This yields a global mean temperature increase in 2100 of 2.8°C (with a range of 1.7 to 4.4°C) for the A1B scenario and 1.8°C (with a range of 1.1 to 2.9°C) for the B1 scenario (IPCC, 2007).
3   Note that temperature increases in mid- and high-latitude land areas will be higher than increases in global mean temperature (IPCC, 2007).

4   Actual investment needs could be somewhat lower (one can imagine costs being half as much) or substantially higher (one can also imagine costs being two to three times or more higher).

5   Even if trends in regional climate could be isolated, attributing them to anthropogenic climate change could be difficult if not impossible for many regional trends.

6   Mendelsohn et al (2000) estimate aggregate regional monetary damages (both positive and negative) without equity weighting. Nordhaus and Boyer (2000) estimates track aggregated regional monetary estimates of damages with and without population-based equity weighting; they do include a 'willingness to pay (to avoid)' reflection of the costs of abrupt change. Tol (2002) estimates aggregated regional monetary estimates of damages with and without utility-based equity weighting.

7   Based on the recently released IPCC report on the science of climate change, such a warming by 2100 is possible but unlikely (IPCC, 2007).

References

Bosello, F. et al (2007) 'Economy-wide estimates of the implications of climate change: sea-level rise', *Environmental and Resource Economics.*

Briscoe, J. (1999) 'The financing of hydropower, irrigation, and water supply infrastructure in developing countries', *Water Resources Development,* 15(4): pp. 459–491.

Burton, I. (2004) 'Climate change and the adaptation deficit', in A. Fenech, D. MacIver, H. Auld, R. Bing Rong, and Y. Yin (eds), *Climate Change: Building the Adaptive Capacity,* Toronto: Meteorological Service of Canada, Environment Canada, pp. 25–33.

Cassassa, G. et al (2007) 'Assessment of observed changes and response in natural and managed systems', in *Climate Change 2007: Climate Change Impacts, Adaptation, and Vulnerability,* London: Cambridge University Press.

Confalonieri, U. et al (2007) 'Human health', in *Climate Change 2007: Climate Change Impacts, Adaptation, and Vulnerability,* IPCC, London, UK: Cambridge University Press

Easterling, W. et al (2007) 'Food, fibre, and forest products', in *Climate Change 2007: Climate Change Impacts, Adaptation, and Vulnerability,* IPCC, Cambridge: Cambridge University Press.

Fischlin, A. et al (2007) 'Ecosystems, their properties, goods, and services', in *Climate Change 2007: Climate Change Impacts, Adaptation, and Vulnerability,* IPCC, London, UK: Cambridge University Press.

Hecht, R and Shah, R. (2006) 'Recent trends and innovations in development assistance for health', in *Disease Control Priorities in Developing Countries,* 2nd Edition, Oxford University Press, New York.

Houghton, J. T. et al (eds) (2001) *Climate Change 2001: The Scientific Basis,* Cambridge: Cambridge University Press.

IPCC (2007) *Climate Change 2007 The Physical Science Basis: Summary for Policy Makers,* Geneva: IPCC.

James, A., Gaston, K. and Balmford, A. (2001) 'Can we afford to conserve biodiversity?' *BioScience,* 51: pp. 43–52.

Johns, T. et al (2001) 'Correlations between patterns of 19th and 20th century surface temperature change and HadCM2 climate model ensembles', *Geophysical Research Letters* 28: pp1007–1010.

Kirshen, P. (2007) *Adaptation Options and Cost in Water Supply,* A report for the Secretariat of the UNFCCC.

Kirshen, P., Ruth, M. and Anderson, W. (2006) 'Climate's long-term impacts on urban infrastructures and services: the case of metro Boston', in *Climate Change and Variability: Local Impacts and Responses*, Cheltenham, UK: Edward Elgar Publishers.

Klein, R. J. T. et al (2001) 'Technological options for adaptation to climate change in coastal zones', *Journal of Coastal Research*, 17(3): pp. 531–543.

Kundzewicz, Z. W. et al (2007) 'Freshwater resources and their management', in *Climate Change 2007: Climate Change Impacts, Adaptation, and Vulnerability*, IPCC, Cambridge: Cambridge University Press.

Leggett, et al (1992) *Emissions Scenario for the IPCC: An Update. Assumptions, Methodology and Results*, IPCC Working Group I, available at: http://sedac.ciesin.org/ddc/is92/.

McMichael, A. et al (2004) 'Climate change', in M. Ezzati, A. Lopez, A. Rodgers and C. Murray (eds) *Comparative Quantification of Health Risks: Global and Regional Burden of Disease due to Selected Major Risk Factors*, Geneva: World Health Organization, available at: www.who.int/publications/cra/chapters/volume2/1543-1650.pdf.

Mendelsohn, R. et al (2000) 'Country-specific market impacts of climate change', *Climatic Change*, 45: pp. 553–569.

Michaud, C. (2003) *Development Assistance for Health: Recent Trends and Resource Allocation*, Boston: Harvard Center for Population Development.

Milly, P. C. D., Dunne, K. A. and Vecchia, A. V. (2005) 'Global pattern of trends in streamflow and water availability in a changing climate', *Nature* 438, pp. 347–350.

Nakicenovic, N. and Swart, R. (eds) (2000) *IPCC Special Report on Emissions Scenarios*, Cambridge: Cambridge University Press.

Nicholls, R. J. et al (2007) 'Coastal systems and low lying areas', in *Climate Change 2007: Climate Change Impacts, Adaptation, and Vulnerability*, IPCC, Cambridge: Cambridge University Press.

Nicholls, R. J. and Tol, R. S. J. (2006) 'Impacts and responses to sea-level rise: a global analysis of the SRES scenarios over the twenty-first century', *Philosophical Transactions of the Royal Society A: Mathematical Physical and Engineering Sciences*, 364 (1841): pp. 1073–1095.

Noble, I. (2007) *Making ODA Climate Proof? Removing Barriers*, Presentation, Washington DC: The World Bank.

Nordhaus, W. D. and Boyer, J. (2000) *Warming the World: Economic Models of Global Warming*, MIT Press, Cambridge, MA.

OECD (Organisation for Economic Co-operation and Development) (2004) CRS Online Database on Aid Activities, www.oecd.org/dac/stats/idsonline.

Parmesan, C. and Yohe, G. (2003) 'A globally coherent fingerprint of climate change impacts across natural systems', *Nature*, 421: pp. 37–42.

Pernetta, J. C. (1992) 'Impacts of climate change and sealevel rise on small island states: National and international responses', *Global Environmental Change*, 2 (1): pp. 19–31.

Raworth, K. (2007) *Adapting to Climate Change: What's Needed in Poor Countries and who Should Pay*, Oxfam International, available at: www.oxfam.org/files/adapting%20to%20climate%20change.pdf.

Root, T. L., MacMynowski, D. P., Mastrandea, M. D. and Schneider, S. H. (2005) 'Human-modified temperatures induce species changes: joint attribution', *Proceedings of the National Academy of Sciences* 102: pp. 7465–7469.

Rosenzweig, C. and Parry, M. L. (1994) 'Potential impact of climate change on world food supply', *Nature*, 367: pp. 133–138.

Smit, B., Pilifosova, O., Burton, I., Challenger, B., Huq, S., Klein, R. and Yohe, G. (2001) *Adaptation to Climate Change in the Context of Sustainable Development and Equity*, IPCC Third Assessment Report, Working Group II, Cambridge University Press, Cambridge, UK.

Smith, J. B. et al (2006) *Honduras Pilot Study Report: Climate Change, Coastal Resources, and Flood Planning in La Ceiba,* Report prepared for the US Agency for International Development, Boulder, Colorado: Stratus Consulting Inc.

Stenberg, J., Johns, B., Scherpbier, R. W. and Edeger, T. T-T. (2007) 'A financial road map to scaling up essential child health interventions in 75 countries', *World Health Organization Bulletin* 85: pp. 305–314.

Stern, N. et al (2006) *Stern Review Report: The Economics of Climate Change,* London, UK: Her Majesty's Treasury.

Tebaldi, C. et al (2006) 'Going to extremes: an intercomparison of model-simulated historical and future change extremes', *Climatic Change,* 79: pp. 185–211.

Thomas, C. D., Cameron, A., Green, R. E., Bakkenes, M., Beaumont, L. J., Collingham, Y. C., Erasmus, B. F. N., Ferreira de Siqueira, M., Grainger, A., Hannah, L., Hughes, L., Huntley, B., van Jaarsveld, A. S., Midgley, G. F., Miles, L., Ortega-Huerta, M. A., Peterson, A. T., Phillips, O. L. and Williams, S. E. (2004) 'Extinction risk from climate change', *Nature,* no 427, pp145–148.

Tol, R. S. J. (2002) 'Estimates of the damage costs of climate change, Part 1: benchmark estimates', *Environmental and Resource Economics,* 21: pp. 41–73.

Tol, R. S. J. (2006) *The Stern Review of the Economics of Climate Change: A Comment,* Dublin, Ireland: Economic and Social Research Institute.

Toubkiss, J. (2006) 'Costing MDG Target 10 on water supply and sanitation: Comparative analysis, obstacles and recommendations', World Water Council, available at www.worldwatercouncil.org/fileadmin/wwc/Library/Publications_and_reports/FullText Cover_MDG.pdf

United States Fish and Wildlife Service (2007) 'Endangered and threatened wildlife and plants: 12-month petition finding and proposed rule to list the polar bear (*Ursus maritimus*) as threatened throughout its range', available at www.epa.gov/fedrgstr/EPA-SPECIES/2007/January/Day-09/e9962.htm

WHO (World Health Organization) (2006) *World Health Report 2006: Working Together for Health.* Geneva: WHO.

Winpenny, J. (2003) *Financing Water for All,* World Water Council, Global Water Partnership.

World Bank (2006) *Clean Energy and Development: Towards an Investment Framework,* Washington, DC: World Bank, available at: http://siteresources.worldbank.org/DEVCOMMINT/ Documentation/20890696/DC2006-0002(E)-CleanEnergy.pdf.

Yohe, G. (2006) 'Some thoughts on the damage estimates presented in the Stern review – an editorial', *The Integrated Assessment Journal,* 6 (3): pp. 65–72.

Yohe, G. W., Lasco, R. D., Ahmad, Q. K., Arnell, N. W., Cohen, S. J., Hope, C., Janetos, A. C. and Perez, R. T. (2007) 'Perspectives on climate change and sustainability', in Parry, M. L., Canziani, O. F., Palutikof, J. P., van der Linden, P. J. and Hanson, C.E. (eds) *Climate Change 2007: Impacts, Adaptation and Vulnerability,* contribution of Working Group II to the Fourth Assessment Report of the Intergovernmental Panel on Climate Change, Cambridge University Press, Cambridge, UK pp811–841

Further Reading

Adaptation Theory

Adger, W. N., Agrawala, S., Mirza, M., Conde, C., O'Brien, K., Puhlin, J., Pulwarty, R., Smit, B. and Takahashi, K. (2007) 'Assessment of adaptation practices, options, constraints and capacity', IPCC Working Group II contribution to the Fourth Assessment Report, Cambridge University Press, Cambridge, UK

Burton, I. (1992) 'Adapt and thrive', unpublished manuscript, Canadian Climate Centre, Downsview, Ontario, Canada

Burton, I. (1997) 'Vulnerability and adaptive response in the context of climate and climate change', *Climatic Change*, vol 36, pp185–196

Burton, I., Challenger, B., Huq, S., Klein, R. and Yohe, G. (2007) 'Adaptation to climate change in the context of sustainable development and equity', IPCC Working Group II contribution to the Fourth Assessment Report, Cambridge University Press, Cambridge, UK

Butzer, K. W. (1980) 'Adaptation to global environmental change', *Professional Geographer*, vol 32, no 3, pp269–278

Denevan, W. M. (1983) 'Adaptation, variation, and cultural geography', *Professional Geographer*, vol 35, no 4, pp399–406

Füssel, H-M. (2007) 'Adaptation planning for climate change: Concepts, assessment approaches, and key lessons', *Sustainability Science*, vol 2, pp265–275

Hardesty, D. L. (1986) 'Rethinking cultural adaptation', *Professional Geographer*, vol 38, no 1, pp11–18

Kane, S. M. and Yohe, G. (2007) 'Societal adaptation to climate variability and change: An introduction', *Climatic Change*, vol 45, no 1, pp1–4

Kates, R. W. (1985) 'The interaction of climate and society', in R. W. Kates, J. H. Ausubel and M. Berberian (eds) *Climate Impact Assessment*, SCOPE 27, Scientific Committee on Problems of the Environment, Paris

Klein, R. J. T. (2003) 'Adaptation to climate variability and change: What is optimal and appropriate?', in C. Giupponi and M. Schechter (eds) *Climate Change and the Mediterranean: Socio-Economic Perspectives of Impacts, Vulnerability and Adaptation*, Edward Elgar, Cheltenham, UK

Liverman, D. (2008) 'Assessing impacts, adaptation and vulnerability: Reflections on the Working Group II Report of the Intergovernmental Panel on Climate Change', *Global Environmental Change*, vol 18, no 1, pp4–7

Parry, M., Arnell, N., Hulme, M., Nicholls, R. and Livermore, M. (1998) 'Adapting to the inevitable', *Nature*, vol 395, no 6704, p741

Scheraga, J. and Grambsch, A. E. (1998) 'Risks, opportunities, and adaptation to climate change', *Climate Research*, vol 11, no 1, pp85–95

Smit, B. (1993) 'Adaptation to climatic variability and change: Report of the Task Force on Climatic Adaptation', occasional paper, Canadian Climate Program, Department of Geography, University of Guelph, Guelph, Canada

Smit, B., Burton, I., Klein, R. J. T. and Street, R. (1999) 'The science of adaptation: A framework for assessment', *Mitigation and Adaptation Strategies for Global Change*, vol 4, nos 3–4, pp199–213

Smit, B. and Wandel, J. (2006) 'Adaptation, adaptive capacity and vulnerability', *Global Environmental Change*, vol 16, no 3, pp282–292

Tarlock, A. D. (1992) 'Now, think again about adaptation', *Arizona Journal of International and Comparative Law*, vol 9, pp169–181

Adaptation, Vulnerability and Resilience

Adger, W. N. (1999) 'Social vulnerability to climate change and extremes in coastal Vietnam', *World Development*, vol 27, no 2, pp249–269

Chambers, R. (1989) 'Vulnerability, coping and policy', *Institute of Development Studies Bulletin*, vol 20, no 2, pp1–7

Corbett, J. (1988) 'Famine and household coping strategies', *World Development*, vol 16, pp1099–1112

Cutter, S. L. (1996) 'Vulnerability to environmental hazards', *Progress in Human Geography*, vol 20, no 4, pp529–539

Downing, T. W. (1991) 'Vulnerability to hunger in Africa: A climate change perspective', *Global Environmental Change*, vol 1, no 5, pp365–380

Frankenberger, T. R. and Goldstein, D. M. (1990) 'Food security, coping strategies, and environmental degradation', *Arid Lands Newsletter*, no 30, pp21–27

Füssel, H-M. (2005) 'Vulnerability in climate change research: A comprehensive conceptual framework', University of California International and Area Studies, Breslauer Symposium, Paper 6, University of California, Berkeley, CA

Füssel, H-M. and Klein, R. J. T. (2006) 'Vulnerability and adaptation assessments to climate change: An evolution of conceptual thinking', *Climatic Change*, vol 75, no 3, pp301–329

Gunderson, L. (1999) 'Resilience, flexibility and adaptive management – Antidotes for spurious certitude?', *Conservation Ecology*, vol 3, no 1

Handmer, J. W., Dovers, S. and Downing, T. E. (1999) 'Societal vulnerability to climate change and variability', *Mitigation and Adaptation Strategies for Global Change*, vol 4, nos 3–4, pp267–281

Klein, R. J. T., Nicholls, R. J. and Thomalla, F. (2004) 'Resilience to natural hazards: How useful is this concept?', *Environmental Hazards*, vol 5, no 1–2, pp34–35

Levin, S., Barrett, S., Aniyar, S., Baumol, W., Bliss, C., Bolin, B., Dagsputa, P., Ehrlich, P., Folke, C., Gren, I. M., Holling, C. S., Jansson, A. M., Jansson, B. O., Maeler, K. G. and Martin, D. (1998) 'Resilience in natural and socio-economic systems', *Environment and Development Economics*, vol 3, no 2, pp222–235

Liverman, D. M. (1999) 'Vulnerability and adaptation to drought in Mexico', *Natural Resources Journal*, vol 39, no 1, pp99–115

Riebsame, W. E. (1991) 'Sustainability of the great plains in an uncertain climate', *Great Plains Research*, vol 1, no 1, pp133–151

Smit, B. and Wandel, J. (2006) 'Adaptation, adaptive capacity and vulnerability', *Global Environmental Change*, vol 16, pp282–292

Swift, J. (1989) 'Why are rural people vulnerable to famine?', *Institute of Development Studies Bulletin*, vol 20, no 2, pp8–15

Yohe, G. and Tol, R. S. J. (2002) 'Indicators for social and economic coping capacity – Moving toward a working definition of adaptive capacity', *Global Environmental Change*, vol 12, no 1, pp25–40

Adaptation and Disaster Risk

Adger, N. and Brooks, N. (2003) 'Does global environmental change cause vulnerability to disaster?', in M. Pelling (ed) *Natural Disasters and Development in a Globalising World*, Routledge, London

Bruce, J. P. (1999) 'Disaster loss mitigation as an adaptation to climate variability and change', *Mitigation and Adaptation Strategies for Global Change*, vol 4, nos 3–4, pp295–306

Burton, I., Kates, R. W. and White, G. F. (1993) *The Environment as Hazard* (second edition), Guilford Press, New York

Green, C. (2003) 'Change, risk and uncertainty: Managing vulnerability to flooding', paper presented at 'Third Annual DPRI-IIASA Meeting; Integrated Disaster Risk Management: Coping with Regional Vulnerability', Kyoto, Japan, 3–5 July

Hay, J. E. (2002) 'Integrating disaster risk management and adaptation to climate variability and change: Needs, benefits and approaches, from a South Pacific perspective', paper presented at UNDP Expert Group Meeting 'Integrating Disaster Reduction and Adaptation to Climate Change', Havana, Cuba, 17–19 June

Sarewitz, D., Pielke, R. Jr. and Keykhah, M. (2003) 'Vulnerability and risk: Some thoughts from a political and policy perspective', *Risk Analysis*, vol 23, no 4, pp805–810

Schipper, L. and Pelling, M. (2006) 'Disaster risk, climate change and international development: Scope for, and challenges to, integration', special issue of *Disasters*, vol 30, no 1, pp19–38

Soussan, J. and Burton, I. (2002) 'Adapt and thrive: Combining adaptation to climate change, disaster mitigation, and natural resources management in a new approach to the reduction of vulnerability and poverty', paper presented at the UNDP Expert Group Meeting 'Integrating Disaster Reduction and Adaptation to Climate Change', Havana, Cuba, 17–19 June

Sperling, F. and Szekely, F. (2005) 'Disaster risk management in a changing climate', World Bank, Washington, DC

Thomalla, F., Downing, T., Spanger-Siegfried, E., Han, G. and Rockström, J. (2006) 'Reducing hazard vulnerability: Towards a common approach between disaster risk reduction and climate adaptation', special issue of *Disasters*, vol 30, no 1, pp39–48

van Aalst, M. K., Cannon, T. and Burton, I. (2008) 'Community level adaptation to climate change: The potential role of participatory community risk assessment', *Global Environmental Change*, vol 18, no 1, pp165–179

Adaptation and Development

Adger, W. N. (2000) 'Institutional adaptation to environmental risk under the transition in Vietnam', *Annals of the Association of American Geographers*, vol 90, pp738–758

Agrawala, S. (ed) (2005) 'Bridge over troubled waters – Linking climate change and development', Organisation for Economic Co-operation and Development, Paris

Apuuli, B., Wright, J., Elias, C. and Burton, I. (2000) 'Reconciling national and global priorities in adaptation to climate change: With an illustration from Uganda', *Environmental Monitoring and Assessment*, vol 61, no 1, pp145–159

Beg, N., Morlot, J. C., Davidson, O., Afrane-Okesse, Y., Tyani, L., Denton, F., Sokona, Y., Thomas, J. P., La Rovere, E. L., Parikh, J. K., Parikh, K. and Rahman, A. A. (2002) 'Linkages between climate change and sustainable development', *Climate Policy*, vol 2, nos 2–3, pp129–144

Bizikova, L., Robinson, J. and Cohen, S. (2007) 'Linking climate change and sustainable development at the local level', *Climate Policy*, vol 7, pp271–277

Burton, I. (2000) 'Adaptation to climate change and variability in the context of sustainable development', in L. Gómez-Echeverri (ed) *Climate Change and Development*, Yale School of Forestry and Environmental Studies and UNDP, New Haven, CT, and New York

Burton, I. and van Aalst, M. (1999) 'Come hell or high water: Integrating climate change and adaptation into Bank work', Environment Department Paper No 72, World Bank Environment Department, World Bank, Washington, DC

Downing, T., Ringius, L., Hulme, M. and Waughray, D. (1997) 'Adapting to climate change in Africa', *Mitigation and Adaptation Strategies for Global Change*, vol 2, no 1, pp19–44

Eriksen, S. and O'Brien, K. (2007) 'Vulnerability, poverty and the need for sustainable adaptation measures', *Climate Policy*, vol 7, pp337–352

Eriksen, S. and Naess, L-O. (2003) 'Pro-poor climate adaptation: Norwegian development cooperation and climate change adaptation: An assessment of issues, strategies and potential entry points', CICERO Report 2003:03, report commissioned by NORAD, Norwegian Agency for Development Cooperation, Oslo

Gagnon-Lebrun, F. and Agrawala, S. (2007) 'Implementing adaptation in developed countries: An analysis of progress and trends', *Climate Policy*, vol 7, no 5, pp392–408

Huq, S., Rahman, A., Konate, M., Sokona, Y. and Reid, H. (2003) 'Mainstreaming adaptation to climate change in least developed countries', IIED, London

Kahn, S. R. (2001) 'Adaptation to climate change in the context of sustainable development and equity: The case of Pakistan', in J. B. Smith, R. J. T. Klein and S. Huq (eds) *Climate Change, Adaptive Capacity and Development*, Imperial College Press, London

Kelly, P. M. and Adger, W. N. (1999) 'Social equity in adaptation as a key constraint in integrating climate policies', paper presented at Second EFEIA Policy Workshop 'Integrating Climate Politics in the European Environment: Costs and Opportunities', Milan, Italy, 4–6 March

Klein, R. J. T. (2001) 'Adaptation to climate change in German official development assistance – An inventory of activities and opportunities, with a special focus on Africa', Deutsche Gesellschaft für Technische Zusammenarbeit (GTZ), Eschborn, Germany

Klein, R. J. T., Huq, S. and Smith, J. B. (2003) *Climate Change, Adaptive Capacity and Development*, Imperial College Press, London

Klein, R. J. T., Schipper, E. L. and Dessai, S. (2005) 'Integrating mitigation and adaptation into climate and development policy: Three research questions', *Environmental Science and Policy*, vol 8, pp579–588

Leary, N., Adejuwon, J., Barros, V., Burton, I., Kulkarni, J. and Lasco, R. (eds) (2008) *Climate Change and Adaptation,* Earthscan, London

Leary, N., Conde, C., Kulkarni, J., Nyong, A. and Pulhin, J. (eds) (2008) *Climate Change and Vulnerability*, Earthscan, London

McGray, H., Hammill, A. and Bradley, R. with Schipper, E. L. and Parry, J. E. (2007) 'Weathering the storm: Options for framing adaptation and development', World Resources Institute (WRI) report, WRI, Washington, DC

Mendelsohn, R. and Dinar, A. (1999) 'Climate change, agriculture, and developing countries: Does adaptation matter?', *The World Bank Research Observer*, vol 14, no 2, pp277–293

Mirza, M. M. Q. (2003) 'Climate change and extreme weather events: Can developing countries adapt?', *Climate Policy*, vol 3, no 3, pp233–248

Pelling, M. (2003) 'Social capital, hazards and adaptation strategies for the vulnerable', paper presented at ZICER Seminar 'Justice in Adaptation to Climate Change', University of East Anglia, Norwich, UK, 7–9 September

Singh, R. (1996) 'Community adaptation and sustainable livelihoods: Basic issues and principles', IISD working paper, International Institute for Sustainable Development, Winnipeg, Canada

Schipper, E. L. F. (2007) 'Climate change adaptation and development: Exploring the linkages', Tyndall Working Paper No 107, Tyndall Centre for Climate Change Research, University of East Anglia, Norwich, UK

Smith, J. B., Klein, R. J. T. and Huq, S. (2003) *Climate Change, Adaptive Capacity and Development*, Imperial College Press, London

Sperling, F. (ed) (2003) 'Poverty and climate change: Reducing the vulnerability of the poor through adaptation', inter-agency report by the African Development Bank (AfDB), Asian

Development Bank (ADB), Department for International Development (DFID, UK), Federal Ministry for Economic Cooperation and Development (BMZ, Germany), Directorate-General for Development of the European Commission (EC), Ministry of Foreign Affairs – Development Cooperation (DGIS, The Netherlands), Organisation for Economic Co-operation and Development (OECD), United Nations Development Programme (UNDP), United Nations Environment Programme (UNEP) and the World Bank

Swart, R. and Raes, F. (2007) 'Making integration of adaptation and mitigation work: Mainstreaming into sustainable development policies?', *Climate Policy*, vol 7, pp288–303

UNFCCC (UN Framework Convention on Climate Change) (2008) 'Climate change: Impacts, vulnerabilities and adaptation in developing countries', UNFCCC, Bonn, Germany

Adaptation and Climate Change Policy

Burton, I., Smith, J. B. and Lenhart, S. (1998) 'Adaptation to climate change: Theory and assessment', in J. F. Feenstra, I. Burton, J. B. Smith and R. S. J. Tol (eds) *Handbook on Methods for Climate Change Impact Assessment and Adaptation Strategies* (Version 2.0), UNEP/RIVM, Nairobi and Amsterdam

Burton, I., Diringer, E. and Smith, J. (2006) 'Adaptation to climate change: International policy options', Pew Center on Global Climate Change Research, Arlington, VA

Burton, I., Bizikova, L., Dickinson, T. and Howard, Y. (2007) 'Integrating adaptation into policy: Upscaling evidence from local to global', *Climate Policy*, vol 7, pp371–376

Fankhauser, S. (1998) 'The costs of adapting to climate change', GEF Working Paper No 16, Global Environment Facility, Washington, DC

Harmeling, S. and Bals, C. (2008) 'Adaptation to climate change – Where do we go from Bali? An analysis of the COP13 and the key issues on the road to a new climate change treaty', Germanwatch, Bonn, Germany

Huq, S. (2002) 'The adaptation COP', *The Daily Star* 3 (1135), 5 November

Huq, S. and Grubb, M. (2003) 'Scientific assessment of the inter-relationships of mitigation and adaptation', paper prepared for AR4 Scoping Meeting, 8 August

Kane, S. and Shogren, J. F. (2000) 'Linking adaptation and mitigation in climate change policy', *Climatic Change*, vol 45, no 1, pp75–102

Lim, B., Spanger-Siegfried, E., Burton, I., Malone, M. and Huq, S. (2005) *Adaptation Policy Frameworks for Climate Change: Developing Strategies, Policies and Measures*, UNDP/GEF project report, Cambridge University Press, New York

Linnerooth-Bayer, J., Mace, M. J. and Verheyen, R. (2003) 'Insurance-related actions and risk assessment in the context of the UNFCCC', paper commissioned by the UNFCCC Secretariat for the 'UNFCCC Workshop on Insurance-Related Actions to Address the Specific Needs and Concerns of Developing Country Parties Arising from the Adverse Effects of Climate Change and from the Impact of the Implementation of Response Measures', Bonn, Germany, 14–15 May

Michaelowa, A. (2001) 'Mitigation versus adaptation: The political economy of competition between climate policy strategies and the consequences for developing countries', Discussion Paper 153, Hamburg Institute of International Economics, Hamburg, Germany

Tol, R. S. J. (2003) 'Adaptation and mitigation: Trade-offs in substance and methods', working paper, University of Hamburg, Hamburg, Germany

Urwin, K. and Jordan, A. (2008) 'Does public policy support or undermine climate change adaptation? Exploring policy interplay across different scales of governance', *Global Environmental Change*, vol 18, no 1, pp180–191

Verheyen, R. (2002) 'Adaptation to the impacts of anthropogenic climate change – The international legal framework', *RECIEL*, vol 11, no 2, pp129–143

Wilbanks, T. J., Kane, S. M., Leiby, P. N., Perlack, R. D., Settle, C., Shogren, J. F. and Smith, J. B. (2003) 'Possible responses to global climate change: Integrating mitigation and adaptation', *Environment*, vol 45, no 5, pp28–38

Index